CRITICAL TIMES

THE HISTORY OF THE
TIMES LITERARY SUPPLEMENT

DERWENT MAY

HarperCollins*Publishers*

HarperCollins*Publishers*
77–85 Fulham Palace Road,
Hammersmith, London W6 8JB

www.**fire**and**water**.com

Published by HarperCollins*Publishers* 2001
1 3 5 7 9 8 6 4 2

A catalogue record for this book
is available from the British Library

ISBN 0 00 711449 4

Set in Birka by
Rowland Phototypesetting Ltd,
Bury St Edmunds, Suffolk

Printed and bound in Great Britain by
Omnia Books Limited, Glasgow

To
ARTHUR CROOK
who saw it all

CONTENTS

LIST OF ILLUSTRATIONS

SOURCES AND ACKNOWLEDGEMENTS

The chief source of the material quoted or cited in this book is the files of the *Times Literary Supplement* itself. For the years from 1902 to 1974, in which the reviewing was anonymous, I mainly consulted the 'marked copies' of the paper in the Times (strictly speaking, the TNL) Archives at Wapping. These are the original copies of the paper in which the name of the reviewer, and often his or her address and fee, were written by hand across each contribution. They were made primarily for the accounts department.

These form the main source of information about the identity of the author of each review, though there is also another record in the so-called stock books. These are notebooks and files in which, each week, the unused copy still in hand was listed, and newly-arrived copy was noted. They are much more difficult to use than the marked copies, since the names given to the articles and reviews in order to identify them were often perfunctory and arbitrary, and usually only the surnames of the authors were noted down. For the staff at the time, of course, this was sufficient. I sought information in the stock books only when there was some difficulty in identifying reviewers from the marked copies, as for instance when the handwriting was illegible or an issue of the paper was missing. For the enormous help they gave me in thus working through over seventy years' issues of the paper, I have expressed my gratitude to the archives staff in the preface.

For the years since 1974, in which the contributions have been by-lined in the *TLS*, I used the bound copies of the paper in the *Times Literary Supplement* editorial office, and thank the present staff for their help there.

For the years from 1902 to 1985, there is a printed index to all contributors and contributions in book form. This consists of *The TLS*

Index 1902–1939 (Newspaper Archive Developments, two volumes, 1978), *The TLS Index 1940–1980* (Research Publications, three volumes, 1982), and *The TLS Index 1981–1985* (Research Publications, 1986). When the latter of these appeared, John Gross, a former editor, wrote in the preface that the files of the *TLS* were now, in Pope's words, 'A mighty maze! but not without a plan.' These indexes only gave names that were published in the paper, so reviewers' names only appear from 1974 onward.

The paper has also always produced an annual index for subscribers to bind up with their copies, and these are generally to be found in sets of the paper in public libraries.

The most important development in indexing the paper and identifying the anonymous reviewers has been the creation, by Professor Jeremy Treglown and Dr Deborah McVea at the University of Warwick, of an electronic database: *The TLS Centenary Archive 1902–1990*. This great index identifies the author of almost every anonymous review that has appeared in the paper, with cross-references to other contributions by him or her, and biographical information where known. Information can be called up by reference to the author of the book reviewed, the title of the book reviewed, and the reviewer. Searches can also be made by reference to the publisher, subject, date and translator, and the review itself can be read on screen. There are also entries, generally without biographical information, for contributions after the end of the period of anonymity, in 1974. The source material used by Treglown and McVea is similar to that which I have used in this book, but I have also drawn on other information that they have uncovered.

In the light of the existence of this database, I have not included in this book any information about the reviews mentioned in the text beyond what is there for purposes of the narrative. There is always enough detail for the reader to identify the review. Readers wishing for further information about any review or reviewer can find it easily and quickly in Treglown and McVea, *The TLS Centenary Archive*, published by Primary Source Media, which is part of the Gale Group (www.tls.psmedia.com).

I am deeply aware of my indebtedness to all the reviewers and other contributors, living and dead, whose writing form the main subject of this book. I am particularly grateful to the reviewers who wrote for the paper anonymously, and are still living, who raised no objection to my revealing their names. A letter that appeared in the *Times Literary Supplement* from Jeremy Treglown and myself, announcing our intention to throw the veil aside in our respective projects, and a circular letter to over a thousand contributors from Treglown, brought objections from only one or two contributors, whose wishes have been respected both in the database and in this book.

I am also grateful to the *Times* archivists for their help in exploring the substantial body of manuscript material relating to the history of the paper that is in their possession.

The letters I have quoted from or mentioned – mainly from the early years in the paper's life – by C.F. Moberly Bell, J.B. Capper, Harold Child, F.T. Dalton, Geoffrey Robinson (later Dawson), W. Lints Smith, H.D. Traill and J.R. Thursfield, are in these archives, as are all the letters and memoranda by successive editors (most of them, in fact, by Bruce Richmond). From Lord Northcliffe's epistolary exchanges with his staff, most of the letters, telegrams and memoranda by Northcliffe, Reginald Nicholson and Campbell Stuart are in the Manuscript Collections of the British Library, which I also thank; however, a few of them (sometimes duplicates) are in the Times Archives.

Also in the Times Archives are the letters I have quoted or referred to by the following, most of them contributors and most of them writing privately to the editor of the *Literary Supplement* at the time: Lord Annan, Sir Isaiah Berlin, Arthur Calder-Marshall, John Carter, Lawrence Durrell, Maurice Edelman, St John Ervine, Geoffrey Grigson, John Hayward, Lord Goodman, Graham Hutton, Lord Lambton, F.R. Leavis, Wyndham Lewis, Sir Nikolaus Pevsner, A.L. Rowse, Roger Scruton, John Sparrow. A.J.P. Taylor and Lord Dacre of Glanton. Unpublished letters by E.M. Forster were shown me by P.N. Furbank, his literary executor, and are quoted by his kind permission.

Alan Pryce-Jones's journals are in the Beinecke Library at Yale University and I thank the Library and especially Vincent Giroud, Curator of Modern Books and Manuscripts, for generous help when I visited Yale to examine them. Permission to quote from the journals was kindly given by his son, David Pryce-Jones, whom I also thank for some personal information about his father.

The poem 'Saporta!' by Edwin Morgan is reprinted here by permission of its author.

Published works that I have quoted from, mentioned or consulted, can be found in the bibliography.

This book was commissioned from me by TSL Education Limited, the publishers of the *TLS*, and I should like to thank the Chief Executive Officer, James MacManus, for his unfailing support. Sir Edward Pickering, the Executive Vice-Chairman of Times Newspapers Limited and John Grigg, author of the latest volume of the history of *The Times*, gave me valued encouragement. The Chief Executive of News International, Rupert Murdoch, has also supported the writing and publication of this book. I was invited to write it entirely as I chose, and this I have done.

Among the many members and former members of the *Times* or *TLS* staff who helped me generously with their reminiscences were: Arthur Crook, to whom this book is dedicated, Alan Pryce-Jones, whom I talked to in America the year before he died, Ferdinand Mount, John Gross, Jeremy Treglown, John Willett, John Sturrock, Charis Ryder, Victoria Glendinning, Caroline St John Brooks, Alan Hollinghurst, Alan Jenkins, Adolf Wood, Ian Trafford, Derek Hudson and Bruce Coward. I also talked to the late Lord Annan, the late Janet Adam Smith, Sir John Ure, Professor John Jones, Sally Sampson, Alan Bell, David Ekserdjian and Donald Cameron Watt.

The book was read in manuscript by Ferdinand Mount, P.N. Furbank and Yolanta May, and in page proofs by Orlando May, all of whom improved it. I also thank Philip Warnock and Denis Lenihan of the Times Supplements Library, and the staff of the Times Picture Library, for their help.

At HarperCollins, I am very grateful to Michael Fishwick, the publishing director, for his enthusiastic backing, and to Kate Johnson, who edited the book, for the care she took over it. Douglas Matthews has produced a characteristically splendid index.

PREFACE

The *Times Literary Supplement* was ninety-five years old, and had printed over 250 million words in its pages, when I started writing this book in 1997. How could one begin to write a history of such a vast endeavour? Early on, I came round to deciding two things. It had, of course, to be a history of the paper's editors and staff, from their literary trials and triumphs to the office comedies. But a history of a journal of opinion had also to be a history of those opinions.

And there were so many different opinions! In the paper's earlier, anonymous years – from 1902 to 1974 – a semblance of unanimity was cultivated by the editors. But the passions and quarrels of the contributors – about poetry or politics or simply questions of taste – were blazing away, always instantly apparent beneath the plain, unsignposted columns of print. They spilt over into the correspondence columns, where everybody could sign their names except for 'Your Reviewer'. And since the end of anonymity there have never ceased to be bouts of openly-declared war.

So there was no hope of giving any kind of analytical summary at any point of 'the paper's view' or the assumptions behind the paper. It had to be a story of the smoke and confusion and endless accidents of the battlefield. Not that, for the interest of the story, that would be a bad thing. However, how, in a book less long than the complete set of bound volumes of the paper, was that to be done?

It was a matter of selection. In the end, this was the greatest challenge that the book presented to me. In order to make it a coherent and enjoyable read I was forced to make constant and anguished sacrifices of reviews and articles. But with every review I have mentioned, I have aimed to give something of its flavour – of its ideas, shrewd or sometimes foolish, its style and metaphor, and its wit, wherever there was any (and there was plenty).

In the anonymous years there was a special interest in discovering who had written the reviews – for I was able to see the 'marked copies' in the Times Newspapers Limited archives. These were the copies in which, for the use of the accounts department, the hand of a long-forgotten member of the *Times* staff wrote each week the names of the contributors across the pages, generally with the fee they were to receive and sometimes with their addresses. Thus I saw 'Miss A.V. Stephen' appear in the pages, to be followed after a proper interval by 'Virginia Stephen' and then 'Mrs Woolf'.

There could have been, then – and could be – many different histories of the *Times Literary Supplement*. I could have chosen innumerable different reviews to mention; other authors of this book would certainly have done so, giving it the stamp of their own pleasures and priorities as I have done.

Nevertheless, I hope I have told its history. This is not an analytical book, yet I think that, as it progresses, a social history, an intellectual history and an individual history do emerge from its tale of accidents and alarms – one that would, in fact, have emerged in much the same way from those histories by alternative authors that I have conjured up in my imagination.

In one way, it is a history of the literature of the twentieth century seen from a particular vantage point. Most of the major works of the century, besides many of the minor ones, are described here in interesting ways by the jostling crowd of reviewers quoted.

At the same time, the book is in part conceived as an anthology of good writing. In the anonymous and the signed years alike, reviewers for the paper have written memorable paragraphs and sentences of which thousands are preserved here.

As for the story of the editors, for that I have interviewed numerous individuals and delved into many books and archives. But three people must be singled out: Eamon Dyas, the head of the News International archive, and his deputy, Nick Mays, gave me three years of constant help, as I turned the marked pages in a quiet room in Wapping. Above all, Arthur Crook – who joined the paper in 1930 at the age of eighteen and was its editor for fifteen years from 1959 – unlocked his rich and wonderful memory for me during numerous afternoons spent sitting in his drawing-room. Many pages in this history would be missing had it not been for those vivid sessions.

Chapter One

The Beginnings

When Bruce Richmond, who had been the editor of the *Times Literary Supplement* for twenty-seven years, was given an honorary doctorate by Oxford University in 1930, one letter of congratulation he received was from a widow he had known for even longer, Mrs Ellen Moberly Bell. It was her husband, Charles Frederic Moberly Bell, who had been the manager of *The Times* on that distant day – Friday, 17 January 1902 – when the first number of the '*Lit Supp*' was published. Replying to Mrs Moberly Bell, Richmond conjured up a vivid memory of that time long past.

The editor of *The Times* in 1902 was George Earle Buckle; the chief assistant editor was J.B. Capper, and Bruce Richmond was the number three on the paper. All three men worked together in the large editor's room in the *Times* offices in Printing House Square, near Blackfriars Bridge, with Moberly Bell himself constantly coming down from his distant eyrie to look in.

The *Lit Supp* had been started – or such was the general belief – as a temporary weekly supplement to *The Times*, a 'makeshift' to mop up book reviews for which there was no room in the paper, because the parliamentary reports had been taking up so much space. J.R. Thursfield, a leader writer who until then had been in charge of the book reviews on *The Times*, was given editorial responsibility for the new venture, with another long-standing member of the *Times* staff, F.T. Dalton, to help him. But soon after the paper began publication, Thursfield went away for two months, and Bruce Richmond took his place. What was left unclear was what would happen when, at the end of March, the first parliamentary session of 1902 came to an end.

In his letter to Mrs Moberly Bell, Richmond recalled what he saw as the fateful moment:

Naturally, in these last few days my thoughts have gone back to the early days of the *Supplement* and its start under the encouragement of the two great men from whom I learned journalism. It is a goodish time ago now; and it is almost a shock to look at the first number with its hesitating announcement that 'During the ensuing session of Parliament' a supplement dealing with books will be published. I well remember my agitation when the last week of the session came: my relief when both your husband and Buckle, immersed in graver troubles, seemed to have forgotten to stop it: my doubts as to whether I ought to remind them, and a note I sent to your husband about it: and then his coming into the room next day at 6, as he usually did, and coasting round & round the room jingling his keys and discussing high matters with Buckle while I sat in my corner, deep in law-reports: and then, without any apparent interruption of his talk with Buckle, a sort of stage whisper as he passed me – 'If I were you, I shouldn't remind anybody.' So I reminded nobody – and here the thing is to this day.

And here the thing has been ever since. That stage whisper of Moberly Bell's, to the accompaniment of jingling keys, seems in retrospect like a mighty gust or roar – for it sent the *TLS* – as we now call it – on its way for 100 years (so far). And Bruce Richmond was to be the editor for thirty-four of those years, until his retirement on the last day of 1937.

Richmond concluded his letter to Mrs Moberly Bell with some thoughts that also take us back to those men in the editor's room in March 1902:

> But it wasn't only at the start that he [that is, Moberly Bell] stood over us. When the hard times came, I always felt I was fighting like Teucer behind the shield of Ajax: and he saved us from many deaths. Dalton and I always hoped we were making the *Supplement* the sort of thing your husband and Buckle would wish it to be. If I am led to think from your letter and from Buckle's that on the whole we have succeeded in that – well, that is for me the best part of the whole business.

Bruce Richmond had joined *The Times* in 1899. He was then a quiet, serious man of twenty-eight, who had been called to the Bar two years earlier and since then had been devilling for an editor of legal textbooks. At Winchester, when he was thirteen, he had headed the school roll, and he had subsequently gone up to New College, Oxford, where he had taken a first class in Classical Mods and a second in Greats. He was to be a constant reader of the classics, and kept a small notebook – which he left, when he died, to the publisher and author Frank Morley – in which he copied passages from Plato and Euripides both as a young man and towards the end of his life. In London, he often organised reading parties of the Greek poets among his friends, and that passing reference to Ajax and the Greek archer Teucer in his letter to Mrs Moberly Bell was absolutely characteristic of his style.

It was a regular policy of *The Times*, under Buckle and Moberly Bell, to recruit as subeditors able young men who had recently come down from the universities – generally from Oxford or Cambridge, and often from Eton or Winchester too – but at twenty-eight Richmond joined the paper at a point quite near the top. He once described the way in which he had been appointed. Writing in 1939 to Stanley Morison, who was then preparing the official history of *The Times* (and who was also in due course to become editor of the *Literary Supplement*), Richmond recalled that

> from '99 to about 1910 I worked in the editor's room with Buckle and Capper, with Bell & Chirol constantly in and out of the room – everything was done by talk – and I have practically no letters from any of them. From Bell all I ever had was a postcard in March '99 telling me to come for a month's trial. I was never appointed to anything: and did my 38 years on that postcard.

The records show that Richmond's starting salary was £33.6.8 monthly, paid from 30 April 1899. The following year it went up to £500 per annum, after a reminder from him.

Buckle, the editor of *The Times*, had had an early career very similar to Richmond's. He too had been educated at Winchester and New College, Oxford, was a classicist, and had been called to the Bar. At Oxford, he had won the Newdigate Poetry Prize, though he never afterwards showed any interest in poetry. He had also become a Fellow of All Souls. In 1884, at the age of twenty-five, he had been taken on by *The Times* as assistant editor, and at twenty-nine he had become its editor.

Since then, this brilliant, high-minded man, with his dense Victorian beard and invariable winged collar, had made himself the guardian of the paper's most exalted traditions – its learning and authority, its impartiality and independence – and, it must be added, its indifference to financial considerations. In spite of all the advances in popular journalism in the last years of the nineteenth century, by 1902 *The Times* had made no real attempt in its pages to attract new readers, or keep old ones, by anything except the seriousness of its contents. This was a policy in which Buckle was completely supported by the chief proprietor of *The Times*, Arthur Walter, a member of the fourth generation of the family which had owned the paper since it began in 1785, though it was a rather inactive family by this time.

Buckle was famous for the speed with which he could digest anything up to the most taxing blue book, his custom of reading every letter the paper received so that he would know what his readers were thinking, and his nightly routine. He would come into *The Times* office early in the evening, go home or out for dinner, return at about ten and instruct the printer what he was to print and the leader writers what they were to say, then, sustained only by siphons of soda water, would correct proofs and write letters till three or four in the morning. He had no other life, apart from his family.

Charles Frederic Moberly Bell – the other of the 'two great men' from whom Bruce Richmond declared that he 'learned journalism' – was dedicated to the interests of *The Times* with equal passion.

Buckle and he were like the captain and the chief engineer on the great ship, and possibly Moberly Bell had the greater power, since all the appointments and finances were in his hands, while the editor occupied himself exclusively with the paper's contents. Moberly Bell had worked as a young man in his father's business in Egypt, and at the same time had been a correspondent for *The Times* there, notably during General Gordon's expedition to the Sudan. Arthur Walter had met him in Cairo in 1889, and immediately invited him to come back to London as its 'assistant manager'. That, at the age of fifty-five, was the title he still had, in what we have seen was the relaxed *Times* way about such matters, but he was the all-powerful manager in everything but name.

He was a burly, energetic man, always in a flowing frock coat, though he limped as a result of an accident he had had in Egypt when he was running to catch a troop train and caught his foot in some railway points. With his typical sardonic humour, he had had the bone that was removed from his leg – the astragalus, a bone which helps to form the ankle joint – mounted as the handle of a walking stick. 'I'll make my astragalus work for me somehow,' he said.

In spite of that attitude to his bone, he admitted 'I'm a bad man to help. I have not the genius of throwing work on to other people.' In fact, he thrived on hard work – sending off telegrams and writing amusing or angry letters and talking on the telephone for long hours every day. He was very punctilious but also liked to flavour all he wrote and said with a salty humour. For instance, his bulging correspondence book for 1902 contains both a telegram to the *Times* correspondent in Peking pointing out that he had written only 1,086 words so far, and owed the paper a balance of 15,914 words; and a letter to a General Webber who wished to see the editor, pointing out that the editor could not see everyone who had a complaint to make. Bell added with zest: 'Imagine the levee of guardsmen we should have to receive!'

He, better than anyone else, knew the serious financial state that *The Times* was in. To a considerable extent, the paper's financial problems went back to the Parnell Affair in 1887–90, soon after Buckle had become editor. The paper had published some letters which it believed had been written by the Irish Nationalist politician, Charles Stewart Parnell, and which indicated that Parnell supported terrorism. When Parnell, who was an MP, protested that the letters were forgeries, the House of Commons set up a special commission to investigate the matter. *The Times* argued its case before the Commission, but Parnell was vindicated, and *The Times* had to bear the cost of almost £250,000 in legal fees – the equivalent of at least £12 million today.

Bell had worked hard to improve the finances of *The Times*. No more than Buckle or Walter did he wish to change the essential character of the paper, and he observed once that 'the better a newspaper is, the fewer people there are to buy it. The more we improve *The Times* the smaller grows the number of readers. If *The Times*, in the interests of the country, is to carry on it must be subsidised.'

But at least he set about subsidising it vigorously. His most successful venture to date had been in 1898, when *The Times* reprinted the ninth edition of the *Encyclopaedia Britannica* and sold it in twenty-five volumes for a total of £14. At the time the *Lit Supp* began, a tenth edition was under way, which would supplement the ninth with nine new volumes and an index volume. Reviews by eminent people of these new volumes would, as we shall see, occupy many pages of the *Lit Supp* in its first year. Later, another less successful venture of Moberly Bell's, the foundation of The Times Book Club, would also leave its mark on the *Literary Supplement*.

Chirol, mentioned in Richmond's letter to Mrs Moberly Bell as another regular visitor to the editor's room, was Valentine Chirol, the head of the Foreign Department, aged fifty in 1902. He, with Buckle and Moberly Bell, was one of the 'three monks' whom Lord Northcliffe came to hate after he bought *The Times* in 1908, and whom one by one he got rid of. For a very long time, though, they were *The Times* itself, flesh of its flesh and bone of its bone. Chirol himself was not such an urbane figure as the others – an uneasy, suspicious man, always glancing about him. But he had an outstanding knowledge of international affairs, which had long been the mainstay of *The Times*'s news coverage.

Chirol was of Huguenot descent, but his father was an Anglican clergyman, the curate of St Paul's, Knightsbridge. In fact all the men at the top of *The Times* had either a clerical or a classical background, and generally both. Buckle's father was Canon Buckle, who had been a Fellow of Oriel College, Oxford, and incumbent of the Oriel living of Twerton on Avon, near Bath. Moberly Bell had a second cousin on his father's side who was Bishop of Salisbury. Richmond's father was the Secretary of the Charity Commissioners. Capper, who was known as the Prince of Accuracy, and read proofs for hour after hour every night, had read Classics at Edinburgh University.

Harold Child was another important member of this group. He had been brought on to *The Times* to write light leaders – about the only concession yet made under Buckle and Moberly Bell to the changing character of newspapers – and was to be a close colleague of Richmond's on the *Lit Supp* over many years. He had been a scholar of both Winchester and Brasenose College, Oxford, and had read Greats; his father was rector of Stratton, Gloucestershire.

It was Child who described this group a few years later in a letter to Lord Northcliffe, when the new proprietor was already beginning to denounce the other-worldliness of the staff that he had bought with the paper. Child seemed able to adopt a freer, even more cheeky tone than the others with the dangerous press lord. In June 1910 he told Northcliffe, 'Some of the "monastery" spirit of Winchester has got into our blood. How can we help being a bit medieval, when our most impressionable years were spent in such a place?' One can see them all sitting there in the editor's room, working very hard, happy and at home with each other until Northcliffe came along to darken the horizon. If we extrapolate from their letters, we can even hear some of their jokes. Capper sneezes, and says it is only a *gelidum* simplex, an old-fashioned cold (*gelidum* indeed meaning 'cold' in Latin, but not the kind that makes you sneeze). Richmond, still feeling very new, says he hopes he can become a real journalist, and not just a young gent of correct and 'illegant' tastes.

Richmond was certainly in his element there. There is another surviving letter from the time when he received his honorary doctorate at Oxford, this time to Buckle himself, now long retired.

> Dear Buckle
>
> Thank you very much – it is a delight to get your letter. And, if you think the *Supplement* deserves this pat on the back from Oxford, I hope you feel concerned in it too. You know where I learned journalism. Some are of Paul, some are of Apollo's. We are of Buckle – & have tried to practise what we learnt.
>
> Yours very gratefully,
>
> Bruce L. Richmond.

But every one of the *Times* giants of 1902 was of Paul and Apollo, too.

How, then, did the *Lit Supp* actually come into being? Its creation was, in fact, more than a mere temporary stratagem for getting rid of the accumulation of book reviews on *The Times*. Another idea of Moberly Bell's some years earlier had been that *The Times* should publish a literary weekly. H.D. Traill, a journalist and writer of satirical verse, was appointed editor, and much of 1897 was taken up in discussions between Traill and Moberly Bell about the character of the new magazine. Many names were suggested, including the *Republic of Letters*, which Traill disliked because he thought it suggested 'news' rather than 'criticism', and the *Reviewer*, which he preferred. In the end the name *Literature* was chosen. Then there was the question of when it should first come out. Traill was keen to get on with it, and thought May would be a good month, 'for the season is not considered over till the beginning of June' – an important consideration, for after the season ended there would not be many people left in London, and the arrival of a new magazine would not receive much attention. Actually, it was to be the end of the year before *Literature* finally appeared.

Traill gave Moberly Bell an account of the competition they would face from other magazines, and his reasons for believing there would be a place for a new one. He thought there was a larger public looking for a serious weekly now than there had been in Matthew Arnold's day. At that time the magazines – the *Saturday Review*, the *Spectator*, the *Examiner*, the *Athenaeum* – were all serious – 'just as now they are almost all frivolous or rowdy'. What has become of that serious public? Traill asked. 'It can't all be changing to the *Spectator*, and of the others the *Examiner* has died, the *Saturday* has gone on the streets,' and though the *Athenaeum* lived on it was an 'improsperous gentleman'. He was sure there must be some public for the new magazine.

The *Athenaeum*, he considered, would be the main rival of his magazine, and with the optimism of a new editor was delighted when he discovered that the *Athenaeum* had been started to kill the *Literary Gazette* – 'and succeeded'. It was a good omen for *Literature*, he felt: he would do the same to the *Athenaeum*.

As for the aim of *Literature*, that would be 'to protect the reader from being overwhelmed by the continually increasing flood of books, and to that end to discriminate more carefully than is usual between books which deserve reviewing in the proper sense of the word, and those which do not'. He would aim at obtaining for the new magazine 'the same position of authority in its narrower sphere as that of *The Times* in its wider sphere'.

No words could express better the conception that Moberly Bell, Thursfield and Richmond had of what the *Literary Supplement* should be when its time came. *Literature* was edited by Traill until 1900, when F.T. Dalton took over the chair. It survived, losing money, until the beginning of the year 1902, when it was sold by *The Times* (for £350 in cash and £150 worth of advertisements) and incorporated with the magazine the *Academy*. The very first issue of the *Lit Supp* announced this sale on its front page, stating that *Literature* had been purchased by John Morgan Richards and that henceforth the *Academy* would be known as the *Academy and Literature*.

The simultaneous demise of *Literature* and the birth of the *Literary Supplement* was not a coincidence, as Harold Child implied in an article about the history of the *Lit Supp* that appeared in it on its fiftieth anniversary in January 1952. Letters exchanged almost daily between Moberly Bell and Thursfield in December 1901 and January 1902 show clearly that the timing was precisely planned, and that the two men were already working out the details of an ambitious new *Supplement* that would carry on where *Literature* had left off.

In fact, these letters indicate that the story that the *Supplement* was invented simply as a 'makeshift' repository for a glut of *Times* book reviews is a legend, propagated by Harold Child in that same fiftieth anniversary article. From the start, Thursfield worried about whether he could get enough material to fill his pages, and firmly stated that he did not want to resort to using reviews of books written for *The Times* the previous year. The two men also discussed whether to bring in Dalton, or another member of the *Times* staff, Harry Hamilton Fyfe, as Thursfield's assistant, and Moberly Bell pressed successfully for

Dalton. He said that Dalton had in the past given him a good deal of trouble, 'but it is only in his manner of doing things and of pressing on me innumerable ideas, some of them excellent and all of them arising from excess of zeal . . . Traill used to say "There's a lot in his coconut when you can get through the shell."'

Certainly Moberly Bell, cautious and devious as he was, was not going to commit himself very far ahead. The 'hesitating announcement' in the first number of the *Lit Supp* only promised that it would be published during the coming parliamentary session – and this would have suited him. He had to step delicately with Buckle, who seemed to be thinking of the *Supplement* as just a few spare pages into which any vaguely literary material could be thrown, and who might not want to commit himself beforehand to anything more permanent, and as separate from the main paper. Moberly Bell was also negotiating at that time with 'three fish who are nibbling at the glittering bait of *Literature*', and would not have wanted to announce plans for a new *Literary Supplement* of his own that might discourage any of them.

We can see, from Bruce Richmond's story of the fateful day, that even he believed that there was no promise of the *Literary Supplement* going on after the end of the parliamentary session – which was indeed in those months a very busy one, since the country was in the middle of the Boer War. (Some of Thursfield's letters turn from *Lit Supp* matters to condemn the British concentration camps in South Africa and deplore the military's disregard for civil liberties.)

Nevertheless, it seems that Moberly Bell intended his new supplement to be a permanent and distinguished addition to the paper. He fussed over it with all the tenderness that one shows a new-born child rather than a temporary expedient. Little though he wanted the essential character of *The Times* to change, he plainly believed that the *Lit Supp* could help its circulation, as it would be given away free with the paper – to be precise, as a supplement 'to' the paper – every week. (Indeed at one point early in 1902 he was contemplating issuing it twice a week.)

The publication of book reviews in *The Times* itself had always been very erratic. In fact, a modern newspaper executive would be astonished at the total lack of anything that might be called layout in *The Times* of 100 years ago. In particular, the outer pages, as they were called – the pages that were printed before the main news and leader pages – were an assemblage of leftover news stories and miscellaneous articles put together by the printer without any sense either of intelligible order or agreeable design – and it was in this extraordinary ragbag that, hitherto, the book reviews of *The Times* had found a home – when they found one at all.

Now, with its simply but attractively laid-out *Literary Supplement*, *The Times*, which still cost threepence, would have something completely new to offer its readers, and something that its penny rivals, the *Daily Telegraph* and the *Morning Post*, could not match. Writing to Thursfield on Christmas Eve 1901, Moberly Bell wrote (expressing sentiments familiar enough to newspapermen a century later, though in language they would not dream of): 'I find *The Times* patronised mainly by older men and alas they die & the Rehoboams come not to our coffers . . . I don't want to abandon the traditions of *The Times* but I want to move with the times.' He must have contemplated that first *Lit Supp*, issued with *The Times* that Friday morning in January, with much satisfaction and high hopes. And within a very short time he would have every reason to be pleased with it.

The *Literary Supplement* was half the size of *The Times*, so that it fitted into a copy of the main paper when that was folded in two. On the front page, the royal coat of arms appeared between the words 'The' and 'Times', which were in Gothic script, and the words 'Literary Supplement' were printed in plain type beneath them. There were three broad columns on each page, and in the first number, which carried no advertisements, a contents list appeared at the head of the first column, followed by the announcements about the sale of *Literature* and the intention to publish the 'Literary Supplement to the Times' during the parliamentary session. It would appear, the announcement said, 'as often as may be necessary to keep abreast with the more important publications of the day', but in fact it has always appeared weekly from that day to this. Later, when publishers' advertisements usually occupied the first column on the first page, the contents list came at the top of column two. The front page of *The Times* itself was then and for many years afterwards wholly given over to advertisements, but that was only to happen very rarely (usually at Christmas) on the *Lit Supp*.

In that first issue, the first book review began halfway down the first column, under the general heading of 'Literature'. In fact in this first number, all the books that were reviewed, including two novels, appeared under this general heading, both in the contents list and in the paper itself. (The other main headings were 'Science', 'Art', 'The Drama' and 'Music'.)

However, from the second number onwards, while the heading 'Literature' stood collectively above every other kind of book, novels and short story collections were normally separated off under a 'Fiction' heading of their own. So 'literature' was conceived of in a very broad way – from politics and history to travel and cookery, and indeed including the criticism of fiction – while fiction, formally at any rate, was not conceived of as part of 'literature' at all. In practice, serious fiction would be reviewed seriously in the *Literary Supplement*, especially as the century went on, but the distinction revealed that a certain puritanical attitude to fiction did still linger at *The Times* (unlike its attitude to poetry, which would be sometimes almost too reverential).

The first book reviewed that week was *More Letters of Edward Fitzgerald*. The publisher was Macmillan, and the price 5 shillings. Giving the price was an innovation – book reviews in *The Times* hitherto had not mentioned that lowly detail, though it did appear in the lists of new books that the paper regularly published. The reviewer was Augustine Birrell, who had been a Liberal MP and barrister, and had won a literary reputation for himself with a volume of entertaining essays called *Obiter Dicta* in 1889, though his critics invented the word 'Birrelling' to mean a kind of 'literary flute-playing'. Later he was to become President of the Board of Education, and then Chief Secretary for Ireland, but lost the latter job unceremoniously when the Easter Rising of 1916 took this flute-player completely by surprise. Interestingly enough, Traill had with some pride got him to write the first of a series of signed columns in the first issue of *Literature*. Were Richmond and his colleagues following Traill consciously in getting Birrell to write the first review in the *Lit Supp*? At any rate, his article in both cases served as something of a guide to readers as to what they were going to get in the new paper.

In *Literature*, Birrell had written of the importance of book reviewing being honest and impartial, without favours to friends. Now, in the *Literary Supplement*, his opening paragraph set out a view of literary success that suggested the way *The Times* would look at the matter. The doors of the Temple of Literary Fame 'swing easily backwards and forwards, and let authors in and out easily enough', wrote Birrell. 'No visible authority presides over this double operation. There are no elections to this Academy . . . The thing settles itself.' This might have suggested that there was not even a role for the new *Lit Supp*! But what it suggested more subtly was that literature was for keen general readers, not for specialists, and that though the new paper would be scholarly and critical, its role would above all be like that of an educated reader, helping other such readers to find the books that were most worth reading.

The rest of the review by Birrell exemplified that role in action, bringing out the charm of the famous recluse's letters with many a literary allusion of the reviewer's own – 'In the essentially ridiculous Fitzgerald greatly delighted, and was as fond as Macaulay of a really bad book. He would copy out the absurd advertisement of a tradesman for the amusement of a friend as conscientiously as if the nonsense were a favourite bit of his beloved Crabbe' – and in its last sentence Birrell struck the policy note firmly again: this volume 'will be added to their libraries by all lovers of good letters and independent thinking'.

Birrell of course reviewed the book anonymously, as would all the other reviewers for the next seventy-five years, except in such special cases as when the book was published by *The Times* itself. Nevertheless the identity of the reviewers would be known to numerous people. Many of the *Lit Supp* reviewers were members of the Athenaeum Club, as were many of the *Times* staff and, no doubt, some of those educated readers with libraries, and they all had plenty of other social connections with one another. So giving Birrell the first review was a decision that would not have passed unnoticed. Oddly enough, though, he never wrote for the *Lit Supp* again: perhaps he did not like anonymity himself.

The second review in this first number was by Sir Henry Craik, an allegedly irascible old civil servant of very conservative opinions who had been Secretary to the Scottish Education Department in Whitehall for the past fourteen years and had been knighted for his good work there. His father had been Moderator of the General Assembly of the Church of Scotland, and he himself would eventually become MP for Glasgow and Aberdeen University, and a baronet. He was said to write his own books on Scottish history between 11 and 2.30 at night, and the book he reviewed was very much in his field, *Scottish Men of Letters in the Eighteenth Century*, by Henry Grey Graham. Richmond throughout his editorship was to apply this principle of employing appropriate reviewers, even though they were supposed to write not just for other specialists but for general readers too.

Craik was not particularly irascible in this review, but had a firmness of critical tone that echoed throughout the first number, and continued to go on doing in the years ahead. Craik found Graham's book 'eminently readable' – but, he added, 'we confess to missing in Mr Graham's pages any attempt to estimate the real worth of the literary work of the men whose personal traits he has drawn with so facile a pen'.

Altogether the first issue comprised eight pages, with eleven reviews under the heading 'Literature'. Thursfield hinted ironically at a certain dullness in a work of rural history, *Scenes of Rural Life in Hampshire*, by the Rector of Bramshott, W.W. Capes. He observed in his review that there was 'fine and mature scholarship' in the book, if not 'the pen of a Green or a Macaulay'. But, he added glancingly, the rector 'would perhaps disdain to be as interesting as they condescend to be'. Those *Times* men could be quite catty.

On the other hand, Alexander Innes Shand, a seventy-year-old military historian and journalist who had written for *The Times* for many years, was unstinting in his commendation of a study entitled *Napoleon's Polish Campaign, 1806–7* by F. Loraine Petre, saying it was 'difficult to overpraise'. Chirol, the foreign editor, gave judicious approval to a study of the Chinese mind, *The Lore of Cathay*, by W.A.P. Martin, president of the Chinese Imperial University, while J.D. Rees, who had retired from the Indian civil service the previous year at the age of forty-seven, attacked a book by William Digby, *Prosperous British India: A Revelation*, saying that the author gives 'elaborate statistics designed to show that our system sucks the life-blood out of India', but 'only has an eye for the demerits of the system'. This was the first of innumerable reviews that would appear in the years ahead expressing a faith in the future of the British Empire.

The other reviews under 'Literature' were a round-up of six volumes of 'Recent Verse' by a classicist and former fellow of Brasenose, now working for *The Times*, T.H. Ward, who had nothing very striking to say about the books, but reminded the poet W.E. Henley that an article in which he had attempted to diminish the fame of Robert Louis Stevenson had 'inspired intense repugnance'; reviews of a book on the life of the clergy, and of a reprint of Leigh Hunt's book about Kensington in the eighteenth century; and short reviews of two light novels, *Sons of the Swords* by Mrs Woods (no further identification given) and *The Velvet Glove* by Seton Merriman. The novel reviews were by a swashbuckling thirty-two-year-old then working as Buckle's secretary, Harry Hamilton Fyfe, the man who had been considered for Dalton's post. Later in the year he went to edit the *Morning Advertiser*, the journal of the Licensed Victuallers' Association, and after being spotted by Northcliffe became a famous war correspondent, besides writing novels himself.

For the first year or two the *Literary Supplement* also took over from *The Times* its surveys of current music, science and other subjects, and as has been indicated, there were some of these in the first number. A survey of 'Science in 1901' was contributed by Hugh Monro Ross, who was working on Moberly Bell's new supplementary volumes of the *Encyclopaedia Britannica*. He declared that the most exciting discovery in 1901 had been the discovery of a new and brilliant star in Perseus, discussed the imminent prospect of wireless telegraphy across the Atlantic, and feared that the increase in underground railways would lead to the subsoil of the City of London becoming 'a solid mass of iron tubes'. The assistant music critic of *The Times*, Robin Legge, said that there had been more British music in 1901, and praised Elgar's *Pomp and Circumstance* as 'a spirited and vivid march', while Ward, the reviewer of the poetry, also praised an etching of Vermeer's *View of Delft* that had just gone on sale. (It was just a year later, incidentally, that Marcel Proust saw the painting itself in The Hague, and 'recognised it for the most beautiful painting in the world'.)

But the most important of these 'arts' pieces was by the *Times* theatre critic, A.B. Walkley. Walkley was to prove himself the star of the first years of the *Lit Supp*, not only in his theatre reviews and articles, but also in book reviews. He was a discovery made by Richmond a couple of years before, and that episode is described by Richmond in the PS of a letter he wrote not long before his death to the *Times* librarian, J.S. Maywood. It gives, incidentally, a very good picture of the atmosphere of the editor's room at night:

> In 1900, or thereabouts, there was a vacancy for a dramatic critic: and I had (with some difficulty) persuaded Moberly Bell and Buckle to try 'A.B.W. of the *Star*'. His first trial was Tree's revival of King John (a bit of bad luck as ABW was never quite at ease with W.S.). It was Buckle's habit, when the night's work was over, to grub about among the proofs that Capper and I had grappled with – and I heard a loud 'What is all this about inspissated gloom?' Not having Dr Johnson at my fingers' end, I made a poor defence – and went home rather discouraged.
>
> Almost immediately, however, ABW got his chance with a ridiculous American drama of 'high life' with a much-boomed incompetent American actress – the grubbing among the proofs was punctuated with shouts of Homeric laughter – and thereafter he went from strength to strength.
>
> What a PS! These tedious old men!

'W.S.' there was of course William Shakespeare; 'Tree' was the actor-manager Beerbohm Tree, and 'inspissated gloom' was Dr Johnson's phrase for the kind of 'thickened darkness' that Shakespeare tried to create in the night scenes of Macbeth.

In this first issue of the *Lit Supp* Walkley actually had three pieces under the heading 'The Drama'. The first was a general article called 'New Theatrical Demands', which argued with his usual pungency that the drama must always appeal first and foremost to the pleasure of the senses: 'To look to the drama for the pleasure of the novel or the pleasure of sheer dialectic is like trying to extract sunbeams from cucumbers.' This was a credo of Walkley's that would often reoccur in his contributions to the *Lit Supp*. Next came a book review – the twelfth and last in the issue. The book was *Shakespeare as a Dramatic Artist*, a history of Shakespeare criticism by Thomas R. Lounsbury, a professor at Yale, and it gave Walkley another chance to make his point. The book had some good qualities, being erudite without being pedantic, but it took the 'bookman's' view of theatrical history, always seeing it as a history of printed texts and opinions, 'never in the constitution of audiences and the actual machinery of playhouses'.

Finally there was a review of a new play at the Avenue Theatre, an adaptation for the stage of Lord Lytton's novel *Eugene Aram*, the story of a sympathetic murderer. It had too many long speeches for Walkley – but he showed his gift for responding to the sensuous on the stage by declaring that Martin Harvey, who played the murderer, 'contrives to put more fateful expression into a walk than any other pair of mortal legs could bear'.

The *Lit Supp*'s first issue ended with three features that would continue in much the same form for many years, and in each case in the same pair of hands. There was a list of new books and reprints which Dalton, rather humbled, was in charge of, and which, once it got going properly, claimed to include details of every book published in Great Britain. This really meant 'every book received for review at *The Times*' and probably even some of those were omitted, by accident or design. Nevertheless it was to become a remarkable list, with short notes appended to many of the books – a colossal labour for Dalton. At the paper it has always been referred to as 'the graveyard'.

F.A. Mumby, who was later to write a classic work on bookselling, contributed notes on forthcoming books. He was able to announce that good progress was being made with Professor Joseph Wright's *English Dialect Dictionary*, and that new volumes in the *English Men of Letters* series would include Leslie Stephen on Hobbes and Augustine Birrell on Hazlitt. Finally there was a chess column, with a problem and some answers to correspondents, who must have written to *The Times*. A letter from Moberly Bell a fortnight later addressed the columnist, S. Tinley, very sternly. 'If there is a single error in the problems they will be stopped,' he wrote. There was to be 'no flummery about "pleasant

Chapter Two

The First Year: 1902

The new supplement of *The Times* was an immediate success. By 9 February, Moberly Bell was already having to fend off a request for free copies from a German professor, telling him that he would have to pay 15 shillings for the next fifty issues of *The Times* containing the *Literary Supplement*, and adding with his usual tart humour that 'we really cannot give away our paper to all friends of England even though their number may not be large'.

In the same month he was telling another correspondent that 'the idea has taken well with literary people who like to know where they may be certain of getting literary news and to get it in a handy form. It also of course lightens the body of the general paper and attracts a special class of advts.'

Publishers' advertisements in fact started appearing in the second issue, and the first column on the first page quickly established itself as a prime site, with the publisher Macmillan one of those leading the way. By June, Frederick Macmillan was writing personally to Moberly Bell that 'I hear the highest commendation of it on every side, and always look forward to Friday's *Times* with unusual interest.'

But there had already been changes on the editorial side. After a month in the editor's chair, Thursfield had gone off for two months, as has been noticed, on a previously arranged holiday – and this was the moment when Bruce Richmond came to the fore.

In his correspondence with Thursfield about Fyfe and Dalton the previous December, Moberly Bell had already mentioned Richmond. 'The sort of man I should like for the post [of assistant to Thursfield] and who may be able to give you valuable help,' he wrote on 12 December, 'is Richmond, who has a really sound judgment on art and music with a very fair knowledge and thorough appreciation of literature.'

On 19 December, he replied to a letter from Thursfield which complained about Buckle's inclination to regard the new pages of the supplement as 'a sort of omnium gatherum into which he could discharge literary and other cognate matter for which he could find no room in other parts of the paper'. 'I don't think you need be discouraged by Buckle's attitude,' he wrote,

It is what I expected at the beginning but we shall be able gradually to change it. Richmond is back and I have very great faith in his quiet, unobtrusive and tactful influence on B in matters literary, musical or artistic.

In fact I shall try & make the fact of your going away an excuse for his delegating to Richmond the editorial control – that is to say, Richmond will be the sort of medium between the Editor & Dalton. The fact that R is continually in the same room as B will give him certain advantages at the starting which you in another room or at Berkhamsted [where Thursfield lived] could not have, and I hope that by the time you get back you will find all running smoothly.

In his biography of Moberly Bell, F. Harcourt Kitchin, who worked with them all on the business side of *The Times*, says that the *Literary Supplement* was actually Richmond's idea. There is no other evidence for that, but reading between the lines of Moberly Bell's letters, I believe that his idea from the start was that Richmond should become the editor of it.

Certainly the young Richmond took full command, and very effectively, within weeks of the launch of the supplement. His conduct of the paper was welcomed by Capper, who was still the number two on *The Times*, in a long letter that he wrote to Moberly Bell on 11 May:

My dear Bell,

Very briefly, what I wanted to say about the *Lit Supplement* was this – During these weeks that Richmond has been taking charge of it, it has begun to make its mark, I believe, among literary people in a way to reflect credit upon *The Times*, and once again to earn for it the beginnings of a literary prestige – How far such prestige would prove, if thoroughly established, to be of cash value to us I don't pretend to discuss – but at least it is a good thing to secure – & if we are to run a *Literary Supplement* at all we ought if possible to run it on lines that will serve this end. Richmond has run it on those lines & with a measure of success that has steadily increased.

The reason of his success is this – that he has regarded it as an organic – or at any rate an artistic whole – an organism in which he has aimed at maintaining, not merely as high a standard of excellence as possible in the individual articles, but, beyond that, a suitable variety of interest & a balance of parts in each issue as a whole.

However, like many journalists, Capper could not praise one colleague without criticising another. He continued:

Dalton entirely fails to grasp this principle & is utterly incapable of carrying it out; and Thursfield, perhaps from different causes, must, I fear, be regarded for practical purposes as equally unable to produce the required result. If you cross examine Richmond tonight about the history of the production of the last number of the *Supplement* you will get some light upon what I mean – ask him in particular his personal views upon the insertion of the review of Brassey's 'Naval Annual', and what was at the last moment selected for omission to make room for it, & the 'principles' upon which that selection was made.

If the *Lit Suppt*, after having trodden the first few steps in the upward path I have endeavoured to describe, so that people to whom such things appeal – (I take Ainger as a representative of the class I mean, for I had a few words on the subject with him at the Royal Lit. Fund dinner) – have begun to look out for it with pleasure & with the expectation of finding *good work*, upon subjects *well chosen*, & adjusted in *well-balanced variety*, *now* falls back to become a mere chance assortment of so many columns of more or less 'literary' matter, a convenient dumping ground for superfluous columns of *The Times* to suit Buckle's convenience, or yours, or anybody else's – then I think it might as well be abolished at once for all the real good it is likely to do.

Of course, in the long run, I fully recognise, its existence must depend on cash considerations, & the connexion between these & the views I have been setting forth I have neither leisure nor competence to discuss here.

One more thing I want to add – It has no direct bearing on the rest of this hurried letter. I have an uneasy impression that I told you not long ago, in answer to your questioning, that I doubted whether Richmond would ever be able to *edit* the Paper, however good a *second* he might be. If so, I wish to withdraw that expression of opinion. My respect for his judgment, his grip of principles & his capacity to direct has much increased of late, & especially since I have watched the way in which he has gone about the *Lit Supplement* work. The qualities he has shown I am convinced are capable of wider application than to purely literary work.

Yrs ever JBC.

Richmond was never to edit *The Times* (which is what Capper meant by his capitalised phrase 'the Paper'), but this letter certainly described intelligently what Richmond was beginning to make of the *Literary Supplement*. If he heard about the letter, he must have been glad of Capper's support – in spite of the scent of office politics (and even, perhaps, of fear of what Richmond's future power might be) that one detects in Capper's words, and in spite, too, of his somewhat patronising attitude towards 'the literary'. 'Ainger', the representative of the literary 'class' whom Capper met at the Royal Literary Fund dinner, was Alfred Ainger, a canon of Bristol and a popular preacher, who had written a life of Charles Lamb – less of a recommendation, perhaps, than Capper realised, though Ainger was later in the year asked to review a book about Lamb for the paper.

This letter of Capper's, although dated only '11 May' without a year, can be firmly assigned to 1902 through the reference to the review of Brassey's *Naval Annual*. And it seems as though Richmond continued to be effectively the editor after Thursfield returned from his holiday. Harold Child's January 1952 article on the history of the paper (which was actually written in 1939 for Stanley Morison's history of *The Times*, but not used) records that the *Literary Supplement* 'was issued for a short time under the editorship of J.R. Thursfield, and then for nearly forty years under Bruce Richmond'.

However, Thursfield remained at least nominally the editor until 18 May 1903, when Bell wrote a formal letter to him stating that

Mr Walter has asked me to write to you to say that he thinks the time has come when we ought to make a rearrangement of your work and salary. His memorandum to me suggests that you should be relieved of all the duties of editorship of the *Literary Supplement*, that you should confine yourself to writing occasional reviews for it, to leading articles that can be written without night attendance and to general articles and advice on naval matters . . . You will I am sure acquit me of anything but regret at having to make a notification which is not wholly pleasant.

Thursfield does not seem to have been particularly unhappy at the decision. When he first took on the editorship, he had already expressed some regret that he would have to come in from Berkhamsted for more than his accustomed two days a week, and after his dismissal his letters to Moberly Bell were perfectly friendly and mainly concerned with his salary. He eventually became a notable naval authority, while his son became an admiral. As for Bruce Richmond, without any formal change being made, he was now incontrovertibly the editor.

Throughout 1902, more and more new contributors were brought in to the paper to produce 'a suitable variety of interests'. They fall, very loosely, into three groups, a division that continued to apply to the *Lit Supp* reviewing team for a long time to come. There were the *Times* leader writers, most of whom went on contributing, but less frequently than in the first few months. There were the other professional journalists and reviewers of the extensive and ever-changing Edwardian world of newspapers and magazines, who made their living in a variety of ways, often fairly hand-to-mouth. Finally, there were the scholars and learned statesmen and church leaders, from whom Richmond soon became very good at extracting weighty opinions and arguments.

Running like a backbone through the *Lit Supp* in 1902 was the series of long, signed reviews of the new, supplementary volumes of the *Encyclopaedia Britannica*. Moberly Bell took it upon himself to invite the people who had been chosen to review these publications that were so dear to his managerial heart, and of course their names appeared in due course at the head of their reviews since it was important that these should be seen to be authoritative and independent. In a letter of 9 October 1902, to Sir Michael Foster, the Professor of Physiology at Cambridge, he asked him if he would review the seventh of the new volumes and gave the line-up: 'Professor Case, Lord Avebury, Lord Davey, Mr Bryce and Senator Lodge have reviewed the five volumes already published, the Lord Chancellor is doing the next, and the remaining three we hope will be done by yourself, the Bishop of Ripon and Lord Wolseley.'

These reviews, the first eight of which appeared during 1902, give a very good idea of many of the issues discussed and points of view that were to recur in the paper in its first few years. The first of them, on 2 May, by Thomas Case, Waynflete Professor of Moral and Metaphysical Philosophy at Oxford since 1889, set the scene by surveying the 'changes of the last 25 years under their chief heads'. Case was in many ways well placed to do this for the paper. He was a deeply conservative man, known both as an opponent of the education of women and a singer of 'merry old songs' in college, yet he regarded himself (as did many men of his time) as a 'Palmerstonian Liberal' or, one might say, a cautious progressive. Buckle, Bell and Richmond would all have thought his opinions worth listening to, though they would doubtless not have agreed with all of them. At any rate, he set a kind of agenda for the new organ in his long article.

Case began with 'the opening up of the world', citing the 'transit of the deserts of Asia' and the 'penetration of the African interior'. Consequently, he wrote, 'human affairs have suddenly assumed a cosmopolitan aspect'. The 'most ominous' outcome of these changes he believed was that England and Russia were now face to face at three vital points – in the north of Afghanistan, the north of China and the north of Persia.

On this point Case's fears were out of keeping with most of the other writers on foreign affairs in the *Lit Supp* at this time, who, as we shall see, already regarded the greatest danger to British interests as coming from Austria-Hungary and Germany. (Incidentally, the contributors at this time almost invariably use the name 'England' for their country, not 'Great Britain' or 'the United Kingdom'.)

Turning to 'scientific discovery' and 'industry' as his next two heads, Case hailed the increase in corn production in India and South America and the development of mining in the Klondike and the Transvaal, as well as the spread of irrigation, roads, railways and telegraphs. But he deplored both the increasing adulteration of food, and the abuse of trade union power, leading to intimidation and the scamping of work. On that 'abuse' he could have been sure of the agreement of most of the voices on the *Lit Supp*, even of those, and they were not a few, who were champions of the working man. Trades unionism – and, even more, the precepts of socialism – were still objects of deep suspicion to the English upper classes.

When it came to 'fine art', Case has little to say in favour of the changes during the previous quarter of a century. 'Democracy makes art popular,' he conceded, 'but popularity vulgarises the arts.' This was an issue that would often, not surprisingly, be debated in the *Lit Supp*, but Case had no doubt where he stood. Music had gone from 'moderated melody and taste' to 'vulgar extremes of levity and bombast', and architecture was now 'an anarchy of style', with design sacrificed to decoration. (I am rather afraid he was thinking of those beautiful 'sweetness and light' houses of the turn of the century.) As for church restoration, that subject of such concern in late Victorian England, he himself liked to dabble in it, and had taken some part in the work on St Mary's in the High at Oxford, quarrelling with the official architect. He took his opportunity here to declare that 'professionals have spoilt far more churches than amateurs with their so-called restorations'.

His main point under 'literature' was: 'May classical literature and archaeology long survive among us!' Under 'morals and religion' he commented that 'an age so cosmopolitan is naturally charitable to toleration, even to the extent of believing that anything is to be tolerated'. He regretted the 'decline of domesticity and discipline, unexpected results of the emancipation of the fair sex', while he thought that moral philosophy itself was 'lost in vagueness, scepticism and paradox'.

His last two heads were 'foreign policy' and 'domestic policy'. On the first he would have found the widest agreement with his views among fellow contributors to the paper, since he thought that the main goal of British foreign policy should be the creation of an imperial federation. This view of Britain's future comes up again and again in the *Lit Supp* in the years before the First World War, not only in reviews but even in poems. At home, finally, Case dryly observed that 'Gladstone, as the head of the Liberals' – who were very obviously not Case's Liberals – 'was the first to avow the policy of judging the interests of a country by the wishes of the people'. Case ended with a warning to his readers that the more the people's wishes came first, the more important the state would also get – a good 'old Liberal' note to conclude with.

Case's views, then, provided a kind of programme of ideas almost at the inception of the new paper against which the ideas of later reviewers can be set. Some of them still find echoes, of course, in the *TLS* today!

The entries in the supplementary volumes of the *Encyclopaedia* ran through them from A to Z, and the other reviewers simply picked out articles relevant to their own interests and discussed those. The range of these reviewers shows what power the new paper commanded.

The second *Encyclopaedia* reviewer, in May, was Lord Avebury, whose mentor as a boy had been his father's friend Charles Darwin, and whose house, High Elms, in Kent was a great meeting place for scientists and statesmen; he was soon afterwards to establish the early closing day for shops and the August bank holiday, which was christened 'St Lubbock's Day'. His volume contained the article on 'Bacteria', and he observed that 'the study of bacteria will perhaps do most to reduce the sad sum of human suffering'. But he expressed agreement with Professor Case about trades unions, arguing that 'if there had been no strikes, our manufactures would have been more flourishing, and wages would have been higher'. He also echoed, perhaps rather smugly, Moberly Bell's joke about Britain having few friends, and gave the reason: 'That the wealth of Great Britain should so greatly surpass that of other nations seems to the non-British mind a violation of the laws of nature.' That wealth was indeed a reality in 1902.

Lord Davey, a judge who had been a Liberal MP known in the House for qualifying and guarding every statement he made, wrote a rather dull piece on the third volume, while the fourth was reviewed briskly by the Conservative MP, James Bryce, at that time President of the Board of Trade. Bryce picked out Leslie Stephen's prefatory essay to the volume on 'The Growth of Toleration': he agreed with Case that the age was more tolerant, but in his unsentimental way judged that 'the change is due not so much to charity as to uncertainty'.

Reviewing the fifth volume, the Massachusetts Senator, Henry Cabot Lodge, complained about English ignorance of other countries, and welcomed the inclusion of some American and Continental writers in the *Encyclopaedia* – at least it informed English readers about 'what they think' abroad, he thought.

Next came the Lord Chancellor, identified only as such; it was assumed that *Times* readers would know who he was (in fact, he was an elderly, uncompromising Conservative, Lord Halsbury). He selected various legal topics, dwelling on the fact that American courts could discuss their country's constitution, whereas with us it was only Parliament which could do that. Sir Michael Foster did, as Moberly Bell had hoped, review the seventh volume, rather optimistically predicting the end of war, because science would enable us to predict accurately the outcome of any war, and 'no nation will spend its money in a fight which it knows that it must lose'. What would happen to a nation which found itself in that unhappy position he did not dwell on.

The last volume to be reviewed in 1902 was also by the man Moberly Bell had hoped for, the Bishop of Ripon, who appeared in the issue of 12 December and turned his review into a Christmas sermon that ended in a more hard-headed and practical way than it seemed to begin: 'The world has needs; the nation has needs. We must redeem the rising generation, who are in danger of growing up feeble, rickety and ill-nourished.'

* * *

Foreign policy loomed large in the *Times Literary Supplement* in its early years. One of the most distinguished figures among Richmond's regular, anonymous reviewers, though his name is virtually forgotten today, was Sir Rowland Blennerhasset – a far-thinking Liberal MP in his sixties. In 1867 he had started a liberal Roman Catholic journal, the *Chronicle*, and was a supporter of a 'reasoned imperialism' for Britain and Home Rule for Ireland. He was a friend of Bismarck and also of many French politicians, and for a number of years Richmond gave him many of the books on foreign policy to review.

In the third issue of the paper we find him reviewing a French book on Austria-Hungary, on which he wrote: 'In proportion as the decay of the Turkish Empire becomes less likely to provoke a general war, the condition of things in Austria-Hungary becomes more and more threatening to the peace of Europe.' In October Sir Rowland returned to the theme in a review of *The Enemies of England* by the Hon. George Peel: 'At present, undoubtedly the most hostile of all Powers to England is the new German Empire.' This was how, presciently, many Englishmen saw the likely shape of things to come and in November Hugh Blakiston of *The Times* foreign department, reviewing a German collection of the Emperor's speeches called *Kaiserreden*, added a warning: in his 'aspirations after Germanic world-power, the Emperor represents a force of public opinion in his Empire with which the statesmen of other countries have to reckon'.

As for the British Empire, it was mainly in poetry that that institution was celebrated in the *Lit Supp* in 1902. This was the year in which Cecil Rhodes died (26 March), the South African War (*The Times* did not yet call it the Boer War) ended (31 May), and Edward VII was crowned (9 August). All of these events inspired verses that the paper published.

The first poem ever to appear in its pages was by Harold Begbie, a thirty-one-year-old novelist and journalist. It was called, with a touch of William Morris mediaevalism, 'Witenagemot', and was a sarcastic attack, strongly reminiscent of Kipling, on MPs. The poet contrasted 'that schoolgirl bickering that tweaks the air' in Parliament with the deeds of 'the great proconsuls who weave/The woof of empery on distal coasts' while MPs were just 'blowing wine-glass epigrams to fate'. 'We spare/Our wisest to our boundaries' he says – he is thinking of Cromer in Egypt and Milner in South Africa – and he believes 'the sense of new-born Empire' calls them not, as you might expect, to stay at their posts but to come home. Although offering some good phrase-making it was rather an absurd poem.

In the issue of 4 April, the week after Rhodes's death, there appeared a poem (by A. Cochrane, but anonymous like Begbie's) about his burial saying that

> *He sleeps beneath another sky*
> *Sleeps in the trackless waste that seems,*
> *Lonely and vast, to testify*
> *To his illimitable dreams.*

Those were also, of course, dreams of empire.

As for the Coronation, the original plan that it should take place on 26 June obliged the *Lit Supp* to come out on Wednesday, 25 June, instead of Friday, 27 June. *The Times* printing presses, it was anticipated, would be needed at the end of the week for more majestic matter. However, at the last minute the King was taken ill with inflammation of the bowels, the foreign guests went home, and the Coronation was postponed until August. Earlier in June the critic John Cann Bailey, who was to be one of Richmond's favourite reviewers for many years, wrote about the 'Coronation Ode' that had been published in anticipation of the event by William Watson. Bailey said the 'Ode' provided 'the right words for the voice of a great nation rejoicing in its strength', but also reminded its readers of 'the solemn tenure on which we hold the glories of our vast inheritance'. He was less enthusiastic in July about the 'Coronation Ode' of the Canadian poet Bliss Carman, finding lines such as 'There are joybells over England, there are flags on London town' lacking in literary qualities; but, always sympathetic to the manly virtues, he granted that it was 'strong, healthy verse'. Finally on 8 August, the day before the Coronation, the paper had another try and published a poem on a poem – a six-line poem by Richard Watson Gilder of New York about Watson's 'Coronation Ode', which declared that 'In this proud pageant of Imperial verse/ Is crowned the King indeed.' *The Times* staff must have fervently hoped that on the morrow would be crowned the King indeed, and that they would not have to come back to the subject a third time. But all went well, even if many of the foreign guests had not returned.

Meanwhile on 11 July there had been a poem 'To Lord Kitchener' by James Rhoades, a schoolmaster-poet well known for his translations of Virgil, which was specifically about the South African War, saying that during the war (in which Kitchener had created concentration camps for the Boers) he had been a 'Doer of deeds, word-sparer', but that when peace came 'out-flashed in magnanimity the Man'.

After this orgy of imperial sentiment, the *Lit Supp* published very few poems for many years. One other reflection of the Boer War came in its signed review, by the American naval captain Alfred Mahan, of the second volume of *The Times History of the War in Southern Africa*, edited by L.S. Amery, in which Mahan said that the main lesson it taught was Britain's 'unpreparedness for war'. It was a pity, perhaps, that in this ultra-imperial year there also should appear a contribution (on 16 May) from T.H. Warren, the President of Magdalen College, who had a passion for Virgil and Tennyson, doubting if the arrival of Rhodes Scholars from the English-speaking lands abroad would be a good influence on Oxford. He feared that a second-rate and provincial medical school would be created in the University in their interest – and 'Will not Greek be abolished to suit them?' Richmond, it seems, was amused to publish this dissident voice from the Oxford heartland.

Domestic politics received less attention in the *Lit Supp* than imperial and foreign affairs. The main paper took care of home matters. But in July a graceful compliment (with a touch of humour) was paid to the new Prime Minister, Arthur Balfour, who had taken the reins of the Conservative government from Lord Salisbury between the aborted and the successful coronations. At the end of that month, a volume of Balfour's essays on non-political subjects appeared, and a Liberal MP and historian, Herbert W. Paul, was invited to review it. He praised Balfour, commenting that 'the Handel essay shows how much, besides golf, he has sacrificed to politics'. Quite a number of Liberal MPs contributed to the *Lit Supp* in these first years, but Balfour remained a hero to it.

The generally independent line of *The Times* on party politics appeared in a review of a book on labour legislation contributed by Arthur Shadwell on 14 April. Shadwell was a striking and unusual figure on *The Times*, to which he had been a contributor on working-class conditions and illness for ten years and would be appointed industrial correspondent in 1908. He was an Oxford graduate and a medical doctor, but he dressed in tweeds and boots, had an untidy grey beard, and spoke his mind plainly and often irascibly – not a typical *Times* man. Nevertheless the views he expressed in the *Lit Supp* reflected the opinions on industrial relations that could be found in the main paper.

Shadwell complained that capital and labour in Britain were now 'at each other's throats'. The trades unions were 'rampantly aggressive' while 'capital makes no serious effort to come to terms'. The ideal for labour relations that he set out was 'a community of interest translated into some form of profit-sharing or payment by results'. That, said Shadwell, was practicable socialism – unlike what he mocked as 'LCC socialism', the kind of radical socialism that could be found among the extreme left of the London County Council and its successor, the Greater London Council. (Meanwhile Shadwell's own happy vision has never come to pass.)

Historical scholarship was strong in these first years of the twentieth century. Richmond brought in one of its outstanding exponents, F.W. Maitland, the great historian of the laws of England, now Downing Professor at Cambridge, to review *Tribal Custom in Anglo-Saxon Law* by Frederic Seebohm. One sentence of his review wonderfully reflects the meticulously detailed criticism for which the *Lit Supp* was to become famous: 'He seems to have neglected certain texts which give the ox in England the low value of 30 pence.' However Richmond did less well in choosing a reviewer for a major historical work that appeared in June, Charles Oman's *History of the Peninsular War*. Richmond's choice fell on Sir Herbert Maxwell, a baronet who by his own admission had spent three years of 'insensate indolence' at Eton and had failed his responsions (or entrance examination) at Oxford, but had subsequently pulled himself together and become an MP and amateur historian. Richmond throughout his career as editor liked to blend the academic and the non-academic writers in his pages, something he could do the more easily since they were all anonymous, but this time he made a bad mistake. Maxwell complained patriotically that Oman had criticised the great commanders in the war too severely, and also disputed Oman's criticisms of Napier, the earlier historian of the Peninsular War. Oman answered Maxwell's criticisms in detail in a devastating letter, and Maxwell was obliged to make a grovelling reply.

What though, about the more strictly 'literary' subjects the paper dealt with at the beginning of its history, and the reviewers Richmond brought in to write about them? They are the subjects that naturally loom largest in the paper in Richmond's day, as they have done ever since. At the beginning of the twentieth century, though, there was a particular wealth of new editions of the earlier English writers, and books such as the highly successful *English Men of Letters* series about them. For years to come they were to provide material for first, or 'lead', reviews. One important reason for their proliferation was the steady increase in the number of English departments, with their professorial heads, in the universities both old and new. The undergraduates needed the books, the professors wrote them, and the *Lit Supp* considered their merits.

All three categories of contributors wrote reviews in this field – the scholars, the 'literary men' (some of whom would have been too modest to call themselves 'men of letters', though they were generally highly educated and very well read), and the leader writers, many of whom were men of notable intellectual calibre.

The one major academic figure who featured in the paper's literary columns in 1902 was Arthur Quiller-Couch, who not only wrote anonymously in the *Lit Supp*, but also wrote pseudonymously elsewhere, and was known to the reading public simply as 'Q'. He had won fame (and wealth) in 1900 with his anthology *The Oxford Book of English Verse*, which is still selling steadily 100 years later. He had also worked on a Liberal weekly, the *Speaker*, and written poetry and some popular light novels. He was another Oxford classics graduate, and only a self-taught scholar in English literature – nothing very unusual in 1902, when there were still so few university English departments, and those concentrated on philology – but he was a genial and incisive man, and though happiest in his native Cornwall, he would be appointed King Edward VII Professor of English at Cambridge by the Liberal government in 1912, after being knighted two years earlier.

The life of the jobbing journalists and reviewers of the turn of the century was well caught in some verses by Charles Graves on E.V. Lucas. Lucas soon became a contributor to the *Lit Supp* and went on writing regularly for it until he became a publisher. (He had begun as a bookseller in Brighton.)

> 'Tis somewhere about '92
> That Lucas burning to enlighten
> An audience fitter and less few
> Packed up his traps and quitted Brighton.
> He gravitated to the Strand,
> That haunt of impecunious scholars,
> And straightway joined the struggling band
> Who drive the painful quill for dollars . . .
> You know the sequel; how he took
> To Lamb and Punch, a dreadful diet,
> And published every month a book
> Until his system craved for quiet . . .

The 'dreadful diet' referred to the fact that Lucas wrote for *Punch* among other magazines, and like Ainger had written a book on Charles Lamb. There is a further glimpse in Graves's book of the dinners of scallops at Lucas's London house, with Joseph Conrad, James Barrie and G.K. Chesterton sometimes among the guests, while Lucas's own book *Reading, Writing and Remembering* gives us a touching portrait of one of the other *Lit Supp* stalwarts, Thomas Seccombe, who had slaved on the *Dictionary of National Biography* as assistant editor to Sidney Lee from 1891 up to the publication of the final volume in 1900, and who unfortunately lived far away in Acton. 'Seccombe', wrote Lucas, 'seemed to me the most overworked man in London, yet always had time to fan a new enthusiasm or to write a long letter. He was kindly and informative, and other contributors to the DNB liked to sit next to him' when they were all working in the British Museum reading room. They would go off to lunch together at the Vienna Café in New Oxford Street.

Then there was Andrew Lang, a prolific author of books on subjects from folklore to cricket, who was already reviewing for *The Times* before the *Lit Supp* began, and whose pungent, rather showy voice was often to be heard in it – 'the greatest bookman of the age' he was once called in the *Lit Supp* itself. Another steady worker who lived by his pen was Francis Gribble, yet another who had a first in Greats from Oxford, and who in the next few years was to produce many light literary works with titles such as *Madame de Staël and Her Lovers* and *Rousseau and the Women He Loved*.

There were five notable women contributors whom Richmond employed in the first years – the novelist Mrs Humphry Ward, whose husband was a *Times* leader writer and also a *Lit Supp* contributor; Constance Fletcher, who wrote novels under the name 'George Fleming', and would be entrusted to review Henry James's *The Wings of the Dove*; Mary Coleridge, of the Coleridge family, and a good poet herself; finally Edith Sichel, and an Englishwoman married to a Frenchman, Madame Duclaux, both of which ladies reviewed numerous books written in French. Mme Duclaux was destined to spot Proust's *Du Côté de chez Swann* for *Lit Supp* readers in 1913.

Perhaps standing slightly apart from these was John Cann Bailey, so admired by Richmond. After his death in 1931, his widow brought out a volume of his letters and diaries that help us to recreate a picture of Bruce Richmond and these early days at the *Lit Supp*. Bailey was the son of a prosperous solicitor in Norwich, and went to Haileybury and New College. In 1887, at the age of twenty-three, he settled down in rooms in the Temple, and for nine years devoted himself to reading, visiting art galleries and seeing friends. He then started writing for the journals. He first met Richmond, who was seven years younger than him, at Duffryn, Lord Aberdare's country house in Wales. They quickly became friends, and it was with Bailey and Campbell Dodgson, later to become Keeper of the Print Room at the British Museum, that Richmond used to dine weekly and read the Greek and Latin classics. They only gave up the custom, says Mrs Bailey, when Richmond's editorship of the *Lit Supp* made it impossible for him to attend.

Bailey describes a 'typical day' in his life at the age of thirty, the 8th of December 1894:

> Breakfast 9.20. Times and letters. Writing at Gibbon (article on), 11.15. 1.20 lunch. Saintsbury Lyrics. Out 3–5pm. Tea with Watson's new volume of poems. Writing Gibbon till 7.15. Dinner at club. Back here 9 to read Lucretius with Richmond and Dodgson. Then at 11.15 went in to F. Smith and had long talk about marriage. Bed 12.30, an hour later than usual.

A little later he reported a dinner conversation between the writer Frank Harris and the dry-witted politician Arthur Balfour. Harris: 'The great curses of modern life are Christianity and journalism!' Balfour: 'Christianity, of course – but why journalism?' However, Bailey himself was a devout Christian, and something of his character is perfectly caught in his wife's remark that his favourite book of devotion after the Bible was Matthew Arnold's notebooks. (He had been very upset by Arnold's death in 1888.) A diary entry for 6 April 1899, when Bailey was contemplating a political career, brings out very clearly how both he and Richmond would envisage the purpose of the *Lit Supp* when it began three years later:

> What Bruce Richmond points out in his letter is that while he hopes to see me in politics, yet there can be no more useful work than that of 'irradiating the humanities', which he assures me I can and do daily accomplish. I hope this is not only friendship's voice, for there is nothing I so wish to be able to believe about myself, and I seriously think that no work in our world can be more sincerely useful.

It was not just friendship's voice, and Bailey was invited to contribute to the *Lit Supp* from the start.

All these reviewers whom Richmond first chose to cover poetry and fiction and other literary works shared in some way this ambition to 'irradiate' literature. Their tone was not so analytical and critical as we are accustomed to in literary criticism and serious reviewing today. The contributors made their discriminations, and were sometimes quite sharp-tongued, but they were essentially *belles-lettristes* and wrote to please. In turn, they asked mainly for pleasure from literature – or if, like Bailey, they looked beyond that, it was either some kind of moral uplift or romantic exaltation that they sought. Their weakness often was that, particularly in poetry, they accepted these qualities at face value, without looking beyond the author's good intentions, and paying attention to his actual use of the language to see how much he had really expressed. The counterpart of this was that they were inclined to criticise too sombre or unromantic a note in what they were sent to review.

It was only later in the decade that a tougher or more radically critical tone appeared in *Lit Supp* reviewing. But we must remember that Richmond had the normal problems of an editor. He could only use what talent was available, and his contributors had to be the kind who could work quickly (the paper almost always reviewed the books in publication week) and who could attract readers without even the fortification of a familiar by-line. In fact, Richmond was extremely resourceful in finding contributors – and when, a little later, writers such as Virginia Woolf or Percy Lubbock turned up – what we might call the first distinctively twentieth-century writers – he was quick to make the fullest possible use of them.

Quiller-Couch wrote several reviews in 1902, including one on *The Essays of Richard Steele*, edited by L.E. Steele, in which he observed that Macaulay had put Steele down in favour of Addison, and welcomed the rise of Steele again. He showed his relative independence most in a piece on C.H. Herford's collection of *English Tales in Verse*, complaining that Herford wanted all tales to be 'works of visionary contemplation', and concluding, with what might even be seen as an anticipation of T.S. Eliot's campaign twenty years later, 'wit in poetry can show a pretty good pedigree; it cannot, at this time of day, be ruled out as unpoetical merely because it does not happen to be romantic'.

Seccombe, who had a steely mind as well as his kind heart, also took a knock at the Romantics in his review of *A History of English Romanticism* by Henry A. Bees, saying that in the end the extravagances of romanticism in European literature eventually descended into caricature. He cited the architect Pugin, who 'wanted Gothic puddings when he came to dine', and a Frenchman who wanted to translate Shakespeare, so to prepare himself came to London, went to a tavern in High Holborn, drank stout and ate *rosbif*. The poet Gautier told him, says Seccombe, that all he had to do now to translate Shakespeare was to learn French.

Seccombe also reviewed the first in the new *English Men of Letters* series, *George Eliot* by Mr Stephen, 'the doyen of English biographers' (the name Leslie is never mentioned once in the review, so naturally did the paper assume that its readers would know who was meant). Seccombe expressed the view that has prevailed in the twentieth century, that *Middlemarch* was the greatest of her books, with 'the substance of 200 novels' in it. He thought that there was 'nothing in fiction more powerfully absorbing' than the relationship between Dorothea and Rosamond.

In August Bailey reviewed another of the new *English Men of Letters* volumes, the one on his hero Matthew Arnold, by the Herbert Paul who had written about Balfour. In it he said that Arnold's 'most permanent contribution to criticism was that he turned its face away from the abstract to the concrete'; but there was no particular sign of that practice in the poetry reviewing this year in the *Lit Supp*.

Nor was new fiction especially well treated. There was a spirited and amusing review by Andrew Lang of Conan Doyle's *Hound of the Baskervilles*, though most later readers of the book would not agree with it. Sherlock Holmes was, he felt 'cast by nature for a hero of short stories, not of so long a tale'. 'As for the hound,' he concluded, 'so long as he was only heard, he was very effective and thrilling. But when once the quadruped comes bodily on the stage, he ceases to excite curiosity, he is only a big dog on whom taxes are paid.' As for Kipling's *Just So Stories*, Harold Child felt that they were 'healthy, humorous and quite unmawkish', but otherwise dismissed them as 'written for little children, not like the *Jungle Book* for both children and adults'.

Arnold Bennett published two novels during the year. *The Grand Babylon Hotel* got a short review from Dalton in Issue No. 2, in which he said little more than that 'the author's cunning keeps the reader's interest'. *Anna of the Five Towns* also got a short review, low in the fiction columns, in which W.J. Lancaster – best known as a writer of adventure stories under the name of 'Harry Collingworth' – acknowledged there was good reading in the life and characters of the manufacturing towns, but said that the 'net result is small' in Anna's own story.

The great novel of the year, Henry James's *The Wings of the Dove*, was reviewed in the first week of September by Constance Fletcher, under the respectful heading, 'Mr Henry James's New Novel'. In one sense, she rose to the occasion well. She started:

> Mr Henry James is to be congratulated. It is a long time since modern English fiction has presented us with a book which is essentially a book; a thing conceived, and carried on, and finished in one premeditated strain; with unbroken literary purpose and serious, unflagging literary skill. *The Wings of the Dove* is an extraordinarily interesting performance.

No remarks, one imagines, could have pleased James better. But then Constance Fletcher entirely abandoned any attempt to show what the book's interest was. It was not just that she did not tell the story. The whole complex interplay of passion and morality, and of social and financial preoccupations, that the novel so marvellously dramatises went completely unmentioned. The reviewer is led off instead into the question of whether the book will do 'for short railway journeys and drowsy hammocks', and then into another byway where she compares a descriptive passage by the popular adventure writer Seton Merriman (from *The Vulture*, reviewed on the same page) with a passage of James's describing a Venetian palace, and labels them respectively 'the realism of impression' and the 'realism of association'. By the time Constance Fletcher made this mock-scholarly distinction, she had no room left to come back to James's real achievement.

Joseph Conrad got even more shamefully treated in the review of the other remarkable fictional work of 1902, his volume of three stories called *Youth*, which contains the great short work *Heart of Darkness*. This went in December to an amiable but very unliterary reviewer, William Beach Thomas, who later became one of Northcliffe's favourite foreign correspondents for the *Daily Mail*. In a very short review, he said that the last of the three stories, *The End of the Tether*, was the best, being a very vivid sea yarn, and that Conrad ought to have started with it, because many readers would 'not get beyond the barren and not very pretty philosophy of *Youth*', and 'more might feel they had had enough horror at the end of *Heart of Darkness*'. This was real drowsy hammock reviewing. But perhaps Richmond felt so too. For much later, when a reissue of *Youth* came out, he gave it to Virginia Woolf to review – and she made full amends.

The star contributor of 1902 was A.B. Walkley, who contributed not only theatre reviews but also many general articles and book reviews. He struck a firm note in the second issue on the subject of railway reading, recalling that Macaulay (still very much in the minds of these writers) began the movement for good railway literature in the 1840s, and praising the proprietor of the Euston Square bookshop, who 'found railway literature brick and left it marble'. But now it was nothing but 'catch ha'penny rubbish and fly-blown remainders'.

He described a lecture by a Frenchman, M. Sylvain, at the Century Theatre, on elocution, L'Art de Dire: 'a portly gentleman, rather like a well-known portrait of Rossini, with a red ribbon in his buttonhole, holding out a minatory forefinger, and declaiming sonorous French alexandrines at a scanty English audience nervously set upon applauding in the wrong places'. It was a good lecture, Walkley wrote, and 'one did not know whether to laugh or weep'.

More than once he came back to his ideas about the place of thought in plays – 'It is not in the theatre that thought awakes feeling – in the theatre feeling strikes out thought.' His most important review was in November, when James Barrie's *The Admirable Crichton* opened in London. He was very enthusiastic about this play in which a manservant becomes the accepted leader of his aristocratic employers when they are stranded on a desert island, only to go back to his old role when they are rescued. He delighted in its irony and playfulness, was 'grateful for its ideas' – 'it shows not only how a new environment but a new hierarchy comes into being' – and finally declared that the acting – especially Henry Irving's – could not be better. He no doubt helped to give the play the success it has enjoyed ever since.

One feature for which the *Lit Supp* has always been famous is its cantankerous letters. They were there from the start. In the second number, the Revd Alfred B. Beaven wrote to complain of errors in the *Dictionary of National Biography*. A reply by the *DNB* editor, Sidney Lee, was printed in the main paper (a practice that was not repeated), but Beaven came back again in the third issue, not satisfied with Lee's promise of a 'corrected issue'. When he had a query, 'Must I write to Mr Lee every time?' the reverend gentleman asked. It would be a heavy burden, he warned, with 'my somewhat peculiar penmanship'.

On 9 May there was a fierce letter from another clergyman, the Revd Churton Collins, Professor of English Literature at Birmingham, mocking a reviewer in the *Athenaeum* who had used some of William Blake's lines in 'The Tyger' as a touchstone for good poetry – 'What a touchstone!' The following week, the *Athenaeum* reviewer replied that if Collins did not recognise Blake as a touchstone, he 'lacks the sense by which poetry is apprehended'. On 23 May Collins declared that 'taken in connexion with the context, Blake's verses are intelligible and excusable as the extravagant and hysterical expression of rapt enthusiasm. Detached from the context, they are mere fanfarade – nonsense pure and absolute.' He added that there were 'too many critics who belong to that hysterical school of which Mr Swinburne is unhappily the founder', and their writings struck a 'falsetto note'. The next week, a great figure came down to join in the fray – none other than W.B. Yeats. Somewhat misreading the correspondence, he observed that Collins thought Blake's lines were 'falsetto', but he had heard his father read the poem as great poetry, and 'I cannot think it less than a cry out of the heart of all wisdom'. Yeats added – a remark that recalls his own lines about Catullus scholars – 'Many a cultivated woman without learning is more right about these matters than all the professors.' Finally, on 13 June, Churton Collins made a rather feeble withdrawal, saying 'I only criticised the lines on their own.' His ferocity had evaporated.

Such was the first year of the *Lit Supp*. From its thirteenth issue, on 11 April, it had felt able to print the words 'First Year' on page one, indicating that it was there to stay. By 30 May it felt obliged to print an editorial note asking clubs, libraries, etc. to allow it to lie on the table for a week, and to bind it separately from the main paper. And how much were the reviewers being paid for their contributions? They all got a standard rate – £3 a column, which consisted of about 1,250 words. If we multiply by forty to get the equivalent sum today, that makes £120 a column, or about £100 a thousand words – a figure very close to what is paid by the *TLS* today. But the columns in 1902 were measured up in one-sixteenths, and paid *pro rata* – that is to say in multiples of three shillings and ninepence. So jobbing journalists and famous statesman alike received cheques for sums such as £3 11s 3d or £6 18s 9d – and, in that era almost without inflation, went on doing so for a long time to come.

Chapter Three

Edwardian Peace: 1903–07

A great event took place on 1 January 1903: the Coronation Durbar in Delhi, at which Edward VII was proclaimed King Emperor. The King himself did not come to India – he was represented by his brother, the Duke of Connaught – and the spectacle was arranged by Lord Curzon, the Viceroy, who was still happily weaving the 'woof of empery' that Harold Begbie had enthused over in the *Lit Supp* the previous year.

Curzon certainly did not want to come home. He and the vicereine, like the royal duke and duchess themselves, arrived at the assembly on an elephant covered with cloth of gold, followed by fifty ruling chiefs. *The Times* correspondent said it was like 'a succession of waves of brilliant colour breaking into foam of gold and silver, with the crest of each wave flashing with the diamonds, rubies and emeralds of robes and turbans' – though after the ceremony *The Times* reminded its readers that 'it is power not pageantry on which our imperial strength is based'.

Meanwhile at home, later that year at a Guildhall banquet, the Prime Minister, Balfour, declared that, as far as external affairs were concerned, it was 'a time of moderate cheerfulness'. In 1904, the Russo-Japanese war would break out, but Britain was little troubled by this conflict, since its main outcome was to leave Russia weakened.

Politics at home were dominated by Joseph Chamberlain's campaign for tariff reform, which mainly meant the reduction of duties on imports within the Empire – a proposal which was to split the Conservative Party, and boost the fortunes of the Liberal Party with its gospel of free trade. The other great issue of the moment was the future of Ireland. Here the Conservatives, or Unionists as they often called themselves, were united against the idea of Home Rule for

Ireland, while it was the Liberal Party which was divided on the question.

Throughout 1903 and 1904 Bruce Richmond was consolidating his position as editor of the *Lit Supp*, further widening his team of reviewers, though he was still working as an assistant editor in the office of the editor of *The Times*. He seems to have been very happy in these years. At the end of November 1904, when advertisements had increased in volume and there had been one or two twelve-page papers, while even a sixteen-page was being mooted, he wrote to Moberly Bell saying he would now best like to have a twelve-page paper with a moderate number of advertisements in it, sinking to eight pages 'in the slack time'. That would give 'ample room for working off our matter', while not being 'too big for convenient reading'.

However, he added that he 'certainly liked the old 8pp. with no or few advts – and think it (from the reader's point of view) the nicest and most presentable – but I only "pined for it"' – obviously in a recent conversation he had had – 'against the 8 pages with 4, 5 or 6 cols of advts'.

In 1903 and for most of 1904 the paper was never more than eight pages long, with four-page issues occasionally, and though advertisements regularly appeared they did not take up too much space from Richmond's point of view. This was the state of affairs he was beginning to 'pine for'.

Books on foreign politics and foreign policy continued to take a prominent position in the paper. Blennerhasset was frequently to be found in its pages, warning against the threat from Germany. In April 1904 he was 'earnestly recommending' a book on *German Anglophobia* by a German author who was friendly towards England, Heinrich Freiherrn Langwerth von Simmern. Von Simmern's book described the deliberate attacks being made in the German press on 'the existence of English power'. These attacks, he said, 'must ultimately lead to a disastrous war'. Hugh Blakiston had not long before reviewed another German book, this one on the Kaiser, and renewed the warning we saw him giving in 1902: 'Are the destinies of Germany safe in the hands of a man whose political insight is not commensurable with his ambition and his energy?'

Rudyard Kipling, already famous though still only thirty-eight, brought out the most powerful paean to British imperialism to be published in these two years, his volume of poems *The Five Nations*, which appeared in October 1903. It fell to E.V. Lucas to review it, and he gave a very clear and accurate account. The book, he said, was 'the message of a publicist (writing poetry) to the English race'. Hitherto, Kipling has 'thrown out incidentally and by flashlight, as it were, expressions of his faith', but here it was set forth in black and white. The book stood 'for the completion of the higher Imperialistic system to which every other of Mr Kipling's books has been a stepping stone'.

Moreover in the past, Lucas wrote, Kipling had shown an impassioned interest in his kind rather than any affection towards them; but now, 'perhaps because he has been nearer the heart of things in his visits to the South African battlefields and hospitals, the interest has become more intimate and more sympathetic ... The ideal of political brotherhood which he sets before his countrymen has a spiritual exaltation that we missed from some of his earlier paeans of Imperial progress.'

This was the book that contained some of the poems by Kipling that became among his most famous, popular and detested – such as 'The White Man's Burden' – and Lucas's review explains very well why that happened. It is interesting to note that the 'five nations' that Kipling wanted to bring together in 'a saner finer brotherhood' through the impact of his poems were never named in the review. Besides 'the old country', they were Australia, Canada, South Africa and India – Lucas assumed everyone would know.

L.S., or Leo, Amery, in these years working for *The Times*, and in the 1920s to become a well-known 'die-hard' Conservative Colonial Secretary, contributed a number of reviews, using most of them to insist on the importance of Britain being well-armed. In a review of *The Army on Itself*, by H.A Gwynne, he declared that with its officers so 'free from conventional prejudice', the British Army could be 'the finest instrument of war the world has yet seen'. He must have been pleased when Thursfield applauded the idea put forward in Amery's own book, *The Problem of the Army*, that there should be an imperial army to defend the Indian frontier. By the time the First World War broke out, however, Amery's aims had not been achieved.

Other domestic matters were confronted in a review, by the Speaker of the House of Commons, of the last volume of the new *Encyclopaedia Britannica*. (Moberly Bell obviously could not get Lord Wolseley.) As when the Lord Chancellor reviewed his volume of the encyclopaedia, the article was by-lined only with the reviewer's official title. Readers were expected to know that the Speaker was William Court Gully, a Liberal MP of long standing who had kept his job in the House under the Conservative government. He took the opportunity in the review to express satisfaction that in recent years 'a far larger proportion of intelligent, educated women have been able to find suitable occupations in which to earn their own livelihood'. So in the course of reviewing the nine volumes, the paper managed to achieve what we might now call a BBC-like balance of opinions on some of the issues of the day.

Politics were also discussed by another regular contributor, the chief writer of legal leaders for *The Times*, Sir John Macdonell, when he reviewed H.G. Wells's *Mankind in the Making*. Wells had won fame before the end of the nineteenth century with his novels such as *The Time Machine* and *The Invisible Man*, and now, as a contentious thirty-seven-year-old member of the Fabian Society, was developing his social and political ideas. Macdonell found the new book a 'really brilliant volume . . . the overflowing of an active, observant mind', but considered that its ideas lacked unity: 'With Marx we know where we are . . . Mr Wells's socialism is of looser texture, and one is never quite certain where his pompom will be heard'. *The Times* was quite happy on occasion to use one socialist to bash another.

But Macdonell took a sympathetic view of the third series of Charles Booth's massive work, *Life and Labour of the People in London*. This new series, in seven volumes, had the subtitle *Religious Influences*. Macdonell said that the chief impression that the volumes left was that 'rectors, vicars, curates, and, indeed, ministers of all creeds are, with rare exceptions, labouring earnestly, to combat the evils encompassing and overwhelming them'. He added that many readers would nevertheless 'close the volumes with a sense of despondency . . . Courage and faith and devotion are apparently baffled in the war with vice and the still more formidable foes, stupidity and helplessness.' Yet there are gains, he said – humanising effects, a sense of present help and sympathy, the dying out of class prejudices – and he concluded by quoting with approval those many clergy who dwell upon 'the astounding goodness of bad people'.

The biggest book of 1903 was by general consent the new *Life of Gladstone* by John Morley. The great Liberal Prime Minister had died in 1898 at the age of eighty-nine, and his policies, especially on Ireland, were still a source of great ferment on the political scene. John Morley, a noted biographer and journalist who was still a Liberal MP and was also currently editor of the *English Men of Letters* series of critical biographies, had been a close associate of Gladstone, and wrote a massive life of his hero in three volumes.

The *Lit Supp* rose to the occasion, giving it the longest review it had yet published – 10,000 words spread across three issues, 6, 16 and 23 October 1903. But it also gave it the review which most clearly so far expressed *The Times*'s allegiance to the Conservative and Unionist Party. The reviewer chosen was a vivacious Irishman, E.D.J. Wilson, who had long been a senior leader writer for *The Times* and had conducted a sustained campaign against the Gladstonian Liberals after they had 'found salvation' (as the obituary of Wilson in *The Times* a few years later ironically put it) in the policy of Home Rule for Ireland.

Though bedewed with compliments to the author ('no other living man could have written it'), the review was nevertheless very critical both of Gladstone and Morley. Wilson made weighty jokes about Gladstone's 'voluminous ambiguities' and Morley's attempts not merely to explain them but to defend them. As for Gladstone's policies, Wilson spoke quite plainly of his 'painfully progressive deterioration as he threw himself into close and active alliance with the Parnellites and their able and unscrupulous leader' – and here Wilson claimed to find even Morley's 'note of admiration becoming forced and shrill'. In the end, the best thing that Wilson could say about Gladstone was that 'in all his family relations Mr Gladstone was admirable, and he was rewarded by an enviable share of domestic happiness and peace'.

In the more strictly literary reviews of these two years, 1903 and 1904, we find the team of the first year all still going strong, and some important new additions. John Cann Bailey was now joined by Arthur Clutton-Brock as one of Richmond's favourites. They were to come fully into their own during the First World War, when they both (especially Clutton-Brock) wrote numerous essays on the right moral conduct for Britain in the conflict, but for the present, along with Harold Child in the office, they took on a great deal of the reviewing of poetry and literary biography and criticism. They were gifted and elegant writers, but all three of them tended to look down on new work from the slopes of Mount Olympus or the Mount of Olives. You catch Bailey's characteristically exalted tone, for example, when in his review of A.C. Bradley's famous book on *Shakespearean Tragedy* (this is early in 1905) he declared that in Shakespeare 'the suffering and death count for little or nothing, the greatness of the soul for much or all', and concluded by asking whether Shakespeare did not have 'a faith that looks through death'.

Thomas Seccombe, as we have seen, was a more robust and down-to-earth reviewer (though a real lover of literature) – and I have a feeling that he was poking a little fun at Bailey when in a lead review in July 1903 on the gypsies' friend George Borrow, he contrasted Borrow's admirers with the lovers of the more gentle and whimsical Charles Lamb. Borrovians, he said, come from a lower social stratum – 'from printers, librarians, booksellers, and others who seldom read books, from indexers, dictionary makers, and such harmless drudges of literature'. (Here, thinking of his years slaving on the *DNB*, he was clearly also having a joke at his own expense.) But 'the cult of Lamb', Seccombe wrote was, 'restricted largely to briefless Templars, to University men and "Oxford M.A.s"'. Seccombe would undoubtedly have known about his fellow reviewer Bailey's easy-going bachelor life as a 'briefless Templar', which he so evocatively described in his diary.

Seccombe was writing many reviews at this time, as were the equally worldly-wise contributors Quiller-Couch and E.V. Lucas. The other major new contributor was Edmund Gosse, who in 1904, aged fifty-five, became librarian of the House of Lords, and was called 'the official British man of letters' by H.G. Wells, although some years earlier he had received a severe drubbing for careless scholarship from the same Professor Churton Collins who had denounced William Blake. (His autobiographical masterpiece, *Father and Son*, would not be published until 1907.)

Gosse had become early in his life an expert on Scandinavian literature, and was over the years to contribute to the paper many reviews of books written in the Scandinavian languages. He had introduced Ibsen to Britain, and in September 1902 had written an amusing letter to the *Lit Supp* stating that Ibsen was still alive, in spite of the fact that it was 'recognised employment for Continental quidnuncs to condemn those eminent veterans Tolstoy and Ibsen to death'.

However, his first long contribution to the *Lit Supp* was on an English subject. In March 1903 a major poetical event took place – the publication of the poems of the seventeenth-century poet Thomas Traherne. They had been found in a notebook on a London bookstall five years before, and their authorship had been established by Bertram Dobell, who had now edited the *Poetical Works*.

Gosse reviewed them. He said that 'the discovery of a substantial body of excellent poetry by a seventeenth-century writer whom no-one ever heard of before is an event of some importance in literary history', and that Traherne's would henceforth be a name 'which can never be expunged from English literature'. He praised the 'brilliant novelty of his images' (though he thought him a 'bad metrist'), and rather surprisingly, considering the general view of Traherne nowadays, he saw him not as a 'Jacobean mystic' but as a poet 'with an ecstatic appreciation of the beauty of physical life', who lifted 'a clear, bold voice in defence of the joy of animal existence'. Gosse commented that this was 'curious in an Anglican divine' – but made no objection. Bailey, perhaps, would have done so.

The other notable poetical event of that year was the publication in October of the first part of Thomas Hardy's epic verse-drama of the Napoleonic wars, *The Dynasts*. This led A.B. Walkley, who was still writing regular theatre criticism for the paper, into a remarkable exchange with Hardy. The book was reviewed by Harold Child, who said it was a 'drama of nations, not a drama of men . . . the men are puppets', and complained: 'Why should the great novelist content himself with the dead fruits of schoolbook history?'

Walkley also wrote a piece about it, riding one of his regular hobby-horses about plays being for acting not reading, and – picking up Child's comment for his own purposes – suggesting that if it was unsuitable for normal production it should actually be performed by puppets!

The following week the paper contained a dignified and amusing letter from Hardy about Walkley's piece. Observing that 'your critic is as absolute as the gravedigger in Hamlet', he asks why the stage-form should be thought bad for reading. 'Because, I understand him to answer, it was invented for the stage. He might as well assert that bitter ale is bad drinking for England because it was invented for India.' Moreover it was a misapprehension, he concluded, that he himself had 'hankerings after actual performance' of *The Dynasts*. 'My hankerings, if any, do not lie that way. But I fancy his do.'

A week later, Walkley was back with a spirited reply. He was only trying to do Hardy a good turn by advocating the performance of his verse drama as a puppet show. But at heart, he said, he was more concerned for the future of the puppets themselves. He thought *The Dynasts* was actually a very fine drama, and indeed a playable one – and he just 'caught with delight' at the chance it offered of bringing good puppet shows back again.

Hardy was allowed the last word. He thought it was creditable to the ingenious mind of 'your critic' to propose 'the quaint and unexpected channel of performance by means of fantoccini, Chinese shadows, and other startling apparatus'. But, though it might seem ungrateful, he was happy just to have written a poem. 'And there, I fear, the matter must remain.'

Walkley also wrote entertainingly about many plays that were performed, including Shaw's *Candida*, where he enjoyed the 'brilliant dialectic' and 'the pleasure of seeing what the players make of their parts',
but thought that it was the kind of play to which the stage presentation
as such added nothing. Harold Child reviewed Shaw's newly-published
play, *Man and Superman*, like Walkley enjoying Shaw's wit but solemnly
warning him that he would never change the opinions of the average
play-going 'Papa Bourgeois' until he could be a little more serious.

Walkley also continued to review books as well as plays, including
one called *The Pleasures of the Table*, by an American, George H.
Ellwanger. Walkley – whose day job was actually as a senior civil servant
in the Post Office – gave a vivid picture of the well-off Edwardian
Londoners who had given up having 'a chop and a couple of potatoes',
in favour of dining at the Café Royal and supping at the Carlton on
the same evening. He also recorded the disappearance of the Chateau
Rauzan '75 from most club wine lists, and the resulting spectacle – as he
claimed – of 'herds of elderly bald-headed gentlemen now perlustrating
London, like the recent processions of the unemployed, asking vainly
for something fit to drink'.

1903 and 1904 were not otherwise particularly notable years for new
poetry, or its reviewing. W.B. Yeats was only mentioned for his volume
of essays *Ideas of Good and Evil*: Harold Child called it the 'essays of
a symbolist', explaining this creed rather sceptically as 'Caves and
waters must not be mere caves and waters'. W.J. Lancaster wrote in
dull, false-poetic vein about a volume of poems by W.W. Gibson and
his sister Elizabeth Gibson: 'His muse goes clad in more fanciful robes
than hers.' Clutton-Brock was funny on the sameness of some poems
by Swinburne to many he had written before: 'One is apt to glance at
a new poem by Mr Swinburne as at another picture by Rubens in the
Louvre.'

However there was a very good long essay by Quiller-Couch on W.E.
Henley, who died in July 1903 after a commanding career as editor of
the *Scots* (later the *National*) *Observer*, and with a reputation also as a
lyric poet. Quiller-Couch drew a vivid picture of this 'large and full-
blooded man', who launched Robert Louis Stevenson and was one of
the first to 'declare Kipling's genius', and who gathered about him a
team of writers who 'cursed with glee everything, good or bad, for
which Mr Gladstone stood sponsor'. Henley 'preached Imperialism
when it was out of season' – that is, under Gladstone – 'and preached
it no less fervently when it swept the country,' wrote Quiller-Couch,
'because he believed in it, heart and soul' – while his *Book of Verses*

in surprising contrast, was a work of 'delicate and almost shy craftsman-ship'. A good *Lit Supp* hero of the time.

One other notable essay on a dead poet was the review of G.K. Chesterton's book *Robert Browning*, by Sidney Colvin, who was the Keeper of Prints and Drawings at the British Museum, and a friend of many writers. He shrewdly observed that Chesterton's qualities were akin to Browning's own – rather mixed: 'a cordial promiscuous gusto, an unpruned fertility of healthy and manly thinking, and a readiness to express his meaning in any rough-and-ready phrase that comes to hand'. For most of his career Chesterton was to elicit this kind of response from *Lit Supp* reviewers.

The major novels of 1903 and 1904 were not very well treated. Beach Thomas was invoked to review both Conrad's book of stories, *Typhoon*, in April 1903 and James's *The Ambassadors* in the following October. Was Richmond trying to find a reviewer who would express the qualities of these complex novelists in straightforward terms for the readers? If so, he was not successful. Beach Thomas said it was 'always an intellectual stimulus to read Mr Conrad' but thought that the best things in the stories were the 'purple passages'. As for *The Ambassadors*, he felt he must say it is 'beautifully done', but all the same 'the cleverness is baffling'. 'The narrative is – where? The denouement – what?' he asked in despair. He was obviously defeated by it.

E.V. Lucas came to the rescue of Conrad in an article soon afterwards on 'Novels of the Sea'. He was a highly intelligent critic, even though he won his fame as a light writer, and here he pointed out that in Conrad 'the sea is the great test, not of practical energy, but of more subtle moral worth. The whole purpose of the Titanic convulsion described in *Typhoon* was to show that a captain who was thought to be a dullard had really just the kind of character that was needed.' This was genuinely getting to grips with Conrad, and in October 1904 Richmond gave him Conrad's next novel, *Nostromo*, to review. But he was disappointed by it. He thought it was a shapeless work, a short story expanded to the length of a long novel. Even so, it was 'a shapeless work by a man of genius'.

Samuel Butler's *The Way of All Flesh* was published posthumously in May 1903. It went to another of Richmond's regular contributors now, a freelance writer called G.S. Street. Once again we find a *Lit Supp* reviewer reluctant to praise a book that does not seem to offer a hopeful message. Street first found the tyrannical father of the story unbelievable, then changed his tack, saying that the story was 'obsolete without being strange' – after all, 'we treat children very differently now'. His real feelings came out, though, when he concluded by saying that the author's philosophy was 'wholly negative' – that the writing was pithy and caustic, and that the author often seemed in despair. Street could not accept a genre of book that in his view was pure satire and denunciation – but in that he seems to have been not unrepresentative of his readers. Once again, it was Virginia Woolf who made amends in another review of Butler's novel in the *Lit Supp* a few years later – while the book itself only took off in popularity in the 1920s.

George Gissing's posthumous novel *The Private Papers of Henry Ryecroft* might have expected a rather similar review at the hands of Miss Fletcher, and she did indeed say of it: 'how well written, how well felt, how well realised, and how infinitely joyless' – but she saw that it was 'destined to command a small but very ardent following'. E.M.W. Grigg – at that time a writer on imperial affairs on the staff of *The Times*, later Lord Altrincham, and the father of John Grigg, a future historian of *The Times* – reviewed Chesterton's *The Napoleon of Notting Hill*. He found it too whimsical and facile, but affably observed that the author's book on Browning was better. Andrew Lang was not much impressed by Erskine Childers's exciting *The Riddle of the Sands*: 'not a novel, but a sketch in naval geography, with adventures, incomprehensible to the landsman, thrown in'. That was the slightly camp note that Lang excelled at. But W.J. Lancaster was eloquent about the 'tenderness and charm' of W.H. Hudson's fantasy, *Rima*, with its 'fantastic little heroine . . . like some fusion of fire and dew, emblematic of spirituality'.

Many other novels, most of them now forgotten, were given short reviews or listed – on 1 January 1904, the paper remarked that some 840 novels had been published in the previous year, 'more than two novels a day, including Sundays'. One that might be picked out among them is one of the many novels Quiller-Couch was producing down in Cornwall at this time, *The Adventures of Harry Revel*, a picaresque tale, full of comic characters, set 100 years earlier in Plymouth. It was another of the books that Walkley took time off from the theatre to review, and he quoted some lines by Miss Plinlimmon, matron of the Foundling Hospital in the story, who had a 'gift of dropping off into poetry':

> *Wounded hero, you were shattered*
> *In the ankle – do not start!*
> *Much, much more it would have mattered*
> *In the immediate neighbourhood of the heart.*
> *The bullet sped comparatively wide;*
> *And you survive, to be Old England's pride.*

46

A good taste, there, of the genteel fun of Edwardian England – with, as Walkley noted, a strong flavour of Dickens about it still.

Richmond was not neglecting fiction from abroad, either, and indeed in these early years was always wanting more space for foreign books. G.W. Smalley, the excellent American correspondent of *The Times*, contributed frequent letters from America which Henry James said once that he always read. Smalley reported in March 1904 on the remarkable voice coming out of the 'uncongenial atmosphere of New York society' – that of Edith Wharton; and three months later Harold Child praised the stories in her book *The Descent of Man* as 'studying new combinations of circumstances, new types of people and new theories of conduct . . . the comedy and the tragedy of them fine and subtle'.

On the death of 'Tchechoff' (so spelt) in July 1904, Francis Gribble was rather cautious about his merits – he 'may or may not have been a man of genius'. However it was certain that for this 'most typically Russian of modern writers' life was 'a battle with no prospect of victory'. With Thomas Mann, the paper was quick off the mark. In April 1903, in a round-up of 'Recent German Literature', Professor J.G. Robertson picked out *Buddenbrooks* as the work of 'a young and hitherto little-known writer' with 'an extraordinarily vivid and attractive style', and three months later, in a similar survey, a Cambridge scholar called Mrs F. Johnson, 'after the success of *Buddenbrooks*', reviewed *Tristram*, the collection of stories by Mann in which one of his most renowned stories, *Tonio Kröger*, was published. She observed that his characters were 'ever conscious of under-achievement . . . a morbid point of view, if you will' but that the author depicts them 'with marvellous vigour and intensity'. That 'if you will' suggests that she – as with some of the other *Lit Supp* reviewers – felt a need sometimes, in these first years of the century, to reach out to and appease the good, healthy Christian readers of the paper, when they were engaged in offering them grimmer fare.

As for Christianity itself, that was under frequent discussion in the paper, and most dramatically in these years after a noted Catholic theologian, the Abbé Loisy, was condemned by the Holy Office for his views. 'Modernism' at this time meant something different from what we understand by it today, i.e. a twentieth-century development in art and literature. At this time it referred to the idea that the Christian revelation was not vouchsafed once and for all, immutably, in the past, but that it was continuing and developing, and that our increasing knowledge had a part to play in that development. Loisy was in this sense a 'modernist'. As Professor of Hebrew in the Institut Catholique in Paris he had expressed ideas about the history of the Bible that the Vatican could not accept, and had been dismissed from his post.

In the *Lit Supp* in January 1904, 'Principal Headlam' came to Loisy's defence. This was the Revd Arthur Headlam, who had just been appointed Principal of King's College, London, and was subsequently to become Regius Professor of Divinity at Oxford, and finally a famously brusque and insensitive Bishop of Gloucester. Here he proclaimed vigorously that 'revelation and reason' can go together, and that Christ was competent to do for the twentieth century what he had done for the age of the Councils. Headlam had managed simultaneously to write a good reference for Christ and aim a good swingeing blow at the Roman Catholic Church.

By the end of 1904, the *Lit Supp* was getting plenty of advertising, but Moberly Bell, ever more desperately aware of *The Times*'s need for revenue, believed it could do even better, and in November decided to put a full-page advertisement in the paper appealing to publishers. The idea did not please the fastidious Richmond, but he expressed his objections to the manager in a letter that was typically delicate and amusing, yet also very strong. Writing on 30 November, he said:

> I do loathe (and from mere prudence distrust) taking a page to exalt & proclaim our own merits to people many of whom would not otherwise doubt them. Of course I see that the *L.S.* must, if possible, be made to pay – But I gather that things have been going better lately – and, if you didn't slay it when every number was a plumb loss, is it necessary just when it looks like going better for us to step down and cadge? If we can't get it to go right, let us rouge and underline our attractions – but I had hoped we were going to get on all right without desperate remedies.
>
> I am not sure that I quite know what the advt. is to be – You say it is 'to exalt our merits as an advertising medium' & is to influence publishers – If so, a page in the *Lit. Sup.* would only bring to the notice of the reader (whom it doesn't concern) in a rather annoying form a fact which we want to bring to the notice of the publisher, and which I imagine your canvassers do bring to their notice every week.
>
> (A suggestion from me, of all people, to you that a business proposal of yours is not likely to achieve its effect strikes me as even more comic than impertinent – and is of course to be taken not as

argument, but as autobiography – a mere confession of perplexity.)

All I mean by all this fuss is that I am awfully disappointed that artificial inflation is prescribed just as I had hoped we were getting stronger without it – But of course if it is necessary, we must away with false shame and hey for the rougepots & belladonna! Please forgive this whine – but I am keen about the *Supplement* –

Yrs ever Bruce L. Richmond.

P.S. Please don't bother to answer this till we meet – you've letters enough to write – A postcard to say the 16 page *L.S.* with our advt. is fixed for Dec 9 will do.

The full-page advertisement did appear on 9 December, headed 'To Publishers'. It announced that the paper 'has attained a circulation which exceeds by several thousands that of the daily issue of *The Times*. It is in demand to this large extent by people who, while not regular purchasers of the daily numbers, take the other publications issued by *The Times*' – there was now also the weekly 'Financial Supplement' – 'and buy the *Literary Supplement* for a penny extra . . . Many of the busy men of affairs who are regular readers of *The Times* habitually detach and reserve it for more leisurely attention than they can give to it in the course of skimming the morning's news, putting it by until the evening, or some other convenient time, in order to read and digest it thoroughly.' The advertisement also included many compliments that had been paid to the paper, by a Justice of the Peace (from near Liverpool), a Chief Engineer of a Gas Company, Major —, Viscountess —, and subscribers from all over the country – 'a valuable addition', 'excellent, sound criticism', 'I am perfectly satisfied with the form and contents', they said. However, looking at subsequent issues, it would seem as though the paper's self-advertisement did not have any dramatic effect on the volume of publishers' advertising it attracted – so it was in the end both unloved and unnecessary.

The year 1905 saw a change in the paper. The first signs appeared of a new phase opening in the life of the literary world, and the most brilliant of these signs was the arrival of the name 'Miss A.V. Stephen' in the 'marked copies' of the paper – still surviving – in which the name of the contributor was written, for the sake of the accounts department, in a bold Edwardian hand across each review. This was Adeline Virginia Stephen, a young woman who would in due course have her name written across many, many more reviews as 'Mrs Woolf'.

Virginia Woolf (as I shall call her) was just twenty-three when she started writing for the *Lit Supp*, and 'Bloomsbury' was just taking shape. In that year she and her brother Adrian moved into the house at 29, Fitzroy Square where so many of the early activities of the Bloomsbury Group were debated and launched. The circle of her family and friends touched that of Bruce Richmond's – Eton and Cambridge, especially, loomed large in the background of both – and her brother Thoby was attracted for a time to a stately beauty called Elena Rathbone whom Richmond himself would marry when he was forty-two, in 1913.

Virginia Woolf had already written a few reviews for the Anglo-Catholic journal *The Guardian*, and had recorded cautiously in her journal on 16 January 1905 that 'Mr Chirol of *The Times* is reading my things with a possible view to asking me to write for the *Times Literary Supplement*'. On 17 January she commented 'If I am taken on by *The Times* I shall think myself justified – and I use my books.' We next get a glimpse of how Richmond operated, for an entry later in the same day reports 'Invited to dine with Crums to meet B. Richmond of *The Times*!'

Nothing was said at this dinner on 26 January. She noted that the hard-working Richmond went back to the office afterwards. But on 8 February she recorded a tea party at Mrs Crum's at which the only person she knew was Bruce Richmond, and 'he very soon came to business'. He asked her if she would write a review for them – 'So I said yes, with joy.'

However, she had no doubt of the inferior quality of the first two books she was sent to review. These were *The Thackeray Country* by Lewis Melville and *The Dickens Country* by F.G. Kitton, two books in the *Pilgrimage* series about places associated with writers. They were 'productions of a pair of scissors', and 'I am not a critic of dressmaking of this kind', she wrote in her journal, but she 'pegged away' at them. In the event she penned a review – printed 'word for word', she noted with pleasure – in which she conveyed these feelings quite uncompromisingly, yet with a brilliant show of intelligence and charm. The late Mr Kitton's mind 'was a unique storehouse of facts about Dickens', but in his book the 'oppressed imagination' had to 'bear an altogether insupportable load before it has followed Dickens to his last resting place . . . A writer's country is a territory within his own brain; and we run the risk of disillusionment if we try to turn such phantom cities into tangible brick and mortar.'

It was the same with the next review she had in the paper. Of a novel, *Barham of Beltana* by W.E. Norris, she wrote in her diary 'nothing whatever to be said about the book so I confined myself to generalities', but in fact she produced a witty and good-humoured analysis of a whole genre of novels:

> He is the type of writer who regards marriage and the events that precede it as the legitimate end of a novel; and when he has satisfactorily disposed of the difficulties that are necessary to make a plot, the sound of marriage bells is the signal for a general handshaking, and we feel that we can all depart in a state of mild felicity.

Richmond knew at once what a star he had found in this young woman. He turned down the third review she wrote for him, about Miss Sichel's book on Catherine de Medici, saying he was sorry that he had misled her, but it really needed to be done by a professional historian – 'to which I cordially agree!' she observed, having found it a struggle (it was reviewed in the end by Constance Fletcher, who lived in Venice with her old mother). However, henceforth he 'pelted' her with books, to use her own word, and in the years from 1905 to 1907 she wrote fifty reviews for the *Lit Supp*. Some of these were of the ephemeral novels that the paper felt it had to cover briefly, but she almost invariably found something memorable to say about them: of *Love the Judge* by Wymond Carey she wrote: 'If we cannot believe that such people lived, we can almost believe that someone thinks they do'; or of *Outrageous Fortune* by Bak, the story of how a woman can live in society without money: 'You draw from it that sense of instruction in unimportant matters which you get by looking from the train window at a flat stretch of the countryside.'

The most important novel she reviewed in these years was E.M. Forster's *The Longest Journey*, which came out in April 1907. Forster, with his own Cambridge background, was by now a figure in, if not quite of, the Bloomsbury set, and as a distinctive new novelist publishing his second novel at the age of twenty-eight must have been of intense interest to her. She found the book

> interesting and living and amusing ... Mr Forster fastens himself again, like some sharp wholesome insect, upon the life of the suburbs and the ideals of those who dwell in red brick villas and in the form rooms of public schools. And in the art of stinging these good people to exhibit their actions in a natural manner he is undoubtedly an expert ... But the jingle which the idols make as they fall, adroitly

knocked on the head by a tap of Mr Forster's pen, destroys the deeper note; there is a sound like the striking of hollow brass.

The *Lit Supp* had failed to review Forster's first novel, *Where Angels Fear to Tread* in 1905: she recalled it and praised it, but stated that she found herself still 'asking as curiously as ever' at the end of this new novel as she had been at the end of the earlier one: 'What will the next book be?'

More perhaps than any other writer, Virginia Woolf found her way to her own ideas, and even into her own feelings, through her reviewing; and while scrutinising Forster's book very intently, she was already doing that here. She and E.M. Forster would remain respectful but wary of each other for the rest of their lives.

Another of Virginia Woolf's young Cambridge friends in Bloomsbury, Desmond MacCarthy, also became a contributor to the *Lit Supp* in 1905, reviewing H.G. Wells's *A Modern Utopia*: he was impressed by the 'well-oiled empire . . . run by a great voluntary order of good men and women' envisaged by Wells as a possible future, but was youthfully uneasy at the lack of passion in it. He did not continue to write for the *Lit Supp*, but made his fame after 1913 as a critic on the newly-founded *New Statesman*.

John Buchan, thirty years old in 1905, and recently back from South Africa where he had been working on reconstruction with the High Commission, wrote a review of a book about that country, arguing that the wellbeing of all its peoples would be best guaranteed by its remaining part of the British Empire. He had already published a novel as a twenty-year-old undergraduate, but his fame was still in the future, as were his main contributions to the paper.

The other really important new contributor was Percy Lubbock, who began at the end of 1904, and was soon writing as frequently as Virginia Woolf was. He was a young man of twenty-six in the year 1905, a nephew of Lord Avebury from yet another circle of friends in Cambridge (where he was just about to be appointed librarian of the Pepys Library at Magdalene), but inevitably known in Bloomsbury. He was said to have fallen in love with Henry James at the age of twenty-one, and was a devoted friend of the novelist to the end of his life. He had graduated from Cambridge with a high reputation as a new critic, and in his reviews for Richmond in these years he certainly justified it by the freshness and vigour of his opinions.

Here he is, writing about Kipling's new stories and poems in *Traffics and Discoveries* – and doing his best to topple another idol:

> All the old gingerbread and naphtha lights as before, it will be seen; on page after page all the old tricks by which the civilian and the landsman are to be bluffed into thinking that the unintelligible technicalities of the Army and Navy, photographically reproduced, make an artistic picture.

And here he is, in 1907, on Henry James's book of travels, *The American Scene*:

> Other masters of fiction, when they write their *sensations de voyage*, generally treat the occasion as a kind of aesthetic holiday . . . Mr James pursues his art as he goes, [and] the dispersed elements of the scene hurry forward to offer their help and to answer his question . . . This crowded, sensitive, intricate book [is] probably the most remarkable book of impressions of travel which we possess.

The same year, incidentally, in 'American Notes', J.D. Barry reported on the presence of Henry James in America, criticising the slovenly diction of American women. As a direct result, a Society for the Study of Spoken English was founded in New York.

William Beach Thomas had by now been relegated mainly to reviewing books about nature and the countryside, and Henry James's last great novel, *The Golden Bowl*, published in 1905, was put into the slightly safer hands of Harold Child. Even so, Lubbock for one cannot have been too pleased with the review, of which Child seems to have missed all the moral implications, saying that the book was 'a fine high-comedy game, exceedingly well played', but that James was not one of the very great artists. Child rose to the occasion better the following year with a powerful but more straightforward American novel, Upton Sinclair's study of the horrific conditions in the Chicago stockyards, *The Jungle*. 'Seldom has so hideous a state of things been exposed so fearlessly and so thoroughly,' wrote Child. He also reviewed one of the notable English novels of the year, the first book in John Galsworthy's *The Forsyte Saga*, *A Man of Property*, in which the author's archetypal bourgeois, Soames Forsyte, was introduced to the world. Child was rather lukewarm about it, but thought nevertheless that 'Galsworthy's career is a matter of some importance to English fiction'.

Conrad's novels continued to go to E.V. Lucas. Virginia Woolf criticised Lucas in a review of one of his light books for trying too hard to make the reader laugh, but he was certainly not frivolous about Conrad, and continued to write beautifully, almost with awe, about him. Of *The Mirror of the Sea* (1906), he said:

> In this study Mr Conrad has come to the sea as an equal. Not that he ever presumes, ever makes light of its vastness and mystery, its terrors and its loveliness; but that seeing all things through a kind of urbane fatalism, coming to life with a high gentlemanliness, a cosmopolitan preparedness and courtesy, he is without fear, without hurry, without noisy wonder, without excitement ... The sea has often met its eulogists. Mr Conrad is its first critic, in the fullest and best sense of the word.

Of *The Secret Agent* (1907), he said that anarchists had hitherto been, in fiction, 'a background for lurid scenes and hair-raising thrills', but now Mr Conrad had come 'with his steady discerning gaze, his passion for humanity, his friendly irony, and above all his delicate and perfectly tactful art, to make them human and incidentally to demonstrate how monotonous a life like theirs can also be.' Lucas, I believe, should not be remembered for his popular humorous books, but for his reviews like these in the *Lit Supp*. He knew what a critic should be, 'in the fullest and best sense of the word'.

New poetry did not feature prominently in the paper in these years. James Joyce's *Chamber Music* (1907) was not noticed. Yeats's *Poems 1899–1905* were reviewed by Arthur Clutton-Brock as part of an article on the Celtic Movement: he said that it was time for Yeats to listen 'rather to the voices of men than to the voice of the wind among the reeds' – advice that Yeats was actually to take before long, though perhaps not because he received it from the *Times Literary Supplement*. Constance Fletcher reviewed the second part of Hardy's *Dynasts* and said that 'Genius and Vision animate the unmelodious and awkward verse.' No dispute erupted this time.

John Cann Bailey wrote an unusually sharp-tongued piece in June 1905 about Robert Bridges, now a venerable figure aged sixty-one. Reviewing Bridges's new long poem 'Demeter', he said 'Bridges can still write a poem occasionally, and here is one.' In his journal on 19 June he mentioned that he had received a letter from Richmond about this review, and his comment on it brings out well his responsible, yet extremely conservative attitude to literature: 'Much pleased with letter from Bruce Richmond on Bridges article. "Wants" to know how I manage to be so interesting and yet "keep to the middle of the road". It is just the praise that pleases me. The thing is to make the true seem new: not the new seem true.' Here was the divide that was to open up increasingly between Richmond's older and younger reviewers – though perhaps it should be said that the younger ones did not so much want to make the new 'seem true', as show that it was true.

Perhaps the most enduring among the other literary works of these years was *Father and Son*, Edmund Gosse's vivid account of his boyhood and his fanatical Plymouth Brethren father. It was published anonymously in 1907, but its authorship must have been widely known. This book went for review to one of the old school, a Canon of Westminster and a writer of religious leaders for *The Times*, Canon H.C. Beeching. He found it 'charming', not an adjective many would have used of this grim if often funny memoir, but this was because he concentrated on the rebellious boy rather than his oppressive parent. He said that he left it to the author's conscience to decide 'how far in the interests of popular edification or amusement it is legitimate to expose the weaknesses and inconsistencies of a good man who is also one's father'. For whatever reason, he was clearly not too keen to look closely at the obsessed and tyrannical ways of Mr Gosse, senior.

The tide in English politics turned strongly in favour of the Liberal Party in 1906, when they won a landslide election. It brought to the fore figures who were to dominate the political scene for the next ten or fifteen years, such as Herbert Asquith and Lloyd George. In May of that year the *Lit Supp* invited John Morley to write a signed article about the great Victorian liberal thinker, John Stuart Mill, for the centenary of his birth on 20 May. The article, which was the second longest that had appeared in the paper so far, running to almost 3,000 words across three pages, was published two days before the anniversary, on Friday, 18 May. Perhaps giving Morley the opportunity to write this piece was seen by Richmond in part as a political balancing act after the critique – which was the longest article so far – of his Gladstone book.

At any rate, Morley's article was a splendidly written eulogy of Mill both as a man and a thinker, praising his 'passionate hatred for either coarse or subtle abuse of power', trying to define his place in the development of social and political thinking (above all, he 'set democracy on its guard against itself'), and not hesitating to allude to recent political events in Britain by declaring that the tide had now turned against 'Neo-machiavellianism – end justifying means, country right and wrong, and all the rest of it' and that 'Millite sanity is for a new season restored'. In fact, this was not a particularly challenging piece politically for *The Times* to run, for many of Mill's ideas as described by Morley were by now as acceptable to moderate Conservatives as they were to Liberals.

Two other important works of recent political history were reviewed by John Cann Bailey, who was as interested in this subject as he was in such themes as the ennobling power of art, and actually wrote about it better. He wrote a long piece in January 1906 on Winston Churchill's life of his father, Lord Randolph Churchill. Winston had become an MP in 1900 as a Conservative, like his father, but in 1904 had gone over to the Liberals over the issue of tariff reform, and was naturally not very popular with Conservative politicians at this time. However, Bailey gave the book a very good review, with just a dig at Winston. He said that Lord Randolph's life provided 'a comedy, a history and a tragedy', and went on: 'It is a pleasure to say that a life so well worth writing has been admirably written . . . Sons have not always proved the most judicious of biographers, and Mr Winston Churchill's warmest admirers would not ask us to think him the most judicious of men . . . But here is a book which is certainly among the two or three most exciting political biographies in the language.'

At the end of the following year he gave an even longer review to a much-anticipated book: *The Letters of Queen Victoria. A Selection from Her Majesty's Correspondence between the Years 1837 and 1861*, 'Published by the Authority of His Majesty the King. Edited by Arthur Christopher Benson, MA, and Viscount Esher, GCVO, KCB. In three volumes. Murray, £3 3s. net.' Though almost abject in his expressions of homage to the late Queen in one or two places, he gave a good and thorough account of her dealings with her governments, and criticised the book itself quite sharply.

He complained that everybody had believed that Mr Benson and Lord Esher were engaged upon a life of the Queen after the royal letters had been placed in their hands, and that 'a volume of selections edited with notes' was not quite the same thing – especially when almost half the letters were written in the third person, which made them very dull to read. The selection of letters was also too much biased towards the political, and did not give much personal impression of the Queen. Even so, the book would 'appeal in one form or another to every reader in the Empire', and it should not have been priced so high. 'It is difficult to overestimate its educational value if it were accessible to the classes who are apt to believe that wisdom lies only in a democracy. But the three volumes which might, one would imagine, have been produced at 10s., and which at a reasonable figure would have sold by hundreds of thousands, are offered to a privileged few at £3.3s.'

A letter in the main paper objecting to the price of the book (it made vague, abusive hints about '30 pieces of silver') actually led to a libel action against *The Times* by the publisher, John Murray. John Cann Bailey's diary gives us an amusing glimpse of this court case, in which he and Richmond appeared for *The Times*. At one point, one of the counsel 'talked so politely of Bruce and me,' Bailey wrote, 'that Bruce whispered "Ought we to get up and bow to the court?"' Richmond also, with characteristic generosity, said to Bailey that he was sure any jury would give such a man as John Murray £10,000 for being accused of being anything but honest. He was not far out: Murray won the action, and was awarded £7,500 damages against *The Times*.

But the *Lit Supp* won its point in the end. A year later, in October 1908, *The Times* in conjunction with John Murray published an edition of the Queen's letters, with the complete text carefully revised, in three crown volumes bound in red cloth for 6s net. This had come about, said a leader in *The Times*, through 'the King's sympathetic insight into the nation's wishes and feelings' – and, it implied, the King's agreement with *The Times* in the matter. The paper was justified in the event, and Moberly Bell must have rejoiced, for over 100,000 copies of the six-shilling edition were sold.

At the beginning of 1905 Moberly Bell was still trying to persuade publishers to advertise in the *Lit Supp*, and a new appeal appeared in the paper on 3 February. This time it concentrated on telling publishers how to write their advertisements:

> Of what does the ordinary kind of advertisement consist? Usually a list of titles and authors, with scraps of criticisms . . . Why should not publishers themselves tell the public what their books contain? A bright, interesting resumé of its contents, presented in the right manner, is the most natural and the most effective means of selling a book . . .

The paper announced that the issue of the following week, 10 February, would, if there was sufficient response from publishers, be increased 'beyond its normal limits' to twenty pages. But this new, rather presumptuous essay in self-advertising was no more effective than the previous one had been. On 10 February, the advertisements all looked much as they had done before, and the paper had twelve pages, as it had often done before.

However, another venture of Moberly Bell's later that year made the whole question of publishers' advertising irrelevant for a time. This was his creation of the Times Book Club in September 1905. Moberly Bell's idea was to start a lending library at which regular subscribers to *The Times* could borrow books for nothing, and buy them at greatly reduced prices after the library had finished with them. This would cost money, but he believed that the increase in the circulation of *The Times* would more than compensate for the loss. Fine premises were opened in Bond Street for the new book club, and indeed new subscribers poured in, though of course old subscribers took advantage of the free offer, too. The Times Book Club was soon able to declare that it was 'the biggest buyer of books in the world'.

What had not been sufficiently anticipated was the violent opposition of the publishers and booksellers to the scheme. The normal trade practice was that books were not sold second-hand at reduced prices until six months after publication, and here was the Times Book Club selling them at very low prices long before that. As a result, most publishers started refusing to sell books to the Times Book Club on trade terms. They also stopped advertising in *The Times*.

This, of course, was particularly harmful to the *Lit Supp*, in so far as it was supposed to pay its own way. Advertisements almost vanished from its pages. But Moberly Bell's blood was up, and he turned the issue of the Times Book Club into a war against rapacious publishers, which soon became known as the 'Book War'.

In the interests of both parties, review copies of new books continued to arrive at *The Times*, and the *Lit Supp* went on reviewing them in the usual way. However, Moberly Bell required the paper to list each week all the books being reviewed that the publishers were refusing to supply to the Book Club on trade terms, preceded by a notice which explained the situation, and concluding 'Subscribers who would co-operate with *The Times* in its efforts to uphold a rule made in their interest may effectively show their disapproval of the publishers' action by refraining, for the present, from asking for the following books at the Times Book Club.' This, of course, was because the Book Club would have to pay full retail price if it was to obtain any of the books in question. Later, the notice in the *Lit Supp* was changed slightly, appearing at the foot of each review and asking subscribers to help *The Times* to 'defeat the Publishers' Trust by refraining from ordering this book so far as possible until it is included in *The Times* Monthly Catalogue'. (So it would appear that some readers went on asking for the proscribed books, and that the Club stood by its undertaking that 'we are prepared to furnish books even at a pecuniary loss if subscribers insist'.)

An unexpected reaction was that some authors, angry in turn with their publishers, advertised their books in the *Lit Supp* themselves. Even more dramatically, in June 1907, with the Book War still dragging on, Bernard Shaw – always enjoying a row – arranged with the Times Book Club itself to bring out a special edition of three of his plays – *Major Barbara*, *John Bull's Other Island* and *How He Lied To Her Husband* – 'thus obviating the inconvenience of his publishers' refusal to supply *The Times*', as an announcement in the paper put it.

The Book War did not end until the spring of 1908, when C. Arthur Pearson, the newspaper proprietor who was by then hoping to buy *The Times*, intervened to restore relations between *The Times* and the publishers, and the paper virtually conceded the publishers' case. But that takes us into the great events, for *The Times*, of that spring, which we shall turn to in the next chapter.

Chapter Four

Storm Clouds over the Empire: 1908–13

In 1908 dark clouds began to form over the *Times Literary Supplement*. In spite of all Moberly Bell's efforts, the financial situation of *The Times* had continued to deteriorate, and the smaller shareholders – the 'proprietors', as they were called – were getting restive. Moberly Bell devised various schemes to inject new money into the paper, but these came to nothing.

At last, Arthur Walter, the chief proprietor, bestirred himself down in his country retreat at Bear Wood, near Reading. Without even telling Buckle or Moberly Bell, he entered into an agreement with the newspaper proprietor Cyril Arthur Pearson, who was the owner amongst many other papers of the halfpenny *Daily Express* (as compared with the threepenny *Times*). Under this agreement a new company 'The Times Ltd' would be formed, into which Pearson's *Express* would be incorporated, and of which Pearson would be the managing director and Arthur Walter the chairman.

Moberly Bell learned of these plans only when he opened his copy of *The Times* in Dover (where he was meeting his daughter) on the morning of Tuesday, 7 January 1908. The night before, Buckle had received instructions from Walter to print on the leader page an announcement of the proposals. Buckle was astounded and outraged – especially outraged, at first, with Moberly Bell, since he assumed that the current managing director must have been in the know and had not confided in him – but he had no option but to do as he was asked.

It is easy to imagine how astonished and enraged in his turn Moberly Bell was. Yet, as one of his colleagues in the management, F. Harcourt Kitchin, puts it, 'he saw the greatest fight of his career opening out before him and his eyes glittered with the lust of battle'. When Kitchin asked him what he was going to do about 'this Pearson business', he replied 'Smash it!'

He immediately launched a campaign to save the paper in another way, and – now without telling Arthur Walter – had soon turned enough of the other proprietors against the Pearson plan to defeat it. Moreover he had found a new purchaser for *The Times* himself. This was none other than an even more substantial press proprietor than Pearson – Lord Northcliffe, formerly Alfred Harmsworth, the owner of the very successful halfpenny *Daily Mail*, and the man who perhaps would change newspapers more radically than any other in the twentieth century.

Moberly Bell's plans went forward in the greatest secrecy. In all the correspondence Northcliffe appeared as 'X' or 'Atlantic'; Moberly Bell appeared as 'Canton', Printing House Square itself was always 'Cenotaph' (perhaps a Northcliffe joke). Until 8 March, Arthur Walter himself only knew that a certain 'X' was making arrangements to buy his newspaper (by that date, Northcliffe felt honour bound to let him into the secret). And on 16 March, for £300,000, Northcliffe, the great, self-made newspaper proprietor of Britain, became the chief shareholder of its greatest newspaper. Another announcement appeared in *The Times* the following morning. It stated that a company would forthwith be formed to take over the publication of *The Times*, with Arthur Walter as chairman, a board of directors consisting solely of existing members of staff – and Moberly Bell as managing director. He had smashed the Pearson plan indeed.

The public, and the staff, were only very slowly to learn who the proprietor of this new Times Publishing Company was. Moberly Bell was at first extremely pleased with his deal. Northcliffe, man of immense and swashbuckling confidence though he was, was undoubtedly awed for the moment by this new purchase he had made, and Moberly Bell believed that by his successful scheme he had both saved *The Times* financially, and preserved it from any interference by its new owner. He was right about the first – but hopelessly wrong about the second, a miscalculation that probably led to his own death in the end from overwork because of Northcliffe's incessant demands on him.

Yet it was to be several years before the full force of Northcliffe's personality, and of his undoubted genius as a successful newspaper man, was to hit *The Times*. For the moment he was content to lie low. In a letter from him to Buckle on 20 June, 1908, three months after he bought it, he wrote 'The paper has, in my view, been so uniformly good for so many days past that I should like to take this opportunity of thanking you and your staff for its alertness accuracy variety and maintenance of tone' – though he added, more ominously, that 'if the present level can be maintained the depreciation which has been continuous since 1868 will be counteracted and eventually the journal will prosper and gain its old place in the respect of the country.' In another letter from him to Moberly Bell, in typically grandiose style, written on 9 July 1908, he declared that '*The Times* in my life is what a yacht or a racing stable is in others'' – that is to say, as long as it is well run, he was happy just to own it and let it be looked after by those responsible. But he did not believe it was well run, and by 1912, as we shall see, he had rid himself of virtually all the 'monks', as he called them – the senior members of the paper – who were now in his employ.

For the time being, the editorial staff went on much as before, and there was no dramatic change in the nature of the newspaper, though the presentation improved, and changes in the efficient running of the company were soon beginning to be felt with the arrival of some of Northcliffe's own management men. Above all, new and better presses were installed.

Nevertheless the old editorial staff were not happy. The world had changed for them, and they knew that the once timeless-seeming character of *The Times* was bound to yield at last in some degree to the commercial dictates of newspaper selling. Moreover the discord that had broken out between Arthur Walter and Moberly Bell was utterly at variance with the newspaper's long tradition of unspoken common purpose. The editor, Buckle, wrote a letter to Valentine Chirol, when he was complaining of some change he disliked in January 1910, which looks back to the mood of 1908, and how most of the staff had coped with it. 'Two years ago we were in a desperate position and we clutched at a means of escape for the sake of preserving the independence of *The Times*. We have secured it for two years and I think we should all be willing to make sacrifices in order to maintain it still . . . We none of us expected a bed of roses.'

Bruce Richmond's *Literary Supplement* went on with no visible changes, but he too was very clearly unhappy. Northcliffe was later to become extremely hostile to him, and perhaps something of that was evident from the start; but in any event Richmond loved the old ethos of the paper with a particular intensity and the change, it seems, was especially painful to him.

We can see from a rather amusing letter of Moberly Bell's to Northcliffe how much Richmond's charm and tact were themselves valued by his old friends. Moberly Bell, who at this time still thought himself to be on good terms with Northcliffe, was writing to him in January 1909. He privately suggested to Northcliffe that the editor, Buckle, should travel abroad more to enlarge his experience, and should also be encouraged to delegate more of his work to others. Buckle, he believed, had

> a disinclination to surrender one atom of authority to others. We all of us like him but it is positively absurd the way we have to conspire to bring before him some perfectly simple matter in a way that shall not render him suspicious. Richmond will come to me and say 'Now I don't think I had better suggest this, but if you would casually introduce the subject to Capper in his presence when I was in the room I think I might be able to join in and say what I think to you' and the probability is that when done in this elaborate and almost childish way he will quite readily agree to what he would have dismissed with contempt if said outright. But please regard all this as very confidential.

Such was Richmond's role in the higher diplomacy of *The Times*. But later that year he was to go through a crisis of his own, very clearly displayed in a series of letters of his to Moberly Bell that have survived.

The sequence seems to have begun (though not all the letters are dated) with a request by Richmond to be excused from working on the Saturday of the Whitsun weekend.

> The four Whitsun days are all the summer I shall get. If I am not obliged (as I hope I shant be) to take a week off my long holiday prematurely, I shall in the ordinary course of things be here in London from Whit Monday till the second week in November on end. So you will forgive me if I put what at first sight may seem an exaggerated value on four days in the country next week!
>
> Yrs with apologies B.L. Richmond.

However, Richmond's unhappiness went far deeper than just the need for a holiday, and he wrote another letter to Moberly Bell on that Whit Sunday, 1909. (It was addressed from the Oxford and Cambridge Club, so it looks as if he might not even have got his weekend in the country!)

His real concern was that, because of the new presses and the way they were being used, there were now too few pages in the *Literary Supplement* to cover the new books properly and promptly. So far in

1909, he wrote, 'we are 40 cols down on last year, which means 30 books unreviewed even if this year's space was to be the same as last year's.' (He was referring here to the fact that in the early part of 1908, there were virtually no publishers' advertisements because of the Book War.) But, he continued, 'the arrears are worse because I assumed we should have more space than last year (and laid in articles accordingly) acting on the general encouragement that was given to enlarge & vivify the paper all round during the last 6 months of 1908 which I did not know was to be only temporary.'

He recalled that in the 'barren' – i.e. advertisement-less – years of 1907 and 1908 'we took to French, German & Italian reviews and current notes' to fill the extra space. And he put forward his concept of the *Lit Supp*: 'a really good paper ought to give its readers reviews of the prominent English books, reviews of a few foreign books, the publishers' advertisements.' But what was the current situation?

In 1906 we gave them the first & third; in 1907/8 the first and second. In 1909 the second and third and half the first. If the *Suppts* of March 18, April 22, May 6, 13, 20 & 27 had been 12 pages each instead of 8 you would have had more Advts and we could have coped successfully with the publishing season which we have largely missed. And here is the root of the bother. Why weren't they 12 pages? In each case I wanted it to be 12, Buckle wanted it to be 12, and you were willing it should be 12. In each case we discussed it with the printer, and agreed it couldn't be done.

He now learned, he said, that the conditions that made twelve pages impossible on those dates were going to last until September, so all that the *Lit Supp* could do was 'draw a very high line for new books – two a week, if possible – work off such spring arrears as we can till September, and then scrap the rest, so as to start the autumn clear'.

Then Richmond opened the full throttle of his passion and eloquence and stated what was really upsetting him:

It is, of course, a bad thing that the efficiency of the *Suppt* should have to be so much regulated not by what I want or by what you want as by what the printer can or cannot do. But it is only a local instance in one corner of the paper of a very dangerous & most lamentable change which is being instilled into the paper as a whole – viz the change of allegiance from editor to printer.

Till a year ago with us, as in any decent paper, the idea was that everybody, printer included, did all he could to enable the editor to produce the best paper he could. The idea now is that the editor & his assistants must all work together as hard as they can to enable the printer to get the paper out. Most of the communications we have received from your side of late are suggestions that if the editor would do this, or would abstain from doing that, the printer would be able to print the paper; and a stranger coming into our room would think that someone or other had made a bet that a particular machine can print *The Times* & that the editorial staff were working to enable him to win his bet.

The dangerous result of this is the practical abolition of that part of our work in No. 8 [the editor's room] that consists in our being Watch Dogs of the paper – things get into the paper every day for which no-one in No. 8 is prepared to be responsible – the rising flood of journalese in the paper is a symptom of it – though it won't be realised till the first libel action.

This same autocracy of the printer, acting in a different way, has lamed the *Supplement*. We haven't retrogressed so much as I said (I admit I exaggerated that) – but it prevented our taking our opportunity of enormously strengthening our position. We have had a big chance this spring, & missed it.

Yrs B.L.R.

In spite of Richmond's slight retraction in the last paragraph of that Sunday letter, the crisis was not yet over. On the Thursday, 3 June, once that week's *Supplement* was finished, Richmond came back to the subject in another letter to Moberly Bell.

He began bitterly: 'I'm sorry to trouble you again over such a piece of deadwood as the *Lit. Sup.* has now become.' But he had now made his plans for the paper, accepting that – in an ironical echo of the circumstances which actually led to the creation of the paper – 'a 12 page supplement is impossible while Parliament is sitting', and that it now appeared 'that Parliament will sit well on into September'. 'However completely we may have lost our position in the literary world,' he went on with a further burst of bitterness, 'I think it would be unnecessarily foolish for us to go solemnly through the autumn publishing-season printing reviews of the spring books. We ought to start October clear of arrears, & keep abreast of things as well as we can (and as we are now going to suppress all French German & Italian reviews we shall be able to do it a little better).' The immediate question he wanted to ask Moberly Bell was, in this case, 'Shall you be willing at the end of September to pay for some 15 or 20 unused reviews? They average $1\frac{1}{2}$ cols each – say £90.' (The rate was still £3 a column.)

The managing director replied straightaway, though not, as we find, in a satisfactory manner, and on 4 June Richmond wrote to him again very fiercely. Moberly Bell had not given him a clear answer to his question, but had produced another set of figures on which Richmond poured scorn:

> My remark about the loss of prestige of the *Supplement* has no less force because you go to the trouble of computing in words instead of in articles. The fact that we've given the public 963,600 words (you say nothing about the Stops) means nothing to me – the *Police Gazette* [a popular crime newspaper of the time] has probably given them 970,000 – and to say that we, who come out weekly, are supplying the public at the rate of $3\frac{1}{2}$ cols. per diem seems to me, though no doubt accurate, a quite unilluminating calculation.
>
> The whole point is how we compare with former years. By reviewing books in a certain way & on a certain scale we achieved a certain position. In the first 21 weeks more than 100 cols have been taken away & you expect us to keep the same position. We cant – & we dont . . .
>
> As to the harm it has done us – it can be compressed into the fact that no one who wants to be abreast of books & literary matters can do so if he only takes *The Times*.
>
> Publishers' advertisements of the spring books are full of quotations from reviews from the other papers – but not from *The Times*, because *The Times* hasn't yet reviewed them. We are even behind the *Spectator*, a thing that had never happened before this Spring.

Finally, the editor of the *Times Literary Supplement* got very personal.

> The endless worries & false hopes over this rotten printing tells, I suppose, on our work too. I always used to edit the *Supplement* with eager delight and an intermittent sense of success & hope; it is now a weekly drudge dogged with a sense generally of failure, always of hindrance. I'm conceited enough to think we should have made it the first Literary Paper very soon. We've muckered a big chance.
> Yrs B.L.R.

There was a final, even more painful letter, undated but apparently from some time later in the summer of 1909. It gives, incidentally, a good picture of Richmond's working life at this time. The occasion was a proposal that he should work longer in the evenings. To this he said:

> On the working days my disposable time averages $3\frac{1}{2}$ hours – I am free from 2.30 to 4.30 and from 7.30 to nine (true, I have more leisure on Thursdays, but that is balanced by my having none what-ever on Wednesdays). Into these $3\frac{1}{2}$ hours I have to cram all prep-aration for my work – the seeing people, the hearing of new ideas, books, music, pictures – all the rubbing shoulders that give a journal-ist stimulus. You can hardly expect me to greet the proposal to reduce those $3\frac{1}{2}$ hours to 2 without cursing God and man – particularly man. However damnable a man's position is, he resents all efforts to make it more damnable – and even a man who is as sick of his job as I am, has enough keenness to hate being made more & more incompetent to perform it.

In fact, he wrote, 'for some time & for many reasons I have begun to think that the office has got out of me all the good it is likely to get: & that the place for a sucked orange is the dustbin & not the shop-window. Even if I liked it I doubt if I could hold on much longer: much less now that I have come to loathe it so, & that the spirit of the office is so changed.'

He concluded by telling Moberly Bell not to worry – 'it wont take me as it took MacDowall [sic] & Blakiston – I watched it break them, but that was because they were caught too young – I had had time to toughen before I began – & though it has broken my spirit it hasn't touched my health. I didn't say I should imitate Blakiston, I only said I envied him. I certainly do. Yrs B.L.R.'

This was a particularly grim set of remarks, for Blakiston – the Hugh Blakiston who wrote some excellent reviews of books about Germany – had committed suicide, supposedly because of the strain of his work in the Foreign Department of *The Times*. (However, Northcliffe and the new 'spirit of the office' could in no way be blamed for this, since Blakiston died in February 1906.) As for McDowall (the correct spell-ing), a Fellow of All Souls and a political leader writer on the paper, he experienced a breakdown in his health and had to leave; he retired to Dorset and became a close friend of Thomas Hardy, and wrote reviews for Richmond for many years afterwards.

The crisis evidently passed. Richmond neither died nor left the paper. The sucked orange got its juice back. Nor in fact, though it had fewer pages for a while, and no doubt temporarily lost some of its standing, does it look at all like 'deadwood' in the perspective of history. By the end of 1909 the *Lit Supp* would have acquired a splendid, varied team of contributors. In fact, only a month after that Whitsun weekend which began it all, in the issue of 8 July 1909, there was an epoch-making review by Percy Lubbock of the collected edition of the novels of Henry James. And much later, in a letter written in 1934, Richmond was able to look back on the whole sequence of years 'from, say, 1906 to 1926' as one when the *Lit Supp* 'got along fairly well' because throughout that period it 'contrived to have two publics: 1) what for brevity I may call the feminine public – books for the drawing room, lending library books, the book of the moment; 2) the more serious reader – books for the study, books to buy, permanent books'.

What did the *Lit Supp* offer its 'two publics' in the years 1908 to 1913? As Richmond said, it did not neglect the popular books – innumerable long-forgotten novels, biographies and books on topics such as golf (with that famously genial *Times* golf-writer Bernard Darwin ruminating in April 1908 on 'the amount of hard thinking that can be concentrated on the apparently simple art of hitting a ball'), motor cars (including a review headed teasingly 'For Moneyed Motorists' in January 1909) and shooting (with Captain Aymer Maxwell reviewing *High Pheasants in Theory and Practice* by Sir Ralph F. Pryce-Galloway in August 1913, and advising readers on how to kill a high pheasant cleanly when it has passed overhead). Such subjects also turned up in weightier reviews, as when Quiller-Couch, robust as ever, asked in September 1909 'Who would not wish to be the first to travel with Dr Johnson in a motor-car?'

Some of these books had full-length reviews in the main body of the paper, and many more appeared in the 'Book List' which the indefatigable Mr Dalton continued to produce, writing short notes on fifty or more books of every kind in most weeks.

The reviewing of the more important literary books was allotted even more clearly to the members of two different camps in these years 1908 to 1913. Obviously Richmond was glad to have them both in his paper.

The 'old guard', as we may now begin to call them, were as strongly represented as ever – John Cann Bailey, Arthur Clutton-Brock, Harold Child, and an important new acquisition who nevertheless fell into this group, the poet Walter de la Mare. There is a very interesting review by Bailey in October 1913 of a book on Walter Pater by the poet Edward Thomas. Bailey said he did not like the book because he did not think Thomas had understood Pater, whose enormous influence around the turn of the century has now been largely forgotten, but whom one can feel at the back of all this group of mainly Christian and classically-trained *Lit Supp* writers. Bailey concluded his review by describing Pater's spiritual state of mind, and it read as if it were the state of mind he himself most passionately aspired to.

Pater's novel *Marius the Epicurean* (which was published in 1885), Bailey wrote, was 'the most penetrating study ever written of the food for the spirit which could be got by a spiritually-minded man out of ancient paganism and philosophy, as well as that which could not be got, and of the manner in which, then as now, sensitive and intelligent men find their approach to Christianity'. In fact Pater's mind had 'a central Platonic quality . . . which can see in art an infinite power of forming life and can yet see that the best and strongest life requires to be controlled by something more entirely free from the action of the senses than art can ever be'.

This vision of the exalted marriage of the religion of art and beauty and of the Christian religion can be sensed everywhere in one of Bailey's major reviews, his article on 4 November 1909, on *Shelley: The Man and the Poet* by none other than his colleague Arthur Clutton-Brock. In it he praised Clutton-Brock for his 'cool, discriminating, unblinded' account of Shelley the man, but his own admiration for Shelley the idealist and poet colours every word he wrote. If 'most young men do not behave as foolishly or badly as Shelley' it was because 'they have not his courage'. Moreover, 'every one who has felt the unique wonder of Shelley must be conscious of a kind of profanation' in saying critical things about him at all. Shelley might not have had the 'sovereign, all-embracing humanity' of Shakespeare, but he was 'a pure untainted spirit in a gross and tainted world, a vision of beauty to those who can see spirits, an ever-working force of hope and love and justice to those minorities to whom in the future the progress of the world will be due'. He was inspired, Bailey concluded, not by 'private joy or fame, but precisely by this hope that through his poetry he might become an energy of life to the best elements in human existence. And before the Mediterranean waters closed over his head that hope had become an undying reality.'

It was a tremendous closing peroration to a review trembling with exalted emotion, and oddly enough Bernard Shaw wrote to him about the review. In his diary Bailey quotes the characteristically pungent Shavian letter: 'Would you mind telling me who you are? . . . It is so exceedingly rare to find an English critic with any power of analysis in psychology – or indeed anything else – that I am justified, I think, in desiring to know which of us is capable of writing that remarkable article on Shelley.' The main thrust of the article was not psychological analysis, so Shaw, like most readers, might have found in it only what he was looking for – or he may actually have been struck by the romantic fervour of it, and analysed his own pleasure incorrectly – but it was certainly a testimony to the power of the piece.

It is instructive to compare Bailey's piece with a review by Virginia Woolf (still Virginia Stephen) of a book on Shelley on 5 March 1908. Virginia Woolf stood at the head of the other group of contributors: the young, brilliant, questioning and sceptical minds. Percy Lubbock was still very actively one of them, while an important new recruit, perhaps brought in by Lubbock, who was a close friend, was George Calderon. All these wrote numerous dashingly intelligent reviews for the *Lit Supp* in the years leading up to the First World War, and in 1908 and 1909 Virginia Woolf was on the page almost every week.

Her Shelley review was of a volume called *Letters from Percy Bysshe Shelley to Elizabeth Hitchener*, annotated and published by Bertram Dobell. These were the letters that Shelley wrote to a country schoolmistress – 'probably the first clever woman he had met' – in 1811 and 1812. He was nineteen when he first knew her, she was twenty-eight. The review really was a brilliant piece of psychological analysis, and read like a short story. Miss Hitchener was 'in need of someone with whom she could discuss the pleasant agitation of her soul'; Shelley could 'pour forth to her, as to some impersonal deity, the surprising discoveries and ardent convictions' which at that age were coming to him 'with such bewildering rapidity . . . The poor schoolmistress took vague alarm when she found to what a mate she had attached herself, what opinions she must embrace; and yet there was a strange and laughable exhilaration in it, which urged her on.' Shelley even persuaded her to come down to Devon to walk and talk with him and to educate his young wife Harriet, but inevitably the relationship soon came to an end. Virginia Woolf ended by imagining that Miss Hitchener 'recovered her senses, and lived a respectable and laborious life at Edmonton, sweetened by the reading of the poets, and the memory of her romantic indiscretions with the truest of them all'.

Of course this was a different kind of book about Shelley from the one Bailey had reviewed, but one can imagine what a spiritual meal Bailey would have made of it. Virginia Woolf would doubtless have agreed with him, if pressed, that writers hope through their work to 'become an energy of life to the best elements in human existence' but one feels she would have hated being drawn into a discussion of such vague, high-minded abstractions.

Richmond gave Virginia Woolf a great variety of books to review, and she tackled most of them with the same precision of definition, vividness of imagery and vigour of judgment. Writing about a book on Burmese Buddhist monks in 1908, she reflected that their faith doubtless 'keeps them happy and makes them unafraid', but asks if this is 'the richest way' for religion to look at the world – 'Does it require any faith so high as that which believes that it is right to develop your powers to the utmost?' There speaks Bloomsbury loud and clear. In 1909, in a long, brilliant essay on the playwright Sheridan (for which she got £10 13s. 9d. – about £530 today), she deftly disentangled his sentimentality from his wit, and concluded with a picture of him as 'a battered Orpheus, still talking divinely'.

She also wrote many long reviews about past novelists, in which, while looking very closely and clearly at their qualities, we also feel her trying to articulate her idea of what her own novels should be. Writing about George Gissing in January 1912, she said that 'a good novelist goes about the world seeing squares and circles where the ordinary person sees mere stormdrift'. Gissing had this gift. 'He had a world of his own as real, as hard, as convincing as though it were made of earth and stone.' It may have been a small world – but it was 'a little world for us to walk in with all that a human being needs'. And on 8 May 1913, now as Mrs Woolf (she had married Leonard Woolf in August the previous year), and with her first novel, *The Voyage Out*, just finished, she contributed a remarkable piece on Jane Austen. She praised her for 'being so fastidious, so conscious of her own limitations, that when she found out that hedges do not grow in Northamptonshire she eliminated her hedge rather than run the risk of inventing one which could not exist'; she found those limitations noticeable only when Jane Austen was saying seriously that such and such people were good – for 'when she is pointing out where they are bad, weak, faulty, exquisitely absurd, she is winged and unapproachable. Her heroes may be insipid, but think of her fools!'

George Calderon's reviews often sparkled on the pages of the *Lit Supp* as brightly as Virginia Woolf's. He was a keen-eyed, dark-featured, swashbuckling figure, who after Rugby and Trinity College, Oxford, had travelled widely and lived for some years in Russia, and finally settled in the 'Vale of Health' on Hampstead Heath. Though he was English, his grandfather had been a Spanish monk and they were descended from the Spanish dramatist Calderón. He himself wrote a number of plays that were performed in London, including the first translations of Chekhov's *The Seagull* and *The Cherry Orchard*. Rather lightly, he held high Tory views, and he was especially hostile to the suffragettes – moreover, he was already forty in 1908 – but his witty scepticism aligned him wholly with the younger group on the *Lit Supp*.

In 1909, we find him teasing G.K. Chesterton over his book *Orthodoxy*. He found Chesterton a 'great entertainer ... no-one else can make his peculiar cakes'. But his journalism, he felt, did not stand up in book form. 'The fact is that Mr Chesterton cannot believe or disbelieve anything, because his organ of belief has been displaced by his organ of preference ... We think, therefore we are; but if Mr Chesterton began to think he could cease to exist; so he writes instead, and we are all the richer for it.' The following year he reviewed a book by Frank Podmore, a virulent opponent of the 'new spiritualism', with its belief in messages from the dead. Unfortunately, Mr Podmore was by now dead himself. Will he now be busy in the beyond, asks Calderon, 'confounding his brother ghosts by denying the genuineness of their messages from the living? Or will he sit down with a chastened spirit to devise some method of proving his continued existence to those he has left behind?'

Calderon also reviewed many books about Russia, and could be just as mocking about them. He took issue, for instance, with Maurice Baring's *Russian Essays and Studies*:

> He chooses almost at random what he will tell us ... We do not care a jot whether the sun, as it was setting on the day that Mr Baring arrived at Yaroslav, 'made for itself a thin strip of gold beneath the grey masses' of cloud, because the same thing might have occurred at Tomsk or Tobolsk or Birmingham. There was no reason in the scheme of the universe why a particular sunset should greet Mr Baring's arrival at Yaroslav; it was a pure accident, and does not appear to have been hallowed by any particular sympathy with Mr Baring's mood at the time.

He also scored a point when, reviewing Aylmer Maude's *Life of Tolstoy*, he asked if Maude 'has Tolstoy's authority for persistently calling the Rostófs of *War and Peace* the "Róstovs"'. Maude was able to reply impressively, in a letter on 1 April 1909, that he had now asked Tolstoy personally about the matter; however, he had to acknowledge that Tolstoy 'pronounces the family name "Rostóf" like the town of the same name'.

Calderon, though by now forty-five, forced his way into the Blues regiment as an interpreter when war broke out in 1914. Percy Lubbock, who wrote a very affectionate book about him in 1921, said 'he was one of the few whom the war found ready, intellectually and morally; his life passed straight into it without a break or disturbance, he seemed to enter into the possession of an inheritance'. He was killed at Gallipoli on 4 June 1915. He must have been one of the most tragic losses to literature of the war. The poet Laurence Binyon (also a regular contributor to the *Lit Supp*, often on the subject of Japanese art) prefaced Lubbock's book with a poem to him:

> *Him now as of old I see*
> *Carrying his head with an air*
> *Courteous and virile,*
> *With the charm of a nature free,*
> *Daring, resourceful, prompt,*
> *In his frank and witty smile.*
>
> *By Oxford towers and streams*
> *Who shone among us all*
> *In body and brain so bold?*
> *Who shaped so firm his themes*
> *Crystal-hard in debate?*
> *And who hid a heart less cold?*
>
> *But that so fearless friend*
> *With his victorious smile*
> *My mourning mood has chid.*
> *He went to the very end;*
> *He counted not the cost:*
> *What he believed, he did.*

On 8 July 1909 Percy Lubbock contributed a lead review of 'the lengthening row of tall grass-green volumes in which Mr Henry James is marshalling his "collected works"'. Appearing as it did in the *Lit Supp*, it marked an epoch in what might reasonably be called the 'Establishment' view of the art of the novel.

This set of James's novels, wrote Lubbock, formed 'a monument of art so fine in quality and at the same time so remote from anything which has preceded it that it has for the critic a double proportion of suggestion and challenge'. First, its 'intricate and highly civilised beauty demands characterisation'. But the challenge went much further. In English fiction, Lubbock declared, we are used to work 'in which the beauties and excellencies are more or less easily detachable from the main fabric . . . We may separate from the generous heap the qualities that please us, as we might pick out the grapes or the apricots from a cornucopia of summer fruit.' (That aptly described much of the *Lit Supp* reviewing of the time.) But in James's novels 'we cannot isolate certain qualities without finding ourselves involved with all the rest' for each of them is 'a densely-woven tapestry, in which style, line, colour and composition are all of a piece, all inherent, all part of one process.' He continued with great sensitivity to pick out many beautiful illustrations of this.

Of course, fiction reviewing did not change completely overnight in the *Lit Supp* after this challenging review. But it made its impact, and novels in general began to be treated with closer critical attention than they had been before. Significant outer signs of this came on 13 April 1911 when the old distinction on the front-page index between 'Literature' and 'Fiction' was dropped and all the books appeared in a single list under 'Literature'. The issue of 30 October 1913 was unprecedentedly billed as a 'Fiction Number', with twelve pages being devoted to a wide-ranging survey of the subject.

In 1913, Henry James himself came on to the scene. His first volume of autobiography, *A Small Boy and Others*, was enthusiastically if rather poetically reviewed by Walter de la Mare on 10 April ('"What Maisie knew" is no more than a trifle compared with what her creator has remembered.'). Later that month James agreed, if not yet to review a new book on Balzac by Emile Faguet, at any rate to read it 'with an eye to possibilities', as he said in a letter to Richmond. By May he was saying he would do the review, but not until June ('I work slowly at this somewhat stricken season' – it had been a very hot May). By 11 June, he was 'packing it down tighter', condensing 'more than 5000 distilled words' into '4000 words even more distilled'.

On 15 June he sent Richmond his 'Balzac paper', and a day or so later wrote one of his most famous letters: when Richmond asked him to cut it still further he groaned 'I have done it *tant bien que mal* – though feeling it thereby bleeds. But it's a bloody trade.' At last, on 19 June, the review appeared – one of James's best-known critical essays, with its subtle account of Balzac's joy in turning the 'jungle' of Paris into art. It was published anonymously, like all the other reviews, but one feels that many readers must have divined its authorship.

There was a touching little coda to these Jamesian events of 1913. On 4 December, Richmond entitled Mme Duclaux's excited review of the first volume of Proust's *A la recherche du temps perdu*, 'A Small

Boy and Others', drawing the elderly master and the rising master together. Meanwhile James promised a survey of the new English novelists for spring 1914.

Joseph Conrad, for all that, did not do particularly well when one of his greatest novels, *Under Western Eyes*, was reviewed by Harold Child in October 1911. Child wrote that 'from its pregnant opening to its terrible, gloomy close it is an enthralling story about real people'. But he never engaged (as E.V. Lucas did) with its arresting moral and political propositions; rather, he was content to say 'we meet strange people' and 'they remain strange till the end', even if 'we begin to understand why they are strange, and that is more than half-way to knowledge'. Child gave the same rather grudging kind of praise to *Some Reminiscences*, Conrad's autobiography, when it came out three months later, calling it 'a delightful book, a winning book, a wise book', yet dwelling mainly on its failure to help us understand Conrad much better.

In 1908, *A Room with a View*, E.M. Forster's third novel, was reviewed by Virginia Woolf, as his previous one had been. She took it seriously – writing that it gives us 'that odd sense of freedom which books give us when they seem to represent the world as we see it' – but she confessed to some disappointment that in the end 'the view is smaller than we expected', due to 'some belittlement that seems to cramp the souls of the actors'. Two years later Lubbock reviewed Forster's next book, *Howard's End*. Forster must have been gratified. In all his three previous books, Lubbock wrote, 'there was an uncertainty of attack and a want of harmony in the method which prevented an exceptionally fine sense of character from making its proper effect', but here 'his highly original talent has found full and ripe expression'. He picked out a 'unique' quality in Forster: 'an odd charming vein of poetry which slips delicately in and out of his story, vanishing the instant it has said enough to suggest something rare and romantic and intangible about the person or the place'. However, Lubbock added, this was 'a refinement which belonged to realism, not romance, for it was simply due justice done to an element in life too momentary and swift for most realism, so called, to overtake'. Here Lubbock lives up to the critical challenge he had himself thrown down in the article on Henry James – and he did as well by Forster in a short review of his volume of stories, *The Celestial Omnibus*, the following year.

The rising new novelist in England at this time was D.H. Lawrence.

The *Lit Supp* missed his first book, *The White Peacock* in 1911, but W.J. Lancaster gave his first great novel, *Sons and Lovers*, a mostly good, if rather short review in June 1913. He described it as 'a complex study of warring loves and passions, containing much beauty, but often overwrought'. He found the sincerity of the book unquestionable, and concluded: 'The toil of existence in village and town, the solace of Nature, the joy of occasional respite from labour are admirably realized and rendered.' This was recognition of the book's novelty – if in rather old-fashioned language, by this time.

Harold Child took charge of H.G. Wells's *Tono-Bungay* and *Ann Veronica* in 1909, characteristically expressing himself more hopeful than Wells had been in the first, a rather Balzacian panorama of Britain, and wondering how typical Wells's portrait of the 'new woman' had been in the second. Lubbock took over *The History of Mr Polly* in 1910 and *The New Machiavelli* in 1911. He thought Mr Polly was a beautifully worked out study of human stupidity and the 'huge and pitiless waste it involves', but felt that Wells had been there before. However, he considered *The New Machiavelli* to be Wells's most important book so far, with its two threads running through 'a seething mass of material' – the political, 'his hero's desire to build a new state', and the personal, 'his failure to adjust to this constructive ambition the passions of his inner life'. (Put like that, it seems a tale still being told very often ninety years on.)

Arnold Bennett received rather meagre treatment, as he usually did in the *Lit Supp*, but Walter de la Mare, in what was for him a surprising tribute to naturalism, said of *The Old Wives' Tale* in 1908 that 'not often comes a book in which every human being portrayed so quietly takes our confidence'. De la Mare also liked Bennett's 'unconquerably young' hero in *The Card* (1911) and *The Regent* (1913).

Calderon was his sparkling, up-to-date self again in his review of G.K. Chesterton's *The Man Who Was Thursday* in 1908 – 'It is full of witty turns, but they are like the flashes of blue light in a tube railway, irrelevant expenditures of motor energy.' W.J. Lancaster enjoyed Beerbohm's *Zuleika Dobson* (the story of the girl for whom the whole of Oxford died of love) in 1911 – 'Oh! Mr Beerbohm, happy in thy quiddity through 350 bland and dulcet pages. Happy in allusion, in reflection, in words exquisite – "omnisubjugant", "inenubilable", "orgulous" – one thing we defy thee to tell us – how it fared with Zuleika at Cambridge.'

But E.V. Lucas, however perceptive he may have been about Conrad's sea, did not appreciate Kenneth Grahame's river: he called

The Wind in the Willows, when it was published in 1908, 'a book with hardly a smile in it . . . Grown-up readers will find it monotonous; children will hope in vain for more fun.' The world, both of grown-ups and children, has long and totally disagreed with him there. However they might have just concurred with poor Lucas when, in his complete misunderstanding of the book, he added that 'as a contribution to natural history the work is negligible'.

In spite of his page problems, Richmond managed to keep an eye on France. Emile Zola died in 1908, and on the day his ashes were transferred to the Pantheon, Francis Gribble wrote an article about the debate that was even then raging about his merits. Many people thought that Zola had 'conquered immortality . . . he had worked at fiction with the brain of a chess master . . . he had painted French manners with a fearless fidelity hitherto unattempted'. But his critics said that that kind of brain was 'more suited for playing chess than for writing novels', and that his pictures of French manners were 'calumnious caricatures'. Gribble left it to posterity to decide between them.

Meanwhile, Mme Duclaux went on assiduously seeking out good new French novels. On 19 August 1909 (one of Richmond's lamentably small issues), she contributed a perceptive review of André Gide's *La Porte étroite* – 'this frail and delicious spiritual story' – while on 4 December she had her great triumph, picking out *Du Côté de chez Swann*, the first volume of Proust's great novel, as an outstanding new work, and catching its quality in brilliant comments. Not only did the novel recover the images stored in the narrator's childhood, which were exhaled here 'as naturally as vapour from a new-ploughed autumn furrow', but it showed the same events through his adult eyes: 'no sooner have we accustomed ourselves to the sun-pierced mist of early reminiscence than the light changes, we find ourselves in glaring noon; the magic glory fades from M. Swann and the fair, frail Odette de Crecy . . .' It is not surprising that Mme Duclaux – formerly Mary Robinson, and now living in France as the wife of the head of the Pasteur Institute – had earlier been known as a poet. She must certainly get much of the credit for the speed with which Proust was taken up and enjoyed in this country.

Poetry fared less well in these years, though they were not especially notable for poetry in Britain anyway. Unfortunately, the *Lit Supp* failed at first to recognise the merits of the one outstanding newcomer, Ezra Pound. Two small books by him fell in 1909 into the hands of Mr Dalton, slaving away on his Book List on the back pages, and got short shrift from him. His note on *Personae of Ezra Pound* was:

> Ezra Pound admires Browning, whom he addresses as 'Old Hip-pety-hop of the accents'. Like Browning he is fond of medieval and Italian themes, and he affects the eccentric and the obscure; but these qualities do not in these pages at any rate, leave much room for beauty.

Dalton's note on *Exultations of Ezra Pound* was slightly kinder, if no more perceptive:

> Mr Pound, though he is not ambitious, and his poems are slight, sings of what he feels, drawing his inspiration mainly from Italy and the Middle Age; and as a composer of metrical music he has an original gift which appeals to the reader the more closely he is studied. Some of his poems have appeared in evening London papers and in the *English Review*.

Not to detect Pound's ambitiousness seems the greatest failure there. Pound's translations of Cavalcanti were reviewed by John Cann Bailey in 1912, but compared unfavourably to those by Rossetti, and Pound himself replied genially in a letter, making the point that he, unlike Rossetti, had been trying to convey the force of Cavalcanti's personality. But for a long time afterwards he continued to receive meagre or no reviews. One hopes that this was not because in 1914–15 he mockingly reprinted in the *Egoist* a number of extracts from what he considered foolish reviews in the *Lit Supp*, heading one instalment 'Inconsiderable Imbecilities'.

The 'Georgian poets' did not get a particularly warm welcome in 1912 either. John Cann Bailey found in many of them a tendency 'to go perilously near the note and methods of the modern descriptive journalists'. Child had played the friendly schoolmaster when he reviewed the first book – simply called *Poems* – of the most gifted of them, Rupert Brooke, a year previously. He had been struck by the 'swagger and brutality' in Brooke's poems – and found his sonnet on love and sea-sickness 'disgusting' – but he thought those characteristics were 'obviously boyish', and detected in him 'a rich nature – sensuous, eager, brave – fighting eagerly towards the truth.' He reminded Brooke that 'swagger and brutality are no more poetry than an unripe pear is fruit'. Clutton-Brock took on his colleague Walter de la Mare's volume, *The Listener and Other Poems*, quite sensitively describing him as 'listening for a music that comes in the quiet hours ... listening for an answer', but rather regretting that he did not try, as Blake did, to give an answer.

John Cann Bailey was more at home with the collected *Poetical Works of Robert Bridges*, published in 1913, the year that Bridges, now a grand old man of sixty-nine, became Poet Laureate. The continuity was clear with the other opinions Bailey expressed: 'It is not for nothing that Mr Bridges is steeped in the poetry of Greece and Rome, above all, in English poetry, that he has made a study of the great Christian hymns, that he is a master of music. All those things make themselves felt in his unfailing sense of language and rhythm, in his incapacity to produce either an empty or a vulgar line of verse, in his grave emotion as of one who has kept company with the ages.'

The lively American, Logan Pearsall Smith, reviewed Bridges's *Tract on the Present State of English Pronunciation* in June 1913, glad that Bridges had raised the question of preserving the beauty of English speech, but wondering if we could actually define what was beautiful in pronunciation and what was ugly. (However, Smith joined Bridges on the original committee of the Society for Pure English when it was founded in Oxford that same year.) Bridges himself also contributed some articles to the *Lit Supp*, in one notable piece in 1911 praising the inestimable literary and moral beauty of the Authorized Version of the Bible, but surprisingly accepting that 'revision will not annihilate the book'.

As for Robert Bridges's predecessor as Poet Laureate, Alfred Austin, no-one had a good word to say for him. When he was appointed in 1896, he was widely regarded as a hack Conservative journalist getting his reward from Lord Salisbury, and Percy Lubbock was severe with the supposedly patriotic poems in his 1908 collection, *Sacred and Profane Love*. He quoted one beginning 'Plotters insolent and vain,/Muster then your servile swarms', and asks where the 'beauty and sacredness of patriotism' is in 'such screaming, pot-and-kettle vituperation'. As for Austin's *Autobiography*, which came out in 1911 when he was seventy-six, the leader writer T. Humphry Ward (husband of the novelist Mrs Humphry Ward) found it interesting when it recorded what eminent people had said to him, but thought that the many compliments to his own abilities that he quoted would better have been quoted by somebody else.

Finally, in the reviewing of French poetry, a new name appeared, that of 'L.S. Woolf' as he appears in the marked copies – Leonard Woolf, the husband from 1912 of Virginia. Poetry is a subject not normally associated with that writer – in fact in the summer of 1913 he was beginning to commit himself in his own mind to the future of English socialism – but he rose to the occasion more thoughtfully than any of the other poetry critics of the paper at this time.

Reviewing Stéphane Mallarmé's poems on 1 May 1913 (when he and Virginia were living in London at Clifford's Inn), he questioned sharply whether Mallarmé was right in thinking that poetry only needed sound and rhythm, not 'verbal signification'. Mallarmé, he wrote, 'lit his lamp, and drew his curtain; he forgot that there had been once, and was still, something on the other side of the curtain, that there was anything in the world but the sheet of white paper and the pen; he forgot that he was a man'.

Reviewing *Cinq Grandes Odes* by Paul Claudel on 18 December the same year (by which time the Woolfs had moved to Asheham in Sussex, after Virginia's attempt at suicide in September), he wrote that simply by employing the rhythm of breathing, Claudel was able to pour forth his thoughts effectively – 'the richness and the rush of words and metaphors and images give the Odes a little of that exhilarating speed that one gets best from flying or from some of the odes of Pindar' (a provocative juxtaposition for one venturing among all the *Lit Supp* classicists). But, he concluded, even where Claudel succeeded, his poetry was scarcely distinguishable from good rhythmical prose. Leonard Woolf was a dependable man who liked to get things clear.

British politics went through one of its major crises in this period. Lloyd George's proposals in his 1909 Budget, with its increased income tax and new land tax, brought the Liberal government into serious conflict with the Conservative-dominated House of Lords. Eventually, after a threat by the government to swamp the Lords with 500 new Liberal peers to get its bills through, the Lords agreed to a Parliament Act in 1911 which gave it power to delay bills, but no longer to prevent their passage altogether.

The Times naturally gave due space to all this, as it did to the continuing battle over Home Rule for Ireland, but very little of either issue was reflected in the *Lit Supp*. Even when King Edward VII died on 6 May 1910, and was succeeded by his son George V, the only reference to the event in the *Lit Supp* of 12 May was an advertisement for the new (and obviously hastily renamed) *George V Prayer Book* by the Times Book Club.

Contemporary politics tended to be reflected only in reviews of books taking larger views of the subject. The most important of these was the first volume of the great new life of Benjamin Disraeli, by the *Times* assistant editor, William Flavelle Monypenny. It was reviewed on 27 October 1910, by John Morley, the author of the Gladstone biography which received so much attention in 1903. Now a Liberal peer, with the title Viscount Morley, he had been in the thick of the battle in the Lords all this year, trying to win the Conservative majority round to co-operation from confrontation. We have his own comment in one of his letters on being asked to write the review:

> By some strange and absurd impulse I promised – to write something for *The Times*, about the new life of Beaconsfield, and I am now engaged in keeping my word. I find that my pen has got rusty, or else I am less easily contented; anyhow it is uphill work. I have a considerable liking for Dizzy in a good many things: his mockery of the British Philistine, his aloofness and detachment from hollow conventions, and so forth. How on earth such a man ever became an extremely popular Prime Minister, I can never tell.

Morley's long review had his by-line on it, the usual policy of the *Lit Supp* when reviewing a book that emanated from *The Times* in any way, but Richmond must have been rather glad too to be able to signal what an eminent reviewer he had caught, for Morley's standing both as writer and statesman was very high at that time. In fact, Morley does seem a little rusty in the piece, or perhaps just overburdened with work.

The review was full of splendid remarks, but it hung rather loosely together compared with his carefully written John Stuart Mill article in 1906. It was not short on praise for Disraeli, though he had died only thirty years before and was leader of the opposing party: 'When he came to the great business of his life, the creation and working of a powerful political party, he showed himself cool, shrewd, patient, far-sighted, practical, full of tactical resource, a consummate master of the fatiguing art of managing men' (that word 'fatiguing' seems particularly heartfelt!). However, Morley was less complimentary about Disraeli's political thinking than his political skills, quoting a flowery speech of his against the Poor Law, and commenting 'We think of the French wit's irreverent jingle about Bossuet's grand periods, that they *resonnent plus qu'ils ne raisonnent*.'

Writing of Monypenny, the author, he was not so much critical as *de haut en bas* about his qualifications: 'He has never sat in Parliament, and the House of Commons was his hero's theatre . . . He has not been a votary in the gilded saloons that Disraeli frequented so systematically and found so adorable, on the principle that in spite of Reform Bills, ballot, and halfpenny newspapers, *C'est toujours le beau monde qui gouverne le monde.*' As for allusions to current political controversy, Morley confined himself to teasing Monypenny for dismissing the Benthamites and Utilitarians as 'insular anachronisms' – 'keeping company, I suppose, in that limbo,' he wrote, 'with Locke and Adam Smith, and lesser English masters of the political philosophy of our Western world'.

So, within the confines of the political debate as it manifested itself in the *Lit Supp*, both Liberals and Conservatives received a good hearing. It was the burgeoning Labour Party which had to take the knocks. Dr Shadwell, still the working man's champion but perhaps even more fiercely anti-socialist by now, wrote a caustic and comic review of Ramsay MacDonald's *Socialism and Government* on 25 November 1909. He praised what he thought was a very 'canny' socialist manifesto, but did not think it would get the author very far:

> We are afraid that Mr MacDonald's fine-spun web will catch neither the common or street-corner bluebottle nor the robust and full-blooded insects of the Social Democratic genus; but *Fabiana subtilis* and *Radicalis confusa* will probably find it highly attractive, and some specimens of *Ecclesiastica sentimentalis* may also be caught.

MacDonald, it might be said, turned the tables on his reviewer by eventually becoming the first Labour Prime Minister – though only, in the end, to be repudiated by most of his party, so perhaps Shadwell had the last laugh of all.

Imperial problems still loomed large in the paper in these years just before the First World War. The final volumes of *The Times History of the War in South Africa*, still edited by L.S. Amery, came out in 1909, and were reviewed on 1 July by H.A.L. Fisher, again with a by-line. Fisher was another outstanding catch for Richmond, a New College historian who would also become an important Liberal minister: as President of the Board of Education under Lloyd George he would bring in the influential Fisher Act of 1916, with its increase in salary for elementary school teachers, and its extension of state scholarships.

Here he described Amery's continuing preoccupation without implying any particular criticism of it: 'in his hands *The Times History of the War* is a history with a mission . . . to defend Imperialism in the past, to make Imperialists in the present, and by displaying not only the virtues but also the faults of British organisation to strengthen the Empire against the perils of the future'. His liberalism revealed itself more, perhaps, in his praise of the reconstruction since the war – 'a manifestation of disinterested endeavour on the part not only of the leading statesmen, but of countless obscure persons, nurses, teachers in concentration camps, repatriation officers, Civil servants, even despised English pro-Boers.'

John Buchan had a chance to shine over South Africa, from which he had returned in 1903; he was now writing novels, working for the publisher Thomas Nelson and also trying to become a Conservative MP, though in his autobiography he said that the glamour went out of politics for him when Balfour retired from the leadership of the Conservative Party in 1911. He wrote a romantic piece for the paper on Cecil Rhodes, evoking his funeral in the Matopo hills when 'as the English hymn was sung over his grave, far down on the slopes could be heard the low hum of many voices . . . the Matabele warriors whom he had conquered chanting after their custom the praises of the dead' (rather like Morley on Disraeli); while a book on Afrikanderisms gave this Scotsman the opportunity to cite the use of the word 'Scotchman' to mean 'a florin' in Natal, 'which commemorates a fraudulent Caledonian who palmed off two-shilling pieces as half-crowns'.

One other book on Britain's role overseas that the *Lit Supp* treated as a major work was *Modern Egypt*, by the Earl of Cromer, who had been responsible for British policy in Egypt for over a quarter of a century of war and complicated indirect rule. Valentine Chirol, the foreign editor, reviewed it over two numbers (5 and 12 March 1908) under the heading 'A Great Page of History'. He said that 'since Caesar wrote *De Bello Gallico*, we can recall no instance of a great Captain of the State telling so fully and unreservedly and with such lucidity and candour, whilst still fresh in the memory of living men, the story of great events *quorum pars maxima fuit*. And Caesar's must have been in many respects the easier task.' Chirol concluded with a sentiment in which he knew many of his readers would concur.

What will be the price to be paid ultimately for introducing European civilisation into these backward Eastern societies is the grave problem which faces us . . . All we can do is to take to heart, humbly and hopefully, the simple piece of advice with which Lord Cromer closes his last chapter: Whatever be the moral harvest we may reap, we must continue to do our duty, and our duty had been indicated to us by the Apostle St Paul. We must not be 'weary in well doing'.

High-minded imperialism was, in 1908, still a powerful presence in the English psyche.

In other fields, Richmond also had his coups. When *Principia Mathematica* by A.N. Whitehead and Bertrand Russell came out in September 1911, he got the leading English mathematician of the time to review it, though anonymously just like everybody else. This was G.H Hardy, another Wykehamist, who was then thirty-four and teaching at Trinity College, Cambridge; he would eventually become Savilian Professor of Geometry at Oxford and write his famous book, *A Mathematician's Apologia*. Hardy admitted that some of the book was 'very difficult indeed', but he encouraged readers to tackle it, saying that all that is wanted is some sort of general familiarity with mathematical ideas. He said that its main thesis was the same as that of Russell's *Principles of Mathematics* – that 'pure mathematics involves no axioms or indefinables beyond those of formal logic'. Hardy made a bold attempt to explain the significance of this thesis in terms intelligible to the general reader, and concluded by saying elegantly that 'it would be insulting to affix the ordinary labels of praise to a book conceived with so far-reaching an object and on so vast a scale'.

The fierce Principal Headlam reviewed the book that first made Albert Schweitzer famous, before the second fame that came to him with his missionary and medical work in Africa. Schweitzer's *The Quest of the Historical Jesus*, translated from the German, was a survey of all the attempts that had been made to 'realise the historical personality' of Jesus, culminating in Schweitzer's own view that Jesus's teaching was just an episode in the history of Jewish belief in the forthcoming Apocalypse. Headlam thought that Schweitzer was a brilliant writer, and that all the German critical theologians discussed in the book could teach us something about Jesus – but as might be expected, he wondered if they had not all just missed the point, which was that Jesus really was the Son of God.

Richmond also snapped up two women writers who were very much in the public eye – Gertrude Bell and Edith Somerville. Bell was the mountaineer and traveller who had been the first woman to get a first in Modern History at Oxford, and had written famously about the Alps and the deserts. Reviewing some books about China, she noted that one author presented the Chinese as contented stay-at-homes, and remarked that 'we Occidentals, who spin down the ringing grooves of change, are apt to forget that grooves can be put to other and less violent uses'. Somerville was the Somerville of the Somerville and Ross (Martin Ross by pseudonym, Violet Martin by real name) who had had such a success with their stories, *Some Experiences of an Irish R.M.*, in 1899. In May 1910 she reviewed for Richmond a book by Dr P.W. Joyce on the 'Anglo-Irish language'. She praised the imaginative use of language by many Irish speakers – and quoted some phrases heard either by Dr Joyce or herself that were 'worthy to sparkle on the stretched forefinger of all time', such as 'The life of an old hat is to cock it' or (a blessing she had heard in Meath) 'May you live so long that a spider would draw you to the grave.'

Finally, a certain drama ran through the pages of the *Lit Supp* in this period connected with the surprising subject of a French saint – Joan of Arc. In April 1908 Mme Duclaux reviewed a new *Vie de Jeanne d'Arc* by Anatole France. She thought well of this book, which took a worldly view of the Maid, acknowledging that she was saintly, but also portraying her as a puppet and a fool who had been used by priests and statesmen. However, the book enraged Andrew Lang, who was a passionate devotee of Joan, and in May he wrote a long, angry letter to the paper, describing it as a long series of sneers against her, not based on facts but motivated by spite.

So Lang sat down and wrote a polemical book of his own, *The Maid of France*, which came out six months later and was reviewed by Sir Robert Sangster Rait, a Scotsman (like Lang) who was then a Fellow of New College, Oxford, and in 1913 was to become the first Professor of Scottish History at Glasgow University. Rait leaned to Lang's point of view that Jeanne was both truly inspired and that she played a major part in her own right in driving the English out of France. In 1911, the French historian Gabriel Hanotaux wrote his own *Jeanne d'Arc*, acknowledging Lang's book and broadly taking the same view as him, and on 18 May Rait reviewed that book favourably too.

In 1912 Lang died, aged sixty-eight, a few days after the publication of a *History of English Literature* he had written. It was reviewed in the *Lit Supp* on 5 September by G.S. Gordon, a young Scots reviewer recently taken on by Richmond, who had been a student under Walter Raleigh at Glasgow, and who, when in 1922 he succeeded Raleigh as Merton Professor of English Literature at Oxford, was said to have got the job largely on the strength of his *Lit Supp* contributions. Gordon made an affectionate and admiring obituary out of the 'melancholy' task of writing the review. He said that Lang was a 'brother of the craft, writing on every subject that touches humanity . . . the greatest bookman of our age, and after Robert Louis Stevenson the best man of letters in the Scottish tradition in the last half century', and he recalled how Lang had cried out that there had never been an age of chivalry, for how could there have been, when no sword leaped from its sheath for Jeanne in 1431?

But writing to Edmund Gosse on 19 November of that year, Henry James made some very different comments on the late Andrew Lang. He blamed him for his 'cultivation, absolutely, of the puerile imagination and the fourth-rate opinion, the coming round to that of the old apple-woman at the corner as after all the good and the right as to any of the mysteries of mind or of art'. As for the controversy over Joan of Arc, 'one feels Andrew again and again bristlingly yet *bêtement* wrong, and Anatole sinuously, yet oh so wisely, right!'

These opinions illustrate vividly just one of the many criss-crossing divisions – high art versus popular reading matter, academic scholarship versus common reader's interests, classical and backward-looking versus provocative and novel, Conservative versus Liberal – that were straddled so generously at this time by the *Lit Supp*.

Chapter Five

War and Independence: 1914–18

Arthur Walter died in February 1910 at the age of sixty-four, and Lord Northcliffe wrote a warm and welcoming letter to his son John – the fifth Walter, now aged thirty-seven – when the latter took his father's place as chairman of The Times Publishing Company. Nevertheless, the press lord was now getting very impatient with *The Times*, and especially with the three 'giant tortoises', as he had begun calling them, Bell, Buckle and Chirol. He had poured money into *The Times*, money made for him mainly by what they would consider the 'yellow' journalists on his *Daily Mail*, but he had seen little change either in the paper or in its circulation – which was only slightly more than the 38,000 it had been when he bought it in 1908.

Northcliffe started overloading the conscientious Moberly Bell with work – at one point asking that relentless letter-writer to send him a copy of every letter that he wrote – with a result that might have been foreseen. Moberly Bell collapsed and died at his desk, his pen in his hand, a letter half-finished, on 5 April 1911. The manager's sarcastic wit stayed with him to the end: the letter was accusing the Asquith Cabinet of legalising burglary and larceny in the new Copyright Bill. He was succeeded by one of Northcliffe's men, Reginald Nicholson, who had already been brought in from Northcliffe's *Daily Mirror* as assistant manager of *The Times*, and was destined to play an important role at a crucial point in the future of the *Lit Supp*.

In January of that year Northcliffe had put a particular strain on all his difficult 'triumvirs', when for the first time he had interfered with the political direction of the paper. The question at issue was the ratification of an international treaty, the Declaration of London, under which nations such as Britain would recognise certain rights of neutral nations in a war. Northcliffe considered that the agreement would seriously weaken Britain and her navy in the event of war, and his other papers were waging a fierce campaign against it. *The Times*, however, intended to support the Declaration.

Northcliffe would not have it. In the end, a compromise was reached – that *The Times* would take up no position at all on the matter. But Chirol and Buckle rightly saw this event as the writing on the wall for them and the paper they believed in.

Chirol resigned in December 1911 (and was knighted on New Year's Day 1912). By now, Northcliffe had introduced into the office a new man called Geoffrey Robinson, who had been the *Times* correspondent in Johannesburg and editor of the *Johannesburg Star*; he was also a Fellow of All Souls and a former Etonian, and had for a time been Alfred Milner's Private Secretary.

Buckle recognised at once that Robinson was intended for his successor; however, he thought that the newcomer should work in the office for two more years before being appointed. But Northcliffe could not wait. Buckle gave in and resigned in July 1912, and Geoffrey Robinson became editor of *The Times* on 24 September 1912 at £2,000 a year (about £100,000 a year in today's money). He was to become a famous editor of the paper, after he had changed his name, for family reasons, to Geoffrey Dawson.

Thus, by the end of 1912 the 'old gang', the 'greybeards', the 'monks' had gone. In fact Bruce Richmond was by now the most senior member of the old 'common room' left. But he was to prove the most resilient of them all, if not without many travails to come.

Northcliffe had never much liked Richmond, or his paper. There is a rather obscure, undated scrawl from him to the new editor of *The Times* describing an encounter with him, which gives the uneasy feel of their relationship.

Writing on his coronetted paper from 22 St James's Place, Northcliffe begins 'My dear Robin' (the form he was always to use when addressing Robinson), and continues:

> I was at PHS today & suggested that *now* was the time to send Mr Bruce to Paris.
>
> Richmond remarked that October was more suitable for getting adverts & I asked what *that* had to do with it.
>
> He replied very impertinently, & incidently (*sic*) untruly, that since the new regime he had been obliged to work with the advertisement department.

I added that such a remark ill became one of those who were implicated in the threats to the publishers as to advertisements that led to their dignified & practical protest against blackmail of that kind.

I should be lacking in my duty to those who with me have rescued the paper from its nefarious ways, & I expressed myself in round terms on the subject hoping that he would retract or resign his position. He endeavoured to explain his statement, *more Hebraeo* & John Walter coming in, then left the room.

It will not happen again. Some things are not done.

Your attached

Chief

It seems fairly clear from this that it was really Richmond's demeanour, obviously very *de haut en bas* while still perfectly correct, that upset Northcliffe and drove him into these insults, vague threats and badly-constructed sentences. The letter is quite different from the crisp and witty letters he usually sent Robin at this time. The fact is that even now he could be intimidated by the remnants of the 'old gang', and in his further attempts to get rid of Richmond he tried to work through Robin and other members of the staff.

On 15 August 1912 – still in the interim between Buckle resigning and Robin taking up his chair – Northcliffe sent this letter to his new appointee:

My dear Robin,

I would suggest that the very first thing you should tackle, in view of the opening of the publishing season, is the *Literary Supplement*.

If you go back to its predecessor, *Literature,* one of the old *Times* blunders, you will find that even then they realised that the chief opponent of *The Times* in the book world is *The Spectator,* with its hundreds of pages of book advertisements annually.

The sphere of the *Supplement* has become more restricted than it was formerly. Practically no more attention is given in *The Times* to the work of living novelists than, until recently, was given to the productions of modern painters. I suggest that Richmond should begin at once to realise that he has responsibilities to *The Times* itself as a whole in the matter of this *Supplement*. As far as it goes, the *Supplement* is much the best thing done in English, but its scope must be enlarged, if we are to compete with *The Spectator, The Nation* and the literary departments of some of the other daily papers. *The*

Times used to have the monopoly of advance announcements of news, but has lost it, and Richmond can hardly be called a news gatherer. When we built the three great Presses at P.H.S. the *Supplement* was specially considered.

The tendency of *The Times* is to sneer at modern work. I do not believe that members of the staff have any of the animosities attributed to them by living writers, but their constant habit of belittling and sneering at much good modern work gives rise to that theory. I do not think Richmond can do what we want. I think you will have to strengthen the staff with an additional hand. Certainly Mr. and Mrs. Dalton have no affection for modern novelists.

The profits of *The Spectator* alone are greater than those of *The Times* Publishing Company with all its *Supplements*. Verb sap. sat.

Chief

This is another confused letter but it shows plainly the drift of Northcliffe's thinking. He desperately wanted more readers for *The Times* and more advertisements in it, but he did not want to be accused of lowering its standards. He needed it to become more popular through means that could still be regarded as respectable. Here he was really flailing about trying to suggest ways in which the *Lit Supp* could do that, while hating its editor and wanting to remove him.

Northcliffe correctly recognised in some of its reviewers a distrust of 'modern' literature, but it was not Ezra Pound or D.H. Lawrence that he was concerned (or even knew) about. It was, rather, the novelists who were talked about – and no doubt managed sometimes to catch his ear – at dinner tables, the ones that Mr Dalton so often briefly dismissed in the Book List. (Incidentally, it seems from Northcliffe's letter as if Mrs Dalton sometimes gave Mr Dalton a hand in his labours.)

Northcliffe bombarded Geoffrey Robinson with letters once he was editor, often morning after morning sending him notes praising or criticising something in the paper. Greater topicality and greater breadth of appeal were his constant and often anguished demands. A famous telegram from Paris read: 'Humbly beg for light leading article daily till I return – Chief'. As for the *Lit Supp*, now he called it 'an admirable intellectual amusement for a few thousand readers', now it was 'inhuman' – but in neither case was it what he wanted. Here he is on 12 December 1912, having still made little headway with it:

My dear Robin

I am quite certain that this morning's Literary section does not make a sufficiently wide appeal.

One thing is certain about the future of the Paper, and that is, that, without lowering the tone, the appeal is to be a very wide one. Otherwise the circulation will be a very small one, and the Paper will stop.

Robinson replied diplomatically the next day: 'I quite agree about the last *Literary Supplement*. A good deal has been done to broaden its basis in the last few weeks, but this is certainly a relapse. I will look into the matter . . .'

1913 came, and Northcliffe's thoughts turned to a further strategy. The two main rivals to *The Times* by now were the *Morning Post* and the *Daily Telegraph*. Both cost a penny, as opposed to the threepence charged for *The Times*. On 5 May, the price of *The Times* was brought down to twopence, and it was advertised as 'The Easiest Paper to Read'. It was not a successful move. The circulation climbed only from 41,000 to 47,000, and slowly at that.

On 28 June 1913 an exasperated Northcliffe told Robin:

I certainly consider that the *Literary Supplement* is one of those things which is causing the lamentable figures that are presented to me every day, and which will sooner or later bring about the great crisis. Richmond has been spoken to again and again about the *Supplement*. Either he is determined not to take any notice, or he is incapable of taking notice. From remarks he made some time ago, I am inclined to think he does not mean to.

I am loath to interfere, but my duty is very plain. My suggestion is that you give Richmond four weeks to improve the *Supplement*, and failing an improvement you can change the editorship. I can quite easily find an editor who will greatly improve it.

One of the fetishes of *The Times* was that the paper increased in sale on the day of the *Literary Supplement*. The figures belie that.

Bruce Richmond, now aged forty-two, proposed to get married that autumn, in spite of all this frustrated fury raging round his head, and Northcliffe brought this particular subject up in a letter on 26 August to Hugh Chisholm, who had been editing the *Encyclopaedia Britannica* and had now just been given the newly-created post of day editor on *The Times*.

> A matter which needs instant attention is the *Literary Supplement*. Bruce Richmond asked Robin if he was entitled to get married, whether, that is, *The Times* will keep him. I have written to him to say, that this entirely depends on his adaptability. His supplement is based, I presume, if it is based on anything, on a *Times* with a very small circulation. It is narrow; often very good, in a narrow sort of way; often very bad, especially lately. There is no life or enterprise in it. If Robin is not back, will you give it your personal attention: if he is back, please help him with it.

Still nothing changed in the *Lit Supp*, except perhaps for the special fiction number, which appeared on 30 October, and was one thing that did please Northcliffe. Richmond got married to his stately Edwardian-style beauty, Elena Rathbone, and continued to edit the *Lit Supp* in essentially the way he had always done.

And now there rose on the horizon the prospect, tempting but terrifying for all parties, of a penny *Times*. Once again the *Lit Supp* got a glancing blow: 'Would it not be wise to inform the leading members of the staff, including Richmond, who issues an impossible Literary Section this morning, that we are about to make the final stand against reduction to a penny,' Northcliffe told his 'Dear Robin'.

But the decision was taken, and by 16 February 1914, Northcliffe had invited Robin to join him in Paris to discuss the 'tremendous undertaking' that was before them, 'quite the greatest business responsibility I have ever undertaken in my life'. There had been intense debates about the appearance and contents of the penny *Times*, including much discussion about Northcliffe's wish that there should be book reviews in the body of the paper as well as in the *Lit Supp*. But the question 'Why should the *Lit Supp* continue in that case?' had hung in the air whilst Richmond's fate hung in the balance.

Two other letters written in February 1914 tell the story of what happened. On 11 February Nicholson, the manager, wrote to 'My dear Chief':

> I have just had an hour's talk with Richmond and impressed upon him the absolute necessity of making the *Lit Supp* more popular. His answer is that he is in every way trying to do this and meet your wishes. To do this he starts out by trying to cover a book in every field and make it as varied as possible.

Take last week. You have Mr Holiday's Reminiscences and New Guinea and the Solomon Islands, the only two books on biography and travel published that week. Outdoor things you have 'Automobilism comes into its own' and 'A Book about Badgers'. For Women 'Old Italian Lace' and 'The Future of the Women's Movement'. Music 'The Flute' etc. etc. and then there are seven books of fiction.

He saw John Buchan only this morning to find out what books were selling most. I have told him to go further with this and see other publishers to find out the most popular books. Since September we have regularly published a column more of fiction.

I know the question of Richmond is a worry to you but need it be? In the future development it will hardly be possible to run the *Literary Supplement* and it must become submerged in the paper and then his services will not be required. Unfortunately Robin clings to him desparately (*sic*) but this can be got over. He has so Robin tells me had much bigger offers to go elsewhere to join a publishing firm I believe.

At this point it seems as if the *Lit Supp* was about to be submerged. But this is the letter Northcliffe wrote to Nicholson on 15 February indicating that Nicholson had by now hatched an entirely different plot – namely, for a separate and independent *Lit Supp*:

My dear Reggie

The responsibility for the weakening of *The Times* newspaper by separate supplements is yours, and one that I personally would not care to accept. I shall do my best to help the *Lit Supp* but you know that I do it against my better judgment and in deference to the wish expressed by you. You will, I am sure, realise that your salary will come greatly into question if your advice proves wrong.

You did not tell me at the meeting on Friday evening that Allison [the head of the advertising department] had spoken to you about the matter. If Allison finds that we are suffering by the insertion of the ads in the *Suppt*, which will have a fifth of the sale of *The Times*, I shall myself engage a Literary Editor of *The Times* (apart from the Editor of the *Lit Supp*) and see that a couple of columns of reviews are inserted in the paper daily.

In most of the offices in which I am engaged, the people concerned with me are willing to take my advice, and your attitude in this matter has been a great surprise to me.

However, you have taken the responsibility and this letter will fasten it upon you. Meanwhile I will do, as I have promised, my utmost to help Freeman & Co. [Freeman, one of the senior editors, had special responsibility for the supplements.]

An advertisement of *The Times Lit Supp* appears in this morning's *Observer*. Who pays for it? We have no money to advertise the *Lit Supp*. You have started on a mad scheme.

But the 'mad scheme' worked, and the 'separate' *Literary Supplement* has been with us ever since.

In the light of Northcliffe's letter, Reggie Nicholson must get the main credit for the saving of the *Supplement* in 1914, just as his predecessor as manager, Moberly Bell, had ensured its continuation after the first few weeks in 1902. However, Geoffrey Robinson played a major role too. Nicholson commented that 'Robin clings desparately' to Richmond, and there is plenty of other evidence that Robinson held the editor of the *Lit Supp* in high esteem as well as being very fond of him personally. Evelyn Wrench, in *Geoffrey Dawson and Our Times*, says that Dawson (as I shall henceforth call the new editor of *The Times*) was 'devoted to him'. Wrench also quotes a letter from Richmond to Dawson at the time of Dawson's first retirement as editor in 1919. (As we shall see, he left and came back again three years later.)

Richmond writes in that letter:

It seems a short time since I sent you a note that was to lie on your breakfast table on the first morning of your being editor. My regret in sending you this one today is tempered by the pleased vanity of the successful prophet when I remember the confidence I then expressed that the traditions of the paper were safe in your hands.

I do congratulate you most heartily on your six years' splendid work – regretfully I congratulate you also on your liberation from what must have been in many ways a beastly job. But anyway you can look back on it with pride – and as one of your staff I hope you will also look back on some sides of it with pleasure.

I want to thank you for being so uniformly considerate to me and my corner of the paper. We are very grateful to you. Good luck to you in the fresh woods and pastures, wherever they may be.

Yours always

B.L.R.

It is clear from this letter how much the two friends had in common, and how much help and support they gave each other. In fact Dawson was a true heir of the 'traditions of the paper' – which would be precisely what brought him in the end to the parting of the ways with Northcliffe. There is also an undated letter from Dawson to Richmond, perhaps a reply to this letter from Richmond, which says: 'The *Lit Supp* owes nothing to me – I wish I thought it did, for it is the most consistently good thing that emerges from P.H.S.' Dawson, moreover, got on very well with Nicholson from the moment of his arrival at *The Times*, and would not have found it difficult to impress his views on him.

As for Northcliffe, in spite of the grave warnings he gave Nicholson, and even the threats he made in his letter of 15 February, he was quite glad to have the matter taken out of his hands in this way. He feared the obloquy of the literary world.

At any rate, he had something else to think about – and something to rejoice about. For the new penny *Times* was an amazing success. The first number came out on Monday, 16 March 1914. Containing all the regular *Times* material, but better laid out and with much light and varied reading in it as well – including book reviews, among them a piece on Henry James's *Notes of a Son and Brother*, and the hoped-for publishers' advertisements – it sold 150,000 copies. In the months that followed, it kept up an average sale of 145,000 copies a day.

Northcliffe had indisputably saved *The Times*. Meanwhile, the *Lit Supp* moved quietly into independence. In its issue of 19 February, given away as usual with the main paper, it carried a notice that it was 'now also sold separately for 1 penny'. The same notice appeared in the two following weeks. On 12 March, the word 'also' was dropped, slightly jumping the gun. On 19 March, the paper simply bore on its first page the words 'PRICE ONE PENNY'.

The *Lit Supp* was out in the world on its own. Nor was there anything in its circulation to confirm the fears of its coronetted owner. At the end of 1914, its average circulation each week since independence proved to have been a remarkable 41,974 copies.

The new penny *Lit Supp* had a different appearance from its predecessor – and not such an attractive one. There were four narrow columns instead of three broad columns, and the margins at the top and bottom of the page became slightly narrower too. This change was introduced on 5 March. The new column contained 950 words instead of the former 1,250 words, and the payment to contributors went down from a basic £3 a column to £2 – so contributors were rather worse off. However the fees were from 1914 onwards more often topped up to the next half a crown or guinea. For a brief period, the paragraphs in the first or 'leading' article were numbered, but this experiment was soon dropped. The number of copies of the paper sold in the previous week was given now at the end of the contents panel.

For a few months, too, short reviews from the new books columns in the main paper were sometimes published in the *Lit Supp* as well, apparently without further payment to the author. However this was hardly fair to the purchasers of both papers, which was probably the reason why this economical practice did not continue for long.

The new penny paper began with a flourish of great names, setting aside for the moment the standing principle of virtually complete anonymity. The leading article on 12 March was an elegant piece of *belle-lettrisme* by Max Beerbohm, with his by-line, on 'Books Within Books' – imaginary novels, that is to say, mentioned in other novels. Plenty of space was given to Henry James, whose art, said Beerbohm, 'can always carry to us the conviction that his characters' books are as fine as his own'. If he owned all those imaginary books, Beerbohm concluded, 'how my fingers would hover along those shelves, always just going to alight, but never, lest the spell were broken, alighting' – an enjoyable beginning to the new era.

The following week the signed lead piece was by Henry James himself, the first part of his promised two-part article on the novels of 'The Younger Generation' (the second part appeared on 2 April). In this famous article, James picked out Hugh Walpole, Gilbert Cannan, Compton Mackenzie and D.H. Lawrence as the most interesting new novelists – with Lawrence, however, 'hanging in the dusty rear'. The review of James's *Notes of a Son and Brother* that had appeared in the main paper was one of those reprinted in the *Lit Supp*; it was by a newly-recruited contributor, Orlo Williams, who was a thirty-one-year-old classical scholar and clerk in the House of Commons and would be a stalwart of the paper for the next forty years. He said that the book was 'an incomparable picture of a leisurely education'.

On 14 May there was a signed article by Edith Wharton, 'The Craft of Fiction', giving her rather Jamesian views on the nature of the novel. This was a real turnaround and also a real coup since, only three years before, Walter de la Mare, reviewing her tragic novel *Ethan Frome*, had said that although it was 'charged from cover to cover with the magic of snow', it was 'a story – at any rate for the over-sensitive – better left unread'. In June, Edith Wharton also reviewed, anonymously, a book by Geoffrey Scott on *The Architecture of Humanism*, observing delightfully that 'Renaissance architecture transcribes in stone the body's favourite states'.

The year 1914 was not a great year for novels, but at the beginning of the year, before the great change, Walter de la Mare had reviewed Conrad's *Chance* in much the same terms as he had used of *Ethan Frome*, commenting that 'romance shines out of a denseness of air and darkness almost insufferable', while Orlo Williams teased the 'fake old Englishness' of Chesterton's *The Flying Inn*, saying that he 'may be right that we shall not be ourselves again till the good old, bluff old, hardy old, sturdy old English spirit returns . . . but the good old English spirit would certainly not understand Mr Chesterton'.

D.H. Lawrence fared better, with a review reprinted from *The Times* of his play *The Widowing of Mrs Holroyd* which praised its 'revelations of the shades and complexities and depths in "simple" natures', while at the end of the year Harold Child reviewed his short stories in *The Prussian Officer*, concluding that 'the world he draws is a world of power and passion, where people are finely alive, if they are not happy'.

The most striking debut of 1914 was that of James Joyce. The review on 18 June of *Dubliners*, his volume of short stories, also appeared in *The Times* that week, but it was only lukewarm: 'The author is not concerned with all Dubliners, but almost exclusively with those of them who would be submerged if the tide of material difficulties were to rise a little higher . . . *Dubliners* may be recommended to the large class of readers to whom the drab makes an appeal.' The reviewer acknowledged that the book was 'admirably written', but evidently did not respond to the beauty, economy and subtlety of this great newcomer's prose.

Another of the signed front-page articles was by Sir Sidney Colvin, one of the leading literary scholars who, during the First World War and especially just after it, would give the paper an enlarged role as the voice of the great burgeoning of textual scholarship in Britain. This article described some hitherto unpublished poems by Keats and letters by his friends, including a poem, possibly addressed to Fanny Brawne, that complained

> *You say your love; but with a smile*
> *Cold as sunrise in September.*

In May, two 'lost sonnets' of Keats followed, this time with a signed commentary by the younger scholar and Professor of English at Birmingham University – Ernest de Selincourt.

One other notable literary article was a review of a book on John Dryden by Charles Whibley – but it is notable mainly for its exclusively aesthetic approach to Dryden's art. Whibley is able to say that Dryden is 'the greatest man of letters that England has ever known', without even mentioning the deep and volatile entanglements of Dryden in the politics of his time that were often his chief motivation in writing his poems. To modern readers, this would be one of the strangest articles that ever appeared in the *Lit Supp*, though Whibley was an esteemed critic at the time.

Richmond's most brilliant new acquisition this year was the twenty-four-year-old John Middleton Murry. This intense, talented young writer had been editing his own poetry magazine, *Rhythm*, while he was still at Oxford, and had come down in 1912 after he met the New Zealand writer Katherine Mansfield. They were soon involved in a turbulent relationship, and in December 1913 had gone off together to Paris, where Murry hoped to make a living. Two months later they were back again – 'with very little but the clothes we stood in', Katherine Mansfield wrote in her journal. But Murry had already published one review in the *Lit Supp* – a survey of some Prix Goncourt winners – at the end of 1913, and now Richmond took him on as a regular reviewer of books in French. It was a relationship with the paper that was to last for forty years, and Murry was soon picking out good French poets (he particularly liked one Charles de Pomairols), defining the nature of contemporary French criticism and discussing the Goncourt brothers and the bluestockings of the Second Empire.

In the months immediately after independence there was not much about British politics or foreign affairs in the paper, but John Buchan, who was by now writing *The Thirty-Nine Steps*, got a chance to praise his (and the paper's) hero, the former Prime Minister Arthur Balfour, in a long anonymous piece on 17 May 1914 – the eve of Balfour's presidential address to the English Association. Buchan praised him both as a humanist, seeking a faith 'a little less chilling to common human blood than the thin air of the Hegelian Infinite', and also as a writer who 'at his best writes the purest prose of our generation', with a clarity 'crystalline rather than watery' and 'in the prose of argument . . . perfect aptness and coherence'.

As for the pleasures of that last spring and summer before the First World War, the *Lit Supp* covered numerous light books. Perhaps Richmond, now he was his own master, was more prepared to do what Northcliffe had wanted. Sir Claude Schuster – a real Bruce Richmond man, educated at Winchester and New College, and now a distinguished civil service lawyer and mountaineer – praised a book on *The Conquest of Mount McKinley*, regretting only the author's 'irritating fondness for the word "rhuksack"'. Bernard Darwin, brooding over a volume of *Noted Murder Mysteries*, remarked that 'a consciously romantic style will drain the greatest murder trial dry of romance in half a sentence'. Erskine Childers, who was already famous for his novel *The Riddle of the Sands*, and who would be executed in 1922 for his involvement with Irish Republicans, contributed a review of *The China Clippers* by Basil Lubbock. These splendid ocean racers were now extinct, he wrote, but 'seamanship still lives, romance never dies'.

E.V. Lucas wrote a piece about the MCC – 'magical initials that cause a thrill in Englishmen the world over'. Eustratius Emmanuel Mavrogordato, the literary-minded barrister who would write hundreds of articles for the paper, reviewed *The Gourmet's Guide to London* by Lt Col Newnham-Davis: 'Gifted with a discriminating palate,' he said, 'he has turned to account a talent which the anchorite would have hidden in his napkin.' Nevertheless, he thought the colonel was a little too laudatory: 'he never mentions, for example, a restaurant where it is forgotten that the chief flavour in a dish comprising sole should be that of the sole itself'. Meanwhile, Walter de la Mare, writing about 'Maps in Fact and Fiction', recommended innocent pastoral pleasures: 'A green meadow may be El Dorado and all the Indies to a simple and unexacting heart.'

When war broke out on 4 August 1914, the *Lit Supp* was prepared for it. Its issue of 6 August led off with a long survey of books of recent years that would help readers to understand the background of 'the crisis'. This was compiled by an up-and-coming historian, Walter Alison Phillips, who had begun life as a professional singer and became Professor of Modern History at Trinity College, Dublin. The war was still, for a few days, no more than a crisis, and on 13 August a T. Fisher Unwin advertisement offered 'A Hint for the Holiday Maker – Buy a Government Ordnance Survey Map', and in the same column promoted Baedeker Guides on the basis that they gave 'the fullest general information about the States involved in the present gigantic struggle'. An advertisement on the cusp of history.

At *The Times*, Northcliffe called for an all-round drop in salaries to meet the rise in the cost of news coverage and newsprint. A letter from Reginald Nicholson to Dalton, still toiling away at the back of the paper on the Book List, said that the management had received 'many voluntary suggestions for the reduction in salaries', that he was sure that Dalton would 'throw in your lot with so many others', and that he hoped Dalton would 'be able to get through these difficult times on a salary of six guineas a week'. This was just over £300 a year, compared with the £650 that Dalton was currently getting. Dalton protested, in the form of a delicately ironic letter accepting the suggestion – 'I understand that I shall receive for the present half my ordinary salary' – and it was put up again to £500 on 1 September.

However, he was to have from now onwards, and for the duration of the war, an unexpected helper. It is often said that Bruce Richmond himself never contributed a review to the *Lit Supp*. In fact, he now started contributing short notices of many books in the Book List – especially light novels, books on law, and books on music. The notices had no critical pretensions; one from these early weeks, for instance, on a novel by William le Queux, read: 'Vigorous but entirely artificial, and its 330 pages would not last much longer than, say, London to Bletchley or Basingstoke.'

The most important innovation in the *Lit Supp* in August 1914 was the series of humanistic sermons on the moral conduct of the war which would be contributed throughout the war's duration by Arthur Clutton-Brock. Clutton-Brock had been for some years now the art critic of *The Times*, but he had also been developing for himself a very high-minded, humanistic religion, and this was now turned to powerful effect. His anonymous articles were invariably to appear as the front-page leads to the paper, and the first, 'The Two Kinds of Courage', appeared on 13 August. Its underlying theme, which was to be the leitmotif of all the subsequent articles, was that Britain was fighting a noble war, but it must make sure that it always fought nobly. In this first essay, for instance, he says:

> We can each of us do something for the soul of England, that, when peace comes again, it may be a treasure unimpaired. We, as a nation, have certain virtues of our own, easier to practise in peace than in war, but more sublime in war than in peace. We are just and kindly and long-suffering. When we are at peace we have a contempt for national vendettas and all the false romanticism that springs from them. Let us keep that contempt still, and still smile at the baser and more fearful part of ourselves that would persuade us to hatred . . . It is because we fight for no national feud that we are applauded, because we have gone to war sadly and without any drunkenness of spirit, like a man who kisses his wife and children at the gate. And we should remember that many Germans have kissed their wives and children so in the last week . . . There is no abstract Germany, how-

ever much the Germans may sing about her, but only a number of Germans, most of them kindly people like ourselves, but cursed by this national romanticism, that is a perverted survival from their righteous struggle with Napoleon . . .

The following week he struck a similar note: '[we have] the spiritual duty to keep our minds calm and clear and our national conscience as steadfast as if we were at peace'. On 10 September he stated, a little more harshly, that Germany had become a machine and that the German people had become marionettes, and that 'the machine must be destroyed' – but 'without anger or desire for revenge, for it is not reasonable to be angry with marionettes'.

Whilst Clutton-Brock's articles held at a distance the horrors of what was going on across the Channel, the newspapers in general were not yet giving a very clear picture of the fighting, partly because of the difficulty of obtaining information and partly because – in the Northcliffe press especially – there was a reluctance to discourage young men from joining up.

The tone of Clutton-Brock's articles was consonant with the mood of the time in many quarters, and as early as 10 September, a letter appeared from a reader, W.W. Greg of Park Lodge, Wimbledon, thanking the paper for them. 'At such a moment as this,' he wrote, 'we ought to treasure as our greatest possession whatever will help us to keep sane, and no man can do a higher service to his country than to help his fellows to face the vicissitudes of war in the spirit which animates the writer of these articles.' However, Greg admitted that 'many ordinarily sober and reasonable people are for the moment possessed with a spirit of timorous hatred that saps in them all power of rational thought'.

Both Buckle and Chirol were brought out of retirement to review some of the instantly-produced books justifying Britain's involvement in the war. They took a harder line than Clutton-Brock. On 13 August Chirol wrote about the *Parliamentary White-book* that told the diplomatic story of the fortnight before the declaration of war – 'The dramatis personae move across the stage almost like automata driven by the evil genius of Germany towards the inexorable catastrophe' – and two weeks later, in a review of two books, one German and one American, about German militarism, concluded that 'if there are any sane Englishmen who, having read the parliamentary White-book, still refuse to believe that this war is being waged by us not only for our national honour, but for our very existence as a free people, let them read these two books, and they will assuredly doubt no longer.' Buckle, in September, applauded the comment of Professor Medley in his pamphlet 'Why Britain Fights': should Germany succeed, she will 'rivet upon civilisation a despotism, organised, suspicious, and ruthless beyond anything which the world even in its most degraded epochs has ever seen'.

For a few months the whole paper was, in its own way, on a war footing. There were innumerable books being rushed out that were more or less closely associated with the war: books on Drake and Napoleon and Garibaldi, books on Boer War generals, books on Serbian legends and Belgian pluck, studies of armies, navies and aircraft (including dirigibles), treatises on military sanitation and war maps. The *Lit Supp* reviewed them all.

Middleton Murry contributed long pieces on the French poetry of the Franco-German war, and on Russian soldiers in fiction (it was only much later in his life that he was to become a renowned pacifist). Thomas Seccombe reported on the soldiers in Thomas Hardy's novels. Walter de la Mare discussed English patriotic poetry, and frankly admitted not much of it was any good, but another contributor quoted a verse from a book called *Soldier Songs of France*,

> *Dixième bataillon*
> *Commandant MacMahon*
> *N'a pas peur du canon*
> *Non, non, non . . . non, non, non!* –

and commented 'Long may the traditional cheerfulness of the French soldier express itself in song.'

The paper also published a number of patriotic poems itself, starting with Robert Bridges's gruesome and facile (and possibly senile) 'Thou Careless, Awake!' on the same page as Clutton-Brock's first article:

> *Much suffering shall cleanse thee:*
> *But thou through the flood*
> *Shalt win to Salvation,*
> *To Beauty through blood.*

Thomas Hardy's 'Song of the Soldiers' – about the men who march away

> *In our heart of hearts believing*
> *Victory crowns the just* –

was not quite so ironic as might have been expected from him. Mme Duclaux contributed a less predictable poem called 'Belgia Bar-Lass' about a girl who used her milk-white arm as a replacement bolt to close a door against an enemy:

> Brave Belgium, Bar-lass of the Western world,
> Thine arm, thy heart, thine act have won the day.

She wrote a rather better comment later on on the death of the French poet Charles Péguy, whose 'one idea was to be a hero or a saint'. She did not much like the 'mighty jog-trot of his later muse', but thought that there could never have been 'a climax more just and adequate for him than his death in battle'.

After October the proportion of non-war books reviewed began to increase again, the most notable of them being the continuation by Buckle of the *Life of Disraeli* begun by Monypenny, who had died prematurely. It was reviewed very conscientiously by John Cann Bailey, but his article, on 26 November, was by no means as sprightly as the review by John Morley of the earlier instalment. He said that Buckle had 'admirably escaped both the opposite dangers of a breach of continuity and of sinking his personality in that of his predecessor', but urged him to use his own political knowledge and insights more in the next volume.

Virginia Woolf had been ill throughout 1914, after her attempted suicide, but she would return to the pages of the *Lit Supp* early the following year. However, Leonard Woolf appeared again in December, reviewing a book called *Jungle Sport in Ceylon*. He had served as a colonial officer in Ceylon and reported that whenever he went to investigate a rogue elephant, 'it was the elephant who obviously considered the writer the rogue, and bolted immediately'.

Another of the toilers at the back of the paper, Mumby, who was still contributing columns of short notes every week on forthcoming books, had a chance to spread himself in an article on 'War and the Book Trade'. He said that the rise in the price of imported paper or esparto to make it from would probably lead to fewer cheap reprints, and that experiments were being carried out to see if paper might be made from bamboo. The gold for gold edges and bindings came from Germany – the art of gold beating was lost in England – but books would look none the worse 'for appearing in more sober garb at a time of national crisis'. The Germans in turn relied on us for the leather for their bindings.

There was a Christmas Books number of twenty pages on 10 December, including John Buchan declaring in an essay on biographies for boys that 'every healthy boy is a hero-worshipper – but also a utilitarian', and four pages of drawings from new children's books, most of them pictures of fairies. On 24 December, the famous classical scholar J.W. Mackail, known (as many men have been) as the most brilliant Oxford undergraduate of his time, took over Clutton-Brock's pulpit with an article on poetic visions of peace. He ended with a sentiment that could have been Clutton-Brock's own – that the greatest peace is the peace of a clear conscience.

In 1915 the *Lit Supp* was still almost completely geared to the war. Clutton-Brock continued to dominate the first page, tirelessly trying to uplift morale and uphold morality at the same time. On 14 January, in 'Christians, Awake!' he wrote about the way in which, on Christmas Eve, British and German soldiers had stopped fighting and answered each other's hymns across the front line, then 'rose and advanced to meet each other as though they had been released from a spell . . . Some say that the darkness became strange and beautiful with lights as well as music, as if the armies had been gathered there not for war but for the Christmas feast'. On 8 April, he reflected almost rapturously on lessons that the war had so far taught: 'Now rich and poor are all volunteers for the same cause, free men now working together – no longer playing apart . . . The new young man will have a sense of beauty where we had only a sense of prettiness; a sense of duty where we only had a sense of honour; a faith instead of our creed; a joy instead of our pursuit of pleasure'. In a poem on 25 February Walter de la Mare wrote:

> *Sweet England, do not grieve!*
> *Not one of these poor men who died*
> *But did within his soul believe*
> *That death for thee was glorified*

But did he really believe it? And if so was he right? The horrors of that first winter of the war were here still being kept at bay.

However, a letter published on 10 June must have gratified Clutton-Brock. It announced that his article of 1 October 1914 – in which he had said 'France is still the chief treasury of all that these conscious barbarians would destroy' – had been read out in the Paris schools because of its 'lofty and masculine frankness'. By now, too, a volume of his articles in which his authorship was acknowledged had already been published under the title *Thoughts on the War*, and a second soon followed.

John Galsworthy took over the front page anonymously on 13 May with an article on 'Our Literature and the War'. He thought, less comfortingly, that the war would not have any beneficial effect on literature, except that when the war was over there might be 'an instant outburst of joyful and sensuous imaginings' and 'a spurt of zest and frankness' – and perhaps 'a masterpiece or two of satire'. As for war itself, he did not think that it raised men's eyes to the stars for very long.

Literature itself was still being conscientiously crafted in Bloomsbury. Virginia Woolf's first novel, *The Voyage Out*, had, to be precise, been finished in 1913, and by the time it came out in 1915, she was, as Hermione Lee puts it, 'in the dark cupboard of her mental illness'. But it received generally good reviews, including a very warm and perceptive one by W.F. Casey in the *Lit Supp* (for which he received one guinea). He called it 'essentially feminine', but he did not mean by that that it was 'sentimental or cynical, frivolous or hard'. What the book had was 'that feminine sort of strength that accepts what is, whether beautiful or ugly ... a quivering eagerness about life, admirably dissembled behind an air of detachment'; its wit too was feminine, 'with its alert scampering from one point to another and the space between taken for granted'. As for the tragic ending, it was desolating but illogical – yet it was made 'almost to seem like the illogic of life', so that was a strength in the book too. This was a review that might have helped in Virginia Woolf's recovery.

Casey, the reviewer, was also a very interesting man. He was a Dublin lawyer who had written plays for the Abbey Theatre in Dublin. When he came to try his fortune in London, Richmond took him on as a reviewer, and he joined *The Times*, ending up as its editor, from 1948 to 1952. Richmond evidently knew his calibre, and gave him *The Voyage Out* because of it.

Leonard Woolf was now working for the *New Statesman*, but went on contributing excellent reviews to the *Lit Supp*. The week after his wife's first work was reviewed he was writing again about Paul Claudel, this time about his book *The East I Knew*. Here he complained that Claudel was so interested in symbols he scarcely considered the reality of the thing symbolised; like Mallarmé's, his meaning was 'perpetually just touching, tickling, and evading one's intelligence, as invisible cobwebs return again and again to brush against the cheek of one walking on a dark summer night up and down a garden path'. Claudel and Sussex seemed to come together in that image.

That autumn also saw the publication of *Art*, by Clive Bell, who was married to Virginia's sister, Vanessa. It was taken on by Clutton-Brock, who had not ceased to write on art as well as the war; he found it challenging and reviewed it at length, but rejected the idea that the 'significant form' of paintings has no connection whatsoever with what they represent. On the contrary, he was provoked to assert that 'representative art is nothing but representation', and that what is significant about form is that it 'makes visible what the mind feels when the eye sees'. A point of view much more sympathetic now than it was eighty – or even twenty – years ago.

There were plenty of poems by soldiers coming out in small volumes, and one by one the paper patted them gently on the head. The first of the enduring 'war poets' was Rupert Brooke, who by midsummer was already dead – a victim of the Dardanelles campaign. His poems appeared in three different books in 1915. His collection *1914, and Other Poems* in fact consisted mainly of pre-war poems; it was sympathetically reviewed on 22 July by de la Mare, who said that Brooke 'lived in perpetual interrogation of the unknowable' and 'made poetry of his questionings', though 'The Old Vicarage, Grantchester' showed how fresh and vigorous his exquisite senses also were. De la Mare ended with the usual threnody, however: 'his life, no less than his poetry, reached its zenith when in the peace and happiness of self-surrender he gave his youth for England'. De la Mare had also picked him out earlier in the year, when he was still alive, in an issue of the poetry periodical *New Numbers*, where he was published along with John Drinkwater, Lascelles Abercrombie and W.W. Gibson. Here de la Mare quoted the whole of Brooke's subsequently famous sonnet 'The Soldier' ('If I should die . . .'), in which he saw the expression – correctly, as it so cruelly turned out – of an 'all-surrendering love'.

Finally, Clutton-Brock – now hogging a great deal of the paper – mentioned Brooke in December in a review of the 1913–15 volume of Edward Marsh's *Georgian Poetry*. He was less enthusiastic, finding in Brooke's verse 'the insecurity of emotion that comes of scepticism' – a scepticism that Clutton-Brock was combating so ardently elsewhere in the *Lit Supp*. In the same review, and with much the same purpose, he regretted the way that as a poet D.H. Lawrence positively encouraged morbidity in himself – it was not, he said, 'the morbidity the artist cannot help'. In yet another review, Clutton-Brock spoke well of Ezra Pound's translations from Chinese poetry in his volume *Cathay*, but called the letter of a river-merchant's wife to her absent husband a 'prose version', not seeing, or not wanting to see, how beautifully expressive in an absolutely poetic way is the variation in the speed and lengths of its lines.

In 1915, the letters page of the *Lit Supp* became very regularly a full page, in a way it had not been before, and a very popular one too, drawing discussions on all kinds of literary and historical topics, from the letters of Horace Walpole to the events at Napoleon's funeral (this latter after some unpublished diaries describing the event were printed in the paper). There was one particularly delightful correspondence to distract readers' minds from the war. It was initiated by a basket maker called Thomas Okey, who took to task Professor Mackail for translating a line in Virgil's *The Georgics*, '*nunc facilis rubea texatur fiscina virga*', as 'now let the basket be lightly woven of briar-rods'. He thought it most unlikely that Roman peasants lacerated their fingers on the prickles of briars (or of brambles, an alternative reading), and suggested that Virgil meant rods of the red willow. A very spirited and learned correspondence followed, with much reference to Pliny's descriptions of shrubs and bushes, and most writers standing up for brambles or briars, though with the prickles removed. Okey was given the last word six weeks later, still insisting that no-one ever dreams of using brambles for baskets, 'even now when, owing to the shortage and enhanced price of willow, we are searching the neutral world for materials'. Richmond must have enjoyed publishing this correspondence; he was writing a piece about an edition of Suetonius for the Book List at the time.

The year ended with a look back to 1715, in a masterly leading article by that A.S. McDowall who had years before had a nervous breakdown and left *The Times*. 1715 was the year in which Louis XIV died. McDowall compared the French king's ultimately unsuccessful militarism, and its outcome in the French Revolution, with the Kaiser's militarism, wondering if there was a possibility after a German defeat of political reform following in his country. 'Will not the adventure, ended on any terms that seem likely, inspire a longing for something different?' It may have taken two world wars, rather than one, for McDowall's hope to have been realised, but in the last week of December 1915, at least some of the readers must have been pleased to find such hard-headed historical and political thinking on the front page of the *Lit Supp*.

The year 1916 was to see some of the worst battles of the war, at Verdun and on the Somme. In January, there was a letter in the *Lit Supp* from 'A Lover of Sculpture' that was seething with hatred of the Germans. The writer took exception to a passage in McDowall's essay in December, where he had mentioned the Kensington Palace statue of William III, defender of Europe against French domination, that had ironically been a gift from the Kaiser. It looked, said the correspondent, like 'some swaggering, swashbuckling soldier of fortune who will sell his German sword to anyone who is prepared to buy it', and he hoped that after the war it would be sent back.

Nevertheless the sweetly moral tones of Clutton-Brock continued to sound regularly on the front page, and were often joined now by those of an excellent Tudor historian, A.F. Pollard, who had written 500 lives for the *Dictionary of National Biography*, and would later found the Historical Association, as well as reviewing historical works in abundance for the *Lit Supp*. In January, he wrote that 'we listen in silence while Americans tell us that it is their duty to remain neutral but ours to do more', and quoted Abraham Lincoln – 'the living must be dedicated to the unfinished work of the dead'.

Another front-page contributor was Principal Headlam. In July, he drew attention to, and praised, a German Professor Forster, who had written an article criticising Bismarckian militarism in a German pacifist paper, the *Friedenswarte*, published in Switzerland. However he acknowledged that it was not surprising that it had 'called up a chorus of indignation' in Germany, and observed that 'we know what we think of Englishmen who at such a time publish in a foreign journal suggestions which, if true, would cut away the ground from the whole case on which the war is being fought'. A statement of rather dubious morality, especially coming from a future bishop.

Sir John Macdonell, who was still writing regularly for the paper, had shown comparable indignation when reviewing Bertrand Russell's *Justice in Wartime* back in April. Russell had suggested that there was nothing to choose between the two sides in the conflict, and that it was only 'the idle rich' who would suffer if we put up no resistance to the Germans. Macdonell said this would be a worthy contribution to *The Prig's Progress*; meanwhile, thanks to the British Fleet, 'Mr Russell may regard with philosophic calm the threat of an invasion'.

On 11 May, John Cann Bailey dutifully reviewed the fourth volume of the Disraeli biography begun by Monypenny, continued by Buckle, but this time complained that there were too few glimpses in the book of Disraeli's private tastes. A month later, on 15 June, the *Lit Supp* published a letter from Bailey saying that he had been unfair to Buckle and that there were more touches of the kind he had asked for than he had realised. Knowing Richmond's deep attachment to Buckle, one feels that there must have been tears in the office in the interim.

The more strictly literary pages of the paper were still completely dominated by the war. Henry James died on 28 February 1916, having taken British nationality the previous year out of a feeling of solidarity with the nation at war. He had received the Order of Merit on New Year's Day 1916. Another recruit from Bloomsbury, Desmond MacCarthy, contributed a front-page appreciation of him on 6 March. He concluded, finely: 'To attempt to express in a sentence the effect of his art upon our lives: he has made us understand better the meaning of intimacy and the beauty of goodness.'

Two weeks later, as the lead piece, there appeared James's signed article 'Refugees in Chelsea', written originally to help raise money in America for the Chelsea fund for Belgian refugees. It evoked brilliantly both the arrival of the refugees in Rye in Sussex, where he lived, and – in the event – the memory of James himself standing at Crosby Hall in Chelsea with the refugees who were sheltered there gathered around him. Belgium was still very much on the mind of the British. In August, the Belgian poet Emile Verhaeren contributed a poem in French called 'Angleterre', saying that we had realised we must emerge from our isolation and had shown that, 'in the heart of the waters', we were glad to feel ourselves a friend of 'a new Europe in a new world'. When Verhaeren was killed by a train four months later, the poet Laurence Binyon wrote ardently: 'We hail that voice which we shall never lose, which in this hour of his country's unimaginable agony speaks from that little remnant of ancient Flanders where the wind blows among the dunes by the desolate sea – the voice of the poet that glorifies all his race, vibrating with the passion of genius, superb in faith for the future.' He noted that Verhaeren would be buried at La Panne, 'that little strip of unconquered country which at this moment is all that remains of Belgium'.

H.G. Wells's novel *Mr Britling Sees It Through* was praised by Percy Lubbock. 'For the first time,' he wrote, 'we have a novel which touches the life of the last two years without impertinence', with its account of how Mr Britling in his time-mellowed Essex village copes with the war.

John Buchan's *The 39 Steps* was hailed as an excellent adventure story by Harold Child in October 1915, and the same month E.E. Mavrogordato was just as enthusiastic about his 'war romance', *Greenmantle*.

Rupert Brooke was frequently mentioned in the paper this year, and two more posthumous books by him were reviewed. The dissertation with which Brooke had won his fellowship at King's College, Cambridge in 1913, *John Webster and the Elizabethan Drama*, was reviewed by Harold Child, who quite properly dwelt on Webster not on Brooke, while Percy Lubbock reviewed his *Letters from America*, and dwelt not on Brooke but on the preface by Henry James, 'the great master of human elaboration and civilised beauty who has just left us'. Lubbock concluded touchingly – and as we know, very personally – 'A valediction from all who care for what is loveliest in nature and man goes to them both.' Robert Bridges's anthology *The Spirit of Man* was hailed by Walter de la Mare as what Bridges wanted it to be – 'a defence and stronghold in times of trouble'. The Poet Laureate also contributed an elaborate tercentenary ode to Shakespeare in the same vein:

> *One with thee is our temper in melancholy or might,*
> *And in thy book Great-Britain's rule readeth her right.*

The swelling generation of 'modernist' poets got some, if not all, of their due. D.H. Lawrence's controversial new novel *The Rainbow* had been ignored in 1915 (as, incidentally, was another novel still revered today, Ford Madox Ford's *The Good Soldier*), but in August 1916 Lawrence's volume of poems, *Amores*, was reviewed by Harold Child, who saw him, not wholly unreasonably, as a man 'whose great desires, left unsatisfied, lead to a half-concealed savagery', but able to write 'tender poems between the storms', and to 'fit manner to matter'. However, Percy Lubbock did not like his prose book *Twilight in Italy*, and said in his usual incisive way that Lawrence, instead of writing about the Italy he actually saw, 'preferred the easier course of discovering the Infinite'.

Clutton-Brock took on Ezra Pound, reviewing the poems in his *Lustra*, and found them loose and ineffectual: as you read them, he wrote, 'you feel as if you had tried to sneeze and failed'; he also noticed his book on Gaudier-Breszka, and found the picture of the sculptor vivid but the Vorticist ideas irritating. Pound himself wrote a review on a surprising subject, *The American Crisis and the War* by William Morton Fullerton (who had been Henry James's friend and Edith Wharton's lover). This book was a rather obscure attack on President Wilson, which Pound in his turn attacked rather obscurely.

As for W.B. Yeats, whose volume of poems *Responsibilities* must now be seen as one of the great books of these years, he was reviewed only rather sorrowfully by Harold Child. *Responsibilities* was published in 1914, *Reveries over Childhood and Youth* in 1915, but they were noticed in the *Lit Supp* only on 19 October 1916, and Child saw them both as middle-aged works in which Yeats 'implied that his creative ardours are over'. The review did not so much praise *Responsibilities*, as make it the occasion to encourage him and tell him 'he has more leaves and flowers yet to sway in the sun'. In that, at least, he must be admitted to have been right – though the poems Yeats wrote after the Easter Rising in Dublin in 1916 might be considered rather sturdier than leaves and flowers, even if not more beautiful.

One of the happiest events for the *Lit Supp* in 1916 was Virginia Woolf's return in the spring to health, and to its reviewing team. She had begun to 'creep about', as she said, at the beginning of the year, and for a while she still spent all her mornings in bed. But in April she wrote an excellent piece for the anniversary of the birth of Charlotte Brontë, which was accompanied by a signed article, with a map, by Marion H. Spielmann on the places in Brussels associated with Charlotte Brontë's stay there. Not surprisingly, with *Lit Supp* readers, the latter article was followed by a letter pointing out what were said to be mistakes in it.

Virginia Woolf also reviewed, among several other books, one that appealed to her famous love of London streets, *London Revisited* by E.V. Lucas. 'For Londoners,' she said, 'there is only one real example of a town in the world – compared with her the rest are country villages.' Nor did Richmond forget her husband's connection with Ceylon, sending him a guide-book, *The Lost Cities of Ceylon* by Miss G.E. Mitton. Leonard observed, in his dry fashion, that the book had 'the dangerous merit of including a little for everyone'.

1917 was, looking back on it, the grimmest and most desperate year of the war, with no end in sight. Clutton-Brock struck a modestly hopeful note in March – 'Already the war must seem like a meaningless treadmill to the Germans, that war which began as a romance of the German will to conquer' – but the mood in Britain was nevertheless sombre, especially in the first months. John Buchan reviewed a volume of letters and recollections of his friend Charles Lister, the son of Lord Ribblesdale, who had died at Gallipoli in 1915, and made it an elegy – romantic in an English way – for a whole circle of friends: 'It was true of him and all the great Balliol brotherhood of the fallen – the Grenfells, Bron Lucas, Raymond Asquith – their hearts were ever loyal to the service of forgotten kings.'

But 1917 was also a year of great events, with America coming into the war, and revolution in Russia. At first the Russian uprising excited enthusiasm, and after the February Revolution, Macdonell, reviewing a book on revolutions, spoke of these 'last marvellous days'. Clutton-Brock, a week later, on 29 March, declared that 'the Germans are fighting against freedom the world over; and Russian freedom new born is a battle-cry against them'. However, by 24 May, A.F. Pollard was asking of the events in Russia, 'Is it indeed a dawn that we see in the twilight, or the gathering gloom of a wasted war?' And he admitted that 'a wasted war' meant, above all, one wasted from the Allied point of view: 'The only test today is the test of war – whatever tends to our victory is good, everything else is bad.' In fact it looked as if the Russians might be giving up the fight against Germany. On 23 August, Pollard was saying that the looming danger in Russia was that of complete social disintegration, with all that would mean both for the Russians and the West. But the fact that Russia had been an ally in the war hitherto had certainly increased the interest in Russian literature, and this year the paper was full of admiring articles on Tolstoy, Dostoevsky, Turgenev and Chekhov. On 1 February, for instance, in the course of reviewing Tolstoy's *The Cossacks*, Virginia Woolf wrote of 'that extraordinary union of extreme simplicity combined with the utmost subtlety which seems to mark both the educated Russian and the peasant equally', and 'the profound psychology and superb sincerity of the Russian writers'.

As for the entry of the United States into the war, Clutton-Brock wrote on 26 April that it 'confirms our faith in the rational order of the universe', and Pollard wrote in August that 'as a portent in human affairs, the Russian revolution pales before it' – the United States had 'made itself bound so that others may be free'. Another sign of the changing world order was a letter from Pollard on 5 July urging the abandonment by Britain of the word 'Empire', because it invoked the ideas associated with the Kaisertum or with Tsarism – ideas he considered quite contrary to those that characterised British rule – 'and it is impossible to describe by a common term antagonistic conceptions'. The war had brought this conflict to a head, so 'let us abolish imperialistic words'.

Pollard also reviewed G.K. Chesterton's *A Short History of England*, but it did not find much favour with him. He said that Chesterton 'stands on his head to proclaim the world is upside down, and fails to realise that that is what he is doing'. The major historical work of the year was John Morley's *Recollections*, which went to John Cann Bailey, by now the principal reviewer of recent political history. He enjoyed the book, partly because of its anecdotes, such as Morley himself having to tell Mrs Gladstone of her husband's resignation as Prime Minister while Gladstone was rattling the dice on his backgammon board, and partly because Morley, while an avowed agnostic, did not like Leslie Stephen's dismissal of the Christian Church as 'an organisation of lying, fraud and crime'.

Stephen's daughter, Virginia Woolf, was in brilliant form in the pages of the *Lit Supp* in 1917. As though she were making up for lost time, she wrote reviews week after week, on an enormous variety of subjects. She was enthusiastic about many different kinds of new writing. She laughed at J.C. Squire's parodies, quoting his version of the nature poet and 'super-tramp' W.H. Davies –

> *I'd rather lie beneath small stars*
> *Than with rough men who drink in bars –*

commenting that the skill of the parody lay in Squire's giving the lines 'an air of artless innocence only a little in excess of Davies's natural expression'. She hailed Norman Douglas's novel *South Wind*: 'Take all the interesting and eccentric people you can think of, put them on an island in the Mediterranean beyond the realms of humdrum but not in those of fantasy; bid them say shamelessly whatever comes into their heads . . . enclose the whole in an exquisite atmosphere of pumice rocks and deep blue waves' – catching all the characteristics of the book with such precision. She mocked a book of over-civilised essays by the American Henry Dwight Sedgwick as 'melodious meditations', and contrasted it with Walt Whitman's preface to the first edition of *Leaves of Grass*, which 'as a piece of writing rivals anything we have done for a hundred years. As a statement of the American spirit no finer banner was ever unfurled for the young of a great country to march under.' She quoted Whitman – giving us a sharp idea of some of her own literary allegiances both in her criticism and her novels: the new writers, or 'priests of men', she wrote, shall 'find their inspiration in real objects today, symptoms of the past and future. They shall not deign to defend immortality or God, or the perfection of things . . .'

Richmond sent Virginia Woolf Henry James's posthumous memoirs, *The Middle Years*, and she wrote a long leading article on it, saying that it sounded like a 'superb act of thanksgiving' to the English world he had lived in – 'with all the creative power at his command he summons back the past and makes us a present of that'. Richmond also sent her new editions of Conrad's *Youth* and *Lord Jim*, no doubt in amends for the inadequate review of *Youth* in his first year as editor (*Lord Jim* had come out before his time, in 1900). In the meanwhile, Walter de la Mare had given an admiring review to *Victory*, and a less admiring one to *The Shadow Line*; but now was the chance for Virginia Woolf to pay full tribute to his 'complex genius' – which she did, along with some tart remarks on the binding of Dent's new edition, with its 'sad green colour, sprinkled with chocolate-brown nautical emblems such as might be stamped on some pamphlet drawing attention to the claims of sea-captains' widows'.

John Middleton Murry rivalled her this year in the frequency, variety and dash of his reviews, and often they shared a page. He mainly reviewed books in French. He fiercely attacked the right-wing writer Charles Maurras, who in his book *Quand les Français ne s'aiment pas* called for a complete volte-face in French policy and regretted that it was not the French who had occupied Belgium. Murry praised the beauty of Paul Valéry's poem 'La Jeune Parque', struggled energetically to interpret its symbolical account of 'the vicissitudes of a woman's soul in the night season' (by its nature obscure, he added), and concluded that 'the genius of English poetry demands a broader sweep, a larger argument'. He admired the 'rare and complex mind' of André Gide, and defined his *sotie*, *Les Caves du Vatican* as 'a kind of clear-headed minor Dostoevsky *de bonne compagnie*'.

James Joyce did much better with his *Portrait of the Artist as a Young Man* than he had done with *Dubliners*. Clutton-Brock was at his critical best reviewing it. He felt compelled to deplore a few improprieties in the book, but only because they would put some readers off, and he wanted it to have as many readers as possible. He said that though the 'whisper of sarcasm' started up about everything in Stephen Dedalus's mind, he was 'not futile, because of the drifting passion and the flushing and fading beauty of his mind . . . Mr Joyce gives us wild youth, as wild as Hamlet's, and full of wild music'. Joyce himself, however, was rather ironical about the review, detecting in it a wish that he should have written about more important people (a comment more apt, in fact, about the earlier review of *Dubliners*). 'He is stating the English preference for tawdry grandeurs,' Joyce responded. 'Even the best Englishmen seem to love a lord in literature.'

A major voice of the future made a brief appearance in January –

Aldous Huxley, still only twenty-two, and staying (as the marked copy of the issue reveals) with Lady Ottoline Morrell, friend and patron of Bloomsbury, at the Manor House, Garsington. He reviewed rather sternly a history of *English Literature from Widsith to the Death of Chaucer*, by an American professor, Allen H. Benham, saying that the extracts from Anglo-Saxon poetry did not adequately display our ancestors' 'Teutonic combination of grossness and melancholy'. In a letter to his father the previous December Huxley described in his typically vivacious way how this review came about:

> I saw Richmond on Monday, who was v. polite and almost infinitely loquacious – thereby very nearly making me miss my train – and I was to study the list of New Books in the *Lit Supp* and send him a p.c. with the names of any I wanted to do: in which case he might or might not give them to me – he cd. not be positive which.

Another great writer of the future also made an appearance in the paper in June 1917, when *Prufrock and Other Observations*, the first, and now famous, book of the young American poet T.S. Eliot, was reviewed by Dalton in the 'New Books and Reprints' section at the back. Dalton was quite baffled by it:

> Mr Eliot's notion of poetry – he calls the 'observations' poems – seems to be a purely analytical treatment, verging sometimes on the catalogue, of personal relations and environments, uninspired by any glimpse beyond them and untouched by any genuine rush of feeling. As, even on this basis, he remains frequently inarticulate, his 'poems' will hardly be read by many with enjoyment. For the catalogue manner we may recommend 'Rhapsody on a Windy Night' [here Dalton quoted twenty-one lines of the poem]. Among other reminiscences which pass through the rhapsodist's mind and which he thinks the public should know about, are 'dust in crevices, smells of chestnuts in the streets, and female smells in shuttered rooms, and cigarettes in corridors, and cocktail smells in bars'.
>
> The fact that these things occurred to the mind of Mr Eliot is surely of the smallest importance to any one – even to himself. They certainly have no relation to 'poetry', and we only give an example because some of the pieces, he states, have appeared in a periodical which claims that word as its title [this was the Chicago magazine *Poetry* founded by Harriet Monroe].

With his need for a 'rush of feeling', Dalton was incapable of detecting the delicately unrushed feeling of these early Eliot poems – or that the 'things that occurred to the mind of Mr Eliot' would in due course be of the very greatest importance to the whole course of English and American literature.

Further poems arising out of the experience of war were making their appearance in 1917, and were received much more enthusiastically than Eliot's. There were 'gallant Mr Robert Graves's hearty chants', as Harold Child put it, both in Graves's volume *Fairies and Fusiliers* and in the anthology *Georgian Poetry 1916–1917*. There was Robert Nichols in the same anthology; in his 'Fulfilment'

> *Was there love once? I have forgotten her.*
> *Was there grief once? grief yet is mine –*

you could 'hear the war in poetry', said Child. Virginia Woolf was deeply struck by Siegfried Sassoon's collection *The Old Huntsman*, declaring that 'what Mr Sassoon has felt to be the most sordid and horrible experiences in the world he makes us feel to be so in a measure which no other poet of the war has achieved'.

However, Bailey and de la Mare must be credited for spotting that, with the death of Edward Thomas in the Arras offensive in April 1917, a most remarkable poet had been lost to Britain. Thomas, who had for many years been writing lightweight books about literature and the countryside, produced a sudden outburst of supremely beautiful poems after 1914. He published a few in his lifetime under the name 'Edward Eastaway', and Bailey picked some of these out in *An Annual of New Poetry, 1917*, calling him 'a real poet, with the truth in him'. De la Mare gave him the greater praise that he merited in his review of the posthumous volume, *Poems by Edward Thomas*, six months later. He said that 'We listen to a kind of monologue, like one of his own nightingales softly practising over its song, as though in utmost secrecy we were overhearing a man talking quietly on to himself', and he quoted in full the now famous poem 'Adlestrop', about the birds singing around the silent country railway station, commenting 'Some time in life the express train draws up for most of us at Adlestrop, and the immortal moment bringing the peace, understanding, and reconciliation which are the recurrent theme of these poems, is ours'. It is de la Mare's usual way of attempting his own romantic evocation of the nature of the poems he is discussing, rather than the closer verbal criticism we are now used to, but it does get near to them.

A book that was reviewed in August marked, in its way, another epoch in the history of the *Lit Supp*. This was *Shakespeare's Fight with the Pirates*, by the other Pollard of these years – not A.F. Pollard, the historian and essayist, but A.W. Pollard, the bibliographer and Shakespeare scholar, who was quite unrelated to him. A.W. Pollard's book was an outstanding and pioneering piece of detective work on the history of the texts of the Shakespeare plays, and some of its material had already appeared in the *Lit Supp*. Its main argument was that the most – perhaps the only – reliable evidence of what Shakespeare wrote was to be found in the *Quartos* that were based on the playhouse manuscripts. All other versions were suspect. Percy Simpson, an Oxford Shakespeare scholar who reviewed the book, said that Shakespearean scholarship had entered on a new phase recently, concerning itself 'not with the poet, but that very prosaic person, the printer'. The supreme merit of Pollard's book was that it faced the problem of the texts squarely and provided bearings for a new advance.

So began one of the first of those great scholarly controversies that were to feature henceforward in the paper's correspondence columns, one of the fruits of the growth of the academic world. Pollard's chief antagonist this time was that Marion H. Spielmann who had written earlier about Charlotte Brontë's stay in Brussels (though in these letters he only signed himself 'S', perhaps because he was engaged simultaneously in another correspondence where he used his name). He was the son of a banker, an amateur, not academic, scholar, but a formidable one and very combative. He could not believe that Shakespeare would not have taken more trouble over the printing of his plays. The argument rolled around for a few weeks, then in October Spielmann triumphantly produced letters he had had from three living playwrights, Arthur Pinero, Henry Arthur Jones and G. Bernard Shaw, all saying they took at least some trouble over the publication of their plays. It did not seem to prove anything about Shakespeare, but it brought the debate for the time being to a stylish end.

Another letter, in May, also looked ahead to the growing importance of academic English studies, discussing problems about the English tripos that was about to be established at Cambridge. Dr F.R. Leavis loomed, as it were, on the horizon. But one set of letters swept the readers far away from current concerns – an argument about whether there used to be crocuses in the Nottingham meadows. This led in turn to two specially written poems being published in the paper, bringing the war back in again. 'In England', by May O'Rourke of the Old Vicarage, Dorchester, said there were crocuses at Nottingham, but

> *The broken flesh that Flanders keeps,*
> *It too may have its flowers,*

while Jessie Bell's poem proclaimed more hopefully

> *There are crocuses at Nottingham!*
> *Young crocus buds at Nottingham!*
> *Thousands of buds at Nottingham*
> *Ungathered by the Hun.*

In 1918, war books were still pouring out, though not in such a flood as they had been in the first years of the war. Arthur Conan Doyle had been bringing out an annual book on the deeds of the British Army, but was taken to task by the Hon. John Fortescue this year for his third volume, *The British Campaign in France and Flanders, 1916*. Sir Arthur, Fortescue said, 'was entirely overweighted by the magnitude and complexity of the Battle of the Somme', and should 'gain himself a clearer conception of such operations before he attempts to explain them to his readers'. But G.S. Gordon, the Scottish professor, enjoyed André Maurois's playful book about the English, *Les Silences de Colonel Bramble*, calling him 'a kindlier Maupassant', and his characters 'the most interesting and amusing group of British officers that we have met in books since the war began'. A new contributor was Aldous Huxley's brother Julian, destined to be a famous zoologist; here he reviewed a book on the history of science, with praise of Newton and Darwin as the two men 'who have laid the basis for all future outlook on the universe, all estimate of man's position therein'.

The takeover of the Russian Revolution by the Bolsheviks brought in another important reviewer, from whom much good work was to come, C.E. Bechhofer. He had been educated at St Paul's School and Berlin University, and at the age of only twenty-four was working at the Board of Trade on the Russian Government Committee, and in 1919 went out to Russia with the British Military Mission. Under the heading 'The Mystery of the Soviets' he reviewed a book called *The Birth of the Russian Democracy* by A.J. Sack, published by the Russian Information Bureau at the Woolworth Building in New York, and gave a long, brilliant analysis of how the Bolsheviks had managed to seize power, though at this stage – in October 1918 – Bechhofer thought they had 'only the authority which mob force can give them in some of the cities'. Dr Shadwell, that friend and scourge of the working man, wrote an article on the centenary of Karl Marx's birth, concluding that 'Marx's name will always remain a landmark, but the tide of economic and social development has flowed away from his scientific system and left it derelict'. He was right, of course, but only proved so seventy years later.

On the literary front, Virginia Woolf was more *engagée* this year even than in 1917. She was again writing practically every week, defending the highest literary standards on every side. Though she had liked J.C. Squire's parodies the year before, she scorned his collection of articles, *The Gold Tree*, saying that he was 'preoccupied with the effort to be smooth, demure and irreproachable' and that 'platitudes spread themselves abroad [in his essays] with an air of impeccable virtue'. She was kinder to Robert Lynd – at least his essays in the sixpenny weeklies 'make us remember the possibilities of his form'.

In fact, Virginia Woolf practically took over the reviewing of poetry in the *Lit Supp*. She advised the young Aldous Huxley to stick to the 'fantastic, amusing or ironical aspects of life' since she felt he had the vocabulary of a poet rather than the inspiration of a poet. She found that the chief thing that Edith Sitwell had to tell at this stage of her career was that the world was 'extremely bright and very noisy'. She commented finely that Siegfried Sassoon's new war poems were 'too fiercely suspicious of any comfort or compromise to be read as poetry; but his contempt for palliative or subterfuge gives us the raw stuff of poetry'. When Rupert Brooke's *Collected Poems* were published, Woolf contributed a vivid tribute to him, again showing the intellectual allegiances of herself and her husband and the best of the Bloomsbury circle:

> Beneath 'an appearance almost of placidity' [Brooke's own words] he was the most restless, complex, and analytic of human beings. It was impossible to think of him withdrawn, abstracted, or indifferent. Whether or not it was for the good of his poetry he would be in the thick of things, and one fancies that he would in the end have framed a speech that came very close to the modern point of view – a subtle analytical poetry, or prose perhaps, full of intellect, and full of his keen unsentimental curiosity.

This year, too, Woolf received another reissued novel by Conrad to review – *Nostromo*. However she did not think this one succeeded. There was a 'crowding and suffocating superabundance' in this South

American story which made it 'one of those rare and magnificent wrecks over which the critics shake their heads' – not, in fact, such a different verdict from that which E.V. Lucas had given originally in 1904.

Her friend Lytton Strachey's *Eminent Victorians* was reviewed on 16 May by the American aphorist who had made his home in England, Logan Pearsall Smith. He thought it had only one fault – it was too amusing: 'Mr Strachey's air of malicious detachment, his mock solemnity, and his Gibbonian style lend themselves so naturally to comic effect that the whole thing becomes really more diverting than any such book ought to be; for, after all, the Victorian age was something more than a joke.'

This review revealed how the Victorian era was, if not a joke, at least receding in the collective memory of the *Lit Supp* as the First World War approached its end, with Bloomsbury driving the process on, as it was elsewhere in England. But Edmund Gosse went into the attack. In a letter on 27 June he complained bitterly of Strachey's portrait of the Earl of Cromer; Cromer did not have a 'subacid smile', on the contrary his conversation was 'copious, stimulating, delicious'; it was absurd to say he took no interest in the East; Strachey had produced a 'pyrotechnical display of satire' but 'what is sparkling should be just'. The author replied coolly the following week that 'it is not always a man's friends who know him best', but he was to get another belabouring in a letter the week after from Mary A. Ward for his 'coarse caricature' of her grandfather Arnold of Rugby. 'Is this a moment,' she asked, 'when the same spirit of sheer brutality which we are fighting in the military field should be allowed to penetrate the field of English letters?'

Yet another Bloomsbury figure, Bertrand Russell, was rescued from the battering he had received in the paper for his ideas about the war, his champion now being D.L. Murray, who was shortly to join the *Lit Supp* staff and in due course become its second editor. Murray was reviewing Russell's collection of essays, *Mysticism and Logic*, commenting that their appearance was opportune – 'for it would be a pitiable thing if this philosopher and mathematician of European fame were to be thought of only, or even principally, as a politician whose ideas have offended the mass of his countrymen'. He praised the 'fundamental stoicism' of Russell's creed, and described him as 'the Cato who upholds the conquered cause of his ideals against the conquering gods of tradition and popular approval'.

James Joyce's play *Exiles*, published in book form, was reviewed not by Clutton-Brock, as Richard Ellman states in his biography of Joyce, but by the poet T. Sturge Moore, the brother of G.E. Moore, the philosopher so esteemed in Bloomsbury. He thought that it revealed 'resources of spiritual passion and constructive power which should greatly cheer the friends of his talent' and we know that he tried, unsuccessfully, to get the Stage Society to produce it.

As for another provocative new writer on the scene, Wyndham Lewis, who had edited the Vorticist magazine *Blast* with Ezra Pound and became the enemy of Bloomsbury, his novel *Tarr* was reviewed by Clutton-Brock, who was horrified, as he was supposed to be, by the unprincipled, blindly functioning characters, but also feared – rightly too, perhaps – that the author was in danger of becoming like them himself.

The war ended with the armistice on 11 November 1918. Clutton-Brock had kept up his noble exhortations to the end, and was rightly given the leading article to write in the first week of peace. In triumph he was faithful to his creed. In his article 'The End and the Beginning' on 14 November, he hailed the victory as the final working out of the moral law, a law in which England had sometimes almost lost her faith but which had now gloriously prevailed. It meant, though, that, if England had proved that it was bearing the sword of God during the war, it must now hold with equal firmness the scales of His justice. Because England had laid aside the weapons of God, Clutton-Brock continued, 'we are not therefore discharged from the army of God to our own devices'. We must 'purify our minds of all base thoughts that would be an insult to the presence and the memory of the dead'. Thus he carried his firm moral note into the peace.

Clutton-Brock had not been without his critics. In Cambridge and Bloomsbury, they were inclined to laugh at him. In a letter to Lowes Dickinson in March 1917, E.M. Forster had remarked, 'How badly Clutton-Brock is doing. He argues as if Nation A can, by beating Nation B, teach it the lesson it desires to teach it, instead of some other lesson which it probably will not desire and certainly cannot foresee. His mind was not thus muddled three years ago. Or has mine grown cocky?' Three months later, Forster is writing to the same correspondent, 'How lamentably Clutton-Brock has gone to pot. "Mutton broth" the little boy next door used to call him, with impish premonition.' Max Beerbohm said, 'I wish Clutton-Brock would take Holy Orders and have done with it, instead of hanging about the vestry "so quietly".'

Even in the *Literary Supplement* itself, he had been criticised. When his book *Studies in Christianity* had come out just three months before the end of the war, that fierce conservative cleric, Dean Inge, had complained in his review that Christianity was not, as Clutton-Brock would have it, 'only a religion of pity and forgiveness'. It was a stern and austere creed, with – in particular – nothing in the Gospels about taking forcibly from the rich to give to the poor. It had only one remedy for social inequalities – to ignore them – and 'Mr Clutton-Brock's counsels of perfection would land us in total economic ruin.'

D.L. Murray wrote an essay on Clutton-Brock after his death, and admitted that he was – though he would have hated the word – a preacher, or at any rate a determined schoolmaster. But he praised the courage of the man who 'in those months of collective hysteria and panic at the early German victories' could make the entreaty 'Do not let us be self-righteous' and remind his countrymen that behind the Germany of the Hohenzollerns there remained a Germany which 'means cradle songs and fairy stories and Christmas in old moonlit towns, and a queer simple tenderness always childish and musical'. Clutton-Brock's boldness, Murray said, might easily have stirred a tempest, but his wisdom made its way. As for Bruce Richmond, his loyalty to Clutton-Brock was total, and he once said that Clutton-Brock had done more to ensure the success of the *Literary Supplement* than any other person. Clutton-Brock died in 1924, writing for the paper and, as we shall see, engaged in controversy almost to the last; but the years 1914 to 1918 had been his years of glory.

Chapter Six

Northcliffe Passes, Eliot Arrives: 1919–22

S o, the Allies had won the war – and the editor of the *Times Literary Supplement* had survived in his job. The average weekly circulation of his new penny paper had been 41,974 in 1914. It had slipped in the following two years, and after the price went up to a penny-halfpenny in November 1916, and to 2d the following March, it fell to a weekly average of 29,398 in 1917. It was around that figure at the end of the war (29,106 was the average for the full year 1918).

This was not spectacular, but not bad for a literary paper while a war was being fought – no doubt Arthur Clutton-Brock had done something for the paper's circulation as well as for the nation's decency and morale – and in 1919 the average weekly sale rose again to 31,864, even though there was a further price rise to 3d in October of that year.

Northcliffe had left the *Lit Supp* alone during the war. He had also remained on good terms with his editor Geoffrey Dawson at the main paper for much of that time. In the first years he was busy campaigning for better political management of the war, and cultivating for himself the illusion that his newspapers were the chief influence in bringing Lloyd George to power. Later in the war he became head of the British War Mission in the United States, and then Director of Propaganda in Enemy Lands – or 'Minister for the Destruction of German Confidence' as an angry German general called him – and threw himself whole-heartedly into those jobs. (The Germans even struck a medal in his dishonour, with his head on one side and the devil on the other.)

But after the war Northcliffe fell out with Lloyd George and the government, and started pressing the editor of *The Times* to support his increasingly megalomaniac vendetta against them. Dawson, like Buckle before him, could tell when it was time to go. (Dawson's change of name, incidentally, had taken place in August 1917, under the terms of an entail in his family that had come down to him through an aunt. A quip that circulated at *The Times* went 'It's strange that a deed-poll under the law/Can change a robin into a daw', but even Northcliffe accepted the change and subsequently called him 'My dear Dawson'.)

Dawson resigned on 18 February 1919, and the foreign editor, Wickham Steed, became editor of the paper. We have already seen Richmond's letter to Dawson on his resignation; Buckle, his predecessor, also wrote him a handsome letter, saying that 'you have established a clear distinction between *The Times* and the other papers having the same Proprietor . . . in the most difficult circumstances, you held the banner of an independent corporate conscience aloft.' However, Buckle added 'What I fear is that all the "old gang", your friends and mine, will follow you into retirement. Richmond, Flanagan [a staunchly Unionist leader writer], Shadwell, Freeman – will any of them remain? And if they don't will the tradition go on?'

Bruce Richmond did not follow Dawson into retirement, though he was almost alone now at Printing House Square; and at the *Lit Supp* the tradition of lofty independence went on undimmed.

During these last years of the war – in spite of Dalton – T.S. Eliot had begun to make his powerful new presence felt on the London literary scene. He had arrived in England from America in 1914, when he was twenty-five, and had quickly made friends with Ezra Pound, who, he said, 'changed my life'. Pound recognised his poetic gifts at once and gave him wholehearted encouragement, and in 1917 the *Egoist*, the magazine edited by Harriet Shaw Weaver but of which Pound was the presiding genius, published the book that Dalton so hated, his volume of poems: *Prufrock and Other Observations*. That year it also published James Joyce's *The Portrait of the Artist as a Young Man* as a book, after running it in the magazine, and in the same year, too, Eliot became assistant editor of the *Egoist*.

By September 1919, when he met Bruce Richmond, Eliot had published another volume, *Poems*, with Leonard and Virginia Woolf at their Hogarth Press in Richmond; he had married Vivien Haigh-Wood, not very happily for either party ('To her the marriage brought no happiness . . . to me, it brought the state of mind out of which came *The Waste Land*', he wrote years later); and after a period of schoolteaching, he had taken a job in the Colonial and Foreign Department of Lloyds Bank in the City, where they encouraged his poetry because they liked their young men to have a successful hobby.

He was introduced to Bruce Richmond by Richard Aldington, who had by now taken over much of the reviewing of French literature on the *Lit Supp*. John Middleton Murry was still contributing to the *Lit Supp* occasionally, but he had resigned from most of the French reviewing, and was now editor of the *Athenaeum*, to which he had given a brilliant new lease of life. In fact he had invited Eliot to become his assistant editor on the *Athenaeum* at £500 a year (£25,000 now), and though Eliot had not accepted the offer, he had contributed some substantial critical essays to the revived paper.

Richard Aldington had been the assistant editor of the *Egoist* before Eliot (he had left when he went into the army), and was as devoted to him as Pound was. He brought Eliot to Richmond's notice because he thought that if Eliot wrote for the *Lit Supp*, it would help to curb the opposition that was growing towards him in some London literary circles.

Just before his meeting with Richmond, Eliot had been on a walking tour with Ezra Pound in France, and had grown a beard there which made him 'look awful' according to Aldington, especially since it was incongruously topped by a Derby hat; and he and Richmond were at first a little uneasy with each other when they met. Richmond also no doubt knew about Eliot's close connection with the hostile Pound. But over a steak and a pint of bitter they were soon laughing together, and in five minutes, Aldington recalls, Eliot had completely captivated Richmond. The editor infallibly knew when he had found someone good, and Eliot was invited to write some leading articles on Elizabethan and Jacobean dramatists. Before long, he and Richmond had become good friends.

Eliot, writing to his mother in October 1919, told her that he has been invited to write for the *Lit Supp*, saying that 'this is the highest honour possible in the critical world of literature'. On 10 November he wrote to tell her that he had given a lecture on poetry in London but that it was chaired by 'a middle aged poetic celebrity who evidently knew nothing about me except that I was supposed to be the latest rage and he didn't understand it and didn't like it'. This was the poet and regular contributor to the *Lit Supp*, Laurence Binyon. In fact, the occasion of the lecture (with its 'heavy fire of heckling') both reflected some of the hostility to Eliot that Aldington was concerned about, and prefigured some later clashes that Eliot would have with the *Lit Supp* itself. But on 18 November he reported to his mother the appearance of his first contribution to the *Lit Supp*, an article on Ben Jonson that has long been regarded as one of the classic literary essays of the twentieth century, with its formidably close and subtle attention to the language of Jonson's verse, and is able to tell her 'the editor was very much pleased with it'.

A few days later he was telling her that 'The *Times Literary Supplement* is a good paper, and not expensive, but you must not expect to find me in it very often. I should only do the "leading article" and no one person writes that more than six times a year'. In January 1920, writing to his friend and patron in America, John Quinn, he gave an interesting picture of the London literary scene as he saw it. J.C. Squire, whom we have already seen being both praised and mocked by Virginia Woolf, had just given up the literary editorship of the *New Statesman*, and founded a new magazine, the *London Mercury*. (The *Egoist*, incidentally, had just come to the end of its life, with another famous essay by Eliot, 'Tradition and the Individual Talent', in its last issue.) Eliot had already, in a letter to John Middleton Murry, written a comic verse about the number of magazines Squire was involved in:

> *And Squire smote the living Rock,*
> *And Lo! the living Rock was wet –*
> *Whence issue, punctual as the clock*
> *Land and Water,*
> *The New Statesman,*
> *The Owl,*
> *The London Mercury,*
> *And the Westminster Gazette.*

(*Land and Water* was the predecessor of today's *The Field*; *The Owl* was a short-lived venture of Robert Graves's.)

Now, in his letter to Quinn, Eliot wrote more seriously about Squire.

> The *London Mercury*, which started with a great deal of advertisement, will I hope, fail in a few years's time. It is run by a small clique of bad writers. J.C. Squire, the editor, knows nothing about poetry; but he is the cleverest journalist in London. If he succeeds, it will be impossible to get anything good published. His influence controls or affects the literary contents and criticism of five or six periodicals already. *The Times* always more or less apart, the *Athenaeum* (and, of less influence, *Art and Letters*) are the only important reviews outside of the Squire influence.

However, by now it was a formidable group of fairly young writers who were opposed to the Squire camp, and before long Eliot would found a new journal, the *Criterion*, as a focus for the imaginative literature and the serious critical thought that in their different ways they all believed in. Meanwhile, in the years 1919 to 1922, the *Times Literary Supplement* gave these relative newcomers plenty of house room – alongside many other reviewers who were anathema to them and to whom they in turn were anathema. It was Richmond's by now established policy of keeping the old and the new voices side by side in his paper.

We have seen how badly *Prufrock* had been received in the *Lit Supp* in 1917 and Eliot would advert to this review later, in 1921. On 22 May 1919, however, Aldington wrote about a short-lived new quarterly called *Coterie*, and picked out Eliot as the 'star turn' among the poets in it. The Eliot poem in it was 'A Cooking Egg' and Aldington spoke of his 'delicate and disdainful mind', praised him as a 'distinguished critic of literature', and said that 'his poetry possesses the charm of a more than superior irony' – quite good characterisation of his qualities.

Three weeks later, on 12 June, Clutton-Brock reviewed his Hogarth Press volume of *Poems*, writing wittily but not very sympathetically about them: 'His verse, novel and ingenious, original as it is, is fatally impoverished of subject-matter . . . He seems to have a "phobia" of sentimentality . . . He is in danger of writing nothing at all, but merely thinking of all the poems he has refused to write.' In a letter to Mary Hutchinson a few days later, Eliot said, 'I wonder who wrote in the last *Times*? He found my joints in one or two places very cleverly.'

In 1920, by which time Eliot was as we have seen a contributor to the paper, his new book of poems, *Ara Vus Prec*, was nevertheless again reviewed briskly – though a little more favourably – by Dalton, in the Book List in February: 'Verses by an able scholar and literateur – whose poetical work may be said to be the most challenging and bizarre of any of the younger bands of the day.' ('Bands' should presumably have been 'bards' – though Eliot would probably have preferred to be called a 'band'.) This time, however, a longer review of the book appeared on 18 March, again by Clutton-Brock, under the heading 'A New Byronism' – but it said very much what he had said before. 'Human voices for Mr Eliot drown everything; he cannot get away from his disgust of them . . . but . . . he does not convince us that his weariness is anything but a habit, an anti-Romantic reaction, a new Byronism which he must throw off if he is not to become a recurring decimal in his fear of being a mere vulgar fraction'.

In April, Clutton-Brock came back to Eliot yet again in a review of *Three Critical Essays on Modern English Poetry*, published by the Poetry Bookshop, to which Eliot was a contributor along with Aldous Huxley and the imagist poet F.S. Flint (also by now a reviewer for the *Lit Supp*). Clutton-Brock claimed that Eliot, who was making a distinction between strictly literary criticism and 'the criticism which is a kind of philosophy', was not appreciative enough of philosophical criticism – 'there is a common belief,' Clutton-Brock wrote rather rudely, 'that criticism of poetry must be left to poets, or to scribblers giving themselves the airs of poets'.

This time Eliot was moved to write a letter in reply, which appeared the following week. He said, modestly, that the reviewer had treated his essay with 'more courteous clemency than this defective composition deserved'. But he went on firmly to say that 'your reviewer's notions of criticism are not much more satisfactory to me than my own', that 'all the best criticism of poetry is the criticism of poets' such as Dryden or Coleridge, and that 'in general, philosophers are as ignorant of poetry as of mathematics, and the fact that they have read much poetry is no more assurance of competence in criticising poetry than their ability to reckon in shillings and pence is of their competence to criticise mathematicians'. Finally he called upon the reviewer to elucidate his use of the term 'philosophy'.

This was the beginning of something of a battle between Eliot and the *Lit Supp*. In May, Clutton-Brock reviewed Aldous Huxley's book of poems *Leda* and remarked that 'many remind one of Mr T.S. Eliot; they express the fact that to the writer life is absurd in its traditional delights and, for the rest, tiresome'. This time Eliot wrote to his mother:

> I do not accept the interpretation of me which the *Times Literary Supplement* is accustomed to make, elsewhere as well as in the review of Huxley's book which you read. I have a very low opinion of this book. Huxley has, of course, like a number of other young men, borrowed a good deal from my poetry. Aldington is an exception – he does not like my poetry, and says so frankly, but I like him none the less.

Eliot contributed another of his notable leads, an essay on Philip Massinger, on 27 May, but in October he was on the attack again in the paper's correspondence column. This time the occasion was an article that had appeared the previous month on Charles Maurras. The reviewer was a writer whom Richmond was now favouring with plenty of work, Basil de Selincourt, who ranged over a wide field of subjects from contemporary sociology to poetry and music. Unfortunately de

Selincourt was not one of Richmond's best discoveries, and wrote in an abstract, pontifical way that was rarely very illuminating. Eliot was more sympathetic to the right-wing Maurras than de Selincourt was, but the main point of his letter was to criticise the quality of de Selincourt's thinking.

'It is in attempting to apprehend your critic's definitions of the terms "romanticism" and "classicism" that my intellect is confused and my serenity disturbed,' he wrote silkily. 'The writer treats romanticism on the whole with disapproval until he suddenly declares that the period of classical production in France was also "a great romantic period".' Perhaps, Eliot concluded, it would be beneficial if we 'forgot those terms altogether, and looked steadily for the intelligence and sensibility which each work of art contains' – a good description of his own practice as a critic.

Clutton-Brock returned yet again to Eliot in a review of *The Sacred Wood*, Eliot's collection of critical essays, in December 1920. He praised the essay 'Tradition and the Individual Talent' but found an 'unconscious malice' in some of Eliot's comments on particular writers. None of this seems to have interfered with Eliot's affection for Richmond; in January 1921 he told his mother that he and John Middleton Murry had fallen apart – 'his articles seem to me to become more and more windy' (in which, alas, there was occasionally some truth) and 'I think him a man of weak character and great vanity' – but that 'Richmond of *The Times* I like very much; and he has the very great advantage of not being himself a writer, so that the element of professional jealousy cannot enter.'

Eliot went on to contribute magnificent (and also now famous) essays on Andrew Marvell, John Dryden and the Metaphysical poets in the course of 1921, but at the end of that year he finally struck out at the poetry reviewing in the paper. In October he wrote to Aldington saying that 'the review of Murry in *TLS* is a revolting mass of torrid tastelessness and hypocritical insensibility'. In her edition of Eliot's letters, his widow Valerie Eliot took this to refer to a review called 'Shakespeare and Love' contributed by Murry on 13 October, but I think it actually refers to a review of Murry's collection, *Poems 1916–20*, in the same issue. 'The review of Murry' does not suggest that Murry is the reviewer but the reviewed – and it seems unlikely, moreover, even if there had been a falling out, that he would have spoken of Murry to Aldington in quite such terms. In fact, the 'review of Murry' was by the egregious Basil de Selincourt. Eliot would not have known this, but applied to him Eliot's words make much more sense.

A few days later Eliot grumbled in a letter to Aldington about four poetry reviews in the *Lit Supp* of books respectively by Pound, Marianne Moore, Edith Sitwell and H.D. (Hilda Doolittle). He did not particularly care for Edith Sitwell's and H.D.'s poetry, but he clearly felt that poets had a common interest in being reviewed intelligently.

Aldington was himself very angry about the review of H.D.'s *Hymen* in the Book List, again by the relentless Dalton, who called her poems 'prose sentences cut into strips'. Aldington had been married to Hilda Doolittle, and though they were now parted, he believed, as he said in a letter that appeared on 3 November, that 'she was the greatest living writer of *vers libres*' and that *Hymen* showed 'a poetic personality both original and beautiful'.

Eliot simultaneously wrote a letter in support of Aldington's general position, but it was not used, perhaps because he had another letter in that same issue of 3 November (signed 'your obliged humble CONTRIBUTOR') in which he answered a point that the great professor George Saintsbury had made about his Metaphysical poets article. (Eliot, unlike Saintsbury, thought that all good poets, not just the Caroline poets, 'thought twice' about their poetry – though he added wickedly that he could not believe that 'Swinburne thought twice, or even once, before he wrote: Time with a gift of tears,/Grief with a glass that ran.')

However we learn something about Eliot's unpublished letter to the paper in a letter to Aldington on 3 November, in which his feelings about the reviewing of his own poetry at last appeared. He says that Richmond may not have printed his letter because 'I complained that all the verse worth reviewing at all had been treated the same way. Damned his policy, in fact. (*My* first book was done to death this way. They only gave me more notice later, either because I had become a contributor or because the Woolfs published my second book.)' But he did not pursue the quarrel any further.

In fact, the end of 1921 marked the end of this close involvement of Eliot with the *Lit Supp* and its activities – a dramatic and instructive saga while it lasted. He was busy now establishing the *Criterion*, in which his own most famous poem, *The Waste Land*, would appear in the first issue, in October 1922. Richmond gave him some help in setting the *Criterion* up, and in May 1922 Eliot wrote to Aldington 'Richmond has been unfailingly kind to me, and about my repeated delays in producing an article about Seneca has been angelic.' Eliot would go on writing occasionally for the *Lit Supp* throughout the 1920s, and the friendship between him and Richmond lasted, with Eliot still going down to parties at Richmond's country house long after the latter had retired.

It was altogether a vigorous poetry scene in Britain in the years just after the First World War. Richmond had many poetry critics at his disposal, too: Dalton, Clutton-Brock, John Cann Bailey, Walter de la Mare, Edmund Blunden, Harold Child and Basil de Selincourt of the 'old school'; Murry, Aldington, F.S. Flint, Edgell Rickword, T. Sturge Moore and Hugh d'Anson Fausset (an arrival we shall hear more of) among the newcomers, but all with their idiosyncrasies and individual tastes. Richmond played his usual game of drawing on them all, not always with the best results but certainly in a way that produced excitement among the *genus irritabile*.

A poet emerging from the past was Gerard Manley Hopkins, who had died in 1880 at the age of forty-four, and whose poems were only now, in January 1919, introduced to the world by his friend Robert Bridges. Clutton-Brock took them on, and stressed their difficulty, but his imagination was fired by them, and in his final paragraph he wrote attentively: 'The poems are crowded with objects sharply cut, and with sounds no less sharp and clashing; you fight your way through the verses, yet they draw you on. There is beauty everywhere without luxury, the beauty that seems to come of painful intense watching, the utter, disinterested delight of one who sees another world, not through, but in this one.' This was a worthy welcome to this newly-revealed, major English poet.

Another volume, in 1922, that sounded as if it was a voice from the past was A.E. Housman's *Last Poems*. However Housman was not dead – he was only sixty-three, and would live to the age of seventy-seven – and the title was only an expression of his melancholy realism. The book was reviewed by that highly intelligent McDowall who had long ago had the nervous breakdown; he was still living near his friend Thomas Hardy in Dorset, and would do some excellent work for the paper in the 1920s. He said that in the poems in *A Shropshire Lad*, Housman's feelings, under a stress of great emotion, 'had poured themselves unhesitatingly into a faultless mould', but that the new book 'does not give the sharp thrill of immediacy so often, or ring so deep'. However, he was sure that Housman's poetry would live because it had 'expressed some passionate moments with the last felicity'.

There were important volumes of war poetry to take in, but Basil de Selincourt did not do very well with his reviews of them. When the posthumous *Poems of Wilfred Owen*, who had been killed a week before the Armistice, appeared in January 1921, de Selincourt gave the dead poet a solemn lesson on the necessity of war and on the poet's 'misplaced moral revolt' – but 'no doubt', he said, 'it was his sensitiveness that played him false'. Nor did de Selincourt show much more sympathy to Isaac Rosenberg, the East End Jewish boy who was killed in action in 1918 and whose *Poems*, brought out by Gordon Bottomley in 1922, received a very patronising review. As for the *Collected Poems* of Edward Thomas, which appeared in 1920, de Selincourt wrote in much the same pompous and indulgent tone about this 'excessively retiring' poet, but did acknowledge that he 'opens up for us a world of strange and refreshing experience'.

W.B. Yeats was now in his fifties, and at last the *Lit Supp* began to acknowledge his stature. Clutton-Brock wrote enthusiastically of his volume *The Wild Swans at Coole* in March 1919: 'In his music he seems to inhabit a world that will tremble away at a touch like reflections in still water . . . Go on, go on, we cry.' In May of that year, de la Mare, lover of simplicity that he was, found Yeats's essays in *The Cutting of an Agate* too 'chiselled, recondite and profound' for any but his little clan of followers; but the poet Edward Shanks, reviewing the *Later Poems* at the end of 1922, came out firmly with the judgment: 'If we consider the whole spread of Mr Yeats's lyrical work, we find in it a steady growth which not many of our lyrical poets have surpassed.'

D.H. Lawrence brought out some *New Poems* in 1919, but Clutton-Brock – sounding almost like T.S. Eliot now – found him too much 'at the mercy of his emotions' in this collection – 'if mere moods, causeless or unexplained, are as interesting as anything else in life, then life itself is uninteresting and one should yawn through it or commit suicide, not write poetry about it'. But, citing the beautiful poem 'Piano', he acknowledged that 'Beyond all doubt Mr Lawrence can write verse, as he can write prose.'

Ezra Pound's *Quia Pauper Amavi* was yet again briskly dismissed by Dalton in the Book List as a 'a strange collection of the commonplace and the recondite'. Another American poet, however, Vachel Lindsay, received a striking if not particularly approving review of his book, *General William Booth Enters Heaven*, from Virginia Woolf. 'There is every reason,' she wrote, 'to believe that America can bring something new to literature; it is high time, we may add, that America did.' This seems a bit unfair, if we remember her reverence for Henry James and her admiration for Whitman, besides the fact that her Hogarth Press had published T.S. Eliot.

However, Virginia Woolf did not find what she was looking for in Vachel Lindsay. She felt he had messages to deliver – 'about Beauty and Temperance and the future of Illinois'. But while 'the poetry may run clear for a moment, at the next the gospel clouds it'. There was a kind of street-corner music in it, but the language was banal – 'pompous, careless, slack, and conventional'. Still, the book had a 'rousing nature' and 'a simple emotional appeal'. There speaks Bloomsbury, loud, clear, condescendingly and wittily.

In fact, these were very important years for Virginia Woolf. She brought out three books, all of which were reviewed in the paper. The first, in May 1919, was one of three small books published simultaneously by the Hogarth Press – the other two were the volume of *Poems* by T.S. Eliot, and an essay by Murry called *The Critic in Judgment*. Virginia Woolf's book, *Kew Gardens*, was a short story illustrated with woodcuts by her sister Vanessa Bell.

Harold Child gave both story and woodcuts an enthusiastic review on 29 May. He said it did not really matter whether Kew Gardens were like Virginia Woolf's account of them, or even whether they existed at all – her 'Kew Gardens' was 'a work of art, made, "created", finished, four square; a thing of original and therefore strange beauty, with its own "atmosphere", its own vital force . . . The more one gloats over it, the more beauty shines out of it.' And he approved of Vanessa Bell's cover – which 'suggests the tulips in a famous Dutch-English catalogue, "blotched, spotted, streaked, speckled, and flushed".'

This review had a tremendous impact. On 4 June the Woolfs came back to Richmond from Sussex to find 150 requests for the book piled up on the doormat of Hogarth House. As Hermione Lee puts it in her biography of Virginia Woolf, from now onwards 'they had a business, and Virginia Woolf had a name'.

In the autumn, her second novel, *Night and Day*, was published, not by her own press this time but by Duckworth. Richmond entrusted her again to Harold Child, who gave this book, too, a very good review in every sense of the word. He drew out the firm shapeliness of the book; he responded with delight to the love affair between Ralph Denham – 'Highgate, strong, raw, ugly' – and Katharine Hilbery – 'Chelsea, mellow, august, exquisite' – who, 'coming together after goodness knows what of queer reluctance and fear and fantasy, are going to make their lives something that shall be true'. And he saw that this was 'a book full of wisdom': in understanding their love affair, as Virginia Woolf succeeds in making us do, 'we understand a great deal more of the age we live in'.

Her third novel, *Jacob's Room*, which came out – confidently published by the Hogarth Press again – in October 1922, went to A.S. McDowall. He had more reservations than Child had had about the previous books, but his review is a brilliantly analytical appreciation. 'It is an amusingly clear and yet enchanted glass which she holds up to things,' he wrote. 'This stream of incidents, persons, and their momentary thoughts and feelings . . . is arrested and decanted, as it were, into little phials of crystal vividness.' Yet he wondered if in this story of the brief career of Jacob Flanders, who is 'absorbed with the half-savage, half-winning absorption of youth', she really created 'persons and characters as we secretly desire to know them. It might be questioned whether her beings, while they intersect, really act upon each other, or whether her method does not condemn them to be external'. Critical but careful reviews like this certainly seem to have helped Virginia Woolf to write 'a deeper, richer book' – to quote Hermione Lee again – when she turned to her next novel, *Mrs Dalloway*. Virginia Woolf herself specifically noted the point about the creation of characters in her diary, though she grumbled that the review, while 'flattering enough', was 'a little tepid'.

Meanwhile, throughout these years, she was continuing to write outstanding pieces for the *Lit Supp*. In November 1919 she praised Max Beerbohm's volume of stories *Seven Men* – 'like some cuttlefish dispersing a silver and crepuscular fluid instead of a dense and a dark, he emits his perfect little disk of fantasy, wit and satire . . . The silvery yet searching light falls with the utmost exactitude into every crease and wrinkle of their faces.' Yet she felt he did the same thing too often. The following February it was Aldous Huxley's stories in *Limbo*. She found them brilliant but, in a way, ineffectual: under his darts, upper-middle-class humbug seemed 'to collapse' – yet when the 'despicable conventions' turned back on him, and asked him to talk about something he actually believed in, he could only stammer. In the end, 'love and death, like damp fireworks, refuse to flare up in such an atmosphere, and as usual the upper middle classes escape unhurt'.

In July 1920 she reviewed Conrad's new novel *The Rescue* (he was sixty-three now), but found that it was 'as if Mr Conrad's belief in romance had suddenly flagged, and he had tried to revive it by artificial stimulants'. Henry James came her way in various forms – his ghost stories, his letters, his posthumous essay about the war *Within the Rim* – and, to use a phrase from that last review, she set out to demonstrate each time that 'he makes us understand what civilisation meant to him and what it should mean to us'.

However, the review of James's ghost stories led her into a little trouble with Richmond, because she used the word 'lewd' in it. He rang her up and she recorded the conversation in her diary for 19 December 1921:

> 'Of course, I don't wish you to change it, but surely that is rather a strong expression to apply to anything by Henry James. I haven't read the story lately of course – but still my impression is . . .'
>
> 'Well, I thought that when I read it: one has to go by one's impressions at the time.'
>
> 'But you know the usual meaning of the word? It is – ah – *dirty* – Now poor dear old Henry James – At any rate, think it over, and ring me up in 20 minutes.'

Virginia Woolf concluded the diary entry 'So I thought it over & came to the required conclusion in twelve minutes & a half.' In fact she changed the word to 'obscene'. But she remained resentful for a while at being censored by the *Lit Supp*, making a New Year's resolution a fortnight later that she would do no more reviewing 'now that Richmond rewrites my sentences to suit the mealy mouths of Belgravia'. However she immediately added in brackets: 'an exaggeration, I admit' – and soon forgot the resolution.

In these years, she also wrote more generally about novels and the literary scene in the paper. She admired Percy Lubbock's *The Craft of Fiction*, but, for all he had done for fiction, she began to wonder if too much of an effort to 'reconstruct, to analyse and dissect' the craftsmanship of novels may not have reduced 'our Castle in Spain to mere rubble'. And she struck a note we have heard T.S. Eliot striking in these pages (and actually herself before him) when in a review of a collection of *Modern English Essays* she wrote that if one reads in bulk E.V. Lucas, Robert Lynd or J.C. Squire – men who 'write weekly, write daily, write shortly, write for busy people catching trains in the morning or for tired people coming home in the evening' – 'one feels that a common greyness silvers everything'. How neat and acute that 'silvering greyness' is – the sparkle that is really dull!

In the immediate post-war years, the two outstanding novelists besides Virginia Woolf were D.H. Lawrence, who was thirty-five in 1920, and (in spite of Virginia Woolf's comments on his short stories) Aldous Huxley, who was twenty-six that year. Edmund Blunden was given

Lawrence's *Women in Love* to review in June 1921. The gentle Blunden did not like it at all. He loathed Lawrence's idea of love, which he said was defined with 'jubilant brutality' in the novel, and altogether he found it a 'dull, disappointing piece of work'. Lawrence himself does not seem to have been much troubled by this review. Writing a few days later from Baden-Baden to his agent, Curtis Brown, he mentioned Lady Ottoline Morrell, friend and hostess to many writers in the twenties, and to some extent the original of the character Hermione in the novel. 'What was poor Ott's nose out of joint for, I wonder' he wrote, 'didn't *The Times* say that Hermione was a grand and sincere figure among a nest of perverse puppies?' Later in the twenties, Lawrence would find a champion in the paper in the form of A.S. McDowall.

McDowall enjoyed the comedy in Huxley's *Crome Yellow* in November 1921 – 'it becomes more amusing as it grows'; Child reviewed Huxley's *Mortal Coils* the following April, and thought that all the five tales in it were clever, but 'four of them want matter worthy of the literary skill that has made them'.

Katherine Mansfield, who was seriously ill with tuberculosis, and often separated from her volatile husband Middleton Murry, saw two postwar collections of her stories published before she died in 1923. (Her first book, *In a German Pension*, published in 1911, had been missed by the paper.) Child liked her volume *Bliss*, published at the end of 1920: the subject matter was dismal, sometimes horrible, he wrote, but they are enjoyable 'because of the beauty, sensuous or spiritual, which she sets to glow in the stuff of her tale'. The commercial short story, he said, just reports, while pretending to create; she 'with the air of dispassionately reporting, is making all the while her own world'. McDowall reviewed her collection *The Garden Party* in March 1922, and said, rather in the same vein as Child, that 'there is tragedy in Miss Mansfield's world, and there are ugly human gestures' but 'a quivering radiance of atmosphere . . . by a miracle, frees her scene from drabness'.

Meanwhile, in October 1921, John Galsworthy had brought *The Forsyte Saga* to an end after fifteen years with the volume *To Let*. 'There will always be conflict in the world between possession and freedom,' Harold Child declared. 'There will always be Forsytes and rebels against Forsyteism . . . It has been Mr Galsworthy's good fortune to live in an era when the successes and failures of Forsyteism were sharply defined; and it has been one of his achievements to give them artistic form in the joys and sorrows of particular persons.' However, Child was not going to allow the idea that the 'possessive' Soames Forsyte was wholly a villain: 'the possessive does well enough,' he said, 'so long as it lives in its own house'.

So Child would probably have liked Lytton Strachey's *Queen Victoria*, which came out in April 1921. D.L. Murray, the future editor of the paper, said that nobody had hit the foibles of Victorianism harder than Strachey in his *Eminent Victorians*, and 'the news that a life of the Queen was to follow suggested a thrust at the very heart of the legend'. But Strachey, 'never deficient in cleverness', had been clever enough to disappoint these expectations. He had 'abandoned satire for interpretation', and had 'caught the gleam' of the mystical light that shone through the 'pure lantern' of the Queen's spirit: 'it falls on his page in rays of wistful beauty', he concluded. This was the kind of sharp and elegant review that in 1920 had brought Murray on to the staff of the growing paper – with his £500 starting salary attributed 'one third to Leaders & Special Writers and two-thirds to *Literary Supplement*', as his staff card put it.

Richard Aldington had also now come into his own as a reviewer and was regularly covering the new French books, while John Middleton Murry busied himself with the *Athenaeum*. Aldington has described in his autobiography *Life for Life's Sake* how he started on the paper, a story that reflects both Richmond's proud independence of spirit and his honest recognition of ability. Aldington, on coming out of the army at the end of the war, happened to have dinner with a rich shareholder in *The Times*, Sir John Ellerman, who gave him an introduction to the editor. The editor in turn sent him with a note down the corridor to Richmond, who looked at the note with annoyance and spoke to Aldington with 'polite insolence'. Aldington presumed that he resented dictation from the financial interests on the paper. However, Richmond gave him some French books to take away.

For three weeks running after that, Aldington brought his pieces in to Printing House Square and carried off some more books, and Richmond always treated him in the same manner. But in the fourth week his demeanour changed. Suddenly he was all geniality, and expressed his hope that his new reviewer liked the work. Aldington supposed that he had finally accepted that this man who had been imposed on him was up to the job – and Aldington went on writing for him for the next ten years.

It fell to Aldington to resume the reviewing of Proust's *A la recherche* which Mme Duclaux had begun so perceptively before the war, and in

August 1919 he hailed the new NRF volume in which *Du Côté de Chez Swann*, the volume brought out by Grasset in 1914, was reprinted along with the new volume *A l'Ombre des Jeunes Filles en Fleurs*. Proust, who was still working on the later books in Paris, was disappointed that Mme Duclaux, whom he knew, had not gone on covering it, but he need not have been. Aldington was lavish in his praise of the 'minute and wonderful character-drawing of Swann, Odette, Norpois, the "I" of the novels, and the members of his family . . . Like many personages of great fiction, they become part of our lives, seem at times even more familiar than our friends.' He said that Proust was not 'modern' in a trivial or vulgar sense, but 'modern' because 'his is a vital intelligence in contact with life' – and, after quoting a description by Proust of hawthorns, he regretted that 'prejudices' made it impossible for him to quote another passage he had chosen: 'That precision which is welcomed as a sign of talent in a description of the behaviour of vegetables is in England censured as undesirable or even disagreeable when applied to the not less interesting yet more complex institutions of human beings'. Did Richmond make him drop this 'undesirable' quotation, but allow him to complain?

Aldington reviewed further volumes of Proust, especially praising *Le Côté de Guermantes*, but when *Sodome et Gomorrhe* came out in August 1922 the reviewer said that 'the fineness of M. Proust's readers is a little strained by their impatience for him to come to the end of his long story'. It is amusing to find that this reviewer was none other than C.K. Scott Moncrieff, who was engaged at that time on translating the great work, but was obviously getting a little bored with the job. However, in the following month Cyril Falls, a regular new contributor, and later a notable military historian, was able to review the first volume of Scott Moncrieff's translation, and announce to those who could not read French that M. Proust has a 'first-class designer for his English dress' – the start of an enduring love-affair between English readers and Proust.

Other French writers were not neglected. In August 1920, Aldington reviewed Gide's *La Symphonie Pastorale*: Gide belonged, he wrote, to that 'genial band of sceptics of whom the most illustrious are Renan, Anatole France and Remy de Gourmont', but in this 'little story' of a pastor and a blind girl he had 'eliminated his scepticism' and it was hard to know what he intended by it. The poet F.S. Flint did a long survey of the French war poets, singling out Claudel among the commentators and Guillaume Apollinaire among the combatants, and showering particular praise on Emile Verhaeren, whose death in 1916 we have already seen mourned in the paper. But in a separate review Flint was impatient with the poet Tristan Tzara, saying that the publication of his Dadaist collection *Vingt-Cinq Poèmes* was like 'the act of the madman who buttonholes you, whispers a few mysterious words and walks off cackling with laughter'.

Aldous Huxley made another appearance, reviewing Romain Rolland's *Colas Breugnon*, a portrait of a Rabelaisian character. He did not think it was a success, because 'this praise of joyous laughter and wine and tripe is not whole-hearted'. Rolland's genius was too different from his hero's – he 'is a spiritual water-drinker', said Huxley. However, Aldous Huxley proved to be one of those writers whom astute editors catch young and make the most of while they can, but who cut away as their fame grows.

Domestic politics continued as a more or less exclusive province of the main paper, even though the *Lit Supp* was now well established as a separate publication. But in many book reviews there are glimpses of the post-war mood and social life of Britain.

In December 1919, Charles Vince, one of Richmond's freelance contributors, reviewed *In the Side Shows*, a reminiscence of the war by Captain Wedgwood Benn – the father of Anthony Wedgwood Benn, and 'a romantic, indefatigable adventurer' according to the reviewer. Vince particularly liked a remark by Benn's batman, when he was charged with some minor offence while the unit was dangerously isolated: 'What I ses is this: there's only a few of us 'ere, let's live in 'armony'. It was 'a remark that should become immortal', said Vince – and it is perhaps one that the author's son has always remembered.

In other ways, the reviewers urged a new amity, or at least forbearance, between the classes, at this time of many strikes. On 2 June 1921, Kenneth Bell, a history don at Balliol and one of the Bell publishing family, discussed the influential book by R.H. Tawney, *The Acquisitive Society*. He agreed with Tawney's view that the troubles of society sprang largely from the fact that men were acquisitive, but did not think that he had much of a prescription for changing things. Who was to tame the tigers of the modern jungle and see that they functioned peaceably as chasers of mice? How were the workers to be transformed into professional men, with 'all the courage of soldiers in warfare and none of their peacetime lethargy'? Tawney, for all his concern for the working man, did not seem to have the answer. For that matter, 'if so much pity and sympathy is going, why should not the man of property have some of it?' – a precise echo of Harold Child's view, quoted above, of *The Forsyte Saga*. In any event, denunciations of the classes by each other were likely to do more harm than good: 'No doubt the rich are greedy and the poor are envious, but is either side likely to do much for society by expatiating on the faults of the other?'

As it happened, on the same page of the paper that week, Francis Gribble was earnestly criticising H.G. Wells's book *The Salvaging of Civilisation* for offering an unrealistic vision of a world state, while 'leaving untouched two of the most menacing problems which the twentieth century will have to solve: the problem of the "rising tide of colour" and the problem of that class war which now cuts across and complicates all the other conflicts'. But John Cann Bailey was more optimistic than either of these reviewers, at least about the future of Britain: reviewing a book on *Traditions of British Statesmanship* by the Hon. Arthur D. Elliott, he continued to put his faith in the 'ancient and inbred honesty, integrity, and good sense of the English people'.

Turning to other areas of notable social change, in 1920 a writer called Gasquoine Hartley attacked the new feminists in a book called *Woman's Wild Oats*, but in the paper Mrs H.A.L. Fisher, the civic-minded wife of the educationalist and politician, came to their defence. She attributed wholly respectable qualities to the feminists: 'a new realisation of the meaning of citizenship, and an even keener sense of duty both public and private'. This was not quite the description of them that even they, I think, would have gone all the way with. Other wild oats – now perhaps being sown more widely – were alluded to discreetly in Canon Barnes's review of a book on *The Control of Parenthood*. It was a 'fresh, clean, and wholesome' guide to the matter, he reported, which 'will help young married people' – while, this Canon of Westminster added approvingly, 'the sensualist will find nothing attractive in the volume'.

As for those traditional pleasures which still engaged some *Lit Supp* readers – hunting, shooting and fishing – change only seemed to make them more enjoyable, as John Buchan pointed out in a cheerful leading article on 'The Literature of Autumn Sport' in September 1920. 'In these days of easy travel,' he wrote, 'we may go to bed at Euston and wake on a western sea-loch; we may sit at the play one evening and be on a Scots moor after breakfast.' And he hailed the rise of the new breed of naturalist-sportsman, 'who sees more in wild life than the raw material of a bag or a basket'.

*   *   *

English political biography continued to inspire long articles in the paper. In March 1920, G.M. Trevelyan's *Lord Grey of the Reform Bill* gave Bailey the chance to praise both the subject of the book – an 'elderly, inexperienced nobleman' who 'carried the country through the greatest crisis it had known since the Revolution' (namely the passage of the Reform Act in 1832) – and its author, the great-nephew of Macaulay, who 'could not but be born with the Whig tradition in his blood, could not but be nurtured in its lore from the cradle . . . The creed of religious and political liberty has always been his creed.'

Bailey took the opportunity to remark, in a way that is now familiar to us in his contributions, that in 1920 the will of the nation was no longer disputed by the Right but by the extreme Left:

> But we did not adopt a French solution of our difficulties 130 years ago, and the English character must have greatly changed if we adopt a Russian solution today. It is not likely that even the earthquake shock of the war has transformed us into dreamers, extremists, or fanatics. After it, as before, England will probably remain the land of common sense, compromise, and practical progress. And if it does, it will never cease to honour the Whigs . . . who gave the country Reform without revolution.

Here was the *Lit Supp* aiming at exerting its usual steadying influence again.

The publication of the last two volumes of Buckle's *Life of Disraeli* three months later also gave Bailey the opportunity to make further amends for the criticism he had made of the previous volumes. In his opening paragraph, he threw in some praise of Buckle as editor of *The Times*, to whose 'wisdom and judgment and high sense of responsibility' its readers owed so much, though most of them would not have known his name when he was there.

A *Life* of a Conservative Prime Minister who held Disraeli in contempt, the Marquis of Salisbury, was reviewed in a leading article the following year by D.L. Murray. The author was Salisbury's daughter, Lady Gwendolen Cecil, and Murray found the book 'illuminating throughout, and in places brilliant'. Two relatives of a more recent Prime Minister, Asquith, were less fortunate in their reviewers, both writing in November 1920. Percy Lubbock, who was still occasionally on the scene, found little to praise in *The Autobiography of Margot Asquith*: the 'whole contents of London' had been open to her for a generation, he said, yet she did not give a clear picture of anybody: 'we peer into that ghostly London of hansom cabs and professional beauties, we peer and are baffled'. She had not proved to be the Saint-Simon of Mayfair. And when Asquith's son (and her stepson) Herbert Asquith brought out a volume of poems, *A Village Sermon*, the new poetry critic Hugh d'Anson Fausset could only find similar things to say. This former choral scholar at King's, Cambridge, who told *Who's Who* that his interests were 'gardening; pondering; singing', reviewed Asquith's book along with the *Poems of Lady Gerald Wellesley*, and advanced a cruel theory. 'We have discovered the cause of world unrest. It is respectable minor poetry: poetry which tells us nothing but that a man is tired, or saw a sunset, or was mildly alarmed, or lived at Constantinople, and, far from transporting us there, settles us more firmly in our chair in an atmosphere of such chill indifference as invites the flames of revolution.'

He accused both writers of 'vague and personal slovenliness' in the way they wrote, and urged them to cultivate 'a more passionate observance and a more scrupulous vocabulary': if they did, the one (evidently Asquith) 'will not again dishonour the sea with platitudes, nor the other languish through weary lines in quest of a dimly pagan Paradise'. So it was not only on Pound and Eliot that the paper turned its fire.

Overseas, the Russian Revolution continued to command most attention. The paper still had Bechhofer writing for it, sometimes for weeks in succession. In 1919 he reported on the events of the Revolution as portrayed in self-justifying books by both Kerensky, the deposed Prime Minister, and Trotsky, but was most impressed and convinced by V. Shklovsy's *Russia Under The Bolsheviks*. 'Anarchy and famine are decimating the Russian people,' Bechhofer wrote in his review of Shklovsky, 'while the men who could save them are persecuted, and the corn that could feed them is rotting in the railway stations'. He quoted with approval Shklovsky's jeers at those 'English Labour people' who say 'The Bolsheviks have made of Russia a Socialist Republic of a high order.' Bechhofer himself criticised a pamphlet and a book by Arthur Ransome, who would later on write the great children's book, *Swallows and Amazons*, but who at this time was a foreign correspondent living with Trotsky's secretary. Of Ransome's *Six Weeks in Russia in 1919* he wrote that Ransome had 'secured some good "copy"' but had not given an adequate statement of conditions in Russia – in fact his book was just an interesting résumé of the Bolsheviks' professions as set out for foreign consumption. In November 1920 Bechhofer wrote very harshly about Upton Sinclair's attack in *The Brass Check* on American journalism and its hostility to Bolshevism – 'Russia is far off,' he observed dryly, 'the American papers are under his nose'.

Bechhofer's own book *Through Starving Russia* was published in November 1921 and a Russian specialist on *The Times* who was revered for knowing thirty languages, Harold Williams, wrote that 'it leaves an overwhelming impression of ruin and despair, illumined only by the red light of fanaticism'. It was hard to be hopeful, Williams concluded, and early in 1922 Bechhofer was writing again in the paper about the torture and shooting in the Soviet prisons by the Che-Ka (as he transliterated the name of the secret police). He expressed a hope that the rulers of Russia would one day be tried.

Bechhofer also contributed in October 1921 a signed letter to the correspondence page, for which he was paid, about current Russian literature and art as he had found it when he went to Russia for his book. He painted a gloomy picture – he had discovered that Anna Akhmatova, 'the best of the younger woman poets', was still in Petrograd, but that many other writers had left Russia or had fallen silent – and he summed up: 'One may say of art in Russia, as of every other independent work of the people, that it is, if not dead, at least moribund.'

However Bechhofer had a new interest – America and American literature – and in May and June 1921 he had written a series of letters, for which he also was paid, on the correspondence page, about American writers. They had a very different story to tell. He discussed H.L. Mencken and James Branch Cabell's *Virginia Stories*, he praised writers of the 'Middle West' such as Dreiser and Sinclair Lewis, he singled out Willa Cather's *O Pioneers* and *My Antonia*; he was enthusiastic about Eugene O'Neill, and he concluded these letters by saying that 'Present-day American literature is of far wider interest and importance than is generally recognised, even in America itself.' In the same issue as his fourth American letter, that of 23 June, R.O. Morris reviewed Scott Fitzgerald's *This Side of Paradise*, calling its characters 'a set of exasperating poseurs', but asking nevertheless whether they foreshadowed a change in America, 'an anti-Puritan phase', and, even though they might be unreal characters, whether they were not 'an omen of liberation'. A slight shift of the centre of gravity of the *Lit Supp* towards the mid-Atlantic is registered in this summer of 1921.

The problems of post-war Europe were tackled in reviews of a number of books on the peace settlement, notably John Maynard Keynes's subsequently famous work, *The Economic Consequences of the Peace*, on 15 January 1920. The reviewer was a distinguished historian of Germany, James Wycliffe Headlam-Morley, who would write frequently for the paper in the next ten years. He had begun as plain Headlam, but had added the Morley on inheriting some Yorkshire property from his grandmother in 1918: shades of Dawson. He was an Eton and King's, Cambridge man, and had been Professor of Greek at Queen's College, London, but had studied in Germany and had a German wife, and in 1899 had published an important study of Bismarck and the German Empire. After that he had become a staff inspector for the Board of Education, and during the war had worked with Claude Schuster (whom we have already met as a reviewer) on propaganda to Germany. He had also been involved in the peace conference, and now had a job that had been specially created for him as historical adviser to the Foreign Office. He would be knighted just before he died in 1929.

Now he praised Keynes for his work at the Paris Peace Conference as chief representative of the Treasury, saying that the book showed that 'throughout the turmoil and complications, the intrigues which necessarily attended these great transactions, he was always able to keep before his mind the great matters which were at stake'. He also praised the 'extraordinary skill' with which Keynes presented the conflict between President Wilson, with his desire for a 'peace of reconciliation and justice', and Clemenceau, with his advocacy of a 'Carthaginian peace' to the immediate advantage of France – a conflict in which Clemenceau was the victor.

But Headlam-Morley thought that Keynes dwelt too exclusively on the economic issues, and did not appreciate the success of the political and territorial settlement, with its mutually agreed determination of new boundaries in Europe. Whether it was a fact to be welcomed or not, wrote Headlam-Morley, 'Germany emerges from the war with her unity undestroyed and her territorial integrity unhampered, except in those districts in which cession of territory was clearly enjoined by the principles of the Peace', and he implied that this was an achievement that Keynes in particular should appreciate.

Incidentally, this was a much more kindly review than *The Times* itself had give Keynes's book ten days earlier. There it was reviewed by the editor, Wickham Steed, and, in the words of the official history of *The Times*, 'dismissed as a piece of pro-German pacifism and a disservice to the Allies, for which their enemies would be grateful'. So, in the spirit of *The Times*, the *Lit Supp* was showing its independence from *The Times* itself.

In September 1920, G.M. Trevelyan, writing in the fine old Whig style that Bailey had praised in his book on Lord Grey, looked back over the half-century to the Venti Settembre 1870 when Victor Emmanuel's soldiers fought the Pope's soldiers and 'Italy entered Rome'. Trevelyan praised the way in which the ideals of the Italian Risorgimento had survived during those fifty years, and still prevailed in post-war Italy: 'parliamentary liberty at home; abroad, nationality as the basis of international peace, might be described as the doctrine of the Risorgimento, and it is thoroughly in keeping with the fundamental kindliness and good sense of the Italian nature'.

Ironically, it was only a month later that Mussolini's Fascisti marched on Rome, and established him as prime minister. But two years after that, in December 1922, when Mussolini's book *Discorsi Politici* came out, it was reviewed very favourably under the heading 'Fascismo'. The writer was an Italian expert, Lacy Collison Morley, and he blandly welcomed the new administration, taking a very different view of the Italians from Trevelyan's: 'the present regime may almost be said to be the only Government that has had the strong moral support of the community behind it since the union of 1870. Economy and discipline are its watchwords with the gospel of work (including every kind of intellectual work) of which its chief has given so fine an example in practice.' Morley declared that 'no-one is more anxious that violence should cease than the Fascisti'. He did notice the 'delight in the trappings of military life' of the movement's young supporters, but dismissed it as simply a 'characteristic of Latin youth'. The review was inspired partly by Morley's vigorous anti-Bolshevism – but it cannot be described as a very far-sighted review.

Finally we have the philosophers of these immediate post-war years. In 1921, the guru of Bloomsbury, G.E. Moore, was brought in to review one great figure from the philosophical era that was just passing, and one from the new epoch. He confessed himself largely baffled by Volume One of J.M'Taggart's *The Nature of Existence*: its 'highly abstract' propositions rested on M'Taggart's own definition of the word 'substance', but understanding that definition was something he had 'utterly failed to do'. But Moore found Bertrand Russell's *The Analysis of Mind* equally unsatisfactory, since 'he does not appear to offer a single argument in favour of his theory'. However, the following year Herbert Wildon Carr, who was the Professor of Philosophy at King's College, London, gave a welcome to Ludwig Wittgenstein, finding that his

Tractatus Logico-Philosophicus 'will appeal strongly to all those who agree with Swift's Houyhnhnm that "the use of speech was to make us understand one another, and to receive information of facts".'

The *Lit Supp* readers also met some curiosities in the paper in this period. On 13 February 1919, they would have been startled by a large panel in the Arabic language, which they would have discovered to be the text of an address by Mr Sefi, of the new School of Oriental Studies, to Emir Faisal of Iraq, on the occasion of his late visit to Britain. It was explained that the literary and poetical expressiveness of the Arabic was impossible to render into English, so the paper had decided to print it in the original language, with just a summary of its import – which was to welcome the Emir, and rejoice at his alliance with Britain. Even in the paper, perhaps, the address was still really being delivered to Faisal.

A more intelligible panel appeared from time to time in 1919 and 1920:

Daily Mail
Million Sale
ORDER TODAY
S.V.P.

It was not clear if the last line was there because Northcliffe thought it necessary to be polite to readers of *The Times*, or because, when spoken in full, it made a nice rhyme. However it disappeared in 1921, when Northcliffe was able to say:

Daily Mail
World's Record Net Sale
Over 1,350,000

Northcliffe continued to ignore the *Lit Supp* in the years immediately after the war. In January 1919, he appointed a new managing director of *The Times*, Lieutenant Colonel Campbell Stuart, a genial and vigorous figure who had worked with Northcliffe as Military Secretary to the British War Mission in the United States. From 1920 Stuart held Northcliffe's power of attorney along with the editor, Wickham Steed, and the chief left him relatively alone for a time. But in the summer of 1921 he was beginning to agitate again, and wrote to Stuart on 6 July that

'PHS is full of undigested schemes – maps, road maps, the *Lit Supp* and the other two supplements. Most of these are absolutely stagnant – notably the *L.S.*, whose sale has decreased a great deal. There is no reason why it should not be 80,000 a week. It should be made a little lighter. I hear constant complaints of their (*sic*) not being enough reviews of books with extracts in them.'

It was the old familiar complaint – but there was truth in the remark about falling circulation. The average weekly circulation at the end of 1918, as we saw, was 29,106, and a year later 31,864, even though the price had gone up from 2d to 3d in October 1919. However the price doubled again to 6d in July 1920, and this was clearly too much for some readers. The average circulation for 1920 was down to 28,896, and for 1921 it was over 5,000 further down to 23,259. It reached its lowest point in this period, 21,205, in 1922, and only revived after Northcliffe's death, when the price was reduced again to 3d in July 1923, lifting the average circulation for that year to 22,761. The sale went on rising after that throughout the twenties.

However the profit figures were better. They are available from 1920, and show a profit of £1,861 in that year, £9,837 in 1921 and £12,214 in 1922, partly due to an increase in advertising.

Richmond's staff also increased in this period. We have seen that D.L. Murray joined the paper in 1920, and in December 1922 there was a new subeditor, Eric St John Brooks. St John Brooks, who was thirty-nine in that year, had been educated at Trinity College, Dublin where his father was a professor of anatomy and where he had been a mathematical sizar, and he had worked for *The Times* since he was twenty-eight. He was an entertaining but scholarly Irishman and was rumoured to have been in love with Katherine Mansfield – which may have helped him on the *Lit Supp*. In his turn, the faithful Dalton would retire in 1923.

Meanwhile Northcliffe had gone off on a world tour, brooding on many schemes. On New Year's Day 1922, now on his homeward jour-ney, he sent a Napoleonic telegram of greetings to 'all the great armies who work for me', and he arrived back in England determined at last to be absolute master in Printing House Square. He bought out John Walter's shares, and was planning to sideline Steed and edit the paper himself. But by March close observers of his demeanour agreed with Steed that he was 'going mad'. His megalomania had reached the pitch where the joke going round *The Times* was that Lloyd George had resigned and Northcliffe had sent for the King.

His assault on the *Lit Supp* began on Monday, 27 March 1922, when he sent a message to Stuart:

> Send for Richmond. Tell him *Lit Supp* deprives *Times* 20,000 weekly readers. Literary side of *Times* very weak since *Suppt* started. Unless he can during present week greatly improve literary side *Times* to my entire satisfaction, shall merge *Supplement* in *Times* beginning with Friday week's number. All important letters addressed to *Suppt* must first appear in *Times*. All important literary news must first appear in *Times* . . . In any case am almost certain to merge *Suppt* in *Times*. It would be an immense advertisement and be greater fighting point. We should lose nothing financially and gain immense amount of advertising. Told Lints Smith [manager of *The Times*, under Stuart] to increase paper by two pages during this greatest crisis in our history. These two pages could easily accommodate *Suppt*. Wire me result of conversation. If unsatisfactory, announce at once merging of *Suppt* with *Times*.

It was ironical that the fault with the *Lit Supp* in Northcliffe's eyes now was not that it was too weak, but that it was too good, and its reviews should be in the main paper.

The same day, Campbell Stuart wired back to Northcliffe at his hotel in Pau:

> Monday have arranged to merge *Lit Supp* in *Times* after issue Thursday week commencing Monday April Tenth. Will make Announcement in this week's issue lit supp & simultaneously Thursday's *Times*. This gives me time to adjust advertising contracts. We must aim at one page books and advertising daily. Campbell

The next day, 28 March, Northcliffe wired: 'Very grateful your efforts . . . Give great prominence to fact *Times* readers will as result merger receive lit supp free but outpoint Richmond many more popular books must be dealt with also.'

However, later that day he wired again: 'Defer announcement merging *Lit Supp* for week to give me time consider Richmond's full plans for *Times*. If he can do both to my satisfaction, Suppt might be continued. Let me have full plan. You are not communicating with me enough. I hear nothing.' (The same day, incidentally, he complained about the report in *The Times* of the visit by Monsieur Coué, the famous French hypnotist, to Eton. Stuart informed him in reply, with some satisfaction, that the report by a 'local correspondent' was in fact by Mr H.V. Macnaghten, the Vice-Provost of Eton.) On 29 March Northcliffe wired: 'No literary literary scheme (*sic*) will satisfy me which doesn't give *Times* first choice everything appearing in *Lit Supp*.'

On Friday, 31 March, a serious Cabinet crisis distracted Northcliffe from these vacillations, but that day Stuart wrote him a long letter on the *Lit Supp* question:

> My dear Chief ,
>
> As to the *Lit Supp*, I sent for Richmond within ten minutes of receiving your wire and replied to you that evening that I suggest after hearing everybody's views that commencing April 10th, we have one page devoted to books and book advertisements every day in '*The Times*' but not as literary as the *Lit Supp*, but absolutely complete. Murray, who is a literary man and Richmond's deputy, can run it in cooperation with Gordon Robbins, who has the news sense. We could reprint all these articles each week in the *Lit Supp* together with a leading article and certain other features which cannot be incorporated into the newspaper proper. That would retain the copyright and the overseas readers. I would, therefore, suggest that we make no suggestion as to the termination of the *Lit Supp* as such, but that we put an announcement in Thursday's *Times* and in Thursday's *Lit Supp* to the effect that commencing on Monday '*The Times*' will have the aforesaid literary features. Will you telegraph me your opinion as to this point because the *Lit Supp* goes to press on Tuesday evening, and it will be necessary to have the announcement in type by then. I have proposed to Richmond that he should act as Literary Adviser to '*The Times*' and generally supervise literature for '*The Times*'.
>
> [Up to this point the letter is typewritten and presumably dictated. The remainder, doubtless for the sake of discretion, is handwritten.]
>
> He is a very competent man and has all the things in his hands, and I do not want him to go to another paper. He quite agrees to this programme. This is my suggestion in the rough. Some day we could merge it in *The Times* (Weekly??) but that can come later.
>
> I know my Richmond and shall not be sorry to see the last of him but this is not the time. I was afraid you thought by my telegram that I was getting rid of him at once.
>
> Yours affectionately
> Campbell

To this letter, Northcliffe replied by telegram on Sunday, 2 April: 'Quite agree excellent suggestion regarding Literature department *Times*. Don't think plan will interfere with suppt but should not wait until April 10. Why not have first page Friday next. We dont give enough extracts from interesting books. Have made this remark hundreds of times'. In the Northcliffe papers there is only one more short message on the subject, another telegram from the Chief on April 4 saying 'Cannot see necessity making any announcement whatever in *Lit Supp*. Will discuss matter with you Friday.' After that, Northcliffe turned his attention to attacking the staff of the *Daily Mail*.

So once again, it seems, a managing director had saved the *Lit Supp*, and by using much the same means as Reginald Nicholson had in 1914 – going along completely with Northcliffe's ideas at first, and then with good timing proposing what was presented as a slight change of plan, accompanied by vague promises for the future. And it had worked again – and again, perhaps, because Northcliffe himself still had misgivings about closing down the *Lit Supp* that the managing director could easily detect. No doubt what remained of the old *Times* establishment also rallied round, as before, in support of Richmond, and Campbell Stuart thought it politic to pay some attention to them, especially if Northcliffe was losing his sanity.

However, it has been widely believed that it was an even closer shave than this correspondence suggests. Harold Child later wrote a short history of the *Lit Supp* for use in the official history of *The Times*, but it was not published until 18 January 1952, when it appeared in the fiftieth anniversary number of the *Literary Supplement*. Child told a slightly different story:

> The number of March 30 (No 1,054) was almost ready for press when a sudden order came from Lord Northcliffe; the next number but two was to be the last, and this death-sentence was to be published immediately . . . Into the leading article on the front page a 'box' was introduced, announcing in italic type that No.1056 (April 13) would be the last number of the *Literary Supplement* . . . But once more the journal was to owe its continued existence to something like an oversight. The order had not penetrated into every department concerned. In one quarter there was some doubt about its validity. Twenty minutes before the number went to press the 'box' was removed from the front page; and the number of April 13 showed no sign of its narrow escape. That summer Lord Northcliffe became too ill to take an active part in his business . . .

In his biography of a later editor of *The Times*, R.M. Barrington-Ward, called *In the Chair*, Donald McLachlan repeats this account, but adds a significant detail: that the 'sentence of death' was actually removed from the front page by order of Campbell Stuart.

In fact, we have seen that on that press day, Tuesday, 28 March, Northcliffe himself withdrew the instruction to close the *Lit Supp* down in a second telegram, after approving of the action in his first telegram of the day. So what seems likely to have happened is that Campbell Stuart ordered the box to be put in on the Monday, and himself had it taken out again after receiving Northcliffe's second telegram on the Tuesday – but quite possibly, as the tradition has it, only twenty minutes before the paper went to press. It was not in that case 'doubt about its validity . . . in one quarter' that caused the box to be removed, it was the managing editor carrying out the proprietor's instruction. It is of course possible that there was some further complication, such as that Campbell Stuart had forgotten about the box, and had to be reminded that it was still there by someone 'in one quarter'.

In any event, Stuart went on successfully to steer Northcliffe in the direction of improving the *Times*'s books coverage without sacrificing the *Lit Supp*, and he can therefore be fairly counted as the third manager or managing director to have saved the paper. Nevertheless, when in later years he himself was accustomed to make that claim, he does not seem to have mentioned to anybody the existence of that second telegram from Northcliffe!

Northcliffe's mental condition rapidly deteriorated after this time, and he died on 14 August. No mention of his death appeared in the *Lit Supp* until 31 August, when a letter from the critic Charles Whibley was published in the correspondence columns praising Northcliffe as 'an eager and assiduous reader'. Whibley was a genuine friend of Northcliffe's, but one feels that the performance must have been staged by Richmond, as a necessary – but all the same sufficient – tribute to his old persecutor.

Richmond must have rejoiced, in fact, to see the end of Northcliffe, and he actually played a small but important role in creating the happy situation in which he would never again be troubled by an interfering proprietor.

This was how it came about. *The Times*'s chairman John Walter wanted to reclaim the option on purchasing Northcliffe's shares after the latter's death, which he had thrown away when he had rashly sold his own shares to Northcliffe earlier in the year. However he did not have the money himself, and was now looking for a wealthy man who would buy and own *The Times* in association with him and allow it to revert to the character it had had before Northcliffe bought it. With Lady Northcliffe's acquiescence, he managed to retrieve the option, but he needed enough money to outbid his chief rival for the paper, Northcliffe's younger brother Lord Rothermere.

Bruce Richmond described, in a letter he wrote to Stanley Morison on 19 May 1939, what he had done to help find the right wealthy man. He thought that the events had taken place in December 1921, but Stanley Morison, in the official history of *The Times*, puts them in June 1922. Richmond wrote:

> At that time rumours as to N's state of mind were rife – and it was also believed that he had several times expressed his desire to give up *The Times*. We understood that by the agreement under which he came Northcliffe was bound, if he wished to sell his interest in *The Times*, to offer it to Walter first.
>
> Thinking that that might happen in the near future and that John W. would almost certainly not be able to buy N's interest, we cast about to find a decent millionaire or two who might (in order to save the paper from an unknown fate, probably Rothermere) be willing to enable J.W. to put up the money, & then make subsequent arrange-ments with him as to proprietorship.
>
> I mentioned this to a very intimate friend – Gen. Neill Malcolm – who mentioned it to Owen [Owen Hugh Smith, director of Hay's Wharf and other companies] – who shortly after told me he thought he had a likely candidate.
>
> So Neill and Owen and I went off to the City, and there saw Guy Granet [Sir Guy Granet, of the American bankers Lee, Higginson, who acted, as *The Times* history puts it, 'in behalf of a man he had known at New College, Oxford'] and Bobby Grant (who has since left the firm & gone to America – but, oddly enough, I met him at Hever last summer and we recalled it all together). We put what I believed to be the situation before them: they said their man was very anxious to save *The Times*, knew quite well that he could never hope to make a penny out of it, and would stand by waiting for us to let them now (*sic*) when the chance came. Nothing was said as to the identity of their man – but Owen felt pretty sure it was Waldorf Astor.
>
> Then, after a few weeks, came the bombshell, that instead of it's (*sic*) being a question of John buying N. out, he had sold his interest to N. – who suddenly became for the first time Proprietor of *The*

Times – but fortunately was already gaga and died before doing anything more.

Then came the dogfight over the body of *The Times* – Cromers, Hugh Bells, Dukes of Devonshire all being sounded. Knowing that Buckle was very keen on the D. of D. scheme & was working for it, I held my hand – but when that failed, and Rothermere loomed larger & larger, I went up to Campbell Stuart's room, and suggested his ringing up Guy Granet – which he did – with, as you say, 'fateful results'.

The 'man from New College' was in fact Major (later Colonel) John Jacob Astor, the youngest son of William Waldorf Astor, the 1st Viscount Astor. He did buy *The Times* and became its chief proprietor – on 23 October 1922, the same day, as it happened, that Bonar Law was called for by the King and began forming a new Conservative government. Geoffrey Dawson returned as editor of *The Times*, and Astor, throughout his years as chief proprietor, never interfered with him or his successors – or with the editors of the *Times Literary Supplement*. It is apt that Richmond's characteristically witty, laconic letter should record the arrival of a new era in the *Lit Supp*'s history – and its reassumption of the old editorial ways.

Chapter Seven

Peace Among the Vile Bodies: 1923–29

Once Astor had arrived, and Dawson had reassumed the editorship of *The Times*, life settled down again at the *Lit Supp*. Bruce Richmond had the confidence of proprietor and editor alike. He had also received, in that fateful month of October 1922, a public honour: he had been made an honorary Doctor of Letters by the University of Leeds. G.S. Gordon, who had once been a pupil of Sir Walter Raleigh's, and was now a professor, said on presenting Richmond to the chancellor that the best literary editors always hid themselves behind their journals, but that the time had come to invite him to 'emerge and endure the publicity of recognition'. The *Times Literary Supplement*, Gordon said, now occupied 'a position of undisputed and ungrudged authority'. It had been 'hospitable both to age and youth, always hating a bad book but always hoping for a good one . . . The attitudes of authority, good will and expectancy were never so happily combined.'

Gordon, incidentally, would go on to become President of Magdalen College, Oxford, where he continued to review for the paper. An Oxford story has it that when a Fellow of Magdalen was told this at High Table one evening, he instantly said, 'I see – the readers of the *Times Literary Supplement* are the Dupes of Richmond and Gordon.'

Back behind his journal, Richmond was now able to forge ahead as he chose. Nevertheless, the 1920s were years of great change for him. One by one, that team he had built up in the early years were dying. Sir John Macdonell, the voice of liberal reason on the paper for so long, had died at the age of seventy-five in 1921. Thursfield – by this time Sir James – who had started the paper off, and had begun his own career as a correspondent on naval manoeuvres for *The Times* in 1887, died in 1923, aged eighty-three. His son would become an admiral, and another naval correspondent for *The Times*. 1923 also saw the early death – at fifty-seven – of the kindly but strong-minded Thomas Seccombe. In 1921, he had gone out to be a professor at Queen's University in Kingston, Ontario, but had been forced to come home because of ill-health. Arthur Clutton-Brock, as we have seen, died in 1924, aged only fifty-six. J.L. Hammond, historian of the English labouring classes, wrote a last tribute to him (signed 'J.L.H.'), concluding: 'His noble language rang strangely in the ears of Europe, when the war had filled Jingo and pacifist alike with its blind bitterness, but it will ring proudly in the ears of England when she stands among the nations at the Judgment Day.' Clutton-Brock's son Alan was already a contributor to the *Lit Supp*, and also the *Times* art critic, like his father, from whom he was sometimes hardly distinguishable in tone.

A.B. Walkley, the dramatic critic of *The Times*, who had made such sprightly contributions to the *Lit Supp* in its first years, died, aged seventy, in 1926. He had angered Virginia Woolf by saying in his weekly column in *The Times* that her unsigned review of Henry James's letters in 1920 had itself displayed some of James's own 'least amiable mannerisms'. The loyal F.T. Dalton, who had shouldered the Book List for so long, manfully if not always perceptively, retired at the end of 1923 and died, aged seventy-two, in 1927. It is to be hoped that he never knew that Virginia Woolf had once called him 'that donkey'.

Sir Edmund Gosse, whose contributions to the *Lit Supp* had mainly been reviews of books in the Scandinavian languages, died aged seventy-eight in 1927, revered above all for his *Father and Son*. But in 1931, when the *Life and Letters of Gosse* by the Hon. Evan Charteris was published, Percy Lubbock expanded affectionately but shrewdly in the *Lit Supp* on a later period in Gosse's life. He described how, in his middle years, Gosse – now librarian of the House of Lords – found himself a popular figure in London social life and 'loved this world – not with the aesthetic and historical imagination that was almost overpoweringly bestowed on it by Henry James – but with frank and gleeful entrancement; archly audacious, elegantly honey-tongued, he courted it and diverted it with all his arts'.

The second of the old *Times* triumvirate whom Richmond so adored, Sir Valentine Chirol, died in 1929, aged seventy-seven. He was writing about India – both his own books, and reviews for the paper – to the end. But a somewhat unseemly mention of him in a letter from E.M. Forster to Joe Ackerley in 1925 reveals that the author of *A Passage to India* (published the previous year) – who probably met him when they were both guests of Robert Bridges in Oxford – saw him as very definitely in the opposite camp to himself and his liberal friends. 'But oh my balls and bum – Valentine Chirol!!' he wrote to Ackerley. 'What must a world be made of that takes such a man seriously and allows him to grow into the shape of Henry VIII?' The third of the triumvirs, Buckle, was still alive, and vigorously editing further volumes of Queen Victoria's letters, each of which got reviewed at length in the paper as it appeared.

Richmond also had to come to grips with a changed publishing and academic scene in the twenties. General publishing was soon thriving again after the end of the war, boosted by the steady growth of an educated and more leisured middle class, and there were books on countless subjects calling out for review. In the first week of 1929, the *Lit Supp* reviewed (amongst many others) books on cave-dwellers, Islamic mystics, the Capuchins, Kirk's explorations on the Zambezi, the Australian navy, handwriting, Brahms's lieder, Hobbes, and old postbags. That year, there were 1,090 pages altogether in the paper, that is to say a steady average of about twenty pages a week.

As we have seen, the circulation had been 28,896 in 1920, but in July of that year the price went up to 6d, and the circulation had fallen dramatically to 21,205 by 1922. In June 1923, the new management brought the price down to 3d again, and the strategy slowly paid off. The circulation rose to 26,734 in 1924, and had climbed to 29,930 by 1929. According to the company's records, profits, which had been £8,880 in 1923, went down to £4,249 the following year, after the price cut, but with the increased circulation (and increasing publishers' advertising) they had recovered to £9,438 by 1929. (One must multiply by about thirty by this time to get the equivalent sum in modern terms.)

The reviewers' fees had also gone up by now to £3 for a column on the four-column page. The fees were still strictly calculated according to the length of the review, and the accounts department is said to have used a ruler calibrated not in inches but in pounds, shillings and pence to make life easier for themselves. Unfortunately, none of these legendary rulers seems to have survived.

The post-war readership had also certainly changed to some extent. Librarians had multiplied with the growth in public libraries, and with its full list of 'books received' the *Lit Supp* was of great value to them. Above all, the rise of English departments in the universities had brought a considerable number of new professionals into being – the academic experts on English language and literature, who had formed only a very small body when the paper began, and who were multiplying in America too.

Not only did they read the *Lit Supp*, but they soon found it to be a perfect organ for publishing their requests for information and their findings in. They were also publishing books, and the review columns began to feature not just new novels and volumes of poems by, say, Conrad and Hardy, but books about the work of such authors written while they were still alive – not to mention books in rapidly increasing numbers on the literary dead. The secondary literature was beginning to match the primary literature in quantity. This phenomenon was also an American one, and the American readership increased correspondingly.

We have seen that Bruce Richmond, looking back at his time on the *Lit Supp*, felt that things changed around 1926. He was thinking mainly of its metamorphosis from a general paper to a rather more academic one. In fact, nothing changed dramatically that year. Perhaps it was just that about that time he became fully conscious of the slow evolution that had been taking place since the end of the war.

But the paper certainly has a different feel in the twenties. There is a touching moment in January 1929 when Edmund Blunden, reviewing a volume of poems by Edgell Rickword that had come out at the end of the previous year, remarks on 'his capacity for pleasure even in 1928'. He was not just thinking of the economic difficulties of Britain in the late twenties; he was thinking of the fact that literature itself had been showing so much more interest in misery and ugliness than in happiness and beauty in recent years. However, by now the 'old guard', where they survived, had largely accepted that the preoccupations of gifted and imaginative writers had changed. A little earlier in 1928, John Cann Bailey, now in his sixties, reviewing *The Classical Tradition in Poetry* by Gilbert Murray, could still beg for 'elevated subjects' in literature, and cry, 'If life be not a great thing, why speak of it at all?' But the clash between the old and the new that was found in the pages of the *Lit Supp* from early in its life to the first years of the twenties was now softened.

The rise in the number of academic works and of light popular books being reviewed added to the impression of diminished liveliness. So many of the books now required only a rather plain summing-up of their accuracy and the workmanlike quality or otherwise of their style.

Richmond during these years was prodigiously successful at finding good, specialist reviewers in numerous fields. But their balanced reviews, almost always well-written, convey little excitement.

The reviews of more challenging books were spread, in consequence, more thinly through the paper. Moreover, the earlier brilliant lights such as Virginia Woolf or Percy Lubbock, or more recently T.S. Eliot and John Middleton Murry, were not contributing so frequently. The last two had spirited magazines of their own to run – Murry first with the *Athenaeum*, and then with the magazine he founded in 1923, the *Adelphi*; and Eliot with the *Criterion*. Nevertheless, when in July 1924, Orlo Williams, the new regular novel reviewer, imagined a modern Socrates sitting in a wine-vault off Fleet Street discussing with the leading modern critics the nature of criticism, it is notable how many of them, in their different camps, were still in some measure stalwarts of the *Lit Supp*: 'Mr Saintsbury, Mr Edmund Gosse, Mr J.C. Squire [the one exception], Mr Middleton Murry, Mr John Bailey, Mr T.S. Eliot and Mr Percy Lubbock.'

In fact, when they appear in the twenties, these writers are mostly contributing long essays, not necessarily linked to a new book. 'Mr Saintsbury', or Professor George Saintsbury, now seventy-six, and recently retired from the chair of rhetoric and English literature at Edinburgh, contributed a signed article called 'Twenty-One Years' on the coming-of-age of the paper on 4 January 1923. It was not a very useful article because, though it asked the question 'What has been the general character of these twenty years and more of English literature?', the only answer it came to, at considerable length, was that it was as yet rather hard to say.

As if by way of compensation, three months later Virginia Woolf wrote a long essay called 'How It Strikes A Contemporary' in which she came out very boldly. First, she sounded a pessimistic note (and gave, incidentally, a very good idea of the literary pecking order of the time):

> If we ask for masterpieces, where are we to look? A little poetry, we may feel sure, will survive: a few poems by Mr Yeats, by Mr Davies [this is W.H. Davies], by Mr De la Mare. Mr Lawrence, of course, has moments of greatness. Mr Beerbohm in his way is perfect. Mr Strachey paints portraits. Mr Eliot makes phrases. Passages in *Far Away and Long Ago* [by W.H. Hudson] will undoubtedly go to posterity entire. *Ulysses* was a memorable catastrophe [not in fact reviewed by the *Lit Supp*] – immense in daring, terrific in disaster

... [We find ourselves] agreeing with the critics that it is an age incapable of sustained effort, littered with fragments, and not seriously to be compared with the age that went before.

Then she suddenly, persuasively, changed her tune:

But there is something about the present with all its trivialities which we would not exchange for the past, however august . . . Modern literature in spite of its imperfections has a hold on us, an endearing quality of being part of ourselves . . . We are sharply cut off from our predecessors. A shift in the scale – the war, the sudden slip of masses held in position for ages – has shaken the fabric from top to bottom . . . New books lure us to read them partly in the hope that they will reflect this rearrangement of our attitude – those scenes, thoughts and apparently fortuitous groupings of incongruous things which impinge upon us with so keen a sense of novelty – and, as literature does, give it back into our keeping, whole and comprehended.

And she left her readers brilliantly balanced on this knife-edge.

She also wrote memorable pieces on Conrad and Hardy after their deaths. Conrad died on 3 August 1924, and Richmond wired her 'earnestly asking me kindly to do a leader on Conrad, which flattered and loyal, but grudgingly [because she was in the middle of writing *Mrs Dalloway*], I did; & it's out; & that number of the *Lit.Sup.* corrupted for me (for I can't, & never shall be able to, read my own writings).' In the article she said that Conrad's early books 'are surely secure of their place among our classics', and she found their genius in the fact that Conrad was able to celebrate his noble, silent men of adventure with the fervour of a lover, and yet, with his 'double vision', wholly understand them too. 'Conrad was compound of two men: together with the sea captain dwelt that subtle, refined, and fastidious analyst whom he called Marlow' – Conrad's narrator.

The Hardy piece, which appeared after his death in January 1928, was a 'refurbishing' of an obituary that Richmond had as a precaution asked her to write in 1919, just before Hardy's eightieth birthday the following year. She made it a statement of her own faith, saying that 'like every great novelist, he gives us not merely a world which we can liken to the world we know, but an attitude towards it, an atmosphere surrounding it, which is of far greater importance and lasts long after the world which the novelist portrays has vanished for ever'.

Other long essays she wrote included a provocative one on the Elizabethan dramatists – particularly provocative since so much space was now being given to them in scholarly articles and letters in the paper – complaining that, apart from Shakespeare, they never give us any solitude – 'all is shared, made visible, audible, dramatic' – and that they leave us craving for Donne, Montaigne or Sir Thomas Browne, 'keepers of the keys of solitude'. There was also a long leader on Montaigne himself – who, she suggested, was one of the only three people who had 'succeeded in drawing themselves with a pen', the others being Pepys and Rousseau. A delightful piece she wrote called 'Geraldine and Jane' about the mid-nineteenth century novelist Geraldine Jewsbury, who had a stormy friendship with Mrs Thomas Carlyle, produced a classic crop of *Lit Supp* letters. One correspondent had found the grave of Geraldine's elder sister in a cholera cemetery in Poona; another had discovered some favourable mentions of her in Dorothy Wordsworth's letters; a third reported a dinner conversation with the Marchioness of Ripon, the wife of the ex-Viceroy of India, who cried out when Geraldine's name was mentioned 'I can never forgive that woman. She took from me Jane Carlyle!'; while the Dean of Windsor revealed that when Geraldine was on her deathbed she received three beautiful letters, on Ophelia, Portia and Desdemona, by 'that gentle woman of genius, so unlike her and Mrs Carlyle, Helena Faucit Lady Martin'.

Meanwhile, of course, throughout the twenties, Virginia Woolf was writing her own greatest novels. It was fortunate for her that Richmond had fallen into the way of sending her books to the intellectually dashing A.S. McDowall, who was still only in his forties. He reviewed in succession her volume of essays (many of which had been published in the *Lit Supp*) entitled *The Common Reader*, and the novels *Mrs Dalloway*, *To the Lighthouse* and *Orlando*. He read them intelligently and praised them all. He said that in her essays, which were published in April 1925, she brought together the gifts of Lamb and Coleridge, combining the impressions received by someone who reads simply for pleasure with a critical standard 'that we never distrust'. Her style was 'as clear as a new mirror, yet with enticing shades as of an old one'.

When it came to the novels, he always saw the point of her experiments. In *Mrs Dalloway*, he wrote in May 1925, 'people and events have a peculiar, almost ethereal transparency', and yet the book was 'outwardly, a cross-section of life'. In 1927, he said of *To the Lighthouse* that its design was 'carried through with a rare subtlety', with every little thread 'woven in one texture, which has piquancy and poetry by turns'. Of *Orlando* – that fantasy of a fascinating personality living through many centuries, sometimes as man, sometimes as woman – he declared in 1928: 'Never, perhaps, has Mrs Woolf written with more verve; certainly she has never imagined more boldly.' The book reminded us that we are 'aware of all sorts of possible selves within us'. The one hint of criticism that he came back to in all these reviews of her novels was that the characters were somewhat elusive to the reader, if not to each other – interacting vividly among themselves but not entirely real to us.

However, in her diary Virginia Woolf complained of her *Lit Supp* reviews. 'As for the *Common Reader*,' she wrote on 9 May 1925, 'the *Lit Supp* had close on 2 columns sober & sensible praise – neither one thing nor the other – my fate in the *Times*'. On 5 May 1927 she noted: 'I write in the shadow of the damp cloud of the *Times Lit Sup* review [of *To the Lighthouse*], which is an exact copy of the Js.R [*Jacob's Room*] Mrs Dalloway review, gentlemanly, kindly, timid & praising beauty, doubting character, & leaving me moderately depressed'. Both brilliant and tortured as she was, it was hard to please Virginia Woolf.

In these years, T.S. Eliot began to get the recognition that he deserved. His most famous poem, *The Waste Land*, was published in the first number of his own magazine the *Criterion* in October 1922, and also in the American magazine *The Dial* a month later. It appeared in book form from the Woolfs's Hogarth Press in September 1923, and was reviewed in the *Lit Supp* that month by Edgell Rickword. Rickword was an excellent critic, and in due course was to bring out an anthology of critical essays on contemporary writers called *Scrutinies*, which in turn led to the foundation of F.R. Leavis's journal, *Scrutiny*.

Rickword gave *The Waste Land* a very intelligent review (called 'A Fragmentary Poem'). In the poem, he wrote, 'we seem to see a world, or a mind, in disaster and mocking its despair. We are aware of the toppling of aspirations, the swift disintegration of accepted stability, the crash of an ideal.' But, he said, 'Mr Eliot's emotions hardly ever reach us without traversing a zigzag of allusion', and he found this disappointing. 'The method suits well the disillusioned smile which he had in common with Laforgue; but we do sometimes wish to hear the poet's full voice.' Nevertheless 'it is the finest horses which have the most tender mouths, and some unsympathetic tug has sent Mr Eliot's gift awry. When he recovers control we shall expect his poetry to have gained in variety and strength from this ambitious experiment.'

No doubt this view of the poem does less than justice to the power and point of its numerous allusions to other writings, something which most of its early readers were slow to take in; but Rickword's review reflected a very careful and affectionate reading of the poem. As the decade went on, the poem was regularly mentioned with increased understanding, and also with a perception of its relevance to the growing force of Eliot's religious convictions. In February 1927, the young Alan Clutton-Brock remarked, *à propos* of some other poets he was reviewing, that 'in *The Waste Land* Mr Eliot constructs out of many rapidly shifting scenes and images a criticism of life, a scale of values, and in short a metaphysical system'. And in December 1928, reviewing Eliot's volume *For Lancelot Andrewes: Essays on Style and Order*, in which Eliot effectively declares himself to be an Anglo-Catholic, Geoffrey West writes of his 'unremitting quest for a philosophy or at least a mental attitude which might square with the complexities, the realities, and in particular the scepticisms of contemporary living,' adding that 'lost in the deserts of *The Waste Land*', it was not surprising that he should 'cry aloud for the security of an established tradition'.

Many of the essays in *For Lancelot Andrewes* had appeared in the *Lit Supp*, and its readers, had they only known he was the author, could have traced for themselves some of the development of Eliot's ideas. Though serious, they were marked by his usual dash and wit. In an article on Machiavelli for the four-hundredth anniversary of his death, Eliot provocatively declared of this legendary villain that 'No one was ever less "Machiavellian" than Machiavelli. Only the pure in heart can blow the gaff on human nature as Machiavelli has done.' A review of *The Outlook for American Prose* by Joyce Warren Beach in September 1926 was very mischievous: 'America is not likely to develop a new language until its civilisation becomes much more complicated and more refined than that of Britain, and there are no indications that this will ever happen.' The Lancelot Andrewes essay from which Eliot's book took its title, also published in the paper in September 1926, spoke of the 'flashing phrases' of this Elizabethan divine 'that never desert the memory'. In one passage by Andrewes that he quotes lies the source of one of his most beautiful poems, 'Journey of the Magi': 'A cold coming they had of it, at this time of the year, just the worst time of the year to take a journey, and specially a long journey in.' Eliot also wrote some shorter, less personal reviews of books for the paper from time to time, such as one on a new scholarly edition of Chaucer's *Troilus and Criseyde*. Perhaps on these occasions, like many other reviewers, he just wanted to have the book.

*   *   *

John Middleton Murry went on contributing both long and short reviews, also using them to develop his ideas. His quick, volatile mind was constantly turning over his beliefs about religion and poetry at this time. One might say he was preoccupied with four beings – God, Shakespeare, Keats and D.H. Lawrence. Richmond did not give him much opportunity of writing about God, but his complicated belief that there was still a Christian God although Jesus was mortal is alluded to in other people's articles. For instance, Basil de Selincourt, reviewing his essays in December 1924, commended his remark 'God is to me a power and an influence which pervades and explains my daily life', but found him rather evasive in defining its means and how he applied it. Katherine Mansfield once said 'John can't fry a sausage without thinking about God.'

Reviewing Murry's novel *The Voyage* in May 1924, D.L. Murray called him 'a taster of souls', and that describes well his desire to get to what he would have thought of as the spiritual essence of great writers. However, Richmond did not give him much opportunity of writing about D.H. Lawrence, either. Murry was engaged in a very entangled emotional relationship with Lawrence in these years and had founded the *Adelphi* primarily to support Lawrence and his work; and Richmond left him to get on with it there, sending most of the new Lawrence books to A.S. McDowall as before.

Most of the plentiful new Keats and Shakespeare books came Murry's way, including the new editions of the plays in the *Arden* and the *New Cambridge Shakespeare* series. However, when his own book on *Keats and Shakespeare* was published in 1925, it was reviewed rather astringently by H.W. Garrod, a don at Merton College. Garrod was impressed by Murry's passion for Keats – who, he said, rather took the book over from Shakespeare – but he was not convinced by Murry's argument that Keats was always 'plotting escape' from the world of the senses to the world of thought, and that in this lay his true greatness. It meant, said Garrod, that Murry had to 'jettison Keats's best poems in favour of the revised Hyperion', which Garrod thought quite wrong. As for Murry's claim that in Keats 'poetry and thought and knowledge are one and homogeneous', Garrod considered such remarks to be pure 'mystification'. Garrod was a classical scholar who rejoiced in suggesting emendations to classical texts, and was said never to go anywhere except to Blackwell's bookshop in Oxford and to the Meadow to exercise his dog, but in due course he was to produce a superb scholarly and critical edition of Keats's poems in the *Oxford English Texts* series himself.

As a taster of the souls of writers, we see Murry at his very best in an article on Chekhov in December 1923: 'The writing of a perfectly free man: a man who has freed himself from all fears and has found that within himself which enables him to stand completely alone. Such a man can afford to love humanity as Chekhov loved it, for he is in no danger of entanglement; he does not love for the sake of being loved.' No doubt Murry's own inner wrestlings are to be detected in that remark; but it was an exquisite comment on the Russian writer too.

Murry could also be simple and jolly. In July 1925 he delighted in Lytton Strachey's Leslie Stephen lecture on Pope, quoting Strachey's remark that in Pope's Pastorals 'the rhythm is that of a rocking-horse; the sentiment mere sugar. But what a relief! What a relief to have escaped from all the profound obscurities of Shakespeare and Mr Eliot.' Murry commented: 'It must be years since a lecture so delicately impertinent was given at Cambridge'. (Eliot, incidentally, reviewed Strachey's *Elizabeth and Essex* in the *Lit Supp* three years later and gave it nothing but praise: we want to read it at a sitting, he said – 'we could no more insert a bookmark until tomorrow than we could see a play by going to a different act each night'.)

Another important acquisition by Richmond in the twenties was the young Herbert Read. He came from what he liked to call a peasant background, and had begun life as a bank clerk. He had gone on to Leeds University, and during the war had become a captain in the Green Howards. After that he had worked for a while in the Treasury and then as an assistant keeper at the Victoria and Albert Museum. He was thirty in 1923, and already had a reputation as a 'philosophical anarchist', and a highly intelligent one.

He wrote a number of long, forceful essays for the *Lit Supp* in these years. They were not in any way wildly anarchist – in fact they were deeply scholarly and well-informed – but they certainly broke some fresh ground in the paper. In November 1925 he wrote a solemn defence – with an unmistakable smile playing on his face – of Smollett's 'indiscretions'. These indiscretions, he wrote

> hover round certain daily physical acts to which we are all subject, but of which only the neurotic are ashamed. It may be that such acts are not a proper subject for humour; but humour being by definition an imitation of the ludicrous in nature, and nothing being more ludicrous than a dignified human being's subjection to these necessities, it is difficult to escape from, at any rate, a logical defence of coprological humour. QED.

The following March he wrote a review of Sir Arthur Quiller-Couch's *Oxford Book of English Prose*. He criticised it first because Quiller-Couch did not regard prose as an art, and in trying to make the anthology 'representative' had included, on his own avowal, many 'quite pedestrian' specimens of English prose. More seriously, the prose that Quiller-Couch evidently liked best was a gentle, reflective prose of 'subjective joys and passive aspirations'. Those qualities, said Read, did not reflect the great spirit of English prose, which was a spirit of 'open candour and of active enjoyment, the life of deeds and of zest in the sensuous quality of our flesh'. Above all, the great masters of English prose were all, in their different ways, dominated by some great passion. Among the writers whom Read cited as his examples were Swift and Newman, Emily Brontë and James Joyce. One can imagine what a different review Blunden or de la Mare – those poets of 'subjective joys' – would have written of this anthology!

In the end, Read went off on an analysis of what he thought were the three main elements in good prose – image, idiom and *ordonnance*, as he called them – and this part of the essay seems more intellectually fanciful. The same can be said of some other ambitious articles he contributed to the paper, such as one on the inadequacy of Descartes or one on poetic rhythm. But there is an air of fine confidence and authority, and a core of hard original thinking, in these essays – something which readers of his much looser later writings as a champion of surrealism will not find. At this early stage in his career he had a reputation for taciturnity – but it was said of him that 'when Read does at last open his mouth, you know there's no more to be said'.

Apart from Virginia Woolf, Aldous Huxley and D.H. Lawrence continued to dominate the novel during the twenties, but there was also one appearance by E.M. Forster, whose greatest novel, *A Passage to India*, was published in 1924. It was reviewed by R.D. Charques, the paper's new regular novel reviewer, who would become the chief novel reviewer some years later – a dark-haired, vivacious and generally kindly man, half-Russian, who peered at people over his large horn-rimmed spectacles. He liked *A Passage to India*, but gave it a rather trite review, hardly noticing the challenge it threw down to ingrained English colonial traditions. He concluded tamely that 'Mr Forster seldom lacks the power to go beneath the surface of the trivial occurrences of everyday life.' Charques also reviewed Forster's little book on *Anonymity*, in which Forster argued that with great literature it does not matter if we know who the author is (he was not concerned with the case of anonymous reviewing), and his *Aspects of the Novel* in 1927, but in both cases Charques did little more than spell out Forster's views.

Aldous Huxley was in Harold Child's hands, and his favour came and went as Huxley's novels seemed to him more or less positive in their attitude to life. Child did not really appreciate the invigorating force of fierce and extravagant satire. Reviewing *Antic Hay* in November 1923, he dwelt on the author's apparent loathing, which he called 'adolescent', of people's bodies, but, like a good Victorian schoolmaster, thought that at any rate it was healthy that Huxley had faced his disgust and 'made a clean breast of it'. In *Those Barren Leaves*, which he reviewed in January 1925, he reported that Huxley was now 'forging ahead. We saw him very lately, in *Antic Hay*, down in the trough of the misery and rage which seize on sensitive souls at odds with the reality they know. In his new novel he is trying his course towards a more real reality'; and he recognised that Huxley was 'an artist in fine comedy'. But in *Point Counter Point* in October 1928 all he could find was an 'asylum of perverts'.

D.H. Lawrence came off best. He still belonged, as Virginia Woolf did, to McDowall, who kept up a stream of praise as Lawrence's books poured out in what were to be the last few years of his life (he died in 1930). In March 1923 McDowall said that the stories in *The Ladybird* were 'studies of the unreasoned, incalculable magnetisms between men and women', recounted with 'ease and mastery'. In May of that year he called *Sea and Sardinia* 'a rich harvest from a few days' travel'. In September he called *Kangaroo* a fine novel, 'written out of plenitude', though he shrewdly observed that 'Lawrence is being drawn beyond art into prophecy'. In December he praised Lawrence's *Love Poems* in which 'he conceals neither the stings of love nor the bewildering smarts of life, but he makes them beautiful'. I think one can safely say that McDowall understood what was best in Lawrence.

In January 1924 he was rather less struck by the stories in *England, My England*, but in May of the following year he wrote that *St Mawr* was 'not only rich with irony and poetry, but succeeds, perhaps more completely than Mr Lawrence has yet done, in expressing those ultimate perceptions of his through symbols' – especially the horse in this novella. He was uneasy again about Lawrence's most symbolic and most aggressive novel, set in Mexico, *The Plumed Serpent*. He said that it was a *tour de force*, but weakened by repetition, which in his 'ruthlessness towards the reader' had 'run away with him', and that it also rang false when he relaxed his control and wrote a sentence like 'the big, florid male, gleaming, was somewhat repulsive to her' – which McDowall commented 'was really absurd'. Orlo Williams – still a clerk at the House of Commons – reviewed *The Woman Who Rode Away* in May 1928 rather less interestingly, saying little more than that some of the stories in it had 'great imaginative power' but that there was also sometimes 'an irritating prosiness'. As for *Lady Chatterley's Lover*, which was first printed in Florence in 1928, that controversial book was not reviewed in the *Lit Supp* until an expurgated edition appeared in England in 1932.

And now another novelist hove into sight – Evelyn Waugh. However Waugh, whose first book, *Rossetti: His Life and Work*, was published in early 1928, when he was only twenty-four, had a bad beginning with the *Lit Supp*. The book was given a lead review of almost two pages by the Irish poet T. Sturge Moore – but the book was little more than a peg on which the reviewer could hang his own ideas. He disagreed with Waugh's rather remarkable claim that Rossetti's *Beata Beatrix* was the most purely spiritual work of European art since the fall of the Byzantine Empire, but he conceded that 'courage in appreciation is always to be reverenced'. Unfortunately, he called the author 'Miss Evelyn Waugh', and said that she 'approaches the "squalid" Rossetti like some dainty Miss of the Sixties bringing the Italian organ-grinder a penny'.

Waugh wrote a haughty but amusing reply the following week. He said he had noticed with gratitude the prominence given to his book, but he had a complaint to make:

> Your reviewer refers to me throughout as 'Miss Waugh'. My Christian name, I know, is occasionally regarded by people of limited social experience as belonging exclusively to one or other sex; but it is unnecessary to go further into my book than the paragraph charitably placed inside the wrapper for the guidance of unleisured critics, to find my name with its correct prefix of 'Mr'. Surely some such investigation might in merest courtesy have been taken before your reviewer tumbled into print with such phrases as 'a Miss of the Sixties'.

He signed the letter 'Your obedient servant, EVELYN ARTHUR ST. JOHN WAUGH'.

But he does not appear to have felt particularly bitter towards the paper, since writing soon afterwards to his friend Henry Yorke (better known as the novelist Henry Green) to congratulate him on his engagement, he said, 'You must be married at once very obtrusively – a fashionable wedding is worth a four column review in the *Times Literary Supplement* to a novelist.'

Worse was to come, though. His first novel, *Decline and Fall*, published later in 1928, was only given a brief review in September by Orlo Williams, who said it was sometimes funny but was not quite as funny as it was meant to be. It did also appear in a Christmas round-up of humorous books by Douglas Woodruff (later, editor of the *Tablet*), who called it 'highly entertaining', but only spared it a few lines; in the same article he gave a much more enticing account of P.G. Wodehouse's latest novel, *Money for Nothing*, concluding that 'a tear-off calendar of cheery insults from his books would make an acceptable present in many homes'. (That was an accolade that, at any rate in later life, Evelyn Waugh would no doubt have particularly liked for himself – not that his insults to people were all that cheery.)

Then, at the end of 1929, the paper made the same mistake about his sex again. In a review of a collection of stories, called *The New Decameron*, Orlo Williams mentioned 'Miss Runcible's Sunday Morning', calling it – very carelessly, considering that he had reviewed *Decline and Fall* – 'a piece of charming frivolity by Miss Evelyn Waugh'. This time the paper apologised.

Waugh's second novel, *Vile Bodies*, in 1930, was completely ignored by the *Lit Supp*. Moreover, in an advertisement for it by his publishers, Chapman & Hall, which appeared in the paper on 6 February it was described as '*Vile Bodies* by ALEC WAUGH'. Alec Waugh was Evelyn's very successful brother, not much liked by Evelyn. In the same advertisement appeared an announcement about Alec's new book *The Coloured Counties*, with the note '1st and 2nd Impressions Sold Out. 3rd Nearly Exhausted. 4th Ready Shortly.' No doubt some junior had failed to notice that there were two Waughs on the firm's list, and the following week the publishers bought space in the *Lit Supp* to make an abject apology to both brothers. After that, the paper's relationship with Waugh improved.

There was another vigorous letter of protest from an author in 1928. In September, C.E. Bechhofer Roberts, formerly known as C.E. Bechhofer, the expert on Russian Communism who had written so many reviews for the paper, brought out a novel about Dickens called *This Side Idolatry*, in which he portrayed Dickens as an extremely unattractive character, and made Dickens's father John the hero. It was reviewed by D.L. Murray, who called this work of faction 'unconvincing' and, what was more, 'an offence against taste'. Bechhofer Roberts came back with a spirited reply. There was a 'sham cult', he said, of Dickens's perfection. Forster, his biographer, had given 'a fantastically false picture of him'. And his family's 'ruthless suppression of evidence' had 'deceived the world'. Bechhofer Roberts stood by his account.

Towards the end of the decade, some of the novelists who were to become well-known in the thirties made their appearance. L.P. Hartley's first novel, *Simonetta Perkins*, came out in November 1925; Wilfranc Hubbard, who had been the Rome correspondent of *The Times*, praised its economy with words, though regretted its suggestions about the 'supplementary functions of gondoliers' and its 'disagreeable description of the Salute'. The summer of 1927 saw Harold Nicolson's first book, *Some People*, and Rosamond Lehmann's first novel *Dusty Answer*, both of which were reviewed by Miss M. Grant Cook, a friend of Richmond's who wrote many of the briefer fiction notices in the paper. She called *Some People* – nine semi-fictional, semi-autobiographical sketches – 'perceptive', remarking, 'What fun young gentlemen in Embassies have, playing pranks,' and she admired Rosamond Lehmann's story of 'a clamorous, lively company of clever young people', pronouncing it an 'intense, self-conscious vivid book' with 'a beautiful quality in the writing'. Elizabeth Bowen must have been disappointed in the autumn by the relatively dampening review of her first novel, *To the North*, that she received from Orlo Williams – but in the end, she was to stay the course much better than Rosamond Lehmann.

In 1929, Richard Hughes's remarkable first novel, *A High Wind in Jamaica*, about a group of children captured by pirates, was reviewed by J.D. Beresford, himself a novelist, who spoke of Hughes's 'astonishing clear-sightedness in the matter of child psychology' and the 'vividness of his pictures' – 'the reader will not welcome interruptions'. J.B. Priestley burst on to the scene as a novelist this year with *The Good Companions*, and Orlo Williams praised its 'rollicking style' but said that 'the characters do not have that intense personality which makes them live beyond the reading'. Priestley had already been reviewing for the paper, and had written a long, appreciative article on a humorous writer very different from himself, Thomas Love Peacock, back in November 1924.

This was also the debut year of Graham Greene – and in June, D.L. Murray gave his novel *The Man Within* one of the best reviews a first novel had that year. He said that this story of a man fleeing from some smugglers whom he had betrayed was 'breathtakingly exciting', yet the author was less interested in the man's outward adventures than in the spiritual adventures of 'the man within'. Greene, he wrote, 'enhaloes his characters with a delicate, translucent mist of psychologising', and 'wields his psychological scalpel with a deftness extraordinary in a first book'. Greene was for ever after to have an affection for the *Lit Supp*.

Three novelists also produced their first notable (though not their first) works in 1929. Another regular fiction reviewer, Betty Walker, said that in I. Compton-Burnett's *Brothers and Sisters* the author 'gets down to the truth of his subject without wasting time on fine phrases'. It was Waugh in reverse; she did not know that 'I' stood for 'Ivy'. J.D. Beresford reviewed J.C. Powys's *Wolf Solent*; he admired the book, but the character of Wolf the pagan mystic left him uneasy. Charles Morgan was now the theatre critic of *The Times*, but was also becoming an ambitious novelist; his *Portrait in a Mirror* received a long review from Orlo Williams which must have helped considerably in establishing his reputation. Williams said that this story of an artist of genius and his idealistic love affair was a 'masterly unfolding of character' in the classic tradition of English prose. 'It has a beauty and a poetry which are reminiscent of George Meredith,' he wrote, and for good measure he threw in a comparison with Proust – though he reassured readers that there was no 'similarity of moral outlook'. This was English fiction and the *Lit Supp* both at their most high-minded – but they both clearly responded to an element in current taste that was looking for something different from the 'contemporary' quality of the other new novels of 1929, and the book was a great success.

At the end of the twenties there was also a spate of novels about the war. The most striking was *Last Post*, the fourth and final volume in Ford Madox Ford's cycle later known as *Parade's End*. Orlo Williams looked back on the four books in January 1928 and gave them high praise: 'This very notable cycle represents the fabric of the English nation and English character under unbearable stresses . . . It has an originality, a robustness and a tragic vigour which make it worthy of inclusion in the great line of English novels.' This was exceptionally warm for Orlo Williams, but many later readers have agreed with him.

A translation of a book that became very famous, *All Quiet on the Western Front* by the German-born writer Erich Maria Remarque, was reviewed by Cyril Falls in April 1929. He found this story of the trenches coarser, or at least franker, than anything you would get in an English novel, but he acclaimed it as a powerful tragic novel. Was there nevertheless a certain chauvinistic satisfaction in his remark that, although some English writers about the war had found the wine of victory bitter, 'it could not have been so bitter as this vinegar of defeat'?

Richard Aldington's war novel *Death of a Hero* followed in September 1929. It was reviewed by Edmund Blunden, whose own fine book *Undertones of War* – autobiographical, not fictional – had appeared at the end of 1928, and had been reviewed by Falls, who had been very moved by its record of civilisation being suddenly cut off when the troops reached the Western front. Aldington's book was a bitter attack on the hypocrisy of his parents' generation as well as an account of the horrors on the front. Blunden was shaken by the 'helpless grief and pity' the novel conveyed so powerfully, and also generously recognised that it went further than his own war book. 'What was behind so many of those faithful faces in the shellholes? Few of us had skill, or leisure, to decipher that.'

In November 1929 the poet Robert Graves also brought out an autobiography which covered the war years, *Goodbye To All That*, and it was given a good review by Bonamy Dobree, best known as an expert on eighteenth-century literature, and later to be professor of English at Leeds, who also contributed many other elegant reviews to the paper around this time. Dobree said that 'one may be certain that the quality of anything Mr Graves writes will make it different from that which other people may write in the same kind; thus the hesitation which might be felt in approaching the autobiography of any other man of 33 is absent with this book', and he went on to call it 'a gay book and a gallant one . . . a courageous appeal to his generation to put the past behind it and to go forward sadder but still hopeful, as individuals who have cast off cant'.

However the following week Graves's *Poems 1929* received a dull review by Alan Clutton-Brock, who was upset by the poet's 'curious and recondite images' but did not try to examine how they were used; and at the end of December, Graves's companion for many years, the American poet Laura Riding, came to his defence in a fighting letter. 'Your reviewer's general complaint,' she wrote, 'seems to be that he finds in Mr Graves's poems an excitement with which his position does not permit him to sympathise. But I do not see how, in all fairness, Mr Graves is to blamed for the emotional inadequacies of your reviewer's position.' It was the first of many letters she was to write to newspapers for many years in this embattled vein.

W.B. Yeats was now being widely recognised as a major poet, and the Irish poet Austin Clarke registered this in his review of *The Tower* in 1928: 'more constantly than in preceding books,' he said, 'there is a quality in these poems which seems at variance with their personal disquiet, a freedom of the poetic elements, an imaginative and prosodic beauty that brings one the pure and impersonal joy of art'. But James Joyce's small collection of *Pomes Penyeach*, published by Shakespeare and Co. in Paris, went to Clutton-Brock, who found an 'urgent sweetness' in some of them but thought that – in contrast with Joyce's 'new way of writing prose' – the language was mostly borrowed from other poets.

New American novelists of the twenties were quickly noticed, but not very quickly appreciated. Ernest Hemingway's first three works of fiction were all reviewed by Charques. He was struck by the 'fresh and sincere psychology' of *In Our Time* in 1926, but troubled by Hemingway's 'unconcern for the conventional features of good writing' and found that the sequence of 'incidents of daily occurrence' lacked the light and shade of drama. When he reviewed *Fiesta* the following year he was most struck by the amount of drink consumed by Americans in Paris, 'which would send most human beings to the grave', and found the 'crude meaningless conversation, often offers of drink or the bald confession of drunkenness, tedious after 100 pages'. Of the fourteen short stories in *Men Without Women* in 1928, he liked two, but he said that in most of them there was 'a mixture of primitive speech and American slang which has one unpardonable failing – it is monotonous'. Orlo Williams came to the rescue in 1929 with his review of Hemingway's novel about the war in Italy, *A Farewell to Arms*. He called it a novel of 'great power', and described it with enthusiasm:

> The events are episodes in a world-agony, not merely the adventures of Bohemians; the characters depicted, with a masterly handling of dialogue, are more interesting than the drunkards of *Fiesta*; the love of Henry and Catherine Barkle, the English nurse, is rendered with an extraordinarily intense simplicity; and the peculiar hopelessness of Mr Hemingway's humour finds an ideal scope in the contrasts and contradictions of war.

It was a review in rather old-fashioned English, but sincerely responsive to a new idiom.

Orlo Williams also reviewed Scott Fitzgerald's *The Great Gatsby*, the first of Fitzgerald's novels to be published in England, in 1926, though Williams noted that the reputation in America of his earlier books had preceded it. He said that it was 'undoubtedly a work of art and of great promise', but he did not really enjoy it. Interestingly, he saw Gatsby, the farm boy who has built up a dream universe of 'ineffable gaudiness' for himself, as 'a Conradian hero, who is lifted above all the evil that he does or seeks by some great elemental loyalty to a dream which in a different world would have been beautiful'. Williams concluded that Fitzgerald 'maintains the necessary emotional intensity' in the novel, but added that 'it needs perhaps an excess of intensity to buoy up the really very unpleasant characters of this story'. Fitzgerald had not broken through Orlo Williams's conservative defences as Hemingway was to do.

As for American poets, Ezra Pound was now being reviewed as one – at any rate, the review of his *Personae: The Collected Poems* in January 1928 was headed 'An American Poet'. It was written by Richard Aldington, but he was not very forthcoming about his old friend. He tells us in his autobiography that at this period he was beginning to turn against 'modernism' in favour of greater simplicity and directness in writing. In the review, noting that much of the book consisted of translations or paraphrases from other languages, he wrote 'Mr Pound seems to have skimmed through half the poetical literature of the world and comes before us laden with strange and disparate spoil, like one of the barbarians returning from the sack of Rome.' However, though there were examples of 'crudity and uncertain taste' in some of the poems, they often possessed 'subtle beauty and quaint energy'. The following winter Aldington was happily playing tennis with Pound in Paris, at the latter's tennis club, and 'getting one or two useful hints from Ezra's conversation' for the satirical passages in *Death of a Hero*.

Robert Frost, meanwhile, was making progress in the *Lit Supp*. In 1923, Edmund Blunden said of his *Selected Poems* that 'he tells good stories but he avoids poetry' – the poems were 'mostly prose in iambic decasyllables'. He quite failed to detect Frost's unemphatic, subtle rhythms. But in 1924 Fausset wrote with pleasure of the poems in the volume *New Hampshire*: 'his characters are sullen with the routine of humble but necessary labour', yet are 'recreated with such a quiet certainty that they will live'.

Marcel Proust, who had died on 18 November 1922, was commemorated in the first *Lit Supp* issue of 1923. A letter had been sent by a large body of eminent English writers to *La Nouvelle Revue Française* for its January 1923 issue, which was entirely dedicated to Proust's memory, and this was reprinted by the *Lit Supp*. It said that 'in *A la recherche du temps perdu* M. Proust seemed to have found, not only his past, but our own past as well, to give us back ourselves, life as we too had known and felt it – our common and everyday experience, but enriched and made beautiful by the alchemy of art'. It is interesting to read the nineteen names beneath the letter, as another reflection of who were thought – at least among themselves – to constitute the top ranks of the literary hierarchy in the years immediately after the war: Lascelles Abercrombie, Harley Granville-Barker, Clive Bell, Arnold Bennett, Joseph Conrad, E.M. Forster, Roger Fry, Edmund Gosse, Aldous Huxley, Desmond MacCarthy, Charles Scott Moncrieff, J. Middleton Murry, Logan Pearsall Smith, J.C. Squire, Lytton Strachey, R.C. Trevelyan, Arthur Waley, A.B. Walkley, Virginia Woolf.

Under the letter, Middleton Murry contributed an unsigned article on Proust. It showed a touch of scepticism about the novel – 'It is hardly congruous to ride through the Waste Land in a sixty horse-power limousine. Nevertheless, it can be done' – and it also to some extent hijacked Proust for Murry's own complex religious purposes, detecting 'a mystical strain in the composition of this *raffiné* of *raffinés*'. But it acknowledged that Proust had already become one of the great figures of modern literature. Not, of course, that the publication of the book was complete yet. There were still three more volumes to come, in French as well as in translation. They were steadily reviewed as they appeared later in the twenties, mostly by Cyril Falls, with his characteristic mixture of acclaim and reservation.

Orlo Williams discovered Italo Svevo in 1926, but failed entirely to see the point of his delicately comic and very original anti-hero in *La Conscienza di Zeno*. He got quite angry with the book's 'interminable bavardage', and insofar as Zeno's clumsy adventures amused him, it was only to the extent of evoking in him 'a wry and contemptuous smile'. He did not perceive that a new type of fictional hero had been launched in European literature.

By contrast, A.W.G. Randall, the young diplomat who was monitoring new German fiction for the paper, proclaimed in 1928 that Franz Kakfa's two posthumous works, *Das Schloss* (The Castle) and *Amerika*, 'strike a new and, we are inclined to think, abiding note in modern German fiction'. He found he had wanted to read *The Castle* twice, finding the 'underlying symbolist intention' emerging more clearly the second time, and he brought out in his review the haunting quality of the book: 'The overshadowing presence of the castle and its hidden inhabitants is wonderfully suggested, and this atmosphere we shall find ourselves vividly recalling when all the incidents in the novel have faded from our memories.' As for *Amerika*, he thought it 'beside the point' to judge it as a realistic representation of American civilisation: it 'should be read for the sudden, and because sudden, sometimes grotesque and irritating flashlights it throws on character and human destiny'.

The scholars for the most part held sway in the correspondence columns. Richard Aldington, in his autobiography, commented that

> I had long since realised that writing on French literature for *The Times* [as he referred to the *Lit Supp*] was no sinecure. At a moment's notice I had to be prepared to turn out a more or less adequate article on any book or author from the Chanson de Roland to the latest Dadaiste freak. It was like holding a chair in French literature, with this difference, that instead of talking to youngsters who knew less than I did, I had to put my views into print to be scanned by thousands of educated people, including a number of hawk-eyed and censorious experts. *The Times* itself was severe about the slightest inaccuracy . . . There was a frightful hullabaloo once when I misquoted Milton as 'Things unattempted yet in prose or verse,' instead of 'rhyme'. When I jestingly claimed that I deserved commendation because I had given a more accurate version of the original line of Ariosto which Milton cribbed, it was held that I had merely added the crime of lèse-Milton to the misdemeanour of misquotation.

Aldington said that he had missed the 'gay twenties', because he was so busy reading and educating himself in order to avoid rebuke in the *Lit Supp* correspondence columns.

It was Shakespeare who still took pride of place in the numerous scholarly articles and letters that appeared in the *Lit Supp* in this decade, with eminent figures such as J. Dover Wilson and W.J. Lawrence foremost among the contributors. The text of the poems and plays, the punctuation, the printing, the performances, and the lives and working conditions of the players, were among many matters investigated and debated. A.W. Pollard, whose *Shakespeare's Fight Against the Pirates* had been one of the founding texts of this great new academic movement, was commemorated when he retired as Keeper of Printed Books at the British Museum in October 1924. R.W. Chapman, another indefatigable scholar, and secretary to the delegates of the Clarendon Press, lauded Pollard's work on the magnificent 'Catalogue of Books Printed in the 15th Century now in the British Museum', which Pollard had initiated twenty-five years earlier and of which five volumes were already completed, with three more to come.

However, in 1921 Bernard Shaw had argued vigorously with Pollard in letters to the paper, suggesting that in the actual conditions of the theatre the passing on of the texts of the plays must have been subject to innumerable hazards that Pollard had not allowed for in his Shakespeare studies, and the issues that he very convincingly raised went on reverberating through the paper.

The texts of other literary works, from the Anglo-Saxon writers to the novels of Robert Louis Stevenson, were often minutely examined in long letters. New scholarly editions of early English works were also often reviewed. In April 1923 we find J.R.R. Tolkien – then thirty-one, with the Hobbits still far off in his future – speaking plainly about 'Hali Meidenhad', an alliterative prose homily of the thirteenth century: this 'edifying' piece, he wrote, reflected a 'ruthless mediaeval concentration on one virtue to the exclusion of all other considerations', and with its portrayal of all men as 'bestial tyrants' was 'more repulsive to modern feeling than anything in Chaucer's Clerk's Tale'. (Now, eighty years later, it might prove less repulsive to some people again.)

One of the fiercest altercations on the letters page so far took place in 1924 when Basil de Selincourt reviewed a new edition of Emily Brontë's poems. De Selincourt, for all his lofty notions, could review very cruelly, and he savaged this edition for its alleged textual errors: the volumes were 'unconscientious, inaccurate and undiscerning'. Clement Shorter, the editor, and C.W. Hatfield, who had collated the text with various manuscript originals, wrote letters in reply, and the argument went to and fro. Hatfield made a firm defence of his readings, except in three places where the original handwriting was in any case indecipherable. Shorter (who had been editor of the *Illustrated London News* and of the *Sphere*) finally took the line of laughing de Selincourt's charges off: 'One of my friends who read your article told me that it had spoiled his breakfast. I enjoyed mine the more from reading it. I have not been writing notes on books for 40 years without anticipating an occasional "Roland for an Oliver". I have not been editing newspapers for thirty-four years without realising that one makes a great many enemies.'

There were also letters attempting to correct accounts of people's lives. Jessie Conrad, the novelist's widow, wrote 'to correct a few of the fantastic statements' about him in Ford Madox Hueffer's (or Ford Madox Ford's) book *Joseph Conrad: A Personal Remembrance*. She denied emphatically that her husband ever 'poached on Mr Hueffer's vast stock of plots' for his own: his books were based on a chance phrase in some old book of memoirs, or some few sentences culled from a book of history or travel, which were then 'nursed in that master-mind . . . to emerge as a finished masterpiece'. Even one of her own suggestions had once been used, she added modestly – but she finished with a fine show of sarcasm: 'I have heard my husband say that he found Mr Hueffer a mental stimulus, but that was in the early days – days before even Ford Madox Hueffer himself became aware of the great dignity he claims – that of being the greatest English stylist.'

There was also an amusing letter from Max Beerbohm in 1925. He had found in *Later Days*, a volume of reminiscences by the 'super-tramp' poet W.H. Davies, a statement that he had once had a conversation with the poet that began with Beerbohm saying 'How long is it since Shaw discovered you?' and Davies replying 'About 14 or 15 years ago, I believe.' After that – to quote Davies's book –

'Oh dear, dear!' exclaimed Max, in an aggrieved voice. 'Oh dear, dear – and has it been going on all this time!' – implying, of course, that it was about time I was forgotten.

'Yes,' I answered, adopting the same serious and aggrieved tone – 'yes, and it is likely to go on much longer too' – implying that my name would not be forgotten for a long time to come.

Even worse, according to Davies, Beerbohm then said something about Bernard Shaw 'helping a lame dog over a stile' – when Davies was, literally, lame.

In the letter, Beerbohm said he remembered the occasion, but he assured readers that he was 'as unconscious of having given offence as I was guiltless of any wish to offend'. If he had said 'Oh dear, dear', 'these ejaculations can only have been meant to express the rather horrified surprise which I, and other middle-aged men, do so often feel at being told that something which seems so recent is in reality a thing of long years ago.' And he had had no idea of Davies's infirmity: 'Let me ask him to believe that the pain I caused him by my careless use of that phrase cannot have been greater than is the pain I feel at his misjudgment of me.' Whatever the truth of the situation, Beerbohm once again showed himself to be 'the incomparable Max' in getting out of it with this accomplished defence.

*   *   *

Everywhere, as the twenties rolled on, there were reflections in the paper of more modern English sights, more modern English tastes and concerns – even if the language of the paper did not always keep up with them. Edmund Blunden was at his oratorical best in March 1929, reviewing a plea on behalf of the National Trust, called *Must England's Beauty Perish?*, by the historian G.M. Trevelyan. The Trust had acquired for the nation a large number of country houses and estates – 'strongholds of peace and populous solitude' – since it was founded in 1895, and Blunden expressed wholehearted support of it. 'The National Trust is a moving and spacious poem of Nature,' he wrote, and he begged for

> the maintaining of a sylvan, tuneful and haunted England . . . Humanity as a whole may be enriched or impoverished accordingly as we decide to meet the incursions and smoke-clouds of a temporary barbarism, or to let the sources of so much happiness and high endeavour become hopelessly polluted . . . There is no time to be lost. All argument is reduced to the shining eye and smiling lip of spring; that angel, surely, is not to mourn her dead loves for ever in the country of her immemorial choice.

It was not the language of twenty-first century fund-raising, but Blunden's passionate attachment to the English countryside rings out in it.

We also find a strong plea for better city planning from H.M. Stannard, who, as we shall see in a moment, was to become the paper's leading voice on European politics in the late twenties and thirties. In April 1924, he described his feelings about Kingsway – 'the one great new street laid out in Central London since the Embankment'. He wrote that it was 'planned with a certain spaciousness, yet it cramps and oppresses the passer-by. The buildings hustle and jostle one another, almost shouting out their individual qualities. The street is not broad enough to bear the crowd of them.' The passage of the street, he felt, was only made tolerable by 'the serenity of Bush House at its southern end'. Stannard also discussed Regent Street, 'of which the whole design has been destroyed', and calls this a civic crime – 'but at least the public conscience has been stung'.

Not far away John Reith was building up the British Broadcasting Company, and in January 1925 C.W. Brodribb, a *Times* man of long standing, reviewed his book *Broadcast Over Britain*. Brodribb applauded the high ideals Reith was establishing for the new medium: 'to apply it to the dissemination of the shoddy, the vulgar and the sensational would be a blasphemy against human nature'. An immediate question was how BBC speakers should pronounce certain words, especially foreign words that had been 'imported and domiciled'. The BBC set up a committee to examine the matter, under the chairmanship of Robert Bridges, who was the founder of the Society for Pure English, and its report appeared in August 1929, when it was reviewed by the word expert Logan Pearsall Smith. He approved of its pragmatic and flexible principles, and noted that though, in general, the committee recommended that imported words such as 'enclave' and 'trait' should be pronounced as if they were English, 'with regard to the word "ennui", since it describes a state of feeling which is still a privilege of the upper classes, Mr Bridges is inclined to agree with Lord Balfour that it should be spoken as a French word'.

British politics hit the paper in 1926, when the General Strike prevented its publication between 29 April and 20 May. On 29 April, C.W. Brodribb made an allusion to the forthcoming strike in a review of a published speech, 'On England', by Stanley Baldwin. He said, paying perhaps a rather qualified compliment to the Prime Minister, that 'at a critical moment, it is clearly no daemonic genius that is at the helm, but a plain Englishman'. On 8 and 15 May there appeared small, duplicated typewritten sheets as a substitute for *The Times* weekly edition, with a few lines 'from the *Literary Supplement*'. The first mentioned one or two books that would have 'claimed notice' if the paper had appeared that week, including John Freeman's study of Melville in the *English Men of Letters* series, while the second recorded that 'practically no books have been published since the strike began', but that 'we have read a few', including Volume IV of the *Cambridge Ancient History*. The paper was back again on 20 May; this was the issue containing Orlo Williams's attack on Italo Svevo. Perhaps the sight of the strikers had exacerbated his contempt for the feckless Zeno.

Just before the general election in 1929, which brought in Ramsay MacDonald as head of a minority Labour government, John Cann Bailey wrote a balanced piece about 'Elections and Electors'. His strongest plea was that the electors should not vote for parties, policies or pledges as such, but choose as their MP 'a man of character and ability', and then respect his right to make his own decisions. 'Your representative betrays instead of serving you' – Bailey quoted his hero Edmund Burke as saying – 'if he sacrifices his judgment to your opinion.' 'That is the true doctrine,' Bailey declared.

The current politician who received most notice in the *Lit Supp* in these years was Winston Churchill, since his four volumes on the war and its aftermath, *The World Crisis*, came out between 1923 and 1929. The first volume, covering the years 1911–14, was reviewed by an interesting character, Admiral Richmond (later Sir Herbert Richmond – no relation to the editor), who had commanded the *Dreadnought* before the First World War, but was always in trouble with the authorities for his cantankerous criticisms of them and his unauthorised articles in the newspapers; he went on to be commandant of the Imperial Defence College and ended up as Master of Downing College, Cambridge. Like the reviewers of the subsequent volumes – Pollard the historian (twice) and Headlam-Morley – he wrote a long, thoughtful piece. Pollard may be quoted to illustrate what they all said in their different ways: Churchill was unashamedly pleading his own cause in the book, but his plea throughout was 'powerful, brilliant, dramatic'.

Other wartime statesman were also bringing out their memoirs, and as usual they got plenty of space in the paper. Headlam-Morley wrote an affectionate account in 1925 of the memoirs of Lord Grey, who had made the famous remark in 1914, 'The lamps are going out all over Europe; we shall not see them lit again in our lifetime,' and resigned as the Liberal Foreign Secretary in 1916. Headlam-Morley portrayed Grey as a very good, conscientious man who was never very happy in his job: 'If men would only be reasonable,' he imagined Grey constantly saying to himself. But he praised Grey's later work for the League of Nations, a body to which the *Lit Supp* gave constant support in the twenties and thirties. John Cann Bailey reviewed the posthumous autobiography of Lord Haldane in 1929 with equal affection, dwelling on his contribution to English education: Haldane's greatest parliamentary success, he said, was as the champion 'before a whole hostile or indifferent House' of the University of London as constituted by the Act of 1898.

The emergence of a great historian of an earlier political scene was recognised when Basil Williams, Professor of History at Edinburgh, reviewed L.B. Namier's *The Structure of Politics at the Accession of George III* in 1929. Williams recognised the originality of this examination of the life history of every political figure of the time, however minor or obscure; he hailed Namier's 'uncanny knowledge of almost every source, both printed and manuscript, in any way bearing on the highways, and even more on the by-paths, of eighteenth-century politics'; and he savoured the pleasures of the book: 'Mr Namier positively revels in the stories he can find to illuminate the characters of the vast assemblage of office-seekers, borough-mongers, "parliamentary beggars" who preyed on the secret service funds, and ordinary MPs paraded before us in his brilliant pages.' Williams's only reservation was that Namier was too cynical: there were also some honourable eighteenth-century politicians, he pleaded, 'unyielding in their devotion to political principle as they saw it'. Namier himself also reviewed occasionally for the paper: he dismissed a German biography of Metternich in 1926 as being 'as heavy as clay, lifeless and unmoulded'.

There was also a scandal over a history review. In January 1923, Philip Guedalla, who was in his early thirties and had already achieved some fame as an irreverent and witty historian (though Lytton Strachey considered him a mere imitator), contributed a review of *Louis Napoleon and the Recovery of France, 1848–1856*, by F.A. Simpson, a pupil of G.M. Trevelyan's. It was a brilliantly destructive piece:

> History (there is no use denying it) is mainly about dead people. But it is the duty of historians to convince us that they were once alive. They were never perhaps more alive in the whole course of the nineteenth century than in the seven years of French history which Mr Simpson covers ... The wild disorder of 1848 was simmering slowly down into an uneasy swell, and a queer crew put out across the troubled waters in the strange, brightly painted Ark of the Second Empire ... But Mr Simpson's eye seems to be fixed a little nervously on the dignity of history. When he has a good thing to say (and he has more than a few) he not infrequently retires to whisper it to his reader in the privacy of a footnote. His grave narrative seems to disdain the bright colours, the quick, undignified movement of reality; and without that touch one may write sound history, but one can never get those seven wild years to live again.

The universities were outraged. Everyone in the business could tell that the review was by Guedalla, and it was considered that he had used his anonymity to sing the merits of the kind of popular history he wrote, and even by implication of a book he had himself written, at the expense of a good academic historian. G.M. Trevelyan wrote a soft but stern reply in a letter the following week, showing clearly that he knew who the author was. Trevelyan accepted that history needed 'picturesque' touches, but said that to ask that such things should be made the principal theme of any history that sought to be literature was to get off the track, for a statesman's policy was far more interesting than the cut of his clothes. He observed that 'we have had a brilliant

example of the kind of history that your reviewer favours in Mr Guedalla's book on this same Napoleon III' – but 'expand such a book to
three or four volumes and imagination sickens at the thought of it'.
And he declared that Simpson's gifts were those required of a book
that aspired to become the standard authority on Napoleon, as well as
appeal to the general reader.

In spite of Trevelyan's defence of him, Simpson did not continue
with further volumes of his work. In fact, he gave up in bitterness at
the review. Over thirty years later, the critic Raymond Mortimer happened to meet Simpson, and on 9 September 1954 wrote a sad letter
about him to Alan Pryce-Jones, the editor of the *Lit Supp* at the time.
Mortimer said that Simpson's life had been wrecked by the review,
which Mortimer suspected had been by Guedalla, although he did not
know for certain. *The Times*, Mortimer said, was 'so rarely downright
rude even to a bad book that everyone thought that Simpson's book
must be very bad indeed'. There had therefore been no reviews of the
book in France, except for a one-line epitome of the *Lit Supp* article,
and hardly any other English reviews. Mortimer quoted from a letter
he had received from Simpson in which he had written: 'I could not
face going through the whole horrible business again . . . I could not
recapture the gusto.'

However it must be said that undergraduates who knew him in his
later years as a history don at Cambridge did not see him as an unhappy
man – rather as one who was enjoying his relatively indolent life.
Richmond himself may have chuckled privately at the review, but it
was a long time before he sent another book to Guedalla. He must
have known that for once he had allowed anonymity to be misused.

On the foreign political scene, there was a new regular contributor,
Harold Stannard. When I asked Arthur Crook in 1999 if he remembered
Stannard, he looked startled and said, 'My God! I haven't thought of
him for fifty years, but now I see him so clearly again! A funny, furtive
little man. Very powerful, because every book he reviewed at 800 words
for the *Lit Supp* he also reviewed for *The Times* at 400 words.'

Stannard reviewed most of the books on Russia and Italy in the late
twenties, and added books on Germany in the thirties. He became the
paper's leading voice in these years on both Communism and Fascism,
and had a rather similar attitude to both.

He was born in Birmingham in 1883 with the name Steinhart, a
descendant of Sephardic Jews who had come from Frankfurt and Metz,

but when he wanted to volunteer for the British army in 1914 he was obliged to change his name. He became a great traveller and an expert on international affairs, writing for many papers, and finally joined the *Times* staff as a leader writer in 1943. But he died four years later, after a heart attack he had when dining at the Private House, John Walter's Georgian home in Printing House Square.

The obituary in *The Times* said that he was a man of 'small stature and extreme modesty', and also a very moral man, 'who could never bear to think that any other human being, however humble, should suffer by any act of his, and never accepted any post or any promotion without first searching his conscience and satisfying himself that he was not thereby keeping out one more deserving and better qualified than himself'.

Perhaps this modesty was one reason why he was for a long time to give the benefit of the doubt both to Lenin and the mysterious Stalin in Russia, and to Mussolini in Italy – and subsequently, at first at least, to Hitler. But in this respect he also reflected a fairly widespread attitude, not only in Britain but across the world. In many people's feelings, the First World War seemed only just to have ended, and the prospect of order rather than chaos on the continent of Europe had an undoubted attraction. Friendship towards the new regimes seemed like wisdom, and also to offer the best hope of curbing any unfortunate tendency in them to a new nationalism and a new militarism. Clearly, Stannard's articles had the approval of both Richmond and Dawson.

Bechhofer Roberts was still contributing occasional reviews of books on Russia, and in September 1929 wrote about a book called *In the Clutches of the Tcheka* by a Finn called Boris Lederholm who had been imprisoned in Russia on false charges of industrial espionage. Bechhofer Roberts did not spare his readers an account of all the horrors of Soviet prison life – hunger, solitary confinement and death threats – culminating in an offer by the authorities to release Lederholm if he would spy on Russian exiles in Finland.

Stannard's tone in his reviews was quite different. Writing, also in 1929, about a book on Lenin by Valeriu Marcu, he said: 'His regime stands today. Whatever verdict history will pass on his theories, it will surely admit that no man in all its records better knew how to get and to keep what he wanted.' And reviewing four American books on Russia in a long article the same year, he lists what he considers to be many encouraging signs in the regime.

He sees the Communist Party as engaged in a ceaseless battle, whose means he often deplores but towards whose end he is not unsympathetic. 'Today,' he writes, 'the party and particularly its secretary, Stalin, has established a supremacy over a Government whose defects in realising its own ideals it is its business to repair . . . A stern party discipline, sternly enforced, can bring disorderly elements to their senses.' And he believes that 'as time goes on and the dictatorship of the proletariat assumes the qualities of an established institution, there is a greater tendency towards moderation and patience'. In schools, he observes, at the instigation of Lenin's widow 'the harsh blacks and whites of the syllabus have been very considerably toned down and the instruction made suggestive rather than dogmatic'.

Stannard even believed that religion was experiencing a revival in Russia. He concluded his article: 'The surviving authors of the revolution . . . have been replaced by men by nature capable of a tenderness towards mysticism, an insight into its quality, a flexibility of judgment towards its expression . . . Today an icon and a portrait of Lenin hang side by side in millions of Russian homes. It may be that their strange conjunction is a symbol of the future.' This was reassuring writing indeed.

By 1929, he is also offering reassurance in his reviews of books on Italian Fascism. In October 1926, writing about two contrasting books on Fascism, both by Italians, he criticised the defender of the regime, Luigi Villari, stating that 'it is not enough to dispose of acts of violence by referring to the few black sheep among the many black shirts', and he defended the critic of the regime, Luigi Sturzo, saying that his book was 'a convincing answer to those Italians who proclaim that a man cannot be at once an enemy of Fascism and a lover of his country'.

However, when he reviewed Mussolini's autobiography in 1928, he praised Il Duce's courage and powers of leadership, and suggested that he had pulled Italy out of the mire; while his review in 1929 of another book by Signor Villari, *Making the Fascist State*, was not this time critical but, rather, neutral shading to approving. Stannard contemplated with apparent equanimity 'the new theory of the State' in Italy: 'No longer would society exist for the individual according to the old Liberal doctrine. On the contrary, the individual existed for society, which acknowledged in turn its duty of developing the personality to be realised in its service. The disciplined Fascist hierarchy was the expression of this emphasis on the State's authority, as was the exaltation of order above liberty'. So 'order' became the watchword here too.

Germany got special treatment in 1929. On 28 April, there was a substantial supplement to the *Lit Supp* on 'Recent German Literature'.

No new writers of consequence were revealed in it, but that was partly because the paper had kept up its regular reviews of German books. The most interesting contribution was a long, unsigned introductory piece by the former editor of *The Times*, Wickham Steed, who had gone on writing widely on world affairs after he was replaced by Dawson.

In 1929, there were still reasons for believing that Germany was reviving as a more peaceable and democratic nation, and Steed said that 'the old Prussian-Hegelian theory of the State as endowed with almost Divine attributes and possessing over individual citizens an inherent authority . . . is giving place to a conception of the State as the organ of a community whose members entrust to it the function of assuring to them the means of personal development'. This may not sound to us a very democratic conception, but Steed seems justified in adding that it was 'the antithesis of the Italian Fascist theory, which subordinates the individual citizen entirely to the state'. He also believed that, though there were impenitent militarists in Germany, there were others who were convinced that the establishment of the League of Nations really marked the beginning of a new era for the whole of Europe.

Harold Stannard too showed that, whatever guarded attraction he may have felt for the new orderliness of Russia and Italy, he also had hopes for the League, when in March 1929 he applauded Gilbert Murray's heartfelt book, *The Ordeal of This Generation*. In this book the renowned Greek scholar, who was chairman of the League of Nations Union, grieved that the world had become 'uncertain and chaotic', but argued that Britain should give a lead to public opinion in the matter of the League – and urged mankind to remember that in the power of reason it had 'an instrument to vanquish every difficulty'. That was the kind of note that Richmond loved to sound in the *Lit Supp*.

In 1924, there was a leading article by R.D. Charques on a book called *Four Centuries of Fine Printing*. The author was a thirty-five-year-old typographer, Stanley Morison, who had been inspired to take up the profession by a 'Printing Supplement' to *The Times* that he had seen on the station bookstall at King's Cross in September 1912. In 1932 he would completely redesign *The Times* and the *Lit Supp*, and in 1945 he would become editor of the *Lit Supp*.

There were already some changes visible in the paper. Publishers' advertisements, especially, had changed their appearance since the days before the First World War, when many of them were not much more than lists of titles in an ill-considered mixture of typefaces with little or no white around them. Now they were much better designed – more airy and spacious, with name blocks for the publishing house and each advertisement more consistent in its style. Victor Gollancz's bold and simple advertisements set a new trend from 1927 onwards. The front-page column advertisement was dropped in 1924; after that there was only a quarter-column advertisement on the front page beneath the contents list.

In the 'marked copies' of the paper on which the contributors' names and fees were written, there was a very visible change. On the Book List, in the old days, Dalton's name (without fee, since he was staff) had been scrawled across whole pages, with only a few other names dotted here and there. Now these pages were being run by St John Brooks, and innumerable short reviews were being written by outside contributors. Among them were early efforts by such writers as Dilys Powell, later to become the first well-known film critic. But their fees were tiny, and the pages are a jigsaw of sums like 7s or 4s 6d.

Titles of articles were still very straightforward; one of the first joky headlines in the paper was 'Coleridge the Less' over an article by Edmund Blunden on Hartley Coleridge on 7 November 1929. It was a long time before another appeared. But there were jokes in the office. John Cann Bailey recorded in his diary a story that Bruce Richmond told him in April 1928. Walter de la Mare had been 'at the gates of death' for three weeks. 'On one of these days, his younger daughter said to him as she left him "Is there nothing I can get you, fruit or flowers?" On which in a weak voice he could just – so characteristically – answer "No, no, my dear; too late for fruit, too soon for flowers."' In fact de la Mare lived until 1956.

Chapter Eight

Richmond's Twilight Years: 1930–37

In the early thirties, the days passed like a ritual at Printing House Square. The front entrance was on Queen Victoria Street, and there in the sergeants' box were to be found the two commissionaires, both with large moustaches, Sergeant Brooker and Sergeant Wilkinson (or 'Wilkie'). In Northcliffe's time a giant sign, 'The Times', had straddled the whole facade of the building above their heads, but that had soon been taken down again after his death.

When either the editor or the manager, Mr Lints Smith, left his house, a message would reach the sergeants. A boy messenger from the room behind the sergeants' box was sent to watch for the Rolls-Royce coming along the Embankment, and would rush back as soon as he saw it. Wilkie would hurry to the lift, crying 'No one gets in.' Brooker would open the main front door for Dawson or Lints Smith; Wilkie would show him into the lift, press the button and send him on his way up – the editor to the first floor, the manager to the third floor; then, if it was opening hours, both the sergeants went round to the pub next door, the Lamb and Lark, for a pint.

On the first floor, the atmosphere was like that of a senior common room. The home and foreign subeditors who worked on the opposite side of the corridor to the editor were nearly all Oxford or Cambridge men, as were most of the reporters and leader writers on the floor above. Many of them had been fellow Etonians. Generally Dawson did not attend the morning editorial conference, but came in in the evening and went round to see his leader writers. It was a kind of parade; his feet could be heard clomp-clomping along the corridor, then he would throw wide open the door of each room he was visiting.

Arthur Crook once saw him come into a leader writers' room where Peter Fleming, still only in his twenties but soon to become a renowned travel writer (and tipped for a while as a future editor of *The Times*), was sitting smoking a pipe with his feet on a table. Dawson stood at the door glowering, with his pug-like face and glaring eyes. All Fleming did was take his pipe from his mouth and say 'Hi-ya, Geoff'. The social atmosphere was very different outside this charmed circle. Here a messenger boy would be sacked on the spot if he dared to take a lift between floors.

Dawson edited *The Times* in a distinctly different way from his predecessors. It could no longer aptly be called 'The Thunderer'. Dawson was very close to the Conservative Party establishment, and especially at the beginning of the thirties saw a great deal of Stanley Baldwin, Prime Minister in 1923 and from 1924 to 1929, Lord President of the Council in the two National Governments between 1931 and 1935, and Prime Minister again from 1935 to 1937. In the thirties, *The Times* fairly steadily supported the government, with Dawson believing that its policies were attuned to public opinion in the country.

In particular, in the first year or two of the decade, the paper was friendly to Germany, expressing a confidence in her economic future and her peaceful intentions in Europe. Dawson himself was more interested in the Empire than in what was happening on the continent, and left a great deal of the paper's policy-making on Europe to the brilliant and loyal Robert Barrington-Ward (another 'Robin' to his friends, and 'B-W' to everyone else), who was to become his deputy editor in 1934, and to succeed him as editor in 1941.

Nevertheless, Dawson was an autocratic editor. He had let the once all-important post of foreign editor lapse when Harold Williams died in 1929, and now held all the reins of power. He wrote many of the paper's leaders himself, and although on his evening parade he encouraged his leader writers, most of whom were experts in their field, to say what they thought, they knew he would scrutinise every word they wrote.

Bruce Richmond no longer sat in the editor's room, but was along the corridor on the other side in Room 5. He shared it with his old colleague Harold Child, who was still held in high regard for his light leaders in *The Times*, and Dr H.C. Colles, the *Times* music critic – a mountain of a man, with a booming voice. Child and Colles wrote there side by side. Child, though not officially employed by the *Lit Supp*, was

Richmond's chief adviser on the merits of the many letters, mainly on textual points in the English literary canon, that were now arriving at the paper, from American almost as often as from British universities.

In the evening, C.W. Brodribb, who read every page of *The Times* for errors every day, took over Room 5. He was the leading classical scholar on the paper, and Richmond also turned to him for advice.

By now Richmond had a typist from the pool, who made carbon copies of his letters, but he always screwed the carbons up and threw them away, as well as tearing up all the letters he received. The staff would sometimes examine the contents of his wastepaper basket to discover his intentions. He consistently refused to have a full-time female secretary, and continued to write many letters by hand. He regarded himself as a *Times* man, and until the end of his life his entry in *Who's Who* described him as an assistant editor of *The Times*, without any reference to the *Lit Supp*.

He, too, was an autocratic editor, though he was always courteous to his staff. But this politeness was accompanied by a markedly remote air – even towards most of the other senior members of *The Times*, whom he would sometimes meet in the editorial dining-room on the ground floor of the Private House.

He consulted no-one on his own staff about what reviewers he should choose, even for the short notes in the Book List, and no books were ever sent out for review when he was away. His experts – whether outside reviewers or leader writers on *The Times* – gathered from time to time in Room 5 to discuss the books. 'I'm in the hands of the pundits,' he told Janet Adam Smith in 1931 when she went to see him about some possible reviewing (which she got, being marked down as a pundit on Scotland). Once Arthur Crook noticed Charles Morgan in Room 5 in court dress complete with sword, just back from a levee in St James's Palace.

Richmond's social life was mostly lived far away from the *Lit Supp*. For him, working for *The Times* was essentially a suitable profession for a gentleman. He did not see publishers, leaving that to Munby with his notices of forthcoming books, and to Norman Gullick, the advertisement manager.

However he liked to know and entertain his leading writers. He had a house in Kensington and another in the country. T.S. Eliot went to stay with him at Netherhampton House in Salisbury in July 1937 (by which time Richmond had been knighted), and subsequently wrote a letter to Virginia Woolf mentioning the Richmonds' 'imperfect drainage'. Later that week Virginia Woolf replied to Eliot, inviting him down to Rodmell, East Sussex, and added: 'Or is every weekend devoted to the Knight's drains?' She kept up the banter when Eliot went to stay with the Richmonds again the following year: 'I'm longing to hear how the visit to the water closet at Netherhampton went off.' She also speculated on who Eliot might have met there – Edith Olivier, the lady mayor of Wilton, the local town? Or Stephen Tennant the fashionable painter, the son of Lord Glenconner?

But in a letter of his that has survived, to R.W. Chapman, the secretary to the delegates of the Oxford University Press, we get an attractive glimpse of the retiring side to Richmond's character, where he describes how one winter's day 'I lunched alone on the top of Snowdon with a wonderful view – & spent misty days revisiting lower haunts. It was splendid.' He was also a great concert-goer in London and a harpsichordist, and for many years served on the Council of the Royal College of Music. In one of those brief reviews that he wrote for the paper during the First World War, he revealed a corner of his feelings when he grieved over the near-impossibility of writing well about music.

In 1930 he wrote to the historian G.M. Trevelyan to congratulate him on his Order of Merit, and Trevelyan replied (addressing him as 'Dear Bruce' though signing himself 'G.M. Trevelyan'): 'I feel somehow that I have done in a smaller sphere what Rosebery was said to have wished to do – get the palms without the dust – while you who do the real work for civilisation are content to labour – and nothing said.' Trevelyan and Richmond had a great deal in common, for both of them were essentially gentle, liberal patricians. However, in that year Richmond did receive another public honour when Oxford, his own university, made him an honorary Doctor of Letters. The university's Public Orator, A.B. Poynton, speaking in the customary Latin, called him an '*examplar humanitatis*' who had for long been a '*hortator, comes, dux*' of students of literature – an encourager, a companion, a leader, with a suggestion in the Latin words of nobility about these roles.

The rest of the editorial staff of the *Lit Supp* worked on the third floor, in a large room where the books for review were kept. With the books themselves another curious ritual was performed. Every evening, the new books were taken down and put on Geoffrey Dawson's mantelpiece so that he could look at them. But people who came into his office when he was out to dinner – leader writers, subeditors, even messengers – would sometimes take one that they liked the look of. When the books came back to the third floor, they were checked against the slips that had already been made for each of them, giving the publishing details, and the slips for missing books were marked with a cross and put in St John Brooks's drawer. From here they were rarely taken out again. Sometimes the person who had removed the book would come in later with a review of it, but some books were never seen again in the office.

Richmond would come up to the third floor to look at the books every week. When they were sent out, they were not usually accompanied by a letter to the reviewer, just by a scribbled note indicating how many words were needed and whether a shorter version was also required for *The Times*. (St John Brooks, who was still running the Book List, now also looked after the book reviews in the main paper, which were more numerous than they had been in the twenties.)

However, Richmond would often write personally to his friends. Two other surviving letters to Chapman must have been typical. In one he explains 'I'm sorry about Boz. I would have sent it: but before I had made up my mind about anything John Bailey floated in, demanding a book to read on his way to Cumberland – So off it went with him.'

In the other he apologises for cutting a review: 'I'm sorry: I don't know how it was that everything in this office seems to have stood still for all Saturday & Sunday – & so your proof was delayed. We had to do our surgery before your proof came back. I hope we weren't very bungle-handed. I return your proof of the full article. We could reclaim the MS if you prefer?' These letters are, I can avow, typical of the letters written by all literary editors.

The deputy editor, D.L. Murray, only came in on Mondays and Tuesdays, mainly to read the page proofs. These had to be cleared by 1 o'clock on Tuesday. He was a tall, heavily-built man, who perspired freely and was always wiping his glasses. In fact he had been rejected for military service because his glasses steamed up. He wrote his reviews at home, and we have seen many examples of what an excellent reviewer he was, always fresh and vivid in expression, and with a great range of interests. We shall see more. He had been at school at Harrow, then won a Brackenbury history scholarship to Balliol, where he took a first in Greats and in 1912 was John Locke Scholar. His first book, which he published that year, was a short study of *Pragmatism*.

In 1930 he was forty-two years old, and had just turned his hand to writing novels. This was why he liked to spend as much time as possible at home in Brighton. His wife, Leonora Eyles, who occasionally contributed light pieces to the *Lit Supp* in the summer holiday season and reflections on women's topics at other times, was writing her novels in the same house. She was also an agony aunt on various Sunday newspapers. As the decade went on she became a more important reviewer. Murray's own novels were mostly well-written period romances, and in Brighton he kept on his carpet an army of toy soldiers, with which he would reconstruct battles that came into his plots. The first, *The Bride Adorned*, which was set in Papal Rome in the nineteenth century, was published in 1929. His most successful book was to come in 1936 – a novel called *Regency*, which followed the fates of four generations of women from the Regency onwards, the first being a mistress of the Prince Regent.

He was therefore not often to be seen in the office. But his presence was felt when he was, for his laughter was as ebullient as his stomach was pronounced. His social world was quite different from the editor's. He was a great friend of the theatre critic, Maurice Willson Disher (or 'Dish') of the *Daily Mail*, and of W. Macqueen Pope (or 'Popey'), who was well-known as an impresario and an entertaining historian of the drama. On Mondays the three of them would go to lunch together or, in the evening, would go to a music hall. Murray liked to tell the story of his first visit to Disher's flat in Doughty Street. In the corner there was a huge assegai spear. 'Dish, why that asseg . . . ?' 'It's for tickling turbulent tarts.'

In 1930 there was one other new member of the staff, who was destined to play a role that none of them – not even he – could have anticipated then. This was Arthur Crook, who had joined *The Times* at the age of fourteen in 1926 as a messenger, and would eventually become editor of the *Times Literary Supplement*. His father was a linotype mechanic on the paper. When he was ten, Arthur Crook had won a scholarship to Holloway County School, but his career there had come to a premature end because of financial difficulties at home. However, he went on studying at night school and reading voraciously. He quickly became known for his speed in delivering messages round London and for the correctness of his spelling, and in 1928 he was taken as a clerk into the Intelligence Department – which is nowadays called the reference library – by its head, John Sidney Maywood. Maywood himself had started on the paper in 1903 as Moberly Bell's office boy.

Crook's self-education continued rapidly in the ID, and after a further two years, Maywood, who liked him, arranged for him to go as a clerk to the *Lit Supp*. Besides wishing to help Crook, he may also have wanted an ally there to help retrieve the review copies, which were supposed at that time to be returned by reviewers, and were then put in the library or sold to staff.

So at the age of eighteen Crook arrived on the third floor of Printing House Square, to sit among the shelves of new books and to tie them up in parcels. Over thirty years later I saw him come out of the editor's office and sit down beside another office boy who was tying up parcels – remarking to him without either show or false modesty, 'I used to do this, so I'll show you how it should be done.'

In 1932 one other notable change occurred. Along with *The Times*, the *Lit Supp* changed its typeface. On 29 September, the *Lit Supp* announced the change in a full-page notice and an article (unsigned as always) by Harold Child. The notice declared that the new typeface was 'specially designed for easy reading . . . with the approval of the most eminent medical opinion . . . In response to the need, under modern conditions, of relieving the eye of all possible strain, a new standard of clearness and legibility will be set up.'

It was indeed a new type, which would be known as the Times New Roman. In the article, Child explained that *The Times* was 'again veering' to what was known as 'old face'. This was a type based on the 'Roman' pen strokes of the Italian humanists, and cut for Aldus, the great Venetian printer of the fifteenth and sixteenth centuries. When *The Times* was founded on 1 January 1785, this was the type it was printed in, but fourteen years later it followed the then current trend and went over to a 'modern face', based not on the pen strokes of the calligrapher but on the fine hair strokes of the engraver's burin.

Now it was going back to a form of 'old face', but one freshly redesigned as suitable for a newspaper. The 'Gothic' title on the front page of *The Times* and of its supplements would also revert to Roman, and the whole paper, said Child, would return to its earlier dignity and beauty. And indeed the *Lit Supp* from October 6 did look much more elegant and was distinctly more legible, though the overall lay-out of its pages remained unchanged. The creator of this new typeface was the typographer Stanley Morison – who would of course become editor of the *Lit Supp*.

*   *   *

During the early thirties, the most remarkable feature of the *Lit Supp* was its long, front-page essays. It had carried these from the start and many have been mentioned, but now there was a particularly good group of writers contributing long pieces, some of them old regulars by now, some of them new discoveries. Many of these essays were on historical subjects, either political or literary. By contrast, the reviewing of new poetry and fiction was mainly in the hands of a regular set of capable but not particularly venturesome reviewers, and the new authors – only a few of whom, admittedly, were writing anything very memorable – were not dealt with especially generously.

Virginia Woolf was contributing less frequently now, but she wrote several brilliant, long essays. She was also getting favourable financial treatment now from the paper. Her fee was first calculated according to its length, like everybody else's – for these long pieces it was generally about £13 – and then, as a privilege exclusive to her, £15 was added to it.

One outstanding essay, published in 1931, was about Elizabeth Barrett Browning's novel-poem *Aurora Leigh*, the story of a Victorian girl with an English father and an Italian mother. It gives us, she wrote, a picture of 'people who are unmistakably Victorian, wrestling with the problems of their own time, all brightened, intensified and compacted by the fire of poetry'. Only novelists could write that kind of thing now, she concluded – 'We have no novel-poem of the age of George the Fifth.'

There was also an essay on 'Fanny Burney's Half-Sister', a wonderful portrait of Maria Allen, the adventurous girl who ran away to marry, on whom Fanny Burney based her heroine in her novel *Evelina*. 'If Fanny had seen more of Maria,' Virginia Woolf observed with a sigh, 'her later books might have been as amusing as her first.' And there was a splendid article in praise of Hazlitt's style in his essays: 'Sentence follows sentence with the healthy ring and chime of a blacksmith's hammer on the anvil; the words glow and the sparks fly, gently they fade and the essay is over.'

As for her own novel *The Waves*, which came out in October 1931, that went to McDowall, who gave it the same kind of praise, mixed with faint regret, that he had given her books before: in her characters 'we are aware of the flickering of that inmost flame of personality – call it spirit or ego – whose place is often vacant even in a novel of character . . . It seems a proof that the matter of fiction can be changed and distilled to a new transparency . . . Yet one feels that its spirits roam through empty places.' All the same, the book was a great success.

Leonard Woolf was not so fortunate. He became very despondent when *After the Deluge*, the first volume of his book on political psychology, got a short, rather dismissive review by Stannard in the *Lit Supp* in the same month.

T.S. Eliot contributed several more of his best essays to the *Lit Supp* in the early thirties, still writing mostly about Elizabethan and Jacobean dramatists – Richmond was sticking to his habits. Eliot subtly drew out, in two essays, the differing achievements of Thomas Heywood and Cyril Tourneur. He found a 'sympathetic delicacy' in Heywood's *A Woman Killed With Kindness*, yet he acknowledged that 'Heywood's is a drama of common life, not in the highest sense, tragedy at all; there is no supernatural music from behind the wings.' By contrast, in Tourneur's *Revenger's Tragedy* he found 'the death-motive, the loathing and horror of life itself' – but he added (perhaps with a defiant hint of his own aim in *The Waste Land*) that 'to have realised this motive so well is to triumph, for the hatred of life is an important phase – even, if you like, a mystical experience – in life itself'.

His *Selected Essays, 1917–1932* and his book *The Use of Poetry and The Use of Criticism* were reviewed, respectively, by a new *Lit Supp* contributor called Alex Glendinning and by Alan Clutton-Brock. Glendinning said that 'we find intelligence and sensibility in a rare combination' in Eliot's best prose writings, and declared that 'it is largely to him that modern poetry owes its release from the oppression of its immediate past'. Yet he did not convey much sense of pleasure in the essays, which had, he said, 'a dryness calculated to promote the utmost sobriety of mind in the reader'. Clutton-Brock also said that Eliot's criticism was 'dry and inconclusive', though he added that these were 'useful and attractive virtues . . . when much criticism is flighty or rhetorical'. Both reviewers felt that Eliot's accounts of individual poets were outstanding, but both were sceptical, in a rather grudging way, about the general ideas he was developing.

Edmund Blunden saw Eliot's *Ash Wednesday* sequence of poems in 1930 as 'pale flowers that spring from the soil of dejection'. Another new reviewer, George Buchanan, reviewing Eliot's religious verse drama *The Rock* in 1934, dwelt mainly on his technical skill – 'a command of novel and musical dramatic speech' – but threw in the melancholy comment that 'he takes a hard view of the Christian struggle'. At least Bruce Richmond showed no favouritism towards his friend in his choice of reviewers.

It took a now-forgotten devotional poet, W. Force Stead, reviewing Eliot's religious pamphlet 'Thoughts After Lambeth', to give him a wholly sympathetic ear:

In *The Waste Land* he expressed the last word of a bankrupt scepticism; in *For Lancelot Andrewes* he acknowledged his acceptance of the long accumulation of the world's wisdom (and its otherworldly experience) which has gone into the making of the Christian religion. He could not rest in the first, and he seemed perhaps not entirely at home in the second; but this pamphlet shows his philosophy and religion in their maturity; he knows why he is a Christian, and why he is an Anglican.

Meanwhile John Hayward, the wheelchair-bound friend of Eliot's with whom he shared a house between his two marriages, felt able to say, in a review of Baudelaire's *Intimate Journals* translated by the twenty-six-year-old Christopher Isherwood, 'that the value of this translation exists solely in the interesting introduction that Mr Eliot has written for it'.

G.M. Trevelyan wrote a long piece about Macaulay's *History of England* in October 1931, when it came out in the *World's Classics* with a copious historical commentary by T.F. Henderson. Trevelyan applauded the fact that the reader could now 'travel safely through the pages of this great classical history without danger of being seriously misinformed by the text on any important point', but he also sprang to the defence of his great-uncle and namesake ('G.M.' stood for 'George Macaulay') on a number of points. He did the same thing when Winston Churchill's book on his own ancestor Marlborough was published. Trevelyan said in a letter to the paper that he had no complaints about the review (which was by General Edmonds, the author of many reviews of books on the First World War), and he acknowledged that Marlborough was a far better man than Macaulay had portrayed him, but he resented Churchill's calling Macaulay a 'liar'. This letter was reprinted in the third volume of Trevelyan's *England Under Queen Anne*, which was published in 1934 and reviewed by Cyril Falls, who wrote that it 'carries along the unlearned with the learned' and 'revives our confidence in English historical writing'.

In April 1934, Trevelyan also reviewed E.M. Forster's book on Goldsworthy Lowes Dickinson, the 'sympathetic, humorous, yet always deeply serious' Cambridge don whom Forster loved and revered, and who had helped to create the League of Nations. Trevelyan wrote of how Dickinson suffered because of the war, 'and continued to suffer after the War when Versailles went wrong and the world went back to its vomit . . . He passed away peacefully before the Hitler revolution came to fulfil his worst fears, and to destroy the last of the Germany of Goethe that he had dreamed of in his youth.' These remarks reflect vividly the change in tone in the paper's attitude to Germany that would take place soon after Hitler assumed power.

E.M. Forster contributed his one, solitary review to the *Lit Supp* on 10 November 1932 – unsigned, just like everybody else's. He wrote about the two-volume edition of Jane Austen's letters that had been collected and edited by Richmond's friend R.W. Chapman. Richmond must have been pleased to get Forster to do it, both for the paper's sake and for the sake of his friendship with Chapman.

Forster wrote a brilliant piece, witty, tart and tender at the same time, in his usual way. He distinguished between two characters, Jane Austen and Miss Austen. Jane Austen was the author of the 'six great novels'. Miss Austen was the author of the letters, which 'belong to another part of her mind . . . Triviality, varied by touches of ill breeding and of sententiousness, characterises these letters as a whole.' He stated this surprising case frankly – and found that in only one letter, a letter to her niece Anna about a novel she has written, do we see 'Miss Austen and Jane Austen for a moment as one person'.

Bonamy Dobree went on writing long, elegant pieces, notably one on Dryden that faced up to the fact of his shifting and apparently opportunistic political attachments, unlike the 'aesthetic' review we saw in 1914. However, Dobree defended Dryden, on interesting grounds: for Dryden, he said, 'politics were good enough matter for a brilliant satire, but in the main he wanted to be left alone to think about literature'. In politics 'there was no certainty, so one had better adhere to what was established'. On that basis Dryden could go from Cromwell to the King, and then stay with the Jacobites – it was 'too much trouble' after that not to be a Jacobite. Dobree argued a very good case, if not quite a convincing one.

Two young Fellows of All Souls were also snapped up for long essays by Richmond at the beginning of the thirties. In 1934, A.L. Rowse, the historian from a working-class family, was thirty-one and John Sparrow, the Winchester and New College barrister whose interests were more literary than legal, was twenty-eight. Much later, they were to be rivals for the wardenship of All Souls, Sparrow winning. Among several leaders that Sparrow wrote at this time was an excellent piece in January 1934 on the seventeenth-century diarist, John Evelyn. He contrasted Evelyn with the vivacious and vigorous Pepys: 'A strange indeterminateness, an almost unholy moderation, ruled Evelyn in small things as well as large. He loved without passion and he disapproved without disgust.' And Sparrow picked out a sinister example of this. Evelyn watched a man being tortured in Paris and 'was not able to stay the sight of another'. Nevertheless, Sparrow comments, 'he stayed out the sufferings of the first malefactor, and recorded them accurately in his evening's diary'. Sparrow's interest in the grisly, which was very evident in later life, clearly began young.

In the same month, Rowse contributed an essay on a subject he would continue to write about throughout his long life: his native county of Cornwall. Here he was reviewing a book on *Cornwall in the Great Civil War and Interregnum, 1642–1660*, by Mary Coate. He evoked the contrast between 'the changes at the centre' and 'the unvarying life of the countryside', saying that it was only the coming of the railways that had changed Cornwall – 'as Cavour said of Italy, the railways "would stitch the boot together in time"'.

D.H. Lawrence died on 2 March 1930. The *Lit Supp* did not devote a special number to him, as the *Adelphi* did, but John Middleton Murry was allowed to write about him now. On 13 March, he put his personal thoughts down 'in haste', as he said, and since they were written in the first person they were by-lined 'From a correspondent'. One imagines that everyone in the world of letters, and many outside, could tell who the correspondent was.

Murry said that Lawrence was the 'most remarkable and loveable man I have known. Contact with him was immediate, intimate and rich. A radiance of warm life streamed from him.' Also 'by a natural magic he unsealed the eyes of those in his company: birds, beasts and flowers became new-minted as in Paradise'. Murry said also that 'his gloom was a massive darkness in which his intimates were engulfed', and that 'in his later years he was induced to think men perverse and wicked when they were merely dull, and he grew exasperated with them'. But the article dwelt mainly on Lawrence's attractive qualities.

It was all the odder that when his book on Lawrence, *Son of Woman*, came out a year later it hardly mentioned these at all. McDowall reviewed the book, and remarked on the paradox. 'This study', he said 'practically excludes the vivid, sensitive, everyday humanity which by the consent of those who knew him made him loveable.' These obviously included Murry. The book was, rather, a compassionate picture of a 'suffering man of destiny' – and a man of destiny who had failed: 'As a leader, with gifts to impel men's minds, Mr Murry holds that he failed, bewildered and betrayed them.' McDowall himself acknowledged that, in Lawrence's books, 'one often feels that he has taken a false road'. But he reminded *Lit Supp* readers of 'the joy in life and expression which Lawrence must also have had, since it shaped itself continually into vitality and beauty'.

In September 1932, McDowall reviewed the letters of Lawrence, which had been edited by Aldous Huxley. In a long article, he analysed the strengths and weaknesses of both the man and the writer – in particular, he did not like 'the drone of the dark gods' in the later work – but he insisted, as we have seen him doing in many reviews during Lawrence's lifetime, on his greatness as an artist. Some of his work would burn away, but not the core, which was 'the relation of his own passionate experience, and his rare perceptiveness of life'. Of all the major writers of the war years and afterwards, it must be said that Lawrence was best served by the *Lit Supp*.

The posthumous works also got thoughtful and appreciative reviews. When *Lady Chatterley's Lover* came out in an expurgated edition in February 1932, Orlo Williams, while regarding the 'shamelessness' of some of the scenes and language as an imperfection, felt that they were necessary to 'the contrast that Lawrence was concerned to draw between the warm fruitfulness of a sexual union in which nothing of feeling or emotion is held back on either side and the cold, selfish unions between men and women that breed bitterness and death in the soul'. He observed that 'like the Ancient Mariner, Lawrence cannot be eluded'. Of Lawrence's *Last Poems*, McDowall said in October 1932: 'In the poems where he faces death there is the essential man, with his confidence touched to a new calmness.' Reviewing the stories in *The Lovely Lady* on 19 January 1933, McDowall was still praising 'the humorous perception of people and things'. But the review of *The Lovely Lady* was posthumous too – for McDowall, Lawrence's loyal champion, had died the day before it was printed, at the age of fifty-five.

Aldous Huxley's *Brave New World* – his great anti-Utopia – was published in February 1932. Orlo Williams, reviewing it, picked on the fact that in this imaginary civilisation birth took place in a bottle. 'Mr Huxley's ingenuity in this kind of fun is extraordinary,' he wrote. A reluctance ran through the whole review to recognise any value, or even any possible prescience, in Huxley's kind of extravagant and sombre satire. It was as though Williams, just like the Clutton-Brocks, father and son, could not see the positive in a negative – every good book had to deliver, in the end, an upbeat note.

There was a feeling of a similar kind in Mavrogordato's reviews of Evelyn Waugh. He said that in *Black Mischief*, in 1932, the African empire that Waugh had imagined offered 'an indefinite number of incongruous combinations for Mr Waugh's inexhaustible and neatly-phrased malice', but he considered it 'an extravaganza written largely about, and presumably for, the bright young people – their elders may find it insubstantial for its length'. Of *A Handful of Dust*, that brilliant, bleak comedy of 1934, he felt that 'whether Mr Waugh's study of futility is worth doing – and doing at such length – is a matter of opinion'. His unstated opinion was clear enough.

Graham Greene, as before, was doing better, even if he was not singled out as particularly remarkable. Perhaps as yet that was fair. J.D. Beresford, in 1930, said that *The Name of Action* was tense and vivid throughout. The following year, Alan Clutton-Brock found *Rumour at Nightfall*, set in 'the remote and exotic atmosphere' of Spain, 'a subtle and elaborate interweaving of brute facts and the reaction to them of tortuous and sensitive minds'. The same reviewer, in 1932, noted that *Stamboul Train* had a more popular flavour than the novels which had preceded it, and thought it 'cleverly done'. It was set on 'one of those trains which run so frequently through modern novels and films, presumably because they provide an ingenious method of cheating the unities' – there spoke the old classicist – but the characters were 'admirably fitted to amuse and interest us during the journey'.

Anthony Powell was making his debut in these years, and his first three novels were reviewed by Alex Glendinning, a young reviewer brought in by St John Brooks. In 1931, the wrapper of *Afternoon Men*, quoted by the reviewer, identified the field that twenty years later would become the principal subject of Powell's novel sequence, *A Dance to the Music of Time* – 'that cross-section of society which is chiefly known to the public through its artists and parties'. Here, Glendinning said, we see that world mainly through its conversation, and Powell 'reproduces the inconsequence and trivialities of its talk with ironic precision . . . and very amusingly . . . but it becomes tiresome after 200 pages'.

Powell could not get it quite right for Glendinning. When *Venusberg* came out the following year, Glendinning wrote that this time 'he builds his background more solidly' – but 'it is perhaps too solid and carefully described a setting for light comedy'. Of *A View to a Death* in 1933 he said that 'humour is still Mr Powell's strongest asset', but that he was 'shy of going very deeply into his characters'.

Waugh, Greene and Powell were the writers who were going to win the palms during the Second World War and immediately afterwards

– along with George Orwell. Orwell's *Down and Out in Paris and London* was reviewed by the *Lit Supp* in January 1933. It went to Murray's wife, Leonora Eyles. One fears that the thinking in the office was that it seemed to be about kitchens, so it had better go to a woman. But she gave it a good review. She observed of Orwell's experiences in the rear parts of Paris restaurants and on the road with English tramps that 'real life can be as surprising as the most fantastic novel'. The book was 'a vivid picture of an apparently mad world, where unfortunate men are preyed on by parasites, both insect and human, where a straight line of demarcation is drawn above which no man can hope to rise once he has fallen below its level'.

Orlo Williams came under fire for his review of Arnold Bennett's novel about a luxury hotel, *Imperial Palace*, on 9 October 1930. Williams imagined the author talking to himself before writing it: 'Well, if So-and-So is attracting the public with interminable novels at 10s 6d each, I can do the same with one arm tied behind me.' Bennett was really angry. In a letter to Thomas Bodkin on 16 October, he wrote 'My many critics say that in writing a *big* novel I am imitating Priestley and following a new fashion. Good God! As if the excellent Priestley were not imitating me in this matter. I got the *TLS* to apologise for their unlawful suggestion that my object in doing *Imperial Palace* was to share in Priestley's booty.' But the *Lit Supp* reviewers of both the old and the new generation had never taken Bennett very seriously. He died the following year, aged only sixty-four, of typhoid he had caught in France.

Charles Morgan's *The Fountain* was highly praised in 1932: this was the sort of book Orlo Williams really liked, with its 'quiet beauty of form', its 'story of passion' and its 'meditations on the problems of the contemplative life'. Williams also gave a good review that year to the first book of a man who was to become an excellent novelist, Joyce Cary. *Aissa Saved*, set in Nigeria, was 'the fruit of a humorous disillusionment on the subject of the white man's success in improving the morals of the black'. Robert Graves's novel of Ancient Rome, *I, Claudius*, was described as 'enthralling reading' by R.W. Moore in 1934. Moore, a classicist, and headmaster in turn of Sherborne and Harrow schools – another very Richmond-ish man – said that it was 'imaginatively unfolded' but also the work of a 'painstaking historian'. Glendinning saw the merit in Samuel Beckett's *More Pricks Than Kicks* the same year: an 'odd book', he thought, but a 'definite, fresh talent at work in it'.

*　　*　　*

As for the American novelists, Richmond found one of his pundits –
J. Kettlewell, a bullfighting expert – to review Hemingway's *Death in
the Afternoon*. Kettlewell declared that 'praise can scarcely be too high
for Mr Hemingway's exposition of the technique of the corrida or his
description of the three-act tragedy that is the bullfight. His prose style
is irritating, his supercharged "he-manishness" is brutal and infuriating,
but his description of the various *suertes* is extremely felicitous.' At the
same time, Kettlewell reviewed a book called *Taurine Provence* by the
poet Roy Campbell, and blamed him for using the word 'toreador' for
a bullfighter. The word, said Kettlewell, meant an amateur, mounted
bullfighter in the seventeenth century, and did not now exist in Spanish.
This led to an animated correspondence, with some writers insisting
that the word was still used, and Campbell himself declaring 'I use the
word consciously and revel in it from the great song in *Carmen*.' The
irrepressible Kettlewell replied that 'I have had the pleasure of knowing
bullfighters, noblemen, bootblacks and waiters, and have literally never
heard the word "toreador", except as a jest thrown at me as an Englishman.'

F. Scott Fitzgerald's *Tender is the Night* received a review from the
critic Geoffrey West much as it might have got from Orlo Williams,
Alan Clutton-Brock or Alex Glendinning. Eight years after his previous
book, he wrote, this new novel 'still displays the mood of disillusion',
as though this fact automatically disqualified it from being a good novel.
'The very title is ominous,' he continued. ' "Tender is the night . . . but
here there is no light", and the narrative is a panorama of wasted or
shattered lives' among wealthy Americans in Europe. The one thing
that inclined him to regard the novel seriously was the 'real tenderness'
in the relationship between the novel's chief character, the psychiatrist
Dick Driver, and his wife and patient, Nicole.

William Faulkner did no better at the hands of Orlo Williams when
he reviewed *Soldiers' Pay* in 1930 and *The Sound and the Fury* in 1931.
Both books had introductions by another Chatto & Windus novelist,
Richard Hughes, and Williams acknowledged the skill in the writing
that Hughes drew attention to. But, in the first novel, it was a 'crude
and fleshy scene' that Faulkner presented in Charlestown, Georgia,
where the characters 'pursue or flee one another in a farandole of desire
or repulsion'. 'Sweat, with sex and death and damnation' overburdened
the story to Williams's mind. As for *The Sound and the Fury*, 'for those
who feel an attraction in the portrayal of pathological delinquency or
find some really tragic effect in the negation of all the fine and kind
elements in young minds no doubt the horrors of this picture will seem

poetical; to others, however, they will appear to be of a kind to which no skill can add any compensating merit'. Gentility still had a strong hold in the Richmond inner circle.

The Scots poet Edwin Muir and his wife Willa were introducing Kafka to the British through their translations in the thirties. *The Castle* (already reviewed, as we have seen, when it appeared in German) was praised in a baffled but submissive way by Charques in 1930: this 'allegory . . . is elusive at times in its spiritual implications, but not more so than is proper in a sceptical or agnostic age'. He praised the Muirs with a firmer note: 'Kafka's prose style, light and flowing and serpentine, is extraordinarily well reproduced by the translators.'

The same year, Charques reviewed the translation of Thomas Mann's *Mario and the Magician*. He gave a good account of this novella, in which a travelling entertainer exercises his hypnotic powers on the people in an Italian village, and these powers seem to swell up and take on the aspect of a greater evil – but Charques missed the palpable Fascist atmosphere in the background. In 1931, Richmond's regular Foreign Office reviewer of German novels in the original, A.W.G. (later Sir Alec) Randall, picked up the Austrian writer Robert Musil's *Der Mann ohne Eigenschaften* (or 'Man Without Qualities'), which the *Lit Supp* would take a special interest in when Alan Pryce-Jones was editor. Randall said that this novel of the last years of the Hapsburg monarchy was 'a brilliant sceptical commentary on and a destructive critical analysis of the philosophy and the mental and social and political prejudices which brought Europe to disaster'.

Madame Duclaux, reviewing some new French novels in 1934, included a short paragraph on André Malraux's *La Condition humaine*, which had just won the Prix Goncourt and was to become one of the most renowned novels of the thirties. She saw it as a specimen of one of the many books now current that were inspired by 'a wish to make the world over anew and form it better, a revolt from formalism, concussion, hypocrisy, the vices of a world in its dotage'. Without saying anything about its plot or its setting in Shanghai, she found an image for it. Like Malraux's other books, with 'their philosophic temper and their chronicle of appalling activities', it reminded her of 'some pure wind-swept sky, divinely blue, dominating a scene of nauseous dustheaps and blackened factory chimneys belching malodorous fumes'.

*   *   *

203

This was very much the image people were getting of the work by the new English poets of the thirties. W.H. Auden, Stephen Spender, C. Day Lewis, Louis MacNeice – all were being mentioned regularly now in the *Lit Supp*. At first they were criticised for sophistication and obscurity – for instance, a brief review by Fausset in the Book List of *Oxford Poetry 1929*, edited by MacNeice and Spender, spoke of 'the brittle play of words' in many of the poems, while in his review of Auden's volume *Poems* in 1931 he wrote 'Mr Auden invites us, so far as we understand him, to discover, amid the horrors and humiliations of a war-stricken world, the "neutralising" peace of indifference. But . . . instead of communicating an experience of value to us, [he] merely sets our minds a problem in allusions to solve.' Reviewing *The Orators* the following year, the younger Clutton-Brock was a little more sympathetic. He found Auden's 'frequent railings and persistent air of disgust' tiresome, but praised his verbal artistry: 'For a poet to be able to say, and say so persistently, "I belong to the post-War generation", without causing a shudder in every sensitive reader, is something of an achievement.' Negative praise, but praise.

By the time Stephen Spender's volume of *Poems* was reviewed, by George Buchanan, in July 1933, the political character of the new poetry was more in readers' minds. 'He intervenes in matters which his Georgian predecessors, happy in the meadows, left over to the politician. He extends love and pity towards the hungry, the unemployed and the oppressed in a fresh and silvery flow.' But this did not trouble Buchanan, for Spender was not obscure, and was likely 'to enter very graciously into the poetic history of our time'.

In 1934, reviewing *New Country*, Michael Roberts's anthology of new prose and poetry, Alex Glendinning noted that all the contributors supported the abolition of the class system, but they did not quite seem to be Marxists, although an article by Spender 'sought to justify the poet's function to the Communist with his distrust of "bourgeois art"'. As for the poems in the book, Glendinning thought that Day Lewis's contributions suffered, 'as poetry, from propagandist intentions', but that 'Mr Auden can afford more than most of his contemporaries to use his talent as he pleases. Even if one discounts the propagandist invective in which he is prolific, a satisfying body of poetry remains; a poetry responsive to the full complexity of the life around it, drawing its movement and images freely from the contemporary world.' This was the best that Auden had done yet in the *Lit Supp*.

Older poets were still doing better. When Wilfred Owen's poems, edited by Edmund Blunden, came out in 1931, he was reviewed again by Basil de Selincourt, whose earlier, rather snobbish sneers now gave way to admiration, if in the language of fifteen years before: Owen's hope was that his readers should absorb 'the impact of modern war on the sensitive and chivalrous mind of modern youth', and that was his achievement. Blunden himself reviewed W.B. Yeats's new volume, *The Winding Stair*, in 1933, calling him a man 'who, with lovely romantic tales, pleased many in his early youth, but who entirely shed that first success, and has earned the right in age to be applauded a second time by the discerning'. Alex Glendinning, reviewing Robert Frost's *Collected Poems* in 1931, quoted the lines

> *On snow and sand and turf, I see*
> *Where Love has left a printed trace*

and commented that 'It is his ability to see that "printed trace" of love on the world about him that gives Mr Frost's subdued utterance an inward warmth and radiance that are rare enough in poetry today.' That was the heartfelt voice of the poetry critics of the *Lit Supp* in the early thirties. They were not ready for what was coming at them.

Meanwhile, in Cambridge, a new school of critics had been emerging. Quiller-Couch, as the Professor of English, had proved as swashbuckling in that occupation as he was in everything else he did. He set up the Final Honours School in English there in 1917, and did everything he could to encourage the students to respond to the books they read and form thoughtful critical judgments about them.

Three remarkable critics grew up under his wing: I.A. Richards, F.R. Leavis and William Empson. They all in their different ways preached the close study of the words that the writer had used, especially in poetry, and they all shared a view of literature as the supreme agent of moral, emotional and intellectual health. They were also all greatly influenced by the poetry and criticism of T.S. Eliot. This was the new seriousness with a bite.

In his *Practical Criticism* in 1929, I.A. Richards gave the results of an experiment he had carried out with Cambridge dons and students, in which they were asked to give their opinions or comment on unsigned poems by both great and minor poets. He demonstrated clearly how badly they read, lazy, full of preconceptions and stock responses they had learned from their teachers, insensitive to the poems' rhythms, and generally preferring the worst specimens.

The *Lit Supp*, though later it was to become the target of Leavis's venom, gave all these new critics' early books a fair welcome. In his review of *Practical Criticism*, Geoffrey West praised Richards's 'beautifully lucid display of the obstacles to understanding', and the way in which he took, 'as his ideal measure of value, the perfect mind rising above disorder and frustration of impulses'. In 1930, Middleton Murry took on another book that was to become famous, Empson's *Seven Types of Ambiguity*. He expressed admiration for this 'exceedingly able young man' – Empson was twenty-four, and had just lost his fellowship at Magdalene for having contraceptives in his room – and was sympathetic to his view that 'the reasons that make a line of verse likely to give pleasure are like the reasons for everything else; one can reason about them'. He also admitted Empson's main point – that 'ambiguity, in the wide and generous sense in which Mr Empson uses the word, is almost essential to poetry'. But he had reservations. With Mr Empson, he said, 'reasons are as plentiful as blackberries', and he questioned how much we gain 'by submitting the admitted ambiguity of poetry to this rigorous analysis'. The danger was that in the 'incontinent' pursuit of so many possible meanings, the ones relevant to the poem as a whole could be obscured.

1932 was the *annus mirabilis* for the third member of the group, F.R. Leavis, and for his wife Q.D. or Queenie, whose work came out of a house in Cambridge they called 'The Criticastery'. F.R.'s *New Bearings in English Poetry* and Q.D.'s *Fiction and the Reading Public* were both published in April, and were reviewed by the *Lit Supp* in successive weeks.

Alex Glendinning said that the argument in F.R.'s book was stripped of everything that was not relevant to it, and 'gains clarity and force from such severity'. He correctly picked out Leavis's main point as the way in which a new poet must reject earlier ideas of the 'essentially poetical' if he is not to be barred from 'his most valuable material, the material that is most significant to sensitive and adequate minds in his own day', and he reported on Leavis's account of how Yeats, Eliot, Pound and Hopkins had each in his own way found access to that 'material'. Glendinning's expression of approval, however, lay more in his sympathetic exposition than in any explicit taking-up of a position.

The following week a new reviewer, Simon Nowell-Smith – a second cousin of Bruce Richmond's who in 1934 would join the *Lit Supp* staff – discussed Q.D.'s book. He greatly admired her 'anthropological' investigation into the history of popular taste and the nature of the contemporary reading public – it was a 'masterly marshalling of evidence', he declared. But he felt she was being too pessimistic when she claimed that it was only the 'conscious and directed effort' of 'an armed and conscious minority' that could break through the 'untutored emotional responses' of a typist with 'a dead life' (like Eliot's typist in *The Waste Land*), and get her to read Conrad rather than Ethel M. Dell. That, nevertheless, was to remain the Leavises' firm conviction in the embattled years to come.

Scholarship rampaged in the correspondence columns, on topics ranging from the pronunciation of Pepys ('Peeps' said the family tradition, 'Pepiz' – said others – was how it was originally written and pronounced) to errors in Tolstoy translations. American and Dominion scholars were more and more prominent – on 17 December 1931, for example, letters from the University of Chicago, Cornell University and the University of Pretoria dominated the page. Reviewing F.N. Robinson's outstanding edition of Chaucer from Houghton Mifflin in 1934, A.W. Pollard commented that in the last thirty years much more work had been done on Chaucer in the United States than in England.

Quiller-Couch sailed in with a letter far removed from the preoccupations of his analytical young Cambridge protégés, arguing that the Lucy of the Wordsworth poems was closely based on his sister Dorothy: every line suited her, apart from the 'poetical assumption of her death and her lover's grief'. A row broke out over why Shakespeare made Falstaff march his ragged army to Bridgewater via Shrewsbury rather than on the straight road through Stratford. Shakespeare knew that that road was too muddy for an army, 'even in his dreams', said one correspondent; Shakespeare did not know that the Stratford road existed at all, said another, less convincingly.

George G. Loane of Woodthorpe complained that the *New English Dictionary* – the original name of the *Oxford English Dictionary*, completed in 1928 – gave inadequate definitions of many words found in Thomas Hardy's poems. He gleefully pointed out, for example, that the NED's definition of 'mothy' – 'infested by moths' – would not do for Hardy's 'mothy curfew-tide', in which the word carried 'no notion of hostility'.

Graham Greene was tempted to send a scholarly letter to the paper in 1931. At the time he was living in a cottage in Gloucestershire writing a book on the seventeenth-century poet the Earl of Rochester, and on 16 April there appeared a letter from him in which he contested the 'legend' that Rochester had had a quarrel with the poet Thomas Otway over an actress, Mrs Barry.

But a much more dramatic correspondence than any of these burst out in 1934. Thomas J. Wise was a well-known book collector and a friend of Edmund Gosse, with whose splendid library Wise's was often compared. He had several times written to the *Lit Supp* drawing attention to the existence of forged publications. But there now appeared a book by John Carter and Graham Pollard called *An Enquiry into the Nature of Certain Nineteenth Century Pamphlets*. This proved that between forty and fifty pamphlets that had in recent years fetched high prices in salerooms were forgeries, and that all of them could be traced back to Wise.

On 12 July Wise wrote a long letter to the paper to 'explain my position with regard to the pamphlets of which the authenticity is challenged'. He claimed that he had got all those pamphlets which had passed through his hands from the collector Henry Buxton Forman, as 'swops' or in lieu of various debts Forman owed to Wise. Wise had sold these through a bookseller called Herbert Gorfin, and 'needless to say' all parties had acted in good faith.

Unfortunately, the following week Gorfin himself wrote to say that though he had regularly sold pamphlets on commission for Wise, the name of H. Buxton Forman had never been mentioned to him as the source of them until 14 October 1933 – two days after Graham Pollard had visited Wise and informed him about the discovery of the forgeries. 'Mr Wise had previously given me a totally different account of their origin,' Gorfin concluded. John Hayward also had a letter in this issue, complaining about the vagueness of Wise's letter, and pointing out that Messrs Carter and Pollard had shown that all the forged pamphlets were probably the work of one man. 'Are we now to understand,' he asked, 'that this individual planted them out in a number of likely and authoritative hands, in order that they might find their way back to those collectors for whom they were originally intended?'

No answer was forthcoming from Wise, and on 23 August there appeared a letter from Lord Esher, saying that 'book collectors throughout the world are still waiting to hear from Mr Wise an explanation of the forgeries . . . Those of us who have bought the forged pamphlets for large sums of money cannot consent to leave the matter where it is . . . Mr Wise played a great part in the distribution of the forged pamphlets, and therefore must be more anxious than any of us to pursue the inquiry.'

Still there was no answer from Wise. It was the most eloquent letter that the *Literary Supplement* never received. Wise was already a sick man, and died three years later. It was subsequently proved beyond

George Earle Buckle, editor of *The Times* when the *Lit Supp* began in 1902 and one of Northcliffe's infamous 'three monks'.

Charles Moberly Bell, manager of *The Times* and another of the 'three monks'.

James Thursfield, first editor of the *Lit Supp*.

Bruce Richmond, editor of
the *Lit Supp* 1903–37.

Portrait of Bruce Richmond
by Frances A. de B. Fottner,
presented to him on his
retirement. It now hangs in
the editor's office.

D. L. Murray, editor of the *Lit Supp* 1938–45, seen here with his stepdaughter.

Stanley Morison, creator of the Times Roman typeface and editor of the *Lit Supp* 1945–47: he had a laugh 'like the bursting of a paper bag'.

Alan Pryce-Jones, editor of the *Lit Supp* 1948–58.

Arthur Crook at the time of his appointment as editor of the *Lit Supp* in 1959.

John Gross, editor of the *TLS* 1974–81.

Jeremy Treglown, editor of the *TLS* 1982–90.

Lord Northcliffe (*right*), chief proprietor of *The Times*, 1908–22, with its editor, Henry Wickham Steed, in the United States in 1921.

Ferdinand Mount, political writer, novelist and editor of the *TLS* since 1991.

John Jacob Astor (*centre*), chief proprietor of *The Times*, with Geoffrey Dawson (*second from left*) dining in the air raid shelter beneath Printing House Square, 1944.

Rupert Murdoch, chief proprietor of *The Times* since 1981, announcing the move to Wapping in 1986.

Reginald Nicholson, manager of *The Times*, who saved the *Lit Supp* in 1914.

Colonel Campbell Stuart, manager of *The Times*, who saved the *Lit Supp* in 1922. (Painting by Alexander Christie.)

Denis Hamilton, editor-in-chief of Times Newspapers Ltd during the Thomson regime.

Printing House Square, the original home of *The Times*. (Drawing by Sydney Jones, 1931.)

doubt that he was the forger of the pamphlets – though Bruce Richmond apparently took a lot of convincing. Wise is described in the *Dictionary of National Biography* as 'book-collector, bibliographer, editor and forger'. John Carter went on to become in due course the trusted bibliographical adviser to the *Lit Supp*.

Other aspects of English life in the early thirties were reflected in the reviews of three books of travel and autobiography that are still being read seventy years later. Mavrogordato teased Peter Fleming about his book *Brazilian Adventure*: it was 'the story of a great adventure by a gifted writer who knows that it was a great adventure' – and as 'great adventures are not done by Old Etonians', which Fleming was, the author 'writhes under the inverted commas romance of it all' and 'fills it with a sense of parody'. J.C. Molony enjoyed *Hindoo Holiday*, J.R. Ackerley's account of his life as the private secretary to an Indian maharajah, written in 'the spirit of Alice wandering through Wonderland'. Walter de la Mare praised Herbert Read's memoir of his Yorkshire childhood, *The Innocent Eye*, which was 'suffused by a serene and wistful light'. De la Mare noted that the only music in Read's childhood came from a small music box and a horse trainer's fiddle, and commented that 'now, no doubt, half a dozen wireless sets comb the circumambient air all day for Bach and jazz'.

Broadcasting was indeed a recurrent preoccupation in the paper, and in December 1933 George Buchanan wrote a front-page review of a number of books on the subject. He predicted that because of the influence of the 'bodiless voices' of the BBC, 'a Southern English manner of speaking may be expected to swallow up provincialism', and though this might be a blow at the picturesque, it 'may not seem an unendurable disaster' because of the increase in mutual intelligibility it would bring. As we now know, his prediction came true only for a short while, if at all. A corrected edition of the *Oxford English Dictionary* (by now so entitled) with a supplement in the same year led the journalist E.D. Osborn to comment on recent additions to the language, including one word whose unintelligibility had been a benign characteristic. He noted that 'tank', meaning a 'moving fortress', was first used in December 1915 – and that 'the authorities approved of the name because, if it leaked out, the enemy would not be provided with anything approaching a description'.

Domestic politics, as hitherto, received little attention in the paper, though there were periodical swipes at socialist theorists – especially at

G.D.H. Cole, who with his wife Margaret was a very influential figure in these years. Hartley Withers, an economics correspondent on *The Times*, reviewing Cole's *Economic Tracts* for *The Times* in 1932, claimed that Cole's proposals were not very precise: 'He tells us that the Socialist ideal is essentially an idea of sociality, which is rather like the Archdeacon who defined himself as one who performed archidiaconal functions.'

There was less ambiguity now in reviewers' minds about what was going on in the Soviet Union. In May 1931, old Dr Shadwell, writing about the Russian Five-Year Plan, spoke of the paralysing effect of the GPU's Terror, the suppression of all freedom, the tragic life of the workers and the 'vice and crime with which Russia is reeling'. A couple of months later, the diplomat and journalist, W.H. Hindle, reviewed a sycophantic book about Stalin written by four leading Bolsheviks, and said that it was 'calculated to make any decent revolutionary sick'. Stalin, he said, was now like 'some monarch of Eastern fable', only known to the people by his rare appearances on Red Square. Bechhofer Roberts was equally withering about Trotsky when he reviewed his *History of the Russian Revolution*: Trotsky claimed all the credit for the triumph of the revolution, but was unreliable about everything he said.

Two English visitors to Russia also got short shrift. Julian Huxley's *A Scientist Among the Soviets* was reviewed by Hindle, who did not like the way in which Huxley admitted the Terror only by implication, and then traced its origins to Allied intervention in Russia at the end of the First World War, and to 'capitalist enmity': Huxley, he said, was 'too ready to praise and trust'. As for the young Malcolm Muggeridge's *Winter in Moscow*, labelled by his publisher 'The Truth At Last', Shadwell declared that Muggeridge 'writes in such an odd way that it is not easy to make out what the truth is': the author seemed to regard 'the whole thing as a fantastic show, equally monstrous and ridiculous' – which, it might be added, was Muggeridge's view of the world for the rest of his life.

Italy was a very different matter. Stannard was mainly in the saddle here, and Mussolini's success with the Italian people continued to impress him. In February 1931, he observed that 'no one who knows contemporary Italy can doubt that the Fascist regime, with its bold attack on modern problems on the one hand and its historical appeal to the traditions of the Roman Empire and the Roman papacy on the other, can and does command a high degree of intellectual enthusiasm'. A year later, in a review of Cicely Hamilton's *Modern Italy*, the Italian expert Cecil Headlam wrote, his tone very much in accord with Stannard's, that 'Signor Mussolini's regime has endured for twice the length of time which he postulated as necessary for rendering it effective and permanent', and observed that 'the most casual onlooker is instantly aware that the Fascist regime has wrought miracles . . . mendicancy has been checked; the tipping system has been regulated; Rome is being rebuilt; the railway system has become as punctual and orderly as any in Europe' (is this where the famous cliché 'Mussolini made the trains run on time' began?). However, Headlam conceded that 'social, political and industrial opposition has been eliminated, and unity is maintained by an intensive culture of patriotic endeavour'.

The *Lit Supp*'s best-known article expressing sympathy for the Italian Fascist regime was Stannard's long review of the new *Enciclopedia Italiana* in the 'Recent Italian Literature' section of 21 June 1934. He acknowledged that Fascism 'repudiates Democracy, because it scouts the notion that principles of government can be determined by counting heads', and that its attitude towards liberalism was one of 'unqualified opposition alike in politics and in economics'. The Fascist conception was that 'development of the individual and of the State must needs go together'. But he had no doubt that 'the lover of Italy is aware of a coherent vitality in the country, whereas fifteen years back he was all too conscious of the abundant but conflicting energies of groups'.

Stannard praised the educational system with its aim of 'making every child realise that he was a member of a great society', and he challengingly described the Opera Nazionale Balilla, the outside-school organisation which had 'peopled Italy with black-shirted children', as 'the first thoroughgoing attempt yet made to democratise the social ideas which underlie the English public school system'. Turning to Mussolini's latest speeches, he rather startlingly compared the way in which 'words are hurled into the place in which they will tell' to 'the effect which so often comes in Hardy's poetry'. It was, all told, a pretty clean bill of health that Stannard offered Mussolini here.

Germany was treated differently again. In March 1931, there was an article by the travel writer Malcolm Letts on 'Unfamiliar Germany' addressed to holiday-makers, praising the small towns of Lower Saxony with their timber houses – 'Nothing, it seems, can stop the building of beautiful houses.' Later in the month, reviewing a rather sombre book on Germany by a German, Eugen Diesel, who grieved that his country was 'wandering in the valley of transition', Shadwell urged: 'Let him be of good cheer. Germany will come through by virtue of those spiritual qualities on which he lays stress.'

But the following March Stannard was seriously considering the argument of another German, Richard von Kuhlmann, that the Germans might be tempted to 'pursue the will-o'-the-wisp of a dictatorship', and from now on the rise of Hitler was closely monitored, in reviews of both English and German books, in the paper. By August 1932, Stannard was drawing attention to the fact that the most important tenet in Hitler's programme was its anti-Semitism, which had already prompted 'amazing examples of extravagances of thought and language'. In March 1933, by which time Hitler had become Chancellor, J.H. Freeman gave sympathetic notice to a book called *Germany Puts the Clock Back*, by Edgar Mowrer, the Berlin correspondent of the *Chicago Daily News*, in which the Nazi doctrine was described as 'a pudding of half-baked eugenics and unbaked economics', and its followers as those Germans who were 'hungry for the return of lost power and prestige'. Freeman was a foreign subeditor on *The Times* who, partly through his reviewing for the *Lit Supp*, would soon become an important leader writer on foreign affairs.

In June of that year, Stannard was again drawing attention to anti-Semitic excesses in Germany, though he was also giving serious consideration to the idea put forward in W.H. Dawson's *Germany Under the Treaty* that there could perhaps evolve 'a union of the British, German and Scandinavian peoples to which the United States might eventually adhere'.

In September 1933, Freeman quoted powerfully from *The Brown Book of the Hitler Terror*, prepared by the World Committee for the Victims of German Fascism, which reported 'over 500 murders carried out by the Nazis since February 3 (the eve of the Nazi electoral triumph), among them 43 Jews shot or beaten to death by the Storm Troopers'. This book also recorded thirty-one contradictions in the official statements made about the fire at the Reichstag in March 1933 – the mysterious event which had led to the Nazis' election victory, after they had claimed it was intended to be the beginning of a Communist reign of terror. (In an article the following year, Stannard described it vividly as 'the great blaze which startled the world and drove a horrified Germany to vote swastika'.) In October, an abridged version of Hitler's political testament *Mein Kampf* was published in English as *My Struggle*, and once again Stannard emphasised 'the fundamental position of anti-Semitism in Herr Hitler's system'.

By 1934 a further aspect of 'Herr Hitler's system' was beginning to loom larger – his threat to peace in Europe. In November of that year, Freeman was reviewing a book edited by Dorothy Woodman (the wife of Kingsley Martin, the editor of the *New Statesman*), called *Hitler Rearms*. Freeman concluded that, if there were no international control of rearmament in Europe, 'the last and worst excesses of the Nazi Reich have, it may be feared, yet to be'.

Against this disturbing background, the *Lit Supp* was itself accumulating troubles. 1930 had proved to be the high point of the paper's circulation. In that year it reached 30,063. Since then it had steadily gone down, and in 1934 the paper sold only an average of 23,945 copies a week. Advertising revenue had also gone down from £30,287 in 1930 to £19,765 in 1934, and profit from £10,962 to a mere £247.

On 27 October 1934, Bruce Richmond sent a long letter to Geoffrey Dawson. 'Dear Editor,' he said, 'May I put before you one or two reflections about the *Literary Supplement*: the position of which, I understand, is now causing considerable anxiety owing to loss of advertisement revenue and loss of circulation – the former, I hope, temporary: the latter, I am afraid, permanent.' He explained why he thought the advertising had gone down, and why he hoped it might come back again. One kind of advertising, of which the *Lit Supp* had practically had the monopoly, had ceased to exist. 'Since the general slump the expensive illustrated book, the edition de luxe, the publisher's speculative complete edition (the Edinburgh Stevenson, etc) has come to an end.' The proof was that for many years the paper had published at Christmas a long article on 'Illustrated Books' and another on 'Finely Printed Books'. For the last two years they had been compressed into one article, and this year both would disappear for lack of material. But 'if the business world recovers in time and such books begin again, there is no reason why we should not recover the advertising as before'.

Secondly, the advertising they had lost had gone to the Sunday papers. However – and here we hear the Richmond voice ring out very clearly – 'their present system of splash advertising is very distasteful to the better publishers, three of whom have told me they only do it "not to be left out": and I think in a year or so a good few of them will tire of it'.

However, the circulation was, he said, a much more difficult matter – 'and the difficulty arises from the fundamental fallacy underlying our existence. The *Supplement* was called into existence to relieve *The Times* itself of difficulties with which *The Times* is no longer confronted.' But nowadays *The Times* could devote as much space as it wanted to books:

The result on the *Supplement* is that, for readers of *The Times*, it is now largely a double instead of a *Supplement* . . . Of recent years many things that the *Supplement* used to have to itself are doubled in the paper: our big centenary leaders used to be rather a feature of the *Supplement*, but no-one wants to read a long leader on Scott, or Lamb or Erasmus or Anselm, immediately after reading as good a one in the paper; then books of travel and generally the lighter 'lending library book' began to be taken into the paper: then (and obviously rightly) novels were taken in, with the result that (except in the rare instance of a novel that is published on a Thursday) the whole of our page of 'New Novels' is for a *Times* reader already stale.

Consequently, Richmond said, the *Lit Supp* had now largely lost 'what for brevity I may call the feminine public – books for the drawing room, lending library books, the book of the moment . . . Even among my own relations I know three households that have given it up.' And with what could it 'supplement' the reading of the reader of the daily paper? – 'theology, scholarship, a few foreign books, some interesting correspondence, and a long list of books which are not considered worth extended notice . . . The position then seems to boil down to this: are there enough people, interested in books but not readers of *The Times*, to keep the *Supplement* going?'

That seemed a fair statement of the case as it was. But how could the lost circulation be recovered? Richmond acknowledged that he did not know how many readers were needed – 'I have never known anything about the finances of the *Supplement*'. But he did not believe 'that ' "new features" (pictures, crosswords, a serial story, special numbers etc) would really have any permanent effect.' What he suggested – 'if the general character and way the *L.S.* is run are to remain roughly the same as before' – was some 'careful judicious pushing'. And he asked if it would be possible 'to delegate the business management of the *Supplement* for a year jointly to Freeman and Bishop'. Patrick Bishop, who was the assistant manager of *The Times*, had 'all the figures at his fingers' ends'. G.S. Freeman – not the Freeman whom we have seen writing on European politics, but a much older *Times* man – had

known the *Supplement* from almost the start – all Northcliffe's edicts and Prior's stunts as to changes of type & heading were done through him – the biggest change of all, from 3 cols a page to 4, was his suggestion to N. – and . . . N. looked on Freeman as the one member of the editorial side who had an atom of business sense . . . I feel that if circulation is to be picked up here and there, a man who has read the *L.S.* from the start and knows the sort of person it appeals to would be invaluable.

Richmond had already written to Geoffrey Dawson quite recently suggesting that he might retire in January 1936, though at that time, he said now, he did not know 'there was a crisis'. But he now asked Dawson to look at that earlier letter again,

and (on the analogy of Spooner's 'Wherever in this lecture I have said Saint Paul please read Alexander the Great') wherever I have said Jan 1936 please read Jan 1935. Salutary changes will be much better started by the excellent team at your disposal than by one who is firmly embedded in a thirty year old groove. Forgive verbosity.
Yrs Bruce L.R.

This offer to resign almost immediately was not accepted, and in fact Richmond stayed on as editor until December 1937. He made one more gesture before the year was out: on 31 December 1934 he wrote a short, melancholy letter to Lints Smith saying 'In view of the condition to which I have brought the *Supplement,* I hope you will consider the question of a reduction of my salary for the coming year.' Lints Smith replied equally tersely on New Year's Day: 'While appreciating the thought which prompts your suggestion, I would be unworthy of my trust if I adopted it. The *Literary Supplement* stands as a great memorial to you, and whatever temporary set-back we are experiencing is entirely due to adverse conditions which we hope will improve this year. With every good wish for 1935.'

So Richmond still had the *Times* establishment behind him. Nevertheless, it was decided that the paper should be lightened and made more popular and easy to read. Richmond acquiesced – but we shall see in due course that, embedded in a thirty-year-old groove though he may have been, he was correct in thinking that such measures would not improve the circulation.

Barrington-Ward had become deputy editor of *The Times* in 1934, and it was he who took the initiative in looking into ways in which the *Lit Supp* might be changed. He took Richmond out to lunch, and assured him that he did not want sweeping changes in the contents – the *Lit Supp* was 'still unique in the world among literary reviews, the only one almost with a true standing in literature'. But he took advice from an old Balliol friend with some contemporary reputation as novelist and reviewer, Denis Mackail, who suggested the use of pictures and the removal of the long lead article from the front page, and from Stanley Morison, who was a very close friend, and besides being typographical adviser to *The Times* had also just finished writing the first volume of its history.

In the event, the main changes that were made were in the layout, under Morison's guidance. There was a polite struggle with Richmond over Morison's wish to abolish the vertical rules between the columns, but Morison won, with the discreet mediation of the new member of the *Lit Supp* staff, Simon Nowell-Smith. The first issue of the paper in its new form came out on 2 November 1935 – a Saturday, for with its new look it had also acquired a new publication day.

The front page went back to three columns, with an advertisement in the first column, and the opening paragraphs of the lead review (which survived) in the next two. Above the advertisement there was a short list of other subjects in the week's issue, while the masthead ran across the two columns above the article. The article itself now had both a title and a subtitle. It gave a very spacious, inviting feel to the page.

Inside, there were still four columns to the page, but these too had plenty of air around them, with many articles now given a title and a subtitle running across two columns, like the lead article. It made the books seem important. The main novel reviews appeared, also well spaced out, under the heading 'The Week's Novels'. The old Book List was now called 'Other New Books' and no longer included the publishing details of the books reviewed in the rest of the paper. The contents list was moved to the back page. And the first tentative use of pictures began, with three small woodcuts on different pages in this issue. Later, fine woodcuts were specially commissioned from artists such as Gwen Raverat.

There was no essential change as yet in the actual contents, though the layout (and the pictures) meant that slightly fewer books were reviewed. However there is a touching letter in the archives from a German, Dr Kurt Fiedler, who lived in Berlin. Since 1930 he had been sending lists of new German books to the *Lit Supp*, and arranging for publishers to despatch review copies of them, but on 21 January 1935, Lints Smith wrote to him to say that the paper had to end its agreement with him, not because of any dissatisfaction with his services, but because 'we are not likely in future to devote very much space to reviews of German works'. This was not because of the international situation, but because there was a plan, subsequently put into operation, to drop the regular weekly column of reviews of foreign books, and just have a quarterly foreign books supplement.

Fiedler wrote back in February saying he hoped the connection could later be resumed, adding: 'Please note that I did not send books only for the monthly cheque you sent me, but for our mutual co-operation. For the time being I cannot quite face the position, that still fewer books should be reviewed.' He concluded: 'If really it is only the financial point of view, please let me know, and I shall of course go on sending you books, without getting any money for it. Please give my regards to Dr Richmond.' A loyal servant of the paper! – and Richmond must have been abashed. Ironically, this change was one that he himself had decided on even before he knew there was 'a crisis'.

One other change of form took place in 1935, though there was no acknowledgement of it in the *Lit Supp*. Bruce Richmond became Sir Bruce Richmond, Kt. We have already seen Virginia Woolf jesting about this event.

The last three years of Richmond's editorship, 1935 to 1937, were marked by various notable occasions. One was the publication of the first volume of *The History of The Times* in January 1935. Its subtitle was *'The Thunderer' in the Making, 1785–1841* and it was described as 'Written, Printed and Published at the Office of *The Times*, 15s.' It appeared anonymously, but in fact had been written by Stanley Morison with the help of many members of *The Times* staff past and present.

J.L. Garvin, the former editor of the *Observer* and a famous thunderer himself, now sixty-seven, was invited to write a signed review of it, which appeared on the front page on 3 January. He praised the founding family, the Walters, but above all he praised the editor after 1819, Barnes, 'the Jupiter of journalism'. Barnes, he said, was for long the Great Unknown of English life and politics, but now, in this new history, 'it is as though an almost living and speaking statue, muffled for a century by some strange decree, were suddenly unveiled . . . The candour, grip and glow of this volume reveal the real life behind the anonymity through the creative decades, and replace the vague pomposities of mid-Victorian homage by an epic of flesh and blood.' Morison must have been pleased by this review, and certainly deserved it. From now onwards he was to becoming an increasingly important *éminence grise* at Printing House Square.

In May 1935 came the silver jubilee of King George V, and to mark the event Philip Tomlinson, a 'Special Writer' on *The Times*, who was to become an important member of the *Lit Supp* staff in 1939, wrote a retrospective essay on the writers of his reign. He could not find any one uniting characteristic of the literature of these twenty-five years – in fact he said that poetry had been 'a battlefield', and that 'a synthesis defies us' – but he asserted that among the novelists 'there was never a period so prolific in output and so abundant in talent, if lacking an outstanding figure'.

It was only eight months later, on 20 January 1936, that the King died. He received more notice in the paper than Edward VII had had on his death, since on 25 January Edmund Blunden contributed a black-boxed poem called 'Elegy' on the front page – but it is an unmemorable piece:

> *An honest King's the noblest work of God –*
> *Now passes one whom all the world termed so.*

Kipling had died two days before the King, and was hailed by Cyril Falls in the same issue as 'a flower of national art in verse and prose', but he too said nothing very new.

The coincidence that Queen Victoria was crowned in 1837 and King George VI in 1937 gave the paper a pretext for having a special issue on 1 May called 'A Century of English Letters', with various surveys of the subject. These included one on the novel from Dickens to Virginia Woolf, in which Orlo Williams notably groaned that by now 'no place, no region of the soul, no murky tract of the subconscious, is safe from the wandering English novelist', and a thorough account by Harold Child of the rich history of Shakespeare scholarship and criticism, in which he properly said that 'the capital achievement of these 100 years is nothing less than a revolution in the knowledge of the text', while in the appreciation of Shakespeare 'sentimentalism has been strangled'.

There was also an American anniversary to celebrate: the tercentenary of Harvard University in 1936. On 26 September, H.W. Horwill wrote a front-page piece on two books about Harvard by Samuel Eliot Morison, who had been Harmsworth Professor of American History at Oxford and was now back 'at his Alma Mater'. Horwill evoked Harvard's early days, with its American Indian students, and hailed the way in which, at the end of the nineteenth century, President Charles William Eliot 'transformed a respectable university into a great one'.

*   *   *

There were glinting reflections in many reviews of the changing aspects of British life. D.L. Murray and his wife Leonora Eyles were both very good on this subject. In April 1936 Mrs Murray reviewed *The Good New Days* by Marjorie and C.H.B. Quennell, and found many things to be glad of in the thirties England they portrayed. In the English village, the old sweet smells of farmyard and bakery might now be drowned in petrol fumes, but in new housing schemes you could see houses 'planned with a view to dignified life, with a pleasant carriage road shaded with trees', and in schools where there were once 'desks so built that only by a miracle was curvature of the spine avoided', you could find 'babies of two or three sleeping in brightly coloured cots, eating at horseshoe tables or romping with a nurse in a clearing'. The previous year, in the same down-to-earth style, when reviewing the latest volume of the *New Survey of London Life and Labour*, she had regretted that there were 'not enough places in London where courtship can be carried on with dignity and safety, and without psychological injury to young lovers through the innuendoes and jokes and interference of their elders'.

Her husband in the same year reviewed John Summerson's book on the architect John Nash, deploring the desecration of Regent Street, that 'Via Triumphalis' celebrating Trafalgar and Waterloo, but glad that in parts of the capital 'there remain the majesty and serenity of those shining panoramas that mounted so swiftly upon the venerable and sooty confusion of the older London'. And he seemed close in feeling to his wife when, reviewing G.K. Chesterton's *Autobiography* in 1936 he confessed that he thought *The Napoleon of Notting Hill* the best of Chesterton's 'fables', especially when it champions 'the beauties of urban construction, the area railings and the chimney pot, glimpsed at

> *some romantic moment when*
> *The wind round the old street corner*
> *Swung sudden and quick as a cab.*

One scholarly letter was in its own way very evocative of the English countryside. Some time earlier there had been a spate of letters debating whether the word 'nook-shotten' meant 'cast into a corner' or 'running out into many corners'. A correspondent wrote to say that he had found a field in Warwickshire called 'Nook-Shotten Close' – and it had nine corners. So he was convinced that the second of these meanings was the correct one.

* * *

In 1937 Bertrand Russell and his wife Patricia brought out *The Amberley Papers*, letters and diaries of his parents Lord and Lady Amberley. They were reviewed by Lord Ponsonby, the courtier who had become a Labour MP, who gave a very vivid picture of these two controversial aristocrats, he a Russell, she a Stanley, who both died young. They took up causes such as women's suffrage and birth control, much to the disapproval of many members of their own milieu. The Duchess of Cambridge said to Kate Amberley: 'I hear you only like dirty people and Americans. All London is full of it; all the Clubs are talking of it. I must look at your petticoats to see if they are dirty.' Ponsonby said that 'as a story of the thwarting by fate of an ideal association of two noble lives, few records of real life can equal it'.

In 1935 the first public edition of T.E. Lawrence's *Seven Pillars of Wisdom* appeared, and Philip Tomlinson welcomed it as a great and extraordinary book, 'with its packed pages of battles and raids, waterless deserts, strange peoples, the antics of rulers and ruled, prophets and robber chiefs, cruelties, sufferings and brief joys'. And he unhesitatingly called Lawrence a hero – not the 'hunter of notoriety' that many people had dismissed him as.

A very different kind of man was still steadily haunting the pages of the *Lit Supp*, John Middleton Murry. Murry had always tried to squeeze out some relevance to himself from every fresh artist and thinker he encountered, and by now he had become, he claimed, a 'Communist', though one whose Communism, he assured his readers, owed as much to Blake, Jesus, Shakespeare and Keats as to Marx.

In February 1935 Geoffrey West reviewed *Between Two Worlds*, Murry's account of his life up to the end of the First World War, which was also the time when his wife Katherine Mansfield's illness was pronounced incurable. West said that the book must take a high place for its unsparing truthfulness, with its self-portrait of the author's negativity, passivity and even self-immolation in those years.

Murry had also claimed that soon after Katherine Mansfield's death in 1923 he experienced an intense, mystical illumination of mind and spirit – which, whatever it was, West said, had led to some very lively writing by him in the twenties and early thirties, such as his book on D.H. Lawrence. But West wondered if his recent 'religious Communist' phase did not reveal in him a return to that tendency to self-immolation, with its call for the 'final liquidation of the ego'.

The following February Harold Child reviewed Murry's book, *Shakespeare*. Child said it was 'rich in ideas and observation which will help the plain man to see more of the beauty and meaning of the plays', but he saw it mainly as 'a gateway into the region where Mr Murry's mind is most at home' – and he echoed West in seeing that region as one where the intellect and emotions are united in a supreme spiritual experience which can only be achieved by 'self-abeyance' and self-surrender. Murry in fact believed that Shakespeare had achieved that state, and that it was reflected in the closing scenes of *The Tempest*, where Prospero lays down his wand.

By 1937, Murry's thoughts had turned to pacifism as the only policy that offered any hope for the kind of pure socialism he dreamed of, and his book *The Necessity of Pacifism* was reviewed by Stannard in August. Stannard quoted Murry's words: 'In defending democracy by war we shall lose it for ever; in defending Christianity by war we shall annihilate it; in seeking socialism by war we shall achieve barbarism instead.' But he did not see any practical future for Murry's ideas, and suggested that by setting up, as he had already done, a kind of monastic farm community, Murry showed that he had really despaired of his peaceful revolution, and was simply hoping to become another St Benedict, 'preserving the relics of civilisation from the barbarism about it'.

At any event, readers of the *Lit Supp* still had plenty of opportunities to watch Murry's thoughts ranging widely through literature to politics to religion – though of course, as most of his contributions were anonymous like everybody else's, they would not have known it unless they could identify the manner and the distinctive opinions.

In January 1935 Murry was approving of Maud Bodkin's attempts, in her *Archetypal Patterns in Poetry*, to find significant underlying patterns of imagery in Shakespeare and other poets, but in April he was deploring I.A. Richards's 'lamentably abstruse' ideas and his tendency to score 'minor logical victories' over poets in his book *Coleridge on Imagination*. A smaller matter was troubling him in April 1937, when he objected in a letter to the spellings 'ecsta*c*y' and 'idiosyncra*c*y', saying that the words should be spelt with an 's'. In June 1937, reviewing *Illusion and Reality* by the Marxist critic Christopher Caudwell, who months earlier had died fighting in Spain for the Republicans at the age of twenty-eight, he was expressing his admiration for the fine minds of Caudwell's generation to whom the theory of Communism had come with the force and fervour of a religious revelation – the 'Shelleys *de nos jours*', he called them, with Marx as their William Godwin. But Murry did not quite go along with them. It was pacifism which by now had taken command of his allegiance.

*　　*　　*

221

Virginia Woolf had lost her dashing cavalier, McDowall, and her new novel *The Years*, in March 1937, went to one of the troopers, Orlo Williams, still a House of Commons clerk, and also a member of a merry literary coterie, including Stanley Morison and John Carter, who lunched together in the Garrick Club and tossed publishing talk around. Williams noted that she had 'constructed a more elaborate framework than usual' for this book, but complained that she had not filled it out with much in the way of dramatic events. However, he caught the tone of the book quite well: 'To her keen sensibility the illuminating moments of life are discontinuous, and the questions that they ask are never answered. Do the hints of refrains – say, the cooing of pigeons or the fall of rose petals – mean that there is a song? . . . When is anything true – then, now or never?'

Virginia Woolf contributed one of her own best known essays to the paper in September of that year, 'The Captain's Death Bed', which became the title essay of one of her posthumous collections, edited by Leonard Woolf, in 1950. It was a study of the early nineteenth-century author of sea stories and children's stories, Captain Marryat, and she was still brooding in it on the nature of fiction, noticing how his pages are full of vivid characters – 'marked faces', she called them – such as Mrs Trotter 'who cadges eleven pairs of cotton stockings', but how also in this 'bright hardness' there is an absence of all the intenser emotions that novels need.

Williams concluded his review of *The Years* with the comment that 'it may perhaps be the conclusion of an epoch in fiction, to which a new age and a new epoch are now succeeding'. Certainly there was a new note in George Orwell's novels, which now loomed up on the scene. *Burmese Days*, in 1935, went to a former colonial officer, G.E. Warrey. He said that the book was symptomatic of the reaction against the conventional portrayal of Burma as just 'tinkling temple bells'. This book was 'steeped in gall', and offered a picture of the town Burmese as 'mainly pimps, professional witnesses and corrupt magistrates'. Here the gall was merited, he acknowledged, 'for these people exist'. But he said indignantly that Orwell entirely ignored the new type of Burmese official, men of high character, and that 'when he says, of their English superiors, that few of them work as hard or as intelligently as the postmaster in a provincial town, he shows he can hardly have mixed with the men who run the country'. The reviewer evidently felt that that was a very good put-down.

Leonora Eyles came to Orwell's rescue in her review of *A Clergyman's Daughter* in the same year, finding that the heroine's life both as a

rector's daughter and as a penniless tramp make 'interesting and exciting reading'. Another regular woman contributor, Elizabeth Sturch,
reviewed *Keep the Aspidistra Flying*, and declared that 'if this book is
persistently irritating, this is exactly what makes it worth reading: few
books have enough body in them to make them irritating'. It was a
depressing account, she wrote, of the hero's shabby-genteel origins and
descent into a more sordid world – but 'the more depressing his theme,
the more efficiently is his skill displayed'.

The Road to Wigan Pier, Orwell's non-fiction book of 1937, went
back to Leonora Eyles. She gave it a long and thoughtful review, the
best Orwell had yet had. She was appalled by the portrait it gave –
backed up by photographs – of 'the conditions under which 20 million
fellow countrymen and women are living today . . . six million of them
on unemployment pay and public assistance'. She picked out his remark
that there were houses in which overcrowding means that 'each human
being has less space for living than is afforded by a public lavatory'.
She did not explicitly go along with his view that 'socialism is the only
salvation', but she gave it a proper prominence, adding that he was
'furious when he thinks of the suffering of millions'. She noted also
that he was not narrow-minded, being also 'sincere in his pity for the
insecure wealthy classes and the harassed middle classes' but she
thought he was unfair to socialist cranks and vegetarians! – and it is
true that Orwell always seemed to hate 'socialist cranks' more than
anybody. This review was a good corrective to the more rosy picture
of Britain that she had sketched in her review of *The Good New Days*
the year before.

D.L. Murray and his wife were really now among the best regular
reviewers on the *Lit Supp*, and Murray wrote a very intelligent review
of Aldous Huxley's novel for 1936, *Eyeless in Gaza*, drawing out its
theme of ultimate deliverance 'by a species of renunciation based on
the study of the great mystics', but adding that 'whatever Mr Huxley
renounces it will not be his modernity', and instancing the form of his
novel, with its interleaving sections of narrative like a Neapolitan ice,
and his 'damning insight into shams'.

His wife in turn took pleasure in Christopher Isherwood's *Mr Norris
Changes Trains*, both in its 'finished, individual characters' and its picture of Berlin just before the age of the Third Reich – it conveyed
admirably 'the tenseness in people living in an atmosphere of financial
and political dissolution'. R.D. Charques reviewed Graham Greene's

England Made Me, finding the story of a charming young blackguard who makes tragic atonement for his sins written 'with power and a fine ironical sensibility', as well as taking an astringent flavour from the implicit criticism throughout of the 'old school tie' attitude to life. Alex Glendinning thought that Hemingway's *To Have and Have Not* was an absorbing and moving adventure story – his 'gift for communicating such emotions as the tough allow themselves has never been more conspicuous'. But Mavrogordato found little to like in Anthony Powell's *Agents and Patients*, in which he said Powell had adopted 'the brisk method of the film extravaganza' and consequently made it difficult to know what the book was about.

Reviewing Dorothy L. Sayers's *Gaudy Night* in 1935, Simon Nowell-Smith expressed his delight in the return of Lord Peter Wimsey, scholar, aristocrat and detective of genius, this time in a book that was much more than just a detective novel; while John Hayward reported in the same year that the publication of P.G. Wodehouse's *Blandings Castle* 'will relieve the anxiety of those who have had no news of Lord Emsworth and Mr Mulliner for two years'. But perhaps the most enthusiastic fiction review of all in this period – in fact, one of the most glowing fiction reviews the *Lit Supp* had ever published – was C.S. Lewis's review on 2 October 1937 of J.R.R. Tolkien's *The Hobbit*.

Lewis, at this time a thirty-nine-year-old English don at Magdalen, and a friend and colleague of the slightly older Anglo-Saxon scholar Tolkien – both of them lovers of mediaeval romance – wrote of this tale of a mythical land that its place was 'with *Alice* and *The Wind in the Willows*'. But it was a children's book 'only in the sense that the first of many readings can be undertaken in the nursery. It will be funniest to its younger readers; and only years later, at the tenth or the twentieth reading, will they begin to realise what deft scholarship and profound reflection have gone to make everything in it so ripe, so friendly, and in its own way so true. Prediction is dangerous; but *The Hobbit* may well prove a classic.' Prediction, in this case, came true.

The letters that Gerard Manley Hopkins wrote to Robert Bridges and to a Church of England friend and poet, Canon Dixon, were published in a fine edition in January 1935, and reviewed by a brilliant young Oxford don who was to become an authority on Coleridge (and edit some further papers of Hopkins), Humphry House. It was Bridges who had introduced Hopkins's poems to the world, but House brought out how much Bridges himself had learned from Hopkins's criticisms of his poems, as well as Hopkins's own love of the 'naked thew and sinew of the English language'. There was also a letter in the paper a couple of months later from L.C. Hopkins, the poet's brother, giving his date of birth, 28 July 1844, a fact that hitherto the world had not known.

In 1936, *More Poems* by A.E. Housman came out, a volume of poems selected by his brother Laurence Housman from unpublished manuscripts. John Sparrow reviewed them admiringly, acknowledging that most of them echoed the well-known poems in the two published volumes, but finding many of them excellent in their own right, with two or three sounding 'the note of passion deep, intimate, undisguised'. Sparrow hinted more plainly at Housman's homosexuality than would have been conceivable a few years earlier.

T.S. Eliot had a letter in the correspondence columns on 10 January 1935. The scholar Geoffrey Tillotson had suggested that the line 'Falls the shadow' in the poem 'The Hollow Men' came from Dowson's poem 'Cynara', and Eliot wrote to say that 'this derivation had not occurred to my mind, but I believe it to be correct, because the lines he quotes have always run in my head, and I regard Dowson as a poet whose technical innovations have been underestimated'. For the title 'The Hollow Men' itself, he added, he had combined William Morris's romance 'The Hollow Land' with Kipling's poem 'The Broken Men'. Eliot's verse play *Murder in the Cathedral* was reviewed in June of that year by George Buchanan, who yet again dwelt on its technical qualities, saying that Eliot had now brought to maturity his dramatic style, 'the chief merit of which lies in his writing for a chorus'.

In October 1936, Alan Clutton-Brock confessed himself alarmed by Eliot's attack on Milton in the volume *Essays and Studies XXI*, edited by Herbert Read, but allowed himself some patronising humour at the fact that Eliot cited a 'difficult passage' in Milton: 'It is amusing to imagine the author of *The Waste Land* wrestling with the meaning of *Paradise Lost*.' By now, though, Bruce Richmond was evidently regarding Eliot as a writer on religious rather than literary questions, and gave his *Essays Ancient and Modern* that year to a *Times* writer on religious affairs, Ivor Thomas. Thomas wrote a considered and appreciative review, finding the essays on Pascal and on Tennyson's *In Memoriam* in particular 'masterly pieces of criticism'. He summed up Eliot's current position: 'Royalism is not openly avowed, but liberalism is frankly denounced; Mr Eliot's style is still classical in its economy, and in his tastes he remains a "lover of beauty without extravagance"; and he is nothing if not Anglo-Catholic, a humble worshipper in the same fane as Hooker and Bramhall, Andrewes and Donne'.

The two plays that W.H. Auden wrote with Christopher Isherwood were reviewed by Buchanan, the first of them, *The Dog Beneath The Skin*, in July 1935, a month after his review of *Murder in the Cathedral*. He noted the ridicule of the Nazis approvingly, but thought that it was often 'riotous and unsubtle ridicule'. The second play, *The Ascent of F6*, a portrait of a thirties strong man, Michael Ransom, who was actually a very weak character, came out in the November of the following year. Buchanan said that the characters in the play were no longer cartoons, but he did not find that Ransom 'absorbs us or is memorable'. He applied a remark of the poet A.E. (George William Russell) to Auden: 'There's no age in his thought.' Auden did better with his collaboration in 1937 with Louis MacNeice, *Letters from Iceland*. This was reviewed by Barrington Gates, who was mainly a travel-book reviewer. He said that in Auden's contributions to the book 'he accepts the discipline of the Byronic stanza (less, it is true, one line) with fine and gleeful virtuosity and has some glorious adventures in rhythm'. Gates thought that MacNeice was 'a more morose rebel . . . his contributions stand beside Mr Auden's like desolate pools unmoved beside a volcano five times as eruptive'; nevertheless he quoted with approval MacNeice's thoughts about the current state of Europe:

> *Hatred of hatred, assertion of human values . . .*
> *Is now your only duty.*

The new poet of these years was Dylan Thomas, whose *18 Poems* in 1935 and *25 Poems* in 1936 were both reviewed by the regular poetry critic Fausset. Fausset was always looking for the spirit shining through matter, the transcendent vision glimpsed behind the mundane, rather than considering carefully what his poets were actually trying to convey through their choice and use of language, so his reviews were all rather similar in tone if different in judgment. He declared that *18 Poems* was as difficult to interpret as a foreign tongue; however 'that he is a poet is certainly proved by the symbolical quality of his language'. Of the second book he wrote that 'those who can only credit poetry with originality if it is also something of a puzzle will find much in this volume to gratify their taste'; however, 'his vivid sense of the correspondence between the forces informing the macrocosm and the microcosm result in some powerful as well as surprising imaginative audacities'. Not one of the most helpful of *Lit Supp* reviews.

F.R. Leavis's influential study of English poetry, *Revaluation*, came out in October 1936, and was reviewed by John Middleton Murry, who recognised that 'Dr Leavis was a critic of no common kind', that he was 'nothing if not discriminate', but that there was a lack of 'excitingness' in his very serious prose. He deduced that what Leavis looked for in poetry was a 'harmonious unity between intelligence and sensibility', and called on him to make his principles more explicit. All in all, he found *Revaluation* a 'wise and suggestive book'. Leavis still had nothing very much to complain of in the *Lit Supp*.

One other book of essays, published in March 1936, was E.M. Forster's *Abinger Harvest*. This got a very warm review from the young art critic, Peter Burra, who in all its eighty richly varied pieces, collected from over thirty years, found 'not a trace of weariness', but who was particularly impressed by Forster's attitude to the current world situation when, in Forster's words, 'existence as it threatens today' was 'a draggled mass of elderly people and barbed wire'. For Forster it was tempting to turn away to loved authors and the consolations of the past – but 'liberty must be defended'.

Liberty must be defended – but how far and by what means? This was a major preoccupation of the *Lit Supp* now, and there were many reviews of books on the general issues of liberalism and socialism, and the state of affairs in Russia, Germany, Italy and Spain.

H.A.L. Fisher's monumental *History of Europe* came out in 1935 and Stannard wrote a paean to the book and to liberalism: the book rang true 'with the authentic note of Liberalism, essentially human, and, when challenged in its essence, uncompromising in its humanism. Such is the spirit of the Liberal tradition which, being vital, endures; and such also is the spirit of European civilisation.' But he wondered if liberalism 'could have averted the age of unreason in which we live'.

A.L. Rowse, reviewing *The Rise of European Liberalism* by Professor H.J. Laski, the influential left-wing thinker at the London School of Economics, also spoke of the shaky state of liberalism in the world, and went some way along with Laski in agreeing that though liberalism had established many freedoms, it had failed to create economic freedom for the masses. Liberalism had also been far too optimistic in assuming that politics was concerned with essentially rational beings. Leadership and authority were in the ascendant in Europe – but Rowse hoped that 'when they have had their day . . . the principle of liberty and the appeal to reason will move to the fore again'. Donald McLachlan, a young leader writer on *The Times* who would eventually become editor in turn of the *Times Educational Supplement* and of the *Sunday Tele-*

graph, was more impatient with Laski's *The State in Theory and Practice*, saying that it just 'gilded the Communist pill'.

Stannard commended Leonard Woolf's book *Quack, Quack*, which was a strong attack on the 'primitive and savage' beliefs – the 'quackery' – that had risen up against reason and civilisation. Woolf's book culminated in a powerful denunciation of Il Duce and Hitler.

There was less about the Soviet Union in the paper at this time, though Bechhofer Roberts wrote a substantial essay in October 1935 on William Henry Chamberlin's *The Russian Revolution, 1917–1921*, defending the foreign intervention that 'did, in all probability, push the frontier of Bolshevism considerably further to the East' and 'prevented the creation of international problems beside which those of the Russian Revolution itself would have seemed of small importance'.

In this period, the historian and political commentator E.H. Carr also began to contribute to the *Lit Supp*. During the Second World War, he would have considerable influence in pushing both *The Times* and the *Lit Supp* into a more sympathetic attitude to Russia (and towards the Labour Party), but it is interesting that in July 1937 he was still denouncing Stalin, asking ironically 'how, except by some mystical process of revelation, are we to know that M. Stalin represents the will of the majority of the inhabitants of Soviet Russia?'

Stannard, in spite of his peroration on liberalism, still felt some attraction towards the Mussolini regime in early 1935, when in a review of Il Duce's speeches he wrote not only of his 'amazing power of grasping a crowd', but also of his 'overpowering sense of public responsibility'. By October 1936, after Italy's invasion of Abyssinia, Stannard was wavering, and gave a mainly sympathetic review to the book *Under the Axe of Fascism* by an exile and a 'man of passionate Liberalism', Professor Gaetano Salvemini. However, this book was mainly about the economic deterioration of Italy under Fascism. Narratives of the war published in Italy by the two commanders-in-chief in Abyssinia, Marshal Badoglio and Marshal de Bono, were reviewed by Sylvia Saunders in December 1936. She gave an impersonal account of the campaigns, but her feelings showed through when she wrote that Marshal Badoglio 'describes the air bombardment he ordered with a rather revolting relish' and that his campaign 'presents itself to the layman as the record of four great massacres'.

A curious sidelight on Italy came in a review on 7 November 1936 of Evelyn Waugh's *Waugh in Abyssinia*. Major L. Athill reviewed it, and was very severe with Waugh, whom he described as 'a most confirmed adherent of the Italian idea'. In Abyssinia after the Italian occupation Waugh was deeply impressed by General Graziani and found a 'contented populace'. He was also enthusiastic about the Italian plan for the Great Trunk Road – in it, he saw 'the promise of order, fertility and peace'. But Athill commented that 'some may say its foundations were laid in arrogance and dishonour'.

Anthony Gishford, a friend of Simon Nowell-Smith's, writing about Franz Borkenau's *The Spanish Cockpit* and *The War in Spain* by Ramon J. Sender in July 1937, remarked that 'the actualities of the Spanish war are still almost as though they belonged to another age'. He gave a sympathetic account of Sender's experiences when 'defending the Republic in the trenches' but noted from Borkenau's book that 'a repressive bureaucratic dictatorship controlled by the Comintern' had already been 'the price of Russian assistance when Madrid's fate hung in the balance'.

Germany was, however, the centre of attention in Europe. A letter on 14 March 1935 signed by, amongst others, Stanley Baldwin and Winston Churchill appealed for help for 'displaced scholars' from Germany, while on 18 July 1935, F.M. Powicke wrote from Oriel College about the difficulties a German Jew, Dr Raymond Klibansky, had been having, 'since the political events of 1933', in bringing out the comprehensive edition he and others had planned of the Latin writings of the greatest mediaeval mystic, Meister Eckhart. A book by Stefan Lorant in May of that year, *I Was Hitler's Prisoner*, had given a graphic account of the cruel treatment of Nazi prisoners including, besides the author, a soldier, a police chief, a bricklayer, a museum curator and a Catholic scholar, and Freeman had called it 'a piteous and searing record of senseless brutality and bestiality'.

But another concern, already noted in 1934, began to appear more insistently from 1935 onward. In August, General J.E. Edmonds, who was working on the official history of the Great War, reviewed the *Berlin Diaries* of an anonymous German general who was very contemptuous of Hitler, but who claimed that the generals and admirals had merely made use of him to obtain rearmament of Germany. Edmonds observed that there was an undercurrent of threats of war in the book, with vivid descriptions of Germany's wonderful new and powerful aeroplanes, her submarine cruiser and her 'green gas', though Edmonds himself did not think that Germany could embark on a major war for many years.

In July 1936, four months after Hitler's invasion of the demilitarised

Rhineland, Stannard, reviewing R.B. Mowat's *Europe in Crisis*, said that 'what alarms the world is not merely the efficiency of Germany's armament, but a doubt as to the purpose which has inspired it'. Was it purely defensive? he asked. In the same month he also reviewed four books under the significant heading 'Keeping Out Of War: Projects for Internationalists', including Aldous Huxley's *What Are You Going To Do About It?* with its proposal of a conference of 'the great monopolistic powers' at which they could settle their grievances and their claims.

In March 1937, the maverick General Wavell, who was to become one of the outstanding military commanders when war came, and who had already written several times for the paper, discussed *Europe in Arms* by the *Times* military correspondent Captain Basil Liddell Hart. The book urged the necessity 'in an armed and restless Europe' for rearmament in Britain too, and Wavell gave it a detailed and sympathetic review.

But by July Freeman was reviewing a book called *Britain Faces* by A.L. Kennedy, a *Times* leader writer, who suggested that if Germany were offered African colonies again as part of a larger settlement she might 'abate her present expansionist ambitions'. Freeman doubted whether she would. But a new phase of history, in which the word 'appeasement' would ring through the air, was clearly on its way.

It was time for Bruce Richmond to retire. After his rejected offer to resign during the troubled time at the end of 1934, he had written to Major Astor in April 1935, again suggesting, as he had already done to Geoffrey Dawson, that he should retire in January 1936, when he would be sixty-five years old. Again he was persuaded to stay, and in fact he retired formally on 31 December 1937, twelve days before his sixty-seventh birthday, receiving an annual pension of £1,000. He wrote to Major Astor to say 'Thank you for allowing me two extra years – and many other kindnesses during my very happy years as a member of your staff.'

It had been an extraordinary career, quiet and regular though the days may have been for years at a time. Single-handedly he had created a great literary organ. The good C.W. Brodribb wrote an article about him in *The Times House Journal* for January 1938, and said that all through his thirty-five years he had been an editor in the truest and fullest sense. 'He has always kept his contributors in order. He has never let them go unscrutinised to say exactly what they fancied; still less has he been in the habit of consigning whole departments of literature to a single reviewer . . . On the contrary, he has always been at pains to keep in readiness a posse of expert writers, some of whom might perhaps not be called on for a year or more; the right man for the right book has been his rule'. He had been 'a diligent reader of books for his own profit and for the sake of his public', and in the matter of English style, 'many and many a time his corrections and alterations have been of a kind which a less conscientious author would not have bothered about'. The *Supplement* could never be too good in its creator's eyes: 'something, it turned out, had fallen short of the ideal; on the other hand, when his colleagues were told that next week's number was going to be really tip-top, they knew that their confidence in the prophecy would not be belied'. Brodribb ended by wishing that 'long may Sir Bruce and Lady Richmond enjoy their new home near Salisbury; and long may *The Times*' – *The Times* itself, note, not just the *Lit Supp* – 'continue to be worthy of Sir Bruce's participation in it'.

It is worth going back for a glimpse of Richmond in Virginia Woolf's journals at almost the mid-point of his years on the paper, 1918 and 1919. In December 1918, a messenger had come to collect an article of hers which she had not quite finished, and sitting over the fire he remarked 'A Christmas number not at all to Mr Richmond's taste. Very unlike the supplement style.' 'Gift books?' she asked. 'Oh no, Mrs Woolf, it's for the advertisers.'

The following March the Richmonds were thinking of taking the Woolfs' house in Asheham for April and May, and Virginia's diaries record several meetings with them. They dined with the Woolfs, who had apparently not seen them for some time: 'Rather an event. But it went off peaceably enough,' she wrote on 15 March. 'I found him mellower & milder & less spruce than I expected, which pleased me in the admiring editor of my works.'

She made several comments on Elena Richmond, whom she had known before her marriage and to whom she as well as her brother Thoby had once been rather attracted, and these bring out very clearly the social and personal tone of Richmond's domestic life in his middle years.

> As for Elena, her distinction in black with a jade jewel is undeniable; her white hair too, on the top of a face coloured like almond blossom; & with all this stateliness & repose an air, if I mistake not, of melancholy, as of hopes not realised & acquiescence accepted instead of something warmer, which slightly touched me . . . He treats her rather as a large magnificent child. 'Oh, you'll like that,' he

remarked when I offered her a bull's eye, and she told me she had noticed a very nice sweetshop in the street. I fancy that Bruce is a kindly & very unambitious man, who has been quite pleased to spend his time in doing kindnesses to poverty-stricken young men & fitting the articles into the advertisements in the *Supplement*, which he says is not such an easy job as it looks.

On another day that month Virginia wrote in a less kindly way about Elena: 'I find her so slow in her mind, so accustomed I suppose to the position of an ornate and handsome ornament that she positively can't understand & scurries in her replies, as if she were a fat spaniel crossing a busy road. And her eyes are without depth.' But in April she visited Richmond in his office and gives a picture of him in more informal vein: 'a restless, vivacious little man, jumping onto a chair to see the traffic over the blind, & chivvying a piece of paper round the room with his feet.' This, one feels, was not a view of him that his staff often had.

He had stayed very much within his own world as editor of the *Lit Supp*. Twenty per cent of the contributors in his time, it has been calculated by Jeremy Treglown and Deborah McVea in their database of reviewers, were members of the *Athenaeum*. Janet Adam Smith told me of a remark Richmond had once made to her husband, Michael Roberts, when Roberts visited him to suggest he might like to see a book she had edited for private circulation, a collection of verse by her godfather W.P. Ker, Professor of Poetry at Oxford. Roberts did not intend to suggest that the *Lit Supp* should review the book, but Richmond looked at it and said, 'This would interest our people.' What struck Roberts was his use of 'our people' – a recognised, faithful band of *Lit Supp* readers and reviewers with whom he felt at ease.

Nevertheless, Richmond had made the most of his often very distinguished circle of friends and acquaintances, and was always on the lookout for brilliant up-and-coming members of it. He relied more than Brodribb had said on a comparatively small group of regular reviewers, but it is easy to forget the relentless pressure of new books coming in to a literary editor's office, and few literary editors have not found relief in regularly assigning some subjects or authors to the same reviewer. This was of course easier in an anonymous paper, where it did not matter if the same contributor wrote several articles in one issue.

Where Richmond was at his weakest was in his treatment of new serious fiction and new poetry. He reviewed it all faithfully, but one feels that he actually had little faith in the merits of most of it, especially after the First World War, and was happy to leave it to reviewers of unambitious mind and of tastes such as he had been brought up with, provided they were reliable in producing the copy and could turn a good phrase. Of course, he recognised the gifts of such writers as T.S. Eliot and Virginia Woolf, and made good use of them, but we have seen that he made no particular point of finding reviewers who would give Eliot's poetry a thoughtful hearing.

Even so, the paper had achieved a remarkable prominence in British life – reflected, for example, in a remark in George Orwell's *Road to Wigan Pier*, published in 1937:

> You and I and the editor of the *Times Lit. Supp.*, and Comrade X, author of *Marxism for Infants* – all of us really owe the comparative decency of our lives to poor drudges underground, blackened to the eyes, with their throats full of coal dust, driving their shovels forward with arms and belly muscles of steel.

Moreover, if we look ahead now to what Eliot wrote in the paper for Richmond's ninetieth birthday in January 1961, it is clear that Eliot held this man with 'a bird-like alertness of eye, body and mind' in sincere reverence. We shall come later to Eliot's remarks in this article on the benevolent discipline of anonymity, and how much he learned from it. He also said that he learned editorial standards from Bruce Richmond, and 'endeavoured to apply them in editing the *Criterion*'.

'I learnt from him,' he wrote

> that it is the business of an editor to know his contributors personally, to keep in touch with them and to make suggestions to them. I tried to form a nucleus of writers (some of them, indeed, recruited from the *Times Literary Supplement*, and introduced to me by Richmond) on whom I could depend, differing from each other in many things, but not in love of literature and seriousness of purpose. And I learnt from Richmond that I must read every word of what was to appear in print.

Eliot concluded: 'Bruce Richmond was a great editor: fortunate those critics who wrote for him.'

Chapter Nine

D.L. Murray Faces the Dictators: 1938–45

In the last issue of the paper in 1937, dated 25 December, D.L. Murray wrote a front-page lead about Charles Dickens's *Christmas Books*. As usual, it was an excellent piece, arguing that in these short books, for all their sugar plums and punch, the 'submerged Dickens' who hated his 'Podsnappian fetters' raised his head more than in his longer works, 'wherein he had more leisure to get cold feet and weave garments of propriety for his figures . . . which is why so many tremendously vital figures boil up in these novels, to disappear, leaving us, alas, barely acquainted with them'.

This well-observed comment on Dickens was to be a swansong for Murray as a reviewer, for on 1 January 1938 he became editor, and wrote very little for the paper any more, apart from occasional editorial comments. Others had been considered for the job. Hamish Miles, the literary editor at the publisher Cape, had actually joined the staff in 1937, with the idea he might be groomed for it, but he died of a brain tumour after four months. Edmund Segrave, the editor of the *Bookseller*, had also been invited to make an application. But Bruce Richmond plumped for Murray, and a committee consisting of Barrington-Ward, Stanley Morison (who was brought in as an adviser) and the advertisement manager offered it to him.

Murray did not really want the job. He was deeply absorbed in writing his novels, and, as we have seen, was happy with the arrangement by which, as deputy editor, he came in two days a week and justified his salary by writing reviews at home. Nor did he like Morison, who had made it clear he was going to propose further changes in the paper. In fact Murray privately called him 'Steiney' Morison after a notorious criminal of the time.

However, he accepted the editorship on condition that he would only have to come in for three days a week, and on 4 February 1938, Morison wrote to Barrington-Ward: 'This week Murray, Simon Nowell-Smith and the Advertisement man of the *Lit Supp* met in my room for what turned out to be a very important confab. Evidently Murray means business. I fancy he will make a literary & commercial success of the thing.'

As it happened, one of Murray's novels, *Commander of the Mists*, a story of Scotland in 1745, had just been published, and was reviewed in the paper on 8 January as the lead novel by Cyril Falls, who called it Murray's best novel yet. In future years, whenever Murray had a new novel out, he would go on holiday and in his absence the regular chief novel reviewer, R.D. Charques, would give it the top spot and pick it as the paper's recommended novel of the week.

Now, under Morison's eye, Murray got down to planning some further changes designed to make the paper lighter and more popular. They were introduced in the issue of 30 April, and constituted a major change in the paper's character and appearance. The front-page article was swept away, to be replaced by a number of short paragraphs called 'News and Notes', with a large picture above them. In this issue, the picture was Van Dyck's portrait of Wallenstein, taken from a book that was reviewed further on in the paper.

Inside, all the pages had large headings: 'World Affairs', 'Historical Biography', 'Travel and Adventure' and so on. As the paper went on, these were invented *ad hoc* and shuffled around as the contents required. The main novels appeared on a right-hand page headed 'Novels of the Week', and the first novel (as well as many of the others) was reviewed regularly from now onwards by the genial, half-Russian R.D. Charques. Other novel reviews appeared further on in the paper.

There was a panel of 'Recommended' books, listing the main titles reviewed in the issue under headings similar to those at the top of the pages: 'Criticism', 'Ballet'. There was also a separate panel of 'Recommended Fiction', with Charques's lead novel headed 'First Choice' (though often he did not like the book at all), and beneath it a selection of a few other novels or volumes of short stories that were reviewed in the issue.

The main article appeared on the left-hand page immediately after the Novels of the Week page. It came to be called the 'middle', and was an important spot in the paper for many years afterwards. Opposite on the right was a page containing the masthead at the top of the first column, with an index to the sections (though not to the individual books) beneath it, and beneath that a new feature: two short leaders on literary and publishing matters, which ran into the second column. After that came the letters, now with rather less space than before.

Short reviews of odd, uncategorizable books appeared at the bottom of any page. The Book List was now called 'Other New Publications', and the back page contained a full index of books reviewed and one or two bibliographical articles.

The overall result was, as was intended, that the paper had a much more popular, newsy, easy-to-read feel about it, with guidance to readers and titbits of information thrown in. The articles on important books were essentially of the same character as before – being mostly written in the first years of the change by the same people as before – though the loss of the long front-page article struck at the weightiness of the overall coverage. Much less space was given to scholarly letters, while popular novels received more space and prominence. There were also more pictures, sometimes of a topical character. For instance, in the second of the new-style issues, on 7 May, following Lady Ottoline Morrell's death, there was a reproduction of a watercolour *Conversation Piece* by Rex Whistler in which she appeared with Lord David Cecil and others.

The leaders were the best innovation. They ranged over every kind of literary topic from the state of poetry to the quality of book production, and after war broke out the following year they gave, as we shall see, an especially strong flavour to the paper. They were often written by in-house people such as C.W. Brodribb, Alan Clutton-Brock and Harold Child, but sometimes if they referred to a book that was being reviewed, they were written by the reviewer himself, who could expand on the subject of the book in a more general way. The fortunate reviewer received two fees in these cases – they might be £4.10s and £1.3s. respectively.

This first issue of 30 April also included a twelve-page supplement on 'Scottish Literature Today', led off by a graceful but rather vacuous signed essay by Walter Elliot, the Secretary of State for Scotland, in which he proposed that 'the true essence of the Scottish literature is the sense of the sky and the seasons', followed by Sir Hugh Walpole (also signed) on Sir Walter Scott (whom Walpole called 'a realist – not a sham verbose romantic') and some good pieces on modern Gaelic poetry, Scots theologians and philosophers and other subjects. There were to be many more special supplements and signed articles from now onwards.

*   *   *

In 1938 the range of the paper was as wide as ever even if the tone was to become lighter, and in the first issue on 1 January there were reviews of books on hymnody, the Spanish humorists, the Rhodesian police, the history of the Althorp and Pytchley Hunt, yoga, eighteenth-century House of Commons procedure, Freud in France, and Shrewsbury School.

There was also a review of Arthur Koestler's *Spanish Testament* by Maurice Ashley, a new member of the *Times* staff who was later to become editor of the *Listener*. It was not a very sympathetic review. In this book, Koestler described the fourteen weeks he had spent in a Fascist prison in Seville under sentence of death, though unsure himself whether that had in fact been the verdict at the court martial: Ashley made the bland comment: 'The agony of uncertainty and the knowledge that many of his fellow prisoners were regularly taken out to be shot were not conducive to peace of mind.' And though he praised the writing in the prison diary, he regretted that Mr Koestler had added a long preface which he regarded as 'mainly Republican propaganda'. A month later, reviewing André Malraux's novel about the Spanish Civil War, *L'Espoir*, Montgomery Belgion described this book too as Republican propaganda – 'but exciting'.

On 30 April (the first new-look issue), Ashley took on George Orwell's *Homage to Catalonia*. He was again rather loftily critical of the Republican side in Spain in his review, calling the conflict that set the Communists and socialists against the Anarchists and the POUM (the Catalan workers' party that Orwell fought with) a 'pathetic party squabble'.

George Orwell himself replied to this review in a letter on 14 May. He said that Ashley, in trying to throw discredit upon the Republican militias, had 'distorted various things I said in order to make it appear that I agreed with him'. For instance, Ashley had said that 'discipline did not exist in the Militia', but the example he had given was Orwell's account of the behaviour of raw recruits on their first day at the barracks. Ashley's reply, printed under the letter, was that Orwell was 'unduly sensitive'.

Books on the Soviet Union went mainly this year to E.H. Carr, who was still very critical of the regime. Reviewing *Assignment in Utopia*, by the American journalist Eugene Lyons, in January he said that 'the army of disillusioned Communists has grown apace these last three or four years' and that Lyons, who went to Russia as a 'near-communist', had come back believing once more in 'justice, humaneness, truth, liberty, intellectual integrity and human dignity – all those abstractions which are anathema to Monsieur Stalin'.

However, it was Germany that was now the centre of attention, especially after Hitler's coup in Austria in March. In May, reviewing Sir Norman Angell's book *Peace With The Dictators?*, Harold Stannard was back in the pages saying, 'If by disarming we leave the road clear for the dictators, we shall have betrayed the hope of building up a real society of nations' and in July, reviewing a book called *Thus Died Austria*, he was once again drawing attention to the outrages committed on Jews.

Nevertheless, after Chamberlain signed the Munich Agreement with Hitler at midday on 30 September, and came back to Britain to declare that it meant 'peace with honour . . . peace in our time', the *Lit Supp*, in tune with the greater part of the nation, breathed a great sigh of relief.

Edmund Blunden wrote a poem especially for the occasion, 'Exorcized', which was printed on the front page on 8 October. It spoke of how men who had fought on the Somme saw 'a ghost which summed the worst they knew . . . come creeping and gathering like a storm above the summer's loveliness'. But now it was possible to say, 'Back to your madhouse, child of hell . . . You find you cannot prowl this way; your very foulness forearmed those who have now checked your matinee, the generous, selfless, wise.'

This note of optimism and, it must be observed, British self-congratulation was echoed in Stannard's review in the same number of *Guns or Butter*, by the well-known diplomat R.H. Bruce Lockhart. Stannard quoted Bruce Lockhart's remark that Nazism was a movement of youth, while in England it was the 'over-forties' who were in power, and commented sharply: 'The "over-forties" have now been able to show that they are still capable of shaping the German national will towards peace.' On 15 October the paper published a Latin version of Blunden's poem by C.W. Brodribb, as though to multiply its majesty and significance; and it was on that note of high hope that the political year ended.

Meanwhile literature had gone its wayward way, and both Evelyn Waugh and Graham Greene had published new novels. Both were reviewed by Charques, though neither got his 'First Choice' top spot. Waugh's *Scoop* in May was beaten by Angela Thirkell's *Pomfret Towers*, while Greene's *Brighton Rock* in July had to give way to Hugh Walpole's *The Joyful Delaneys*.

Charques nevertheless enjoyed *Scoop*, saying that it was ingenious, satirical and extremely funny, with 'more than a single good laugh or character to the page'. He also said that there was 'a good deal of subtly flavoured excitement' in *Brighton Rock*, 'this story of gangsterdom in Brighton' but he could not take it very seriously – he said that 'the more squalid scenes appear to have truth on their side', but by way of contrast to those he would have preferred 'the ordinary virtues of humanity to pub-crawling good nature or theological complexities'. Charques had a great gift for cutting literature down to size, and he was to do that in the *Lit Supp* for seven more years now.

Alan Clutton-Brock weighed up the achievement of Dorothy Richardson in her twelve-volume sequence *Pilgrimage*, the first thoroughgoing 'stream of consciousness' novel. Everything was seen through the heroine Miriam's eyes, he said, and this was a technique that could be misused, but here it gradually made a substantial and coherent picture quite different from 'masculine realism'.

New, or newish voices in fiction were V.S. Pritchett, whose stories in *You Make Your Own Life* were greeted with delight by Georgina Battiscombe (later a well-known biographer), who said he had 'the urgency and vitality of Mr Hemingway with none of his barbarism'; Rex Warner, whose novel *The Professor*, about a liberal-minded academic who finds hatred is more necessary than love to preserve freedom in a Fascist state, was called 'an arresting tract for the times' by Charques; and Stevie Smith, whose novel *Over the Frontier* was described by John Hayward as 'acting on one like an unfamiliar, rather bitter but stimulating cocktail'. However John Hayward, who was now writing frequent reviews of novels, dismissed Christopher Isherwood's *Lions and Shadows* as 'lacking depth and shape'; he was happier with P.G. Wodehouse's *Summer Moonshine*. Wodehouse, he said, had no-one to equal him in ingenuity, but he warned that an alarming crack had appeared in the 'supposedly impregnable structure of his social system': a baronet had been reduced to 'that last infirmity of noble purses – the turning of his seat into a paying guest house. It is to be hoped' – Hayward concluded – 'that Mr Wodehouse will refrain from pursuing this unhappy theme into the peerage.'

On the Continent, very different forms of anxiety prevailed. Montgomery Belgion gave a good review to *La Nausée* by Jean-Paul Sartre, 'a notable new writer' situated 'midway between Céline and Kafka': he said of the chief character, Roquentin, that 'monotonous as are Roquentin's days, he is enacting an intense drama – the drama of a human being who is sickened by an awareness that he does no more than exist'. This was one of the first whispers of French existentialism on our shores, and not a bad whisper. Belgion would subsequently contribute many more reviews of French books.

Meanwhile, Edwin Muir reviewed Max Brod's biography of Kafka in its German-language publication in Prague, identifying the underlying anxieties in all Kafka's novels and stories as springing from his obsessive relationship with his father.

There were more poems in the paper from now onward, though to begin with they were still mostly linked to special events or occasions. A light poem by Louis MacNeice, 'Departure Platform', headed a 'Summer Reading Section' on 9 July – a more explicitly sexy poem than the *Lit Supp* had yet seen, hinting at holiday activities:

> *The distance opens like a mouth to meet us*
> *Wantonly tongue to tongue.*

It was followed by a delightful prose piece in more traditional vein by Walter de la Mare, called 'My Mind To Me . . .' and decorated by a Rex Whistler mermaid. Travel, de la Mare said, can even be a twilight expedition to the nearest pillar-box, 'with an evening star that seems in its serene and solitary beauty to have been awaiting the assignation until that very moment'. A different sort of assignation from MacNeice's.

Cecil Day Lewis's collection *Overtures to Death* was praised in characteristically negative vein in October by Alan Clutton-Brock – he had 'escaped from the hesitations, obscurities and hidden meanings that belong to the poetry of his time'. However Clutton-Brock did acknowledge that the poems were 'dreadfully apposite at the moment', being written 'under the stimulus and fear of death by air raid'. W.H. Auden's *Oxford Book of Light Verse* was reviewed by Anthony Bertram, a general reviewer for the paper, who thought that he had extended the idea of light verse too far by including folk-songs, broadsheets, epigrams and so on, but nevertheless concluded that it was 'one of the liveliest and most original anthologies ever compiled. There is punch in these pages, if not *Punch*.'

Literary criticism also loomed large this year, with a series of three articles by Orlo Williams on 'Present Discontents'. The literary scene was painted here with a broad and not very illuminating brush, but the articles led to a letter from Middleton Murry saying that with the disappearance of many literary magazines and changes in the newspapers 'the decline in the amount and quality of reviewing has been catastrophic since 1914', and that 'book reviewing is a vanished profession'. He noted that people wanting to take up the profession of literature now often went into teaching, but that 'a kind of paralysis appears to descend upon the man of letters who takes to teaching literature'.

F.R. Leavis replied to this letter. He said that he believed that graduates with critical intelligence ought to go into university teaching, but that they were in fact not the kind of applicants who got the jobs. Universities wanted a different kind of academic ability. It was not a matter of critics being spoiled by teaching – for 'what critics have ever been allowed to teach?' Leavis's own current struggles in Cambridge could be seen looming up behind this letter.

Orlo Williams also reviewed Virginia Woolf's pamphlet 'Three Guineas', which was nominally about how women could help to prevent a war, but ranged over the whole question of women in the professions and as public figures, and especially as professional writers. Williams gave this essay almost unreserved praise. He described Virginia Woolf as 'the most brilliant pamphleteer in England', and said that the pamphlet 'might mark an epoch in the world's history' – though he thought that the road to women's equality – and the struggle of women to bring peace to the world – might be harder than even she imagined.

One unlikely and remarkable article in July this year was a signed review by the theatre director Gordon Craig of a book on the actress Eleonora Duse. It was published in Rome, and written by Olga Resnevic Signorelli, who gave a portrait of the actress in Rome during the First World War, after her great days were over – but 'to be sorry for Duse would be as though one were sorry for a hurricane' wrote Craig. Craig also described the author's daughters, who had come under La Duse's influence – 'like three small princesses from Bali, going here or going there, ever stately and beautiful diminutive figures in a city of huge arches'. This was not quite the sort of scene that the Treasury civil servant, John Beresford, was alluding to when, in the same month, he wrote of the newly-discovered diaries of the nineteenth-century Welsh country parson Francis Kilvert, 'He understood the importance of little things in life.'

Yet another supposed 'little thing' was the subject of a classic *Lit Supp* scholarly letter in May. Harold Temperley of Peterhouse, Cambridge reported that Napoleon was not so short as was commonly supposed.

A friend had measured the height above the floor of the spyholes through which Napoleon had watched the sentinels from his prison on St Helena. It was 5 foot and $^{13}/_{16}$ of an inch. Allowing for four inches above his eyes, that made Napoleon 5 foot $4^{13}/_{16}$ inches tall. He was not a pigmy.

In the first half of 1939, there was much uneasy reflection in *Lit Supp* reviews on the Munich agreement. E.H. Carr and Donald McLachlan (who this year became editor of the *Times Educational Supplement*) were the main contributors on this subject. Carr, reviewing a book called *Fallen Bastions* by G.E.R. Gedye, a former *Times* correspondent in Austria and Czechoslovakia, said that he understood Gedye's bitterness at 'the partition of Czecho-Slovakia by the Power which he had come to hate more than anything else in the world', and admitted that 'an arguable case can be made out against British policy last September'. But he believed, as he wrote in a review of *Munich and the Dictators* by R.W. Seton-Watson, that that policy had been 'the only solution that might preserve peace'.

Reviewing some French books on Munich, Carr noted approvingly that Jules Romains's *Cela Dépend de Vous* 'defends the Munich settlement on lines familiar in this country – that it would have been impossible for Great Britain to fight for frontiers so incompatible with the principle of self-determination' – meaning there was a German majority in the part of Czechoslovakia that Hitler seized – 'that war would have been fatal to democracy, that a peace based on conciliation is the sole hope for the future, and so forth'. In July, reviewing Churchill's reprinted articles in *Step by Step, 1936–39*, he praised Churchill's role as 'a gadfly to awaken the country from an orgy of somnolence and chatter', but also observed that 'the later articles breathe a reasoned hope that the situation can be, perhaps has been, saved'.

In February, McLachlan reviewed an adulatory biography of Hermann Goering by Erich Gritzbach (with a sympathetic preface by R.H. Bruce Lockhart), and though he mocked it and stressed Goering's ruthlessness, he found Goering 'a good deal more human than some of his colleagues'. In March, he reviewed the unexpurgated edition of Hitler's *Mein Kampf*, which had just been published in English by Hurst and Blackett. He said that 'it would not be surprising if this publication increased sympathy for those ideas of Herr Hitler which do not immediately threaten our own interests in the world', and that it 'will make every Liberal search his heart for the replies to its bold and brutal challenges'. There was a great deal of interest in the book in Britain: an advertisement in the paper indicated that it had been the January choice of the non-party National Book Association, who stressed – for what it was worth – that their previous choice had been Neville Chamberlain's speeches, *In Search of Peace*. Meanwhile Harold Stannard went on alerting readers to the treatment of the Jews in Germany. Writing in August about *Six Years of Hitler: The Jews Under the Nazi Regime* by G. Warburg, he said, 'This is a terrible book – as grim a record of man's inhumanity to man as has ever been written.'

The *Lit Supp* had intended to sponsor this year the annual meeting of intellectuals in Pontigny, where they would discuss – as Middleton Murry put it in a signed article on 26 August – how to defend democracy, Christendom and 'the supremacy of the person', in a world of 'potential savagery' where that defence would inevitably have to be conducted 'by a mechanical and indiscriminate massacre of persons'. Murry's pacifism was struggling to survive but was now being very much put to the test.

The British end of the Pontigny conference had been mainly organised by Arthur Crook, now twenty-seven, as one of his first major responsibilities on the paper. But his next was to cancel the arrangements, for the German invasion of Poland on 1 September and Chamberlain's declaration of war on Germany on 3 September swept the conference away. That mechanical and indiscriminate massacre had begun.

The prevailing note in the paper now changed. Philip Tomlinson, a man of fifty-seven who had been on *The Times* since 1925 and on the *Lit Supp* since May 1939, had started writing many of the notes and leaders. He was a quiet, pacific man, but in his writing he now found another voice. On 2 September, in anticipation of the events of the next day, he wrote a leader in which he declared that if literature were to cease, 'the soul of Europe perishes', and that 'the task, the policy, of the *Literary Supplement*, as for the writers and publishers, from beginning to end, must be to tend the lamp and man the strongholds of the mind'. On 9 September, the writer E.M. Almedingen wrote to say that the inspirational value of Tomlinson's leader was immense, and urged that it should be reprinted as a pamphlet. On 16 September, the paper published another poem by Edmund Blunden, 'A Window in Germany: August 1939', describing a peaceful rural scene by the Weser, and Tomlinson's leader this week contrasted the similarly peaceful scene in England the morning war was declared – 'Bees were murmurous in fair gardens . . . There was a golden exhalation in the air' –

with 'the abyss into which the world is thrown by the insatiate lust for power of a dictator.'

In this same issue of September, John Middleton Murry published the first of three signed articles called 'Democracy's War Problems' in which he took up a position not unlike that of Arthur Clutton-Brock in his First World War articles: 'Let us not deceive ourselves into the belief that because we are fighting against evil things we, as we are, embody the good. That is not given to men, or nations.' But pursuing his latest line of thought, he went on to argue that mankind had reached the point where it was in danger of destroying itself because it had become the slave not the master of the machine, and, looking beyond the war, called for a complete reorganisation of society where the benefits of the machine were given to all.

In 'News and Notes', and in leaders, Tomlinson kept up his fierce anti-Nazi commentary: Hitlerism was the vilest system of government to afflict mankind for centuries, and life on the terms conceded by Nazism was not worth having. By 16 December, Donald McLachlan, reviewing Hermann Rauschning's *Hitler Speaks*, had abandoned his cautious attitude to Nazi Germany, and was calling Hitler 'a symbol of evil things' – though still insisting that 'as a critic of democracy he has his points'.

But Harold Child had the last word this year, in unqualified but confessional vein, in his 'Thoughts for Christmas': the previous Christmas, he wrote, 'we were uneasily watching the movements of the evil beast which we were ostensibly committed to considering harmless, knowing full well in our bones that it can never be trusted. We need no longer wheedle and humour it, nor pretend that foul offences committed within its own territory are no concern of ours. We are at open war with it, pledged to fight it to the death; and the new candour lifts a load from our conscience that was heavier than all the loads that warfare lays upon our nerves and spirits.'

W.B. Yeats died in the South of France, aged seventy-three, on 28 January 1939, and on 4 February the poet Austin Clarke wrote a long 'middle' about him. Yeats had never had such a good review in the paper before. Clarke spoke of the 'intense and brilliant personality' that dominated his poetry, and of his two distinct reputations, the earlier one in which he 'lured the senses with an unearthly music' and the later when, in his 'last and greatest period' of 'intricate and metaphysical poetry', he appealed both to 'those of guarded conservative taste and those whose sympathies are progressive and not infrequently impatient'. In an accompanying leader in the same number he said that Yeats had succeeded Thomas Hardy as doyen of English letters – he still used the word 'English', though both he and Yeats were Irish. In July, Clarke wrote a review of Yeats's *Last Poems* in similar terms.

By now, Yeats, Eliot and Pound were acknowledged as the 'typical poets of the age', as Middleton Murry put it when reviewing Edwin Muir's *The Present Age from 1914* in the Cresset Press series, 'Introductions to English Literature'. These were poets who in this age of 'incessant social disintegration . . . turned to the past to have some criterion of coherence . . . Mr Eliot's grim sentence in *The Waste Land*, "These fragments I have shored against my ruins", is symbolic of the condition of the consciousness of the age.'

In fact, in the first issue of 1939, on 7 January, Eliot was quoted sympathetically on his decision to close down the *Criterion*: 'In the present state of affairs – which has induced in myself a depression of spirits so different from any other experience of fifty years as to be a new emotion – I no longer feel the enthusiasm necessary to make a literary review what it should be.' Nevertheless, Eliot felt it was all the more essential that 'authors who are concerned with that small part of "literature" which is really creative – and seldom immediately popular – should apply themselves sedulously to their work, without abatement or sacrifice of their standards on any pretext whatsoever'.

Certainly he was still applying himself sedulously to his work, with three books coming out in 1939. George Buchanan, who was still getting the poetic drama to review, echoed Murry's words about Eliot when in March he said of *The Family Reunion*, where the Furies come to haunt a modern family, that 'he has visited the world of the dead and is bringing back what he needs to enrich the modern age'. But Buchanan did not like the play, commenting that 'the poet must keep his eyes on his own brief day lest, ironically, the world of the dead will cease to help him'.

Middleton Murry reviewed Eliot's *The Idea of a Christian Society* in November, but used the book mainly to urge his own idea that we needed a community of Christians to 'contend against the demonic forces of a machine age'. Eliot did best this year in the *Lit Supp* with Alan Clutton-Brock's review of his comic poems, *Old Possum's Book of Practical Cats*, which had, said Clutton-Brock, 'the quality of suggesting another world – the secret world of cats, parallel to, but never touching, the normal life of human beings'.

A third major writer to command attention in 1939 was James Joyce, whose *Finnegans Wake* was discussed on 6 May both in a review by R.A. Scott-James (who had been the editor of the *London Mercury* for the previous five years), and a leader by Tomlinson. Both of them acknowledged his fertility of invention and his gusto – he is 'almost savagely satisfied with the thrilling spectacle of life as he sees it in all its sordidness' wrote Tomlinson – and both were more disappointed than severe about the difficulty of understanding his book, with its 'distorted words . . . heaped together in tangled skeins' as Scott-James struggled to express it.

As for the younger poets, W.H. Auden's poem about Edward Lear – 'And children swarmed to him like settlers;/He became a land' – appeared with a frieze of Lear characters by Bip Pares round it on the first page of the Spring Books supplement, while his poem 'Spain' was picked out by Hugh d'Anson Fausset as the most remarkable in the collection *Poems for Spain*, edited by Stephen Spender and John Lehmann. But after Fausset said of Roy Campbell's long poem praising Franco's fighters, 'Flowering Rifle', that 'it flings down a crude challenge to "liberal" democracy', Campbell wrote back fiercely but amusingly to the paper to say that he was more concerned with social conditions than the left-wing poets were: 'You cannot expect a whole foreign race to die tamely of hunger for the British publishers, poets and reviewers just to ensure a record crop of best sellers.'

Anthony Powell's *What's Become of Waring* was judged a good joke by a regular novel reviewer, Mrs H. Tiltman; Joyce Cary's *Mister Johnson* was called a brilliant novel about Africa by Georgina Battiscombe; Graham Greene's novel *The Confidential Agent* was dismissed as exciting but trivial by Charques. Charques was more uncertain about *After Many a Summer* by Aldous Huxley, who appeared to have been liberated from personality and time into union with God – the novel was 'the perfect bloom of Huxley – pessimism, a graveyard aroma of the flesh, an enveloping glory of corruption and decay that induces a shudder and is all the more oppressive for being translated by Mr Huxley into a bliss of mystical experience'. Reviewing William Faulkner's *The Wild Palms*, Charques asked, 'Why grow lyrical over the inglorious weakness of our blood and state?' – though he made it his First Choice – but Jan Stephens praised John Steinbeck's *The Grapes of Wrath* for 'his understanding of character, the candour and forcefulness of his dialogue and his mastery of climaxes'. Incidentally, Charques disappeared into the country without leaving an address in the first week of the war, and in his absence this review by the South African journalist Jan Stephens occupied the First Choice spot on 9 September. Charques came back the following week, was forgiven by Murray, and resumed his column.

Two *Times* books were also reviewed. J.L. Garvin came back to review the second volume of *The History of The Times, 1841–1884*, 'a crowded and living chronicle . . . as full of portraits as the Garrick Club', but above all the story of the great thirty-six-year-long editorship of John Thadeus Delane. Murray's old friend Disher was brought in to review *A Poor Player*, the autobiography of Harold Child, long a faithful servant of *The Times* and destined in the next few years to contribute many excellent 'middles' on past literary figures to the *Lit Supp*, for which he was now writing more than ever. The book told the story of Child's life in the 1890s as an actor at the Royal Strand Theatre, where he had specialised as a 'monocled masher' (or favourite with the ladies). Then he had 'turned critic' – and the rest was his life on *The Times*.

The changes made in the paper in November 1935 had not lifted its circulation. By the end of 1937 the annual figure was down to 22,529. The further changes made in April 1938 were equally unsuccessful. By the end of 1939 it was down to 19,974. It would be not at much more than 17,000 in 1940 and 1941, but it picked up a little in the later years of the war, reaching just over 22,000 again by the end of 1944.

However, the war helped the paper commercially, in spite of these relatively low figures. From the first issue in 1940 and throughout the rest of the war it had only twelve pages, so it was much cheaper to produce. Also, because of paper shortages, most newspapers gave much less space to book reviews during the war years, and publishers used the *Lit Supp* relatively more to advertise their books in.

The paper also worked much more closely with the publishers than it had under Richmond. In its 'News and Notes' columns in July and August 1940 Philip Tomlinson vigorously argued the case for not subjecting books to purchase tax and for allowing the publishers to have more paper. He employed several arguments: the high cultural argument that ideas must continue to have full and free play, the political argument that books served Britain by putting her case in America and other foreign countries, and the commercial argument that the future of the publishing trade was gravely endangered. A leader in the issue of 3 August 1940 by the young historian Felix Fries, who would be killed two years later, said: 'England has become the tiny fortress of liberty on the edge of an enslaved Europe . . . Is it opportune at such a time to quench the torch of freedom?'

Fortunately – and no doubt in part because of the *Lit Supp*'s campaign – this particular torch was kept alight. Geoffrey Faber, the president of the Publishers' Association, was able to say, on 7 September, in an introductory article to a special 'Export Number' (itself a label reflecting the interests of the book publishers) that two dangers to the book trade had been averted, though only as a result of the most strenuous efforts: 'We are now assured of an adequate supply of paper; and at the eleventh hour we have secured the exemption of books from the purchase tax.' In October, the paper was able to announce the further good news that the British Museum Reading Room was open again, the manuscripts having been removed to safety.

The war of course continued to dominate the pages of the paper in 1940. The publishers were bringing out a constant stream of books about the progress of the war, insofar as censorship allowed, and titles such as *Inside the Gestapo*, *I Was Graf Spee's Prisoner*, and *Germany: Jekyll and Hyde* were steadily and informatively reviewed.

The events leading up to the war were still of absorbing interest to Britain, and Donald McLachlan reviewed *Failure of a Mission*, a memoir of the years 1937–39 by Sir Nevile Henderson, the British Ambassador to Germany, who had tried to bring about no less than six attempts at negotiation with Hitler. McLachlan concluded that Nazism being what it was, Henderson had been bound to fail. Maurice Ashley, reviewing a book by D. Walter Smith about the Prime Minister, Neville Chamberlain, accepted the author's argument that the guarantee to Poland 'may not have given us peace, but it gave us the next best thing, the boon of time'. Ashley, who was writing in January, also remarked that Chamberlain's courage 'guides us now and will surely direct us towards victory' – not foreseeing that Churchill would become Prime Minister four months later.

Other men's eyes were already turning to the post-war years, on the assumption, perhaps not always a very confident one in 1940, that Germany would lose the war. W. Ivor Jennings brought out a book called *A Federation for Western Europe*, which drew up a plan not unlike some people's goal for the European Union today: the *Times* leader writer Dermot Morrah called it 'an essential starting point'. Morrah also commended books making similar proposals by Sir William Beveridge (*Peace by Federation?*) and Lord Davies (*A Federated Europe*), but observed that a common government would need 'a common loyalty ultimately transcending the national', and that 'with all respect to the enthusiasms of the Pan-Europa movement, no such common loyalty is discernible today'. Morrah was less friendly towards Leonard Woolf's *The War for Peace*, praising his 'usual sweet reasonableness', but scornful of his proposal 'to reform the League of Nations by increasing its power to make law, and depriving it of the little force at its disposal'. Woolf protested in a letter that he had been advocating regional forces in place of an international force.

Philip Tomlinson continued to write leaders looking at the morality of war from different angles, and at Christmas there was a notable signed article by Sir John Squire, the old literary enemy of T.S. Eliot, whose magazine the *London Mercury* had – like Eliot's *Criterion* – ceased publication the previous year. It was called 'Men and Monuments: A Plea Against Senseless Reprisals', and called on the government not to bomb the great architectural glories of Europe. 'If we destroy St Mark's or the roof of the Sistine Chapel,' Squire wrote, 'we shall have prospered no better in this war and will have stained our record.' Those Italian monuments were in the event untouched, though Germany did not fare so well.

Sir Bruce Richmond made his last public appearance in June 1940 with the publication of his only book, an anthology called *The Pattern of Freedom in Prose and Verse*. It was an expression – still through other men's words – of all that he had believed in during his years as editor of the *Lit Supp*. It was reviewed in a 'middle' by his old friend and colleague C.W. Brodribb, who praised eloquently the way Richmond exhibited, under the shadow of the new despotism, 'the many rich and diverse qualities which flow from the possession and exercise of freedom . . . until Freedom is seen to be a condition which is all-comprehensive and all-necessary for man's well-being'. Alongside the great classical expounders of freedom, Milton and Wordsworth, Burke and Mill, Richmond included writers whose books he had sent out for review in his own time, such as Eliot and D.H. Lawrence, and also loyally included some of his favourite contributors, such as Arthur Clutton-Brock and even Basil de Selincourt. As a monument to cultured English liberalism the book is still an excellent read today.

R.D. Charques – obviously wholly forgiven for his disappearance – was now writing more and more for the paper. He reviewed George Orwell's collection of essays *Inside the Whale* in April, and quarrelled with almost everything in it – the 'irrelevancies' of Orwell's political comments on Dickens, the over-seriousness of his essay on boys' weeklies, the 'ignorance' of English history that it displayed. However in an accompanying leader called 'The Communist Cult', he agreed with Orwell that the writers of the thirties who flirted with Communism were victims of middle-class unemployment – or as Charques epigrammatically put it, 'the Communism of Bloomsbury was the patriotism of the deracinated' – adding sourly that they nevertheless had also 'an incurable habit of mental superiority'.

In December he reviewed, much more sympathetically, Arthur Koestler's *Darkness at Noon*, that brilliant novel about the arguments and techniques by which Communist dissidents in the Soviet Union were induced to confess their guilt before they were shot. He called it 'a remarkable book, a grimly fascinating interpretation of the logic of the Russian Revolution', which 'possibly comes as near the truth as anything written about the Moscow trials of a year or two back'. Not long before, reviewing a volume of Stalin's speeches, he had written 'the growing likeness between the Soviet regime and the Nazi regime is dreadfully plain to the honest and informed observer'. But Charques would display a very different attitude towards Stalin and Soviet Communism, once Russia joined the side of the Allies.

Another notable novel of 1940 reviewed by Charques as his 'novel of the week' was Graham Greene's *The Power and the Glory*, about the Mexican 'whisky priest' who is in the end loyal to his faith. He called it one of the boldest of Greene's novels, expertly done, but was not sympathetic to the idea, as he saw it, of concealing Catholic salvationist doctrine beneath the devices of the thriller – 'perhaps one needs to be of the author's religious persuasion to feel complete imaginative sympathy'.

There was also an apocalyptic poem called 'Lullaby' by Edith Sitwell – 'Red is the bed of Poland, Spain' – and a milder one by Dorothy L. Sayers rejoicing that England (as this country was still being called) was fighting the war alone, in her old way –

> *The single island, like a tower*
> *Ringed with an angry host.*

The most important poem of 1940 was T.S. Eliot's 'East Coker', over which Philip Tomlinson shook his head sadly, saying that its portrait of 'a terrible, bleak meaningless world of hollow men' was 'the confession of a lost heart and a lost art'. It was certainly different in tone from his own rousing leaders. However, F.R. Leavis wrote in with cool anger to protest, saying it was 'not permissible in a serious critical journal to write in contemptuous condescension of the greatest living English poet . . . The present seems to me a particularly unhappy time for such an exhibition in the *Times Literary Supplement*: our riches of spirit are surely not so superabundant that we can countenance it.'

W.H. Auden's new collection *Another Time*, which contained some of his most famous poems, was reviewed by Fausset, who commented on its 'more resigned note', reflecting 'a civilisation falling apart rather than its revolutionary climax'. He picked out the poem 'Lay your sleeping head' as 'a satisfying example of the simplicity won through complexity' but greatly disliked the 'irresponsible callousness' of Auden's ballad 'Miss Gee'.

Charles Marriot, the *Times* art critic, said that Virginia Woolf's *Roger Fry* 'takes a very high place as biography', and remarked on Fry's 'enormous influence' as an art critic – 'the greatest since Ruskin'. Reviewing Herbert Read's *Annals of Innocence and Experience*, Philip Tomlinson contrasted it with his earlier book *The Innocent Eye*, which was 'a wistful look back from our regimented, robot world to a life of vivid individualism on a moorland farm in Yorkshire'. The new book was altogether sterner stuff, describing the development of Read's belief that 'the highest manifestation of the immanent will of the universe is the work of art'. Read's earlier precision of mind was fading.

There were several delightful essays by a new contributor, Peter Quennell, including one on Philip Gosse's *The Squire of Walton Hall*. The squire was Charles Waterton, the cranky Victorian naturalist who looked like an Edward Lear creation, especially when he was up in the treetops, reciting Horace or Virgil to a windswept rookery. Quennell regretted, as Tomlinson had done, that 'the eccentric, like the individualist, has fallen upon evil days'.

Murray, the editor, took up his pen to review Middleton Murry's new book, *The Betrayal of Christ by the Churches*. He was plainly getting exasperated by Murry by now, and Murry dropped out of *Lit Supp* reviewing for a time after this. Murry, in blaming the churches for their failure to preach 'the common brotherhood of men and their common sonship to God', also implied that the English were responsible for the coming of war and the Nazi barbarities. Murray would have none of this: 'the English people know they are simply *not* responsible'.

Murray also commented in a leader on a comic squabble that broke out involving Bernard Shaw. Lord Alfred Douglas had written a book, *Oscar Wilde: A Summing Up*, which had been reviewed by Harold Child. Douglas was still protesting against Wilde's imprisonment, but Child pointed out that Wilde had committed 'a forbidden act punishable by law', and said that, 'misled by Bernard Shaw', Douglas had confused crime with vice.

Shaw wrote in to protest, and Murray described in his leader what happened next.

> Writing with the accent of a man stirred to almost uncontrollable rage, Mr Shaw began by a personal attack upon our reviewer, described by him as 'in the mental condition of the simplest agricultural labourer as regards the most vital and famous clause in Magna Carta' . . . To his reference to Magna Carta, the relevance of which was challenged last week by Mr G.M. Young in a letter which so far he has not considered worth answering, Mr Shaw added references to the trial of the Seven Bishops and to Fox's Act, the relevance of which is equally obscure; and concluded with the assurance that apologies were due to Lord Alfred, but that he 'forgave' the reviewer.

However, Murray did not leave it there. He analysed Shaw's letter:

> It reveals three characteristics with which we have grown painfully familiar during the past few years. A topic suitable for cool discussion is transferred at the outset to the realm of passion. A disputant who has the temerity to differ from the enraged controversialist is promptly stripped of his right to the ordinary courtesies of debate, and presented in vituperative caricature. Lastly in place of reasonable argument, which can be followed and weighed, a salvo of resounding irrelevancies (or fantasies) is exploded upon the bewildered followers of the debate . . . This is the very technique whereby the friends of Hitler in Germany besiege the world with their clamour that he invaded Poland to maintain the peace of Europe, and the friends of Stalin in England deafen us with the assertion that he is resisting a Finnish invasion of Russia . . . In a nation which has been taught that it is dishonourable to suffocate reason with passion, even over a relatively trifling dispute, the technique of Goebbels and Stalin will find no field.

That was both Murry and Shaw disposed of in favour of Britain.

Simon Nowell-Smith had left the paper for war service on 1 September 1939, and remained officially on the staff, but did not return. He resigned at the end of 1944, and went on to become librarian of the London Library. Arthur Crook joined the RAF in October 1940, but came out for health reasons and returned to Printing House Square in April 1941.

This gave Crook the opportunity that led eventually to his becoming editor of the paper. Under the threat of German air raids, all the other staff would hurry off each day to catch the 4.30p.m. train from Farringdon to get back to their homes in the country. Crook, however, would stay in London, often doing firewatching and sleeping in Printing House Square, and more and more responsibility was left to him – writing paragraphs for 'News and Notes' and in due course editing the column, arranging reviews, reading proofs (where he often found terrible mistakes). Murray liked and respected him, and in September 1941 made him editorial assistant. At this time he often worked for long hours in an office that was like an office of the dead.

The first issue of 1941, 4 January, began with a comment on the bombing at the end of December of the Guildhall, which, it said, had 'suffered more grievously than in the Great Fire . . . The new orderers bade farewell to the year 1940 by writing in letters of flame their distaste for the civilisation represented by the City of London.' However, it was also able to report that there had been 11,000 new books in the previous twelve months, a figure which exceeded by several thousand the total published in the first full year of the First World War. The Christmas of 1939 had been one of the poorest in the history of the book trade, but at Christmas 1940 the demand for books was much brisker again.

War books were as numerous as ever. One that received special attention in August was a collection of German political speeches from the last 150 years, *Thus Spake Germany*, which had a preface by Lord Vansittart arguing that there was nothing new in Nazism and that German militarism had always been the menace. Wickham Steed, brought in to review it, said that 'assuming we want a better world and therefore a better Germany, this book shows us what must be avoided'. Murray contributed an accompanying leader, in which he said more dramatically that 'We publish on the page opposite one of the gravest reviews that it has ever been the duty of this Supplement to undertake.' The book demonstrated that Hitler was a medicine man stimulating a sub-rational frenzy, and that it was 'not simply false doctrines that have to be exploded but a pre-rational disposition that has to be broken up'.

A very different sort of war book was *For My Enemy Daughter* by Murray's wife, Leonora Eyles. She had a daughter who had married an Italian and gone with him to Rome, and had heard nothing from her since Italy entered the war. Her book consisted of nine long letters about her life and her ideas, 'so that if she were killed during the war her daughter would still hear her voice'. It was reviewed by the novelist Storm Jameson, who was a friend of the Murrays and was now contributing regularly to the paper: she said that 'for its deep wisdom, compassion, sanity and its tough English temper, this book is one not only to be read, but to be pondered and lived with'.

Incidentally, Mrs Murray was always very kind to the young Arthur Crook, and when he had an attack of Bell's palsy just before the war, he went to stay with the Murrays in Brighton for a while. He had to wear a chain across his mouth to keep the muscles round it from going slack, and he recalls her addressing him firmly: 'What do you think caused this trouble, Arthur? Was it sex?,' and himself mumbling through his chain, 'I don't think so.'

The German invasion of the Soviet Union on 22 June 1941, and the consequent enrolment of the Soviet Union among the Allies, wrought a change in the paper. From now on it was to adopt a softer tone in its comments on Soviet Communism. Reviewing *Russia and Ourselves*, by the influential left-wing publisher Victor Gollancz, on 9 August, Charques joined with him in mockery of the British Communist Party and its volte-face. A day before the German attack, Ivor Montagu had been insisting that 'the talk of an attack was moonshine – and, alternatively, that if in fact the attack came off, it would be by arrangement between Mr Churchill and Hitler!' But as soon as the Communist line had switched from anti-war to pro-war, the cry of the secretary of the British Communist Party, Harry Pollitt, was 'All behind Churchill!'

Nevertheless, Gollancz's book was about 'the tremendous opportunity created by our comradeship in arms with the Soviet Union', and Charques said that it had 'a ring of earnest and conscientious moderation'. He made a few cautious noises about the 'illiberalism' of the regime in Russia, but there were no more rude words about Stalin, and no attempt to question Gollancz's statement that 'the foundations of Socialism have been well and truly laid in Russia'.

At the end of August Charques reviewed Edmund Wilson's book on Lenin, *To the Finland Station*. He said it was 'finely written', and described Lenin's success in the internal divisions of the early Communist leaders as that of the practical man over the theoretical, making no attempt at any criticism of Lenin.

Moreover when in October a new edition came out of Sidney and Beatrice Webb's *Soviet Communism: A New Civilisation*, Charques said that its view that Stalin was not a dictator and that the USSR was a political democracy was 'exaggerated', but his chief criticism was merely that 'The effect of Mrs Webb's pleading is too often marred by the narrowness and extreme positiveness of her theoretical exposition.' Meanwhile in September, Sir Bernard Pares, who had been Professor of Russian History both at Cambridge and London, and had spent his life trying to interpret Russia to the British, had contributed a long signed piece on 'Links with Russia: Points of Cultural Kinship', in which he observed that 'many a young and energetic Russian, trained in the bracing school of administration developed by the Five-year Plans, especially among backward peoples of Asia, will approach his task in very much the same spirit of friendliness and common sense as our administrators in India'. That would give the British people a common ground of understanding with Russia.

The note of 'common understanding' with the United States was not being forgotten either. An Anglo-American number in April had a historical survey of 'Common Ideals' by G.M. Trevelyan, and a boxed message from the American Ambassador in London, John G. Winant, in which he said that 'Common ideals are not made by wishful thinking; they come from an understanding, not only of the problems common to nations working together, but of the thoughts, feelings, history and culture of their diversified peoples. It is for that reason that the Special Anglo-American Number of the *Times Literary Supplement* merits our special attention at this time.' The United States would of course enter the war when the Japanese bombed Pearl Harbor in December.

There were some special signed articles about literature and the war. In January, Lord David Cecil regretted that so little that could be called literature had been written in Britain since the outbreak of war – the muse of letters had only a faint voice among the thunderous beating of right and left wings. Drama seemed to have stopped with the closing of the theatres. 'It takes more than a world war to stop Mr Huxley or Mr Wells', but neither of them had revealed a new side to his talent. 'We have had no fiction from Mrs Woolf, Mr E.M. Forster, Mr Forrest Reid, Miss Elizabeth Bowen, Miss Compton-Burnett or Mr Christopher Isherwood' – it is interesting to see what his roll call of interesting novelists was in 1941 – 'nor has any new novelist appeared of a calibre to compensate for their absence.' It was poetry which had proved the most fruitful branch of letters – Auden, MacNeice and Sassoon and Ruth Pitter had all brought out books, 'while Mr T.S. Eliot in "East Coker" has produced his finest work, combining the breadth and originality of *The Waste Land* with the still beauty of his later religious lyrics' – but apart from Eliot, none of these poets had produced 'anything to raise our opinion of their talents'. Lord David suggested that what writers needed was a new 'stability of vision' – like most prescriptions for writing, a completely unhelpful one.

In September it was the turn of J.B. Priestley to tackle 'The Cultural Problem'. Priestley by now had a great reputation as an inspiring and patriotic broadcaster as well as a novelist. His more optimistic view was that in the past, 'an undemocratic England gave us, with some exceptions among individual creators, an undemocratic culture. No Greekless dentists need apply' – but that the war was changing all that. Shades of the future here.

On 28 March 1941, Virginia Woolf died, drowning herself in a river near her Sussex home. Orlo Williams wrote a full-page epitaph for her on 12 April, calling her 'a great artist, who pursued her vision with unswerving integrity', and summarising her purpose in her writing as 'to try to make life stand still at the significant moment'. An accompanying leader by Philip Tomlinson also praised her, but saw her death as the end of an epoch – an epoch characterised by an excessive self-consciousness and even a tendency to self-torture among writers, as well as a love of hidden meanings that were only accessible to the initiated. He thought that 'the shocking reality of war' was changing all this, and like Priestley welcomed the fact.

However there was a novel by Virginia Woolf yet to be published, *Between the Acts*, and Charques contributed a 'middle' on this on 19 July. He too said that 'hers was a cultivation that excluded much else . . . she shrank instinctively from forms of goodness and beauty other than those she had absorbed into her own private vision'. But he called her last novel 'a rare and sometimes haunting book'.

James Joyce, who died on 13 January, received a similarly qualified farewell from Philip Tomlinson on 25 January: 'He was a poet and a master of English prose when he chose to write so that he who ran could read; instead, he decided to occupy years of his life in throwing at us masses of incomprehensible words from which he who reads them runs!'

Elizabeth Bowen actually had a novel out only a few days after Lord David Cecil's article regretting that there had not been one from her. This was *Look At All Those Roses*, which Charques described as a story of some clever, charming or unhappy pre-war souls, adding somewhat sadistically that they were 'ripe for some shattering ordeal of society or revenge of nature'. Joyce Cary had two novels in 1941, both also reviewed by Charques. In February there was *A House of Children*, which Charques called 'a captivating account of childhood on an Irish lakeside' – he liked the 'well-bred, healthy children' who were 'nearer the heart and understanding than the perkily adventurous or tough little products of the East End of London of whom he wrote in his previous novel'; in December there was *Herself Surprised*, than which Cary had written 'nothing livelier or more telling', with its heroine like a new Moll Flanders.

Yet again it was Charques, mammoth scribbler of the paper, who reviewed Ernest Hemingway's *For Whom the Bell Tolls*, the story of Robert Jordan, an American volunteer on the Republican side in a guerrilla episode of the Spanish Civil War. Charques found it 'an episode full of drama that rings very true . . . The excitement gathers pace, and through it all Jordan's personal drama, the drama of a civilised soul on the losing side in war with only courage to sustain his hope of victory, has pathos and poignancy'.

The first collected English edition of Proust's *Remembrance of Things Past*, including the translation by Stephen Hudson of the last part, 'Time Regained', went to D.W. Brogan, a brilliant writer who was now establishing himself as a leading contributor to the paper on both French and American history and politics.

Brogan called it 'one of the two or three important novels since the end of the productive career of Tolstoy', comparing it with Saint-Simon's memoirs of Louis XIV's court in its unflattering – even unjust – portrait of the old aristocracy, but also observing that Proust's Faubourg Saint-Germain was like 'a vast Drones Club', and noting how the theme of the novel, 'the dissolution of society and the discovery that its unbridgeable gaps were always being crossed', had been echoed when Pierre Laval's daughter married in 1935 into the House of Noailles – something that 'would have infuriated Saint-Simon and fascinated Proust'.

A new historian from Magdalen appeared on the scene with the publication of A.J.P. Taylor's *The Habsburg Monarchy, 1815–1918*. The great Wickham Steed was asked to do this, and gave it a thorough but often critical review on 22 February. The following week Taylor replied in a typically acerbic and witty letter:

> Your reviewer objects of my book that it is not based upon 'first-hand observation'. To this charge I must plead guilty. I never met the late Prince Metternich; by gross carelessness I did not witness the revolutions of 1848 . . . I was not presented at the Hofburg . . . But greater men than I have also erred. Macaulay never saw James II and Gibbon never even visited Constantinople. Yet Gibbon saw more deeply into the degeneracy than did any monkish scribbler

of the 11th century, and Macaulay understood the spirit of Stuart despotism better than did any Roman Catholic sycophant of the time . . .

As for poetry in 1941, Philip Tomlinson called Auden's *New Year Letter* 'erudite and entertaining' – though without looking at all closely at it – but he did not let up on T.S. Eliot, in spite of Leavis and Lord David. Writing of 'The Dry Salvages', he complained that Eliot was silent on the war and merely offered a 'horrifying vision of volitionless stuffed men', concluding that 'the impulse of his work has spent itself'. This time it fell to a colleague of Leavis's on the journal *Scrutiny* to write a letter in reply. L.C. Knights declared that those readers who had admired him were not now dejected, as the reviewer had said they were, but felt that they had got something of permanent value from Eliot's poetry.

Finally, Lord David Cecil's plea for new writing in the war received something of an answer in a poem published on 24 May 1941. This was an exquisite little poem by a twenty-six-year-old soldier, Alun Lewis, called 'Raider's Dawn' – which was to be the title of his only book of poems, published in 1942 (he was killed in Burma two years later). In its measured delicacy, to my mind it is the first really good poem that the *Lit Supp* published.

> *Lovers waking*
> *From the night . . .*
> *Recognise only*
> *The drifting white*
> *Fall of small faces*
> *Into the lime.*
>
> *Blue necklace left*
> *On a charred chair*
> *Tells that Beauty*
> *Was startled there.*

In 1941 Geoffrey Dawson retired with some reluctance as editor of *The Times*, and Robin Barrington-Ward replaced him. Two of 'B-W's' closest friends were Stanley Morison and E.H. Carr. They were destined to have a growing influence both on *The Times* and the *Lit Supp*.

Morison, who was fifty-three in 1942, was still technically the typographical adviser to the paper, but he was consulted on many other matters too, and he fostered Barrington-Ward's sympathy with the Labour Party and its post-war hopes and intentions. Carr, who was fifty, was Professor of International Politics at Aberystwyth University. He was generally regarded as a cold but brilliant man. He had been seconded at the beginning of the war to the Ministry of Information, and at the behest of Barrington-Ward had also started writing leaders for *The Times*, with some of which Geoffrey Dawson had been distinctly unhappy. One such leader that was widely noticed on 5 December 1940 spoke strongly, in a Labour-minded way new to *The Times*, about the two great scourges – war and unemployment – that must be abolished in the 'new social order'. In 1941, Barrington-Ward appointed Carr an assistant editor of *The Times*.

In March 1942, Carr's book *Conditions of Peace* was published, and was given a long review in the *Lit Supp* by J.H. Freeman, who was still a senior leader writer on *The Times*. The review appeared under a three-decker headline: 'Towards A Constructive Peace. From the Old World to a New Order. Rebuilding Shattered Europe.'

Freeman drew out an important point about Carr. Carr felt that the epoch of capitalist laissez-faire was over in history, and even now he felt some sympathy towards both Stalin and Hitler for leading the world on to its next stage. Hitler, Carr said in this book, had at least performed 'the indispensable function of sweeping away the litter of the old order'. After the war, the essential task of the 'new democracy' – for Carr was careful to call it 'democracy' – would be to 'make political rights effective over economic power'. This would mean strong governments acting in the name of the people, and 'substituting welfare for wealth as their main purpose'. The future, in short, was Socialism and even Communism.

Freeman, who as we have seen already was a moderate supporter of Labour ideas, gave a cautious welcome to Carr's book. His doubts lay more in his tone than in any substantial explicit criticism – for instance, he seemed to hint at rather too great an attachment to power and even violence in Carr, when he wrote that: 'Professor Carr destroys illusions as remorsely and, in a sense, as gladly as Mr Keynes did 22 years ago.' However, Freeman took the opportunity in this review to criticise those writers like Victor Gollancz who, from a left-wing viewpoint but going much further than Carr, were questioning whether the Germans were really responsible for the war at all.

John Middleton Murry had been busy devising complex arguments along similar lines to Gollancz, and this time it fell to Philip Tomlinson to rebut them. Murry's book *Christocracy*, lamenting the world's turning away from Christ, came out in July, and Tomlinson was as angry about it as his editor Murray had been about Murry's previous book. He quoted in derision Murry's statement that Hitler was 'simply the statesman who has tried to solve the problem of unemployment . . . by turning the great German nation into one vast army'. As for Murry's declaration that, in spite of all Britain's faults, he believed there was still more of the substance of a Christian society in Britain than in any other great nation, Tomlinson observed that 'this should be reassuring, but perverse Britain may not be duly grateful'.

When it came to the question of Russia, Charques quite frankly said, in a review of a batch of books in March, that 'since June 22 of last year almost all of us in this country have been proved wrong on the subject'. We were wrong because 'we persisted in evaluating the gains of the so-called Russian experiment by Western European and not by Russian standards, with the result that we had still to discover the political cohesion and the moral solidarity of the peoples of Russia under Soviet rule'. Clearly, now that the Soviet Union was an ally, he was not going to go on making such a foolish error.

What was happening to France was of great interest now to the paper, and would feature more and more in its articles. Denis Saurat – Professor of French at King's College, London, and director of the Institut Français – gave a long review to the first substantial book on General de Gaulle, written by Philippe Barrès, the son of the French nationalist writer Maurice Barrès. Saurat said that de Gaulle 'represents the rebellion of the ancient spirit of France against undeserved catastrophe and foul aggression'. Denis Brogan gave a more analytical account of events in France when he wrote an obituary of the writer Léon Daudet, the son of the Provençal writer Alphonse Daudet. He admired the younger Daudet as a cruel humorist, but thought he shared with the nationalist Charles Maurras 'a great responsibility for French disunion, for the Anglophobia of the *bien pensant* classes and for their equally suicidal faith in Mussolini'.

This new preoccupation with France would come out especially in a new series of articles that began on 31 October 1942, called 'Menander's Mirror'. These were written by Charles Morgan, and soon built up a strong following. They took up all kinds of literary topics, sometimes in a manner to draw readers' minds beyond and away from the war, sometimes relating them closely to current events. They had a high-minded, moralising tone, but were rich in fascinating allusion. The first one was appropriately called 'In Search of Values', but perhaps too oratorically came to a conclusion with the questions 'What is worth dying for?' and 'What is worth living for – and in what order?' Later essays would be more specific, generally reaching rather conservative conclusions.

Morgan, incidentally, was paid £5 a column for 'Menander's Mirror', but the strictest application of the rules was applied even to him, and for his three-column article he would sometimes receive £15.1.9, sometimes £14.12.0. If the article was a little short it would be bumped up by spaces and rules for which he was not paid. With the arrival of 'Menander', the 'News and Notes' on the front page also came to an end, to be replaced by a short and often rather scrappy article under the picture.

The novel of 1942 in retrospect was Evelyn Waugh's *Put Out More Flags*, although it failed to be chosen as the *Lit Supp*'s 'Novel of the Week' and was reviewed not by Charques but by Mavrogordato, who was still soldiering on as a reviewer. He said that Waugh's vision of his fellow creatures was limited to their defects, but was not obscured by political prejudice: left-wingers would savour his portrait of the upper classes, but would be damped by his picture of evacuee London children arriving in the countryside – they were loathsome! A dire review.

'Little Gidding', the last of T.S. Eliot's 'Four Quartets', came out in December 1942, but this time the poem went not to Philip Tomlinson but to Hugh d'Anson Fausset. Eliot did not gain much by the change. Fausset quoted the passage about being redeemed from fire by fire, and approved of Eliot's realisation of how hard it was to choose between the two fires, but complained that this spiritual debate 'tends to reduce the music of poetry to the dry discourse of the moralist and the intellectual'. Fausset also alluded unfavourably to Eliot when he came to review Alun Lewis's volume of poems, *Raider's Dawn*. As usual, Fausset made no comment of any interest on the language of the poems, and was mainly exercised by what he saw as their pessimism. He said that this young soldier-poet had 'the tragic vision', but 'in the darkness he is often not far from the waste land where horror has no meaning'.

The fiftieth anniversary of Tennyson's death on 6 October 1942 was doubly commemorated, four days later, with an article by G. Wilson Knight on Tennyson's 'mystic imperialism', and two photographs taken specially for the paper of the woods round Aldworth, the poet's favourite scene in his last years.

Finally, George Orwell made two contributions to the paper this year. He wrote a 'middle' on Bernard Falk's *The Bridgwater Millions*, the story of how the wealth of the Dukes of Bridgwater had been spent.

Orwell concentrated on the 3rd Duke, who built the Bridgwater Canal between the Wortley collieries and the Manchester coal wharves, and gave a vivid picture of him 'watching the long procession of black barges' on the canal with 'an aspect as grim, sober and devoid of brilliance as the northern industrial landscape he was helping to create'. But he drew no moral or political conclusions in this review.

However, a letter he wrote was in fighting form. He complained about a review of a novel, *The Sword and the Sickle*, by an Indian writer, Mulk Raj Anand, contesting the reviewer's opinion that the author wanted to stir up hatred against English people. It was quite true, as the reviewer had said, that the novel was 'anti-British', but only in a political sense, and 'if Mr Anand makes it plain that he is anti-imperialist and thinks India ought to be independent, is he not saying something which almost any English intellectual would echo as a matter of course?' Orwell could not know, presumably, that the reviewer was himself Indian, Ranjee G. Shahani. Shahani replied firmly that Europeans were denigrated in the novel 'by innuendo and oblique reference'.

1943 was Menander's year on the *Lit Supp*. Writing a full-page article each week he was able to cover a great deal of ground, and he provoked frequent letters to the editor. An article on 13 February called 'An Expectant Silence', about the absence of war poets, produced a letter the following week from Stephen Spender. He agreed that there was a need 'for a poetry of generally shared suffering and generally shared hope'. But, he said, reflective poetry about the war can only be written if poets are granted leave to withdraw temporarily from the endless interruptions of war-time tasks. He himself, though his notebook was full of odes, was only asked by the Ministries or the British Council to write propaganda pieces. 'In a society where every function of every one's life has been pigeon-holed and arranged from morning to night,' he concluded, 'I cannot see what place there is for a Keats, a Leopardi, a Wordsworth, a Hardy.' This seemed rather a feeble-spirited complaint in the middle of a war.

An article Menander wrote in the same number as Spender's letter produced a more robust letter on 6 March from George Orwell. Here Menander was discussing the poems of the French Communist poet Louis Aragon, and argued that his political beliefs should not make the reader deaf to the music of his poetry. Menander also used the occasion to object to an article that George Orwell had written in Cyril Connolly's magazine *Horizon*, in which Orwell had said that 'translated into political terms, Yeats's tendency is Fascist': Orwell, said Menander, had been overcome here by his 'irresistible political itch'. Orwell replied that poetry does not exist in 'a sort of watertight or rather thought-tight world of its own' – and he pointed out that he had been saying for years that the best writers of 'our time' had been reactionary in tendency.

Answering another point raised by Menander, Orwell defended his dislike of the word 'loveliness'. He claimed that certain words, if not inherently ugly, could be 'vulgarised by association, and I object to a word like 'loveliness' because in our age it inevitably calls up a picture of pink sunsets, Dorothy Lamour, soft-centre chocolates etc.'

This led to an amusing exchange of letters. Lord David Cecil wrote to say that Orwell was a 'word-snob', and Orwell replied this time that if being a word-snob meant thinking one ought to fight for decent English, then he was one. David Cecil had said that any words if used aptly would assume dignity. Orwell said, 'What about "love-nest"?' He would give five shillings for a sentence and 7s 6d for a line of verse in which the word love-nest 'assumes dignity'.

David Cecil came back with two entries he had written, which he did not put forward as examples of good writing, but in which he claimed 'love-nest' was disinfected of its vulgar associations. The sentence was: 'The lady's eyes were at once so tranquil, so radiant, that a poet once compared them, in his phantasie, to two love-nests or bowers of Cupid, whither the little god would betake himself to rest, when wearied with roving the world on his impish sport.' The verse line could be imagined to be taken from a poem on the Nativity in the Hopkins manner: 'Oh but praise for the winter-white heaven-hallowed love-nest, dove-nest of Mary's son.'

Unfortunately, the correspondence lapsed after this, and it is not known whether David Cecil got his 5s or his 7s 6d. In my view, he did not earn the money.

The call for a new poetry went on resounding through the paper this year. In December, Menander was still making the complaint we have often heard *Lit Supp* poetry critics making, that 'the modernism of the thirties found itself lost in a desert of negation'. But there was one article in this vein that took a somewhat different tone, a signed article in September by Storm Jameson. It was called 'Literature Between the Wars', and – quoting a poem by Edith Sitwell – it too called for 'the warmth of the affirming sun' to be felt again in English literature. But the author did recognise two 'bold figures' between the wars – T.S. Eliot and James Joyce – who, she said in a fine remark, 'forcing their imagination to accept the fact of disintegration, wrote about it as natives'.

The day-to-day events of the war did not get much notice in the paper, since everything was filtered through reviews of books, and 'News and Notes' had now gone. Menander wrote about French literature and the state of France in several of his articles. He told two melancholy tales. Reviewing the autobiography of André Maurois, translated as *Call No Man Happy*, he regretted the change it revealed in this old friend of England, who in the First World War had written *Les Silences du Colonel Bramble*. The book, which evoked so beautifully Maurois's childhood and youth and 'the awakening of an acute intellect', showed Maurois now acquiescing without protest in the capitulation of France in 1940, though the book was written in America in 1941. Menander also reviewed *Le Silence de la Mer*, by Vercors, a book published clandestinely in France, which told the story of a German quartered in a French house. The German, von Ebrennac, who is a composer, speaks of his love of France and his longing for peace. Yet he does not regret the war, and believes that France will recognise that the Beast that has conquered her, will, with her love, become a pure knight who will save her. Menander saw it as a parable of the 'hysterical idealism' of even the best Germans, and felt that it rang true.

Charques's adulation of Russia surfaced from time to time in the paper, notably in an article called 'Heroes and Martyrs of the Soviets', but it was the politics of Britain after the war that was now in the foreground of discussion. The Beveridge Report had come out, with its identification of the Five Evil Giants that needed to be slain after the war – want, disease, ignorance, squalor and idleness – and many politicians and thinkers who were to become Labour leaders were writing books. They were mostly welcomed by the paper. The *Times* leader writer J.V. Radcliffe gave a sympathetic account of *The Britain I Want* by the working-class Labour politician Emanuel Shinwell with its 'intolerance of social wrong and preventable hardship' and its call for public ownership. Freeman was very impressed by Harold J. Laski's *Reflections on the Revolution of Our Time*, which argued – very much as Carr argued – that capitalist democracy had had its day and that the future belonged to a planned society.

Even the Roman Catholic individualist Dermot Morrah was struck by two books about Stafford Cripps, the austere future Labour Chancellor of the Exchequer, saying that 'it may well be that his vigorous pursuit of a clear-cut and passionately desired social ideal will do more than the thought of any other man to determine the ground on which the post-war political battle will be fought out'. However, he uttered a note of warning in his review of *Wartime Speeches* by Herbert Morrison, the future Labour Home Secretary – 'his conception of the method of planning suggests that the arbitrary powers necessarily vested in a war-time Ministry of Home Security have generated a decidedly authoritarian, if not quite totalitarian, temper of mind'; and in the same issue, 2 October, Menander asked how many collectivists there were 'who will not see that in the corruption of German and Italian collectivism there is a criticism of all collectivism, whatever its name', observing that 'as soon as the German system became anything but an enablement and protector of individual free will, it became corrupt and an instrument of man's self-destruction'.

Charques still dominated the novel reviews in 1943, besides the paper's pronouncements on Russia. He admired, perhaps surprisingly, Arthur Koestler's psychoanalytical attack on revolutionary idealism, *Arrival and Departure*, saying it had 'a hundred times as much of the peculiar meat of modernity in it as there is in the run of contemporary novels', but he was not so impressed by Graham Greene's *The Ministry of Fear*, 'another of his tensely atmospheric thrillers', but 'more far-fetched than usual'.

Two books by new American women novelists also received his attention. He scorned Carson McCuller's Southern novel, *The Heart is a Lonely Hunter*, saying 'Make your characters sufficiently singular, enigmatical and even freakish, and you can easily claim vast and explored significance for what they do or say', but he called Mary McCarthy's New York novel, *The Company She Keeps*, 'a clever essay in fiction, up to date, amusing, sophisticated'.

Meanwhile an English woman novelist was having a great success on the wireless. Dorothy L. Sayers had told the story of Jesus in her play *The Man Born to Be King*, and R. A. Eddison wrote that 'Miss Sayers and the BBC have done the English world a great service by presenting the story with fresh realism.' The author used 'a kaleidoscope of kinds of language', but the result was satisfying 'because the story is one that belongs to eternity as well as time'.

The Allies invaded Europe in May 1944. There was some terrible fighting ahead, but victory seemed in sight. At the end of April, Philip Tomlinson wrote a middle article about Edmund Blunden's new book *Cricket Country*. The review was an outpouring of joy by Tomlinson at this 'glorious salutation to a glorious game' by his old friend Blunden, appearing in a year 'when the light fades over the field and the pitch crumbles under the tramplings of a sterner game'. Tomlinson said that 'all England, all human affairs, poetry, pictures, music, love, hoops and roundabouts, are disclosed in this vision of cricket's maze and winding labyrinths', and they were 'healing reminders of the sweetness and light that have been and could be'.

After the liberation of Paris, there was a rapturous leader (on 26 August) written at Murray's request by Storm Jameson. She was living at that time in Murray's house with him and his wife, and knowing what great feeling she had for France, he sat her down to write it. She described the scene in her autobiography: 'I had had to force back tears when the Marseillaise, violent and triumphant, sprang from the wireless, but as soon as I started my thousand words, genuine feeling withdrew, and all I wanted to do was to write as much as possible like Giraudoux at his best and least metaphysical.' In fact, she wrote some moving if rhetorical words:

> To have heard that Chartres was safe brought an overwhelming relief; Orleans and the Loire were freed, and we thought of Péguy. Paris – but what is it we feel, and what has been released? Not only the capital of great France, not only the passion of a people. Paris is free; that is, a source to which the world has turned naturally for ideas, a path which the thought of humanity has learned to take almost by instinct – an instinct for the just measure, the courageously human – is once more open. What we feel is more than joy, other than relief. It is perhaps simply the light.

The week after, Brodribb contributed another, more archaeological leader about France called 'Duke William's Land'. He described how the place names in Normandy that had kept coming up in the news since the invasion on 6 June – Falaise, the Orme, Mortemer, Angers – 'gives to this campaign the feeling of stepping back into feudal England', and reflected that to the descendants of the great Norman barons of the Conquest taking part in the invasion 'there must have been a sense of home-coming to their own history'.

Brogan wrote a brilliant review in August of some books about the state of France, including Raymond Aron's *L'Homme Contre Les Tyrans*. Brogan tried to explain, if not forgive, the 'treason of so many French clerks' and the 'ignominious contrast between the resistance of the French people and the acceptance of the German triumph of 1940 by so many of the intellectual élite'. Some of the latter, he thought, were positively attracted by 'the passionate faith of the Nazis', when the pre-war Third Republic had 'failed to provide a political authority adequate for the reconstruction of French economic life'. He followed Aron in arguing that nevertheless 'the survival of civilisation is not impossible . . . We are not bound to pass into the hands of the officers of a totalitarian state communism or the agents of a new international of cartels'.

'What to do with Germany' was the title of another article this summer (reviewing a book of the same name by an American, Louis Nizer). In this article Freeman wrote approvingly of Nizer's proposals that the whole German officer class must be swept away and that the Allies must take on the task of the re-education of Germany – 'de-mentalisation' going hand in hand with disarmament – but also that Germany should be granted the means to enjoy economic wellbeing again. Meanwhile Charques was praising a *History of Anglo-Soviet Relations* by a Mr and Mrs Coates which tried to show how misguided anti-Bolshevik sentiment in England had been. Charques declared – in very E.H. Carr-like tones – that '1917 was in line with the entire logic of Russian historical development', and that there was now 'no alternative to Anglo-Soviet collaboration that will secure peace for Europe'.

On the home front, the second and most famous of Sir William Beveridge's reports, 'Full Employment in a Free Society', came out in November. It was given an extremely thoughtful review by François Lafitte, a *Times* leader writer and expert on industrial relations brought in by E.H. Carr. Lafitte went along with its argument that 'there is nothing in the nature of an unplanned market economy which guarantees that it will attain full employment except by chance, temporarily and at infrequent intervals', and, to the extent that he agreed with the goal of 'abolishing idleness', consequently accepted the need for planning. He also accepted the argument – which he said was now 'economic orthodoxy' – that it was only the State that can set up a demand for the products of industry that will make use of the whole manpower of the country. He cited Beveridge's remark that accepting the idea that the State must take on this responsibility meant 'crossing a line from the old Britain of mass unemployment and jealousy and fear to the new Britain of opportunity and service for all'. But Lafitte firmly posed the two questions that arose from this: 'Can a free society cross this line?' and 'Can a free society refuse to cross the line and remain free?' This, he said, was 'perhaps the fundamental dilemma confronting twentieth-century Europe and America' – and, it may be added, one that goes on confronting them in the twenty-first century.

G.M. Trevelyan's *English Social History* came out in August 1944. Brodribb, reviewing it, correctly predicted that this 'homely history of everyday life' would be read for a long time to come. 'How well,' he exclaimed, 'has the Master of Trinity shepherded the great, ordinary novel and newspaper reading public through the pages of English history!' The new book, 'as human as history can ever be', was written 'with all Dr Trevelyan's customary skill and fervid, passionate and sometimes pitying love of his country'. Beveridge's 'new Britain' seemed already to be announcing its arrival both in Trevelyan's book and in Brodribb's recommendation of it.

Another great Cambridge figure and hero of the *Lit Supp*, Sir Arthur Quiller-Couch, died in May 1944. Harold Child wrote an obituary of him, commending his view that literature is 'a common human activity' concerned with 'the abiding elements of human life', and so 'must take in the whole of human life, man not only as individual person but also as citizen' – opinions that were heretical and abominable, said Child, to the *fin-de-siècle* advocates of art for art's sake. Q's only mistake, in Child's view, was his high-handed way, in the *Oxford Book of English Verse*, of leaving out lines or stanzas that he did not like.

For its 30 September issue, the *Lit Supp* managed to get hold of Q's 'last essay, last testament', as Tomlinson called it in an accompanying leader – an article expressing Q's dislike of Basic English. (A.L. Rowse claims in his autobiography that it was he who was instrumental in getting the article into the *Lit Supp*'s hands.) It was a spirited last testament, inspired mainly by the fear that C.K. Ogden and I.A. Richards would attempt to get Basic English substituted for 'true English'. Q was particularly indignant about Basic English limiting itself to eighteen verbs, which according to Richards could 'translate adequately more than 4,000 words of full English'. 'A few mere nouns may serve for taking a railway ticket,' Q wrote, but 'in all civilised speech the verb is the very nerve of a sentence' and 'in matters of intellectual or emotional persuasion the verb takes charge'.

Incidentally, it was during the war that there began in the *Lit Supp* itself a certain slackening off of formal, classical structure in the composition of the sentences. It was not the verbs that had started to disappear but the relative pronouns. In earlier *Lit Supp* pieces there was almost always a full battery of appropriate 'thats' and 'whichs' in any complex sentence. For example, from Murray's own review of John Middleton Murry's book in 1940, the sentence 'The English people know they are simply *not* responsible' would, in Richmond's day, almost certainly have read: 'The English people know *that* they are . . .' Now such sentences as Murray's were becoming more common.

Harold Child returned to Q when Q's *Memories and Opinions: An*

Unfinished Autobiography came out in December: Child evoked with delight Quiller-Couch's literary boyhood – such as reading *The Tempest* among some brambles into which it and he and other books and children had been tipped when a wheel came off his father's dog-cart – and said that the description of his grandfather's old house and dairy farm at Newton Abbot 'will set some of his readers aching with regret for the England that was'.

Still in Cambridge, Dr Leavis had brought out his book *Education and the University* – and still Leavis could have no personal complaint against the *Lit Supp*, for Brodribb in a leader applauded his concern that university English studies should develop in students 'such a power of critical thought as shall help to guide the community in all matters where disciplined thought is needed'. The subject of Leavis's book, concluded Brodribb, was nothing less than the mental health of the nation.

As for another notable university man, the great bibliographer A.W. Pollard, who died in March, a letter from a woman who knew him, Miss M. St Clair Byrne, told a touching story of his reply when someone mentioned his 'international reputation': all that that meant, he said, was that 'ten old men in different countries of the world have heard of one's work and don't approve of it'.

The double act of Charques and Fausset were still in charge of the fiction and poetry respectively. Charques enjoyed Virginia Woolf's posthumously published short stories in *A Haunted House*, but kept up the old *Lit Supp* complaint: 'She sensed beauty wherever beauty was to be found and held it for a moment in the rhythm of her prose; but there was nothing sufficiently earthy in her habit of mind to enable her to join the moment to the rest of human experience.' But in *Mrs Dalloway* and *To the Lighthouse*, at least, she surely did exactly that. Charques also found Joyce Cary's rumbustious portrait of the elderly artist Gulley Jimson in *The Horse's Mouth* too experimental, though he conceded it 'a droll sort of punch'.

Two war poets received appreciative notices. Fausset said that 'in Sidney Keyes's death during the last days of the Tunisian campaign, poetry lost one of its most gifted practitioners'. The 'lyrical passion' in his poems had 'a solemnity at once heroic and heartbroken'. Philip Tomlinson took over the obituary notice of Alun Lewis, and commended the irony that mingled with 'his sense of beauty's fragility in a world of violence'.

'Menander's Mirror' appeared every week in 1944, and Charles Morgan spread his net wide, very often writing some kind of inspiring, commemorative article. For instance on the first day of the year he described the potent inspiration still to be found in Westminster Abbey, the kind of morally-weighted descriptive writing in which he was at his best:

> Go there on an afternoon in this fifth winter of war. It is Sunday. Outside, a bleak drizzle is falling on the half-deserted streets. Many of those who now enter by the west door might not have gone in but to shelter from the increasing rain ... The afternoon Service is ending. For a little while an assembly of fighting-men and civilians waits at the barrier, looking in upon the shadowy congregation and the lighted altar. When the barrier is taken down, they flow on into the transepts, to the poets in the South or to the statesmen in the North, seeking, it would appear, in many instances, some monument that they have previously decided to visit. They find it, read the inscription, stand there for a time – then, turning away, hesitate, are at a loss; but their being at a loss for a particular direction becomes at once their opportunity to discover the whole Abbey, to feel its response, to be received into it, and they move henceforth with as lively and tranquil a wonder as a man has in a wood which, in youth, was his own, and is now both deeply familiar and half-forgotten.

Or again, Morgan wrote about Madame Duclaux, the reviewer for many years who was the first to write about Proust in the paper, and who had died in the Auvergne on 9 February – a death not reported in England until two months later. He evoked her Victorian girlhood in a house where Pater and Gosse were visitors, when she was still Mary Robinson – the daughter of G.T. Robinson, editor of the *Art Monthly Review*. He went on to praise her personal charm and her brilliance as a critic – 'her method was always to break down the ring of fashion or prejudice by which a living writer might be surrounded ... to relate his work to his intention, then to the achievement of the masters. Thus, with perfect relevance, she would quietly confront Claudel with Aeschylus.'

Menander also tackled issues such as the desperate need for more paper to be allotted to publishers by the government. This was a matter rumbling through the letter columns at this time as well, with one bookseller, S.R. Fuller, of Clifford Street, London, listing authors whose works were in constant demand but of which no copies were available: 'Jane Austen, the Brontës, John Buchan, E.M. Forster, D.H. Lawrence, Somerset Maugham, Kipling, Axel Munthe, Beverly Nichols, Mary

Webb, Galsworthy, Tolstoy, Dostoevsky, Ibsen, R.L.S., Cecil Roberts, Conan Doyle.'

When a collection of Menander's articles, called *Reflections in a Mirror* and acknowledging Morgan as the author, was published in December, it was reviewed in a signed article by Storm Jameson, who also made the point, in her dramatic way, about the paper shortage. Total war, she wrote, may have made inevitable the perversion of imagination and intelligence to the need to kill or simply to survive.

> But need it have made it impossible for us to buy new books unless we wait on the bookseller's doorstep on the day of publication, or old ones unless a supreme piece of luck takes us into an out-of-the-way shop where an only remaining copy has been hidden? This triumph of Dullness sharpens our gratitude for any counter-blow. We must regard it as such when *The Times* clears a weekly space in its shrunken *Literary Supplement* for the speculations of a subtle and detached but not unprejudiced mind, and places no restriction on it.

She went on to say that the surface of 'Menander's Mirror' was clear, while its depths held 'a rich interplay of wit and memory' – and found the mirror's only blind patch 'its insistence on the aridity of the writers of the twenties and thirties. (Or is this only the counter-prejudice of a critic who finds their aridity infinitely preferable to their soft core?)'

D.L. Murray wrote an accompanying leader about Menander. He said that he believed the paper had been right to give him enough space 'to develop his themes without hustle or abbreviation', and noted that 'his "belief in continuing grace", as Miss Storm Jameson phrases it on the page opposite, has been vindicated by the continuous lightening of the sky since the black days when he took up his pen with such courageous serenity'. He added that 'the volume of correspondence that has flowed into our office on the subject of his essays has shown the wide and heart-felt welcome accorded by our readers to this enterprise'.

Perhaps, in this last sentence, David Murray was cheering himself up. For when he wrote it on 9 December he already knew that his editorship of the *Lit Supp* was coming to an end.

Ironically, he had learned this fact from Charles Morgan. He had bumped into Morgan one day about this time, and Morgan had said 'So you're leaving the paper?' Murray was totally nonplussed: he had heard nothing. It transpired that Stanley Morison had asked Morgan if he would be interested in editing the *Lit Supp*. Morgan had said no, but he had naturally assumed that Murray was aware of the situation.

Murray, according to his friend Storm Jameson, was mortified by the discovery and the way it had come about, and went back to the office to write an immediate letter of resignation. He soon learned that Stanley Morison would be his successor. On 10 December, he wrote from Hove, where he now lived, to Simon Nowell-Smith, whom he had always hoped would take over the editorship. He said that he was retiring from the position early in the New Year, and knew whom Barrington-Ward had chosen to succeed him, but had been asked not to mention it yet. He had not been consulted about the decision or even given an opportunity of expressing an opinion. He went on: 'When I took over the editorship in 1938, which I could not have done without your invaluable help, I told you that if my recommendation was sought when my time came to go there was only one person I should recommend, and I have never swerved from that position. I should not like you to think that I had changed my mind or made any different suggestion. Simply, I was not consulted.' To Crook, Murray said, 'Sorry, Arthur, I'm afraid it's Steiney.'

Behind this story lay a number of conversations between Morison and Barrington-Ward about the *Lit Supp*. Neither was happy about its character now, even though many of its features had been introduced at Morison's behest. Murray's administration and judgment had both come under criticism at various times, as when 'Baudelaire' had been spelt 'Beaudelaire' in a Menander article, producing a magisterial rebuke from T.S. Eliot, or when Noël Coward's memoir of entertaining the forces had been given a front-page review. Besides Charles Morgan, John Sparrow, still a major in the Coldstream Guards, had been sounded out as a possible candidate, but in the end Barrington-Ward had invited Morison to take the editorship, and Morison, with some hesitation, had accepted.

Murray may have been deeply hurt by what was in effect his dismissal; nevertheless, he had things to console him. He had never been a full-time editor, and in the meanwhile he had become a best-selling novelist. The *Lit Supp* itself once carried an advertisement for a novel of his that read 'Cure your blues with light-hearted D.L. Murray', and included a picture of Murray jumping over a hedge on a horse.

Moreover, he had kept the paper going throughout the most difficult years of the war, with the London Blitz to contend with, and with many writers who might have reviewed for him away in the forces. He had loyally followed the lines set down when he became editor, and though the evidence did seem to be (and later even more clearly appeared to be) that the lighter paper was not so popular, its circulation had risen again, after a low point of 17,455 in 1941, to 22,063 in 1944 – only a few hundred copies fewer than it had been in 1937, the year before he took over.

His own contributions, though not numerous, had always been among the best things in the paper. The *Lit Supp* had also responded, through its reviews and leaders, and through Menander's articles, to all the great political and social debates set off by the war. However, Murray's greatest weakness had been to let Charques write so much – often half-a-dozen articles in a single issue. As we have amply observed, Charques reviewed a large number of the best novels that were published during the war, and was very grudging in his assessment of most of them. Charques was also allowed to write very uncritically about the Soviet Union after it entered the war, outdoing in this respect even E.H. Carr – whom, it must be feared, he was anxious to please. Murray was, it seems, also mistaken not to seek another main reviewer of poetry than Hugh d'Anson Fausset, whose interests 'gardening; pondering and singing' were pure and delightful occupations, but perhaps not enough for a critic of twentieth-century poetry.

David Murray – that 'good-humoured priest, large, soft, delicate in mind and manner', as Storm Jameson described him – left his editorial chair on 31 January 1945. In February, the black-suited Stanley Morison swept in.

Chapter Ten

Stanley Morison's Hard Read: 1945–47

Stanley Morison, who was fifty-five when he became editor of the *Times Literary Supplement*, was a striking and imposing figure, with a laugh as loud as D.L. Murray's – 'like the bursting of a paper bag', Alan Pryce-Jones called it. Pryce-Jones also described his appearance: 'He was tall and very thin. He stooped. He dressed in black, down to a stringy black tie, though on one day each year he wore a tie adorned with bathing belles. His eyesight was poor, so that he needed thick glasses, which were encased in wire.'

He was one of those mainly self-educated men of high intelligence who sometimes take thought and learning more seriously than those who have been brought up to be at ease with them. His father had been a commercial clerk in East London, and though Morison went to Owen's, a good Islington grammar school, he left at fourteen. Once, when a woman sitting next to him at a dinner party of Mrs E.H. Carr's asked him where he was educated, he replied, 'His Majesty's Prison, ma'am' – for he had been a conscientious objector in the First World War, and from 1916 to 1918 had spent much of his time in jail or in work centres, reading and growing tomatoes.

By 1916 he had also been converted to Roman Catholicism, and had taken his first steps on what was to be a distinguished career as a typographer. Before the war he had got a job on the *Imprint*, a new printing trade journal, and by 1919 he was 'Designer of Printed Matter' at Francis Meynell's Pelican Press. He went on to design new type for the Monotype Corporation, to become typographical adviser to Cambridge University Press and, as we have seen, to redesign *The Times* in 1932, and thereafter take charge of its typography and evolve into a general adviser to its editors. He had also, by the time he became editor of the *Lit Supp*, completed two volumes of *The History of The Times*, showing himself to be a powerful and cogent writer, and had almost finished the third volume, taking the story to 1912.

Before accepting the editorship, he had written a memo to Barrington-Ward, asking that he should also be appointed, as Bruce Richmond had been, an assistant editor of *The Times*. The memo even included a veiled threat: 'Promotion to the first place on the *Supplement* of a man who has not risen to a responsible position on the parent paper is hardly the best way to secure loyalty and discipline.' However, although he was granted the status of assistant editor, he was not given the formal title.

In fact, he had his critics on *The Times*. When Barrington-Ward, who had not had a particularly distinguished academic career, remarked, as Morison went out of the room, 'There goes the most intelligent man I know,' some of his colleagues thought him foolishly overawed, while the Catholic leader writer Dermot Morrah, who was also the Arundel Herald Extraordinary (and sometimes had to be helped into his great cloak in the office), always called Morison 'that unfrocked Jesuit'.

Nevertheless, Morison accepted the job, confident in his relationship with Barrington-Ward, and at once set about making major changes to the *Lit Supp*. The vigorous and good-humoured reforming spirit in which he approached this task can be seen in a letter he wrote to Mrs Carr in March 1945, a month after he had taken over: 'Would you like to attempt a weekly literary rag with three debilitated assistants, a secretary in hospital with pneumonia, and an arrears list of reviews dating back nine months?' He said that he had found there were two sorts of reviewers. First there were the hacks, who could always be relied on to give a summary of the book and leave the reader without any particular taste in his mouth, and whom 'I shall probably be taught by experience to prefer'. The second kind were the non-hacks, who could always be relied on to rise superior to the author they were reviewing, and show off their own knowledge. Both sorts sent their reviews in late, and if their review was questioned could not answer it because they had already sold the books. 'The best reviewer of the book is the author,' he concluded. 'I asked an author the other day whether he could suggest anybody who would review his book – thus giving him the chance to do it himself. Unfortunately he was such an English gentleman that he did not even like such a question being put to him, so I had all the trouble of finding an alternative.'

Morison was not an admirer of St John Brooks, who still ran the 'Other New Publications', and it was not long before he heard St John Brooks expressing a feeling of weariness and a longing to retire. He offered to arrange a speedy retirement for him, and brought in Kathleen Dowding, a woman of thirty-five, to take the book list over from him. She arrived in July 1945, with a heavy task ahead of her, since Morison now wanted all 'worthwhile' books noticed in it again, not just the selection that it had offered in Murray's time.

Tomlinson was no great favourite of Morison's either, but he stayed with the paper until 1947, and was largely instrumental in bringing in Morison's other new appointment in 1945, Edmund Blunden. Blunden had of course been a contributor closely associated with the paper for years, but it was only now that he joined the staff. He was in need of a job, since he had just lost his Fellowship at Merton College, Oxford, for having a love affair with a student. (Subsequently Blunden divorced his wife, the writer Sylva Norman, and the student became Clare Blunden.) He arrived in the office in June 1945, aged forty-nine, with a high reputation as a poet and critic, though after two years he was given leave to go and teach again, under the auspices of the Foreign Office, in Tokyo, where he had already had a spell lecturing at the university.

Tomlinson was delighted by Blunden's arrival at the *Lit Supp*, and the two shared a table facing each other, engaging in much jesting conspiracy. Tomlinson was sometimes rather somnolent after returning from lunch, and once he fell forward, fast asleep, with one of his hanks of hair covering the inkwell. Blunden leaned forward and gently parted the hair, and went on dipping his pen into the ink.

Arthur Crook also recalls Blunden passing a note to him during a dull meeting in a week when there had been a tame commemorative poem by the poet laureate, John Masefield, published in *The Times*. The note read:

> *Missing Words Competition*
>
> May Destiny, allotting what befalls,
> Grant to the newly-born a . . . .
> A guard more sure than wealth and more majestical,
> Assign to him, Fortune, a third . . . .
>
> Junior competition: Give your reasons for suspecting that the missing words are not 'choice of shawls' and 'tricycle'.

These staff changes strengthened the paper. But the main change that the *Lit Supp* experienced with Morison's arrival was the crowd of brilliant and learned new contributors he brought in. In the memo to

Barrington-Ward already mentioned, he had spoken of his intention 'to render the *Supplement* a critical and constructive medium of thought which would deserve recognition, in due time, as a literary institution', and to use 'the best critical pens available to deal with the output of philosophical, religious, political and historical works, while giving poetry, biography, memoirs, art and art history, and fiction their due'.

He was not troubled by the fact that his new plan for the paper was the exact opposite of the one he had imposed on Murray in 1937. His boast before the year was out was that 'I've made the *Supplement* hard to read again.'

In his second issue, 10 February 1945, Morison dropped the crossword, and to make the point more clearly did not even print the solution of the previous crossword. He also dropped the panel of 'Recommended Books' – that was also too frivolous for him. A month later he introduced what he thought was much more appropriate, a full index of 'Books Reviewed' on the leader page.

It was also announced this week that 'Menander's Mirror' would henceforth appear fortnightly, and on 28 April readers were told that Menander would be suspended after the present issue. Charles Morgan's last article, in this issue, ended on a grim note. He said that at the end of the First World War, most men looked forward to the resumption of a life not greatly different from their former life, and differing, where it differed, in being freer, less threatened, more active and light-hearted. But now 'no-one who is neither a gangster nor a dupe believes that an abundant paradise will spring from this chaos . . . What has been done must be paid for, and the debt is long'. That was the mood in Britain with which the war in Europe ended the following month.

The following March, Morison also made a typographical change, putting the paper into five columns instead of four. He calculated the number of words gained at 3,598 per issue, and was very pleased with this, since the paper was still generally restricted to twelve pages each week. The change also raised the question of payment, and Morison was able to persuade the management to go on paying the contributors at a basic rate of £3 a column. This was a distinct improvement in their pay, for there were now only 750 words to a column instead of 900. (£3, incidentally, was equivalent to about £90 now, so the contributors were getting the modern equivalent of about £120 a thousand words – slightly more than they are fifty years later.)

From the day of his arrival, moreover, Morison bumped up the fees of many distinguished or favoured contributors. On the marked copies, the fee is shown as a sum calculated strictly according to the £3 a column rule, with a further sum written beneath it, and the total initialled 'S.M'. Morison usually put the fee up to a round sum so that, for example, Namier one week received £19.12.0 + £5.8.0 = £25, and C.V. Wedgwood another week received £12.6.0 + £7.14.0 = £20. Morison felt it was too degrading to send pernickety figures to his best writers, and in any case felt the need to pay them more.

Those contributors were the heart of the matter. It must have given Morison enormous pleasure that in only his fourth issue, 24 February 1945, he was able to lead the correspondence columns with a learned letter about Swinburne's copy of Middleton's plays from Kenneth Muir at Leeds University, which began: 'In the *Times Literary Supplement* of June 17, 1939, Professor Larsen called attention to a copy of Bullen's edition of Middleton . . .' It was as though Morison's paper were simply continuing where the *Lit Supp* had left off before the war, and the lightweight years could be expunged from its history.

Morison opened his pages wide to Namier, the refugee art historian Nikolaus Pevsner, E.H. Carr – of course – and D.W. Brogan, outstanding young scholars such as A.J.P. Taylor, Noel Annan, Anthony Blunt, the economist Graham Hutton and the historian of France David Thomson, and leading members of *The Times* staff old and new such as Dermot Morrah, Iverach McDonald and T.E. Utley. The short front-page article was quickly dropped, and a long lead piece restored, now often running over on to a third page, while the long 'middle' was preserved intact. Meanwhile the scholarly letters began pouring in again, many of them once more from the United States.

Namier, who was a close friend of his, was a backbone to the paper in Morison's three years of editorship. In April, before the war had ended and while the Russians were over-running Eastern Europe, he was championing the cause of an independent Poland with 'its natural frontiers on the Oder and the Baltic'. In July, reviewing at length Hugh Seton-Watson's classic book *Eastern Europe Between the Wars*, he argued that although the old ruling classes disappeared from Europe because they were not equal to their task, their countries were nevertheless the poorer for the loss of them – and he welcomed the news that some 'younger members of the highest nobility' took part in the Czech resistance movement, and were about to enter the service of the Czech Republic. 'If they do and are fully accepted, Czechoslovakia will have achieved a reconciliation of social radicalism with historic traditions.'

Namier sketched out in such articles the possibilities for the restoration of a 'civilised Europe', before the shadow of Russia had fallen clearly over the Continent – exactly the kind of review that Morison wanted in the *Lit Supp*. Namier also wrote some powerful reviews of books on Germany and the Germans: these reviews offered grim warnings to the victors, urging them not to forget (as in one article headed 'The Road to Nuremberg') that the war had shown that there was such a thing as 'a Belsen of the mind and the spirit'. These articles can be set against the criticism often made of Namier that, though he was a master of historical detail, he could not take larger views of historical change.

E.H. Carr was also given his head by his old friend Morison, and allowed to argue left-wing, verging on Communist, propositions. For instance, in a review of *The Children of Light and the Children of Darkness* by the Protestant theologian Reinhold Niebuhr – which itself proclaimed the merits of a distinctly socialist form of Western democracy – Carr asked if such a form of government, though it may be suitable for 'the sheltered world of American bourgeois civilisation', was dynamic enough for a shattered Europe, which needed 'a more positive, more specifically social vindication of democracy'.

Where Carr was looking was obvious from such pieces as an article on 'Marshal Stalin' in the month the war in Europe ended, which concluded with an admiring portrayal of the Russian leader, 'who has emerged both as a more commanding and as a more human figure . . . at the height of his authority and activity . . . with an era of social and economic expansion ahead such as the world has never known'. In 1947, reviewing Christopher Hill's *Lenin and the Russian Revolution*, Carr openly praised Lenin for the 'compound of consistency and flexibility' with which he had implemented his revolutionary policies – and implicitly praised Stalin for continuing those policies with the same skill. In another long article about Alexander Herzen, and the 'revolution of the intellectuals' that he inspired in nineteenth-century Russia, Carr's final accolade for Herzen was the elementary Marxist one that 'his thought was a necessary step in the development of the Russian revolution'.

Morison really, it seems, just liked this kind of vigorous argument, and having quite a strong socialist bias himself, felt that Carr's views – in holding which he was far from alone in the world of the late 1940s – were well worth publishing. Moreover Carr was still writing leaders for *The Times* which, if not so explicit as some of these reviews, were still coloured by the same opinions. But Morison was by no means inter-

279

ested in making the *Lit Supp* a left-wing journal. He wrote very little for the paper himself, but when President Roosevelt died in April 1945, he contributed an eloquent leader. Morison, the old master typographer, who had always lived with print, hailed Roosevelt's famous 'fireside chats' on the radio as inaugurating a completely new era in communication. But Morison also praised Roosevelt for the help he gave writers and scholars during the Depression, through his Works Project Administration. 'The world leader who set "freedom of expression" first among the human freedoms had already sent his country to the aid of economically crippled writers, poets and dramatists,' Morison wrote. 'It was Lincoln and Whitman who held open the door of immortality when Roosevelt strode across the stars to join them.'

'Freedom of expression' did mean more to Morison than any of the views that were expressed in the exercise of that freedom. Just as prominent as Carr in his reviewing team – besides Namier – were Denis Brogan and David Thomson, who held much more liberal views than Carr. In the second month of his editorship, Morison sent Carr's book *Nationalism and After* to Brogan, who opined that Carr, in his impatience with nationalism and its crimes, was far too ready to believe that it was on its way out in the world. Brogan took the opportunity to suggest slyly that the Soviet Union itself was just a 'super-national' state, and one, moreover, of a particularly horrible kind.

The following year, Brogan reviewed Bertrand de Jouvenel's book *Du Pouvoir*, and here he put up a plain liberal warning against the dangers of 'The Saviour State', as his review was headed: 'All the movement of the age has been towards the uncritical exaltation of State power. Where today are the Pluralists, the guild Socialists, the Anarchists? Reduced to tiny sects or transformed into uncritical acceptors of the saviour State. It is not only in France that the old wariness of the State, and the lesson of not putting unlimited trust in princes or parties, has been forgotten.'

Contemporary France was in fact the main subject of Brogan's reviews, and in April 1945 he discussed with notable knowledge and insight the trial of Charles Maurras, who had been condemned for treason in France soon after liberation. Brogan suggested that it was his perverted monarchism that had led Maurras – who actually hated Germany even more than he hated 'Protestant, liberal, triumphant England' – to give his support to Pétain after the German invasion: 'Government by one man, even a senile and heirless man, was better than the "headless state", as he called the restored republic at his trial.' This review led to an odd letter protesting against François Mauriac's views on the Dreyfus case, and Brogan had to point out in a reply that the letter-writer had confused Mauriac – 'one of those libertarian Catholics most detested by Maurras' – with Maurras himself. The French philosopher Gabriel Marcel also wrote an article, two years later, arguing that some of the French who had supported Pétain had believed that under this honest man the country could undergo a kind of spiritual purification, while waiting to take up arms again. They were *patriotes de la collaboration*. But he acknowledged that they been under a 'vast illusion'.

There were many other assaults of varying character on totalitarianism. Carr was certainly not having it all his own way in the *Lit Supp*. The thirty-year-old Noël Annan, just back from serving in the British Control Commission in Germany, and now a Fellow of King's College, Cambridge, gently regretted Arthur Calder-Marshall's failure to see, in his book on Yugoslavia, *The Watershed*, how repressive the Communist regime in that country was, and urged this pre-war left-wing writer, who had fought in Spain, to recognise that the political watersheds had changed since then.

Harold Stannard, who had been such an important political writer before the war, and would die in December 1947 at the age of sixty-four, took a rather amusing line on one of the most influential post-war books, Karl Popper's *The Open Society and Its Enemies*. He wholeheartedly agreed with its devastating attack on totalitarianism in any form, but said that Popper was less clear on what the 'open society' should do, apart from occasional experiments in social engineering to make it freer still. He said that Popper should not be surprised 'if few followers are attracted to a leader who assures them not only that the way is long but that it leads to no Tipperary'.

Victor Kravchenko's *I Chose Freedom*, with its graphic account of Soviet labour camps and the power of the NKVD, was hailed by Iverach McDonald as deserving 'a front place in the library of Soviet studies'. And in October 1946, David Thomson put very clearly what he called the current 'unanimity of general policy' of all the major parties in Britain and France. This was at the end of a review of A. Ramos Oliveira's book, *Politics, Economics and Men of Modern Spain, 1808–1946*. Thomson defined this widespread liberal view as follows: 'Only by the recovery of the vision of a society of free and equal citizens, enjoying rights freely because they are equally enjoyed by all, is democracy likely to meet successfully the challenge of totalitarian collectivism.' This was a very fair account of the state of mind in which Western Europe approached the Cold War that was just beginning.

As for Britain itself, the strongest recurrent note in the paper was precisely an appeal for the people and the parties to work together. Reviewing a string of political pamphlets in June 1945, just before the first general election that there had been for a decade, Donald Tyerman deplored the fact that the purpose of most of the election literature was simply 'to assist candidates and their supporters to blacken the record of their opponents'. This stricture applied as much to the Conservative Quintin Hogg as to Labour's Konni Zilliacus and Aneurin Bevan.

On 8 March 1947, when the Labour government's White Paper, the Economic Survey for 1947, was published, H.F. Carlill wrote a long lead, 'The Call to a New Britain'. This was immediately after two weeks when the paper did not appear – apart from a single page incorporated in *The Times* itself – because of the economic situation, especially the shortage of fuel, that winter.

Carlill was a retired civil servant from the Board of Trade whom Morison had discovered and encouraged as a writer – Morison was good at bringing out unexpected qualities in people. In the White Paper, Carlill said, the great economic crisis had now received official recognition. Though he disliked its dry figures and toneless style – 'Armageddon expressed in algebraic equations' – this document was 'the most fateful publication that the *Literary Supplement* has needed to record since the Blue Book of September 1939 on the declaration of war against Germany'. It was the first time that a British government, or perhaps any government, had attempted to 'exhibit the nation's resources and needs as a whole, and the material which must be moulded into a coherent plan'. It was a dismal catalogue of losses, arrears, deficiencies, maladjustments – 'the *damnosa hereditas* of total war'.

As for what it called for – and Carlill agreed with that call – that was nothing less than a national revival – 'a great constructive effort by all the British people'. That meant not only economic and intellectual mobilisation but also a moral one. Patriotism, courage and above all a higher social morality were needed. 'Austerity is certain to be our portion for a long while to come. Let it be the austerity of a lean, athletic people passionately reforging a great destiny.' The note was almost Churchillian – and the article received such an enthusiastic response from readers that it was immediately reprinted as an eight-page pamphlet, price 2d.

Two rival historians of post-war Britain were now becoming prominent – the left-inclined A.J.P. Taylor and the right-inclined H.R. Trevor-

Roper. In June 1946, Taylor reviewed Harold Nicolson's book, *The Congress of Vienna*. Nicolson wanted to draw parallels with the end of the First World War, and also with the current state of peacemaking in Europe, but Taylor did not think that those parallels were very close; however, it was interesting to watch statesmen at work on the perpetual task of adjusting national interests to international needs, 'for this interest does not change even when they were not engaged on exactly the problems which threaten to baffle their successors'. He engaged himself in the current argument over peacemaking in an article on 'The Degradation of Germany' the following spring, when he complained of the victors' failure to agree on any policy for Germany, and declared that they had one imperative duty – 'to remain united and so prevent a new Hitler from seducing the Germans'. Meanwhile Trevor-Roper's memorable book *The Last Days of Hitler* had been published, and R.W. Cooper, a *Times* sports journalist who had become a war correspondent and covered the Nuremberg trials, said that his account of Hitler's death 'in the clammy darkness of the air-raid shelter' – which so many people, especially among the Germans, were reluctant to believe in – was a 'convincingly argued narrative'.

Apart from Marxism, would Morison attempt to infiltrate Roman Catholicism into the *Lit Supp*? This was another thing that some people in Printing House Square were concerned about when he was appointed, and there was particular alarm when on 6 October 1945 he published an article to commemorate the conversion of John Henry Newman. Not only did the reviewer say that 'After having rendered signal and lasting service to the Church of England, he still had the second half of a long life to devote with unfaltering loyalty to the service of a greater church', but the article was also accompanied by two photographs, especially taken for the paper, of Newman's surplices and hood, with one of the surplices on a bust of Newman. The photographs were taken in Birmingham Oratory, and Arthur Crook had had the task of arranging the vestments – while the compositors thought that the photographs looked like pictures of a barber's shop, and hung them up with the caption 'Next, please'.

However, Morison was able to tell his critics that the article had in fact been written by a Church of England clergyman, Canon Francis Hutchinson of Worcester, and Barrington-Ward, having spoken to Morison, wrote in his diary on 8 October: 'I assured Morison once more of my confidence that he wd see fair play to all religions. Felt sure he was making a great thing out of the *Suppt.* and did not want him to prejudice himself with some suspicious readers by the kind of inexpediency produced last week.'

In fact, when Ronald Knox's new translation of the New Testament came out the following April, it was quite sharply criticised by a regular theological reviewer, the Revd Hedley Sparks, late Professor of the Interpretation of Holy Scripture at Oxford. Sparks greatly admired the style of the new version, but regretted that Knox had been obliged by the Catholic hierarchy to translate it from the Vulgate Latin approved by Pope Clement VIII, not from the Greek, so that it was a translation of a translation. Moreover, the Clementine Vulgate was sometimes an incorrect translation, and though Knox knew this, he had only amended it by adopting readings from earlier Vulgate translations – 'pinning his faith to a Latin text, even when he knows it is probably wrong'. And where he had found all the Vulgate texts wrong, he had sometimes left a passage deliberately ambiguous. So the translation, Sparks concluded, was 'hardly an unqualified success'.

Morison's pleasure in such give-and-take in the discussion of religious, as much as political, matters comes out in some letters he exchanged with the Irish dramatist St John Ervine when he was writing an article to celebrate Bernard Shaw's ninetieth birthday. Writing from his house (called 'Honey Ditches') in Seaton, Devon on 6 April 1946, Ervine promised the article within a week, and added 'I go to Belfast at the end of the month for a draught of Orangeade . . . Have you ever pondered on the fact that whereas the national emblem of the poor Irish Papist is an insignificant weed, the shamrock, the emblem of the Ulster Protestant is the lovely Orange Lily?'

Two days later, Morison replied: 'I hope we may meet after your visit to Belfast. I was under the impression that you had a conscientious objection to going near the place but stoked up as you will be with nice fuel for the anti-Papist controversy I should find you extra good value.' On the same day (such was the speed of postal delivery then) Ervine wrote back: 'What makes you think I have a conscientious objection to going near Belfast? Eire, yes, but the Six Counties, no. Never again, so help me God, shall I defile my feet by setting them on Eireann soil. But I glorify myself as often as I can by going home to Ulster.' Far from being offended by these smears on his Church, Morison wrote 'Come up and see us in the first week of July and I will add the fare to an unusually fat cheque.'

1946 saw the publication of two books that were to become standard reading for older schoolchildren and undergraduates – not to say innumerable adults – for many years to come. They rode the crest of the wave of that revived passion for learning and understanding that swept through Britain in the immediate post-war years. These were Bertrand Russell's well-timed *History of Western Philosophy* and E.V. Rieu's prose translation of *The Odyssey* for the new Penguin Classics series. Morison saw their likely impact and gave them both long reviews in the paper.

However, the *Lit Supp* review of the Russell book was a cautionary one. The book went to Dr J.B. Hawkins, the parish priest at Esher, who was highly sceptical of its basic contention that 'All definite knowledge belongs to science.' It meant, he said, that Russell had excluded from consideration at least half the questions which occupy the chief attention of philosophers, and implied that most philosophy was moonshine. Moreover, there was a contradiction in it. Russell displayed a profound respect for the personality and rights of the human individual. But how could one have that respect for a mere 'bundle of sense-data'? The book, said Hawkins, was eminently readable, full of wit and acumen, but its 'agnostic empiricism' was not enough to satisfy men's needs: 'while we owe him a debt for entertainment, we must turn from him and look for something of greater weight and substance'.

By contrast, the new *Odyssey* got a wholehearted welcome from R.W. Moore, the classicist headmaster of Harrow School (who had tried to create in Harrow itself the atmosphere of a small university town). Moore said that Rieu had 'brushed away all the cobwebs of traditional phrase, whether literal or archaic, and his approach is fresh, direct and clean of line . . . He who would evangelise must go into the market-place and speak in the language of the people.' Best of all, the book cost only a shilling – and was to be followed by many more Penguin Classics. His generation must recognise that the cherished translations of their youth had not worn well.

One more publishing venture that would have a long post-war life was also under way at Allen Lane's Penguin Books – Nikolaus Pevsner's *Buildings of England* series, which would open the eyes of the English as never before to the wealth of their architectural heritage. The first of the chunky volumes would not appear until 1951, though Pevsner had been working on them since 1945; meanwhile Morison snapped him up to write many learned and lively reviews of art and architectural history.

He reviewed Sacheverell Sitwell's *British Architects and Craftsmen* in July 1945, welcoming the author's plea for a less parochial spirit in the treatment of British architecture, and regretting England's unnecessary 'inferiority complex' on the subject. He observed that critics had been worried by the seemingly illogical fact that the British revived great Palladian architecture in their country houses at just the same time as they were inventing the picturesque garden, and suggested, in his characteristically witty way, that Palladian and picturesque belong together in the English character 'as tails and tweeds in our way of dressing. English life would be drab without the one, unbearable without the other.'

This review, and another in 1946 of Fiske Kimbell's *The Creation of the Rococo*, both led to spirited argument in the letters columns about the nature of rococo and baroque. Replying to a correspondent who said there was no real distinction between them, Pevsner attempted a definition: baroque was an active, expansive, conquering, dramatic style, found in Bernini and Rembrandt and Wren; rococo was the style of the aperçu, witty, playful, sophisticated, neither too profound nor too systematic, and found in Guardi, Casanova, Voltaire, Lord Chesterfield and Horace Walpole. Charles Marriott, now the *Times* art critic, added his contribution in a letter: 'For practical purposes, would it not be enough to say that Rococo is fricasseed Baroque?'

These debates set the scene for many later arguments on matters of art and architecture in the *Lit Supp*. John Betjeman and Osbert Lancaster also started writing in the paper now about architecture – and Betjeman was already implicitly crossing swords with Pevsner in a leader called 'The New Pedantry' that he contributed in September 1947. 'The introduction of professionalism into such subjects as literature, architecture and art too often turns enjoyment to ashes,' he wrote, and he regretted that 'the vanity of prefixing "Doctor" or "Professor" to a surname and some letters after it' had crept from Germany and America into Britain. For years afterwards Betjeman would grumble about Pevsner, 'that dull pedant from Prussia', both in articles and private letters.

A cartoonist with a sharp eye for buildings and interiors and what they expressed about people, Osbert Lancaster took on *The Castles on the Ground* by another noteworthy architectural writer of the time, the champion of modernism J.M. Richards, but he confined himself to observing, with a rather detached irony, that the British would always want a Jacobean inglenook rather than a labour-saving operating theatre: 'man cannot live by plumbing alone'. Anthony Blunt, later to be better known as a spy than an art historian, also appeared in Morison's pages. Reviewing John Rewald's *The History of Impressionism*, he gave a formidable account of how much the Impressionist painters had taken from their predecessors – 'from Courbet an interest in country subjects and a new breadth of handling . . . from Corot the study of the different effects of light at different moments of the day . . .' – but he concluded that Zola was right to observe that 'they had deliberately eliminated all interest in human beings and human emotions'. The Impressionists were not for him – though he did not give any hint that the Socialist Realists were.

In the programme for the *Lit Supp* that he had proposed in his memo to Barrington-Ward, Morison seemed to give a somewhat lesser role to poetry and fiction than to learned studies and political works – and, to begin with, that order of priorities certainly showed in his paper.

The reviewers of literary subjects remained much the same people, and Morison's new appointment, Edmund Blunden, started writing regular leaders of a very much more old-fashioned kind than the contributions such reviewers as Namier and Carr, Brogan and Pevsner were making. Blunden's leaders often struck a note very like that of Charles Lamb's essays over a century earlier, suggesting that the good old writers – Kit and Ben, or Noll and Bozzy – were still sitting around in tavern or coffee house, where one could always call in and have a chat about books with them.

No doubt Morison astutely calculated that he did not want to lose too many readers by his cultivation of 'hard' contributions, and literature could to some extent be exploited to add a lighter or cosier touch to the paper. However, he was also very alert to current intellectual moods, and he jumped at the chance, when it came, of appointing as his deputy a dashing writer and critic who knew many of the other younger writers – Alan Pryce-Jones.

Pryce-Jones, who was thirty-eight in 1946, had been at Eton and Magdalen, and before the war had been John Squire's assistant for several years on the *London Mercury*. He had worked in intelligence at Bletchley Park during the war, after which he had ended up as a lieutenant-colonel ('a basic rank by 1945 for those who had been in the army more than five years,' he said, with his usual way of making light of anything he achieved), and now, married to an Austrian woman and with a son, he was looking for a job. He was very well-connected socially, far outside the world of letters; it was said that he appeared among the list of guests at every function reported on the Court page of *The Times*, or if he did not, it was he who was meant by the words '*et al*'.

Pryce-Jones joined the *Lit Supp* staff in November 1946, and gave a vivid description in his journal of his first day on the paper:

Opposite me Edmund Blunden is reading *The Times* of 1826. He is like a knobbly, charitable little bird, neither clean nor dirty, non shaved non unshaven. Not much talk – but what there is comes out with a most charming, immensely gentle, radiance. He is writing an article on Test Cricket for the Church of England Newspaper, I gather. Beside him is Philip Tomlinson – equally small and kind – dictating a small, kind letter. Whatever I wear I feel my clothes are wrong. If I put on a dark suit it looks like the suit of an interloper who has thrown in his lot with the editor. If I wear tweeds they are the wrong kind of tweeds, too weekendish or too gay. I hide my umbrella behind a tin-box, because I ought to be carrying a mackintosh. I feel like a family solicitor, or shareholder, or dilettante – anything but an unobtrusive new-boy.

On the facing page of his journal he added a comment on Blunden that reflected the same unease – an unease, half attraction, half repulsion, that he perhaps never entirely lost in all the years he was editing the *Lit Supp*. Certainly after these entries his journal continued to be almost entirely about his travels and his social life, with only very occasional references to his life on the paper:

> Extraordinarily ugly hands, Edmund Blunden's. A heavy spatulate thumb, and the kind of dead red which goes uneasily off to white at the wrists when the sleeve is rolled up. Yet, with this clumsy member, a beautiful script is formed, and fast-written, too. (Is not a *beautiful* handwriting compensation for some essential deficiency?)

He became assistant editor and the recognised heir to the editorship in July 1947, and editor on 1 February 1948, exactly three years after Morison.

After Pryce-Jones joined the paper, the reviewing of poetry and fiction changed its character as he brought in new people and new ideas. In fact the arrival of contributors such as John Betjeman and Osbert Lancaster was mainly due to him. But Fausset remained one of Morison's poetry critics for a while. In Morison's first week as editor, Fausset reviewed George Barker's *Eros in Dogma*. He was far more attracted to the new Romantic poets than he had been to their thirties predecessors, and said that although Barker was 'too self-intoxicated and self-torn a poet to possess the power which possesses him, the expression of that power, even when he almost frenziedly assails the inexpressible with a torrent of realistic images, is formidably his own'. A month later he reviewed W.H. Auden's new volume, *For The Time Being*, and acknowledged development in it. There were still 'elaborately ironic pyrotechnics' in the two long poems in the book, but the serious-ness of his theme sounded through – 'the search for a way out of the intellectualism that splits experience into two unreal halves ... the abyss which opens up before the disintegrated soul'. The review perhaps reflected his preoccupations more than Auden's.

Blunden took over much of the poetry reviewing when he arrived in June 1945. In August, he wrote a good, well-informed middle on the two war poets, Sidney Keyes and Alun Lewis, though it did not entirely free itself from his usual deftly-expressed generalities – 'If both have something to say of death,' it concluded, 'both have a place among the poets who have said a word for love.' In November, he gave a long, admiring review to Walter de la Mare, who was now in his sixties, declaring that 'the light on his pilgrimage is derived, if any poet's ever were, from a changeless heaven'. In January 1946 he reviewed *New Bats in Old Belfries* by John Betjeman, calling him 'the John Clare of suburbia and upriver places, and not least happy in North Oxford'. Professor Garrod, a colleague of Blunden's at Merton College, Oxford, reviewed Blunden's own book on Shelley in May 1946, praising the author's 'fine narrative talent' but asking 'why, in this mid-twentieth century, so much set on so many of Shelley's ideals, so socialistic, so scientific, so free-thinking, in this striving age the striving Shelley seems to live less than less likely poets?' Garrod asked the question, but – as a leading Keats scholar – he did not seem so much to mind the fact.

A young critic, A.M. Hardie, expressed admiration of Dylan Thomas's *Deaths and Entrances* in March 1946, but did not do much more than characterise it – 'the earlier symbolism and "surrealism"' remained, he said, but there was 'more clarity and fervid observation with a picturesqueness of language and imagery'; while in May he applauded the 'mastery of many moods' of yet another of the predomi-nantly romantic post-war poets, Henry Reed, in his collection *The Map of Verona*. These books won their fame through other means.

The important new poetry critic was G.S., or George, Fraser. He was an ebullient Scotsman who had published poems in a neo-romantic vein during the war, but was also acutely alert to other possibilities in contemporary poetry, and well schooled in the critical ideas and style emanating from Eliot and Leavis. In 1946 he was thirty, just married, and making himself at home in London's post-war Bohemia, with many poets among his friends.

In fact it was Blunden, who had met him at a dinner of the Poets' Club, who invited him to write for the *Lit Supp*. His first assignment, in August 1946, a middle on Osbert Sitwell's second volume of memoirs, *The Scarlet Tree*, was a difficult one, but his account of its wit and fun went down well, and he became a regular contributor to the paper for the rest of his life. However, it was a little later, under Pryce-Jones's editorship, that he really began to exert his influence.

R.D. Charques went on rampaging among the novels for a time after Morison was appointed. He hated Aldous Huxley's *Time Must Have A Stop*, both for its 'cynical japing and jibing' about people and for its confident, mystical apprehension of eternity. 'It seems a little odd,' wrote Charques, in March 1945, 'that so incommunicable a sense of indwelling superiority should lead him to write a novel about human beings at all.' Philip Tomlinson backed Charques up with a leader in the same issue regretting that Huxley 'scorns all human effort at betterment'.

Charques was no more happily struck two months later by Arthur Koestler's *The Yogi and the Commissar*, which he felt did not 'give a balanced impression of Russia' – in fact, it was no more than a 'furious excoriation'. The following May he was equally derisive about Elias Canetti's story of the downfall of an obsessive scholar, *Auto da Fé* – 'the professor has no existence whatsoever', and the whole book was a 'ponderous and trivial caprice'. Henry Green's *Back* in November 1946 was 'negligible in substance' though it had a 'low-pitched veracity of dialogue'. One novel he did enjoy was Simenon's *The Shadow Falls*: he called Simenon 'a chilly anatomist of our blind desires', and said that if he was 'not quite in the great family of French moralists . . . his resources go a long way beyond crime and detection'.

The novel reviewed by Charques during these three years that has endured best with readers is Evelyn Waugh's *Brideshead Revisited*, which came out in June 1945. He did give this a more considered notice. He noted Waugh's claim that the book was an attempt to 'trace the workings of the divine purpose' in a half-paganised English Catholic family, and was doubtful if Waugh had been successful in doing that. But he found the novel extremely amusing – 'Mr Waugh's humour is of several kinds – the ribald, the oblique and sophisticated, the intellectually astringent – and each is paraded with a careful and flowing ease'

– and he thought the Oxford scenes were 'very well done in their way, though it is a rather lordly way'. However 'in general Mr Waugh seems to have had his style cramped by a too obviously preconceived idea'. Waugh himself noted in his diary that 'most of the reviews have been adulatory except where they were embittered by class resentment' – was there a touch of this in Charques's use of the word 'lordly'?

By the time Mr Waugh's next novel was published, another man, brought in by Pryce-Jones, had taken over as the chief novel reviewer. This was the novelist Anthony Powell. He had left Eton too early for Pryce-Jones to have known him there, but they had often met during the war on night duty in the cellars of the War Office. The reviews Powell now started writing for the *Lit Supp* were in principle more sympathetic to the novel and to novelists, but he was carefully analytical, and could be very critical too, and Waugh, though a friend of his since Oxford days, might have been no better pleased with his piece in December 1947 on the new book, *Scott-King's Modern Europe*, than with Charques's review of *Brideshead*.

In this short novel about the visit of a teacher of classics to a totalitarian state, Powell approved of the author's strong individual voice at a time when, he said, many writers seemed to speak with the voice of a group, and liked the 'almost cantankerous' satire on the world of VIPs and jacks-in-office, which was 'concise, witty, making its points with hammer-blows'. But he thought that there was a certain inconsistency in Waugh's approach at two levels, the realistic and the satirical, and would have liked more of the lighter, naturalistic side, such as the treatment of headmaster, boys and common room.

Powell wrote a number of other reviews in that autumn of 1947, and many more after Pryce-Jones became editor. One other notable review that year was of *The Light and the Dark*, the first novel in C.P. Snow's *Strangers and Brothers* sequence. In characteristically judicious tones, Powell said that it was 'a painstaking and readable account of university life seen from high tables. It would give a foreigner a fair idea of the types he might meet and the opinions that he might hear expressed in such circles. With personal relationships the author is less at home . . .' Powell himself would soon start work on his own, twelve-volume novel sequence, *A Dance to the Music of Time*.

Another contributor Pryce-Jones introduced was the lively and original author of novels and travel books, Rose Macaulay – later Dame Rose Macaulay. A middle article she wrote on Ivy Compton-Burnett's novel *Manservant and Maidservant* on 22 March 1947, marked a turning point in the *Literary Supplement*'s treatment of fiction – as Murray's old friend Willson Disher said in a congratulatory letter to the paper on 19 April: 'By giving a place of honour in your paper to the review of a novel you have removed a long-standing reproach against the conservative practices of English literary criticism.'

Indeed this was the first time that a new English novel had been given a full-page article to itself in the paper. In due course, such treatment – which became a regular feature of the paper – came to be regarded by novelists as a sign that they had 'arrived'. Rose Macaulay's inaugural fiction 'middle' was also an excellent article in its own right. She wrote that Compton-Burnett's novels, with their 'macabre atmosphere of melancholy domestic unkindness, resentment, fear and intrigue, lightened by the éclaircissement of wit and humour', were the opposite of mid-Victorian family tales. The sensation they gave us was 'as if, after reading Keble's *Christian Year*, we should say a Black Mass'.

Ronald Lewin, who later became a popular military historian, also contributed some novel reviews in 1947. In January, he wrote that 'more should be heard about the young American author of *Dangling Man*', that is Saul Bellow, whose first book this was: 'Avoiding the Scylla and Charybdis which catch most transatlantic novelists, it is neither hard-boiled nor flagrantly romantic. It is simply an account of an ordinary man's experiences elevated, by imagination, into an individual work of art.' He was equally correct in his prediction for Philip Larkin when he reviewed his novel *A Girl in Winter* in March (in the same issue, in fact, as Rose Macaulay's article): the author was 'a young man with an exceptionally clear sense of what, as a writer, he means to do and how to achieve his ends . . . His novel has a pleasant ease and gives many indications of promise.' Two major writers of the next decades were coming into sight here and well spotted.

Pryce-Jones himself wrote a number of reviews of novels. In fact he had, nominally, done a long piece on Christopher Isherwood's *Prater Violet* in September 1946, but it was not so much an article about that one novel or that one writer as a general survey of the writers of the thirties. Oddly enough, in its own metaphorical, post-war idiom, it takes a view of that decade not so different from that of most of the older *Lit Supp* reviewers. Pryce-Jones chose W.H. Auden's *The Orators* as representative of the thirties in its dry, stony character: 'The explosions of Mr Auden's vitality throw up mineral fragments of enchanting shape and colour; it is the animal and vegetable elements which are missing from a world which . . . never conceives a population except in terms of a moraine left by, while the glacial flow of circumstance is watched by a small party of friends shouting their private jokes up the valley'. Since then, he wrote, we have seen the thirties writers groping for faith, and 'the interest of the next few years lies in the prospect that one or two will find hope and charity as well'.

As for the French 'existentialist' novels, Alick Dru reviewed Sartre's *Les Chemins de la Liberté* in October 1946, and Gabriel Marcel reviewed Camus's *La Peste* in August 1947. Dru was a friend of Anthony Powell's, and the original of the narrator Nick's languidly intellectual wartime friend Pennington, in *A Dance to the Music of Time*. The Sartre review appeared as part of a brilliant survey of existentialist shades and groups extending 'from the atheistic right of M. Sartre and Professor Heidegger to the Christian personalists of the left who number M. Mounier and Gabriel Marcel, and Professor Jaspers who provides the centre.' (Dru did not elaborate on this provocative association of Sartre with the right, though it comes out in his stress on the influence of Nietzsche on Sartre.)

In the end, Dru was not convinced by the novel's attempt to represent Sartre's idea of existential freedom, though he tried carefully to define the nature of that supposed freedom. 'Sartre refuses to interpose the dream world of reason and Olympus between himself and the horrors and terrors of existence . . . The liberty of M. Sartre's heroes is indeed to be nothing.' But this liberty, Dru wrote, was itself 'a purely literary victory'. 'A suspicion exists,' Dru added in his delicate way, 'whether "the choice" that is put before the individual who would "exist" is really quite so terrible as Sartre depicts it. So terrible a choice can hardly be open to all men, as it surely must be, unless French existentialism is to sink into an esoteric mystery.'

Gabriel Marcel – who in turn was a friend of Dru's – was much more impressed with Camus's *La Peste*, which proposed a very different response to those 'horrors and terrors'. It was a work of 'sober maturity'; it showed 'a handful of individuals who react each in his own way to the incomprehensible evil' of the plague in their city, which 'little by little turns above all to a sickness of heart'; and it seemed to appeal in the end for 'a sainthood without God'. 'Firmness and unvarying beauty of style make of this novel a work of art in the most venerable sense of the phrase.'

The drama of the Wise forgeries went on reverberating through Morison's editorship. On 28 April 1945 P.H. Muir, a leading antiquarian bookseller, reviewed a book that had been published in New York, *Letters of Thomas J. Wise to John Henry Wrenn*. The editor of the book was Miss Fannie E. Ratchford, the custodian of rare books at the University of Texas, where the late John Henry Wrenn's books and correspondence were now held. Muir said that Miss Ratchford's book showed clearly that Wise had faked title pages in books that he had sold to Wrenn, and had falsified bibliographical works in order to cover his deceptions. 'The full malice of the transactions is appreciated only when it is remembered that they were made not as between a trade bookseller and a client, but as between one friend and enthusiastic bibliophile to another.' The revelations made Carter and Pollard's charges 'finally irrefutable'. Wise, known in his time as 'decent, jovial, and an ardent lover of books', emerged as 'a crafty and unscrupulous bookseller'.

On 1 June 1946 there was a signed article by Carter and Pollard following up the book they had published twelve years earlier. This was an extended review of a University of Texas publication called *Between the Lines: Letters and Memoranda interchanged by H. Buxton Forman and Thomas J. Wise*. In this article, Carter and Pollard reproduced from the book part of a letter from Buxton Forman to Wise, with Wise's handwritten interlinear comments. It clearly proved the complicity of the two men in producing forged copies of a book of Ruskin letters. At last Carter and Pollard were able to say – what they had not said explicitly in their book in Wise's lifetime – that he was the forger of the rare Victorian pamphlets that they had shown to be forged. 'Wise,' they wrote, 'is at last convicted.'

One issue still hovered in the air – was Edmund Gosse in any way mixed up in the matter? Miss Ratchford had claimed in her book that she had found a correction in the margin of a forged proof sheet that was in Gosse's handwriting. Muir in his review said that that the evidence was not strong enough that this correction – the single word 'mangoes' – was written by Gosse.

On 28 September 1946, Blunden came to Gosse's defence in another signed article in the paper. He had examined the evidence, and wrote: 'I knew his handwriting well. That word is not in his hand.' Blunden had shown his loyalty to a friend who, he declared, 'was not the man to smile on knavery'. But Muir had also said: 'The vanity of Gosse, his irresponsibility, his passion to hear himself applauded and, worst of all, his complete lack of serious principle regarding life or letters are faults admitted by his best friends.'

In January 1946, twelve months after he was appointed editor of the *Lit Supp*, Stanley Morison wrote another of his powerful memoranda to Barrington-Ward. He pointed out that over this period the circulation had risen from 22,340 to 30,000 and that the circulation department were of opinion that it could sell 35,000 if the paper were available. The weekly profit, due to an increase in advertising, had increased from £120 a week to £330.

There had also been an increase in the reading matter of 22 per cent, and when the change from four- to five-column make-up took place the figure, he predicted, would go up to 37 per cent. That, he wished to point out, made a great deal more work for him. He needed another subeditor because he was now having to help a great deal with the routine work: 'I am in danger of becoming a bottleneck.'

The main result was that he had been unable to make any progress with *The History of The Times*. Volume III needed cutting and checking, and he had only written the first four chapters of Volume IV, down to 4 August 1914, leaving twenty more chapters to write 'to close the enterprise'. He would therefore like to revert to the pre-war plan by which he had assistance at his disposal – a whole-time assistant and one or two part-time assistants. However, even that might not solve the difficulties regarding his burdens, and perhaps a more radical solution was called for – that there should either be a new editor for *The History*, or that he should have a new deputy on the *Literary Supplement*. Tomlinson and Blunden were a sufficiently strong writing staff, and Crook discharged admirably the duties of make-up man and general assistant manager, but there was no-one in the department capable of taking his place.

This was the memo that led to the appointment of Alan Pryce-Jones to the editorial staff in November 1946. After that, Morison could spend more time again in the little former boxroom, at the top of the Private House, where he had long enjoyed having his office. But on 17 June 1947, Morison wrote a further long memorandum to Barrington-Ward, this time raising the question, as he put it, of 'What Price Jones?'

The situation now was that Tomlinson was being retired at the end of the month from his unofficial position as assistant editor, and that Blunden was going off to the Far East at the end of July. It had been agreed in March 1947 that Pryce-Jones should 'in due but undefined time' take over the editorship from Morison, but Morison's conversation with him on the subject had been 'reserved and no mention was made of terms'.

Now, however, David Astor, the editor of the Sunday newspaper, the *Observer*, had intervened with the offer to Pryce-Jones of 'an important and lucrative position' on that paper. Morison said that he had asked Jones (as he called him) to stay, and to placate David Astor by saying that Morison 'would not oppose his offering a job to, say, Charques'. (So Morison was quite happy to throw Charques to the wolves.)

However, 'as expected, this device failed. Jones is the most brilliant combination of the creative writer and accomplished critic now functioning. He is experienced, disciplined, reliable and versatile. David Astor, in fact all the Astors are peculiarly well situated to appreciate Jones's qualities. The offer to him was renewed and the pressure on him increased.' Hence the position was that 'in addition to losing Tomlinson on 30 June and Blunden on 31 July, I might lose Jones on 31 August'. (How Morison relished, one feels, the drama of that sentence.)

Morison went on to say that 'now that I am satisfied that the paper is appreciably healthier in point of quality and revenue than it was when I took charge, I regard myself as entitled to hand over responsibility – of course, to the right man. I considered it as my duty to find a man whose talents for the job are greater than my own. The man who fulfils all the requirements is Jones. The *Supplement* needs him. From every aspect, therefore, to let Jones go to the *Observer* would be reckoned a major error of judgment.'

The memorandum had its required effect. A fortnight later, on 1 July, Pryce-Jones was appointed assistant editor and his salary went up from £600 to £800 a year. Six months later, he became the editor, at £1,750 a year plus £250 expenses allowance. But Morison had been right about the pressure that David Astor had put on Pryce-Jones to join the *Observer*. Writing on 15 March, Astor said that he was making a 'passionate appeal' to Pryce-Jones, 'at the end of a long and fatiguing Saturday' to reconsider joining the *Observer* 'before you wall yourself in at PHS for ever'. It was a clever appeal to Pryce-Jones's love of freedom and travel, though it did not succeed.

Morison was happy to retire. He had made the *Supplement*, as he put it in a letter to the manager, C.S. Kent, 'not only a better threepennyworth than it was in 1944, but a more remunerative property'. But he had only achieved this by 'the hardest work I have ever placed at anybody's service'. Barrington-Ward and Astor agreed that Morison could resume his work as 'historian, typographer-in-chief and "Special duties for the editor"', at the same salary of £2,500 a year that he had been getting when he was editing the *Lit Supp*. This arrangement was the last thing that Barrington-Ward was to do for his old and close friend Morison, for he died on 29 February 1948, four weeks after Morison left the *Supplement*.

Before his departure, Morison had been able to print one review that must have given him special gratification – Namier's review on 6 December 1947 of Volume III of *The History of The Times: The Twentieth-Century Test, 1884–1912*, published by *The Times* at 21 shillings. Above the heading on the review was Max Beerbohm's cartoon of the editorial staff of *The Times* rushing up to Lord Northcliffe as he cries: 'Help! Again I feel the demons of Sensationalism rising in me. Hold me fast! Curb me if you love me!' The heading ran 'The End of the "Old Gang" at Printing House Square. By L.B. Namier, FBA, Professor of Modern History in the University of Manchester.'

The book was written anonymously, so Namier could not praise Morison personally, and he had one or two criticisms to make – the book concentrated on European politics at the expense of home politics, it sometimes forgot it was a history of the newspaper when its attention was riveted on events, and it allowed the editor, Buckle, to be overshadowed by Moberly Bell and Chirol. But the 'confidential correspondence' of Printing House Square was blended with the contents of *The Times* into 'a coherent survey which will make this volume rank high among works on international history'.

And now, before picking up the threads of Volume IV of *The History*, Morison was going to America with Gavin Astor, the chief proprietor's son, for a holiday. There was a dinner at the Garrick to welcome Pryce-Jones to the editorship, there was a letter from T.S. Eliot reproaching Morison for leaving the paper – and then, in his unvaryingly black suit, he was gone.

Chapter Eleven

The World Pours In: 1948–58

When Alan Pryce-Jones joined the paper, he took over a little room that Arthur Crook had hitherto worked in. This room had a door out into the corridor as well as one into the main editorial room, and Pryce-Jones would slip away when he felt like it through this outer door without a word – perhaps to lunch at the Beefsteak or the Garrick (to both of which clubs he was elected in 1948), or at The Travellers', where he had long been a member and where the secretary was an old Oxford friend.

His two assistants on the paper now were Kathleen (or Kay) Dowding – subsequently Mrs Nixon – and Arthur Crook, who sat where Blunden and Tomlinson had previously chuckled away together; and there was also a subeditor, R.H. (or Bob) Hill, who had recently been transferred from *The Times* to the *Lit Supp*.

Kay Dowding was appointed an assistant editor on 1 February 1948, the day Pryce-Jones became editor, and Arthur Crook was appointed as an assistant editor in 1951, working on the same footing as Kay Dowding after that, until she left at the end of 1955. In the first three years of Pryce-Jones's editorship, Crook was paid an extra one-and-a-half guineas each week to write the 'Books to Come' column, since his salary could not be officially increased.

Kay Dowding now no longer wrote all the material in the 'Books Received' section. Crook, Hill and Pryce-Jones's secretary, Teresa Girouard (the sister of the architectural historian Mark Girouard) contributed many of the notes, and outside contributors were also brought in again. Kay Dowding played a big part in these years in building up the coverage of children's books, with frequent special children's book sections.

Pryce-Jones's arrival inaugurated a very good period for the *Lit Supp*.

He was a relatively young man, and belonged to a wide social and literary circle. He knew the value of the powerful figures that Stanley Morison had brought in as reviewers, and gave such writers as Carr, Namier and Carlill as much work as Morison had given them. But he was also acquainted with a wealth of younger writers and would-be writers, besides innumerable well-placed people in other spheres, amongst all of whom he went cheerfully recruiting for the paper. Altogether some 1,600 new reviewers were brought into the *Lit Supp* during the eleven years of his editorship.

A light-heartedness danced through its pages between the more serious reviews, and these in their turn reflected a wide range of social and political opinion. The paper was also getting bigger again. It was still twelve pages a week when Pryce-Jones took over, but three years later it often had sixteen pages a week. And Pryce-Jones was given a very free hand in the way he edited it. 'It was all very informal,' he told me. 'There were no crises. I don't know if my colleagues knew I was related to the Astors but they always fell in with my ideas.' One feels they knew. To be precise, the chief proprietor of *The Times* had married a first cousin of Pryce-Jones's mother – and Pryce-Jones's autobiography, *The Bonus of Laughter*, is packed with stories of visits to Astor houses and adventures with Astor brothers.

Not that he held them all in great respect. Meeting Mrs J.J. Astor in August 1946, a few months after he had started as editor of the paper, he recorded in his journal that she 'looked like a pretty little undercook. The vast diamond on her finger had stuck like a fish-scale. Why be rich if it leads no further?'

He himself came of a family of landowners, soldiers and courtiers. His father, a gentleman-at-arms, and his mother lived during the later part of their lives in Henry VIII's Gateway in Windsor Castle, and further back in his ancestry was Lord Grey of the 1832 Reform Bill. In the late fifties, his diaries regularly record dinner at Windsor with 'Mama, Papa, Queen, Queen Mother'. At Eton, he considered himself to have arrived just too late for the best generation of the 1920s – Anthony Powell, as has been mentioned, Harold Acton, George Orwell and Cyril Connolly among them – but he came to know most of them soon afterwards. At Oxford he made many new friends, particularly Osbert Lancaster and John Betjeman – who called him 'Boggins' or 'Bog', and later referred to the *Lit Supp* in his letters as 'Captain Bog's Weekly'. 'Bog' was also Maurice Bowra's name for him.

In fact Pryce-Jones was only at Oxford for two terms, since he was rusticated for climbing out of the college at night when he had already been 'gated' for not working and not paying his bills – and after that his angry father would not let him go back. So it was that in 1928, at the age of eighteen, he joined the *London Mercury*, and started enjoying the London life of the twenties and thirties: 'To look back on those days from a safer plateau more than fifty years later,' he wrote in his autobiography, 'is to be blinded, as if by looking too long at the unshaded sun.' Then marriage in 1934 to a young Viennese woman, from a family of wealthy assimilated Jews, opened a whole new European society to him, and a long period of personal happiness.

In 1938 we find him dining with Christopher Isherwood, Stephen Spender and his wife Inez, Cecil Day Lewis and Cyril Connolly, and observing them all sharply. He noted in his journal Isherwood's 'very quick light eyes, with a look of fear in them. He constantly gives the impression of doing sums in his head, except that instead of figures it is possibilities which are being weighed and added, enemies subtracted, personal success reckoned, dispassionately, at compound interest. Seduced more boys than any other individual in Berlin, one is told with aghast admiration.' He referred to Spender as 'a dreary old thing suffused by flashes of gaiety', but found him 'quite obviously the truest poet among all these people'. Inez Spender was 'an Oxford blue-stocking, pretty and disconsolate. Why do people listen to him and not to her?' Day Lewis, he thought, 'a memorial. A cape gooseberry. There is no trace of poetry left, no fire.' Cyril Connolly was 'quick under the fat, disloyal, an admirable destroyer' – though, after the war, Pryce-Jones was to write very affectionately of him and the dinners of pheasant and Haut-Brion they would have together at White's – 'There is in the world no-one nicer to dine alone with.'

Another entry tells of a different milieu. In August 1942, in one of numerous breaks from his wartime duties, Pryce-Jones was at a lunch at the Connaught Hotel given by the 'the princess E. de Polignac', with Lady Crewe, Lord Derwent and Bogey Harris among the other guests, and observed 'We might have been under a glass shade on the mantel-piece, clockwork toys repeating the motions of 1939. For already 1939 is spoken of as a park wall, like 1914. The building estate creeps up to September 3rd, and the value of the acres within is rising out of proportion.'

Without any special emphasis, but on occasions when it was appropri-ate, Pryce-Jones's *Lit Supp* gave off vivid reflections of that social world he was so much involved with. He himself reviewed the book of mem-

300

ories of Maurice Baring, the writer son of Lord Revelstoke, that Laura, Lady Lovat edited, with its evocation of life among the great families of late nineteenth-century England, in his first month as editor. 'The little pictures glow with the warm afternoon light of a Terborch,' Pryce-Jones wrote of Baring's own reminiscences of his childhood world, 'an appropriate light for a society which was gracefully, if a little vaguely, awaiting its eventide.'

Anthony Powell, who, from being chief novel reviewer, was now appointed fiction reviews editor by Pryce-Jones, was also fascinated – as his novels show – by the complexities of English society, and he too could be tempted away from his very energetic novel reviewing by such books. In March 1948, he reviewed *The Social Structure in Caroline England* by David Mathew, and took pleasure in defining those men of the Welsh marches – his own part of the country – who were 'not quite squires, and not quite yeomen' as the 'lesser-lesser-gentry'. In May of the following year he reviewed *Burke's Peerage*, and compared the recent political peerage with the noblesse created in the previous century by Napoleon. 'Will there be a tendency in several generations,' he speculated mischievously, 'for descendants of Labour peers to identify themselves with an older aristocracy, and by degrees to become absorbed in what has always been something of a family affair? More unlikely things have happened.'

Pryce-Jones once said to me, 'Evelyn [Waugh] and Cyril [Connolly] were not anonymous people', but he did get Connolly to write an anonymous review for him, on 6 January 1950, about an aspect of London society that intrigued him. The book was *Recollections of Logan Pearsall Smith* by Robert Gathorne-Hardy, who for sixteen years was the disciple of 'Logan . . . the Chinese sage, old, bald, angry and ironical, yet infinitely delicate and wise.'

Connolly – a famously Chelsea man – evoked beautifully that pre-war world 'in which people of independent means, living beside each other in creamy Georgian houses, devoted their lives to art', with Chelsea as their centre – 'leafy, well-to-do, fig-ripening Chelsea, from Carlyle Mansions to Ebury Street, where a good luncheon-party would last till lamp-lighting', and 'the strange, spell-binding quality of Logan's talk echoed in his listeners' ears for many months afterwards like a Balinese gong'.

Just before Pryce-Jones became editor, on 24 January 1948, the *Lit Supp* had reviewed Lewis Namier's book *Diplomatic Prelude, 1938–39*.

The events leading up to the war had now become an obsessive interest with Namier, and the reviewer, J.F.D. Morrison, agreed with Namier that in those immediate pre-war years 'the rest of Europe had neither the faith, nor the will, nor even sufficient repugnance to offer timely, effective resistance' to Hitler. It had been 'a failure of European morality'.

So it was natural to offer Namier for review the first volume of Winston Churchill's history of *The Second World War: The Gathering Storm*, when it came out in August that year. Namier retold the story of Churchill's political life between 1919 and 1940 very vividly, not surprisingly praising Churchill's efforts to prevent the outbreak of a Second World War while the nations 'meandered into the abyss'. He expressed his admiration of Churchill as both man and writer: 'below stubborn pugnacity and a brilliant, imaginative versatility appear great emotional intensity, intuitive insight, and warm human feelings: factors in his greatness . . . But, sensitive and impressionable, he steps back to gain perspective: and wide horizons open . . .'

This review, however, caused Pryce-Jones some trouble, since he dashingly arranged for the American Houghton Mifflin edition to be reviewed, several weeks before Cassell brought out the English edition. Sir Newman Flower, the chairman of Cassell, exploded, and a day or two later Pryce-Jones received from Colonel Astor's secretary Flower's letter demanding that Pryce-Jones should be sacked for impertinence to a great British firm.

However, Astor was away, and his secretary asked how she should reply. 'It gave me great pleasure,' Pryce-Jones wrote later, 'to write to Sir Newman, pointing out that, since I had to answer his letters to our chairman demanding my ouster, it would save trouble all round if he confined his correspondence to me.'

The next two volumes of Churchill's book went, incidentally, to A.P. (or Patrick) Ryan, who would later become deputy editor of *The Times*, and also its literary editor when in 1953 it started having a substantial book page of its own again. Of Volume II, *Their Finest Hour*, in July 1949, Ryan wrote vividly that Churchill took 'shape like a king in an old story dispensing justice, personal and direct, under an oak tree. A massive common sense seems to guide him. The humblest suppliants will get their rights and the largest brass hat will not protect its wearer from getting a bloody crown.' Of Volume III, *The Grand Alliance*, the following July he said: 'All who were grown up in 1941 will be confirmed that Mr Churchill was a genius as commander-in-chief of a nation fighting for its life.'

Namier, meanwhile, was continuing to receive books on the immediately pre-war days. Reviewing the official documents on foreign affairs relating to Germany and Czechoslovakia in 1937 and 1938, he gave a withering portrait of Neville Chamberlain just after he had signed the Munich agreement: 'The businessman and administrator was winding up a broken concern. Of the "pity and fear" of that night he felt nothing' – and next morning, Namier added bitterly, Chamberlain remarked that he had had a 'very friendly and pleasant talk' with Hitler.

Namier also got involved in one of the most epic clashes yet in the correspondence columns of the *Lit Supp*, when he reviewed the memoirs of Georges Bonnet, the French Foreign Minister on the eve of the war. Namier charged that Bonnet was very reluctant to go to war, and was not, as he presented himself, 'Résistant No. 1' in France. Bonnet wrote a letter almost a page long defending his policy of 'patience and prudence' in 1938 and 1939.

Then the debate took a different turn. In 1938, did the Poles propose to discuss with the French an offer of help from Poland to Czechoslovakia? Bonnet denied it – but Namier said tersely that 'the Polish offer, for what it was worth, was first torpedoed by Bonnet the statesman, and next obliterated by Bonnet the historian'. An objective observer would, I believe, have judged that Namier, over-vehement though he may have been, had the better of the argument with the French statesman.

In August 1950, there was a special number – one of a series of grand surveys that Pryce-Jones had introduced – called 'A Critical and Descriptive Survey of Contemporary British Writing for Readers Oversea'. Here A.J.P. Taylor wrote, anonymously, the 'History' article, and singled out Namier for his importance as an historian. However he concentrated in this piece on Namier's studies of eighteenth-century English history, attaching a seminal importance to his now famous book *The Structure of Politics at the Accession of George III*, which 'could no more be ignored than *The Origin of Species* could be ignored in a discussion of biology'. That book 'showed principles and parties as they appeared to the working politicians of the time, rather than as abstract creations of political philosophers'.

Taylor also observed that, though there were no obvious 'schools' among contemporary English historians, only individual writers, there was an increasing consciousness among them of society and social issues, and most historians no longer, like an earlier liberal historian such as H.A.L. Fisher, saw men simply as individuals. Taylor was generally regarded as an historian of the Left, but he nevertheless sounded a warning note here: the notion 'Tell me a man's class and I will tell you how he believes' could, he said, be overdone.

Taylor picked out as notable new historians the Christian moralist Herbert Butterfield, and Keith Feiling, whose *History of England*, he said, was not exactly Tory, but was concerned to show how the past worked rather than, like G.M. Trevelyan and the Whig historians, how it was preparing the present. Taylor also mentioned the new interest among British historians in the history of Europe, citing Brogan on France, and – quite rightly – 'Barraclough and Taylor on Germany, Taylor on the Hapsburg Monarchy'.

Taylor's own new book in 1950, a collection of essays called *From Napoleon to Stalin*, was reviewed by E.H. Carr. Carr used the occasion to promote again his belief that the era of collective man had arrived and that the liberal era, with its belief in the importance of the individual, was over. Nor was it generally true, he said, that the individual had been collectivised against his will. 'He has sought the support and protection of the collective group because, in the highly organised mass society of the modern world, he could not stand or work effectively in isolation.' Carr used Taylor's essays to try to illustrate this point, but he conceded that if Taylor's book read like an obituary for liberalism, Taylor's own deepest roots were nevertheless in the liberal tradition.

Carr was scornful of the Communist Party of Great Britain, with its 'slavish imitation of Soviet methods and of Soviet policies', as he wrote in a review of *The Case for Communism*, a Penguin Special by the old Scottish Communist William Gallacher. But he was still awed by the sheer triumph of Stalin, whom, he wrote, it was not profitable to discuss in terms of praise or blame, but who now, as he approached the age of seventy was 'at the pinnacle of his own and his nation's power'.

When Carr wrote about F.I. Dan, the Menshevik leader, commenting that Dan recognised that 'socialism could not be realised in a free democratic form', he received an enthusiastic letter of support in the paper from the Balliol left-wing historian, Christopher Hill. Hill supported Carr's view that we 'should not assume that democracy must take the forms appropriate to a capitalist society'.

This in turn provoked a letter from a surprising quarter – none other than John Middleton Murry. After living in his private commune during the war years, he had now turned violently against Communism, at least as it was practised in Soviet Russia. He wrote that 'to say, as Mr Hill says, that it is difficult to refuse the name "democracy" to the Russian system is ridiculous. It is a moral and intellectual obligation to do so.'

In fact Murry had just brought out a book called *The Free Society*, in which, as was noted by J.M. Cameron, a lecturer (and later professor) in philosophy at Leeds, Murry had renounced his pacifism and was now actually proposing a preventive war on Russia. Cameron did not at all go along with this, but he did write that 'the fall of Czechoslovakia back into darkness shows us the challenge' now being presented by Russia.

Finally, seeds of Carr's later clashes with Isaiah Berlin were being sown in a leader called 'The New Scepticism' that Carr wrote in June 1950. Commenting on an article that Berlin had contributed to the American journal *Foreign Affairs*, he mocked Berlin's 'nostalgia for the comfort of eighteenth and nineteenth century rationalism' and his advocacy of 'less Messianic ardour, more enlightened scepticism'. This was not what Carr – who now sometimes gave lectures and lessons to the staff of *The Times* – wanted for the world at all.

In the universities, there was a good deal of annoyance that Carr got all the books on Russia to review for the *Lit Supp*. But as in Morison's day, there were plenty of other voices to be heard in the paper. One of these was T.E. (or Peter) Utley.

Utley, later to become a well-known political writer on the *Daily Telegraph*, had actually been discovered by Carr, who to his credit had introduced him to Morison. Through Morison's influence he was soon taken on as a consultant to *The Times* on political and religious matters.

He was totally blind, and Morison found him a small room on the ground floor where he worked with a devoted secretary, Bernadette Folliot – one of many young women who helped him with his blindness by reading to him over the years. Arthur Crook would sometimes go down and have tea with him in the afternoon, and he became godfather to Crook's daughter. Utley himself married Dermot Morrah's daughter.

Pryce-Jones soon made him a leader writer on the *Lit Supp*, and here he regularly expressed opinions very different from Carr's. He was a Christian conservative, and a leader he wrote on 'Liberty' on 10 July 1948 puts his position very well. Actually, like Carr, he thought that liberalism had grown weaker in the world, but his answer was not collectivism but Christianity:

> While the Christian argument for freedom derives from the idea of man as morally responsible, the liberal argument rests on the precarious ground that he is happier when not under restraint. The voluntary renunciation of liberty in many parts of the world during

the last 20 years has made it increasingly hard to sustain this liberal assumption, and once it has been abandoned the liberal case for freedom soon collapses.

The Christian, on the other hand, is not primarily interested in happiness. He asserts that men have a moral duty to claim and exercise freedom. It is for this reason that while Mill's liberalism has slowly degenerated into collectivism the Christian Churches have emerged in the unfamiliar role of champions of civil liberty.

Pryce-Jones himself converted to Roman Catholicism in 1950. He had already given evidence of his faith in an article he elected to write the previous year on the quatercentenary of the Church of England's *Booke of The Common Prayer*, though his emphasis in the piece was on the Prayer Book's importance in the history of English prose and poetry. 'The phrases of the liturgy,' he wrote, 'have echoed like a ground bass under the whole of our literature,' while 'there must be, over the centuries, a vast concourse in cathedral and parish church, in chapel and schoolroom, which, without ever being aware of its affinity, perhaps even despising the name of poetry, has experienced exactly the effect of the noblest extension of a poetic faculty, on kneeling to the words of administration, on repeating the general Confession, on hearing the collect for Ash Wednesday.'

And what of that other god – *The God That Failed?* Peter Calvocoressi reviewed that famous collection of essays in February 1950. Arthur Koestler, Ignazione Silone, Richard Wright, Louis Fischer and Stephen Spender, all of whom had at one time been Communists, wrote here about their reasons for rejecting Communism, while the Oxford don Enid Starkie wrote about André Gide's similar change of heart. The root cause for their defection, Calvocoressi said, was not merely negative disappointment, but 'the very same active indignation which had thrust these men towards Communism in the beginning. They rebelled against the exaltation of party discipline above truth and justice; against the dethronement of the individual conscience and the individual judgment.'

As for the straightforward political defence of Western liberal capitalism, that fell often into the hands of the economist Graham Hutton. He received many of the books on America for review, and in November 1948 paid a notable tribute to the United States. Reviewing the memoirs of Cordell Hull, the US Secretary of State from 1933 to 1944, and the *White House Papers of Harry L. Hopkins*, he discussed at length the record of the 'middle of the road' President Roosevelt – the New Deal, the ruling out of extremisms, the refashioning of democracy and the end of isolation. He concluded that the books he was reviewing 'make you realise how much everyone in the world owes to a few leading American citizens: Roosevelt and his trusted aides'.

One other notable article on foreign affairs should also be mentioned from these years: Sir Duff Cooper (later Viscount Norwich) on *Trial and Error* by Chaim Weizmann, the first President of Israel. Duff Cooper said that in the unhappy history of mankind there were no sadder pages than those which record the sufferings of Jewish people, and hailed the miraculous date of 15 May 1948 when the United States recognised the provisional government of the State of Israel. He said that Weizmann's book might be called *The Second Book of Genesis*. Duff Cooper received an exceptional fee for this review of £50 (now worth about £1,000) – £12.18s.6d according to normal lineage rates, plus £37.1s.6d extra, as the figure appeared in the marked copy.

Anthony Powell was now an important figure on the paper. He came in every Thursday, and he and Pryce-Jones ran through the new novels together. Then they went out to lunch together at the Travellers'. Powell himself reviewed a novel almost every week, and sometimes more than one. He also sent the other novels out, often in batches which the reviewer would write about in a single article, covering perhaps three books. Between them Pryce-Jones and Powell brought in many good new contributors to the fiction pages. Powell was paid £350 a year for the editorial work, plus £3.3s 0d a week for his main novel review.

The most important novel of the end of the forties was George Orwell's *1984*, which was reviewed in a middle in June 1949 by Julian Symons, the poet, critic and crime novelist, who was then in his late thirties. In his biography of Orwell, Bernard Crick said that 'Anthony Powell steered it into comprehending hands'.

Symons wrote a classic 'middle', setting the new novel amongst its predecessors, and gave it an admiring, if slightly solemn and restrained review. He said that Orwell's picture of society in 1984 had an 'awful plausibility', and that the book's argument about power and corruption was conducted 'at a very high intellectual level' and with 'sobriety and subtlety'. But he thought the book was marred by 'a schoolboyish sensationalism of approach', and especially did not like the rats in Room 101 which finally break Winston Smith's will – rather surprisingly, he felt them to be comic rather than horrific. However he gave thanks for 'a writer who deals with the problems of the world rather than the ingrowing pains of individuals'.

Orwell himself had contributed a 'middle' to the paper the previous year, in which he wrote about an anthology of new American stories and poems called *Spearhead*. He did not find much to praise in it, observing that 'where American writing particularly excels at this moment is in literary criticism and in political and sociological essays'. He was to die in 1950, and Anthony Powell reviewed his posthumous collection of essays, *Shooting an Elephant*, in October of that year. The review naturally had something of the character of an obituary, and Powell wrote, with his usual careful intelligence, that

> like many – perhaps most – writers who hold our attention, Orwell never resolved within himself a number of contradictory enthusiasms and prejudices; but, unlike some of his fellows, he was determined that these inconsistencies, instead of being concealed or skated over, should be emphasised to the full to demonstrate the difficulties in honest behaviour.
>
> This desire to speak the truth on all occasions made him sometimes an embarrassment to political associates; and there can also be no doubt that he had in him a kind of puckishness that delighted in showing up human inconsistencies, and was not really sympathetic to workaday life as such. Such an approach requires a severe standard of personal integrity.
>
> Orwell possessed this integrity in the highest degree. But in his efforts to be a saint he was sometimes surprisingly unaware of how people not greatly interested in saintliness lived, and what it was, and was not, reasonable to expect from such ordinary people.

The other major 'novel of ideas' of 1949 was Aldous Huxley's *Ape and Essence*. This was reviewed by the popular philosophy professor of the radio brains trust, C.E.M. Joad, who made the phrase 'It depends what you mean by . . .' a joky catchphrase in Britain for a while. His review itself contained a distinct dose of ambiguity. He thought that this picture of human society after the third world war, in which contemporary man is symbolised by baboons, was 'the most frankly horrible book that Mr Huxley has produced', and that he 'chastises mankind with a hatred that knows no pity'. Yet he found that the denunciation was 'of the highest order', and that *Ape and Essence* was 'the most powerfully moving book that has appeared since the war'.

*   *   *

Anthony Powell reviewed novels both by the known and the unknown. He would analyse their strengths and faults, as he saw them, in a punctilious and responsible way, showing no indulgence to either category of writer. He clearly felt that whatever the differences between novels – and he enjoyed novels of many kinds – they needed, in order to be wholly satisfying, to contain fully developed, convincing characters.

Reviewing Graham Greene's *The Heart of the Matter* in a middle article in May 1948, he posed an interesting question about characters, such as Scobie in this novel, who are influenced by religious belief. Was Scobie, the British colonial officer in West Africa, driven to suicide by his creed or his character? The same question, he said, could be asked of the fate of Pinkie, the young criminal, in *Brighton Rock* (in fact the article was called 'West African Rock').

In French Catholic writers such as Bernanos, he thought, the main interest lay in religious belief and its consequences, not in human character, but in Greene's religious novels he thought that the characters were at their best fully created and their actions could at least equally be explained by what they were as individual human beings – and he plainly approved of that. He concluded his review by saying that Greene was a writer 'whose powers of development, in style and attitude of mind, seem to show an ever-renewed vitality'.

A new voice in fiction was Angus Wilson. In 1949, Bernadette Folliot, Utley's assistant, had reviewed his first book, *The Wrong Set*, and reported that 'these 12 stories of vice and stupidity in the suburbs and provinces are well worth reading'. But Powell, the following year, was more doubtful about Wilson's second volume of stories, *Such Darling Dodos*, which he described as portraying a 'seedy world of quarrelsome spinsters, dons, retired eccentrics and suchlike set against a background of rectories and boarding houses'. He found two faults with them: Wilson was 'not fastidious in his manner of writing, jokes following one another helter-skelter whether good or bad', and, above all, 'the weakness of the satire lies in doubt whether the people satirised are truly like this'.

A lighter book that scored a success in 1949 was Nancy Mitford's *Love in a Cold Climate*. Powell reviewed it in an equally judicious manner. 'Miss Mitford's people,' he said approvingly, 'possess an authenticity not always achieved by novelists whose characters are drawn largely from families of the Peerage.' But, he warned, 'Miss Mitford's wit and facility are both so abundant that they need constant discipline'.

He was less complimentary in 1950 about *Helena*, the novel about the mother of the Roman emperor Constantine, by Miss Mitford's (and his own) good friend Evelyn Waugh. He thought that Waugh had tried to pack too much into a brisk fable, and that there was too tenuous a thread between 'the horsy schoolgirl in Britain and the eccentric dowager seeking the True Cross'.

The new novel reviewers were men in their late twenties, some of them already becoming known as novelists or poets themselves – among them, Alan Ross, the future editor of the *London Magazine*; Julian Maclaren-Ross, presiding drinker at the Wheatsheaf pub in Soho, and later model for the figure of X. Trapnel in Anthony Powell's *A Dance to the Music of Time*; Erik de Mauny, the BBC correspondent in Moscow; the elegant critic Francis Wyndham, and the effervescent critic Maurice Richardson.

It was Mrs Marie Hannah, though, who reviewed Evelyn Waugh's other novel of this period, *The Loved One*. In a middle article, she set this novel about an animal and bird graveyard in California in the context of his earlier books, and hailed his vocation, which was, like Coleridge's *Ancient Mariner*, 'to warn, to startle and affright the Wedding Guests'. His enemy was the materialism of modern society, and what was shocking 'in this gruesome little tale is not the preoccupation with corpses but the fact that the live characters are virtually indistinguishable from the dead ... He has given us a satire, witty and macabre, ominous and polished, which strikes straight at the heart of the contemporary problem'.

Julian Maclaren-Ross wrote a similar retrospective middle on Henry Green, pegged to his new novel *Concluding*, about a day in the life of an old, deaf state pensioner. He found the purpose of the novel obscure – it might be intended, he thought, as a study in anti-climax. It was 'principally his qualities as technician and stylist', he said, 'which in a decade of undistinguished prose' – this was in December 1948 – 'make this writer remarkable'.

In 1950 a posthumous novel, *A Voice Through a Cloud*, won a great deal of acclaim which Erik de Mauny also lent his voice to in the *Lit Supp*. The author was Denton Welch, who after a lonely childhood had fractured his spine in a bicycle accident and then suffered thirteen years of chronic illness until he died at the age of thirty-one. The novel was largely autobiographical, and de Mauny wrote of its 'dark, tormented background of sinister ambiguities' and the 'effortless brilliance' of the writing. However, Welch has been almost forgotten. By contrast, the first novel of Barbara Pym, who was much later to be judged a considerable writer after Philip Larkin and Lord David Cecil spoke up for her, had a poor review. This story of an archdeacon and his wife was called *Some Tame*

Gazelle, and Bernadette Folliot said it was as restrained as its title suggested. It just 'flowed on cheerfully with little wit and much incident'.

Earlier novelists got some good reviews. Maurice Richardson reviewed some reprints of E.W. Hornung's Raffles novels, and vividly contrasted the life style of the gentleman burglar with that of Sherlock Holmes. 'Mrs Hudson could be relied on for bacon and eggs, a chop, or even a partridge; there were spirits in the tantalus, smokeable cheroots for those who funked the shag' – but Raffles drinks Steinberg 1868, Pol Roger and Château Margaux, and dines on *jambon de Westphalie au champagne*, while afterwards 'the smoke from the eternal, fat, juicy Sullivans (the cigarette "which is the royal road to a cigar") hangs in thick blue coils on the night air'.

Francis Wyndham welcomed the revival of *The Real Charlotte* by the two Irish ladies known as Somerville and Ross. They had become known, he wrote, for 'vigour, warm humour, bracing weather and a sharp eye for obvious absurdity' through their very popular book *Some Experiences of an Irish R.M.* But this earlier novel about a rich Dublin girl, portrayed with 'the pitiless irony of the social analyst', was even subtler than Balzac's *La Cousine Bette*.

Among American novels, Hemingway's *Across the River and into the Trees*, his first book for ten years, was highly praised by C.M. Woodhouse, later a Conservative MP for Oxford, and an historian of Greece. The reviewer had not liked Hemingway's early books, but in *A Farewell to Arms* and *For Whom the Bell Tolls* he had thought the stories were carried forward by genuine emotions – love, courage, fear – and in this book, the third in the same vein, 'at last he knows his own strength'. Norman Mailer's long story of a wartime campaign on a remote Pacific island, *The Naked and the Dead*, got a less enthusiastic review from Alan Ross, who said that Mailer's 'virtue and limitation are that he leaves nothing out'. Anthony Powell enjoyed Lionel Trilling's study of left-wing intellectuals in New England, *The Middle of the Journey*, because the author was 'dexterous in presenting the peculiar combination of arrogance and imbecility found at certain levels of intellectual life'. And – Powell's *sine qua non* – nearly all the characters in Trilling's novel were 'remarkably convincing'.

In August 1950, Powell reviewed André Maurois's *The Quest for Proust*. His own novel sequence, *A Dance to the Music of Time*, has often been compared to Proust's novel, and though there are of course many differences, a remark he made in this review does seem to apply aptly to his work. He said that Proust's book 'curiously resembles a poem in the manner in which its cadences convey the ebb and flow of the imagination and the will' – and Nick Jenkins, representative of the imagination, and Widmerpool, representative of the will, might be seen as the two poles on which *A Dance* turns.

Powell was less appreciative of Albert Camus's remarkable novel *The Plague*, when it came out in translation – differing here from Gabriel Marcel, whose admiring review on its first appearance we have already noted. Powell took once again the kind of view that we have already seen him expressing. The symbolism of the plague in Oran was achieved by a strict adherence to realistic incident – but 'any suggestion of symbolism in a novel tends to make it hard for characters set in a realistic background to come alive'. He thought, too, that the suggestion that disasters such as a plague 'make the way of duty clear to many who would otherwise have little idea what to do with their lives' was 'a distinctly romantic doctrine'. Powell also reviewed the English translation of Mann's *Doctor Faustus*. Here he thought that 'none of the characters ever comes alive' – and that the narrator was 'a bore of the first water'.

Robert Musil's novel *Der Mann ohne Eigenschaften* – 'The Man Without Shadows' – got very different treatment. In fact, it was one of Pryce-Jones's discoveries – and he thought of it as one of the justifications for his travelling about so much while he was editor. In 1949 two friends he had met abroad, Eithne Wilkins and Ernst Kaiser, brought into his office the only fragment still in print of this massive Austrian novel about the year 1913–14 – a privately published, posthumous third volume. Though virtually unknown, it was obviously a masterpiece, and on 28 October 1949 Kaiser and Wilkins contributed a long 'front' to the paper in which they compared Musil with Proust and Joyce – except that, with his inimitable ring of authority, his strength and lucidity, he was not so 'sick' as them.

'Close acquaintances,' Pryce-Jones wrote later, 'suggested that to invent a writer and his work was going too far. But Secker & Warburg thought differently. They commissioned a translation from my contributors, and it was the success of the English version which launched Musil in Central Europe and added a name to stand beside Proust and Joyce and Thomas Mann.'

There was one further episode with a novelist worthy of mention. Pryce-Jones, just before he became editor, invited Wyndham Lewis to lunch at the Travellers' to see if he could be persuaded to write something for the paper. Anthony Powell, who was also invited along, described Lewis's appearance at this lunch in his memoirs as 'big, toothy, awkward in manner . . . in his white shirt and dark suit he looked like a caricature of an American senator or businessman'.

Lewis agreed to write a 'front', on a subject now apparently lost to record, but did not realise that as it would be published anonymously he could not use the word 'I'. This necessitated quite a lot of rewriting in the office when the article arrived. When he sent Lewis the proofs, Pryce-Jones wrote an accompanying letter saying that all he had done was to make the article 'fit easily into our scheme of anonymity', and that he had tried not to 'alter the colour of your writing in any way'.

Lewis's reply to this and Pryce-Jones's further letter are, respectively, classics of authorial paranoia and editorial tact.

> Studio A,
> Kensington Gardens Studios,
> 29 Notting Hill Gate,
> London W.11.
> Feb. 10th 1948

> Dear Pryce-Jones,
> Before last night the galleys you sent me had remained unread. – To push your spiteful joke so far as to print what you have fooled about with of mine would of course precipitate an immediate action against the newspaper for its sins responsible for you. – As it is, the article can be suppressed: in which case the cheque would be due just the same. Or I can eliminate from the text the first person wherever it occurs.
> On the second galley (132) I stopped reading when it became clearer at almost every line that it was your idea to be very offensive. I had however read enough to admire, among your transformations, the femininely placed *very*, 'on the very title page' (bottom of first galley): to note how infinitely more elegant the word 'comprise' is than the word 'is' (galley 132): and to mark your really radical improvement of one of my unworthy sentences, from which emerged your masterly 'emphatically an archipelago'. This fills me with awe: obviously those two words were brought into the world to coalesce – '*emphatically* an *archipelago*' – but they awaited your fairy wand to effect the graceful conjunction. – You are fond of the word 'emphatically' I expect?

313

Thus to draw your attention to three out of all the changes made in my text is not, however, retaliatory. Its purpose has been to demonstrate how alien an element has been introduced into the text, apart altogether from questions of mechanical improvement or the reverse.

Sincerely,

Wyndham Lewis

February 10, 1948

My dear Wyndham Lewis,

The question is really very simple, and certainly does not deserve a quarrel. It depends on two basic propositions:

(a) You have something to say.

(b) We should like you to say it in this paper.

If you look up the letter that came with your proofs, you will see that I have made no bones about acting as Beckmesser: that, unfortunately, is a corollary of proposition (b). But it is because we want to give our readers the chance of learning what you have to tell them that we think it worth asking you to reconsider your reactions – for surely two meetings have made it perfectly clear that we have none but the friendliest feelings towards yourself and your work?

I suggest that we go through the proofs together after luncheon one day – for on second thoughts you will surely agree that a signed article does not turn into an unsigned one simply by deleting its signature. The alternative would be very unwelcome to me. It would amount to your replying that you have nothing to say to the reader of the *Times Literary Supplement* (which I don't admit!) and that you would like your typescript sent back with, naturally, a cheque.

I hope you may prefer the gentler course of luncheon and talk.

Yours sincerely,

[no signature on the file copy]

In the end, no article appeared. However, in 1954, in a 'Special Autumn Number' in which authors wrote signed articles about their favourite works, Wyndham Lewis did contribute a piece on Matthew Arnold, in which he advanced the extraordinary opinion that no greater poetry had ever been written than the concluding song of Callicles in Arnold's 'Empedocles on Etna'. Even this led to some trouble, for Lewis sent back his cheque for 25 guineas, stating that it must have been sent him in error and implying, of course, that it was not enough. It was firmly returned to him by Pryce-Jones's secretary – but Pryce-Jones took some trouble over getting grants for Wyndham Lewis from the Royal Literary Fund and the Civil List.

In Pryce-Jones's first number as editor, 7 February 1948, the author Philip Toynbee took Virginia Woolf to task for her criticisms of the thirties poets in an essay in her posthumous volume, *The Moment*. He quoted her as saying of Auden, Spender and Day Lewis that 'The bleat of the scapegoat sounds loud in their work, and the whisper of the schoolboy saying, "Please sir, it was the other fellow, not me."' Toynbee called this 'a ludicrously obtuse analysis of their motives'. But just over two years later, on 25 August 1950, Alan Ross, voice of the younger poets, was in turn pouring scorn on them. 'The movement initiated by Auden, Spender, MacNeice and Day Lewis,' he wrote, 'which wore every international problem like a heart on its sleeve, has ended by one of its members putting the Atlantic between him and his conscience, another vowing silence for a decade, a third being broken down on the wheel of broadcasting (the great leveller) and a fourth returning to pasture among the proprieties and conventional manner-isms of an earlier social era.' (The four being characterised by Ross in the order in which they are mentioned.) Fighting talk from a new generation! But though there were many new poets writing, no war or post-war British poet apart from Dylan Thomas had received much acclaim yet, and 'the Movement'– the anti-romantic tendency in British poetry – was still a little way off.

From this issue onward – it was the special number on 'Contemporary British Writing' in which appeared A.J.P. Taylor's round-up of historians – the *Lit Supp* gave poetry notable encouragement by regularly publishing new poems, chosen mainly by G.S. Fraser, who kept a particularly close eye on the younger hopefuls. In this issue there were poems by Blunden, Alan Ross and Roy Fuller, who each received 3 guineas, besides a 'non-copyright' stamp in the copy of the paper that was marked up for payment, which meant that the paper itself claimed no copyright in the poem.

Pryce-Jones himself reviewed the *Selected Poems* of his old friend John Betjeman. He was somewhat circumspect, observing that 'those who are insensible to the "mushroomy, pine-woody, evergreen smells" round Camberley, or insecure on the finer points of Anglican variety, will make little of him', but going on: 'Granted this premise, however, it is impossible not to admire the freshness of Mr Betjeman's art . . .

He needs very little: an old tennis racket, a bicycle seat, a pair of shorts, a defective chapel stove, a Morris Eight or an encaustic tile – from such prosaic ingredients a wholly original and often enchanting poetry is wrung.'

Pryce-Jones also spotted a new poet whose first volume, *Season Ticket*, had been published in Alexandria, where he was lecturing at the university. This was D.J. Enright, whose poems, Pryce-Jones said, 'concerned with the life of Alexandria . . . are admirably made for the poet's purpose. They move forward, they arrive precisely at the intended point.' He hoped that the English public would have a chance of judging this 'most interesting poet' by a method less cumbrous than sending to Egypt for his work – and in subsequent numbers often gave it that chance by publishing Enright's poems himself.

One unusual poet who had first become known for her novels, Stevie Smith, was well characterised at the end of 1950 by a young member of the staff that Pryce-Jones had recently brought in as an editorial assistant, a former Guards officer called David Tylden-Wright. (He would in due course become an important reviewer of novels for the paper.) Reviewing her book *Harold's Leap*, he said that she 'chants of a world that seems as cracked as the window pane through which she peers'.

Alan Ross's eyes were meanwhile turning to America. In August 1950 he reviewed Robert Lowell's *Poems 1938–49*, in a careful and serious piece of writing. He found some of the poems obscure, but 'whereas in most American verse the obscurity is due to a thinness of content, in Mr Lowell the opposite is true' – any given passage contained, 'like a vitamin pill, a great deal of boiled down energy'.

In Lowell's poetry he found a feeling for place, with a consciousness of the past, of family ties and of an inherited landscape; a belief in the validity of Christian symbols as references to be used in poetry; and 'a repetitive mnemonic use of certain familiar subjects, such as the sea, graveyards, saints' days and conventional religious themes, to bind together the various elements in his poetic memory and induce the sensation of unity and permanence', all of which gave the work 'the force and undidactic cleanness of real poetry'. This was not a bad attempt at a first analysis of Lowell's poems, and certainly helped them to acquire the great standing they later had in Britain.

G.S. Fraser did much the same for John Berryman. He wrote that in his collection *The Dispossessed*, Berryman 'attempts to give, what a poet should give today, something like an all-round, commanding view of the human situation'. He added that in America there was now to be had quite elaborate textual criticism of contemporary verse – and that the poets were helped by it. Literary criticism was growing in prestige in these post-war years.

Maurice Bowra, the famous Warden of Wadham College, Oxford, reviewed in April 1949 the revised edition of Maurice Baring's *The Oxford Book of Russian Verse*, with a supplement by D.P. Costello. He said 'it is melancholy that the Russian people, with its instinctive love of poetry and its great achievement in it, should now be compelled to strangle its natural gift and write mechanically to order'. And he was not pleased with Costello, whom he found too sensitive to existing Russian opinion, placing poets who had been publicly disclaimed, like Akhmatova and Mandelstam, in as bad a light as possible, 'as if they really deserved the hard words said about them'. However later that month G.S. Fraser was not much kinder about Bowra, calling his book *The Creative Experiment* – about seven major European poets – 'popularisation at the very highest level'.

As for eyes turned to France, they were on Juliette Greco's songwriter, Jacques Prévert. Stephen Ullman said that his book of poems *Paroles* derided the bourgeoisie, but with delicate and bantering irony; he also remarked on Prévert's influence on the British cinema, through the naïve, unhappy, restless people portrayed in his screenplays for films like *Quai des Brumes* and *Les Enfants du Paradis*. Cinema-goers of that time may still think of these films as great classics – but find their influence on British cinema harder to trace.

T.S. Eliot's modest-sounding book *Notes Towards the Definition of Culture* was discussed at length by H.F. Carlill in December 1948. He said that Eliot 'sets out to be as dry as his title', but ends up by giving us a 'whole philosophy of civilisation . . . a poetic vision of a human community as a progressively intricate system of societies each with its own character and qualities but overlaid and interdependent – the family, the region, the sect, the nation, even the trade, even perhaps the club and society'. Carlill picked out for especial attention one element in this vision: Eliot's remark that 'It is essential for the preservation of the quality of the culture of a minority, that it should continue to be a minority culture.' Reading between the lines, Carlill said, that meant that the social classes should remain separate. But Carlill made, as might be expected, a democratic objection to this. Wording it gently, since he felt considerable respect for Eliot's book, he put forward a further vision:

Only some of us can be scholars or artists or saints; but it is hard to think that we cannot all have some idea of and some respect for truth, beauty and goodness. Even the dustmen's elite might sing or at least listen to madrigals ... There is an ethos, a sensibility, that one can imagine permeating a whole community and becoming part of the tradition of every member of it.

Fifteen months later, Eliot's play *The Cocktail Party* (which by this time had already been performed at the Edinburgh Festival and in New York, and was soon to have a success in London) was reviewed in the *Lit Supp* by the excellent dramatic critic of *The Times*, A.V. Cookman. Cookman thought that this drawing-room comedy in verse, with a spiritual point to make, was very successful. He went so far as to say that the scene in which the young heroine, Celia, 'a cocktail-drinking girl ... bares her spiritual misgivings and strivings in the Harley Street consulting room' was 'perhaps the finest scene in modern poetic drama'. Stage performance had also made the purpose of the verse clear: it was 'not to paint scenery in the Elizabethan way, nor to make verbal patterns, nor to create emotions in excess of the matter under discussion, but to give the dialogue the finest possible precision and intensity ... The auditor need not notice the versification. He is meant only to be aware of the higher charge of energy which has entered the scene.'

F.R. Leavis, with his own vision of the importance of a literature that was imbued with intelligence, imagination, and moral insight, was also given high praise for his finest book, *The Great Tradition*, a study of the four novelists who he thought had created and sustained that tradition – Jane Austen, George Eliot, Joseph Conrad and Henry James. It was reviewed in a middle by Dr R.G. Cox, who had been one of his pupils. He concluded that 'Such an urgent concern to see the novel fulfilling its highest potentialities, such an awareness of the responsibilities of criticism, and so delicate a sense of discrimination between genuine imaginative grasp and its counterfeit – these form a combination of qualities rare at any time and vitally important today. It is hardly too much to say that Dr Leavis has thrown more light upon the aims and methods of the novel than any previous critic.'

G.S. Fraser gave a useful general conspectus of the state of Anglo-American literary criticism when he reviewed Geoffrey Grigson's anthology *Poetry of the Present* in May 1949. He said that there were macroscopic critics like Maurice Bowra who 'dispose of three or four tendencies in three or four pages'. Now there were also many microscopic critics such as the American, Cleanth Brooks, who 'in three or four pages, unravel the subtleties of three or four lines'. Dr Johnson and T.S. Eliot were both kinds of critic in one. As for Geoffrey Grigson, whose 'brisk impatience makes him readable', but who was somewhat arbitrary in his likes and dislikes, he was 'a critic of the middle distance'.

A major, long-awaited philosophical book came out in April 1950, Gilbert Ryle's *The Concept of Mind*, and Pryce-Jones got an outstanding new Oxford philosopher of the linguistic school, J.L. Austin, to review it. The book's purpose was to demolish the myth of 'the ghost in the machine' – the idea that we have a body, which is in space, and a mind – the ghost – which is not in space and has its own private career.

Austin's opening remark about the book has become famous in philosophical circles, where everyone no doubt knew that he had written it: 'A quite unusually high percentage of it is true, the remainder at least false.'

He went on to say that this assault on traditional, Cartesian dualism by Ryle, 'the *philosophe terrible*', was acute and illuminating, but in the end it only added up to 'a quiverful of miscellaneous and original arguments'. Ryle himself had compared his argument to 'the subtle folding of a winter's snake', but, Austin commented, 'perhaps the rapid darting hither and thither of the summer reptile might be a more exact analogy'.

Nevertheless, he said, Ryle's racy, untechnical and idiosyncratic manner of writing would make the book readable to non-philosophers, and 'all save those who have never learned to suspect solemnity will join in his enjoyment of his numerous jokes . . . *Le style, c'est Ryle.*' Austin's review itself was an outstanding example of difficult philosophical argument made lucid and enjoyable.

Another spirited, philosophical review appeared at the end of the decade, when Anthony (later Lord) Quinton reviewed several books on Wittgenstein in May 1959. He wrote that 'Wittgenstein's basic conviction is that the task of philosophy is negative, a matter of elimination or cleansing. . . Both thought and life, as things are, are corrupt and sophisticated; thinking is perverted by metaphysics, the conduct of life by the system of respectable pretence embodied in conventional morality. . . The primary need is to get back to the simple, ordinary, straightforward beginnings. . . His view of life has something in common with that of George Orwell, in its emphasis on honesty and decency, and with that of D.H. Lawrence in its prophetic denunciation of the complexities and contrivances of bourgeois life.' A text for the looming sixties?

Art and architecture continued to get the substantial coverage they had had under Morison. One notable article in 1948 was a review by the sixty-seven-year-old Clive Bell of Maurice Malingue's book on *Gauguin*. 1889 was Gauguin's 'year of grace and glory', Bell said: instead of the 'infinite diversity of subtle tones' that the Impressionists had used, Gauguin was now offering broad patches of strong, contrasted colours, and stylised forms – but, said Bell, 'he seems conscious of monitory spirits in the background, Pisarro and Cézanne, and doubtless it was their presence which held in check the rhetorical upholsterer lurking in the ex-stockbroker'. Bell was still writing with the old Bloomsbury vividness and dash – as well as its snobbery.

In June 1950, Sir Philip Magnus reviewed the report of the Gowers Commission set up by the government to consider the future of 'Houses of Outstanding Historical or Architectural Interest'. He wanted the houses preserved, but he had one warning. He was suspicious of special tax arrangements for them. The commission, he observed, showed a disposition, to which he was not favourable, 'to include within its definition of a unified work of art, not only a designated house and its listed contents, but the owner also'.

As for the history of literature, Frank Morley reviewed with gusto Boswell's *London Journal, 1762–1763*, edited by Frederick A. Pottle – the first volume for the general public of the great haul of Boswell papers which had all begun with a letter in the *Lit Supp* on 29 July 1920 from Professor Tinker of Yale, asking if owners of Boswell letters would communicate with him. This led to the discovery of an ebony cabinet stuffed with Boswell papers at Malahide Castle, followed by many more caches in the house and outbuildings, and then the turning-up of yet more Boswell material at Fettercairn House – altogether 'the most fantastic literary story of our time'. Yale University had in the end acquired everything.

Morley said: 'Here is immortal Bozzy at his delicious prime: up in the clouds, down in the dumps, momentarily pious, frequently not . . . There never was a document more close to the heart-beat of an insecure and eager man of twenty-two.' But he too had a warning: the text of the journal was unexpurgated: '"High debauchery", in Boswell's phrase, was debauchery with genteel ceremonial; "low debauchery" was debauchery without. There are instances, not always pleasant, of both kinds.' The warning, unsurprisingly, did not stand in the way of the book's success.

On the Letters page, the most striking debate in this sphere was over the contention of the Canadian scholar Leslie Hotson that the reference to the 'mortal moone' that 'hath her eclipse endur'd' in Shakespeare's 'Sonnet CVII' was not, as had been generally thought, to Queen Elizabeth, but to the crescent-shaped fleet of the Spanish Armada. This would mean that the sonnet, and certain other related ones, could be dated back to 1589, when Shakespeare was twenty-five. The Letters page had one of its great set-piece battles over this in the ensuing weeks in 1950. Did not the language of the sonnet show that it came from the same period as *Measure for Measure*? Could Shakespeare, as a young man in his twenties, have portrayed himself as being in the autumn of life? John Sparrow found a typically obscure reference in support of Hotson, a description of the Spanish Armada as a crescent moon in a book published in Leiden in 1619.

After the appearance of Pryce-Jones's first issue as editor of the *Lit Supp*, W.F. Casey, who was editing *The Times* during Barrington-Ward's last illness (B-W was away on a cruise from which he never returned), wrote to congratulate him and to make one suggestion. Casey did not like the use of the word 'we' in anonymous reviews, where it meant 'the collection of all us correctly educated friends'. Such usage was always 'in danger of getting close to archness'. This seems to have been practically the only attempt at interference from *The Times* that Pryce-Jones had to contend with in his time as editor.

The circulation of the *Lit Supp* rose rapidly in the first three years of his tenancy of the chair. From an average of 42,116 copies a week in 1948, it went up to 49,061 in 1950 – a supreme year, the highest annual average it has achieved in its 100 years of life. But in March 1951, the price, which had been 3d ever since June 1923, went up to 6d.

Circulation quickly dropped again, and the overall average circulation for 1951 was down to 44,876. By the end of 1952, average weekly sales had dropped to 41,924. The circulation stayed within 2,000 copies of this figure, sometimes up, sometimes down, for the remainder of Pryce-Jones's tenure of the editorial chair. At the end of 1958, just before he left, it was 39,225.

Nevertheless, the *Lit Supp* continued to be a very lively paper. The fifties saw numerous controversies in its pages, and the rise of a new generation of writers who were welcomed with a warmth that new writers had not always been accorded before.

There were also many more fat, special issues, including two regular children's books numbers a year edited by Kay Dowding. These were produced mainly, it must be said, at the instigation of the advertising department, who could usually round up all the publishers for them. Frank Derry, who was the advertisement manager for all the supplements, was also the man who first saw the possibility of getting substantial advertising from American publishers in the paper if American readers were cultivated more and the paper was promoted more strongly in the USA. He went out to the States in his bowler hat and smart blue suit, with a rolled umbrella, and made an enormous impact on the publishers himself. From his time on, American publishers' advertising has made a significant contribution to the *Lit Supp*'s income.

The special numbers gave an opportunity both for surveys of the British scene in fiction, poetry and so on, and also for *tours d'horizon* of foreign literatures, such as the paper had rarely published before. They were helpfully informative and brought in many foreign contributors, even if they generally lacked the critical sharpness of the reviewing of individual books. Notable examples included the fifty-six-page supplement, 'The Mind of 1951', on 24 August of that year, which included surveys of writing from Catalonia to New Zealand and declared itself to be 'published throughout the world'. It also printed fourteen new poems by English poets, from D.J. Enright's delicately ironic 'The "Black" Country'

> So shall we call it the Grey Country, out of deference.
> But Grey is slyer than Black: 'Why, I am practically white' –

to Edith Sitwell's sweeping 'Gardens and Astronomers' –

> And happy as the Sun, the gardeners
> See all miasmas from the human filth but as the dung
> In which to sow great flowers.
> Tall moons and mornings, seeds and sires and suns.

Edith Sitwell got 12 guineas, Enright – like most of the others – got four.

Another impressive special number was the French issue of 26 March 1954, in which A.J.P. Taylor singled out for special praise the historian Fernand Braudel, who urged historians to 'leave their books, know life for themselves – know every aspect of human existence', and in whose history of the Mediterranean 'the forces of nature, the spirit of the period and finally the political events are all bound into a single whole'. Many experts on France contributed to the number, such as the Leavisite critic Martin Turnell on Marcel Jouhandeau, Robert Speaight the actor-scholar on Claudel, and the young Olivier Todd on new writers in France. Conor Cruise O'Brien, who was at that time an Irish diplomat and had just published a volume of criticism called *Maria Cross*, under the pseudonym Donat O'Donnell, wrote an article in which he examined the 'key word in contemporary French criticism – *la conscience*', meaning, as he said, both 'conscience' and 'consciousness'.

He thought that in French it was now a 'fatigued word', which had too often been used 'as a moral shock-word in the Stalinian rhetoric', and that too many French writers had become mere *directeurs de conscience*, who 'instead of refining or enlarging consciousness' were 'simply infesting minds with slogans'. This was a good example of one of the uses of anonymity, for O'Brien could not easily have written such a challenging article under his name while he was still in the Irish Foreign Service.

On 6 August of the same year, there was a 'Special Autumn Number' called 'Personal Preference', in which thirty writers chose their favourite – preferably modern – book. The identities of this group give an idea of some of the figures whom Pryce-Jones esteemed among the established generation, just before the appearance of such writers as Kingsley Amis, Iris Murdoch, Philip Larkin and Ted Hughes. Many of them were, as well, regular anonymous contributors of reviews to the paper.

Classifying them roughly (for several of them could appear in different camps), there were the novelists Clemence Dane, L.P. Hartley, Storm Jameson, Rosamond Lehmann, Wyndham Lewis, Rose Macaulay, Charles Morgan, William Plomer, J.B. Priestley and Rex Warner; poets were Edmund Blunden, Norman Nicholson, Alan Ross, Stevie Smith and Stephen Spender; historians and biographers were Roger Fulford, Margaret Lane, C.M. Woodhouse and Alan (A.J.P.) Taylor; art critics and historians were Clive Bell, Douglas Cooper and James Pope-Hennessy; literary critics were Erik de Mauny, G.S. Fraser, Raymond Mortimer, Robert Speaight, Philip Toynbee and Francis Wyndham. There were also the philosopher Stuart Hampshire and the economist R.G. Tress.

This was the issue in which, as we saw earlier, Wyndham Lewis proclaimed the unrivalled greatness of the song at the end of Arnold's 'Empedocles on Etna'. Alan Taylor chose – magnanimously, it may be thought – Hugh Trevor-Roper's *The Last Days of Hitler*. Stephen Spender abjured surprise and nominated the poems of Auden and Dylan Thomas. Two contributors – Storm Jameson and Rose Macaulay – chose books by the historian of the Crusades, Steven Runciman. Margaret Lane chose R.W. Chapman's essays. Alan Pryce-Jones observed in an introductory article that only two of the choices were works by young writers – Keith Douglas's posthumous poems, picked out by Alan Ross, and *A Share of the World* by the young novelist Hugo Charteris, which was Francis Wyndham's favourite.

Another special number followed hot on the heels of this one – 'American Writing Today', which came out on 17 September, had 100 pages (including, thanks to Frank Derry, numerous full-page advertisements by American publishers) and was priced on the cover at 50 cents as well as 6d.

It was the new American poets and critics who got most attention in this issue. Edith Sitwell commended the poet Theodore Roethke to British attention, and there were new poems – painstakingly assembled by Pryce-Jones – by Randall Jarrell, Wallace Stevens, Marianne Moore and Robert Frost, among others. They got $20 each, apart from Frost who got $30. The English critic Geoffrey Moore – a consultant for those special numbers – described John Crowe Ransom, Robert Penn Warren and Cleanth Brooks as the successors to Richards, Leavis and Empson, and especially praised the work of R.P. Blackmur, who 'makes us feel the critic is honest and exact', while the young American scholar Sam Hynes added the names of Yvor Winters and Allen Tate. A new galaxy of critics was being introduced to *Lit Supp* readers. More generally, Kenneth B. Murdock wrote of the passing of English influence on American literature, while Graham Hutton remarked that in the great American melting pot, 'what seemed for so long – particularly in literary terms – without form and void is now suffering the pangs of formulation'.

There was a further special number of the *Lit Supp* on 18 January 1952 – its fiftieth anniversary edition. This consisted mainly of reprints – still anonymous – of past reviews. T.S. Eliot wrote privately to Pryce-Jones to say 'how delighted I was to see in the jubilee issue the original review of *Prufrock* transformed from the small pica in which it took its place in 1917' – a very good-humoured letter if one recalls what Dalton had said in that review.

This jubilee issue also included a brief history of the paper, in which the names of some of the reviewers from its early days were revealed, and some of the books they had written about were named. This was a posthumous article by Harold Child. It had been written for Stanley Morison's *History of The Times*, but Morison had decided against using it partly because it named names, and partly because he decided that he would not, after all, cover the *Times* supplements in his book. The article came in handy now.

Anger also streaked and rumbled across the paper in these years. John Sparrow, in particular, had grown more keen on controversy than ever. He also liked literary detective work, and on 2 July 1954 contributed an article suggesting that Jane Austen had met the Reverend Sydney Smith at Bath, and had based the character of Henry Tilney in *Northanger Abbey* on him. However when a correspondent wrote in with 'six helpful observations' for him, suggesting other contacts that Jane Austen might have had with Smith, Sparrow 'disclaimed the profferred support'.

The following year, on 29 April, Sparrow displayed his forensic powers to the full. He wrote a long, devastating review of a book by Tom Burns Haber of Ohio State University entitled *The Manuscript Poems of A.E. Housman: 800 Lines of Hitherto Uncollected Verse from the Author's Notebook*. This was a collection of 'chips from the author's workshop', as Sparrow put it, and he started by expressing his profound disapproval of Haber for publishing them at all, since Housman had asked for them all to be burned. Then he turned his attention to Haber's transcriptions of the manuscript.

The attributes needed for such work were, he said,

> the patience to disentangle and rearrange the material; an eye capable of reading so much of the text as is decipherable; accuracy in transcribing it where it is clear; a becoming humility where it is doubtful; and an ear so attuned to the poet's voice that it can tell, where the eye is defeated, what he must, or might, or could not possibly, have written. Perhaps it is not unreasonable also to ask that an editor of Housman should be capable of understanding Latin and of writing English. Of these attributes Mr Haber has none, in any adequate degree, except the first.

Sparrow went on to give many examples of places where he believed Haber had misread the text, and also of his use of unintelligible words such as 'omnipathy' and 'congelation'.

Haber wrote back to assert that his readings were accurate – though only taking Sparrow up on one point – and to accuse the reviewer of 'peculiar animosities'. The reviewer replied with another very convincing argument for a misreading, and a declaration that he knew 'nothing whatever about Mr Haber except what can be gathered from his published work'.

A letter from the novelist E.M. Almedingen on 19 October 1951 stirred some interest. She said that when she read Katherine Mansfield's stories she 'got a curious sense of walking through once well familiar rooms', and concluded that Katherine Mansfield had plagiarised ideas from Chekhov. In particular, she argued that the story 'The Child who was Tired' was taken substantially from Chekhov's story *Spat Khochetsia* ('Sleepy' or 'Sleepyhead'). John Middleton Murry wrote back protesting that in 1909, when his wife wrote her story, there was no English translation of Chekhov's story in existence. However other letter writers showed that it had appeared in English in 1903, and that there was also a German translation, and the general conclusion of the correspondents was that Katherine Mansfield was at any rate influenced by the Chekhov tale. E.M. Almedingen came back to assert that, in any event, it was 'not a minor matter'.

A poem by Rose Macaulay produced a more comic protest. The poem described the fall of Trebizond to the Turks in 1465, and the Turkish press attaché in London wrote on 12 August 1955 to say that it was offensive, since it spoke of the Turks as 'barbarians' when in fact the Ottoman Empire was very tolerant in the fifteenth and sixteenth centuries. Rose Macaulay replied to say that it was not she who was speaking in the poem, but 'the imagined ghosts of the defeated Byzantines', who would in any case have used the word 'barbarian' of all non-Greeks. There was no more reason for modern Turks to take offence than for her own compatriots to complain if a Turkish poet had described fifth-century Celts bewailing the capture of their city by the barbarian English.

Anthony Powell went off in 1953 to be the literary editor of *Punch* under Malcolm Muggeridge. During the previous year or two he had been reviewing less often for the *Lit Supp*, and Julian Symons had emerged as the leading novel reviewer.

Powell had meanwhile been working on his superb sequence of novels, *A Dance to the Music of Time*, and the first volume, *A Question of Upbringing*, appeared at the beginning of 1951. It was reviewed in a 'middle' on 16 February by Julian Maclaren-Ross – who, as has been noted, was to appear amiably if startlingly transformed into the writer X. Trapnel in a much later volume. It would have been difficult for Powell to have portrayed his reviewer harshly, for the article was lavish in its praise. Maclaren-Ross was (as we can now know) astute in his predictions of the future careers of such characters as Widmerpool and Stringham, and declared that 'whether considered as a study of the obsequious and self-seeking, a brilliant comedy of manners (there are passages in the book which cause one to laugh aloud) or as an analysis of the doom of youth, it cannot fail to be regarded as a triumph'.

Julian Symons was as enthusiastic about the second volume, *A Buyer's Market*, which he reviewed in June 1952. He said that it was 'written with great distinction, and marked throughout by a fine comic sense . . . But above and beyond the sureness with which individual characters are drawn is the author's evident capacity for indicating and commenting with great perception and subtlety on changes in the social structure of English life . . . which, if it can be enlarged to deal with events in the thirties, will make this book one of the fictional landmarks of our time'.

Symons was not disappointed, in May 1955, by the third volume. *The Acceptance World* did indeed 'depict a fragment of metropolitan society in the very early 1930s', as well as 'analysing modern love'; it was 'written with the serpentine distinction characteristic of Mr Powell's later style, and shows his infallible sense of social ironies'.

Symons showed his mettle as a social observer himself on this occasion by getting a 'small worried feeling that some of the local detail belongs to a slightly later period': he instanced Surrealism as a topic of conversation in England, the use of 'Trotskyist' as a general term of denigration, and the participation of writers in unemployed demonstrations as typical, rather, of the late thirties. 'But these,' he ended, 'are the merest rufflings of a general contentment in finding the mores and emotions of a particular group in a particular period so beautifully recaptured.' By the time of the fourth book, *At Lady Molly's*, in October 1957, he was content to recommend readers to 'sit back and unabashedly enjoy the varied felicity of each volume'.

The other major work of fiction that began to appear in the fifties was Evelyn Waugh's trilogy, *Sword of Honour* (as it came to be called). Powell himself reviewed the first volume, *Men at Arms*, in September 1952, making his points judiciously one by one, as usual. Its theme, he said, was the impact of the war – and more especially of the army

– on a middle-aged civilian with a romantic approach to the circumstances in which he finds himself. He declared straightaway that it
contained passages as funny as any in *Decline and Fall*, but went on to
say that on its serious side he thought that the edges of Guy Crouchback's character – the civilian in question – were slightly blurred. However the misadventures of Guy's brother officer, Apthorpe, were to be
'enjoyed in the fullest and richest manner'.

David Tylden-Wright reviewed the second volume, *Officers and
Gentlemen*, in July 1954. He observed that Guy had reverted to the
mild, melancholy cynicism he had displayed before the outbreak of war
temporarily gave him a sense of purpose, but that his creator – whose
prose was as delightful and dexterous as ever – had now 'a deepening
capacity for fusing entertainment and experience'. He cited the way in
which Waugh 'painted a tragic and moving picture of the Cretan disaster without ever deserting his humorous and satirical standpoint'.

Waugh paused – or was halted in his tracks by his own weird
psychological experiences – to write *The Ordeal of Gilbert Pinfold* in
July 1957. This got a dustier response from R.G.G. Price, later author
of the *History of Punch*, who called it a thin little tale and opined that
Waugh, though a comic writer of immense talent, was essentially a
lightweight who had suffered from being bracketed with writers such
as Graham Greene – it was time 'people stopped treating him as a
failed Mauriac'. The final volume in Waugh's trilogy would not appear
until 1961, when Arthur Crook had become editor of the paper.

Graham Greene himself, meanwhile, had received rough treatment
from Miss Folliott in September 1951 for his novel *The End of the
Affair*. She thought it 'uninspired and rather humourless'. Poor Waugh
and Greene – they seem to have had their reviewers the wrong way
round for these last two books.

However David Tylden-Wright came to the rescue in his review, in
December 1955, of *The Quiet American*. It was more, he said, than a
report on the Indo-Chinese war transposed into fiction. Its particular
excellence lay in the way Greene 'builds up the situation finally to
explode the moral problem which for him lies at the heart of the matter'.
The problem was: has the Graham Greene-like character, Fowler, older,
disillusioned and joyless, the right to condemn Pyle – the 'quiet American' working for Economic Aid in Vietnam – 'whose misguided idealism
makes him a force as well-intentioned but as potentially dangerous as
Robespierre when he instituted the Rule of Virtue'? Tylden-Wright was
glad that this time Greene was concerned with a moral rather than a
religious problem: 'He has moved on, taking with him his immense

capacity for discovering new variations of human imperfection.' In October 1958 Christopher Sykes, the radio producer and friend and biographer of Evelyn Waugh, was equally enthusiastic about Greene's comic gift in *Our Man in Havana*: 'the misunderstandings multiply with the facility of themes in a Bach fugue'.

As for Aldous Huxley, whose novel *The Genius and the Goddess* appeared in August 1955, he received a sad dismissal from Noel Annan. Annan said that the theme of the book was 'how fatuous and inexpert human beings are in the solemn business of improving themselves in their short span in the world' – but that its author sounded just like 'one of those beloved old clubmen who tell us that the country is going to the dogs'.

Novelists whose reputation was, on the contrary, consolidated in these years were Tolkien and Beckett, C.P. Snow, L.P. Hartley and Angus Wilson. Alfred Duggan, himself making a name as an historical novelist at this time, reviewed Part One of *The Lord of the Rings* in July 1954, and said that it was as though the 'jolly, rather Philistine creatures . . . the Light Programme types' of *The Hobbit* had intruded into the domain of the Nibelungs. Frodo, from being 'a greedy young hobbledehobbit' had become a noble Paladin. But the book embodied 'a coherent, complete and detailed mythology' and was written in sound prose and with rare imagination. G.S. Fraser made the case for Beckett in February 1956: he 'uses his enormous skill to reduce readers to a state of tired disgust and exasperated boredom', and yet he unexpectedly raises the dignity of mankind, for 'questing and expectation do give life dignity, even though the expectations are never answered'. These views make us feel a long way from the days of John Cann Bailey.

Francis Wyndham reviewed Angus Wilson's first novel *Hemlock and After* in a classic 'middle' in August 1952. His two volumes of short stories, *The Wrong Set* and *Such Darling Dodos*, wrote Wyndham, had established him already as an intelligent and accurate scourge of vulgarity who had 'to a marked degree the mysterious quality of readability'. The novel clarified the point of view which dictated the stories: it was an ambitious moral work, a 'savage exposure of corruption in a disintegrating society' which also showed 'the tragic inadequacy, in the face of this, of the liberal humanist'. (A book to please E.H. Carr? That we do not know.)

Wyndham also reviewed L.P. Hartley's most successful novel *The Go-Between*, in November 1953. 'For all his delicate perception of social nuances and witty appreciation of social absurdities,' Wyndham wrote, 'he is the least frivolous of writers. A sense of evil, more potent when imprecise, gives his work a moral strength and implies a standard of virtue.'

Powell was the reviewer again, in July 1951, of what has probably been C.P. Snow's most popular novel, *The Masters*. He observed that whereas the don used to be portrayed in novels as 'an intensely conservative figure, vague, eccentric, oddly dressed, probably snobbish' – like Powell's own fictional don, Sillers, one might remark – 'nowadays only the snobbery, as a fictional attribute, remains. Otherwise, we are shown him, on the whole, as left-wing, small-minded and grasping'. Snow's combination room was 'certainly not an engaging community', but the book gave an excellent account of at least one side of university life.

The three new novelists of the fifties who quickly established a reputation were John Wain, Kingsley Amis and Iris Murdoch. The *Lit Supp* did well by all of them to begin with.

John Wain was the first to get in with his *Hurry on Down*, reviewed by Julian Symons on 9 October 1953. Symons called it 'a fresh and amusing novel about the adventures of a young petit bourgeois hero attempting to escape from the restrictions of class and cash', and hailed Wain's 'grasp of comic effects, which range from some fine inconsequential farce, through skilfully treated social irony to an uncomfortable facetiousness'.

When Alan Ross reviewed Amis's first novel, *Lucky Jim*, on 12 February 1954, he put it in a larger context that rightly included Wain. Amis's young lecturer, Jim Dixon, 'short, round and bespectacled, and a day-dreamer with a robust sense of farce', was 'the anti – or rather sub – hero who is beginning to figure increasingly as the protagonist of the most promising novels written by young men since the war – in, for example, the work of Mr Ernest Frost, Mr William Cooper, and Mr John Wain – an intelligent provincial who, after getting a scholarship and an Oxford or Cambridge degree, finds his social position both precarious and at odds with his training.' But these characters, Ross continued, did not aspire to more assured social standing. On the contrary, they were 'vastly aware of the comedy of life, are irreverent about those who have to bolster their self-esteem by constant reference to their official positions, and delight in their own ludicrousness'. He found *Lucky Jim* 'richly comic' and 'very promising'.

However, Isaiah Berlin wrote privately to Pryce-Jones saying that *Lucky Jim* 'lowers me more than I can say'. No doubt it was a realistic and even gifted description of certain conditions of life, but he could not bear the images it forcibly brought up to him, and he was taking it like medicine in doses. At least it had left him more reconciled to his own life, because this life of another university teacher had made him realise what the alternative might be.

Symons took over Amis's second novel, *That Uncertain Feeling*, in September 1955. He was just as enthusiastic as Ross had been, saying that he was 'that rarest of writers, one who can make us laugh', that he treated the class struggle as a joke, which was one of the main reasons for his success, and that 'he remains well out from the rest of the field of young English novelists'.

Rayner Heppenstall, a racy but learned Bohemian, who was now contributing more and more regularly to the paper, reviewed Amis's third novel, *I Like It Here*, in January 1958, and also compared him with Wain. He treated them essentially seriously, as two writers who, though both very funny, were 'hot on the scent of humbug' and 'groping after a rock-bottom decency'. Amis, he said, was 'the defter and more engaging comic writer, but Mr Wain has been the pioneer', for *Hurry on Down* came out a year before *Lucky Jim*, 'and first established what became known as the Movement'. (Here Heppenstall was slightly misleading, since the name the Movement was mainly applied to the new poetry – though the boundary was blurred, as Wain and Amis were both poets in the Movement vein too.)

Amis early in his career revealed his combative spirit by writing to the paper after what he called this 'amiably-toned though intermittently incoherent' review had appeared, objecting to the suggestion that he had in any way derived the plot of *Lucky Jim* from Wain's novel. He had read *Hurry on Down* when it came out in August 1953, he said, but *Lucky Jim* had already been accepted for publication in April 1953. Heppenstall replied, asking why Amis was so curmudgeonly – he had not been trying to show that Amis was 'just an old copycat', he was 'concerned to do Mr Wain credit, not Mr Amis discredit'.

Meanwhile, Julian Symons had revised his opinion of them both, and in April 1959, commenting on a volume of current articles called 'Protest', remarked that Wain and Amis had become trivial. (Wain had by now written two further novels called *Living in the Present* and *The Contenders*.) The jokes in which they had 'first indulged themselves were the jokes of serious writers', but now it seemed as though nothing mattered to them as long as 'you were a decent chap in your personal relationships'. This was not enough for the socially conscious Symons.

Iris Murdoch's first book was a little volume on Sartre which Dr Hawkins reviewed on 15 January 1954. He observed that 'Sartre displays in its sharpest form the antithesis of God and cosmic absurdity', and called her exposition of this theme 'remarkably penetrating'. Richard Ollard, later to become known as a popular historian, reviewed her first novel, *Under the Net*, in the July of that year. He said that this 'picaresque novel about a lazy but gifted writer' revealed a 'brilliant new talent', with 'a remarkable sense of timing which makes her comic scenes extremely funny'. (The following week John Bayley, her future husband, who – as he describes in his memoir, *Iris* – was just at this time falling in love with her, contributed a poetry review, in which he declared with the kind of apt and idiosyncratic metaphor at which he was so good that John Heath-Stubbs in his poems was 'stylish, and always fully on duty'.)

In her second novel, *The Flight from the Enchanter*, two years later, David Tylden-Wright perceived a different characteristic – that under the superficial mockery there was 'a vein of quiet, earnest, Bloomsbury pessimism' and that though the book was extremely funny, it was nearer to tears than laughter. Her first book might indeed have been thought akin to Wain's and Amis's, but not her second, which pointed more in the direction in which she would develop. Her third novel, *The Sandcastle*, was also reviewed by Tylden-Wright, in May 1957. He thought that this book was 'much more securely tethered by the demands of the story and the desire to make the characters not only interesting but realistic', and felt that the relationship between Mor the schoolmaster and Rain, the artist visiting his school to paint the headmaster, 'comes out as a very real one'.

The Bell, her fourth book, was promoted in the now characteristic *Lit Supp* style to being reviewed in a 'middle'. Marigold Johnson, the wife of the journalist and historian Paul Johnson, was the author, and gave the book high praise. She described how, in the story, a group of foolish idealists trying to live in a William Morris-like utopia is broken up by the inner force of their own romantic hopes and passions, and found in it the lesson that one should not be dogmatic about how people should live. It was the product of a 'brilliant imagination'. With this novel and her next, *A Severed Head*, in 1961, Iris Murdoch perhaps reached the peak of her reputation. She characteristically got into no rows with the paper. Pryce-Jones had met her in France in 1957 and noted 'Iris Murdoch very fair, silent . . . yet holding back something, rather than protecting vacancy'.

Julian Symons hailed another important debut when in September 1954 he reviewed William Golding's *Lord of the Flies* – 1954 was in fact an outstanding year for new British fiction with Amis, Murdoch and Golding all appearing on the scene. Symons called *The Lord of the Flies* a 'remarkable fantasy' about the reversion to primitivism of the schoolboys in the story, beautifully constructed and with the various children just sufficiently individuated. And 1957 saw the debut of three more novelists who were eventually to achieve literary fame. In February, Tylden-Wright reviewed *Justine*, the first volume in Lawrence Durrell's *Alexandria Quartet*, enjoying Justine's 'demented course of erotic experience' and remarking that Durrell was 'one of the few writers who can convey the elusive feeling of happiness'. Later that month Siriol Hugh-Jones reviewed Muriel Spark's *The Comforters* more cautiously, calling it a Pirandello puzzle with some bizarre characters in it, while in May, Tylden-Wright said that V.S. Naipaul's *The Mystic Masseur* was 'promising'. A literary career of another kind was launched in April 1953 when Ian Fleming published his first James Bond novel, *Casino Royale*, which Alan Ross called 'exciting and extremely civilised'. Ian Fleming himself contributed a thoughtful discussion of racial problems to the paper on New Year's Day 1954 when he reviewed Fernando Henriques's *Family and Colour in Jamaica*. However, by April 1958 P.J. Stead, a regular reviewer of crime fiction, was dismissing Fleming's *Dr No* as 'rejuvenated old tricks'.

A new galaxy of American novelists was also starting to shine bright in the fifties, and the *Lit Supp* was much more attuned to such a phenomenon than it had been in its earlier history. The new star was John Updike, and his first novel *The Poorhouse Fair* was greatly appreciated by the Irish novelist, Anthony Cronin, who was now starting to review regularly for the *Lit Supp*. Writing in March 1959, he said that this story about an old people's home, set 200 years in the future, was 'perfectly real, humanly true and humble' and 'coloured by a spirit of sad unillusioned comedy, perfectly in keeping with the subject of old age . . . If larger issues lurk behind it, they wait their turn.'

Julian Symons called Saul Bellow 'a considerable talent writing on a major scale' when he reviewed *The Adventures of Augie March* in June 1954. This was 'colloquial, complex, powerful writing,' he said, even if it was 'rather like that of an Argus-eyed machine, which observes all but interprets nothing'. Mary McCarthy's reputation in Britain leaped on the publication in 1953 of *The Groves of Academe*, with its 'unrelenting pressure of intellectual wit' as Julian Symons put it. Symons said that 'the truth of this picture of the American academic world, with the effect of the current political witch hunt on its life, must be taken on trust', but that she was 'unique among women novelists in England and America in being able to sustain a whole novel on this level'. That reputation was sustained by *A Charmed Life*, her satire in 1956 on a psychologically-minded America where, as David Tylden-Wright put it, people 'not only cannot see or think straight, but cannot even feel direct emotion without discounting it as the product of some complex or other'.

Carson McCullers had put the anguished distaste of her earlier *Lit Supp* reviewers behind her, and reviewing a reprint of *The Heart is a Lonely Hunter*, published first in 1940, Julian Symons said that 'from her preoccupation with freaks and with human loneliness she makes fictions which touch and illuminate at many points the world to which all art makes, however obliquely, its final reference: the world of literal reality'. Obliquity was understood now; indeed, as the wheel of taste spun on, the Movement was saying by now that it had become far too highly rated.

As for the great Southerner, William Faulkner, his *Requiem for a Nun* was set among his other novels in a 'middle' by Julian Maclaren-Ross. 'Lust, masquerading as, and mistaken for, love is the theme of many of Faulkner's most compelling stories,' he said – but pride was the ruling passion of his characters. Maclaren-Ross saw Faulkner's work as a *roman fleuve*: 'his imaginary county and the characters with which he has populated it are intensely real, and therefore subject to the changes, both subtle and drastic, which age and time bring to most human beings; changes not always credible at first in the light of our knowledge of the persons affected, yet seeming, on reflection, to have been predestined from the start'.

The novel from the European continent that most excited the world in these years was probably Boris Pasternak's *Dr Zhivago*. It was reviewed on 5 September 1958 by John Willett, who would in due course become deputy editor of the paper as well as a leading Brecht scholar. Willett praised the 'great freshness' of the novel, but was careful not to make Cold War propaganda by suggesting that it was simply an anti-Soviet book – 'nobody who sees so much ever finds it easy to make up his mind', he observed. However in October the Russian scholar Gleb Struve wrote to ask why Willett had not mentioned that the book could not be published in the Soviet Union.

As for Thomas Mann, who died in August 1955, he had left the years of *Lit Supp* disdain behind him. His comic novel *Confessions of Felix Krull, Confidence Man*, which had been published in its final form in German the previous year, was reviewed in its English translation in November 1955 by Erich Heller, an outstanding scholar and critic of German literature living in England.

Mann had begun it – and published a fragment of it – as long ago as 1911, and went back to it again forty years later – 'one of the more astonishing cases of invisible mending recorded in the history of literature' wrote Heller. Heller found in it a wonderfully sustained double vision 'which unflinchingly comprehends at the same time the joke in the serious business of living and the utter seriousness of the joke'. It was like Verdi's *Falstaff*, he thought. It contained 'the rarest blending of rare qualities: substance, depth, humour and the utmost virtuosity'. Yet no erudition was needed to enjoy it, for it created 'that happy and light-hearted illusion of simplicity which emerges from the consummate mastery of art over its complex material'. However, he thought that the book was almost impossible to translate, and that like one of Felix Krull's victims, Madame Houpfle, in the English version it had been robbed of all its jewellery.

Meanwhile, the Movement was beginning to be talked about by late 1954. The loosely defined label had first been applied mainly to Kingsley Amis, John Wain and Philip Larkin, who had in common that they were all young men from relatively modest backgrounds who had been at St John's College, Oxford, and were all now writing poems that broke with the florid or portentous manner of Dylan Thomas and Edith Sitwell, in favour of regular verse forms and plain sense delivered with ironic humour.

The *Lit Supp* was lucky to have G.S. Fraser in charge of the poetry at this time. He found himself in sympathy with these Movement poets, yet was also quite able to criticise them. Already, in February 1954, he had reviewed Kingsley Amis's volume of poems *A Frame of Mind* in the paper, observing that Amis was reacting against the neo-romanticism of the 1940s, and that though his manner was sometimes 'tough', modesty and good feeling underlay it. Fraser noted that writers such as Philip Toynbee and the poet Dannie Abse had already begun to criticise the new anti-romantic tendency in English poetry.

In April, a batch of pamphlets under the general title of the 'Fantasy Poets' was published. The poets were Thom Gunn, Anthony Thwaite, Louise Bogan, Donald Davie, James Price, Philip Larkin and Kingsley Amis, a list which included most of the core poets of the swelling

Movement – notably Gunn, Davie, Larkin and Amis. Fraser noted the prevalence of irony in their tone, but perceptively singled out Larkin, some of whose poems, he said, 'show that he can touch us more profoundly when he drops, as he can afford to, the ironic shield'. In May Alan Pryce-Jones, reviewing a batch of three poets, picked out D.J. Enright – whose first pamphlet, it will be recalled, he had praised – as the one with the greatest potential power, 'both moving and funny and advancing both in skill and interest', in his new book, *The Laughing Hyena*. Enright was another poet who would now be broadly associated with the Movement.

In September, in the course of reviewing a book on Ezra Pound and T.S. Eliot by Richard Aldington, Fraser remarked that 'lesser, more traditionalist poets like Empson or Graves now provide young poets with more practical working models than those two great experimental masters'. And in December Gordon Wharton, an excellent new poetry critic on the paper, who was a notable champion of the new lucid and ironic manner and the reversion to traditional forms, hailed the publication of Thom Gunn's first collection *Fighting Terms*.

1955 saw the publication of two collections by Movement poets, Philip Larkin's *The Less Deceived* and Donald Davie's *Brides of Reason*. Larkin's book was undoubtedly the outstanding new volume in this whole period, and received its due appreciation in the paper. The poet Michael Hamburger – who from his own work might have been judged a member of the romantic camp – was unstinting in his admiration. He did not make much attempt to define the character of Larkin's poems, but said that he was 'a poet of quite exceptional importance', with 'a mature vision and the power to render it variously, precisely and movingly'.

Donald Davie's book was overlooked by the paper, though back in 1953, reviewing his volume of criticism *Purity of Diction in English Verse*, Professor Garrod had noted Davie's appreciation of 'a civilised moderation and elegance' in the best eighteenth-century poetry.

In June 1956, reviewing John Wain's book of poems, *A Word Carved on a Sill*, Gordon Wharton judiciously summed up the situation as he saw it at that point.

> It is almost impossible to mention John Wain's name without becoming involved in a discussion of what is called 'the Movement'. We might agree, at this stage, that 'the Movement's' friendlier critics have been more nearly right than its hostile ones. Those who praised, say, Miss Elizabeth Jennings, Mr Thom Gunn, and Mr Philip Larkin

for their economic use of language, for their 'purity of diction', have been nearer the mark than those who saw in their work a period of dull conformity. For, certainly, the books of poems these three young writers have so far published show that a few commonly held notions about poetry do not necessarily mean a common practice.

Wharton went on to say that though Wain too used strict verse forms and had 'a nervous reserve about saying too much', there was a 'Wain tone' that distinguished him as an individual too, and that the best of the poems here were 'beautiful in that they are strong and well-proportioned'.

The publication of two anthologies, mainly of work by these poets, in that summer of 1956 was the high point of the Movement. These were *New Lines*, edited by Robert Conquest, and *Poets of the 1950s*, edited by D.J. Enright and published in Japan, where he was now teaching. They were reviewed together on 13 July by G.S. Fraser, who gave a very rounded view of the whole Movement scene.

He repeated his point that the poets in the two volumes were in conscious reaction against the prevailing neo-romantic fashions of the 1940s, and tried to identify what as a result, they had in common. They were all 'makers rather than bards', all careful craftsmen, all speaking in 'a quiet though usually a reasonably confident tone of voice', and their poems tended to be reflective rather than directly lyrical. On the whole, their temper of mind was 'humanistic rather than religious, liberal rather than radical or reactionary, cool rather than fervid, pragmatic rather than systematic, sceptical rather than enthusiastic, empirical rather than transcendental . . . a traditionally English temper of mind'.

But Fraser said that it was surprising to find that temper of mind put forward as a typically poetic one, and on the introductions to the volumes by the two editors he commented: 'In their humanly very justifiable fear of the irrational, of the transcendental and the unmeasured, are they not turning their eyes away in shocked horror from some of the deepest springs of poetry? Their liberal moralism, taken too seriously, might seem likely to cut a young poet away not only from direct lyricism, not only from the invocation of unseen powers, but from the tragic sense of life.'

However, there was not really any need to worry. Their range of tones and styles was 'much more various than recent polemics about the "new movement" might have led the ordinary reader to expect' – and 'the best poems in these volumes do, after all, reach for absolutes, restlessly'.

In fact, of course, the best poets in due course went their own way – and Fraser and the *Lit Supp* can take some credit for helping them, by printing much of the poetry that they went on to write. Fraser himself, indeed, brought out an anthology of poems called *Poetry Now* at the end of 1956. It was sent for review to D.S. Carne-Ross, a classical scholar and poet who favoured the camp that was hostile to the Movement, and who said scathingly that 'the English have returned to careful, learned, sensitive, minor poetic forms that befit a culture in decline'.

Fraser's anthology also produced an outburst of arguments in the letters column about whether the neo-romantics, the Scots, and various other groups had been properly represented in it. On 4 January 1957 there was a letter from D.J. Enright that brought these arguments to a comical – but firm – end. He said that

> Faber & Faber are good enough to commission an anthology of 'New Poetry'; Mr G.S. Fraser is industrious enough to edit it; the *Times Literary Supplement* goes to the trouble of reviewing it. And straight-away an uncouth dog fight breaks out in the correspondence columns. Somebody has only one poem in the book, somebody hasn't even one, somebody else oughtn't to be in it at all. There are too many (too few) (no) Empsonites, there are too few (too many) Scottish, Irish and Welsh! Ya! Favouritism! Riddling rotter! Lallans loon! Grr! Did poets of the past – the ones we know of – really go on and on in this petty way? . . . The common man doesn't read much poetry. Perhaps he has read some of these 'Letters to the Editor'.

So the Movement passed on into history. Meanwhile, the thirties poets were not getting a very good press. Auden was still in the hands of Dr R.G. Cox, who said of *Nones*, in July 1952, that Auden's talent 'was continually dissipated in irresponsible facility and incidental cleverness', and of *The Shield of Achilles* in January 1956 that he was 'groping towards a Christian vision' but 'lapses back into eclectic reminiscence, irresponsible smartness or a display of miscellaneous knowledge'.

Stephen Spender's main publication in this period was his autobiography *World Within World*, which Pryce-Jones reviewed in a 'middle'. It was an admiring yet teasing review, very much a Pryce-Jones piece: he thought that there was 'a streak of the absurd in Mr Spender's quest for so many high things at once: ideal friendship, great art, personal absolution, fulfilment simultaneously in service and in privacy', though he acknowledged that Spender knew that before the reader did; and he felt that at the age of forty Spender had still not 'resolved his personal equation as Arnold or Gide resolved theirs'. However, he believed that the book would survive 'as required reading in the tragi-comic story of the liberal decline' – for Spender was 'far closer to his Liberal forebears than a cursory judgment might suggest'. Spender himself contributed a review in 1951 of *Mid-Century American Poets*, edited by John Ciardi, in which he helped to advance the fame of Robert Lowell in Britain by calling him 'the outstanding poet of his generation'.

The British neo-romantics who had succeeded the thirties political poets were still getting some praise in the fifties. In August 1957, in 'Mr Barker's Bite' – another of the increasing number of joky headings – the poet Burns Singer, who was also now appearing quite often in the paper, defended *The True Confession of George Barker* against the charges of obscenity that some critics had levelled at it, and praised Barker's vision, which 'embraced pettiness and nobility', even though he displayed 'ludicrous extravagance in his vocabulary'.

Dylan Thomas died in America in 1953. The following February, Julian Symons reviewed his very successful radio play, *Under Milk Wood*, about the events between one night and the next in the Welsh seaside town of Llareggub (to be read backward as well as forward), a town that had fallen 'head over bells' in love. Symons said it was 'the most gaily gruesome of bawdy rhetorical fancies', and not really much more than that, but it was 'a fitting epitaph for a man who played in such a masterly way with words'.

As for the coming generation, the leader of these was undoubtedly Ted Hughes, who was quite unlike the Movement poets from the start, but whose first book, *A Hawk in the Rain*, received a rather grudging notice from the poet Patric Dickinson. Dickinson said that Hughes was a countryman with real roots, but that his idiom was not startlingly original, not did his poems have any strikingly individual rhythm. As far as the *Lit Supp* was concerned Hughes's success was yet to come.

In the early 1950s William Empson published two important volumes on poetry and literary criticism. R.G. Cox paid homage to this 'mind of extraordinary intellectual agility' in a review in June 1952 of his new book *The Structure of Complex Words*, praising his contribution to the theory and history of language, but suggesting that 'no theory will do the critic's essential work for him, however useful the set of analytical tools it provides. Even the critic who invents the theory and the tools must be judged in the end by the sensitiveness of his response to the work of art.'

G.S. Fraser had no doubt of Empson's 'sensitiveness' when he reviewed his *Collected Poems* in October 1955. The 'middle' that Fraser wrote was one of the very best of his many poetry reviews. In Empsonian manner, he took a detailed look at a 'short and moving' poem called 'Let it Go', written during the Second World War ('It is this deep blankness is the real thing strange . . .'), and showed persuasively that 'the poem is about deciding not to go mad, or about being grateful to Nature for her odd, her sometimes rather flat and depressing ways of stopping us going mad . . . Though it deals with a mood of apathy, the poem does not express such a mood. It expresses a firmness of mortal decision.'

Fraser observed that 'many young poets have in the past five years or so been profoundly influenced, and rightly so, by admiration for Mr Empson's "tone of voice"; its assurance, its moderation, its sanity. But some of the verse produced by this discipleship has been, to say the least, prosy. Mr Empson is a master of the line that makes its point by not making it, by a sort of terse reticence . . . His enormous vogue among the young is anything but a fad.'

Empson himself wrote a number of admirable letters to the paper at this time. One especially, about Hopkins's poem 'The Windhover' on 20 May 1955, is a classic example of his subtle yet commonsensical reading of poems, suggesting that Hopkins was contrasting here the 'unconscious grace' of the kestrel's flight with his doubts as to 'whether his severe Jesuit training had only crippled him'. He doubted what another correspondent had suggested, that the poet was gloating over the bird's savagery, and – liberal rationalist that he was – added that he disliked the current keenness of Christian apologists to recall 'the stark roots of primitive human sacrifice and their place in Christianity'.

Dr F.R. Leavis had hitherto received excellent reviews from the *Lit Supp* for his books, but in February 1952, when his collection of essays *The Common Pursuit* was published, Pryce-Jones himself wrote one of his teasingly critical 'middles' about it. He acknowledged that Leavis was 'a critic of high and admirable purpose', but he had two complaints: that Leavis was dogmatic ('he is liable to try to polish off an argument with a phrase rather as, in different circles it might be done by throwing a saucepan') and, above all, that he did not take pleasure into account as a reason for reading books. Leavis, he said, was certainly not a lowbrow – but neither was he a highbrow, for highbrows 'find themselves looking at pictures, hearing music, reading in other languages, travelling, correlating as far as possible the whole plan of a civilisation in which the English faculty at a university occupies only one corner'.

That was a definition of a highbrow which was wickedly tailor-made to apply to Pryce-Jones himself – and he invented for Leavis the word 'flatbrow', meaning someone who carried on intellectual activities 'with a conviction of mission, a devoted ardour and a fundamental misunderstanding of the nature of literature'.

That was carefully calculated not to improve relations with the doctor. And it was at about this time that, according to Pryce-Jones's son David, a lorry drew up outside the paper containing the complete set of a new multi-volume Chinese encyclopaedia in Chinese. 'Send them off to Dr Leavis,' the editor told his secretary, 'with a note saying it's a suitable book for him to review and could we have 10,000 words on it by next Thursday.' Along with occasional critical remarks about Leavis in leaders by George Fraser, Pryce-Jones's 'middle' was enough for one to understand the increasing number of letters the paper received from Leavis about hostility and misrepresentation in its pages.

Traditional, less controversial literary scholarship also continued, of course, to appear and be reviewed regularly in the *Lit Supp*. John Sparrow expressed unreserved admiration in September 1953 for R.W. Chapman's edition of Dr Johnson's letters, saying that 'few scholars can have lived longer or more intimately with the subject of their study' and 'none has escaped more completely the deadening touch of pedantry', while in 1951 Dr Garrod cautiously welcomed the first volume in the revised Arden Edition of Shakespeare, *Macbeth*, edited by Kenneth Muir: 'it begins again, with the omens fair'. The sprightly old don had more fun in 1957 reviewing Geoffrey Faber's reverential life of Benjamin Jowett, the Master of Balliol who according to the popular Oxford rhyme about him said, 'What I don't know isn't knowledge.' Garrod questioned the breadth of his scholarship and said that 'his grand passion was ordering the lives of other people . . . In the practicalities of arranging other people's lives there was never such an expert.'

Wars and revolutions continued to be a battlefield – and E.H. Carr continued to take up many columns of the paper. Now, however, he had another learned apologist for the Russian Revolution alongside him: Isaac Deutscher, the champion of Trotsky rather than Lenin and Stalin. The first volume of Carr's enormous *History of Soviet Russia*, which appeared early in 1951 – *Lenin and His Rise to Power* – was dismissed rather peremptorily by the American Arthur Schlesinger as 'an act of faith rather than of analysis', and Carr wrote twice to the paper in protest without getting an answer. However later volumes were reviewed by Deutscher, who unhesitatingly called it a great work, but who suggested, in his review of Volume III in June 1953, that Carr was sometimes 'carried away by his sound respect for Realpolitik and his contempt for illusion' – a judgment we can well sympathise with in the light of what we have seen so far. In Deutscher's equally respectful review of Volume IV the following year, it is amusing to see him pursue this one dissenting note by suggesting that Trotsky was the real hero of the book, who 'in spite of Mr Carr's deliberately unimaginative language' emerged from it as 'the great precursor, the originator of ideas the realisation of which lay in the future, the first brilliant and determined advocate of planned economy'.

Carr in turn reviewed Deutscher's biography of Trotsky, and in the same way paid him many compliments, while in turn urging his own views on Deutscher. He judged the book to be 'biography' of a high order – but, after all, it was only biography, and good biography was necessarily bad history, since 'it concentrates the spotlight on individual idiosyncrasies rather than on major social forces'. However, the two pro-revolutionary historians of the Soviet Union stood side by side against the challenges – notably from Leonard Schapiro and Robert Conquest – that were destined before long to come their way. Meanwhile, Michael Oakeshott, who would take over Harold Laski's chair at the London School of Economics and become the intellectual hero of the Conservative Right, wrote with glancing irony about a series of radio lectures that Carr gave, published in 1951 as *The New Society*: 'If you want to be an individualist or to enjoy some personal freedom (in the old, out-of-date sense) in the new collectivist, equalitarian, mass society . . . you must be prepared to live in the interstices of the society and put your trust in its imprecisions.'

Carr reviewed books by many other leading figures of the fifties, mostly critically. In *The Price of Revolution*, by his old enemy D.W. Brogan, in 1951, he saw 'the victory of the table-talker over the political analyst'. Reviewing a reissue of Leonard Woolf's pre-war political study, *After the Deluge*, and a new work *Principia Politica*, in October 1953, he portrayed Woolf's belief in reason and progress and liberal democracy as no longer relevant or adequate: 'The far-reaching alterations in the map of the world which appear to herald the decline and fall of western Europe are watched with very different emotions in other continents, where they seem to open up new avenues of opportunity.'

In a leader the following month he described Isaiah Berlin's essay

'The Hedgehog and the Fox' as 'brilliant', but dissented from its conclusions. Berlin had quoted the Greek poet Archilochus's remark 'The fox knows many things, the hedgehog one big thing' and had divided thinkers and artists into foxes and hedgehogs. Aristotle, Shakespeare and Montaigne were foxes, who were content just to portray the manifold diversity of life, Plato, Hegel and Dostoevsky were hedgehogs who sought for one unifying vision or principle, while Tolstoy was a fox who wanted to be a hedgehog – and Berlin preferred foxes. Not so Carr. He believed all great artists and thinkers 'refused to be foxes, and staked their lives and their art on the quest for a guiding principle of unity in the diversity of storm and stress in which their fate had been cast'.

Carr struck similar notes in his review in November 1954 of A.J.P. Taylor's *The Struggle for Mastery in Europe, 1848–1918*, saying that Taylor would be in the front rank of living historians if he would shed his distaste for ideas and recognise that 'history would not be worth writing if it had no meaning', and also in his review of Hugh Trevor-Roper's *Historical Essays* in November 1957, where he mocked Trevor-Roper's 'detestation of that strangely composed Satanic trinity, Roman Catholicism, Marxism and Professor Toynbee', and his 'cultivated aloofness from a world that eludes his wavelength'. Isaac Deutscher, for his part, provoked the historian Hugh Seton-Watson to wrath by his review in October 1953 of his book *The Pattern of Communist Revolution*. The anti-Communist Seton-Watson replied that he did not claim to be neutral in the Cold War but could not agree with the reviewer's 'curious opinion' that no-one could make a contribution to scholarship who was not neutral. Deutscher replied to that by saying that the partisan could only make such a contribution 'to the extent to which he controls his partisan emotions'.

The hostile historian of the Soviet Union, Leonard Schapiro, brought out his book *The Origin of the Communist Autocracy* in May 1955, and this went not to Carr or Deutscher but to C.M. Woodhouse. He acknowledged Carr's history as being more comprehensive, but he observed, as may be thought more importantly:

> It has been so far the peculiar triumph of Marxism to have succeeded in prescribing not only the spectacles through which Marxists will view history, but also the spectacles through which their rivals and opponents will view history. Mr Schapiro's special merit is to have made his own spectacles. They are of very simple design, and very familiar in other less controversial fields of historical study. They

are perhaps as near as any we shall be offered in our lifetime to those that will eventually be worn by future historians of the Bolshevik Revolution.

As for D.W. Brogan, table-talker or not, in reviewing Raymond Aron's *L'Opium des Intellectuels* in September 1955, he wrote a very amusing article about the Marxist intellectuals of the village of Saint Germain-des-Prés, 'far from Roubaix or even Billancourt, not to speak of Coventry, Detroit or Dusseldorf', standing in their church porch offering their all to the idealised French workers, for whom to their distress it was either 'not enough, or not wanted, or casually accepted as a great beauty accepts the homage of a gawky if interesting worshipper'. Brogan was thankful that in Britain – as Aron himself noted – poets and novelists were not expected to have opinions on economics and politics, and 'Mr Anthony Powell is not asked his views on the central banking system because he has written *The Acceptance World*'.

Meanwhile in May 1952 the young journalist Peregrine Worsthorne contributed an article that anticipated his later renown for saying the unexpected as a columnist on (and subsequently editor of) the *Sunday Telegraph*. He complained that books about Russia were about nothing except Soviet prisons. In fact there was so much written on the subject that 'gentle maiden ladies, for whom Brixton is only a name on an omnibus and Dartmoor a breed of pony, can rattle off the prison routine of Moscow's Lubyanka and the geography of the labour camps in the Arctic Circle'.

The other historians were not slow to enter into controversy. A.J.P. Taylor remarked in a survey article in 1952 that 'some regret has recently been expressed in Germany that "anti-German" writers (Namier, Taylor, Trevor-Roper, [Max] Beloff) have a monopoly in commenting on recent history. It is unlikely that the writers would recognise themselves under this common description; perhaps the facts are not particularly "pro-German".' Certainly he did not hesitate to attack another 'anti-German', namely F.H. Hinsley, whose *Hitler's Strategy* he reviewed in January 1952. Taylor argued that Hitler was not susceptible to the rational analysis that, he claimed, Hinsley applied to his motives: Hitler was 'a gambler who recognised no limits', and a book about him needed to convey the 'atmosphere of world-shaking lunacy he lived in'. Hinsley complained bitterly in a letter about the 'strident and hysterical appeal' of the review, Taylor's distortions of what he had written, his love of anecdotes, unsupported assertions and theatrical phrases, and his 'three sneers for my academic status'.

Hugh Trevor-Roper also entered into disputes with gusto – notably into a long-running debate over Arnold Toynbee's Reith lectures in the spring of 1954. The Catholic author Douglas Jerrold had quarrelled with Toynbee over what he saw as the diminished importance that Toynbee – as a very ecumenical Christian, quoting Pope Pius XI – had attached to Western Christianity and civilisation, in comparison with other faiths and cultures. Trevor-Roper intervened with a tart and sceptical letter. 'Mr Jerrold appeals from history to religious dogma, Professor Toynbee from history to ecclesiastical authority . . . If we are to deduce any useful lessons from history, we should not subject the entire content of history either to a single miracle doubtfully recorded nearly two thousand years ago or to the obiter dictum of a twentieth-century eccelesiastic.' Trevor-Roper also wrote a very critical article for the paper in March 1957 about Spain with its 'hatred of change': 'How many excellent projects dissolve uncompleted into dusty nothing! How many ideas, once adopted, degenerate into mere moods, emotions, sensations! . . . We are back where we were, swallowed up again in that ancient, unthinking conservatism which still dominates, even today, that Oriental society.' Conservative he may have been, but not of that kind.

Isaiah Berlin contributed a review in March 1953 of a *History of Russian Philosophy* by N.O. Lossky. He took to task with more gentle humour the two main types of the history of Russian philosophy that were currently being written: Soviet histories, with Marx and Lenin 'soaring above the categories, omniscient and infallible' and 'a motley collection of more or less left wing critics and pamphleteers tacked on'; and émigré histories, 'their pages often no better than directories of the names of third-rate metaphysicians and theologians'.

His own book, *Two Concepts of Liberty*, was reviewed by the young philosopher Richard Wollheim in February 1959. Wollheim did not enter into polemics, but gave a careful, sympathetic exposition of the book's fundamental idea – that there was a supposed 'positive liberty', a set of rights and opportunities that society could try to give its members, but that such attempts were all too often made by authoritarian regimes and at the expense of the much more important 'negative liberty', which simply allowed people to live as they chose, and as best they could, without any obstacle other than those of accepted law and morality being put in their way. This was perhaps Isaiah Berlin's most important and influential book, a turning point in the slow restoration of liberal thought in the world.

*   *   *

From the time he became editor, Pryce-Jones did everything he could to increase the fees paid to reviewers. He went much further than Morison in adding extra sums to the official payments based on column inches, and sometimes whole pages of the marked copy in his first few years are covered with these double lines of figures in red pencil, all signed 'APJ'. In practice, this came to mean paying about £4 a column instead of the official £3; £10.10s 0d for a leader; £18.18s 0d, for a 'middle'; and special rates for a front-page article. But these changes in payment only began on a regular basis in August 1953, when the 'middles' and leaders were fixed officially at those figures, and £4 a column became the norm for the rest of the paper. Novels were often reviewed now in batches of three, and in this case the reviewer generally got an extra guinea. After this, Pryce-Jones did not have to authorise the payments personally, apart from exceptionally large ones to distinguished or demanding contributors, and the accounts department could take out their rulers again.

There were various staff changes. 'Eddy' Blunden came back from Japan and rejoined the staff in June 1950, at the age of fifty-four. By 1953, when he left again to become Professor of English Literature in Hong Kong, it was calculated that he had written over 1,000 articles for the *Lit Supp*, though the great majority of these had in fact been contributed before Pryce-Jones became editor. Pryce-Jones did not give him very many books to review. His ex-wife, Sylva Norman, an authority on the Romantics, appeared in the paper as often as he did now.

G.S. Fraser went out to Japan in the summer of 1950 to take up the university teaching post that Blunden had just vacated. He returned to England in 1953 – just in time for the onset of the Movement – and resumed his role as chief poetry critic and adviser on the selection of new poems for publication, though he was on a retainer, not on the staff. The young Guardsman David Tylden-Wright, who had come in at the suggestion of the chairman, Colonel Astor, and gone on to become an excellent reviewer of fiction, left the literary world to take up the life of a country gentleman.

Later in the fifties, Pryce-Jones brought the author James Pope-Hennessy on to the staff, partly at the behest of Harold Nicolson, who said that he was on the verge of bankruptcy. Pope-Hennessy wrote a number of good reviews, but he did not stay long, since the *Times* staff were scandalised by his wild homosexual private life – which led, in the end, to his being murdered. John Richardson says in his book *The Sorcerer's Apprentice* that one summer when Pope-Hennessy was working in the *Lit Supp* office, he became so obsessed with the sight of a bare-chested labourer sweating in the street outside that he could not keep his mind on his work. He tore a twenty-pound note in two, gave one half with his telephone number on it to the man, and told him to come and collect the other half – as he did. (However, when I talked to Pryce-Jones about my intention to write a history of the *Lit Supp,* when he was almost 90, he said to me: 'Don't forget to put Jamie in.')

There were changes in the editorship of *The Times* itself in these years, but the *Lit Supp* and its editor were not much affected by them. Casey – who so long ago had written that perceptive review of Virginia Woolf – succeeded Barrington-Ward as editor in April 1948, but it proved to be too late in his career – he was sixty-four – for him to be able to bring any great vigour to the job. Pryce-Jones in fact said to me of him, 'Delightful but hopeless man – did nothing except have a glass of port.' Casey was succeeded in 1952 by Sir William Haley, who had begun his career as a telephonist on *The Times*, then had joined the *Manchester Evening News*, where he had worked his way up to being managing editor, and now came back to *The Times* after eight very successful years as Director-General of the BBC.

Haley was an energetic editor, with a particular interest in books, but he gave Pryce-Jones no trouble apart from occasional admonitory memos about the need for great accuracy in the paper. He consulted Pryce-Jones closely over the development of a proper book page in *The Times* – an idea that Casey had launched – and A.P. (Patrick) Ryan, when he became the first literary editor of *The Times*, depended a great deal on the *Lit Supp* – and especially on Arthur Crook – for ideas and reviewers. A memo from Pryce-Jones to Haley in January 1955 suggests that the *Times* book page should have an essay written each week by the same person, 'who could build up a personality in the same way as Desmond MacCarthy and Robert Lynd did in the past'. This may well have been the seed of Haley's decision to write a regular article himself, which he subsequently did under the name of 'Oliver Edwards'.

Items in the paper sometimes had a history behind them that the paper itself did not reveal. One was the case of the three dots, in which Robert Graves and Joshua Podro threatened a libel action against the *Lit Supp* after a review appeared on 9 February 1954 of their book *The Nazarene Gospel Restored*. In this book they tried to show that Jesus was an 'apocalyptic Pharisee' whose message was neither unorthodox nor original, and that the four Gospels were piracies from a single authentic tradition about him that had been orally preserved in Aramaic by the Apostolic Church in Jerusalem. Professor T.W. Manson, the Moderator of the General Assembly of the Presbyterian Church, poured scorn upon the book in his review, calling it 'reckless and uncritical'. For example, he said that Graves and Podro invoked the lost Nazarene gospel to prove that their portrait of Jesus was correct, then used their portrait in order to 'restore' that gospel.

There was a sharp correspondence in the paper after this between Graves and Podro on the one hand, and the reviewer on the other, which centred in the end on a remark in one of Manson's replies. The letter that Haymon & Lewis of College Hill Chambers, EC4, delivered by hand to *The Times*'s solicitors on 17 June 1954 must have been one of the most learned expositions of biblical textual scholarship ever penned by solicitors.

Graves and Podro had quoted Galatians IV.14 in one of their letters. There were two versions of this text, each containing a different Greek expression at a certain point ('We assume that your clients' contributor's knowledge of the Greek Testament,' Haymon & Lewis dryly commented, 'is sufficiently extensive for him to have been aware of these two versions'). No-one knew which version was the correct one, and in their Greek quotation in their letter, Graves and Podro had omitted either expression, as being 'of no materiality', and had substituted three dots. They had given an English translation which assumed one of the expressions to be the correct one, giving the reading 'the temptation to sin which was in my flesh'. (The other expression would have given the reading 'your trial in my flesh'.)

If the reviewer, said the solicitors' letter, 'had been applying his mind fairly and without bias, he could not have failed to appreciate to which text our clients made reference. Instead of that, he thought fit to allege that the three dots had been used to camouflage the suppression of the second expression, "your trial in my flesh", and to imply that our clients had behaved in a grossly unethical manner – clearly a defamatory imputation against the integrity of our clients'. They would issue a writ if there was not a retraction of this libel and a suitable apology.

Pryce-Jones – apparently with the backing of *The Times*'s solicitors – urged on the manager that this letter should not even be acknowledged, but that 'we should await what may come with a calm mind'. However, Graves and Podro stuck to their guns, and over a year later, worn down, the *Lit Supp* agreed to publish 'an explanation'. It appeared on the leader page on 22 July 1955, and was not much of a climb-down. The reviewer maintained, it said, that the interpretation of the passage as 'your trial in my flesh' was correct, 'and that it is the view prevailing generally and adopted by textual critics and commentators of repute . . . The authors have read into the correspondence a charge against them of unethical procedure in adopting [the text that they did]. Such was not our intention.' However the paper conceded 'that a certain small body of opinion in this country would support the authors' choice of reading' – and (though this was not announced) it agreed to pay £275 plaintiffs' costs.

Another drama behind the scenes in which the *Lit Supp* played an active and important part was the break-up of what was known as 'The Book Ring'. Some cautious letters in the paper from booksellers towards the end of 1955 drew attention to a dishonourable but time-honoured practice among many antiquarian booksellers. At book auctions, especially country sales, they would choose a bidder and agree not to bid against him in order to keep the prices down, then share out among themselves the profits that were made when the books were resold. This of course cheated the vendor of the true value of his books, and cheated innocent auctioneers over their commission. It had been an illegal practice since 1927, but no cases had been brought (except – in a different sphere of life – for an inglorious fiasco against some scrap-metal merchants), though in the book trade it was known that some even of the most respectable dealers were guilty. In particular, there had been considerable private scandal over a big sale at Lowther Castle.

Articles on the subject appeared in other papers, and through a member of the Antiquarian Booksellers' Association, the *Lit Supp*'s bibliographical expert John ('Jake') Carter managed to get hold of some actual documents and even a catalogue of purchases and purchasers. The question was, should the *Lit Supp* go ahead and publish this information? Arthur Crook was keen that it should, but Morison, Pryce-Jones and Carter were reluctant to pillory members of the trade by name.

Eventually an article was written, and set up in type – and a copy of the proof sent to the President of the ABA. It did the trick. The ABA asked for a chance to put its house in order, and just before the September 1956 Congress of the International League of Antiquarian Booksellers announced its adoption of measures which would stamp out the ring in Britain and reverberate abroad. On 14 September 1956 the *Lit Supp* was able to publish a quietly triumphalist leader, congratulating the ABA on grasping 'with commendable courage, a nettle far more prickly, more deep-rooted and more proliferant than most of its critics realised'.

Pryce-Jones's wife died in 1953, to his great grief. He even contemplated going into a monastery. After that, he began to travel abroad more. He justified his frequent absences from the office by the increased knowledge it gave him of literary developments, and of potential contributors, in other countries, which was indeed reflected in the pages of the paper. In May 1956 he tried to get the fees for reviews increased again. In a memo to the manager he cited conversations he had had recently with two contributors, Christopher Hollis and Peter Quennell, both of whom 'confirm what I have been fearing: that payments we make to our reviewers have lagged behind all literary papers of equal standing . . . and it looks as though a day will come when we shall find it impossible to fill our columns unless we fall into line with e.g. the *Spectator*'. He also observed that *The Times*'s own book page was paying 70 per cent more than the *Lit Supp*, and suggested that the latter should now pay a flat rate of a guinea per 100 words. A column (for which contributors normally received £4), contained about 750 words, so a reviewer was currently paid something over £5 a thousand by contrast with Pryce-Jones's proposal of £10 a thousand. This time his suggestion was not taken up, and the fees remained the same.

However at the luncheon with the manager which followed this memo, an important step was taken to improve the financial position of the paper, namely to raise the advertising rates by 50 per cent from November, 'and in order to do this as gracefully as possible, to hold a luncheon for the principal publishers a month in advance', as Pryce-Jones put it in a further memo recapitulating the decisions reached. The advertising rate, as the advertisement manager for the periodicals department, Frank Derry, pointed out in a letter to the publishers in October, had been held at the same relatively modest figure, with only one increase, for more than fifty years. The audited average of sales was 43,388 copies a week in 1955 – 'one of the highest figures in its history' – and an average of 16,244 of these copies were sold abroad, 'again one of the highest foreign sales ever achieved'. The new rate would be £3 a column inch for displayed advertisements. In fact, advertising by the publishers held up after this decision.

In September 1958, writing to the editor of *The Times*, Pryce-Jones noted: 'I assume that we are all agreed that the essential purpose of this paper is to hold its own intellectually and financially without making any great contribution to the net profits of Printing House Square.' This was a very fair statement of how the *Lit Supp* was still regarded in the Astor regime, and Pryce-Jones can be said to have achieved that purpose as editor.

He had enabled it to do more than hold its own intellectually. Sometimes he failed to get a contributor he wanted: when he sent A.J.P. Taylor the autobiography of Clement Attlee he got it back with a note saying: 'I can think of fewer books drearier than the memoirs of Lord Attlee and am therefore unable to review this', and when Arthur Crook sent a book at his behest to Rose Macaulay with a slip saying: 'Alan thought that this might amuse you,' the slip came back with the words added: 'He is wrong. R.M.'

However, he brought in an extraordinary range of contributors, and in the years of his editorship the paper became a serious, modern, intellectual journal discussing freely the issues of the day in a way it had never quite been before.

Nevertheless, even in the relaxed atmosphere of Astor's Printing House Square, a growing casualness in Pryce-Jones's attitude to his duties began to raise eyebrows. Arthur Crook loyally held the fort when Pryce-Jones was away, taking on more and more responsibility without complaint, but even he was astonished one morning when an urgent message arrived from the British Council which made it plain that Pryce-Jones and Anthony Powell had set off together that morning on a six-week Council tour of South America. Pryce-Jones had never said a word about this to Crook. Even on the evening before, he had just waved him his usual cheery 'Good night, Arthur.'

Towards the end of the 1950s Pryce-Jones was constantly out of the office. Among other things, he was very busy broadcasting, including being a regular member of 'The Critics' on the BBC's Third Programme. He seems, in fact, to have been considering the possibility of becoming the Controller of the Third Programme. It was about this time that John Betjeman made his famous remark that Captain Bog had had to ask a policeman the way to Printing House Square.

He was also very slack in answering letters, holding that 90 per cent of letters answered themselves. There is an anguished letter to him from John Carter when he was about to resume his position as bibliographical adviser in 1955 after a break:

> My dear Alan,
> I have a distaste for unilateral correspondence. But I am now within six weeks of my return to the bookish world, and I cannot

conveniently wait any longer for a reply from you to earlier letters asking for some firm word about our arrangements for my assumption of a hand in the conduct of the back page . . . I seem to remember that in 1946 I had a magisterial letter of appointment from the Manager. In 1955 I would settle cheerfully for an unmagisterial line from the Editor, if he would brace himself to indict it. Yours ever,

John

More seriously, Monsignor Vince, an occasional reviewer of theological works and a friend of Francis Mathew, the *Times* manager, became very angry in due course about Pryce-Jones's failure to answer his letters. He wrote to Mathew, and showed his letter to Stanley Morison, who – in spite of Haley's desire to keep him at arm's length – still held an ill-defined position of some power at *The Times*. Morison was disturbed by Vince's letter, and though of course he must have known a good deal about the situation already, Vince's remarks seem to have pushed him into writing a letter himself in October 1958, to Mathew, a friend of his too (all three men were Roman Catholics). It is rather a sad letter when one recalls the 'What Price Jones?' memo he had written eleven years before.

Dear FM

It's very embarrassing for me to have to say that V's [Vince's] criticism is a mild form of what I hear outside.

There is no substitute for an editor. No doubt, as an absentee editor APJ is outstanding – but it isn't enough.

I hear nothing but praise for Crook who does a very good best and is most loyal to his nominal 'chief'. But the present situation cannot be justified – most especially as the figures are bad – and likely to be worse.

A remedy must be found. Nothing will make APJ return to the *Suppt*. He is a writer, not an editor. You know that I have the highest admiration for his talents. But we must somehow find a means to 'promote' him.

And quickly

SM

I suggest you have a candid quarter of an hour with H[aley].

'Quickly' was perhaps not quite the word, but Pryce-Jones's resignation followed. He gave up the editorial chair at the end of June 1959 – by which time his salary had reached £2,250 a year – but he still kept a retainer of £500 a year, plus £15 a thousand words for any contributions to *The Times* and its supplements. This arrangement lasted until February 1962, and he did contribute from time to time to the *Lit Supp* for a while after he left.

I doubt, however, whether he was sorry to go. As a young man, he had dreamed of becoming a concert pianist, but once he had realised he would not get to the top in that profession, he had decided he wanted to get to the top in another – and as a very successful editor of the *Lit Supp* for over ten years he had done that. Also, with the freedom he was allowed there, he had made the most of his time socially and in his personal life. Nevertheless in his eighties he once told me, surprisingly, that he had been happy in Vienna and happy in America, but had never really felt at home in London. After leaving the paper, he wrote theatre reviews for a while for the *Observer*, often going abroad to review foreign theatre, but in 1960 he decided he would move to the United States, and he lived there, in New York and Newport, for the rest of his very long life.

So Alan Pryce-Jones had gone; and Arthur Crook's moment had come.

Chapter Twelve

The Gaiety of Nations: 1959–74

In 1959 Arthur Crook was forty-seven. He had been on the paper for over thirty years, and no-one in Printing House Square knew more about the ways of this strange animal than he did. Everyone connected with the *Lit Supp*, from the *Times* management to the reviewers, was fully aware that he had edited the paper for long stretches during Alan Pryce-Jones's absences, and Pryce-Jones himself was determined that his ability and loyalty should be rewarded with the editorial chair. Stanley Morison and William Haley – who must have remembered his own modest beginnings on *The Times* – both concurred in the choice, as did Francis Mathew. Bruce Richmond – whom it was felt necessary to consult, but whom Crook imagined being incredulous at the proposal – was visited by Crook's supporters and won over.

When Haley called Crook into his office to tell him he had been appointed, he looked at Crook with his penetrating light blue eyes, and said, 'It's a make-or-break job, you know.' But Crook knew that he wanted it, and that he could do it. Stanley Morison commented in his dryly human way: 'I got him the job because he was so good to his mother before she died.' The only old colleague who did not congratulate him was R.D. Charques, who was now a special writer on *The Times*. When they passed in the corridor, all he said to Crook was: 'There's a nemesis to charm, Arthur.'

In fact, Crook's charm was an essential element in the success that now awaited him. He was open with everybody, he enjoyed his position, reviewers became good friends, and his staff liked him and were loyal to him because he gave them a very free hand in their various responsibilities. He also shared his pleasure in editing the paper with them. One of my own most vivid memories from the short time I worked for him in the early sixties was his way of coming out of his office holding a newly arrived review or letter that had particularly amused him, and reading it out to the whole open-plan office for their delectation.

The staff knew too that he would stand up to the management when necessary, and moreover that, with his long familiarity with almost everybody on *The Times*, he generally knew precisely how to get his way. One item among the papers from his time as editor reflects the atmosphere in the office. Among his early appointments was Alexander Cockburn, the son of the radical journalist Claud Cockburn, and himself to become a well-known columnist on the *Village Voice* in New York. In the *Lit Supp* files there is a 'Memorandum from the Administrative Office' announcing that the marketing manager has now completed the reorganisation of his department and that he has appointed a promotion manager, *The Times*; a promotion manager, periodicals; a studio manager, and so on. Attached to it is another memorandum – this one from Cockburn. It announces that the appointments manager (Mr A.C. Crook) has completed his 'managerial designation survey' of the *Lit Supp*, and that 'the manager of Editorial Management is Mr Arthur Crook, the manager of Subeditorial Management and joint occasional manager of Page Proof Production is Mr A.C. Cockburn, and that the joint occasional manager of Page Proof Production and joint manageress of Actual Production and manageress of the *Times* book page is Miss C. Ryder'. It adds that 'staff should be addressed by these titles and not by their names. In this way much confusion will be avoided.' Crook would greatly have enjoyed pinning these papers together and putting them into his archive.

At the same time, he had a very clear idea of his position. He had long since overcome the limitations of his early education. He was now a man of wide acquaintance, confidence and authority. But he knew that he spoke no foreign languages – something Morison had rubbed in in the past, even suggesting in his idiosyncratic way that Crook should take classes in mediaeval Latin – and since he particularly wanted to enlarge the international character of the paper he knew he needed staff that would serve him there.

He quickly appointed Anthony Curtis as his deputy, but after a year and a half Curtis moved on to become literary editor of the *Sunday Telegraph*. Crook then made what proved to be his most brilliant appointment – John Willett as deputy editor. We shall see what Willett did for the paper in a moment.

The Miss C. Ryder mentioned in the archives was Charis Ryder, who had joined the paper as Pryce-Jones's secretary after she had graduated from Oxford in Greats. She had become the lynchpin of the paper, holding the production side of it together, and continued to do so throughout Crook's editorship. A.P. Ryan, with whom she also worked on the *Times* book page, hoped she might become Crook's deputy, but she did not want to take on that further responsibility.

In his first few years Crook also brought in a number of young men as subeditors – besides Cockburn, they included Piers Paul Read, later a very successful novelist, and Nicholas Bethell, a Russian scholar who as Lord Bethell became a very active Member of the European Parliament. A little later Crook gave a job to the fiery rationalist Nicolas Walter after he had been sent to prison for two months for shouting at Prime Minister Harold Wilson in church.

The gesture had impressed Crook, but he was not well rewarded for his act of faith. James Morris wrote to ask if there was an anarchist on the paper, because on a proof he had received he had found the name 'Kropotkin' added to a list of people he had mentioned in a review. It transpired that Walter was in the habit of dropping anarchists' names into reviews that he subbed, not changing the author's meaning – where the reviewer wrote, for instance, 'unlike Tolstoy' he would simply add 'or Kropotkin' – but giving his heroes some publicity.

The genial atmosphere in the office extended equally to the world of contributors. The *Times* archives are full of letters expressing thanks to Crook for merry lunches, from Hugh Trevor-Roper's description of almost missing his train, 'Like a diver panting over the gunwale on his return from the sea-bed, I scrambled into my carriage spouting red liquid (in my case Old Madeira) from eyes, nose and ears, and lay there exhausted till we entered harbour at Oxford,' to the declaration 'I never meet you without feeling that I am a much more splendid and wittier fellow than I am. What art you have!' which came from Maurice Edelman, a Labour MP who often reviewed political books for the paper. Graham Hutton, the paper's arch-defender of free markets, sent a poem after a luncheon in the Blue Room, where *Times* guests were entertained at the top of the building:

> *In re comestibile, scilicet lunch,*
> *The top of* The Times *packs a terrible punch;*
> *There,* Times *men and other top people lap up*
> *The next morning's menu or next week's* Lit. Sup.
> *The fare and the fowl and the verbal ingredients*
> *Accord with Establishment rules of obedience;*

Thus manner and matter, of substance or not,
Combine to provide what no others have got!

while Gavin Astor wrote to Crook to thank him for finding so many people to invite to the parties.

Crook also took on John Hayward, the wheelchair-bound landlord of T.S. Eliot in Chelsea, on a retainer of £250 a year, to advise him on the publication of scholarly letters. Hayward sent in his reports in comic form, drawing large headings such as 'NO x 1000' over letters he thought should be rejected, and signing himself as 'Pres. Society for the Protection of Yeats', 'Editor of The Dunciad', or 'Your friend Johannes'. One envelope is addressed with the space between 'Arthur' and 'esqre' filled with a long, elegant drawing of a shepherd's crook.

However, Crook also had, like all good editors, a touch of mischief in his make-up, and he liked the smell of battle to waft quite often across his paper. In a letter to the Canadian poet and novelist, Margaret Atwood, who was involved in a literary controversy, he urged her to try to remain above the battle, but acknowledged that 'you sometimes need wings to avoid being shot at by both sides'. However he liked using those wings. He showed his independence early in his editorship. At the beginning of November 1960, the ban on publication of the unexpurgated version of D.H. Lawrence's *Lady Chatterley's Lover* came to an end after a dramatic court case, and in the issue immediately following, the *Lit Supp* published a brilliant long review of it by Rayner Heppenstall. Haley in *The Times* had come out against the book, but the *Lit Supp* went swiftly ahead.

Heppenstall quoted James Joyce's remark, hostile both to the novel and to the fuss that was made over it: 'a piece of propaganda for something which, outside Lawrence's country at any rate, makes all the propaganda for itself'. But he argued that the book was much more than that. He said that in fact it offered a sane view of English society (or, he added, of British society, since Lady Chatterley herself was a Scottish girl). Above all, it portrayed an idea of sexual fulfilment that was 'tender, candidly sensual and healing'. The four-letter words were only a 'top dressing'.

However, Heppenstall thought that the enemies of such fulfilment, as Lawrence envisaged them, were less well depicted, especially Chatterley himself. Lawrence had tried to embody in the one character both the intellectual enemies – the 'trilling semi-eunuchs' – and the class enemies, but 'the magnate and the intellectual do not fit together in that one wretched frame'. But Heppenstall concluded categorically that

357

'young persons of either sex were the last out of whose hands this book should be kept' – adding that the worst it could do to them would be to make them a little over-solemn. No doubt it was also unwise, he said 'to scamper around in the rain gathering forget-me-nots'.

The paper maintained a similar liberal but unsentimental stance on censorship throughout Crook's editorship. However in August of the year after the trial, John Sparrow was allowed a certain amount of mischievous taunting of the liberals. He had already written a study of *Lady Chatterley's Lover* in which he had argued that Lawrence was covertly describing anal intercourse between Lady Chatterley and the gamekeeper at one point – an article which he had shown to Crook, describing it in a letter as 'Lady Chatterley's Haunches: An Essay in Posterior Analysis'. This article was published in *Encounter*.

In the *Lit Supp* he wrote a long review of the transcript of the trial which had been published by Penguin Books. Here he acknowledged that the argument used by the prosecution that the book 'tended to corrupt or deprave' was impossible to maintain, and had been almost bound to fail in court. Where he had his sport was in suggesting that if the prosecution had argued that the book was an offence against public decency they might have had more success. Would not the ordinary reader be disgusted by 'the profuse descriptions of male and female pudenda' and (here he gaily rode his hobbyhorse again) 'by the allusions to the "two entrances" and to "love all ends on" that betray so clearly an anal obsession in the author'? (What, though – one might ask further – would the ordinary reader think about Sparrow's own 'clearly betrayed' obsessions?)

However in the same article he also reviewed Lord Radcliffe's Rede lecture on censors, and he ended by applauding Radcliffe's warning about the new 'controllers' of what the masses should hear and see and read – the 'huge and monopolistic engines of production' of information and entertainment. 'The outlook,' Sparrow concluded, 'is not a bright one for those who care for quality or are interested in the independent flowering of thought or of the arts.'

Nine years after the trial, in July 1969, Julian Symons came back to the subject of Lady Chatterley in a review of several new books on obscenity and censorship. He made it the occasion for the *Lit Supp* to print the word 'fuck' for the first time, quoting Richard Hoggart at the trial as using it in the course of his submission that 'one of the things Lawrence found most worrying was that the word for this most important relationship had become a word of vile abuse'.

Symons observed that though the trial had taken place less than a decade before, it 'took place in a different world'. Though at the time Gerald Gardiner had assured the trial jury that victory for the book would not mean that 'these words can be used by any scribbler writing any kind of novel', by now, Symons wrote, ' "any scribbler" can use any word and describe any act in any novel with little fear of prosecution'. In other words, the sixties – with sexual intercourse beginning, in Philip Larkin's words, in 1963 – had come and almost gone – and 'the gains that have been made, the liberties that have been won, are of enormous value in helping us to understand the nature of the modern world and of human psychology'.

However, Symons thought that the liberal 1959 Obscenity Act was still not very satisfactory, and he suggested that the law might be further reformed along American lines. In the American trial at which *Lady Chatterley* had been acquitted, the scope for expert evidence was clear, and critics such as Malcolm Cowley and Alfred Kazin who had defended the book in court had not had to rely on such 'over-solemn' arguments as Hoggart's. Since then, moreover, the Supreme Court had decided that a book could not be condemned for obscenity unless it was 'utterly without redeeming social value'.

But he had a word of warning too: 'In words begin responsibilities', and 'artists should be their own censors'. He regretted the anti-intellectualism seen in 'the present cult of instant sensation, instant art, instant revolution', which could play no part in changing society. If that were pursued far enough, it would 'bring the whole force of the state down to crush the freedoms so painfully won'.

The need for self-censorship had also been stressed by John Willett in a review of William Burroughs's novels on 14 November 1963 that had set off a long and lively correspondence under the heading 'Ugh!' Willett, though generally in favour of free and open debate, had been nauseated by Burroughs's *The Naked Lunch*, which he thought was like wading through the drains of a big city: 'Look out: here it comes ... ectoplasm, jelly, errand boys, ferris wheels, used contraceptives, centipedes, old photographs, jockstraps, turnstiles, newts, and pubic hairs ... If the publishers had deliberately set out to discredit the cause of literary freedom and innovation they could hardly have done it more effectively.' He reached the same balanced conclusion as Symons: 'Any juryman can vomit, but only one verdict can clear up the mess: that of the book world itself.'

Dame Edith Sitwell, now seventy-six and in the last year of her life, made a characteristic contribution: she was delighted by Willett's review, and added: 'The canonisation of that insignificant dirty little book *Lady Chattterley's Lover* was a signal to persons who wish to unload the filth in their minds on the British public. As the author of *Gold Coast Customs* I can scarcely be accused of shirking reality, but I do not wish to spend the rest of my life with my nose nailed to other people's lavatories. I prefer Chanel [No.] 5.' But Anthony Burgess weighed in on Burroughs's side, declaring that authors did not always like what they wrote about, and that he was nauseated by the content of his own novel, *A Clockwork Orange*, while Burroughs wrote on 23 January 1964 to say that his work actually contained a moral message about drugs. Willett commented that 'Burroughs's intention is less obvious than he thinks' – and gave a round-up of the debate the following week in an amusing leader in his typically under-solemn style, called 'Whither Ugh?'

Issues, rather than individual books, now often dominated the pages of the *Lit Supp*, and, as in the case of obscenity and censorship, sometimes got well thrashed out between the reviewers and the letter-writers.

John Sparrow was the source of much of the controversy during these years. He liked to take on delicate moral or legal questions and treat them provocatively with his keen forensic mind. ('I am going to introduce you to the most devious man I know, apart from myself,' Alan Pryce-Jones had said to Crook, just before he first introduced him to Sparrow.) He was now the Warden of All Souls, and a steady stream of letters came to Crook's office from the college – not only from Sparrow, as we shall see, but also from Isaiah Berlin and A.L. Rowse.

In April 1964 Sparrow wrote a long article about Hannah Arendt's *Eichmann in Jerusalem*, the book in which she had coined the phrase 'the banality of evil' and portrayed the SS mass murderer who had been tried by the Israelis not as an unimaginable monster but as a small, squalid figure whom it was all too easy to imagine. This portrayal, plausible though it was, had outraged many of Arendt's fellow Jews, especially in America.

Sparrow took her to task more for her criticism of the Jewish Councils in Germany who, in trying to protect Jews, had in Arendt's view effectively collaborated with the Germans. Here, he said, her fairness of mind and powers of sympathy had deserted her – and he flung a few insults at the same time at her friend and supporter, 'the egregious Miss McCarthy'. Mary McCarthy, not surprisingly, came back at him, with a long letter in June in which she said that the reviewer, like so many of Arendt's critics, had done no more than engage in 'a sort of treasure-hunt for damning sentences' – and she accused those critics in their turn of 'a conspiracy of banality'.

Sparrow also offered the *Lit Supp* a long article in the same year on the Profumo affair, in which the British minister, John Profumo, had become involved with call-girls and possible spies, and then lied to the House of Commons, but the article took a much more indulgent line than *The Times*, and Haley would not allow it to be published in the *Lit Supp* in spite of all Crook's efforts – one of Crook's few defeats. He and Sparrow had better luck with Sparrow's long study of the assassination of President Kennedy, which analysed and rejected the claims of the conspiracy theorists, and was published in the paper in December 1967. Sparrow, Crook told me, was 'not exactly a great deliverer' – and this article took months before it was delivered, during which Crook received continual bulletins about how the 'great work' was getting on.

There were two letters in which Sparrow scored notable triumphs. On the last day of December 1964, the *Lit Supp* published an article by G.S. Fraser about the Scots poet Hugh MacDiarmid. It was followed by a letter in which the writer Glyn Jones pointed out that – 'no doubt through some inadvertence or forgetfulness' on the poet's part – a description in verse of a pigeon's skull by MacDiarmid was identical, word for word, with a description by Jones of a seagull's skull in one of his short stories.

MacDiarmid wrote to say that he must either have memorised the words or written them down, and subsequently thought them to be his own. He had apologised to Jones – but 'such things occur'. Correspondence raged after that over the question of whether it was legitimate for a poet to take other people's words and turn them into poetry. But Sparrow had the last word when he wrote to say that he had discovered that it was not MacDiarmid who had put the words into verse, but the Welsh poet Keidrych Rhys, who had done it as a literary experiment or *jeu d'esprit*, and had sent MacDiarmid the result. Rhys wrote in to say that Sparrow was right.

The other letter was about one of Sparrow's own books (of which there were not very many), a study of monumental inscriptions called *Visible Words*, which was generously reviewed by the art historian Edgar Wind in March 1970. Sparrow must have found out who the reviewer was, although Crook had told him nothing – as, it must be said, was his absolutely invariable practice even with his closest friends when their books were reviewed.

Wind had made a few criticisms, including one relating to Botticelli's painting *The Madonna of the Magnificat,* in which (in Sparrow's words in his letter) the reviewer 'reproves me for suggesting that the Child with his finger indicates the word 'humility' in the book in which his Mother has been writing . . . No well-behaved child, let alone the Divine Child, would point with the middle finger.' But, Sparrow wrote, the significance of the gesture as he described it was originally pointed out to him by Professor Edgar Wind – and he added, in private triumph, or triumph to share with his friends: 'I am sure your reviewer would be the first to acknowledge the weight of that authority'.

Sparrow also invented a monumental inscription – or at any rate, a memorial poem – for Maurice Bowra, who died in July 1971. Sparrow's poem was printed in the *Lit Supp* on 23 June of the following year. It imagined Bowra as 'seizing God's high sceptre' once he got to Heaven. Its concluding lines were:

> *Send us to Hell or Heaven or where you will,*
> *Promise us only, you'll be with us still.*
> *Without you, Heaven would be too dull to bear.*
> *And Hell will not be Hell if you are there.*

Finally, Sparrow twisted the literary world by its tail, with semi-serious intent, in a letter published in the paper on 18 January 1974. It followed a signed article that had appeared two weeks earlier by John Bayley, who had just been appointed the first Warton Professor of English at Oxford. Bayley had proposed the idea that Shakespeare's 'man right fair', who is a close but rather mysterious associate of the poet in his relations with the Dark Lady in the Sonnets, is not a person at all, but a jesting personification of the poet's own *membrum virile*, 'the Shakespearean penis'.

Sparrow's letter suggested that, in the same way, the 'one talent that is death to hide' but is now 'lodged with me useless', in Milton's sonnet 'On his Blindness', was not his literary gifts, as was generally thought, but his procreative powers, 'rendered useless by the unhappy outcome of his marriage'. There were letters of protest, notably one from the Oxford professor Helen Gardner, who deplored the publication of such a fanciful interpretation of a sonnet which could be so inspiring to schoolchildren. But on 1 March, Sparrow contributed a 'Viewpoint' article to the paper in which he admitted the whole thing was just a parody of John Bayley's article, written because he thought critics were now too eager to read a sexual significance into perfectly simple and innocent passages in literature.

A last word this time came from William Empson, who had evidently enjoyed the episode. He said in a letter: 'The poor Warden deserves respect for appearing so firmly in a white sheet, having to explain, while accepting rebuke for, a very good and clear parody. The only shame attaches to those who rebuked him, or presumed that solemn lies must always be told before the children.' However, many readers must also have noticed and chuckled at this further revelation of the Warden's own obsession with sexual innuendo.

Dr Leavis became more involved with the *Lit Supp* during Arthur Crook's years. Soon after Crook became editor, Leavis sent him a lengthy mimeograph giving an account of the misunderstandings, insults and neglect that he and his journal *Scrutiny* had suffered at the hands of Pryce-Jones – and sent another copy of it before long. He also sent it round the academic world. However in July 1963, just after his official retirement, a long letter he had written to the paper on 'Research in English' was published as part of a special number on criticism called 'The Critical Moment', and in November of that year the Cambridge don, S. Gorley Putt, wrote an appreciative review – subtitled 'Dr Leavis's Monument' – of the twenty-volume reissue of *Scrutiny*.

'Research in English' received some criticism in letters from other Cambridge teachers of English, notably Ian Jack, who mocked what he called Leavis's 'complacent parochialism' and asked: 'Have all the most distinguished scholars and critics been products of the Cambridge English Tripos?' But Gorley Putt in his review acknowledged that part of the strength of *Scrutiny* had been that it was an 'uncomfortable organ', dealing wounds and receiving them, and he ended by declaring unreservedly that it had left a lasting legacy in the 'brilliant series of literary assessments by a handful of hard-working critics which in effect presented an entirely fresh approach to the history of English literature'.

Yet Leavis's battles were far from over. An address which he had given at the University of Wales on university education, and which was published in the *Lit Supp* on 29 May 1969, contained a reference to the novelist Margaret Drabble, deploring the fact that she had been able to get a starred first in English in Cambridge without, as he understood, doing any work. She wrote an ironical letter in reply, saying, 'How strange that Dr Leavis should see fit to invoke my lightweight name in a discussion as serious as one on the future of English in the Universities: a subject which he claims as the most important preoccupation of our time' – and stating that she found his remark 'an insult to three years of very hard work'.

But it was in the following year that the exchange of big guns sounded through the paper. Leavis's earlier clash with C.P. Snow over the latter's Rede lecture at Cambridge in 1959, 'The Two Cultures and the Scientific Revolution', had taken place elsewhere. Snow's lecture was published in *Encounter*, and Leavis's reply – the Richmond lecture at Cambridge in 1962, 'Two Cultures? The Significance of C.P. Snow' – was published in the *Spectator*. But now the dispute flared up again in the *Lit Supp*.

Leavis began it with a lecture at Bristol University, called ' "Literarism" versus "Scientism" ' that Crook published in the issue of 23 April 1970. It attacked the idea that computers could in any way replace the human mind and imagination, and, as so often before, proposed D.H. Lawrence – 'a voice of wisdom, human insight and sanity' – as a model for life, literature and university education to follow. But it also contained some personal barbs, directed here not only at Snow but also at Noël Annan, now the Provost of University College, London, who, Leavis implied, thought of the university merely as some kind of ever-humming industrial plant, and even went along with those people who dared to believe that computers could write poems.

Annan was invited to reply in the following issue. He rejected all the charges, and made his own case for universities as the home of a pluralistic intellectual life. But Leavis, he wrote, 'wants unconditional surrender to his own definitions and judgments' – which in any case he expressed in 'cliché and jargon'.

Annan also complained that Leavis's 'personal animosity puts a strain on your temper and humour', and from now onwards the argument – good though it was, in fact – became enveloped in personal feeling. C.P. Snow was also invited to write an article in reply, which appeared on 9 July. He repudiated, as he had before, the suggestion that he saw no difference between literary and artistic culture on the one hand, and scientific culture on the other: for one thing, there was progress in science, but no 'progress' of that kind in humanistic culture. As he had said in his original lecture, he simply wanted them to understand each other better.

However, he in turn gave a good deal of his article up to attacking Leavis, asserting that Leavis was not very accurate or truthful, though he was 'abnormally free with words such as morality'. At one point in the continuing debate, Annan was even considering whether to sue Leavis for libel, but Crook averted this turn of events by a spirited move.

He happened to have staying with him in his house the Anglophile American historian John Clive, who also contributed reviews to the paper. Clive went swimming every morning at the Swiss Cottage baths, where he always found Annan swimming too. Crook went to the baths with him, plunged in – not greatly to his pleasure – and contrived to bob up just as Annan was doing the same. 'Now what about this libel action?' he asked casually as they went back to the changing rooms – and in the friendliness of the swimming baths in the early morning the matter was allowed to rest.

The publicity department made the most of this controversy, advertising the Leavis lecture with which it started by announcing 'Leavis takes up the cudgels against Lord Annan ... C.P. Snow comes in for a few swings of the club'. They were magisterially rebuked for this in a letter to the *Lit Supp* from some Bristol University teachers of English, including Henry Gifford and Christopher Ricks (also both contributors), who wrote: 'What world are we living in when the *Times Literary Supplement* delights in pre-reducing to personalities and sensationalism all possibility of urgent impersonal thought about the problems of our time?' It might however be thought that the personalities themselves had made some contribution to this process.

Leavis went on harassing and haranguing Crook until the end of his editorship. It is hard not to agree with another remark made by Gorley Putt, this time in a review of Leavis's Clark lectures, *English Literature in Our Time and the University*, in November 1969:

> Yehudi Menuhin makes us love the violin while playing it, not by using his bow to beat the heads of inattentive listeners or incompetent critics. Dr Leavis makes us value literary criticism of a high order by *doing* it, as in the best pages of these lectures. The point has surely been reached when, more acclaimed at last than he seems able to credit, he could with honour leave the rest to time.

The historian A.L. Rowse also became very angry with the *Lit Supp* for its treatment of him. His book *William Shakespeare* was reviewed in December 1963 by John Crow, a brilliant if eccentric lecturer in English at King's College, London, whom Crook had found. Crow had once written a newspaper boxing column called 'From the Crow's Nest'. He liked to wear a nightgown in bed, and the story was told of him that one day he had been driving through a country town and seen some fine specimens hanging in a shop window. He went in and bought one, and as the shop assistant was wrapping it up, he said, 'This is a great day for us, sir.' 'Why's that?' 'It's the first time we've sold one of these to a living man, sir!'

Crow had a fine sense of the nature of literature, and was appalled by what he considered the reckless and insensitive way Rowse had simply used Shakespeare's work as evidence for theories about Shakespeare's life. Rowse argued that the Sonnets were direct evidence for Shakespeare's private life and were not just a 'literary exercise'. Crow argued fiercely and wittily that the alternative to their being autobiographical was 'not their being a "literary exercise" but their being dramatic – telling a story that is imagined'.

Unfortunately Crow made one or two mistakes in his review, for instance confusing 'Erasmian' with 'Erastian', and Rowse fell violently on these errors in his letter of reply. But Crook would not let Rowse publish a further letter, in which he repeated his claims for his book, cited private letters (including one from Harold Macmillan) that had praised it, and renewed his attack on the reviewer's 'coarse sensibilities, blunt perceptions and intellectual obtuseness'.

Rowse's second biography of Shakespeare a decade later, *Shakespeare the Man*, in which he advanced the theory that Emilia Lanier, the daughter of a court musician, was Shakespeare's 'Dark Lady', was reviewed by the great Shakespearean scholar, S. Schoenbaum in April 1973. Schoenbaum wrote more silkily about it, but was just as firm as Crow: this was 'mystical scholarship'. There was no record of any sort linking Emilia Lanier's name with Shakespeare – and surely it was the 'imperatives of art' that had dictated the complexion of the Dark Lady? However, Rowse, with 'the powerful force of his personality' had certainly enlivened the scholarly scene, said Schoenbaum: 'Who else could have made a conjecture about the Dark Lady matter for feature articles in newspapers throughout the world?'

It was in part, no doubt, because the *Lit Supp* had become such an accepted forum for literary discussion that Ted Hughes chose it to publish his dislike and disapproval of the memoir of his wife, Sylvia Plath, that Al Alvarez included in his book about suicide, *The Savage God*. Hughes's letter was published in the 'Commentary' column of the paper (a feature that had recently begun) on 19 November 1971. He said that he had not been consulted about the publication of Alvarez's book. His wife, he said, had 'tried briefly to find more of a friend in him [Alvarez], showing him some of her poems, in the winter of 1962–3', and in early 1963 he himself had described some details of her suicide to Alvarez, since he was a friend of both hers and mine, who lived nearby, who presented himself in the role of consoler, and who did seem to understand and be private . . . I told him only a few of the details, and what I told him I distorted, since I was trying to work out many explanations for myself.

He has misremembered even what I told him. His facts are not only extremely fragmentary, they are mostly wrong, and at best mis-leadingly interpreted. His need to dramatise the whole episode to special effect is evident enough . . . His 'facts' are material for fiction, second-hand scraps, glimpses and half-experiences, re-surfacing after seven years, imaginatively reshaped and acceptably explained to the author. They have nothing to do with the truth of an event far more important to Sylvia Plath's family than to Mr Alvarez or any of his readers.

He asked Alvarez and his publishers to withdraw the piece from any wider circulation, 'acknowledging that it is wrong'.

Alvarez replied courteously but with a note of steely firmness. 'I did not consult Mr Hughes,' he wrote, 'for a simple reason: I was not writing a memoir of him. I was writing about Sylvia Plath as a person – I think, a genius – in her own right. I was also writing about the girl as I knew her during a period in which she was living mostly on her own.' He said that he had told the facts as he knew them truthfully, and his only distortion was that he suppressed all mention of the personal situation between Syl-via and her husband during the last months of her life, out of consider-ation for the feelings of the living. 'I took great pains to handle the tragedy as delicately as I could. The impartial general reader of my book must be the final judge of my success in doing so.'

This letter – hinting as it did at matters that the memoir itself had not touched on – cannot have brought Hughes any comfort. His sister Olwyn wrote to the paper the following week, politely expressing her hope that Alvarez would at least completely rewrite the section on Sylvia Plath for future printings of the book. So began her attempt, which was to go on for many years, to combat what she and Hughes considered to be distorted accounts of the relations between Hughes and his wife, which culminated in 1998 in the publication of Hughes's poems about his marriage, *Birthday Letters*.

As for the realm of politics and international affairs, there were natur-ally numerous disagreements between contributors, authors and correspondents here. As in the past, of course, much of the debate was at one remove from the events, since the paper rarely commented on current affairs outside the fields of literature and publishing until they were mentioned in books that came later.

E.H. Carr still received for review many of the books on recent Russian history. One can see why he was still held in esteem from the review of Part Two of his massive work, *Socialism in One Country*, by C.M. ('Monty') Woodhouse in the first issue of 1960. Woodhouse, who often wrote about European, especially Greek, affairs for the paper, was the Conservative MP for Oxford at this time, later becoming a junior minister, but he felt compelled to say that Carr's account of Stalin was 'the definitive portrait of the most extraordinary man of our time', and that the book as a whole was a 'vast mosaic in which every pebble is carefully fitted into place'.

However, there was still a continual buzz of letters in the paper objecting to what the correspondents – most of them anti-Communist historians – considered his biased reviews, especially his shorter pieces. When Max Beloff, Max Hayward (the co-translator of *Dr Zhivago*), George Katkov, Leonard Schapiro and others criticised as 'grossly misleading' Carr's severe review of S.V. Utechin's *Everyman's Concise Encyclopaedia of Russia*, 'Your Reviewer' replied airily, 'Either your correspondents have studied the work less carefully than I did, or are less allergic to the tendencies it reveals.'

Of course, Carr's opinions were also of interest to general historians, and he received a more wide-ranging rebuke for one of his reviews, from the standpoint of scholarship, in a letter in March 1966 from the Tudor historian G.R. Elton (who pretty clearly knew or had deduced who the reviewer was). Elton was famous for his fiercely argued – and on the whole successful – attempt to show that the Tudors were not despots, and every word was weighed and loaded in this letter of his:

> Your reviewer seems incapable of supposing that changes of opinion or interpretation could ever stem from anything but changes in the historian's personal politics, a view so cynical as perhaps to argue that your reviewer must also belong to 'the right'. Of course, one understands and sympathises with the feelings of a man who finds the cherished generalisations acquired in the possibly distant past under severe attack from the progress of research.
>
> Since by an historical accident most of the legends or misconceptions current in history were, in the years between the wars, created by people of 'left wing' opinion, the present setting right of error

may indeed appear to be the work of wicked Tories. The present generation of historians is overwhelmingly concerned with the truth of the past, and relatively indifferent to the implications of that past for the present.

A.J.P. Taylor was also attacked for letting his political allegiances colour his historical judgments – but this time, surprisingly, from the Left, in the shape of Isaac Deutscher, who by now evidently regarded Taylor as a false friend. In June 1961, after Woodhouse, reviewing Taylor's *The Origins of the Second World War*, had asked why Taylor had not been given a professorial chair at Oxford – he never was, incidentally – Deutscher wrote to point out that whereas at the end of the war Taylor was arguing that Germany was exclusively responsible for the war and that all Germans were guilty, 'now, no German, not even Hitler, was guilty'. In 1945, in accordance with the Allied policy of 'unconditional surrender', he supported the dismemberment and deindustrialisation of Germany; now, he was in harmony with the dominant mood that favoured Western alliance with Germany and German rearmament. This was a 'truly Orwellesque rewrite of history', said Deutscher. By the 1960s, intellectual allegiances were becoming confused.

Deutscher, too, went on reviewing for the paper under Crook; but a new voice had appeared to report on what was currently happening in the Soviet Union. This was the measured and well-informed voice of Alexander Werth, a foreign correspondent who had gone out to Russia in 1941 with an Allied mission and had survived the siege of Leningrad. In April 1965 he published a 1,100-page book, *Russia at War 1941–45*, which – said Major-General M. Prynne in his *Lit Supp* review – because of Werth's 'unique experience and generally sound assessment of a number of highly controversial questions' was 'the best general history, in English, of the Russian war to date'.

Werth had considerable feeling for the Russian people. He had scant sympathy for the regime, but was not a Cold War warrior. Some of his best reviews were of Russian artists and writers, including one on Prokofiev's autobiography in March 1962, after the composer's posthumous rehabilitation in Russia, and one in January 1964 on 'Grandpa' Kornei Chukovsky, the children's writer, who with his 'faultless sense of language' had written a book attacking Russian officialese – though Werth pointed out that he sometimes pulled his punches, for instance treating Lenin as a great master of the Russian language.

Isaiah Berlin, incidentally, knew Chukovsky, and wrote to Crook saying that the Russian had thanked him warmly for giving him a subscription to the *Lit Supp*, but that he knew nothing about it. In fact, Crook had arranged the subscription after Chukovsky had written an article for one of the special numbers – and was, in a way, rewarded by the comment in Chukovsky's letter to Berlin, 'I should very much like to know who is the conductor of genius who directs this entire many-toned orchestra – and compels it to sound so symphonically'.

Werth, Willett and Bethell between them kept up a good commentary in the mid-sixties on the fortunes of literature and art in the Soviet Union, though generally without doing more than brush against the larger political issues. In January 1963, Bethell welcomed the appearance of two items in the issue of *Novy Mir* the previous November: Solzhenitsyn's sixty-three-page novella *One Day in the Life of Ivan Denisovich*, with its 'ghoulish yet fascinating details' of life in a Siberian 'corrective labour camp', and Viktor Nekrasov's article on Italy, with its 'glimpse of the unseen bright side of the capitalist world'. In the same month, Werth described the ovation that the twenty-nine-year-old Andrei Voznesensky had received at a poets' evening in a Moscow stadium, also in the previous November, and wondered if 'his experimentalism, his originality, his youthful, disrespectful verve' would survive the poison gas coming since then from the Central Committee of the Party.

In April Willett deplored Khrushchev's speech of 8 March in which he attacked these and other Soviet writers and artists. He called it 'perhaps the longest and most pernicious speech on the arts to come from any twentieth-century politician' – far more comprehensive even than Hitler's speech when opening the Haus der Deutschen Kunst in 1937, and echoing its very words in places. Willett hoped the speech would not be 'a mortal blow'.

By September, Bethell was able to report that *Novy Mir* had, after all, published another story by Solzhenitsyn in its July number, and in January 1964 he praised the paper's editor, Aleksander Tvardovsky, for the magazine's unusually vigorous defence of Solzhenitsyn against the attacks of the diehard paper, *Literaturnaya Gazeta*. Khrushchev seemed to have 'called the hunt off'. And when the fortieth anniversary number of *Novy Mir* came out in January 1965, Werth joined in the praise of Tvardovsky – 'the top liberal and de-Staliniser among Soviet editors'. But of course it was an uneasy peace, and Solzhenitsyn had to publish his later, great works abroad.

In October 1967 Werth wrote a powerfully dismissive review of *Twenty Letters to a Friend* by Stalin's daughter, Svetlana Alliluyeva.

'Seldom,' he wrote, 'if ever, has such a world-wide fuss been made about a book of such mediocrity and of so little historical value.' He particularly criticised Svetlana's attempts to shift the blame for 'the worst horrors of the Stalin regime – the mass-deportations, the mass-arrests, the mass-shootings, in most cases of party members' from her father to Beria. Werth observed that the year of the worst nightmare, 1937, coincided with a time 'when Stalin was a particularly affectionate father to his then eleven-year-old daughter'. The following October, the Soviet expert Michael Duncan hailed Robert Conquest's massive and pioneering study of *The Great Terror* – 'Stalin's cold terror', the reviewer called it, adding that 'if the monument to those unjustly repressed, promised by Khrushchev, is ever to be erected, it will need to be of mammoth proportions'.

That same spring of 1967, in April, the *Lit Supp* had also published some extracts from Solzhenitsyn's *Cancer Ward*. In September, *Cancer Ward* was reviewed by David Gallagher, a young scholar whom Crook had brought in primarily for his knowledge of the new South American literature, but who also took on reviews of Russian books. Gallagher praised Solzhenitsyn's act of heroism in publishing this account of his country, with its horrific vision of the average citizen living his life in 'unthinking stupor' and of death in the end striking down both the 'brazen optimists and the rotten bullies' of Soviet society. In November, Gallagher had similar things to say about Solzhenitsyn's *The First Circle*, with its 'suffocating picture' of the Soviet Union under Stalin in the 1940s.

However, the paper got into trouble in October 1970, when John Sturrock, who had by then effectively succeeded Willett as deputy editor, complained in a 'Commentary' article that, since the award of the Nobel Prize that year to Solzhenitsyn, the Kremlinologists had been using his name and work for propaganda purposes. *Encounter*, which was an openly anti-Communist magazine, denounced the *Lit Supp* for this article, and one correspondent to the paper asked: 'Is there some Western Zhdanov living in the shadows?' However, in January 1971 the *Lit Supp* replied that it was in no way critical of Solzhenitsyn, just his exploitation by 'over-zealous opponents of Russia'.

In any event, the following October, N.J. Anning, of the School of Slavonic and East European Studies at London University, wrote a long, admiring review of the Russian language edition of Solzhenitsyn's *August 1914*, making only a literary, not a political, criticism of it when he said that Anna Akhmatova might have been right to suggest Solzhenitsyn lacked 'great imaginative vision'. He was a 'scientist-novelist', said Anning. What he did have was 'outstanding powers of observation, memory and cross-reference' and a 'polished, innovatory and distinctive style', and he had 'made up for his years of enforced silence with prodigious and savage fluency'. In February 1974, in the last weeks of Crook's editorship, Anning was registering the news of Solzhenitsyn's arrest and deportation from Russia, and hailing the Russian language edition of the first part of his *Gulag Archipelago*, with its 'angry and harrowing montage' of 'how the terror spread'. Robert Conquest, who had also written to criticise the *Lit Supp* at the time of the *Encounter* attack, should have been appeased.

Crook and Isaiah Berlin had been introduced to each other by John Sparrow at All Souls, and after that Berlin kept up a correspondence with Crook throughout his editorship, sometimes delicately suggesting reviewers whom he might like to consider (or alternatively urging him not to use Carr), sometimes congratulating him (as on Sparrow's review of *Eichmann in Jerusalem* – 'the best piece on the whole tormented topic'), and sometimes complaining gently.

Berlin, rather like T.S. Eliot in earlier days, certainly did seem to come in for a lot of criticism in the paper, considering what good relations he had with the editor. He took particular exception to a leader written in April 1966 by the historian Geoffrey Barraclough, who was an advisor to the paper on several special history numbers.

In this leader, Barraclough had remarked that Berlin held the view that 'common-sense and good judgment' were all that were needed 'to understand the workings of human beings'. In his letter of reply Berlin said that this was a complete misrepresentation of his views. He believed that history needed whatever it could obtain from any source of empirical knowledge. What he did also believe, however, was that 'the work of integrating the data provided by the sciences into a credible account of past human experience had not (at any rate as yet) proved reducible to a method governed by a set of principles or laws (or models)'.

However, Berlin characteristically concluded his letter by saying that he had no serious grievance, and wrote only to set the record straight. In a personal letter to Crook, he said he had realised that the article could not be by E.H. Carr, as he had first thought, but was obviously by someone wiser, such as Barraclough (he had evidently guessed, or found out!) – 'or', he added more sharply, 'by some other furious man, anxious to get into a fight, and knock something down, and blow something up'. 'Let it all blow over', he concluded in amicable style. 'My only concern was to clear myself of a grotesque charge.'

Berlin himself contributed a long article on the early twentieth-century French political philosopher, Georges Sorel, on 31 December 1971. He observed that Sorel had 'the moral fury of perpetual youth', and that he was in revolt against 'the rationalist ideal of frictionless contentment that repels the young today'. But a year later he took objection to another article in the *Lit Supp*, a review in December 1972 by Professor Richard Freeborn, a Turgenev scholar, of the Romanes lecture on Turgenev's *Fathers and Children* that Berlin had given in Oxford in 1970.

The lecture presented Turgenev, who had become a hero of Berlin's, as the most desirable kind of voice for liberalism in a radical epoch. However Freeborn's review dwelt more on alleged errors, or misleading uses, of scholarship in the lecture, and Berlin said that he 'could not allow to pass unchallenged . . . imputations of dishonesty and of culpable ignorance'.

There was an exchange in January between Berlin and Freeborn, in the course of which Freeborn rather curiously wrote 'I wish Sir Isaiah the utmost vigour of mind and heart in the New Year'. Afterwards Berlin wrote to Crook saying that he knew who had written the review – and deplored the reviewer's reply with its 'appalling pseudo-joviality'. He added that John Sparrow had been inciting him to send the paper a further letter with a lot of quotations about 'free born' Englishmen from *Areopagitica* – but he would be magnanimous, and not expose the professor 'as he deserved'. Berlin was always modest and courteous in his public exchanges, but one can see from these two episodes that the fire sometimes raged beneath.

Two very critical reviews also became famous in interested circles, although in the event they did not lead to any great argument on the letters page.

One – in November 1970 – was by Geoffrey Grigson, poet and critic and the founder of the thirties magazine *New Verse*, and was a severe attack on the poetry of Cecil Day Lewis, who at that time was Poet Laureate. Grigson had always been a champion of W.H. Auden, but never of Day Lewis, who, he thought, displayed that 'gentlemanly, amateurish, idle attitude' towards poetry that Vronsky in Tolstoy's *Anna Karenina* displayed towards painting. The result was poems 'so flat you could cycle on them'. Yet 'how often such verse' – and this was his more general point – 'without felicity, without emotive cadence, illumination or independence, without tension, offering no surprise of recognition, no turning of corners, no uphill or downhill . . . has enjoyed an extensive, if doomed honour!' He called for the nature of this verse to be 'quickly recognised, for the health of literature'.

In the hothouse world of the poets it was, of course, soon widely known who had written the review. The paper published some letters of protest, but Day Lewis himself did not reply. It was known that he was deeply hurt, while Grigson, in a letter to Crook, ruefully reflected that he had probably cut his throat again:

> My dilemma is that all the laureated and knighted persons who might direct an of course deserved Civil List pension of £10,000 a year in my direction, are former victims, all the Betjemans and Day Lewises. Years ago, going through the wood outside this window, my daughter asked me, Do cuckoos bite? I said they didn't, but I think I gave her the wrong answer.

The other article, just over six months later, in June 1971, was by Edgar Wind, and it was the world of art scholarship that was set chattering feverishly by this one. Wind had been asked to review E.H. Gombrich's biography of Aby Warburg, and the situation brought two great tyrannosauri of art history into confrontation over a third.

Aby Warburg was a German scholar of the turn of the century whose subject, as Wind put it, was 'the cultural significance of pagan revivals as sources both of light and superstition' in Reformation and Renaissance Europe. He had built up a magnificent library, arranged as a kind of guide to civilisation, which was now in the Warburg Institute of London University. Gombrich was currently the director of the Warburg, and had been pressed into writing a book about which he had many misgivings.

Wind, Professor of Art at Oxford, had a profound respect for the memory of Warburg, and considered that Gombrich had completely failed to take the measure of the man. He might have been indulgent towards John Sparrow and his book on inscriptions, but here there was no place for indulgence. Gombrich had evidently found the writing of the book uncongenial, but he had made his choice – and 'one must discard one's sympathy and say what has gone wrong'. He wrote a devastating review.

Gombrich, he said, had seen and presented Warburg as a tortured figure. Through rummaging too much in the great mass of notes and unfinished drafts that Warburg had left behind, he had come to think of Warburg as a 'man lost in a maze'. He had lost sight of the real

Warburg – a master craftsman, a writer of economy and elegance, a citizen of the world, a man with a glorious sense of humour who had been known as a 'ravishing dancer' in his youth. In fact, Warburg's animal vitality was at the root of his 'marvellously exact comprehension of folk festivals, whether in Renaissance Florence or among the Pueblo Indians'. But as a result of Gombrich's preoccupation with Warburg's 'pullulating swarm of ephemeral notations', the great man had emerged, instead, 'like a spectre, in the now fashionable guise of a tormented mollusc: shapeless, flustered and jejune, incessantly preoccupied with his inner conflicts and driven in vain to aggrandise them by some unconquerable itch for the Absolute'.

Wind went on to make many detailed criticisms of the book. Gombrich did not reply. The art scholars – who of course knew to a man who had written the review – nodded their heads sagely after their first excitement, and, most of them, sadly agreed that Wind was right.

John Willett joined the paper in November 1960 as part-time deputy editor, and stayed till January 1967, retaining after that a connection with the paper in various capacities until November 1975. He was forty-three when he joined the staff. He had been educated at Winchester and Christ Church, and after the war, when he served in intelligence, he had worked for a while as a leader writer on the *Manchester Guardian*. He had also become a great expert on Bertolt Brecht, and his book *The Theatre of Bertolt Brecht* had been published to acclaim in 1959. He lived in a handsome Georgian house in Hampstead, but dressed very casually, by contrast with Arthur Crook, who always wore beautifully cut suits. In fact when Richard Boston, who was employed as a subeditor for a time by Crook, went for his job interview, he thought the man standing by the editor's desk was the window cleaner until this figure – who was Willett – started asking him about Beckett, Ionesco and Astérix. Willett was a man of 'infinite curiosity', very ready to give an airing to new ideas in art and literature, but by no means always convinced by them, and capable, as we have seen in the 'Ugh' controversy, of taking a very strong line against things he disapproved of.

He was interested in design and typography, and also in the experiments with typographical art and the so-called 'concrete poetry' – concentrating on the visual effect of the words on the page – that were frequent in the 1960s. He brought in artists such as Kitaj, Morandi and Kokoschka to design covers for the special numbers, and published some of the typographical art in the paper, such as that of Richard Hamilton. In January 1961, not long after his arrival on the paper, he was saying of Hamilton's typographic version of Marcel Duchamps's *The Bride Stripped Bare by her Bachelors, Even*:

> Point of. this
>   ty pographic ecCentricity
>   *not* **easy** (?difficult) to see

Nevertheless his interest in these subjects continued, and in August 1964 we find in the paper a poem-letter by the witty Scots poet Edwin Morgan to a French 'new novelist', Marc Saporta:

> Saporta!
> O satrap!
> O Sparta!
> Oars tap.
> O, a strap?
> A pastor?
> Pa Astor?
> Ps! Aorta . . .

That 'Pa Astor?' must particularly have amused the staff of the paper, whose proprietor may have been paternalistic but was not conspicuously paternal – and whose son, Gavin, two years later was to sell *The Times* and its supplements.

Another of Willett's interests was the new Liverpool school of joky, performance poets and the paper even published a poem by one of them, Adrian Henri, on the death of T.S. Eliot in January 1965:

> *I'd been out the night before & hadn't seen the papers or the telly*
> *& the next day in the café someone told me you were dead*
> *And it was as if a favourite distant uncle had died . . .*
>
> *For years I measured out my life with your coffeespoons . . .*

(There would also be weightier appraisals.)

The paper was also quick, with Willett there, to take an interest in the new technologies of communication and the new media. The early guru in these matters, the Canadian Marshall McLuhan, himself contributed an article to an issue devoted to the 'Printing and the Mind of

Man' exhibition in London in July 1963 (an article subsequently reprinted in his book *Understanding Media*), while already in March of that year George Steiner had reviewed McLuhan's *The Gutenberg Galaxy* for the paper.

From about this time, Steiner was regularly invited to review books by the controversial new thinkers. As an outstanding polymath, he could be relied on to be aware of most of what was going on in the world of new thought, although his own weighty and epigrammatic style added a challenge to the reader over and above that already provided by the authors he wrote about. He was also a tenacious controversialist. In one of his letters to Crook about the Turgenev argument, Isaiah Berlin remarked, 'George Steiner may at any moment feel moved to join in, and then, in the words of a Russian proverb, the entire forest will be on fire again'.

A quotation from Steiner's review of *The Gutenberg Galaxy* shows both his sharp perception of what was new and important in McLuhan, and also his somewhat oracular manner:

> Mr McLuhan posits that western civilisation has entered, or is about to enter, an era of electro-magnetic technology. This technology will radically alter the milieu of human perception, the reality-coordinates within which we apprehend and order sense data. Experience will not present itself serially, in atomised or linear patterns of causal sequence, but in 'fields' of simultaneous interaction. To offer a very crude analogy (and the process of analogy may itself be a vestige of an earlier logic), our categories of immediate perception will shift from those at work in an Ingres drawing to those we experience in a Jackson Pollock.
>
> But we are unready to master the new spontaneity, randomness, and 'totalisation' of the electronic experience-field, because print, and all the habits of feeling and thought print has grafted on the western mind, have broken the creative, primal unity of the senses. By translating *all* aspects of the world into *one* sense only – the reading eye – the printing press has hypnotised and fragmented western consciousness. We lie rigid in what Blake called 'Newton's sleep'.

Steiner questioned many points in McLuhan's thesis, but when he reviewed his *Understanding Media* a year later, in August, he said that McLuhan was a 'real modernist. He belongs to that small group of radical dreamers and thinkers – Canetti, Paul Goodman, Lévi-Strauss, Adorno, Queneau – who are trying to realise and explore the altered conditions of modern existence.' Marshall McLuhan himself contributed a review of a book of essays, *Communication and Language*, edited by Sir Gerald Barry and others, in March 1966, reiterating (though anonymously here, of course) his main arguments, and in September 1967, Willett reviewed a whole batch of McLuhan books that had all been issued together, including *The Medium is the Message*, reaching the conclusion that McLuhan's vision was 'surely right in its essentials', even though his argument was slapdash and full of weak or missing links. In this manner the *Lit Supp* registered the laying of a foundation stone of much of the culture of the later twentieth century.

Above all, Willett, a French as well as a German scholar, opened up the paper much more welcomingly even than in Pryce-Jones's day to the art and thought that was coming from the Continent. The special numbers were particularly important here. They fairly soon fell into a regular pattern, usually with one in the spring and two in the early autumn, the first autumn one (sometimes called the 'overseas' or 'export' number) being mainly about Britain, and the second – timed to coincide with the Frankfurt Book Fair – about foreign, predominantly Continental literature. (The tradition of the 'Frankfurt number', another invention of Frank Derry's, survives to this day.) They grew into very fat issues, some of eighty pages, with numerous full-page advertisements by publishers both British and Continental, in those long-gone days when publishers still believed that advertisements sold books.

They were, as in Pryce-Jones's day, often general surveys of developments in different fields. Richard Hoggart wrote a signed review of one of them, *The British Imagination*, when it subsequently appeared in book form in March 1961. He complained that it was like 'thirty little biscuits each topped with tinned anchovy' – and especially with the early ones there was some truth in the criticism. These brief round-ups of different topics did not give much scope for thought; however they were at least always informative.

One of the best of the autumn pairs also appeared in book form, as *The Critical Moment* (which was the title of the first part, on 26 July 1963; the second part, on 27 September, was called in the paper 'Critics Abroad'). This was where Leavis's lecture 'Research in English' was published; it also included articles by two figures who were now looming very large in their own countries, Roland Barthes and Umberto Eco, and was no doubt the first that many British readers had heard of them. Each tried to give a clear account of their difficult reflections on the peculiar semantic systems constituted by poems and novels.

But there was also a strong sceptical note to be heard in the paper about these new structuralist analysts of language, which came out most notably in an article by the London University lecturer (later professor), John Weightman, in June 1966. Roland Barthes had been attacked by another Frenchman, Raymond Picard, who in a book called *Nouvelle critique ou nouvelle imposture* had accused him, especially in his book *Sur Racine*, of producing pretentious critical cant.

John Weightman surveyed the quarrel, remarking that not since the heyday of Sartre's quarrels with Camus had there been such a flapping of wings in Paris, and that in the turmoil almost all the themes of contemporary French intellectual life had been brought to the surface – 'Existentialism, Marxism, Freudianism, Structuralism (both linguistic and anthropological), the psychology of mythic substances, the nature of rhetoric . . .' and so on. 'One can imagine Racine's bewilderment,' Weightman added, 'if he could be made aware of all these complexities.'

However, Weightman acknowledged that Barthes developed his ideas with great subtlety and talent. The main point, he said, was that for Barthes the subject matter of a work of literature was 'an ever-changing mass of different, linguistically stimulated associations . . . which, being ever-changing, does not really exist' – so it was no use looking for its meaning in any simple sense, or bothering with any such naive ideas as working out the author's intentions. All this was 'most seductively expressed . . . an abstruse siren song' that seemed 'far more profound than M. Picard's brisk common-sense'. But it was to that brisk common-sense that Weightmann was drawn in the end, feeling that at any rate a great deal of *la nouvelle critique* just 'draped itself in a philosophico-poetic profundity'.

George Steiner wrote several times about the anthropologist Claude Lévi-Strauss, notably in a review of several books, including the English translation of his *Anthropologie Structurale*, in April 1966. He saw Lévi-Strauss's influence on the post-war life of ideas in France as second only to Sartre's, with his notion that the ways in which different societies did things had not just developed for practical purposes, but were a kind of inherited code or language, reflecting the way the society saw things, that could be analysed structurally in the way ordinary language can be.

When, two years later, in January 1968, Annette Lavers reviewed the psychological theories of Jacques Lacan in his *Ecrits*, she firmly associated the anthropologist Lévi-Strauss with the predominantly linguistic theorists, Barthes, Lacan and Foucault. And she said that the cartoonist was not entirely wrong who had shown them all as 'savages concocting in one melting-pot the philosophy of our time'.

However, Michel Foucault was reviewed in the paper not by a literary or linguistic analyst, but by an empirical scientist, the Professor of Psychiatry at the Maudsley Hospital, Sir Aubrey Lewis. In a front-page piece in October 1961 on his *La Folie et la déraison: Histoire de la folie à l'âge classique*, Lewis just cut through the Frenchman's 'abstruse reflections' – with which he said the book was 'overloaded' – and applauded it simply as an excellent piece of historical scholarship on the way the 'insane' had been treated in France. This was particularly ironic in the light of Foucault's pervasive doubt about whether anything that passed for information was reliable at all.

For reviews of the currently revered German thinkers, George Lichtheim, another weighty figure, was brought in alongside Steiner. Between them they provided good accounts of the Marxist literary critic, George Lukács, and of the subtle Marxist analyst of culture, Theodor Adorno.

Steiner, writing in February 1962, tried to disentangle the more personal and imaginative elements in Adorno's ideas about music and poetry from the orthodox dialectical materialism out of which they grew, while in June 1964 he criticised Lukács's collapse into the 'hollow immensities' of his great scheme of Marxist aesthetics – 'a charnel house of metaphysical bones' – while praising the acuteness of his comments on individual novelists in his earlier works. There was nothing, Steiner said, in Lukács's latest theories for 'the young artists and intellectuals of eastern Europe who are asking whether there is anything left of life and incitement in the Marxist legacy'. (One wonders, however, if there were not more such 'young intellectuals' by this time in Western than in Eastern Europe.)

Lichtheim, in September 1967, elegiacally portrayed both Lukács and Adorno as Marxist intellectuals who had been forced to realise that Communist revolution had not changed the world, and so had returned to 'the familiar role of contemplation' – with fairly unsatisfactory results, he seemed to think, in both cases.

Among the German novelists of these years, we find Günter Grass being especially singled out for attention. The poet Michael Hamburger reviewed the English translation of *The Tin Drum* in October 1962, and *Hundejahre* in September 1963. He had had no doubt of the power of the writing in both books – it had an 'unencumbered and uninhibited zest absent from German ever since Grimmelshausen's time'. But he was not at ease with the tone of *The Tin Drum*, where he was disturbed by the 'moral neutrality' of the author towards Oskar, the monstrous dwarf whose adventures in Germany through the pre-war, wartime and post-war years were so undeniably engrossing. He was more unreserved in his praise of *Hundejahre*, which he said was 'by far the fullest and most convincing critique of Nazism yet achieved in fiction'. Grass had achieved this by 'de-mythologising, de-heroising and de-demonising that phenomenon . . . exposing its vulgar shoddiness from the inside' – though in a far more fantastic and comic way, it might be added, than Hannah Arendt had done in her Eichmann book.

Among the French novelists, Natalie Sarraute, Alain Robbe-Grillet and Raymond Queneau received notable attention. In January 1960, Rayner Heppenstall commented amusedly on the fact that there were no proper names in Sarraute's novels, though in some a *je* did 'eke out the *il* and *elle, ils* and *elles*'. When in the end some characters did receive names, he felt it was 'under protest from Mme Sarraute'. However, added Heppenstall, 'what passes as novel-writing here is at present so abject that the merest flicker from abroad is likely to be seen as a ray of hope'.

John Sturrock, reviewing her novel *Les Fruits d'Or* in July 1963, was untroubled by the anonymity of her 'characters'. This book was about the reactions to a novel of a collection of unidentified reviewers and readers. He said that we never learn much about this fictional novel itself because it has 'vanished into a mist of critical commonplaces and prejudices', emanating from such types as the man who knows the author and the man determined to classify the author into a literary school. Sturrock admired the convincing way in which this ironical book – Sarraute's book, that is, not the one she was writing about – showed 'the iceberg nature of literary judgments, only a tiny fraction of which peep above the surface', and which are in fact 'counters in a different and more serious game, in which person plays person'.

Sturrock wrote this review four years before he joined the paper, which was in July 1967 – after which time the new French criticism and fiction were in general treated more respectfully in the paper. Sturrock was a great admirer of Barthes in particular, and in due course became one of the leading interpreters for the British of the new French thought.

John Russell Taylor, who was the film critic of *The Times*, reviewed Robbe-Grillet's *L'Immortelle* in September 1963. He found this *ciné-roman* an unsatisfactory work, since it was the author's attempt to put into words the images he had already created in a film of the same name, 'of which they are only a stumbling, cumbrous, incomplete description . . . much ado, to convey very little'. John Weightman was no more highly impressed in December 1965 by Robbe-Grillet's novel *La Maison de rendez-vous*, a 'glacial exercise in sadistic tensions' set in a Hong Kong brothel. The author supplied the reader with the elements of a melodramatic story, but 'he arranges them in such a way that they cannot be unscrambled'.

Weightman suggested that Robbe-Grillet should 'give up pretending that art has to be as incomprehensible as life, and come out into the open as a precise and gifted eroticist'.

However, Raymond Queneau, in the hands of Sturrock in May 1967, got a much better reception. Sturrock surveyed his work – the wisdom that, he said, Queneau put into the mouth of clowns – in a long article. Sturrock argued that in his insistence that we cannot in the end know reality, Queneau had been practising 'structuralism' for thirty years before Lévi-Strauss's 'recent apotheosis', and also that he had been deliberately undermining his own novels long before Robbe-Grillet started doing it. He cited the moment in Queneau's absurdist novel *Zazie dans le métro* when 'everyone and everything is described as being no more than a dream of a dream, "un délire tapé à la machine par un romancier idiot (oh! pardon)"'.

British fiction in these years was not doing anything so absurd – in either of the ways that the word might be applied to the French writers. However, E.M. Forster, who died in 1970, had left behind his novel about homosexuality, *Maurice*, and in Britain it was thought daring when his publisher, the old firm of Edward Arnold, brought it out in October 1971.

It was reviewed by an American professor of English, Samuel Hynes, who visited England nearly every summer and became a major contributor to the paper.

Hynes was in no way troubled by the subject of the novel, but thought, on the contrary, that the author was too much troubled by it. Forster had written the book with a very human purpose – to show that happy homosexual love was possible. But, Hynes said, he was not frank or realistic about homosexual love, and certainly not 'liberated'. His attitude to it was 'guilty and regretful . . . an Edwardian view of homosexuality'. Maurice, the homosexual hero, 'accepts his condition, but he disapproves of it, and so, one gathers, does Forster, for at the end he turns from the real, social world, and sends his lovers off into a sentimental world of romance, like two Scholar Gypsies.' The book added nothing to Forster's achievement as a novelist. However, Hynes added charmingly, Forster would probably not have minded that judgment – 'he would rather have had the kind of immortality that rests, not on words or deeds, but on the constancy and intensity of affections'.

Another book that excited scandal was Nabokov's *Lolita*, published in Britain only after a court case in November 1959. Julian Symons reviewed this story of Humbert Humbert and his obsessive sexual passion for a 'nymphet'. He enjoyed its 'rich sense of the comic and absurd', and far from being upset by it, he thought that 'scenes that might be tedious and unpleasant become under Nabokov's hand uproariously funny'. However it was 'not – as critics with a worthy wish to attack the rigid laws of censorship say – a great novel . . . We are meant to find tragedy in Humbert Humbert's flight across America with the Lolita whose youth he has so remorselessly destroyed – but we can never accept the clownish Humbert as a tragic figure.'

The older generation of British novelists was still in favour. When Graham Greene's autobiography *A Sort of Life* came out in September 1971, along with a new *Collected Edition* of his novels, it was again Sam Hynes who was asked to review them. He said that Greene was a major English novelist, who had done what he aimed to do – 'he has expressed a religious sense, and created a fictive world in which human acts are important . . . His art is perhaps little comfort to the religious, for it offers no confirmation of comfortable words, and if it celebrates, it celebrates minimal virtues. But art has other things to do besides comforting and celebrating; it can feed our imaginative lives by insisting that the religious sense exists, in this world, in Brighton and Tabasco and Indo-China. No-one has done that better in fiction than Graham Greene.'

Julian Symons went on reviewing and delighting in Anthony Powell's *A Dance to the Music of Time*, from the fifth novel, *Casanova's Chinese Restaurant*, in June 1960, which led him to predict that future students would be set questions like 'Who poured the sugar over Widmerpool's head?' to the eighth, *The Soldier's Art*, in September 1966, where he dwelt on the military comedy – the fiddles, intrigues and plotting for promotion. The next three volumes went, however, to the poet Alan Brownjohn, who when he reviewed *The Military Philosophers* in October 1968 seemed to think that the narrator's quirky, personal vision of events was rather a limiting factor, but by the time he reached Volume XI, *Temporary Kings*, in June 1973 was saying that Powell had 'never combined high comedy and the sense of impending tragedy so powerfully'.

Evelyn Waugh published *Unconditional Surrender*, the last volume of his *Sword of Honour* war trilogy, in 1961, and in 1966 John Willett reviewed Waugh's revised edition of the whole trilogy on 17 March – just before Waugh's death on 10 April. It was one of the very best of Willett's contributions to the *Lit Supp*. The trilogy now read, he said, like 'a large and very fine novel, whose scale and seriousness are offset by a remarkable lightness of texture'. Waugh had written that it was a description of the war as it was experienced by a single uncharacteristic Englishman, but Willett thought the aspects covered were all fairly representative of 'the war we waged'.

But he was amused by Waugh's remark that when he re-read it he realised that he had written 'an obituary of the Roman Catholic Church in England'. 'It would hardly be more far-fetched,' Willett commented, 'to call it a study of the servant question.'

He went on to show wittily how servants could be said to dominate the book, at first cheering up the hero, Guy Crouchback, then deteriorating in quality, then acknowledged as having their own rights. 'And the name of this study? *Active Service*? *Divine Service*? Never mind. For it is not the book that Mr Waugh has in fact written, any more than is "the document of Catholic usage of my youth" which he now feels he has produced.' Yet 'the test of a first-rate work of fiction is that each re-reading should reveal fresh aspects, undetected threads, new implications' – and 'this the trilogy fulfils'.

As for C.P. Snow, Crook sent the novel that his name is most often associated with, *Corridors of Power*, not to a literary critic but to a British ambassador, Sir David Hunt, who wrote for the paper on many subjects from the classics to military history. Hunt had been an Oxford don, a soldier, and Private Secretary to both Attlee and Churchill, and was at this time the High Commissioner in Uganda. In his review, in November 1964, he pronounced with tolerably acceptable authority (though because of anonymity that would not have been known to readers) that 'C.P. Snow's picture of the operation of a ruling class and a senior bureaucracy is near enough to the mark.' He only questioned one or two small points of detail, such as 'the phrasing of a parliamentary question, or the waistcoat to be worn by a Minister when sworn on the Privy Council'.

Some of the next generation of novelists were not doing quite so well, however, in the *Lit Supp*. Iris Murdoch published eleven novels during the period of Crook's editorship, but many of them puzzled the reviewers. In June 1961 G.S. Fraser said that her novel *A Severed Head* was a brilliantly enjoyable book, with a dazzling surface of wit like

Congreve's *The Way of the World* – but 'one feels there is a central, large and simple meaning which one has, somehow, just missed'. In September 1963, Antony Cronin, the Irish novelist, spoke of the 'bewildering facility' with which the characters in *The Unicorn* fell in and out of love with each other, 'sometimes in the course of the same day, nearly always without prior warning', while in September 1966, the scholar and critic Miriam Allott, reviewing *The Time of the Angels*, said 'Miss Murdoch's intricacies appear to run nowhere but into the sand'. However, Marigold Johnson, in February 1973, avowed that 'the reviewer considers *The Black Prince* to be Miss Murdoch's *Hamlet* – a novel in which she comes to grips with the crucial questions that have preoccupied her ever since *Under the Net*, and in which, more passionately, densely and eloquently than in any previous book, she restates her philosophical position, in the form of a question: "Can there be a *natural*, as it were Shakespearean felicity in the moral life?"'

Angus Wilson published four novels in the same period. Randall Swingler, normally a genial writer, did not like *The Old Men at the Zoo*, writing in September 1961 that 'there is an unpleasant recurrence of unnecessary and therefore ostentatious nastiness running through the book', but Wilson's most ambitious novel, *No Laughing Matter*, fell into the hands of an admirer, the critic and journalist D.A.N. Jones, who wrote in October 1967 that 'this rich novel is about laughter, what things it is proper to laugh at, and in what style,' and concluded his review by praising 'the modesty and gracefulness of this deeply serious history of our century, conceived in terms of class individualised'.

As it happens, I reviewed three of Kingsley Amis's novels while Arthur Crook was editor. I greatly liked *One Fat Englishman*, of which I wrote in November 1963 (when I had just joined the staff of the paper for a couple of years): 'It is a small book, no bigger than a man's fist – but it plants that fist with precision and force square in the belly of the fat English publisher who is its main character. This is satire of a wit and intelligence that class it with the best.' I also liked *I Want It Now*, about a successful television interviewer called Ronnie Appleyard, approving in October 1968 of its 'brilliant portrayal' of the 'degenerate moeurs' of the television studios, but less convinced by the reformation of Ronnie through the influence of a strange, frigid girl. *The Green Man*, a ghost story about a pub landlord, I found in October 1969 to be a 'ramshackle book, though full of good things'. Martin Amis, Kingsley's son, published his first novel, *The Rachel Papers*, during his eighteen-month stint on the paper as an editorial assistant. It was reviewed in November 1973 by another up-and-coming writer, Lorna Sage, who said that it was about the 'social and sexual free-for-all of well-heeled London', and was 'scurrilous, shameless and very funny'. It won the Somerset Maugham Prize in 1974.

After the great debut of *The Lord of the Flies*, William Golding was giving his readers more difficult philosophical allegories to contend with. Sam Hynes tackled several of them. Of *The Spire*, Golding's story of a fourteenth-century priest who feels called by God to build a cathedral spire, Hynes said (in April 1964) that the spire itself was the most vivid presence in the book, not any of the characters. In fact the spire could be seen as 'a symbol of the novel that contains it, because, though the book lacks sufficient fictional foundations, yet it stands'. In June 1967, on the publication of *The Pyramid*, a novel set in Wiltshire in the 1920s to 1940s, Hynes said 'one greets with relief the appearance of Golding's least philosophical, and most modest, novel'.

But V.S. Naipaul's reputation was growing. When his novel *A House for Mr Biswas* came out in September 1961, the *Lit Supp* reviewer, the poet and critic Burns Singer, said 'the hunt for the Great West Indian Novel is on' – and in fact this novel has generally been regarded, ever since, as the winner of that title. However Singer was more sceptical about it. He approved, rather dryly, of the picture of life in Trinidad that 'this enormous, rambling, picaresque book' contained: 'few social investigators could have given us as vivid an account of the housing conditions as Mr Naipaul'. But he thought that the main character, Mr Biswas, who is trying to build a house, was 'rather a stupid little man . . . almost a tragic figure, but never quite', and found it hard to believe either in Mr Biswas's Herculean labours to get his house built, or the psychological penetration that Naipaul had endowed him with.

After that Naipaul did much better in the paper, which indeed must now have helped to consolidate his great standing. The novelist Thomas Hinde reviewed his novel about surburban England, *Mr Stone and the Knights Companion*, in May 1963, and found it wholly convincing, with Naipaul 'very funny about his characters . . . but handling them very gently'. D.A.N. Jones greatly admired *The Mimic Men* in April 1967. This memoir of a Caribbean politician exiled in London was, he thought, a true 'Commonwealth novel', with its portraits of many citizens of former British dependencies, all of them wanting to be aristocrats but unsure what traditions to select, and all feeling their doubts about their rank and status as 'a huge, tragic wound'. In October 1971, the poet Ian Hamilton (now on the staff of the paper) praised *In A Free State* (the collection of three linked stories that won the Booker Prize that year) both for its 'desolate vision' of uprooted people across the world 'yearning for a home that isn't home', and for the fact that Naipaul did not allow that desolate vision to 'devalue the absurd, ugly and, at times, heroic efforts that are made to mitigate it'. Meanwhile A.H. Hanson, who normally wrote about British social issues, gave a very enthusiastic review in September 1964 to *An Area of Darkness*, Naipaul's account of his visit to India, the country his family originally came from: 'this truly dark book,' Hanson wrote, 'contains more of India than has ever been encompassed in so few pages'.

The mid-sixties also saw black African novelists making their claims with new vigour, and Chinua Achebe's novel *A Man of the People* was especially singled out. Ken Trodd, a young critic who later became a television producer, said that Achebe's political thinking was misty and ambiguous, but that the novel was a triumph of documentation: 'nearly all the most telling and odious features of recent Nigerian life are here'. In August 1966, John Barnard hailed *In Praise of Older Women*, a novel by a Hungarian émigré, Stephen Vizinczey, for its 'cutting and ironical commentary on human pretension and frailty'.

After Iris Murdoch, Muriel Spark was the British woman novelist winning most esteem at this time. In September 1963, Marigold Johnson enjoyed *The Girls of Slender Means*, her novel about 'young ladies of respectable country background and poverty in a Kensington hostel', set in what Miss Spark managed to portray as a Golden Age – 'the cratered, blacked-out, austerity London of summer 1945'. The novel was 'splendidly witty', and 'her provocative, anarchistic asides about sin and salvation melt so blithely and neatly into the narrative that even Mr Waugh would approve their sophistication'. The novelist Anthony Burgess, who had now started to write quite frequently for the paper, was less satisfied in October 1965 with her long, ambitious novel, *The Mandelbaum Gate*, set in Jerusalem during the Eichmann trial: 'The Mandelbaum is slow in delivering its almonds.'

Another brilliant young reviewer on the paper was Francis Hope, who as we shall see was to die young. He was a great admirer of Margaret Drabble's novels. In April 1967, he said that her fourth novel, *Jerusalem the Golden*, written at the age of twenty-seven, was 'an impressive addition to an already impressively consistent oeuvre . . . It would be over-generous to compare Miss Drabble with George Eliot, but not totally ridiculous. If people in 50 years' time want to know what it was like to be a young woman in the 1960s, this novel, like her others will tell them.' In March 1972, he said of her novel *The Needle's Eye* that she wrote with a rare passion, a passion for justice. 'She has what Sartre recommended for a novelist: moral obsession' –

which in this book was given its head. However he did not enjoy this story of a rich married woman in London quite so much as some of the others: the 'flights of lyricism in pursuit of moral feelings' were in danger of sloppiness, while after apparently shaping course for a catastrophe, in the end, when the heroine decided to patch up her marriage, Miss Drabble shied rather unsatisfactorily away from it.

In 1972, John Berger, best known till then as an excellent, Marxist-orientated art critic on the *New Statesman*, won the Booker Prize for his novel *G*, but at the prize-giving dinner created a scandal and some humour by lambasting the food company Booker, the founders of the prize, alleging that it exploited its Caribbean sugar workers, and announcing that he would give half (but only half) the prize money to the West Indian revolutionary group, the Black Panthers. His novel had been reviewed in the *Lit Supp* in June that year by David Caute, a novelist himself regarded as left-leaning, and (until he resigned in dramatic, slightly Berger-like style) a Fellow of All Souls.

The novel, as Caute put it, was about an Anglo-Italian Don Juan of the turn of the century who is presented both as 'a radically alienated product of bourgeois hypocrisy' and 'a type of existential hero completely devoid of bad faith'. He said that Berger was 'a humanistic Marxist who believes that the artist's proper duty is to overcome the fragmentation, alienation and despair endemic to a decadent bourgeois culture'. However this modish novel did not entirely satisfy Caute, especially in its more experimental aspects – 'employing and rather over-taxing many of the devices used in recent years by Sarraute, Sollers, Butor and the other novelists who have said farewell to naturalistic certainty'. One comes away from *G*, he concluded, 'as from many modern paintings: provoked and stimulated, yet baffled and faintly resentful'.

Incidentally when the art critic and connoisseur Douglas Cooper had reviewed Berger's collection of art reviews, *Permanent Red*, ten years earlier, in January 1961, he had claimed that Berger was, for political reasons, untrue to his own perceptions, saying that 'time and again, Mr Berger feels obliged to focus on paintings whose subjects have a social significance, where his eye would appear, on the evidence of much that he writes, to tell him that other pictures are better painted and also better as works of art'. It was a much kinder judgment than Cooper made on most other art critics.

There was also one novel review, in March 1967, whose significance could only have been seen by an eye far in the future. Mary-Kay Wilmers gave a very disobliging review to Ferdinand Mount's first novel, *Very*

Like a Whale. She said that it had an insipid hero, and that the only bits of interest were those which described the functioning of a merchant bank. It could not have been foretold that a quarter of a century later, Ferdinand Mount would be the editor of the *Lit Supp*, and Mary-Kay Wilmers the editor of its chief rival, the *London Review of Books*.

T.S. Eliot's last important appearance in the paper in his lifetime was at the time of the publication of the *New English Bible*, in the spring of 1961, when he was seventy-three. This new translation was discussed on 24 March both by the Revd Hedley Sparks, who said that it was too elucidatory, with the translators trying to convey what the original texts meant, not what they actually said, and by Marghanita Laski, who said it was 'a sad weakening', with 'a loss of profundity and beauty'.

On 28 April, Eliot wrote to the paper to approve of Marghanita Laski's review, and to object in particular to the description of Mary in the new version as a 'girl', not a 'virgin', in Luke I.27. Writing again two weeks later, he said the point was 'Did the learned committee of translators believe that Saint Luke believed in the virgin birth?' If so, why had they used the word 'girl'? There was much subsequent philological and theological debate in the letters pages. On the whole Eliot seemed to carry his point that the English word 'virgin' was the right one to convey the meaning Saint Luke intended, and five years after his death, on Christmas Day 1970, C.H. Dodd, one of the editors of the *NEB*, wrote to say that they had accepted his argument, and changed Luke I.34 from 'I have no husband' to 'I am still a virgin.'

In the wake of Eliot's death in January 1965, apart from Adrian Henri's poem, there was an eloquent leader by G.S. Fraser, on 7 January. Fraser said that 'for many readers, Mr Eliot's death will be like the death of part of themselves, the death of the shock and exhilaration of one's first insight into the gulfs and heights, the bewildering threats and promises, of life'. Of *The Waste Land* he wrote 'it is not his greatest poem, but his most interesting poem, as *Hamlet* was Shakespeare's most interesting play'.

The Waste Land itself was to make an appearance in the *Lit Supp* after Eliot's death. One of Crook's notable gifts as an editor was his ability to get interesting unpublished material for the paper, such as, in August 1968, the diaries of Sir Sydney Waterlow. These included Henry James's reply when he was asked by Mrs H.G. Wells, at a fancy-dress ball, 'Oh, Mr James, *will* you dance the Sir Roger de Coverley with me?': 'With reserves, dear lady, with reserves!'

Crook's biggest scoop in this field was to get Eliot's wife, Valerie, to let him publish part of the missing manuscript of *The Waste Land* in the *Lit Supp*. The manuscript had been given by Eliot to John Quinn, his American benefactor, and had ended up, sold by Quinn's niece and more or less forgotten, in the Berg Collection of the New York Public Library. Valerie Eliot was first informed that it was there in the summer of 1968, and Crook heard about it through the curator of the Berg Collection, Dr Lola Szladits, whom he knew. They were asked to keep the news secret until the Library issued a public statement on 25 October 1968.

Valerie Eliot owned the copyright, and was offered a sum around $60,000 to publish it by an American publication; but she was a friend of Crook's, she wanted it to be published first in the *Lit Supp*, and she let the paper have it for £100. A facsimile of the opening of the first section of the poem, 'The Burial of the Dead', with holograph markings, appeared in the *Lit Supp* on 7 November 1968, the day the manuscript went on show at the New York Public Library, and there was an article about its history by Dr Donald Gallup called 'The "Lost" Manuscripts of T.S. Eliot'.

After his death, sharp attacks on Eliot had begun, particularly over his relationship with his first wife Vivienne, and it had been argued that what *The Waste Land* was really about was the poet's hatred and fear of women. However, in December 1971, when the whole 'Waste Land' manuscript was published in book form by Faber, the poet and critic Donald Davie wrote a subtle essay in the *Lit Supp* using the drafts to defend the poem, acknowledging that such feelings were to be found in it, but arguing that to single that element out was entirely to mis-understand the character of the poem. The *Lit Supp* might be said to have rallied round T.S. Eliot in the end.

W.H. Auden died in Vienna at the beginning of 1973, and Clive James, who set out in life as a literary critic – for years he was planning a book on Louis MacNeice – wrote a review which stood as an obituary on 12 January. On the whole, Auden had not been getting good reviews from the *Lit Supp* in his last years – of his volume *Homage to Clio*, in August 1960, R.G. Cox, keeping up his criticism, had said that 'much of it is simply dull' – though Geoffrey Grigson had found various occasions to write in praise of him, and published a poem to him in the paper on 2 February 1967 to celebrate his sixtieth birthday, calling his poetry 'an extra fine light in our darkness'.

Clive James wrote a good piece, ostensibly about Auden's book *Epistle to a Godson*. He regretted Auden's attempt to suppress and alter his earlier poems, and also that critics had not protested much about it: 'no strong movement arose to challenge Auden's assumption that these youthful poetic crimes were committed by the same self being dishonest, rather than a different self being honest' (an early example, incidentally, of the kind of witty antithesis on which much of James's later career in television has been built).

James saw this desire of Auden's to change the past, and also the loss of 'ambiguity, resonance, areas of doubt and discovery' in Auden's later poetry, as the triumph of an impulse towards control that had been there from the start: 'he was already trying to discipline, rather than exploit, the artistic equivalent of a Midas touch . . . the parkland of imagination was what he annihilated'. But James paid his tribute to 'Auden's magic' in those years long past when he first became 'the hero of the young intelligentsia'.

In a leader in August 1966, Ian Hamilton noted that among the poets Ted Hughes, Thom Gunn and Philip Larkin were by now 'the reigning triumvirate'. Hughes's first book had received a rather curmudgeonly review, but G.S. Fraser, reviewing his next book *Lupercal* in April 1960, said it was startlingly better than his first. Hughes was not afraid of grand themes: 'he looks for the numinous and finds it in the blind, instinctual thrust of the animal and vegetable worlds . . . the most perfect short poem here is about a snowdrop'. In February 1964, when Hughes's volume of children's poems, *The Earth-Owl*, appeared, Fraser observed that 'Birds and beasts of prey, fierceness and obstinacy and violence, the fact that we do in the end live in a universe in which everything survives by eating everything else are what have gripped Mr Hughes's imagination. At the same time, he has not only "high spirits and hopefulness" [which Hughes had attributed, in an essay, to Keith Douglas] but at the same time a roaring and clownish sense of burlesque humour'.

By July 1967, Anthony Thwaite, reviewing the collection *Wodwo*, could say that 'at thirty-seven, Mr Hughes is widely taken to be the best British poet since Dylan Thomas . . . a classic of our time', but he thought that in this book Hughes seemed 'temporarily to have lost his certainty of tone' (presumably he meant that he hoped it was temporary), and that the poem 'Wodwo' itself, when read aloud, seemed 'irretrievably though unintentionally comic'. Ian Hamilton took the assault further in his review of *Crow* in January 1971. Hughes had brought a 'fond exactitude' to his earlier poems about animal behaviour, but it had always been worrying that there was no 'complex or subtle personality' detectable in them. Now, in *Crow*, all the reader got was 'a cosy, unperplexing wallow' in a territory where Hughes could unload his obsessions, a world 'drenched in blood, racked with agony, devastated by numerous varieties of violence'.

Thom Gunn's book *Moly* was reviewed in April 1971 by Terry Eagleton, who in due course would become a vigorous exponent of his own brand of Marxist and structuralist criticism, winning many enemies in the process, especially after his appointment as the Warton Professor of English at Oxford in succession to John Bayley. He used his review to look back at Gunn's work in terms already distinctly abstract: Gunn's poetry had always been concerned with discovering 'a kind of poise which would preserve the self's intactness from the invasion of a gloomy Sartrean *néant*' but in *Moly* 'Gunn's sense of what sustaining "poise" involves seems to have been significantly modified . . . it is by rooting himself responsively in the flow of natural forces, not by fending them off, that man can master them'. Eagleton cited as an example the surf-riders in one poem:

> *It is the wave they imitate*
> *Keeps them so still.*

But it was Philip Larkin who had loomed up as the finest poet to come out of the Movement, and the *Lit Supp* rose to this fact. In March 1964 Anthony Thwaite hailed the publication of *The Whitsun Weddings*. Larkin's previous book, *The Less Deceived*, Thwaite wrote, 'was widely recognised as the outstanding poetic product of the 1950s'. Since then, Larkin had continued to produce his 'rare and fine poems', and *The Whitsun Weddings* contained thirty-two of them, 'of which ten are among the best poems of our time'. The poems ranged across 'a whole emotional human landscape which can take in compassion, violence, humour, love, a sense of order and a sense of waste. Together they present the finely imagined and expressed distillation of a remarkable poetic personality.'

The outstanding new voices were Sylvia Plath and Seamus Heaney. Sylvia Plath, already married to Ted Hughes, had appeared quietly on the scene in 1961 with her book of poems, *The Colossus*. It was immediately noticed by G.S. Fraser, who said that she had 'a real gift for creating images which are at once sensuously vivid and dramatically disturbing'. But he also commented that her writing was 'elusive and private, as if what the poems were "about" in a prose sense is very much her own business'. By the time I reviewed her collection *Ariel* in November 1965 she was dead. I quoted her line 'All the gods know is destinations', saying that 'nearly all of her poems are full of these gods, inexorable and often terrible forces driving through her mind and body regardless of any consequences; and the first accomplishment of *Ariel* is that it makes their existence real'. Yet there was another quality in some of the poems: 'an ability – ability with language, ability of spirit – to confront the horrors not only with a precise description of them but also with a slangy bravado, to make mocking caricatures out of them at the very moment that they threaten to suffocate her'. In that, in her life, she had not succeeded. But I concluded (and still think) that *Ariel* was 'one of the most marvellous volumes of poetry published for a very long time'.

Alan Brownjohn reviewed the first book of poems by the Irishman Seamus Heaney, *Death of a Naturalist*, in June 1966, calling it a substantial and impressive collection, in which the best poems had an 'unforced fidelity to his rural experience'. By the following month, Heaney had been roped in to write about the Welsh poet R.S. Thomas for the paper. He wrote, in something of the style and brogue of his own poems, that 'Thomas aims at a sparse lyric note and keeps his muse spancelled most of the time on a few God-fearing acres'.

Clive James reviewed Heaney's next volume *Door Into the Dark* in July 1969, praising his 'poetic intelligence' and the 'dense beauty of his technique' but worried by the fact that the poetry was all pretty desperate stuff – 'I will show you fear in a tinful of bait'. In Heaney, he said 'Things live; animals almost live; humans live scarcely at all.' In December 1972, Anthony Thwaite looked back to this book and said that though it had plenty of bogs, bulls and buckets, 'human beings were getting a bit more of a showing in it'; but in turn he thought that the new volume *Wintering Out*, skirting as it did round the grim situation in Heaney's native Ulster, gave the impression of being a transitional book. So both Hughes and Heaney were now getting a rougher time from the paper – though Thwaite noted that some of Heaney's poems published recently in periodicals spoke more 'from the centre of the bitter conflict'.

Other new British poets reviewed (there were many more) included Ian Hamilton (poetry editor after 1965) and Geoffrey Hill. The American critic Irvin Ehrenpreis, reviewing *The Visit* in July 1970, saw Hamilton's theme, in his 'unpredictable but beautifully placed images', as 'the futility of tenderness, the poet's incapacity to relieve the afflictions of those he loves'. Terry Eagleton, in August 1971, said that Geoffrey

Hill's *Mercian Hymns* hoard their words frugally, 'with the sparseness of a primitive economy, thus forcing each phrase to flex its potential to the full' (a good Marxist image) – but that this stringency resulted in a 'tight-lipped, poker-faced emotional anonymity which, one guesses, would weary if the book were not as brief as it is'.

Meanwhile, Al Alvarez had for some years been urging the claims of a poetry that went 'beyond the gentility principle', and Ian Hamilton gave Alvarez his support in a leader in March 1967, though the following February Denis Donoghue lightly teased Alvarez, for whom the only heroes were 'masters of risk' and 'the only respectable game' was Russian roulette.

In practice, it was mainly the American poets, and especially Robert Lowell, who benefited in Britain from Alvarez's campaigning. In fact, it was in the sixties that new American literature began seriously to receive attention from British readers, and also from the *Lit Supp*. There had been a very successful special number on 'The American Imagination' in November 1959, and in October 1960, John Gross – then a young don at Cambridge and later to become editor of the paper – was writing in a review of the new 'Writers and Critics' series of paperbacks that 'it is a sign of the times that three of the first four writers should be American'. These were not new writers – they were Ezra Pound, Henry James and Wallace Stevens – but Gross's remark had a wider application, and indeed Stevens was still not at all well known in Britain. (The fourth writer, incidentally, was Robert Graves.) As regards America, things were about to change.

In October 1960, comparing Lowell's two volumes *Poems 1938–49* (reviewed as we saw by Alan Ross in 1950) and *Life Studies* (which had just come out in Britain), G.S. Fraser said that whereas the poems in the first book reflected a rebellion against a tradition, the poems in the second book 'express, in their more easy, relaxed, ironical and sometimes humorous mode, a kind of recognition of the tradition, or at least a forgiveness of ancestors.' However, Fraser added, when the two volumes were read together, it was hard, 'for all one's admiration for a major gift, not to be reminded of the young man who kept banging his head against a brick wall because it was so pleasant when, finally, he stopped'. All this anguish was more to Alvarez's taste than to Fraser's.

A review of *For the Union Dead* which I wrote in July 1965, and which appeared under the heading 'Eastern Personal Time', was more wholehearted in its admiration. I wrote: 'The technical accomplishment of these new poems is outstanding, the revelation of personal feeling in some of them is of the utmost delicacy and candour. Loss, failure and guilt are major themes, but there are also some intensely moving poems of pity and love.'

The scholar and critic Denis Donoghue was also enthusiastic in August 1967, when he reviewed *Near the Ocean*. He acknowledged that Lowell, unlike Wallace Stevens, found no consolation for his despair in the beauty of the earth. 'Mr Lowell is not consoled. He is not assuaged by April's green. To every hint of joy there is an immediate reply, a denial.' But in the title poem, in particular, he felt a richer 'interpenetration of private and public feeling' than before, and an idiom that was 'weighty, in an Augustan sense, but not, in any sense, heavy'.

However Ian Hamilton, reviewing *Notebook* in December 1970, marked a turning point: 'Lowell's powers of language have degenerated into a ready-for-anything rhetorical machine: you name it, I'll write it up with urgent vigour.' Clive James, reviewing *The Dolphin*, *For Lizzie and Harriet*, and *History* – three volumes that had all come out together – in August 1973 was dismayed by their fragmentary quality, but felt that Lowell's talent was 'still operating, and majestic' and wished he was making more of it. As Hamilton had said in his review, 'life slips, and with it life's applause'.

Another American poet who received considerable attention at this time, with several batches of his poems printed in the paper, was John Berryman. However, if the reviewers were fascinated by Berryman, they were not entirely delighted by him. Ehrenpreis, in July 1968, said that the 'staccato fury of language and syntax' in Berryman's *Sonnets* – a sequence about a lacerating love-affair – were no more than 'a shop-window for a display of Mr Berryman's technique'. Reviewing *His Toy, His Dream, His Rest: 308 Dream Songs* in a long article in June 1969, Clive James tried to tease out the nature of their complexity, finding that there were moments which made one 'feel like kicking the book about the room', but also that at its best the *Dream Songs* was 'a voice near your ear that you listen to, turn towards, and find that you must turn again; a voice all around you, unpinnable to a specific body; your own voice, if you had lived as long and could write in so condensed a way'.

There were also kind words, up to a point, for Richard Wilbur in June 1963, when Burns Singer, reviewing *Advice to a Prophet*, said that he was an 'imposing, elegant figure . . . who would obviously be pre-pared to eat his boots on a desert trek rather than trifle with a participle or insult an adverb'; and for Theodore Roethke after his death, when Clive James, reviewing his *Collected Poems* in July 1968, said that a slim volume of his love poems, ruthlessly chosen, stood a good chance of lasting.

The American novelists also got a careful hearing in these years. Saul Bellow continued to be seen as an outstanding figure, though he was not spared a touch of irony. Thomas Hinde, reviewing *Herzog* in February 1965 said that the hero 'asks himself most of the fundamental questions which a modern American might ask', and although it was a 'big, untidy and sometimes difficult book, its untidiness is in part a measure of its quality, for it contains enough ideas and themes for a dozen lesser novels'. *Mr Sammler's Planet* was reviewed with considerable panache by Francis Hope in July 1970. He said that Bellow had 'the ability to make philosophy sing, but also the temptation to make a singsong into a philosophy'. However, if he had campus fans, 'he is prepared to shed them now. Through his aged mouthpiece, he dins in the two lessons that young American radicals neglect: that the past is a valuable heritage, and that things can go terribly wrong.' Hope summed up: 'Mr Bellow's planet has a thin atmosphere, like mountain air; but the views are magnificent, and even ennobling. Some people feel nearer to God up there, or at least to Meister Eckhart. Almost all will feel better for the climb.'

John Updike also continued to get well reviewed, though progressively less so. In September 1961, Thomas Hinde called *Rabbit Run* a 'successful and alarming novel'; in September 1963 Martin Bax, reviewing *The Centaur*, called Updike 'one of the best, if not the best, of the American prose writers at work today'. Marigold Johnson, reviewing *Couples* in November 1968, said that the scenes in 'the all-American dreamtown of Tarbox' – the basketball afternoons, the bathroom flurry, the children on the beach and the Sunday morning sermon – were much better done than in any other domestic American fiction, but that the central situation of the two lovers fell as flat as any American pancake, because 'the words of lovers are incurably ludicrous in print, the difference between one orgasm and another impossible to convey in words'. Ian Hamilton, reviewing *Rabbit Redux* in April 1972, thought it was too 'plump and comfortable'.

Mary McCarthy's most popular novel, *The Group*, which appeared in November 1963, was disliked by K.W. Gransden, who had been literary editor of the *Listener*: she had written a collection of case histories on the sex war, he said, but it was documentary rather than analysis. She had 'taken some striking and revealing photographs, and written some amusing captions' – but 'the photographs, for all their glossy finish, obstinately refuse to come to life'. Marigold Johnson was much happier with *Birds of America* in September 1971: Miss McCarthy charted the tragi-comic enlightenment in Paris of her nineteen-year-old hero, Peter Levi, 'in Voltairean mood', and the result was 'an enormously enjoyable, intelligent, civilised novel'.

Philip Roth was the new star of the decade, and when *Portnoy's Complaint* burst forth, in April 1969, Harold Beaver (one of the *Lit Supp*'s new British scholars of American literature) gave it an enthusiastic, racy review, unshocked by the spectacle of Alexander Portnoy 'enthroned on the lavatory, masturbating'. He called it 'the most zany, zestful novel Philip Roth has written . . . a *cri de coeur* from a Jewish adolescence, a casebook of the Jewish blues', with its hero who, 'while everybody else has been marrying nice Jewish girls, and having children, and buying houses, and (in his father's phrase) putting down roots, has been chasing women, and shikse women to boot!' Where Bernard Malamud, Beaver wrote, 'has explored fables of the quest for fatherhood achieved, for adult responsibility won through suffering, Philip Roth has triumphantly turned the tables. His is the anguished comedy of Jewish fatherhood evaded and perverted.' (However, an admiring review in a faraway British literary newspaper cut no ice at all with an appalled Jewish New York.)

Harold Beaver also praised Jack Kerouac's novels, in May 1962, as 'hymns to the flux and flow and endless human diversity of life', while in September 1963 Burns Singer wrote a long article on James Baldwin's novels. Singer said that 'Mr Baldwin would seem to be almost the only American Negro who has succeeded in learning the white man's language without losing some portion of his racial integrity in the process . . . Among humanity he makes no distinctions, because he is on very good terms with humanity.'

An historian won his fame in the *Lit Supp* of these years: Richard Cobb, who had acquired an extraordinary knowledge of everyday life in France, both in the present and the past, and whose fascination with the subject could be felt in practically every line he wrote. Anyone could identify his style, so he was anonymous only to readers who were oblivious to modern history; eventually he became Professor of Modern History at Oxford.

He expressed his creed, characteristically, in a review of a novel by Georges Simenon, in December 1968. In his Inspector Maigret novels, he wrote, Simenon had the eye both of a detective and an historian, 'constantly and attractively reminding one that history should be walked, seen, smelt, eavesdropped, as well as read: the historian, too, he seems to say, must go into the street, into the crowded restaurant, to the central criminal courts, to the *correctionelle,* to the market, as well as to the library'.

Cobb's distinctive approach and style (never far from a French word) were already in evidence in one of the first pieces he wrote for Crook, a review in November 1963 of the memoirs of a French peasant woman, Marie Besnard, who had been accused of poisoning eleven of her relatives. 'Famous murder trials light up the years,' he begins, drawing a wonderful picture of the scenes and events, from the village in the Basses-Alpes where 'we are never far from the death-bed, plates of cold soup, *pots de chambre*, vomit, death rattles, funeral dinners both hot and cold . . . someone dying in the big bed upstairs under the enormous red feathered quilt' to the successive trials and the 'macabre comedy in the journeyings, to and fro across France, of intestines, livers, stomach linings, gall-bladders, kidneys, bile-ducts, all finally inextricably mixed up in one another's jars . . .'

Even when engaged in controversy (which he often was, hating the 'Gothic jargon' of sociologists and the 'grimly statistical' work of some French historians), he was led off into similar evocations of French life. In August 1966, after John Sturrock had contributed an article about the anti-Semitic novelist Céline, Cobb wrote a letter calling Céline 'a master in the literature of hatred', and went on: 'Céline's style is like bad breath, it has the seedy, decayed odour of a slippered *retraite* of the rue des Plantes, the tomblike stiffness of narrow coffin-shaped rooms crowded with buffet and chairs *faux Henri III*, the hopeless ugliness of Nanterre, Arcueil and Bobigny.' Language itself was like a town, a street, a room in France to Cobb.

There was also a sharp dispute in the paper in May 1966 between an English historian who had made himself a master of statistical investigation, Lawrence Stone, and the historian J.P. Cooper, who reviewed Stone's book *The Crisis of the Aristocracy, 1558–1641.* Stone believed he had learned important facts about the degree of wealth of the upper classes and its influence on seventeenth-century British history, and saw his statistics as the 'bony skeleton of his book', but Cooper thought he had not given enough evidence of how he reached his figures for other historians to be able to check them: 'Professor Stone shuts his statistical skeleton in an opaque cupboard . . . He should not complain if others hear it rattling.'

The other historian who wrote extensively for the paper under Arthur Crook, was D.W – later, Sir Denis – Brogan. He often wrote about earlier American history; but contemporary American history, like English politics, was mostly treated at one remove, after the event, as books came out. Brogan's prevailing note was one of watchful sympathy with successive American administrations. For instance, reviewing the first volume of Eisenhower's memoirs in November 1963, he wrote:

> The assassination of President Kennedy has lent a graver interest to his predecessor's memoirs ... For quite a long time now the President of the United States has shared with the Chairman of the Soviet Council of Ministers the power of destroying the whole human race – a power that doubtless will sober even the most light-hearted and light-headed candidates for the White House or the Kremlin. And it must be noted that President Eisenhower, like President Kennedy, steadily refused to be panicked into using or even threatening to use the power that science had, possibly unfortunately, given them.

Just as the British government supported America in the Vietnam war but never engaged any of its troops in it, so the *Lit Supp* restricted itself mainly to criticism of the literature of the war. There was an excellent review by the novelist and playwright Simon Gray of Norman Mailer's *The Armies of the Night* in September 1968. Gray appreciated greatly the candid comedy of Mailer's account of the Washington Peace March in October 1967, when writers such as Mailer and Robert Lowell found they could not go as far in their protest as the Quakers who reached 'the last rite of passage' in a jail in Washington. The 'incomparably human Mailer – Mailer louche, Mailer nervous, Mailer bold and Mailer cerebral' – teaches us, said Gray, that 'for most of us the conscience is not a pure and separate instrument, but captive to our egos ... He knows that the war in Vietnam is a barbarous war, a war in which American atrocities abroad are defended by American atrocities at home, and he condemns it as best he can, with all the cutting edge of his style. But most of us are like him in that we could not go to "the last rite of passage" either.' D.A.N. Jones was much more disappointed by Mailer's novel, *Why Are We in Vietnam?*, the following April: its story of young American men, not in Vietnam but on a hunting trip in Alaska, was just 'a miscellany of moods emanating from the private parts'.

Student protest in America was approached more obliquely in a review by A.H. Hanson in February 1969 of two British books, *New*

Revolutionaries edited by Tariq Ali and the New Left publication *Student Power*, edited by Alexander Cockburn and Robin Blackburn. He found the British contributors to these books a 'pretty provincially-minded lot', compared with Eldridge Cleaver, who 'in a "Black Panther" contribution of stark brutality, boasts of his party's determination to encompass the "total destruction of America" should "total liberty for black people" be refused'. On that, Hanson's comment is: 'No one who is not himself a fanatic of comparable single-mindedness can imagine that these are the men who hold the keys to the solution of the agonisingly complicated problems of the modern world.' *A Theory of Justice*, John Rawls's majestic attempt to devise a new form of social contract that would yield a standard for judging the degree of justice in a society, was welcomed by the British sociologist, W.G. Runciman: 'it will exercise a significant and perhaps lasting influence on the central questions of political philosophy with which it deals'.

Other, colourful reviews lit up the years like Cobb's murder trials. In January 1961, Siriol Hugh-Jones, a delightful writer who died young, reviewed *Mrs Dale's Diary*, the book based on the popular radio programme about a doctor's wife. 'May Mrs Dale's kettle never boil dry,' she wrote. 'Pepys had more gusto, Boswell a wider vision and Bashkirtseff a more flamboyant sensibility, but Mrs Dale has an audience of five million. Thank heaven she had that restful Christmas.'

In November that year, Rebecca West teased the ageing Leonard Woolf when she reviewed *Growing*, the second volume of his autobiography. 'He represents himself as swimming against the tide,' she said, 'when in fact he was swimming with it.' But there was nothing wrong with that: 'we like a hero to be a rebel'.

Norman Shrapnel frequently contributed reviews of books on contemporary English life; a notable one was an amiable piece on Baden-Powell, a biography by William Hillcourt and Olave, Lady Baden-Powell. Shrapnel respected, in a somewhat amused way, the 'great movement . . . Utopia, moral gymnasium, bolthole' that the Chief Boy Scout of the World had founded, and informed his readers that Baden-Powell also had an underestimated gift – 'a powerful gift for the absurd, sometimes taking us right out of the world of Mowgli and lifting us into the healthier world of Alice'. At one international jamboree, B-P was asked what he would like as a present, and said that all he needed was a pair of braces.

> After the more serious gifts had been produced – a Rolls-Royce with trailer, a commissioned portrait in oils and a large cheque – the

The Queen Victoria Street façade of *The Times*, after Northcliffe emblazoned it with the paper's name.

The old *Times* building making way for the new in the early 1960s.

Harold Child, a member of the editorial staff of *The Times* for forty-three years, most of them on the *Lit Supp*.

Edmund Blunden, poet, scholar and member of the *Lit Supp* staff, playing cricket in a friend's garden in St John's Wood.

Anthony Powell, novelist and the fiction editor of the *Lit Supp* in Alan Pryce-Jones's time.

John Willett, Brecht scholar and deputy editor of the *TLS* in Arthur Crook's time.

Cartoon by Max Beerbohm of Lord Northcliffe with the Printing House Square 'monks' coming to his rescue, 1911. *Northcliffe: 'Help! Again I feel the demons of Sensationalism rising in me. Hold me fast! Curb me if you love me!'*

"It all started with that trial subscription to the T.L.S. Then came that Nigel Nicolson book, the smoking jacket and pipe, the pint of bitter, and, bingo, little West Tenth Street has become Bloomsbury."

The *TLS* becomes chic in the USA: cartoon by Everett Opie from the *New Yorker*, 20 May 1974.

The first front page of the *Lit Supp*, 17 January 1902.

The first signed review on the front page of the *TLS*, 7 June 1974.

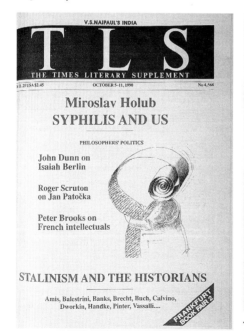

'Syphilis and Us', Treglown's controversial cover, October 1990.

The first issue of the *TLS* to be printed on the Wapping presses, 9 August 1991.

Virginia Woolf, one of the most important reviewers in the paper's history.

T. S. Eliot pictured with his mother, to whom he wrote proudly about his first contributions to the *Lit Supp*.

Charles Morgan, novelist and contributor of 'Menander's Mirror' during the Second World War.

John Sparrow, Warden of All Souls and pugnacious contributor.

Lewis Namier, historian in the opposite camp to Carr.

E. H. Carr, radical left-wing reviewer who enraged many scholars and readers.

Isaiah Berlin, political philosopher and contributor.

Two rival historians of post-war Britain: A. J. P. Taylor, on a visit to Blackpool, and Hugh Trevor-Roper.

F. R. and Queenie Leavis: often at war with the paper.

D. J. Enright, poet and provocative reviewer.

braces were duly and solemnly presented. B-P hung them round his neck like an order of chivalry. 'Now,' he told his mighty audience, 'I have everything I want in this world.' He was prepared.

Roger Fulford, a country squire and learned amateur historian, was the natural person to review the new impression of Frederic Boase's *Modern English Biography*. He picked out George Smith, the public hangman in the 1860s: 'With one hand he took life – he hanged 60 people; with the other he saved it – he was a cow-doctor', and the 12th Lord Lauderdale, who after making his living as a railway porter, celebrated his unexpected succession to the earldom by sallying forth after grouse on 12 August 1884, and was immediately struck by lightning and killed. Fulford was also complimentary about *The Young Lloyd George*, by John Grigg, who 'wins the confidence of his readers by an unrelenting pursuit of the truth' – something very necessary, since 'the impression of himself which Lloyd George fostered needs some adjustment from the facts'.

Other notable events took place throughout the sixties. On the sixtieth birthday of the paper in 1962, a great party was held in Astor's house, 18, Carlton House Terrace. When Alan Pryce-Jones had organised celebrations for the fiftieth anniversary, there were two parties, one in this house and one in the *Times* boardroom, but everybody felt they had been invited to the inferior party, so this time Crook decided that there should only be a single event. At the beginning of the party, Astor took up a position at the head of the stairs to greet the guests, with Crook beside him, and since Astor had a wooden leg and had found a comfortable stance – and perhaps because he did not particularly want to mingle with the guests – he did not move from his place for the whole of the evening. Consequently Crook could not leave his position either. He had his first drink only after the party, when he joined Willett, Cobb and Dan Davin, a New Zealand writer who worked for Oxford University Press, at a restaurant in St Martin's Lane. They were far in advance of him in this respect – and Cobb arrived home that night to find he had lost his shoes somewhere on the way.

There were also other landmarks in these years. Bruce Richmond died on 1 October 1964, aged ninety-three, and the death was announced in the paper on 8 October with a single unsigned comment, written by Arthur Crook: 'He left behind him one cardinal rule: the right man for the right job.' The paper's tribute had already been paid by T.S. Eliot on Richmond's ninetieth birthday. His wife Elena, fancied so long ago by both Virginia Woolf and her brother Thoby, died six days later, and on 29 October there appeared a couplet by 'O.L.R.', Richmond's brother Olliffe:

> *Epitaph for Bruce and Elena Richmond, October 1 and 7*
>
> *In death he knew no parting, nor could she*
> *have parted, but in peace kept company.*

Arthur Crook arranged the memorial service at the church of St Andrew's by the Wardrobe, next to the *Times* offices.

Richmond's successor, David Murray, had been unhappy in his last years, especially after his wife died after thirty-two years of marriage in 1960, and he committed suicide two years before Richmond's death, on 30 August 1962, at the age of seventy-four.

Stanley Morison, who had supplanted Murray, died on 11 October 1967. At the Requiem Mass at Westminster Cathedral the service sheet was printed, as he had wished, in a version of his own *Times* type. When the biography of Morison by Nicolas Barker appeared in September 1972, it was reviewed by his old friend and colleague, E.H. Carr, who praised his 'towering personality, with its inexhaustible intellectual fervour embracing both the broadest syntheses and the minutiae of scholarship'. But Carr also saw him as a tragic figure, saying that for Morison – as for Bernard Shaw – 'the sparkling epigram, the odd mixture of self-mockery and ostentatious self-assurance, the outrageous paradox, served as a façade for a hidden hollowness and emptiness at the core'. He quoted some words of Morison after Eric Gill's death: 'He believed in certain things – what? The fundamental basic things. The man, the woman, the child, the family, all of which he bore out. No wife, no child, no family, my golly, I mean I can see at once, without any further argument, I mean, how remote I am from the realities he faced and did.' Carr commented: 'Morison was by destiny, not by choice, a solitary.'

Arthur Crook went on steadily following the maxim he had attributed to Richmond. As throughout the history of the paper, there were innumerable books, scholarly and less so, that were still being despatched to appropriate reviewers. Arthur Calder-Marshall wrote to Crook asking him for just the occasional book to review, not too many, 'just a soft, dew-like fall'. As yet another sample of that steady coverage under successive editors, on 2 July 1964 there were reviews of books entitled *Greek Temples, Theatres and Shrines*; *Cypriot Bronzework in the Mycenean World*; *Egyptian Ornament*; and *The Authenticity of the Rhesus of Euripides*.

Scholarship was growing ever more wide-ranging and minute, and with the growth, especially, of university departments of literature, the increase in the volume of secondary works was also notable. The poet D.J. Enright drew attention to this development in a letter on 14 May 1971. He said that now he was back in England after many years teaching English literature in countries 'rather amusingly called undeveloped', he found British students of English somewhat jaded. There was so little excitement left for them in the study of literature. Students were always being directed to Casebooks, Heritages, Critical Guides, Views, Readings, Studies, with the result that they no longer discovered treasures for themselves. 'Text-books, it would seem, are the only books.'

Of course, some of the secondary works were superior to these student guides. In any event, the number of academic works calling for review in the paper was steadily growing, and the emphasis of the paper was inevitably to some degree changing too.

One department that was a triumphant success in these years was the children's books department. Kay Dowding, later Nixon, built up the twice-yearly children's books supplement into an incomparably wide and well-written survey of a genre that was at its peak in Britain in these years, with many well-known children's writers contributing anonymously. The section often ran to forty-eight pages, and was the only part of the paper that was heavily illustrated, generally with line drawings from the books reviewed. After Kay Nixon left, the supplements continued under the guidance of Charis Ryder, with the help of Anthea Fairfax-Jones, and towards the end of Crook's editorship, under Julia Eccleshare, who became in due course a successful children's publisher herself.

John Carter looked after the weekly reports on book sales and bibliographical matters that were also a remarkable feature of the paper, and which appeared on the back page until 1967. A recurring problem here, however, was that Carter also worked for Sotheby's, and, as Crook put it in a letter to him on 6 August 1965, 'I have had a good deal of private criticism about the way in which the back page is supposed to have "plugged" Sotheby's to the disadvantage of other sales houses.' Crook greatly admired Carter's work for him, though he was amused once when he told Carter that he was taking John Willett on, and Carter said, 'Is he one of us?' 'What do you mean?' asked Crook. 'Is he a scholar and a gentleman?' 'I wouldn't know because I'm neither.'

However Crook went on to say in his letter that he had not bothered Carter with these criticisms about his back page articles, 'because they have been, I'm sure, flimsy and unfounded'. He just wanted Carter not to give these critics 'large doses of ammunition'.

Carter wrote back, in his fine hand, to say that he valued Crook's candour, but that it was difficult for him because 'Sotheby's produces (in an average season) ten times as much interesting material as all the other book auctions put together'. He suggested in the time-honoured way that they should 'talk it over', and 'if you can think of an authoritative and unbiased counsellor to join us, so much the better'. But two years later Carter was still grumbling to 'My dear Arthur' that references to Sotheby's were being cut out of his articles and sometimes, he claimed, making nonsense of them. He signed himself 'Your always obedient, if sometimes fretful servant, Mr Editor.'

As the sixties went on, changes took place at *The Times*. The old Printing House Square, other adjacent *Times* buildings and even the Private House were all pulled down, and the *Lit Supp* found itself in a modern, open-plan building facing Queen Victoria Street.

Colonel J.J. Astor, by now Lord Astor of Hever, went abroad to live in the year of that sixtieth anniversary party, 1962, since the Conservative budget of that year had made his American assets subject to British death duty. Before this he had already transferred most of his shares in *The Times* to his eldest son, Gavin, who had also succeeded him as chairman in 1959.

The Times itself was not prospering, and in 1964 started to modernise and expand, though with inadequate resources. The most dramatic change while the Astors still owned it was the appearance of news instead of advertisements on the front page on 3 May 1966, along with the institution of a diary and a political cartoon.

The *Lit Supp* meanwhile, on its own scale, was still doing well, and continued to do so throughout the sixties. Its weekly circulation had gone down to just over 40,000 by the time Pryce-Jones left in 1959, but by 1963 it had reached 43,344 again. The following year the figures began to be audited by the Audit Bureau of Circulation, but no significant difference from the paper's own figures emerged. The readership swallowed a rise in price from 6d to 9d in October 1963 (the first increase since 1961), with the 1964 circulation figure coming in at 43,425, and swallowed a further increase to a shilling in November 1967, with the 1968 figure reaching 44,068. It was never to reach this height again. After a rise in price to two shillings in October 1970, it fell just below 40,000 in 1971, and after a rise, with decimalisation, to 12p (or approximately 2s 5d in the old money) in September 1972, it came in at 38,148 in 1973.

It is notable how in the sixties the proportion of overseas sales increased, accounting for almost half of the 40,000 or so total. Of these overseas sales about two-thirds were in the United States, where there had been energetic promotion of the paper ever since the very successful special number, 'The American Imagination', in November 1958. In 1961 Arthur Crook paid a four-month visit to the United States as a Kennedy Fellow, on the back of 'The American Imagination', leaving John Willett in charge. He travelled over much of the States, meeting editors, writers, academics and publishers, and managed while there to sell the reprint rights in the *Lit Supp* to date for $50,000. He went again in 1965, coming back to report, among other things, on the closeness with which the paper was read there, especially in the universities, and on the competition now coming from the *New York Review of Books*, which had been largely modelled on the *Lit Supp*.

Publishers' advertisements were at a steady level throughout these years, with the special numbers still exciting enthusiasm, though some British publishers had misgivings about American publishers coming into the paper and advertising books that they themselves were publishing here. There was also a dramatic growth in the use of the *Lit Supp*'s advertisement columns by libraries of all kinds for their 'Situations Vacant'.

Contributors' fees went up in 1961 to a basic £6 a column, with Crook, like Pryce-Jones before him, soon starting to top them up again. Like his predecessors he regularly tried to get the management to increase the fees. In one document he observed that 'To make it viable the *TLS* has for years been run on a shoestring . . . We pay John Sparrow £40 for a front-page article (4,500 words) involving a great deal of scholarly research; the *Sunday Times* pay him the same amount for a straightforward review of 600–800 words. Any worthwhile *TLS* review is based on personal friendship or acquaintance, or on a hard sell.' In his report on his second American trip he says, 'To go on persuading some of the best brains in the country to write anonymously for us at £6 a column becomes progressively harder. Dr George Steiner, for instance, an American don who has contributed a good deal to the *TLS*, points out that his brilliant piece on Lévi-Strauss took three months to prepare; that we paid him £35; that the *Herald Tribune* rate for the piece would be not less than $500; and that in that paper he would have had his signature. This is a particularly pertinent example, since this article was widely praised at Yale and Harvard as a model *TLS* front-page piece.'

In all these circumstances, there was not a great deal of pressure on the *Lit Supp* to make changes as long as the Astor reign lasted. Nevertheless there were some other innovations in the paper, besides those we have already mentioned, in the first half of the sixties.

In January 1961, an occasional series called 'Live Words' was introduced, in which the scripts of new plays were discussed, usually by John Russell Taylor. Paperback round-ups also began – we have already noticed John Gross doing one of those in October 1960, and both he and John Crow went on doing them regularly.

In December 1964 a feature called 'The Living Language' began. The idea was 'to examine and record some of the extensions of English that are now taking place, often under the influence of its Commonwealth, transatlantic and other overseas users. This is almost the opposite of the policy pursued in France, where writers, critics and academics are anxious to detect foreign neologisms and denounce any innovations that detract from their language's purity.'

Various writers were asked for their opinions on the idea and whether they would contribute. Anthony Burgess said: 'I regard this sort of thing as fundamental as well as fascinating and you can rely on me to send something in.' (He did.) I.A. Richards wrote: 'All success to it.' Anthony Powell answered: 'I think it sounds a very interesting subject, but I am always a bit doubtful, from a novelist's point of view, of examining too closely how you do it. There has to be a certain impulsiveness, like making love.' Evelyn Waugh wrote: 'I am sorry to say that I am totally out of sympathy with your project. A few new words are needed for scientific gadgets. Otherwise there is no honourable reason for departing from the diction of Arnold and Newman.'

The feature was conducted by Marghanita Laski, an indefatigable contributor of examples of word use to the *Oxford English Dictionary* (and also at this time of reviews of crime novels, of which she read one a night, to the *Lit Supp*.) In introducing the series she observed that it was impossible to predict which new words would survive and which would not. The *OED* in 1927 had excluded the word 'usherette', while at the Oxford University Press she had heard someone say of 'brainwashing': 'It'll never take.' The series became a great success, with many readers contributing, and William Empson joining in to say 'Everyone who writes can do a good deal towards the upkeep of the language.'

There was, however, an unfortunate event in 1964. Sir Alec Randall had written a review (headed 'Jairmany Calling!') of a book called *Lord Haw-Haw – and William Joyce* by J.A. Cole. In it he had written 'Joyce was sentenced to death, as was Julian Amery.' The proofreading at the *Lit Supp* was generally meticulous, but on this occasion no-one noticed the error, nor did the reviewer when he was sent his proof. It was, of course, John Amery, not his brother Julian, who was sentenced to death for treason after the war.

However, it was one of William Haley's pleasures to read the *Lit Supp* as soon as the first copies came off the press on Wednesday night, as he did on this particular Wednesday night, 11 November 1964. He noticed the error immediately, stopped the distribution of the paper, and had the whole run printed again with the reference to Amery omitted.

Randall apologised unreservedly to Crook and Crook to the management, and Crook also went to see Julian Amery personally to apologise. Amery wrote to Gavin Astor to say that though his legal advisers had told him it was a plain libel, he recognised that what was printed was a result of negligence and not malice, and that every possible attempt had been made to retrieve the mistake once it had been spotted. Accordingly he did not propose to take any further action unless the reference should be taken up by other papers with damaging consequences. Amery's wish was to avoid any kind of publicity in connection with his brother, and in the event the episode passed almost unnoticed.

At *The Times*, in spite of the changes and some rise in circulation, the financial position grew worse, and in September 1966 the Astors sold the greater part of their holding to Lord Thomson of Fleet, the Canadian-born press lord who already owned the *Sunday Times*. The two titles were put into a new company, Times Newspapers Ltd, under an editor-in-chief, Denis Hamilton, who had for the previous five years been the exceptionally successful editor of the *Sunday Times*. Haley retired as editor of *The Times*, and became the chairman of the new company, while William Rees-Mogg became the new editor of *The Times*. The *Times Literary* and the *Times Educational Supplement* were part of the deal, but from now onwards their editors were responsible not to the editor of *The Times* but to Denis Hamilton.

Thomson gave guarantees that 'the special position of *The Times* throughout the world will now be safeguarded for all time'. Nevertheless, further changes soon started appearing in *The Times*. In January

1967, the personal column, which had been moved to page 2 when advertisements came off the front page, was transferred to the back page. Pictures, which had been on the back page, were moved inside the paper. The diary, which had been on the leader page, was moved opposite, so that more space was available for leaders without unduly cramping the letters. Above all, the principle of anonymity was breached, with many correspondents henceforth allowed a personal by-line on longer articles and despatches.

This more modern approach to presentation in the main paper did now begin to put pressure on the *Lit Supp*. Crook's editorial independence was still guaranteed, but he accepted the need to make some changes. Privately he told Rayner Heppenstall, who had been a radio producer, that it was like ITV taking over the BBC, but that he had not lost his 'unfailing optimism'.

Subheadings such as 'Art' appeared again for a while at the head of the pages, though as before this produced difficulties, with headings such as 'Seascapes' sometimes having to be invented. More signed articles, usually of a newsy or scholarly nature, started appearing on the centre spread, and from October 1967, in a new feature called 'Fifty Year Rule', reviews from the past were reprinted with the reviewers' names now revealed.

Another new feature in October 1967 was called 'Commentary'. This was generally published in addition to the leader, and contained several short paragraphs reporting on literary and cultural events, usually with some approving or disapproving observation.

John Willett left the paper in January 1967 to go and live in France, though he remained a consultant on and off until 1975, and returned to the staff for a time between 1969 and 1971. Most of Crook's early recruits, including Alexander Cockburn, Nicholas Bethell, Piers Paul Read and myself, had left by now. Edmund Blunden, aged sixty-nine, had reappeared as an adviser in 1965. The two main members of Crook's editorial staff from 1967 onward were Ian Hamilton, who had joined at the end of 1965, and John Sturrock, who joined in July 1967, and who deputised when Crook was away. These two wrote the majority of the new Commentary paragraphs, and both enjoyed introducing a combative note into them, as into the leaders.

A particularly vigorous attack was made by the *Lit Supp* on the Literature Panel of the Arts Council. This began in October 1966 with a leader called 'The Panel Game' written by John Willett, and was resumed at the end of 1968 by Hamilton and Sturrock. The main criticism of the panel that the paper made concerned its awards to individual writers: the 'first aid' it handed out had not led to any better books being written, and too much money went to 'dunces, charlatans and scroungers'. Cecil Day Lewis, at that time chairman of the panel, replied to the first attack on the ITV programme *This Week*. On the occasion of the second attack Lord Goodman, the chairman of the Arts Council, wrote a characteristic letter to Arthur Crook, dated 5 December 1968:

> Dear Mr Crook
> I rarely see the *Times Literary Supplement* but from time to time have a report on its antics.
> I have been shown this week's Commentary and do want to express my great sympathy with you that, having culled all the evidence given to the Committee on Estimates, you could alas find nothing better to serve your cause than a statement from me that (i) as magazine publishing was largely in the hands of cartels and large groups, the Arts Council must encourage independent publications as much as possible; (ii) that we must encourage experiments, and (iii) that we must not discourage experiment, even if it runs counter to our notions – albeit they are moral notions.
> It is good of you to make my views on these subjects known to your readers, even though you bang away with your characteristic misrepresentations on other scores. I will honestly try to furnish something more to your taste in some future pronouncements.
> Also I hope you would not believe that I seriously suspect that the policy of the *T.L.S.* may from time to time be influenced by the fact that it is owned and published by a large group or cartel. The notion crosses my mind only very rarely.
> Kind regards
> Yours sincerely
> Goodman

But the paper did not relent.

Besides its Commentary comments, the *Lit Supp* was also rather more abrasive in its reviewing of fiction and poetry in the later sixties. We have already seen this reflected in the progressive decline in the esteem shown towards Ted Hughes, Seamus Heaney, Robert Lowell and John Updike. It was mainly due to the influence of Ian Hamilton, who had already won for himself a reputation as a severe and teasing critic on his own poetry magazine, the *Review*. Hamilton also brought on to the *Lit Supp* from the *Review* such excellent critics as Clive James and Francis Hope, who had similar standards to his, if a less cutting style. Hope was killed in an aeroplane crash in March 1974. In 1969 he had published in the paper a sad, ironical poem called 'Departure Lounge', about a journalist waiting in an airport for his flight on a foreign assignment, 'a breathing space . . . between paid and unpaid lies', the unpaid lies being the lies to his wife:

> *Must go: they've called my plane.*
> *Don't think me sad. I use*
> *Regrets like travel pills*
> *Or duty-free champagne.*
> *This time I'll take the booze.*
> *But grief would do. It kills*
> *The pain, it kills the pain.*

But the most conspicuous change in the paper after the Thomson takeover was its change of name. In the first issue of 1969, on 2 January, the paper appeared on the bookstalls with the letters 'TLS' on its masthead. The name '*The Times Literary Supplement*' was printed in smaller letters at its side.

The name *TLS* had in fact been in use for some while by the new generation of reviewers and readers. No doubt it reflected the general tendency in modern times towards brevity and succinctness in speech, not to say towards the use of acronyms. The usage must also have been encouraged by the fact that since 1963 a series of books had been appearing from Oxford University Press containing some of the best reviews of the previous year, and called *TLS*, *TLS2*, *TLS3*, etc. As for this book, we have now used the name '*Lit Supp*' in it for the last time.

The circulation of the *TLS* held up and even increased in the later sixties, and only dropped slightly after the price rises in the early seventies. According to the management's calculations, it also registered a small profit every year. Nevertheless, relations between Crook and the management slowly worsened.

A publishing director, Derek Jewell, was appointed, and was soon irritating the *TLS* staff with his constant suggestions about editorial content. Above all, doubts about whether the anonymity of reviewers should be continued were regularly expressed on the management side. On this, to him, fundamental principle of the paper's policy, Crook stood absolutely firm.

On one occasion the editor-in-chief, Denis Hamilton, showed his attachment to the *TLS* in a curious way. The suggestion had been made that the Thomson organisation might buy the *Bookseller*, and Hamilton asked Crook to take its owner, Haddon Whitaker, and its editor, Edmund Segrave, to lunch in order to sound them out. Crook had been authorised to suggest a figure of £75,000, but Whitaker was not tempted. However, the meeting left Crook with the idea 'What if the boot were on the other foot? How much is the *TLS* worth?'

He took an opportunity when going to see Hamilton to ask him if the Thomson organisation might consider selling the *TLS*. Hamilton dipped into his pocket, took out a visiting card with his name on it, and slowly wrote on it:

The *TLS* is NOT for sale.
It is beyond price or reach.
January 26 1968

At times, Crook thought Hamilton's attitude to him was 'Go on being the rebel you've always been.' But there were also contrary indications. Once, Oliver Woods, the personal assistant to Hamilton, took Crook aside and said: 'Denis Hamilton doesn't like you arguing with him all the time. When we hear you and Willett coming up the stairs to the meetings, it's like "Enter Fortinbras with trumpets blaring."'

Another awkward occasion was when Crook and Ian Parsons, the chairman of the publishers Chatto & Windus, gave a dinner in the Garrick Club for two publishers who had both been in business for fifty years, Hamish Hamilton and William Collins. There were fifty diners, and the two guest publishers were seated at opposite ends of the table, since they did not particularly like each other.

When Denis Hamilton heard about the dinner, he expressed annoyance that he had not been invited. Crook was genuinely astonished, and told the editor-in-chief that he had supposed that he was invited to far too many such occasions to want to hear of another. But Denis Hamilton had come from a relatively modest background, and in spite of his great success in journalism still took pleasure in mingling with members of what he considered the Establishment.

At any event, one day towards the end of 1973, Crook heard from an acquaintance that Jack Lambert, the literary editor of the *Sunday Times*, had been telling people that he had been asked if he would consider becoming the editor of the *TLS*. It was disagreeably reminiscent of the way in which D.L. Murray had heard that he had lost his job.

Crook spoke to Lambert, who said that he had in fact been approached by Derek Jewell, but had told Jewell that he was not interested.

Shortly afterwards, Denis Hamilton asked Crook to come and see him, and informed him that John Gross, then literary editor of the *New Statesman*, had been appointed editor. The new appointment was announced in the *TLS* of 19 November 1973, and readers were informed that the new editor would take up his position in the following April.

Crook was due to retire in 1977. He was invited to stay on at full salary until then, as an adviser with an office of his own, and accepted this, though in the event his advice was never called on. Later he regretted this arrangement, deciding that if he had accepted redundancy he would have got a much better financial deal, since he had been with *The Times* all his working life.

Crook continued to edit the paper up to the end of March 1974, and indeed one of the liveliest events in the paper's history, the Milton spoof by John Sparrow, took place in that period. John Sparrow's admission that his letter about Milton had been a hoax appeared in a new signed column, called 'Viewpoint', which had been inaugurated in 1972.

Crook wrote the Viewpoint in the last issue of his editorship. He said that it was only the second time ('discounting an entry reporting some libel proceedings best forgotten') that his name had appeared in print in the *TLS*. He gave the first entry in full – a letter from him in the *TLS* of 11 August 1945, about the replanting of rose bushes on Edward Fitzgerald's grave in 1917 from 'corresponding bushes' to those that had died there the year before. And he used it to convey some of his feelings about his departure:

> The purpose of republishing this little piece of one-upmanship? Perhaps to point out that nothing (or no-one) is irreplaceable; to emphasise that 'corresponding bushes' can quite easily reproduce themselves with something of the perfumes and flavours of the origi-nals; to echo a hope that a rose by any other name . . . ? But the analogies mustn't be pushed too far. Who cares today how fare the flowers on Fitzgerald's grave? Yet it is surely important that somebody should. Just as it is vital to remember that the *TLS*, like some other English things, was 'started as a makeshift and continued through an oversight'.

(This was at any rate the legend on the paper.)

He went on to re-tell, briefly, the history of the paper, to make his last stand for anonymity ('In the last resort any serious journal surely stands or falls on the appeal of its contents and not on the names of its contributors') and to thank that 'long line of colleagues, contributors, and correspondents most of whom became my friends', as well as 'publishers all over the world', the printers, and the paper's readers 'who never failed to spot the fault that the rest of us missed'.

What he could not say was what he said to me at the age of eighty-seven, that he had 'loved the *TLS* as people love a woman'; or that – as I say now – he gave the *TLS* more of his life than any man in its history.

Chapter Thirteen

Coming Out: 1974–81

In the summer of 1973 John Gross was approached out of the blue by Denis Hamilton. He was invited round to Hamilton's London flat and informally asked if he were interested in editing the *TLS*. Two months later the same thing happened, and a further two months elapsed without any communication before, yet again, he was invited to call on Hamilton. A week or so later he was offered the job and accepted it. The announcement of his appointment was made in November, but Anthony Howard, the editor of the *New Statesman*, wanted Gross to work out his three months' notice period as literary editor there, and it was the beginning of April before Gross arrived at the paper.

The overwhelming decision confronting him was whether or not he would continue anonymous reviewing. Hamilton raised the question from the start, but told him that the decision was up to him, and that he should not decide in a hurry. However, it was obvious that within the Thomson organisation there was strong pressure for the paper to change over to signed reviews. Derek Jewell was certainly pushing for such a change, believing it would make the paper much easier to promote and sell. Arthur Crook's opposition to the idea must have been a factor in the management's decision to replace him, for even if there was no certainty that a new editor would bring about the change, it was certainly the case that while Crook was there there was very little hope of it.

The principle of editorial freedom had become well enshrined in the British press in recent years, apart from being of long standing at *The Times*, and was one of the factors that enabled the new editor to make his own decision about anonymity. Perhaps more important was the fact that Hamilton was a cautious man, who was proud of his position in the larger world he had moved into – where, for instance, he had become a trustee of the British Museum. The *TLS* was a monument of that world, and he respected it and cared about it. He was genuinely unsure whether a change to signed reviewing would be for the better.

At the same time – and for the same reasons – he would have been listening to the arguments against anonymity that were coming much more strongly by the early seventies from the academic world. These arguments were not invariably of the highest moral character. The *TLS* was inevitably becoming more of an academic journal, and academic reputations were becoming more affected by it. An unfavourable anonymous review could not be contested so easily as a review by someone whose name and status were known. On the other hand, a signed contribution to the *TLS* could help advance a man or woman's academic career. At present that could generally be achieved only in the form of a letter to the editor.

In Richmond's years, anonymity had simply been taken for granted at *The Times*. The paper, and its *Literary Supplement*, were decidedly not regarded as assemblages of individual opinions, but as organs of a collective judgment that gave them their authority – and also imbued them with a certain mystique, gratifying to their editors and contributors, and alluring to many of their readers.

Nevertheless, the issue had rumbled around ever since the paper began. There had been a notable discussion of it in 1938, when Stephen Spender had (with a certain irony) contributed a signed article in favour of anonymity. It was called 'A Plea for More Anonymity', and it was an attack on 'the growing tendency in literary journalism today to emphasise the importance of the signature at the bottom of a review, rather than that of the paper itself as an organ of opinion.' He continued:

> The reader glances at the front page or brightly-covered cover and reads a few names he knows, followed by names he does not know, John Podge, Clement Marleybury, Young Suckle, for example. Perhaps he reproaches himself for never having heard of these stars before; perhaps with a sigh he realises he must assimilate three new stars within an already blazing firmament . . . The whole system of signed journalism rests on the modern fallacy that the expression of the writer's personality is always a good in itself. Actually it is far better for writers to arrive at certain generally accepted critical standards, and to write in a style that does not over-emphasise the critic's own personality but concentrates on the work which is being criticised . . . There is nothing degrading about a certain amount of anonymity;

in fact, it is more stimulating to live up to the standard set by an intelligent group of writers working under a brilliant editor than always to be working, in public, for oneself.

These were views that the paper naturally welcomed – though they were rather surprising views coming from such an un-anonymous writer as Spender, a man very much in the same camp in that respect as Connolly and Waugh. C.W. Brodribb wrote in the same issue an accompanying leader – naturally unsigned – in which he too applauded 'team-work and the unified point of view which effective editorship, out of pride in its organ, aims at maintaining'.

The questions that both these writers begged were, of course, whether it was possible in the twentieth century to talk of 'generally accepted critical standards' or feasible to talk of a 'unified point of view', however hard Richmond and his colleagues had tried to achieve such things.

In Alan Pryce-Jones's time, in late 1957 and 1958, there was a run of letters attacking anonymity, with F.W. Bateson, an Oxford don who had several years earlier founded the journal *Essays in Criticism*, leading the campaign. In an article about the *Times Literary Supplement* published in his own journal, he argued that 'the worth of an opinion varies with the degree of respect we have for the holder', so it was necessary to know reviewers' names. In the *Lit Supp*, in a letter to the editor, he declared that 'even with the eyes of Argus one could not detect each and every perversion of critical justice some of your army of reviewers occasionally commit', while another correspondent, B.A. Wright, simply declared that most of the paper's reviewers were unlearned, worthless, misleading and brutish. Pryce-Jones himself wrote two unsigned leaders in reply in the course of this debate. He maintained in traditional *Times* fashion that the 'disembodied voices' of the *Literary Supplement* added up to a better and more disinterested debate than an assemblage of signed reviews – and added, in his own gleefully provocative style, that 'the collector of autographs can, after all, visit our neighbours'.

A more modest but perhaps more powerful defence of anonymity than the standard *Times* view appeared in T.S. Eliot's article in honour of Bruce Richmond's ninetieth birthday in 1961. This article emphasised the quality of writing that anonymity encouraged, under a good editor. Eliot wrote:

I am firmly convinced that every young literary critic should learn to write for some periodical in which his contributions will be anonymous. Richmond did not hesitate to object or delete, and I had always to admit that he was right. I learnt to moderate my dislikes and crotchets, to write in a temperate and impartial way; I learnt that some things are permissible when they appear over one's name, which become tasteless eccentricity or unseemly violence when unsigned. The writer of the anonymous article or review must subdue himself to his editor – but the editor must be a man to whom the writer can subdue himself and preserve his self-respect. It is also necessary that the editor should read every word of what he prints; for he is much more deeply inculpated in what he prints anonymously, than in what he prints over the writer's name.

Arthur Crook firmly held to the view that anonymity produced better reviews. No doubt his belief in anonymity reflected, in part, the fact that he had been accustomed to it all his working life, and in part, too, the fact that he was a past master at dealing with it. Jokingly, he used to say that the editor of an anonymous paper had an exceptionally interesting life, since it was necessary to know everything about the love affairs, the ambitions, the friendships and rivalries of one's contributors, in order to be sure that their contributions were written with complete disinterestedness. Seriously, he accepted the responsibility that Eliot spoke of, as his predecessors had done – they had all been remarkably successful, for the most part, in keeping out of the paper the exploitation of anonymity by reviewers for personal ends.

Crook's main platform in defence of anonymity was the view he expressed in his farewell Viewpoint: 'In the last resort any serious journal stands or falls on the appeal of its contents and not on the names of its contributors.' And he was particularly proud of his skill at getting outstanding contributions from people who would not have been able to write them if they had not been anonymous. In a memo to Denis Hamilton arguing for the continuation of anonymity in the paper, he wrote:

> Signed reviews would also mean the loss of some excellent reviewers for certain kinds of books. The sort of person I have in mind is someone like Sir David Hunt, who while High Commissioner for Cyprus, wrote a remarkable review of an account of that island which he could never have written under his own name. There are other Civil Servants who would hesitate or be unable to express themselves under their own names; MPs who would hesitate openly to criticise their parties; Roman Catholics or Anglicans who would

417

feel the same about their churches; not to mention the excellent extra services we receive from the staff men of other newspapers.

Crook was also very punctilious about never revealing the names of reviewers to anybody, and there was an amusing example both of the point he was making to Hamilton, and of this scrupulousness, when Lord Chalfont wrote a review for the paper in May 1965. As Alun Chalfont, he had been defence correspondent of *The Times*, and Crook had often used him as a reviewer, but now he was a Minister of State at the Foreign Office. Crook persuaded him to write a long review on a batch of books about the Cold War, and was so careful about preserving his anonymity that even in the marked copies of the paper the word 'Anon' is written across this review. On this occasion Crook no doubt informed the head of the accounts department privately of what the fee for the article would be and who it was for. I was only able to identify the author from the stock book – the list, revised each week and kept in the editor's office, of reviews that had come in and not yet been published.

In fact, however, people often did know, in one way or another, who had written a review, and a failure of anonymity caused Crook some bother in November 1962. There was a very critical review that month of Conor Cruise O'Brien's book *To Katanga and Back*, which was an account of O'Brien's experiences in Katanga in 1961 and a criticism of the United Nations' actions there. He himself had been the representative there of the Secretary-General of the United Nations, and at the end of 1961 had resigned from the UN, after differences with them, and become Vice-Chancellor of the University of Ghana.

The author of the review was Brian Urquhart, who had had overall responsibility for the UN in Katanga in 1961–62, and was still at the UN. Getting him to write the article was, in a sense, a coup for Crook. But Urquhart described O'Brien as 'intensely egotistic' and 'patently mercurial', and strongly disputed his account of the events in Katanga, which was a short-lived state that had been formed out of part of the old Belgian Congo.

O'Brien had no difficulty in finding out who the author was. A letter from him appeared in the paper on 2 February 1963. He said that the review was written in 'vituperative vein', and continued:

> Many of your readers will have formed the opinion that this article, issued with the authority of your respected paper, represented a corroboration, from an impartial and objective source, of the United

Nations Secretariat's case against my book [in a public attack which had appeared shortly before the review].

The article in question cannot be taken to corroborate the Secretariat's case because it is written (as your reviewer did not seek to disguise from me) by a serving official of the Secretariat, who was concerned with the publication of the Secretariat's original attack on my book.

My purpose in writing this letter is not to engage in any controversy with you or your reviewer on the substantive issues involved, but simply to point out why the review in question cannot be accepted as being an impartial critical assessment.

I leave your readers to reach their own verdict on your reviewer's defence of the institution to which he belongs.

A note from Haley to Crook a few days later commented: 'I think, if this closes the matter, the *Literary Supplement* can consider themselves well out of what might have been a mess.' In fact, the exchange did nothing to interfere with the personal relationship between Crook and O'Brien, who began after this to contribute to the paper again.

John Gross did not make an immediate decision about anonymity. From his first issue, on 5 April 1974, he introduced more signed articles than there had been before, but the bulk of the paper remained anonymous. There was a large backlog of unsigned articles, especially reviews of academic works, that he did not want to discard.

He was very aware of the arguments against a change. When he was appointed, he received many letters of congratulation, most of them urging him to abandon anonymity. But some, both from his friends and from correspondents unknown to him, spoke up in its favour. Lawrence Durrell said that though anonymous reviewing was obviously often bitchy, 'for the most part it gave the feel of impersonality and cold summing up of books. One knew too that the spirit of fair play wasn't entirely dead, and that if one were writing anonymously one would lean over backwards to be impartial and fair to the work.' Nikolaus Pevsner thought that the advantages of anonymity were greater than the drawbacks. 'This will probably be reflected in more limited reviewing. I am thinking of cases where one's friends have written bad books. Anonymously one could point that out without being catty. If the review is signed the reaction will simply be to refuse to review it.'

Another argument against the signing of reviews that he heard from a number of correspondents was that it would lead to a more exclusive use of 'big names', with the 'little names' being dropped. Gross acknowledged to himself that there might be an editorial temptation in that direction, and also a reluctance to use a good, long piece as a lead if it was by someone unknown to the world. But he could also see that some of the letters asking him to keep anonymity were simply from people afraid of losing their position as reviewers on the paper if it were abandoned.

At heart, he told me, he knew that the introduction of signed reviewing was inevitable. And the main argument for it, in his view, was the one he eventually put forward in his signed leader, 'Naming names', in which he announced his decision on 7 June:

> The case against anonymity is a relatively simple one. There are many occasions on which a reader is entitled to ask on what authority a judgment or opinion is being advanced. There are even occasions when the whole import of a review depends on knowing the identity of the reviewer. Above all, critics should be prepared to be held directly responsible for what they write . . . As Kingsley Amis has put it, once you decide to name names there is always the temptation to start naming NAMES . . . The age demands superstars, intellectual acrobats, personality cults, instant-opinionators, and no age has ever demanded them quite so voraciously. But an editor can at least be aware of the pressures, and try to resist them . . . if the possible drawbacks of abandoning anonymity seem to me so many risks which have to be faced, it is primarily because I feel that the principle of accountability comes first . . . Today, at all events, we have naming of parts.

So the 'principle of accountability' was adopted. Now came the question of how Gross was to implement it. He wrote to all the existing reviewers that he was aware of, telling them of his intention, and asking them if they would agree to have their name on any further review they wrote. He did not particularly want to drop any of them, though some were overlooked. Irvin Ehrenpreis, for instance, who had been reviewing a good deal of the new poetry, received no more, and wrote an aggrieved letter. Gross had to explain that he had simply not known about him. In general, once the decision had been made to abandon anonymity, the reviewers acquiesced without a murmur.

Until almost the end of the year, however, the paper remained a curious patchwork of signed and unsigned reviews. The first signed lead review appeared on 7 June, the same day as Gross's leader 'Naming names'. It was a review by Denis Donoghue of *William Empson: The*

Man and His Work by Roma Gill, and was accompanied by a large picture of Empson. The following week, there was a signed lead by the philosopher Quentin Skinner on John Passmore's *Man's Responsibility to Nature*: Skinner asked the still-unanswered question: 'How can we apply the coercion needed to avoid pollution without imposing it in a totalitarian way?' On 21 June the lead was a signed review by John Bayley of Philip Larkin's volume of poems, *High Windows* – a review we shall return to. The new style had been established.

Meanwhile, the number of unsigned reviews each week began to diminish. The last appeared on 13 December 1974, and the honour of being the last anonymous reviewer went to a writer on gardens, Camilla Sykes, who contributed a short piece on a book in Spanish, *Jardines de España* by the Marquesa de Casa Valdes. It bore the title 'Terrain in Spain'.

When I say this was the last anonymous review, I mean the last to appear that had been commissioned as an anonymous piece under the old regime. Other anonymous pieces appeared for some special reason in later years, for instance in the 'Books in Brief' columns, but in principle, from the issue of 7 January 1975, all reviews in the *TLS* were signed with the author's name.

John Gross was thirty-nine when he became editor of the *TLS*. The son of a London doctor, he went to the City of London School and Wadham College, Oxford, and had been a Fellow of King's College, Cambridge from 1962, when he was twenty-seven, until 1965. In 1969 he had published a book, *The Rise and Fall of the Man of Letters*, that was widely enjoyed and won the Duff Cooper Memorial Prize that year. Arthur Crook had at one time given him a regular paperback column in the *TLS*. When he became the editor of the paper, he had been working as literary editor of the *New Statesman* for just a year.

The staff that he inherited consisted of John Sturrock, who became his deputy, and who kept that position throughout Gross's editorship; Martin Amis, who looked after the poetry and fiction reviewing, but left the paper at the end of 1974, the year in which his first novel, *The Rachel Papers*, won the Somerset Maugham Award; Nicolas Walter, chief subeditor, who also left towards the end of 1974; and Patrick Carnegy, a German scholar and expert on music, who had been brought in in 1969, and left in 1978, later becoming the dramaturge at the Royal Opera House. Peter Porter, the Australian poet long domiciled in England, who had been brought in by Crook, stayed as Gross's poetry adviser. An early new recruit to the staff was Mary-Kay Wilmers, who had been deputy editor of the *Listener*, and took over the fiction reviews when Amis left. Soon afterwards Adolf Wood joined the staff with responsibility for several areas of interest, including reference books and the Middle East. Oscar Turnill looked after production, sitting at a table in the middle of the main room. Victoria Glendinning, Rosemary Dinnage, John Ryle, Galen Strawson, Michael Neve, Keith Walker and Michael Trend came in at various points on varying part-time agreements, writing for the paper and all joining in the enormous weekly task of checking, subediting and rewriting.

Many years later, when Alan Pryce-Jones died, Gross observed that he had accomplished the feat of making the paper 'chic'. Gross himself was prepared, in the Stanley Morison sense, to make the paper difficult – at least to the extent of carrying long articles on complex topics where he thought it necessary – but he succeeded to a considerable extent in making it chic as well.

Gross also had a good eye for original and entertaining items appropriate to the character of the *TLS*. It was not his intention in general to serialise new books in the paper, but in October 1974, when he had been there six months, he published two pages of drawings by Osbert Lancaster from a new book called *The Destruction of the Country House*. Lancaster's drawings included memorable views of the Mansfield Park School for Girls, with feverish hockey going on where Jane Austen's Fanny had dreamed, and of Chesney Wold, in deepest Dickensian Lincolnshire, where solitude with dusky wings once sat brooding, but where now the Rural District Council's housing records were stored, and the menacing footsteps on the terrace led to pile-ups on the motorway that passed in front of it.

The following month Gross printed some of the fruits of a major spoof. The MP Humphry Berkeley had, back in 1948, when he was still an undergraduate at Cambridge, sent a long series of letters to headmasters of various public schools, signed by an 'H. Rochester Sneath', who introduced himself as the head of another, small public school. They were full of gratuitous advice about the running of the recipient's school and references to eminent friends who had spoken well of it. 'Sneath' had received increasingly baffled, and then increasingly angry, replies from most of the real-life heads. Now Berkeley had published all Sneath's letters and the replies to them in a book called *The Life and Death of Rochester Sneath*, and Gross snapped some of them up quickly for the paper.

At Christmas that year he had a feature called 'I remember, I remember', in which twenty-one writers recalled the favourite books of their childhood. Similar light-hearted surveys appeared from time to time after that, and there was one in January 1977, on the seventy-fifth anniversary of the paper, called 'Reputations revisited', for which authors were asked to nominate the most overrated and underrated books of the past seventy-five years. (The novelist Frank Tuohy wrote the following month to say 'This section was most interesting. It was an amusing idea to request comments from several writers with reputations long overdue for downward revision.')

'Reputations revisited' had one remarkable outcome. Both Lord David Cecil and Philip Larkin spoke up in it for a forgotten novelist, Barbara Pym. Larkin said that her six novels published between 1950 and 1961 gave 'an unrivalled picture of a small section of middle-class post-war England', while David Cecil said that her 'unpretentious, subtle, accomplished novels, especially *Excellent Women* and *A Glass of Blessings*, are for me the finest examples of high comedy to have appeared in England during the past seventy-five years'.

This created quite a stir in the press. It transpired that Barbara Pym – now in her sixties and living with a sister in Oxfordshire – had had the last novel she wrote turned down by Jonathan Cape and for fifteen years had written nothing more. Philip Larkin followed up his nomination of her with a long article in the *TLS* in March describing 'The world of Barbara Pym', in which he said that what stays with the reader after he has enjoyed 'the satire, the alert ear and the exact eye' is 'the underlying loneliness of life', and 'the virtue of enduring this, the absence of self-pity, the small, blameless comforts . . . not a world likely to have held its own in the Swinging Sixties'.

That autumn, Macmillan reprinted the two novels named by Lord David Cecil and published a new one by her, *Quartet in Autumn* – all of which were reviewed enthusiastically in September by a new, regular novel reviewer, Anne Duchêne, who called her 'an expert in loneliness and High Anglican comedy'. And Barbara Pym resumed her career as a novelist.

Another entertaining note was struck in the series of reviews by Alastair Forbes that now began to appear in the paper. Ever since the war, Forbes had been the friend of a remarkable number of people in the social, political and literary world. When he wrote reviews of biographies of such people – or even of autobiographies – he frequently showed a better knowledge of them than the authors themselves. Nor did he hesitate to display the wealth of his acquaintanceship. It was not every contributor who could say, when reviewing a book about

Noël Coward (as Forbes did in October 1976): 'when shortly before he became President, I was dining in a New York restaurant with Jack Kennedy, I earned his gratitude by taking him up, at his request, to introduce him to Noël, who was dining at another table'; or, when reviewing *A Part of My Life*, the autobiography of the philosopher Sir Alfred Ayer (as he did in June 1977), could remark of a woman whom Ayer had wooed expensively and in vain in 1946, that he had suffered from the same 'bolting *femme fatale*'.

He had, too, a fund of light anecdotes about his friends, such as one he recorded when reviewing (in February 1975) *The Siren Years*, the diplomatic diaries of a Canadian ambassador, Charles Ritchie, who had been the lover of Elizabeth Bowen.

Once, in Paris, when Ritchie had told Lady Diana Cooper that he felt unloved, she instituted a Ritchie Week,

> which was devoted to proving to him the contrary. 'Vive Ritchie' was chalked up by night on many a Paris wall . . . and there was a culminating ball, given in the house of Lord Hood, at which Duff Cooper made a speech in which he said 'we have been suffering from an embarras de Ritchie'. Perhaps Mr Ritchie will let us have his account of this and other jolly incidents in a subsequent volume. One can't have too much of a good fellow or good writer like Ritchie.

Not everybody, it must be admitted, liked such smart stories, or what they considered the name-dropping that went with them – although Forbes always said, and was believed by his friends when he said, that he never dropped a name he did not know. His editors always had to be on the alert for libel in his articles, or at least for a bit of mischief-making in what some might regard as bad taste. When Forbes mentioned the 'predilections' of the murdered James Pope-Hennessy in one review, his brother, Sir John Pope-Hennessy, took great exception to it. Although he was a frequent contributor of art historical reviews to the *TLS*, he wrote to the paper in November 1976 calling Forbes a 'gossip columnist about the dead' and stating his opinion that 'even in the context of the Times Sexological Supplement' what Forbes had written was 'surely the quintessence of the second-rate'. Such chances had to be taken with Forbes. Gross also had to tidy up his sprawling sentences, stuffed with parentheses, and to contend with rows and arguments with him. But he went on employing Forbes as a reviewer till the end of his editorship.

Joky – usually punning – headings also became more common in the paper, with John Sturrock responsible for some of the best of these. In Gross's very first issue there is a review of Leni Riefenstahl's photographs from the Sudan headed 'Sudan Death', and a review of a Brian Aldiss novel headed 'Aldiss and Heaven Too'. The front page of the paper was restyled later in 1974 to advertise the contents in poster style, usually with an amusing drawing, while the full contents list – longer now, as the paper increased in size – was transferred to the back page.

At the same time, inexorably, the growth in the number of academic books went on, with a corresponding growth in the number of academic reviewers in the *TLS*. The ending of anonymity made this latter development much plainer, especially when brief biographical notes called 'Among this week's contributors' were introduced.

It was not long before Geoffrey Grigson reacted to this state of affairs. In April 1975 there were several letters objecting to a proposal by Michael Foot (subsequently dropped) that there should be a 'closed shop' for writers on newspapers, and on 16 May Grigson joined in the correspondence to say that another class of persons was already driving out writers, namely dons. He pointed out that there were at least sixteen academics writing reviews in the issue of the *TLS* for 25 April, all of them salaried, and all 'pushing out writers who live by writing'. He also attacked the quality of writing by academic contributors, singling out Denis Donoghue for a review of Josephine Miles's *Poetry and Change* in which, he said, 'nearly every sentence in his five columns is blown up with stifling clichés, in pedantic balance, culminating in arcane announcements fit for an academic's Pseuds' Corner'. On 30 May Donoghue defended himself, pointing out in turn the clichés in Grigson's letter (including 'stifling clichés'); but Graham Greene wrote in the same number in support of Grigson.

Grigson's letter had in fact not been grouped in the correspondence columns with the letters about Michael Foot's proposal, but appeared under its own heading 'Grigsoniana'. Greene, addressing the editor, said that this title suggested that Grigson was an eccentric 'when he writes of your own closed shop', and added his own comment on academic criticism, saying that George Steiner, 'in an unusually lucid piece of writing on John Cowper Powys, seems to assume that "a wealth of symbolic incidents" is necessarily a desirable quality (desirable of course it is in the academic market for theses and Litt.Ds). You will find a lot of us Grigsonians as we struggle through your no longer anonymous columns.'

In fact, as his book had made plain, Gross particularly valued good writers who were not academics, or, if they were academics, had the range and style of the best 'men of letters' of the past. Questions of literary and philosophical importance were now being discussed more and more in a difficult, abstract vocabulary, especially in France and increasingly in America, and if the *TLS* was to be the serious intellectual journal he wanted it to be, they were questions that had to be addressed, and the vocabulary had to be admitted to its columns. The steady disappearance of the men of letters was particularly ironical at this point in the history of the *TLS*, in the light of the attachment to them that Gross had shown in his book.

But the preferences in his taste were emphasised in the way one name loomed up again and again in the paper at this time: Lionel Trilling. For Trilling was the American critic who had most successfully combined the discussion of tough literary and intellectual issues with a fine sensibility and a graceful, humane style.

In April 1975, John Bayley reviewed a reissue of *The Middle of the Journey*, Trilling's one novel, published in 1948 (and favourably reviewed then by Anthony Powell, as we saw), to which Trilling had now added an introductory essay. The novel was a subtle study of the Communist mentality in America, embodied here in a couple called the Crooms, whose rigidity of mind and political intolerance is shown in the end to derive from their fear of death. They resent the preoccupation a sick friend has with the subject: death, it might be said, is reactionary, an impediment to progress, and they do not want any dealings with it.

One character in the book was based on Whittaker Chambers, the ex-Communist who had denounced a government servant and former friend of his, Alger Hiss, as a Communist agent, and who was at that time hated intensely by the American Left. The portrait of Chambers had, in the end, excited more interest in the book than anything else, but Bayley praised it very highly as a novel, with its 'turmoil of ideas, guilts, intellectual anxieties and vulnerabilities encapsulated there like dust and flies in a polished block of amber', and the Crooms themselves 'beautifully realised in their sunny and strangely sinister idyll'.

Bayley of course saw the book's contemporary political force. Trilling, he said, believed that 'art could and should try to correct the aberrations which those who lived by ideals and the will to power had showed themselves capable of making', and Trilling himself remarked in his introduction that Chambers, absurd figure though in some ways he was, had come to the aid of the book with his experience of 'the reality which lay behind the luminous words of great promise' that emanated from the Communist intellectuals of the West. However, Bayley concluded that 'when the noise of time has died down completely, *The Middle of the Journey* may well be regarded not as a marginal creation of a political controversy, but as one of the most original humanist novels of its generation'.

Trilling died later that year, and on 21 November, the paper published a short poem by Robert Conquest, 'Lionel Trilling, 1905–75':

> *What weaker disciplines shall bind,*
> *What lesser doctors now protect,*
> *The sweetness of the intellect,*
> *The honey of the hive of mind?*

And Trilling continued to make his presence felt in the paper posthumously. His wife Diana, who was also a writer, was a friend of John Gross's, and in March 1976 she gave the *TLS* the text of a lecture, 'Why We Read Jane Austen', that Trilling had written but never delivered because of his illness before he died. Gross published in full this wide-ranging discussion of whether humanism could justify its belief in 'the moral instructiveness of past cultures' – a question which grew out of the discovery that a group of American students reading Jane Austen with him had no real concept of what a servant was. Trilling tentatively argued in the lecture that this humanistic belief could be justified.

Diana Trilling herself wrote a vigorous letter to the paper that December. The English writer Richard Mayne had reviewed sympathetically the book *Scoundrel Time* by the American journalist Lillian Hellman, and had asked, 'Does anyone care – did anyone in his senses ever care – whether the author of *The Children's Hour* and *Watch on the Rhine* had naive ideas about the Soviet Union?' 'Yes,' wrote Mrs Trilling, 'I cared. My husband, Lionel Trilling, cared. And most of our friends, all of them supposed to be in their senses, cared . . . And just as I and my friends cared about the death of freedom under Soviet tyranny, we cared about the freedom guaranteed by the United States Constitution when it was infringed by the House Un-American Committee and Joseph McCarthy. Freedom is indivisible: must I, at this late date, repeat this to Mr Mayne?'

When her own book of essays, *We Must March My Darlings*, came out in England in February 1978, it was reviewed by a Cambridge don, George Watson, who was slightly mocking about the Trilling couple: they were, he said, 'to put it grossly, Marxists who turned conservatives, who moved by way of Freud and D.H. Lawrence towards a love of civilised order in the Arnoldian style. In the end, the hallmark became civility. By 1950 both had come to think it the highest social good, if widely interpreted.' But he was prepared to acknowledge that 'what the West urgently needs, as Mrs Trilling rightly and momentously insists, is a responsible intelligentsia'.

A lecture on feminism by her, 'The liberated heroine', that she had given at Columbia University, took up almost five pages in the issue of 13 October 1978. She saw the sexual liberation of women, in fiction at least, as a new tyranny:

> Should there be no man immediately available, another woman must be at once provided, or some mechanical instrument of gratification – vibrators are endemic ... So arduous is the heterosexual enterprise of liberated heroines that they must have recourse to soothing baths in baking soda, so monumental is their responsiveness that it is to be measured not by the shaking of the earth but by the crash of planets. In point of chic, the multiple female orgasm has somewhat the same place in present-day liberated fiction that casserole cookery had in Mary McCarthy's *The Group*.

Trilling himself made a delightful appearance in a review of Edmund Wilson's letters in November 1977 by Joseph Epstein, editor of the *American Scholar*. Epstein noted that Wilson and the ten-years-younger Trilling had met in the men's room of the New School of Social Research in New York when Trilling was writing his book on Matthew Arnold – 'a book that no-one seemed to want at a time when everyone else was swept with radical politics' – and Wilson had encouraged him to go on with it. 'It is impossible not to picture them,' wrote Epstein, 'the past half-century's two most important critics, trough to trough.' And Robert Langbaum, reviewing the critic Alfred Kazin's book *New York Jew* in November 1979, quoted a remark by the author that perhaps echoed, in a more aggrieved way, what George Watson had observed about the Trillings. When he first met him, Kazin had bristled at Lionel Trilling's manners, feeling that he had 'never met a Jewish intellectual so conscious of social position, so full of adopted finery in his conversation'.

The prominence of the Trillings in the *TLS* illustrated the new editor's interest in American intellectual life generally – as well as the increasing use the paper was now making of American writers.

Gore Vidal contributed a long article 'The fall of the house of fiction' in February 1976. Reviewing a collection of essays, *The Theory of the Novel*, edited by John Halperin, he scorned the idea that you could say '*the* novel' – there was no such thing (and therefore equally you could not say '*the*' theory) – and dismissed the claims of two recent novels that had been much praised. He said that '*Giles Goat Boy* is a very bad prose work by Professor John Barth ... Whatever Professor Barth's gifts, humour, irony, wit are entirely lacking from his ambitious, garrulous, jocose productions', while Donald Barthelme's *The Dead Father* was 'written in a kind of numbing baby talk ... Hopefully, as Professor Halperin would say, the book will self-destruct once it has been ritually praised wherever English is taught.'

Meanwhile in October 1975, David Lodge (whose own novel, *Changing Places*, came out that year) reviewed the new novel by Saul Bellow, *Humboldt's Gift*. He did not think it was so successful as *Herzog*, which had succeeded by the 'fine madness' of the hero and the device of having him write long letters in his head. Charlie Citrine, the hero of the new book, was, like Herzog, 'a spiritual questioner tragi-comically burdened with public and private worries', but this time he had been overindulged by his creator, and the alternation between his 'densely allusive metaphysical speculations' and the 'racy, low-mimetic narrative' was not so satisfying. (Gore Vidal had, incidentally, quoted the description of Bellow by Leslie Fiedler, in one of the essays in the book he reviewed, as 'a present-day practitioner of the Art Novel of yesteryear' along with Updike, Moravia and Robbe-Grillet. 'This is an odd grouping,' said Vidal, 'but one sees what he means.')

Russell Davies was no more satisfied with Philip Roth's first Nathan Zuckerman novel, *My Life as a Man*, when he reviewed it in November 1974. He felt that the savage humour of the novel left one feeling that one was being 'browbeaten into laughing more derisively than one would like'. Alison Lurie's *The War Between the Tates* was one of the last novels to be reviewed anonymously, in June 1974. The reviewer was Rosemary Dinnage, soon to join the staff, who called the book 'very cool, funny and didactic', though she thought that insofar as the war was between males and females the description of it was biased: the nice men were impotent and the potent men were nasty or stupid. Alison Lurie wrote to John Gross later saying she thought the review was 'kind and intelligent ... I should love to thank your anonymous reviewer too if I knew who they were ... it is certainly nothing anyone should blush to acknowledge.'

Lisa Alther's *Kinflicks* had been one of the few new novels mentioned favourably in Diana Trilling's article – she said that the vibrator in this novel 'precipitates one of the few truly funny scenes of liberated fiction' – but Germaine Greer, the very voice of the liberated female at this time, was much less respectful when she wrote about it in a special women's issue in August 1976. Greer said that this 'picaresque novel of a *femme moyenne sensuelle*' was neither the voice of liberated woman nor the voice of female wit, and 'to clear the fogged brain of the flicker of *Kinflicks*, 500 words of Dorothy Parker will suffice'.

In September 1975, *Hearing Secret Harmonies*, the final volume of Anthony Powell's *A Dance to the Music of Time*, was published in the UK, and John Bayley, six months after his Trilling piece, wrote another long review (illustrated with Mark Boxer's drawings of Widmerpool), surveying the sequence as a whole, and finding intense enjoyment in it. He thought that what was remarkable in Powell was that he could be as wholly accurate and illuminating about real life as Tolstoy or Stendhal, and yet as wholly and superbly fanciful as P.G. Wodehouse. He had the gift of 'disembarrassing us from the natural defences we need to carry on our non-fictional existence. We should run a mile from a real Alfred Tolland, Bob Duport or Mrs Maclintick: in the pages of the novel we cannot have too much of their company.' He concluded: 'The author as God can only create his own universe, and we can be grateful that Anthony Powell has done so.'

Later in the seventies, Powell published two volumes of memoirs. John Russell, best known as an art critic, reviewed the first of them, *Infants of the Spring*, in October 1976. He enjoyed it greatly but said that it had stiff competition from Powell himself. This autobiography of his early life could not, by its nature, compare with the 'fullness, resonance and wealth of cross-reference to Powell's personal mythology' with which Eton and Oxford were portrayed in the first volume of the novel: 'The music of time is on the players' desks, but the players themselves may not come in today.' Alan Bell, later the librarian of the London Library, reviewed the second, *Messengers of Day*, in April 1978. He discouraged readers from trying too hard to identify the originals of Anthony Powell's characters: 'mere spot-Dancing limits appreciation of the autobiography'.

The other leading novelist of Powell's generation, Graham Greene, brought out his spy novel *The Human Factor* in March 1978, when T.J. Binyon (a don and crime writer who often reviewed the crime novels for the paper) compared it unfavourably, on the whole, with the spy stories of another writer: 'With this novel, Graham Greene has ventured into territory previously explored by John le Carré. If the map he has brought back is sharper in its outlines, surer in its delineation of major features, than those of le Carré, it lacks their detailed topography, their shading and their relief . . . it is thinner, drier, almost skeletally schematic.'

The Murdoch-Amis-Spark generation were now taking on the lineaments of respected middle age. The reviewers, always looking for a stick to beat authors with, at least lightly, had already started to compare them with their earlier selves. However, in April 1975, Stephen Wall, who was a don at Keble College, Oxford, was impressed by the portrait in Iris Murdoch's *A Word Child* of Hilary Barde, a bitter man who had retreated into a routine which was 'a prolonged parody of order and lucidity', taking endless rides on the London Underground, and who now had to 'reconcile himself to contingency' and start seeing other people as real. In this novel, Wall thought, she 'comes as near as she has yet done in reconciling what she feels to be the demands of art with what she also senses as the beautiful recalcitrance of ordinary life'. Michael Irwin, reviewing *The Sea, The Sea* (which won the Booker Prize) in August 1978, had more reservations about her. Her novels were 'marvellously entertaining' but, as here, she attempted too much in them, with her 'clutter of Buddhas and quotations from *The Tempest* and so on'. It was as though she 'had tried to achieve power by wiring hundreds of torch batteries together'.

In May 1974, Russell Davies found a 'grisly forthrightness' in Kingsley Amis's novel about old men, *Ending Up*. The brutal relish with which, he wrote, Amis 'deprives the seniors of their citizenship . . . is indicative not only of his characteristic determination to look life squarely in all the organs and orifices which may pack up first, but also of the fear that results when he does so.' But four years later, in September 1978, Karl Miller found in *Jake's Thing* – the story of a man whose libido has failed – 'all the virtuosity of Amis at his comic best'. Amis appeared to have come through that crisis. As for Muriel Spark, her novel *The Abbess of Crewe* did not find favour when it was reviewed by Gabriele Annan, Noël Annan's wife, in November 1974: this story of upper-class nuns was 'too silly'.

V.S. Naipaul's novel *Guerrillas* was reviewed in September 1975 by D.A.N. Jones, who had so much liked *The Mimic Men*. The new novel was about a Caribbean writer, James Ahmed, who is a supporter of Black Power, and who has been sponsored by white people in Britain, but who becomes involved in a murder back in Trinidad. Ahmed seemed to be based on a West Indian writer, Michael X, who was in fact hanged for murder.

Jones had once been asked to help Michael X write his autobiography, but had turned the offer down because he thought his writing was 'bloodthirsty gibberish'. But he applauded Naipaul's attempt here to understand Ahmed's motives. He felt the book had Naipaul's customary incisiveness, and explored people's feelings about race, sex and power 'in a spirit that is by no means condemnatory, but is not vaguely all-forgiving, either'. He was particularly pleased by this because he thought Naipaul had sometimes written provocatively about racial questions.

Margaret Drabble's novel *The Ice People* was seen by Michael Irwin in September 1977 as a bold attempt to diagnose the current ills of England, with its cast of a dozen people of different background in the mid-seventies, but he thought it was less poised, less fastidious than usual. Margaret Drabble's sister, A.S. (Antonia) Byatt, brought out a substantial novel, *The Virgin in the Garden*, in November 1979, and was destined to become as successful as her sister, in later years of famous rivalry. However, Irwin, who reviewed this novel too, thought the prose was stodgy and that the author was committed to her ideas rather than to the imaginative life of her story.

A new woman novelist, Beryl Bainbridge – a Liverpudlian and a former actress – had been having a considerable triumph, and was a prolific writer in the seventies. In September 1973, Marigold Johnson (still anonymous, of course) had reviewed her first big success, *The Dressmaker*, and said that it 'adumbrated in one grim little tale the cataclysm that war created in working-class society'. Nellie, the dressmaker who lives in a poky little Liverpool terrace house with her bewildered adolescent niece Rita, was 'a frightening, perhaps pathological character' to whom the author gave 'Zolaesque tragic status'.

In November 1974, Susannah Clapp, who along with Karl Miller and Mary-Kay Wilmers had just left the *Listener*, reviewed the new Beryl Bainbridge, *The Bottle Factory Outing*, about two women sharing a bedsit in London. She said that the portrayal of the women's 'sardonic, Siamese-twin existence' was a triumph, though 'the outrageousness of the black comedy, the flirtation with spookiness and the bizarre make this a less controlled novel than *The Dressmaker*'. In October 1976, Francis Wyndham wrote that in *A Quiet Life*, Beryl Bainbridge had 'eliminated the teasing element of Grand Guignol which hovered round her earlier novels' and had achieved an effect of complete credibility in its story of a family living in a small house near Southport. The theme of the book was 'the intolerable tension of family life, the mutual rape of sensibility recurring from hour to hour'; the period was immediately after the Second World War – 'an era in which Beryl Bainbridge, with her infallible memory for the subtlest of its minutiae, seems to find her purest and most potent inspiration'.

However Michael Irwin, reviewing *Injury Time* in September 1977, complained that 'in the longer run there is only a bleak and limited interest to be derived from watching pathetic people endure indignities', suggesting she should attempt a more expansive project. The following year Beryl Bainbridge seemed to rise to this challenge with *Young Adolf*, in which she imagined that Hitler stayed in Liverpool as a young man. The American novelist Diane Johnson reviewed this novel very enthusi-astically, in a long article, saying that 'we believe this account of Hitler, because of its manner, detailed and confident, and because it does not insist too stridently in foreshadowing the later reality'. But the author did make the suggestion, 'no doubt not entirely mischievously', that the real horror might have had its origin in the England of 1912, when Hitler watched the poor people in a Liverpool street stand passively as the authorities came to take away from their parents some children who were living in squalor. 'Let the minority act with enough authority,' one character tells him bitterly, 'and the majority will walk like lambs to the slaughter.' 'It is a lesson,' Diane Johnson commented, 'young Adolf will remember.' She thought the book was Beryl Bainbridge's 'most ambitious treatment yet of the serious concern and conviction that underlie her comedy'.

Two other novelists making a reputation were David Lodge and A.N. Wilson. David Lodge, a university teacher who was an expert on the new critical theory, but in no way a slave of it (as his reviews have shown), quickly established himself as a very funny writer, but like Beryl Bainbridge with an underlying seriousness. His novel *Changing Places* was partly about the *TLS* itself: two lecturers in literature, one English, one American, have swapped jobs at their respective universi-ties, and the American, Zapp, has found evidence suggesting that the Englishman is responsible for a villainous anonymous review of his work. Comic difficulties ensue. D.A.N. Jones's comment on the book's moral (in his review in February 1975) was that the different kind of liberalism of each man 'is exactly what is needed in the alien territory'.

Ferdinand Mount, who was at this time political correspondent of the *Spectator*, was also now occasionally reviewing novels for the *TLS*, and in May 1977 had warm words for A.N. Wilson's first novel, *The Sweets of Pimlico*, about a Cambridge girl who is picked up by an elderly foreign gentleman. The plot, he wrote, was not just a neat device for keeping the reader's attention but 'the real motive force of the enterprise'; the author's cool manner at first seemed excessively plain, 'then you begin to scent hidden ironies, unwelcome surprises'. His only complaint was that Wilson seemed to have picked up from Iris Murdoch, to whom the book was dedicated, the habit of 'assuming that any old sexual hang-up, however casually described, will convince the reader provided that it is freaky enough'.

Finally, among the novelists of the seventies, three stood out as being in the front line of the new fiction: Martin Amis, Ian McEwan and Salman Rushdie. When Martin Amis's *Dead Babies* was published in October 1975, Michael Mason found a comparison between him and his father:

> Both Amises do a special line in describing the heroic degree of suffering and temporary mutilation that human beings are prepared to inflict on their own organisms in pursuit of pleasure. In Martin Amis's new novel there are passages about what certain characters endure before, during and after sex and drugs that recall Jim Dixon's crapulence and the high drama of Roger Micheldene's nostrils.

But whereas Kingsley Amis used drinks and snuff-taking simply to create wonderful comedy, Martin Amis 'represents our contemporary practices with drugs and sex as sad and horrific'. A new young critic, Blake Morrison, wrote in rather similar vein in April 1978 about Martin's next novel, *Success*. It displayed 'an old-fashioned Swiftian disgust of human anatomy . . . he skirts the genres of romance and soft porn, but derives much pleasure from debunking them, from speaking of what in those genres must always go unspoken (ugliness, dirt, age, excreta, self-disgust).' The novel was 'a presentation of city life in its sadness'.

Ian McEwan's first book, a collection of short stories called *First Love, Last Rites*, was welcomed by Gabriele Annan in May 1975. There was a feeling of impending evil in them; the atmosphere was tangibly real, and 'the behaviour of the characters springs naturally from what they are, while what they are emerges from their behaviour'. But she thought he was heavy-handed with his symbolism.

Caroline Blackwood, a writer herself who was also the last wife of Robert Lowell, reviewed McEwan's next story collection, *In Between the Sheets*, in January 1978. She thought he was an original writer, with (like Martin Amis) an obsessive horror of the human body, but unlike Gabriele Annan she found that 'his determination to shock can make his dialogue absurdly tortured and the stories too contrived'. He was

434

in favour again in September 1979 with Blake Morrison, who reviewed his novel *The Cement Garden*, about four children left alone to fend for themselves, and called him one of the best young writers in Britain today. However, Morrison's praise seemed somewhat ambiguous when he said that in this novel 'the morally extraordinary [is] made ordinary by the indifference or perfunctoriness of the telling'.

As for Salman Rushdie's first novel, *Grimus*, in February 1975, about Flapping Eagle, a renegade Red Indian who is given the blessing or curse of immortality, David Wilson called it 'a convoluted fable about the enduring need for myth and its constricting effect on the individual'. It was an ambitious, and strikingly confident first novel, but 'is this dryly entertaining intellectual conceit any more than an elaborate statement of the obvious decked out in the mannerisms of Oxford philosophy?'

Two popular novelists were noticed approvingly. P.D. James, who at this time was reviewing thrillers under the general heading 'Criminal Proceedings', and who was herself to become an extremely successful crime writer, welcomed the arrival in September 1975, in Colin Dexter's *Last Bus to Woodstock*, of a new Oxford detective destined to achieve world fame on television, Inspector Morse. Morse, she said, was 'inordinately unpredictable, irascible and introvert', but 'no doubt he will grow on us'. She was right.

The writer E.S. Turner reviewed Jeffrey Archer's *Not A Penny More, Not A Penny Less* in September 1976, noting that he had written the book to retrieve the million dollars he had lost in a Canadian business collapse, and calling its story of four men cheated out of a million dollars who resolve to steal the money back 'a bright idea'. It was written with a 'curious racy innocence', but there was too much name-dropping of a kind thought to lend authenticity. 'The firms of Krug and Bernard Weatherill will be delighted.'

James Joyce's *Ulysses* made a curious appearance in April 1976, when S.S. Prawer, Professor of German at Oxford, wrote about a German translation of it by Hans Wollschlager. He complained about 'the introduction of analities where the English text gave no warrant for them', such as the translation of 'on my own-i-o' as *auf meinem Popoooniooo*. Prawer, who regularly reviewed German books for the *TLS*, produced his copy so swiftly and reliably after he was sent the book that he was known on the paper as Steam Ship Prawer.

A Russian controversy hit the paper when Gross published, in October 1974, a translation of an article by Alexander Solzhenitsyn about the authorship of *Quiet Flows the Don*, which it was always supposed was written by Mikhail Sholokhov, winner of the Nobel Prize for Literature in 1965. Solzhenitsyn lent credence to the idea that in fact it was by Fyodor Dmitriyevich Kryukov, a novelist who died in 1920 leaving a box of manuscripts, and whose name it had been forbidden to mention in Russia for fifty years because in the Civil War he had been secretary of the Cossack Assembly. Nothing was resolved but argument raged for a while.

Solzhenitsyn's own work was steadily praised in the paper, and brought in some new Russian scholars as reviewers. In April 1976, Michael Scammell applauded his 'frontal assault on Lenin's myth' in *Lenin in Zurich*; in May 1978, Kyril FitzLyon reviewed *Kolyma*, and mused on why the Soviet government 'squandered its human resources' in the Arctic death camps the book described; in September 1978, Geoffrey Hosking, reviewing the third part of *The Gulag Archipelago*, which told the story of the rebellions in the camps, said 'this will be the most valuable part of the entire work' and 'testifies to the resilience of the human spirit'. In the same issue as Hosking's review, E.H. Carr appraised Norman E. Saul's *Sailors in Revolt: The Russian Baltic Fleet in 1917*, calling it 'an immense muddle'.

There was also a long, brilliant article by Max Hayward in May 1976 on two books that had been published in Russian in London by the dissident writer Andrey Sinyavsky, under his pseudonym 'Abram Tertz'. He had been sent to a forced labour camp in 1966 for the stories he had published abroad under that name, but while there he had managed to write a book on Pushkin and begin one, now finished, on Gogol.

Hayward, reviewing these books, contributed a fascinating passage on the Pushkin book:

> Sinyavsky's essay goes far to explain the uncanny power that poets have exercised not only over the minds of the Russian nation, but also over the minds of even its most oppressive rulers. It was Pushkin who first created the aura of authority which surrounds them – Stalin hesitated to kill Mandelshtam, and shrank from touching Pasternak and Akhmatova. It was thanks to Pushkin that the Word, embodied in poetry, became almost sacrosanct, evoking a feeling akin to religious awe . . . For this reason, in the Soviet period one or two poets were able to survive as the repositories of alternative values.

The apogee of British poetry in these years was Philip Larkin's collection *High Windows*. John Bayley, again, was called on to review it, in June

1974. The review, as we saw, was the third of Gross's new signed front-page articles. Bayley gave a very subtle and penetrating account of the poems, characterising their qualities in his own inimitable way. The intimacy Larkin offered, he wrote, was that of the lounge-bar, never that of the psychiatric couch, and 'Larkin is careful never to let us know what happens between our odd meetings in that lounge-bar . . . Wordsworth or Robert Lowell we have with us always, as one of the family; and very boring their company can be.'

Larkin, he concluded, 'updates the fundamental aesthetic' that Spenser, Keats and Matthew Arnold all took for granted,

> that the business of poetry is to delight and console, to calm and to satisfy, above all to entrance into completeness the inadequacy and the 'disagreeables' of living. It is to the interest of many writers now to assume the opposite: that what is boring or squalid – or, worse, merely grossly familiar – should be faithfully enlarged and underlined in any art that is honestly and fearlessly 'with it'. They do so because they are incapable of achieving that paradox of transmutation which this poetry displays, on a scale as spacious and felicitous as that of its many English predecessors.

The *TLS* also published Larkin's last major poem. John Gross told me that perhaps the most thrilling moment of his editorship was when he opened a letter one morning and found that it contained the poem 'Aubade':

> *I work all day, and get half-drunk at night.*
> *Waking at four to soundless dark, I stare.*
> *In time the curtain-edges will grow light.*
> *Till then I see what's really always there:*
> *Unresting death, a whole day nearer now,*
> *Making all thought impossible but how*
> *And where and when I shall myself die.*
> *Arid interrogation . . .*

It was published in the paper on 23 December 1977. Larkin wrote in characteristic style to Barbara Pym: 'The *TLS* is going to print my in-a-funk-about-death poem in their Christmas number. The death-throes of a talent.' After that, Larkin wrote only a few slight *vers d'occasion* before his death in 1985.

Many other English poets were reviewed, and published, in the paper, but few were admired as much as Larkin was. The eighteenth-century scholar, Claude Rawson, reviewing Keith Sagar's *The Art of Ted Hughes* in March 1976, said that his claim that Hughes was a major poet of the first rank was 'a sign of the incurable provinciality of the English literary scene today', while the following July, a new poetry critic, Oliver Lyne, reviewing *Gaudete*, Hughes's long narrative poem about a clergyman who makes love to all the women in the parish and is killed by outraged husbands, found it perplexing, though he liked the manner in which it went 'with cinema's way of suggestive particularising' from one picture to another. Lyne got more enjoyment out of D.J. Enright's collection, *Sad Ires*, in January 1976 – it was 'subtle, controlled and textured' – while in August 1978, Blake Morrison, in a review of Enright's kindly, ironic version of the events that took place in Eden, *Paradise Illustrated*, observed approvingly that 'in poetry as in politics the role he has most relished is that of the sharp-tongued, unfettered liberal, deflating current pieties and often brushing up against authority in the process'.

Anthony Thwaite, writing in August 1975, called Seamus Heaney's *North* 'by far his best book'. He quoted the 'unusually intelligent blurb', which said 'Heaney has found a myth which allows him to articulate a vision of Ireland – its people, history and landscape', and commented that the new poems 'have all the sensuousness of Mr Heaney's early work, but refined and cut back to the bone. They are solid, beautifully wrought, expansively resonant. They recognise tragedy and violence without despairingly allowing them to flog human utterance into fragments.'

Thwaite also compared Heaney's poems with Geoffrey Hill's *Mercian Hymns* – 'both works allow the play of cold imposed order on native earthy resilience, and also see custom invaded by anarchy'. Christopher Ricks, who was now Professor of English at Cambridge, made a powerful case for Hill's poetry in a lecture published in the paper in June 1978, 'Geoffrey Hill and "The Tongue's Atrocities"' (which won the George Orwell Memorial Prize in 1979). Ricks called him 'the best of those English poets who entered into adult consciousness in the post-war world' (Hill was born in 1932), and argued he had written 'the deepest and truest poems on the Holocaust . . . poems on this atrocity which are honourable, fierce and grave'.

Here Ricks was in full admiring vein, as he was also when he reviewed *The Composition of 'Four Quartets'* by the Oxford professor Helen Gardner, calling it 'simply and subtly the most inaugurative work of Eliot studies that we have – or are ever likely to have, since the only substantial manuscripts still unpublished are of work rejected by this most boldly discriminating of poets'. Helen Gardner's book was a study of the 'Four Quartets' manuscripts, and Ricks observed that while the 'Waste Land' manuscript 'included and ministered to melodrama' through the thrill of its loss and discovery, and through the suspense of watching Ezra Pound 'question the diseased parts' when Eliot was writing it, the 'Four Quartets' manuscript offered an 'intense transparency' through which to see 'the work of a poet at the height and depth of his powers'.

Ricks quite frequently appeared in the paper in scourging vein, too – as in August 1977, when he said of J.A. Cuddon's *Dictionary of Literary Terms*, in which he had found many errors: 'It is likely enough that three-quarters of the things said even in this book are true. But which quarters are they?'

One other significant volume of English poetry was a posthumous selection of C. Day Lewis's poems made by his publisher and colleague at Chatto & Windus, Ian Parsons. The *TLS* review, in February 1977, took the form of a more or less explicit apology for the devastating review of Day Lewis's poems that Geoffrey Grigson had written in 1970. Sam Hynes, the American, was brought in to redress the balance. He said in his first paragraph that he thought the reviewer's assault (his anonymity was naturally preserved) had been in 'crude and vicious' terms, and had not been so much a review as a literary mugging. He made a case for Day Lewis as a 'private, lyric poet' – clearly in 'the Hardy tradition', which went back to Wordsworth and John Clare, but with his own individual mark.

New American poetry was now getting much greater notice in the *TLS* than it ever had before. This was especially noticeable in the summer of 1977. The American poet Anthony Hecht wrote about other American poets a number of times, and the note sounding in the paper on every side was upbeat. Of 'Geography III' by Elizabeth Bishop, who would die two years later aged sixty-eight, Hecht wrote in August of that year, that

> hers was a poetry of isolation and loneliness, without either the stoicism and desolation of Hardy, or the wistfulness and self-mockery of Philip Larkin. Instead there is an infinitely touching valour, a gallantry that is the more impressive because it is maintained in full knowledge of the odds against it, and with a breathtaking cheerfulness

... Hers is about the finest product our country can offer the world; we have little by other artists that can match it and it beats our cars and films and soft drinks hollow.

In May Hecht had praised Richard Wilbur's *The Mind-Reader*. Wilbur, he wrote, had 'a superb ear for stately measure, cadences of a slow processional grandeur, and rich ceremonial orchestration'. He also had 'an unfeigned gusto, a naturally happy and grateful response to the physical beauty of life, of women, of works of art, landscapes, weather . . .' And earlier that month George P. Elliot had written admiringly of Hecht's own poems in *Millions of Strange Shadows*. 'What matters to Hecht,' he said, is 'the passionate need to praise and, in the old high sense, to communicate . . . In effect he says, "Not all the glory has been lost beyond recovery to ruin and museums. Much of it is still alive in the world, some of it in the English language itself. Let me show you." And he shows us.'

Two exiled Russians also elicited praise. In August 1979, Henry Gifford, Professor of Russian at Bristol University, surveyed the Russian poems of Josef Brodsky, and challenged the Americans by suggesting that 'it could be that the best poetry from America in recent years is the work of this Russian'.

In January 1977, Gifford had been more cautious about Nabokov's heavily annotated translation of Pushkin's *Eugene Onegin*. Nabokov was 'a master of English, but a capricious one; he rides it hard, and sometimes the language groans under him.' But as a feat of scholarship Gifford thought it was 'stupendous'. Robert Lowell wrote a letter to the editor about this translation later in the month: 'The impression it makes on me,' he said, 'is of fascinating eccentricity. I think Nabokov has perhaps done the opposite of what he intended. A remarkable original English (American?) poem flickers and glows behind his weird pre-Wordsworthian words – an unsought reward for his breathless research to be accurate.' Nabokov could make what he might of that.

In 1977 the first volume of P.N. Furbank's magnificent biography of E.M. Forster was published, and reviewed in July by Samuel Hynes, the second in March 1978 by Noël Annan, who (like Furbank) had known Forster well in Cambridge. Hynes dwelt on the extraordinary fact that although for the first thirty years of his life Forster had a very dreary existence – 'the suburbs, the aunts, the Italian *pensiones*, and the half-hearted young man who lived his life among them . . . an existence empty of the things that one would ordinarily consider matter for art' – nevertheless 'this was the period of Forster's greatest productivity' as a novelist. Annan dwelt on Forster's eventual discovery of love with an Egyptian tram conductor in Alexandria and then with a young policeman in London, Bob Buckingham, to whom he remained faithful for the rest of his life; and on his slow rise to a 'curious eminence' among a circle of liberal-minded friends and admirers, mostly outside the fashionable literary world.

Hynes had previously articulated in the *TLS* his reservations about Forster's tendency to sentimentality and his 'self-denigrating irony', whereas Annan felt quite abashed by the contemplation of Forster's 'lifetime of moral self-cultivation', as Furbank put it. But both had unstinting praise for Furbank's book: Hynes speaking of the 'frankness, sympathy and unfailing tact' with which it was written, Annan calling him a 'masterly biographer . . . As with invisible mending, you cannot detect a stitch in the narrative . . . He has told the truth without reservation, but without vulgarity, affectation, archness, facetiousness and those other lice which crawl over the pages of less serene biographers. Is he just and does Forster stand before us as he was? Indeed he does.'

Annan ended with a fine display of his admiration and affection for Forster – in which a certain unease about this man who went his own unfashionable way can still be detected. Obloquy, he said, would overtake Forster in the age that had followed him:

> The presumption of an artist whose desires rose no higher than a cuddle with a policeman will be duly punished . . . His morality, which was once thought to be subtle, will be portrayed as the unction of a narrow and vanished middle class; and the persistent intrusion of his whimsicality and of his voice addressing us, and as often as not dressing us down, will be contrasted unfavourably with the detachment of Jane Austen. Amid much self-congratulation (especially at Oxford) the critics will issue an expulsion order to deport him from the island.
>
> But it will never be served. The news will get about that he has emigrated. He will be found pottering about on the slopes of Olympus.

Annan's wife, Gabriele, was full of praise in April 1977 for Christopher Isherwood's memoir of his life and homosexual adventures in the thirties, *Christopher and His Kind*, in spite of the fact that 'he covers ground that he and others have covered before, and that no doubt will be covered until there is not a blade of grass left on it, when the PhD herd have moved on from the overgrazed 1920s'. She thought Isherwood was the funniest living English writer since the death of Evelyn Waugh – 'funny-dry, that is, not funny-fantastic'.

In July 1978, Mary Lutyens, the daughter of the architect Sir Edwin Lutyens, reviewed a reprint of *Prisons and Prisoners: Experiences of a Suffragette*, by her maternal aunt Lady Constance Lytton. She provided some vivid reminiscences of 'Aunt Con', after she had had a stroke:

> I remember her tall, thin, drooping figure dressed in a purple velvet housecoat (purple was the dominant suffragette colour) with a lace collar, her suffragette medals always pinned to her chest, her right arm hanging useless, dragging her right leg round the house while she made heavenly Japanese flower arrangements. I thought her very beautiful; she had violet eyes and abundant black hair, now with a good deal of white in it. With her gentle voice and manner and chuckling laugh, I have never known anyone more entirely feminine. Her other activities, apart from writing, were peeling white grapes for her white Pekinese and polishing all the coins that came her way until they shone with their original brightness . . .

And in October 1975 Lord Lambton reviewed Lord Hailsham's *The Door Wherein I Went*, taking a rather sceptical view of the thoughts of this other Conservative peer: 'His beliefs are set out in a series of chapters which might not bring him first-class honours at a university today. God and Christ and the Holy Ghost are put in the witness box, are fed convenient questions, are aided by convenient witnesses, and leave the court triumphant.'

Unfortunately, Lambton was outraged by some rewriting that was done the following year to a review by him of Lord David Cecil's *Library Looking Glass*, and after that would not write for the *TLS* any more. Lambton said that from reading the published review carefully, he had concluded that it had been rewritten by a young Frenchman, German or Dutchman who bred horses and liked telling dirty fishing stories. Gross replied that it was he himself who had edited the piece, and he congratulated Lambton – genially rather than sarcastically – on 'placing' him with such 'uncanny accuracy'. But Lord Lambton did not relent.

Among the historians, Christopher Hill, Master of Balliol, found himself the object of a superficially friendly but in fact very severe attack in

October 1975, when he published his volume of essays, *Change and Continuity in Seventeenth-Century England*. An American historian, J.H. Hexter, praised Hill's 'monumental' productivity and erudition, 'truly Pelion piled upon Ossa'. In this book Hill supported, broadly speaking, the arguments of Max Weber's *The Protestant Ethic and the Spirit of Capitalism* and R.H. Tawney's *Religion and the Rise of Capitalism* on a 'venerable and lively topic', the relation between Calvinism and economic progress. Freed from the restraints of the Roman Catholic Church and left to their individual consciences – the argument ran – the Calvinist merchants were able to find sanction in the accepted practices of the market-place for the 'unremitting pursuit of gain': 'By a happy concatenation [Hexter wrote] such merchants and industrialists, sure in their faith, enjoyed the extraordinary providence of getting richer and richer with God on their side – or so they believed. Or at least so Dr Hill believes they believed.'

Hexter went on to demonstrate, or so he believed, that Hill only managed to support this contention by an extremely selective use of the mass of evidence he had assembled. He said that, as an historian, Hill was a 'lumper', as opposed to the other type of historian, the 'splitter'. The splitters like to point out divergences and draw distinctions, and shrink away from systems and general rules. They 'rather like accident and untidiness in the past'. Whereas 'the lumping historian wants to put the past in boxes, all of it, and not too many damn boxes at that, and then to tie all the boxes together in one nice shapely bundle'. Hegel, Marx, Spengler and Toynbee were lumpers, and Christopher Hill was a lumper too.

Hill, in his long letter of reply, said that Hexter's splitters 'are so busy making qualifications that they forget that anything actually happened', whereas he continued to believe in 'tackling big questions and advancing theses' – just as he thought other influential historians of the seventeenth-century, such as Tawney, Lawrence Stone and Hugh Trevor-Roper, had done. As for his own argument, he could not accept that he had in any way distorted the evidence, and submitted his case, as historians must, to the judgment of other workers in the field.

Among the other correspondents on the subject was Richard Cobb, also of Balliol, who wrote a loyal letter of support for his colleague. He acknowledged that he, in Hexter's terms, had to be regarded as a splitter, but he objected to Hexter's remark that Hill used his sources in 'the service of lumping, in such a way as to ensure that mere people will never get in the way'. Cobb said that Hill wrote with elegance, humour and sympathy about, among many other subjects, 'mere people' – and all that he knew about Oliver Cromwell, he knew thanks to Dr Hill.

Another subject of debate was the nature of family life in earlier centuries. Lawrence Stone had now carried his statistical investigations into classes other than the English aristocracy, and had formed an opinion of the kind of family relationships that were found among them. He did not believe that there was very much personal affection between husbands and wives, or between parents and children, any-where in early modern Europe, and when he reviewed Edward Shorter's *The Making of the Modern Family* in May 1976 he congratulated the author on his documentation of the harshness of family life among the French peasantry in the late eighteenth and early nineteenth century. He contrasted it with 'the false romantic glow' about the past that suffused, he said, Peter Laslett's book *The World We Have Lost*, with its picture of 'the circles of loved, familiar faces'. But he deplored Shorter's lyrical tone – the tone of the new 'counter-culture' in America – when he described the 'erotic revolution' of those same years in France. What Shorter hailed as the advent of sexual liberation was just the onset of an epoch of massive female sexual exploitation.

The Oxford historian Keith Thomas reviewed books on the subject by both Peter Laslett and Lawrence Stone in October the following year. He found flaws in the work of both men. In Laslett's *Family Life and Illicit Love in Earlier Generations*, based on the work of the Cam-bridge Group for the History of Population and Social Structure, he thought there was now too heavy a dependence on statistics, by contrast with the 'more obviously seductive' *The World We Have Lost*. In the new book, 'Mr Laslett analyses the outcome of millions of acts of copulation, but scarcely ever refers to any actual people, save for a Devonshire family of congenital bastard-bearers, appropriately named Hoare, and one solitary bastard – Nimrod Laslett.'

Stone's book was *The Family, Sex and Marriage in England, 1500–1800*. Stone acknowledged a growth in affection and intimacy among families in the eighteenth century, but Thomas thought he was wrong not to concede any 'common humanity' to men and women of the Tudor and the early Stuart period. However he admitted that the history of the emotions was difficult territory.

Richard Cobb went on writing beautifully about France. In May 1977 he contributed a piece about René Clair's films, and their truthful evocation of the mood of Paris before, from about 1934, the atmosphere darkened:

Clair is *the* poet of the Paris night: a bluish sensuous night of dark velvet, carrying a whiff of powder and the promise of adventure . . . a period when the night was still democratic and *à la portée de tout le monde*: areas of impenetrable black, picked out by the yellowish headlights of the black and red G7 taxis, contrasting with the brilliant milky-white lights of a café: curtainless windows, dimly lit, silhouetting a woman undressing, and adding a further shade of yellow. A café in which *le père la Tulipe* and *Jojo la Terreur* might encounter, at the Bar, a *noceur*, in white tie, a runaway accountant, or a lovesick *monsieur décoré,* not a flight of fantasy, but an accurate representation of a limitless sociability that did exist, especially between midnight and four in the morning, in the 1930s, and that even partially revived in the 1940s.

Cobb also introduced a personal note into a review he wrote in July 1977 of Simon Schama's *Patriots and Liberators: Revolution in the Netherlands 1780–1813*: 'When I was a child my parents used to say that the Dutch were the only foreigners who were in any way at all acceptable: "They were the most like us", meaning the middle-class, Protestant English. After reading this outstanding book, I cannot help hoping that we are the most like *them.*'

Schama, who was to become a renowned popular historian with his books on the French Revolution and Rembrandt, had already been a contributor to a Dutch number of the *TLS* on 28 November 1975, when he had written a three-page survey of recent Dutch work on history. He had picked out especially 'one of the masterpieces of post-war historical writing in Europe', A.M. van der Woude's *Het Noorderkwartier*, a study of the land north of Amsterdam and Haarlem – in the seventeenth century, 'a luminous, serene world where meadows are interlaced with canals and ditches, houses still have little moats in front of their gardens, blocks of peat are piled up alongside the edge of fields', but where the balanced economy of dairying, marine services and small manufacturing collapsed into dereliction, with 'even the gloomy redundancy of those industrious bakers who had specialised in the production of ship's biscuits'. Gross still looks back on that article by Schama as one of the best he published.

In November 1978 there was a dramatic hiatus in the life of the *TLS*. The paper closed down for a year.

Gross had had a difficult time with the production side of the paper ever since he arrived. First there had been the move of the whole *Times* organisation, soon after his arrival, from Printing House Square to a new building – called New Printing House Square – in Gray's Inn Road, next door to the *Sunday Times*. The old Printing House Square was sold to the *Observer*, and the transaction was meant to improve *The Times*'s deteriorating financial situation, but it was not wisely handled and made the situation worse. Gross found it difficult to get management agreement to his taking on new staff, except on a part-time basis, and because the trades unions controlled the employment of secretarial staff he could not even choose his own secretary. One secretary, on the day she arrived, threw away the notice board where Gross pinned up souvenirs and *aide-mémoires* behind his desk.

Above all, the seven print-related unions exercised – as John Grigg, the historian of *The Times*, has put it – a virtual *imperium in imperio* in the printing of the papers. They displayed no particular hostility to the *TLS*, but their restrictive practices and, effectively, their blackmail of the management caused the paper continual problems. For instance, Gross found it very difficult to get proofs of articles and reviews much in advance of their use in the paper, and this made it difficult to send proofs to contributors, especially in America, and get them back in time. The use of the transatlantic telephone was still uncommon – it was still both unfamiliar and expensive.

For the first five years of Gross's editorship – until the stoppage – the circulation of the paper remained around the figure that he had inherited, that is to say between 38,000 and 39,000. In a series of six small price rises between 1974 and 1978 it had gone up from 12p to 28p, but the readership weathered this.

In 1977 the *TLS* lost two issues because of industrial action by the printers spilling over from *The Times* – the issues of 16 and 23 September – but the crisis for *The Times* and its supplements came in November 1978.

This was the 'winter of discontent', when the Labour government under James Callaghan was also battling with the trades unions, and Mrs Thatcher was promising to break their power if she were elected, as she was in May 1979. *The Times* had lost three and a half million copies in 1977 through unofficial strikes, and militancy was still growing in the unions. *The Times* newspapers were also overmanned. In April 1978, the Thomson Organisation formulated a set of proposals for a new disputes procedure, the introduction of new technology and a general wage restructuring. It also indicated that if it could not reach agreement with the unions on these matters, it would close the papers down on 30 November 1978.

The union leaders continued to resist – many of them knew they would have no future if the proposed changes went through – and unofficial action went on, with even bigger losses of *The Times* than in the previous year. On 30 November, the publication of the papers was suspended. The last issue of the *TLS* before the stoppage was on 1 December – it had been printed before the deadline. It gave no notice that the paper would not be appearing the following week – and many anxious letters arrived from America in December.

No-one knew how long this state of affairs would last. Some books were sent out; some reviews came in; a log was kept of important books in every field. The staff came into the office on a rota. In the upshot, like the journalists on *The Times*, they had twelve months on full pay without much work to do. John Sturrock went off for part of the time to America. Blake Morrison, who joined the paper to look after the poetry and the fiction reviewing only a month before the shutdown, had a year to write his book on The Movement.

From June 1979 onwards the *Times* management and union representatives had been in negotiation, and on 11 November – 'a suitably symbolic date' says Grigg – an agreement was reached which gave the printers and associated employees a significant pay rise in return for an unenforceable undertaking on such matters as manning and reliability.

The *TLS* was by now prepared for starting again. It returned on 23 November, and Gross wrote an unsigned editorial, in which he announced that there would be about forty articles surveying the most significant books that had come out between the closedown and, roughly speaking, September. Books that had appeared since then would generally be reviewed individually, in the normal way.

The first survey articles, which appeared in this issue, consisted of three on different aspects of British history, and one on Latin America. Others continued well into the New Year. There was a new style for the contents list on page two, with the reviewers' names down the left in small capitals followed by details of the book or books they were reviewing, and there were some new features, including a quiz with a prize of £10 in which readers were invited to identify three quotations. Gross announced that there would now be a regular, signed 'Viewpoint' article, while 'Commentary' would occupy more pages and contain more reviews of the arts. ISBN numbers of books would also be given.

'But,' wrote Gross, 'the essential character of the paper will remain unchanged: books, and book reviews, must always be the first and much the largest concern of a Literary Supplement.'

The first two years of the 1980s, which were the last two years of Gross's editorship, saw the issue of French structuralism come more to the forefront in Britain, and also saw the publication of some striking new novels.

In the seventies, the paper had wrestled manfully with all the 'new' thinkers, all of whom were concerned in different ways with the nature and power of language. In the commercially-inspired Frankfurt number of 4 October 1974, the 'Critical Theory' of the Marxist-inspired Frankfurt School was examined sympathetically by Jeremy Shapiro of the California Institute of Arts. The three main figures – Theodor Adorno, Max Horkheimer and, most recently, Jürgen Habermas – had all attempted to produce sophisticated Marxist critiques of culture that took into account the changing nature of capitalism. In their eyes, the language of the prevailing culture was often a subtle weapon of repression. In September 1976, John Searle wrote a long, questioning article about the influential American linguistic theorist, Noam Chomsky, and his belief in a 'Universal Grammar' that was an innate feature of the human mind. Searle was attracted by the idea, but not persuaded it was true.

However, it was the new French thinkers who continued to command most attention, especially Jacques Derrida and Jacques Lacan, though Lacan was not treated very sympathetically. In 'Commentary' on 28 July 1978, Eric Homberger, a lecturer in American literature, gave an amusing account of the Sociology of Literature Conference earlier that month at Essex University. He presented it as a battle between the followers of Lukács the old Marxist, most of them male, and the Lacanians, decidedly female, many of them from Yale and Columbia, and now firmly in the ascendant.

Homberger said that the Lacanian papers were no doubt only fully comprehended by others similarly skilled in the mysteries. In the current French style, authors were out of fashion, being just more or less unconscious vehicles for language, and it was texts that were in: the Lacanians tried, precisely, to produce 'a psychobiography not of an author, but of a *text*'. However, wrote Homberger, to do this was

> to venture into territory where no association is too far-fetched, no
> metaphor too fanciful . . . The Lacanian literary performance invites

448

a critical fantasia upon certain themes or associations which may well be central to a 'text'. But as long as the 'text' is treated in this way, as the autonomous 'given', within which one searches for a 'dispersed subject', the old-fashioned left will wonder what all this has to do with the class struggle.

The following month, a conservative English philosopher now becoming increasingly more prominent, Roger Scruton, made a much fiercer attack on Lacan and the private language or 'metalanguage' of the new criticism, in which – rather as Homberger had described – any association could be presented as though it contributed to the textual analysis, and nobody was in a position to judge if that claim were meaningful or true.

A letter from Sollace Mitchell of Brasenose College replying to Scruton on 22 September offered, perhaps, a clearer distinction between the English and the French views of language than any of the longer articles. For the English, he said, 'language is a formal system controlled and used by the individual', whereas for the current French thinkers, it was 'a vehicle of cultural and sexual order that formulates and dominates the subject'.

In the English view, human beings were in charge; in the French view, human beings had to find out what was in charge of them – and that was, the power of the language they were born into, a power of which they were often quite unconscious. This view, of course, owed a great deal to both Marxist and Freudian ideas about human beings' unawareness of their own situation.

The whole matter erupted in Britain in January 1981, when an assistant lecturer in English at Cambridge called Colin MacCabe failed to get an upgrading, and it was believed by some of his colleagues that this was because of his Marxist and structuralist sympathies. The row that followed got into the press, and in February the *TLS* took the opportunity to ask a number of literature teachers what they thought about 'Modern Literary Theory: Its Place In Teaching'.

Denis Donoghue, Henry James Professor of Letters at New York, said 'it was easier in Leavis's day' (Leavis had died in 1978). Leavis believed that the central activity of an English department should be literary criticism, and that philosophy, history and sociology were only vital when they contributed to that. That was something it was now harder to believe. George Steiner, who had become Professor of English and Comparative Literature at Geneva, naturally wanted the new European thinkers to be taught in the curriculum at Cambridge, and scorned the 'planned parochialism' of much of the English teaching there. Malcolm Bowie, Professor of French at Queen Mary College, London, came out firmly in support of teaching the new ideas:

> When the brilliant generation of French theorists now loosely known as 'the structuralists' began to emerge, British academics in the relevant fields froze, read nothing and said nothing. As Lévi-Strauss, Lacan, Barthes, Althusser and Foucault became increasingly difficult to ignore, and as it became clear that they were not nine-days mandarins but the initiators of powerful and versatile research techniques, silence was followed by much vociferous complaint and even, here and there, timorous attempts at flirtation.

Bowie thought that the time had now come for proper consideration of the way in which writers such as Foucault and Lacan continually asked themselves, 'On what authority do I do as I do?' – a question which he thought all scholars and critics should ask themselves.

Malcolm Bradbury, Professor of American Studies at the University of East Anglia, said that in fact structuralism had been widely taught for fifteen years, and had been in 'constant and profitable struggle with the tradition of British moral empiricism', which was 'still as evident as ever in the insistent realism of our reviewers and readers, and the unspeculative nature of many of our writers'.

Roger Scruton, who was a Reader in Philosophy at Birkbeck College, London, stood up for the 'central' Cambridge tradition of Coleridge, Arnold, Richards and Leavis, with their concern for human values, as against the 'ether of uninteresting abstractions' in which the French critics dwelt. John Bayley, Warton Professor of English at Oxford, characteristically saw all the claims for literature that theoretical critics made – Leavis and Trilling, as much as the French – as just so many 'magical principles', and said that the important thing was that everybody should read for themselves. Gifted teachers who could help to give their students eyes and ears flourished best under a dispensation which did not take 'English' too seriously: 'a highly theoretical or ideological environment occludes them,' he said, using a favourite word of his.

During this period there also occurred a number of disputes among or about actual novelists. Novels – and novel reviews – were becoming more difficult pieces of writing as the French influence, *pace* Malcolm Bradbury, began to bite.

1980 saw drama at the Booker Prize. It was well known before the night of the prize-giving dinner that two novelists out of the six on the short list were in serious contention for the award: William Golding and Anthony Burgess.

One of the books reviewed in the first issue of the *TLS* after the stoppage was Golding's novel, *Darkness Visible*. Frank Tuohy welcomed this first book by him for eight years – a study of evil, the story of a child mutilated in the Blitz – and said that it displayed 'in episode after episode an intensity of vision without parallel in contemporary writing'.

In October 1980 Golding published another novel, *Rites of Passage*, which was set on a British ship sailing to Australia during the Napoleonic wars, with two sharply contrasting main characters, a swashbuckling young man of good family in the eighteenth-century mode, and a poor parson of early nineteenth-century sensibilities, who learn important lessons from each other after various sexual escapades. T.J. Binyon called it 'a class novel and *Bildungsroman* combined', and said that if readers compared it with the rest of Golding's work, they would feel 'amazement at the variety and range it demonstrates' – although he found its 'elaborate system of correspondences and parallels' puzzling. This book was soon being considered very seriously by the Booker judges.

The week after the review of *Rites of Passage* appeared, Jeremy Treglown (who had recently joined the paper, and would succeed Gross as editor) reviewed Anthony Burgess's 'enormous and enormously impressive new novel', *Earthly Powers*, the life story of a writer who seemed to be based partly on James Joyce, partly on Somerset Maugham. Its main theme was 'the great tragic theme, the difficulty not just of averting evil, but of recognising it' and this was worked out through a number of 'appalling surprises, including one particularly audacious fictional coup'. Treglown felt he had to tell the story to make his points, but like a newsreader giving a football result before the replay of the match on television, at one point he warned the reader 'not to read the next paragraph if you don't want to know what happens'. Treglown was moved to declare that Burgess was one of the most ambitiously creative writers working in English, and it appeared that some of the Booker jury were thinking the same.

On the night of the Booker dinner, the jury were still arguing over these two candidates until the guests were due to go in. Golding was there, but Burgess had apparently said that he would not come if he did not win. The outcome: he never came. At any rate he had had that *TLS* review.

The suspense over the Booker Prize in 1980 made it more widely talked about, and the following year the prize received much more attention in the media than it had had previously. 1981 was the year in which Salman Rushdie published his novel *Midnight's Children*. This was long before the Iranian *fatwa* called on Muslims to kill him for his alleged blasphemy (following the publication of his novel *The Satanic Verses* in 1988); but *Midnight's Children* still caused great excitement.

It was the most ambitious example the British had yet had in their own language of the 'magic realism' they had met in Latin-American novelists such as Borges and García Márquez. The Oxford don Valentine Cunningham gave it a long review in May 1981, and said that 'what makes it so vertiginously exciting a reading experience is the way it takes in not just the whole apple cart of India and the problem of being a novel about India but also, and this with the unflagging zest of a *Tristram Shandy*, the business of being a novel at all'. Saleem the narrator, chutney-maker-in-chief at the Braganza pickle works, born on the midnight stroke that gave India her independence, pickles the history of his times in his own blend of fact, fiction and fantasy, and (with a nod to the French thinkers) in his 'play of signifiers, of textualities'. 'He becomes India herself,' said Cunningham – and it was 'a remarkably dextrous performance'.

Midnight's Children won the Booker Prize that year. It was also the year in which the judges started writing more freely in the press about their meetings. Hermione Lee, who was one of the judges, did this in the *TLS* at the end of October. She said that the judges had read seventy-three novels and discussed all of them, and she urged that, 'as Britain's only major literary award', the Booker should be taken seriously. She wrote appreciatively of Rushdie's 'twentieth-century Indian epic': it was not a piece of writing in 'the formal, controlled literary tradition in which the writer disappears behind masks', it was 'a huge, verbose, arm-tugging narrative, bursting with the presence of the writer at play'. But she did not reveal which book she had voted for.

She also mentioned another novel on the short-list, Ian McEwan's second novel *The Comfort of Strangers*, about a young English couple on holiday in Venice, and called it 'spare, cool and alarming'. This novel was reviewed in the *TLS* by Lorna Sage in October in the course of a long, sympathetic article about McEwan's work as a whole. She described how in this book the young couple's rediscovery of each other in the 'decaying labyrinth' of Venice opens up for them 'an ancient chamber of horrors' of sexual cruelty, but saw the book as going further than the 'polymorphous fantasies' of his earlier short stories. It attempted to place private fantasies in a context of public issues – in this case some of the problems of sexual politics – and she hoped his fans would not want him to climb back into the pram.

There were first novels in these years by two writers who would quickly win fame, Julian Barnes and Anita Brookner. However, the novelist Paul Bailey expressed disappointment in Barnes's *Metroland*. Writing in March 1980, he said that after reading Barnes's television reviews in the *New Statesman*, he was looking forward to the book, but this account of a young man growing up 'traipses over well-worn territory, the territory of a thousand apprentice works'. Anita Brookner, writing about a similar subject in *A Start in Life*, did better with her reviewer, Anne Duchêne, in May 1981: 'her story deals very directly and tenderly with a narrow but more or less universal seam of experience, that period in which one is disengaging from one's parents . . . her writing is healthy and elegant'.

Alice Thomas Ellis – who was Beryl Bainbridge's friend, and (under her real name, Anna Haycraft) also her publisher at Duckworth – had already published several novels, but her 1980 novel, *The Birds of the Air*, was particularly well received. Jennifer Uglow, reviewing it in August, said that, 'beneath its elegant and often very funny surface', this story of Home Counties life was 'almost overburdened by urgent blasts against modern society . . . One is confronted by the forces of death, love, hatred and sex in the suggestive context of Christmas, a feast at once pagan, Christian and capitalist.' Readers who just wanted a story would find a mixture richer than they bargained for.

V.S. Naipaul and Graham Greene both had new novels. Naipaul's novel *A Bend in the River* was reviewed by John Ryle on 30 November 1979, the second issue after the return of the paper: it was a study of a deracinated man, a Muslim African trader on the River Zaire, and Ryle said this old theme had 'never before been explored, even by Naipaul, with such sombre passion'. T.J. Binyon, writing the following March, called Greene's *Doctor Fischer of Geneva*, a tale about a mysterious, millionaire manufacturer of toothpaste, 'a sharp, glittering, wryly comic novella: not a word wasted, not a false step made'.

The American novel that made most impact in the *TLS* at the start of the eighties was Norman Mailer's *The Executioner's Song*, which was reviewed at length by David Lodge in January 1980. He greatly admired this 'true-life story told as a novel' (in Mailer's words) about the seventies murderer Gary Gilmore who insisted on being executed because he thought the sentence was just. Lodge said that at a time when 'the classic realistic novel has been so assiduously deconstructed and to an extent discredited by contemporary criticism . . . *The Executioner's Song* demonstrates the undiminished power of empirical narrative to move, instruct and delight, to provoke pity and fear, and to extend our human understanding.' This recommendation was all the more telling, coming as it did from a novelist who had also written at length about French structuralism.

For a special crime fiction number in June 1981, Gross managed to get both Kingsley Amis and Philip Larkin to contribute articles. Amis praised the books of John Dickson Carr, the master of 'that classic rarity, the tale of detection in which detection is seen to take place, and crimes of majestic and multifarious impossibility are shown at last to have been possible after all'. Larkin looked back fondly to Ian Fleming's James Bond novels, where 'England is always right, foreigners are always wrong', and 'life's virtues are courage and loyalty, and its good things a traditional aristocracy of powerful cars, vintage wines, exclusive clubs, the old *Times*, the old five-pound note, the old Player's packet'. He regretted that Ian Fleming's hero, James Bond, had now been handed over by his publishers to John Gardner, whose new Bond novel, *Licence Renewed*, 'despite his sincere and conscientious efforts, just will not come to life'.

The start of the decade saw little improvement in Ted Hughes's reception in the paper. In January 1980, the poet Peter Scupham reviewed Hughes's *Moortown*, in which the title sequence was a record of his farming experiences in Devon. He found a tenderness in it, but a tenderness 'overmatched by a kind of verbal assault and battery which deafens and can deaden the reader's response', while the poems were written in a 'solid, lolloping free verse', full of awkward run-ons and arbitrary line-lengths. Seamus Heaney came off better. The American critic Harold Bloom, writing in February 1980, said that in his new book, *Field Work*, Heaney's eye was 'as clear, through discipline, as the air bubble in an icicle'. Bloom was glad that Heaney had not become simply a poet of the Northern Ireland Troubles, as he was earlier on the verge of doing, but had gone south, where he could 'set free his imprisoned thoughts' and become an even finer Irish poet. Yeats must be Heaney's precedent, and in the grandeur of the poem 'Kinship' in this volume, Bloom believed he had already acquired 'the authentic authority of becoming the voice of his people'.

As for 'mere people', there were plenty of them in the paper. Virginia Woolf, it seemed, could not stay out of its pages. The sixth volume of her letters was reviewed in October 1980 by the American literary scholar Phyllis Grosskurth, who launched a fierce attack on Leonard Woolf. She found no 'note of real tenderness' either in the suicide notes Virginia left for him, nor in his own account of his relationship with Virginia. She believed that Leonard regarded his wife's suicide as inevitable and had made no serious effort to prevent it – indeed, she claimed, his treatment might have hastened her death. This brought forth a storm of protest from John Lehmann, Quentin Bell and George ('Dadie') Rylands. John Lehmann said that one of the central concerns of Leonard's life was the wellbeing of Virginia. Rylands called Phyllis Grosskurth's ideas 'pestilential rubbish', though 'doubtless wishful thinking will deafen her to anything that Quentin Bell or an Ancient such as myself can say'. However, she did not change her opinion.

There were three voices from Oxford. In October 1980, Isaiah Berlin published in the *TLS* his now famous recollections of his meetings in Russia in 1945 with Boris Pasternak and Anna Akhmatova. He saw Pasternak in his dacha in the writers' village of Peredelkino: Pasternak's voice was 'something between a humming and a drone . . . each vowel was elongated as if in some plaintive aria in an opera by Tchaikovsky, but with far more concentrated force and tension', and he told Berlin about the novel he was writing, which would be 'new, luminous, elegant, well-proportioned, classically pure and simple – what Winckelmann wanted, yes, and Goethe'. This was of course *Dr Zhivago*.

Berlin met Anna Akhmatova in her room in Leningrad – a meeting bizarrely interrupted by the voice of Randolph Churchill, who was in Russia as a journalist, screaming Berlin's name in the courtyard down below – and they talked far into the night. 'The account of the unrelieved tragedy of her life,' wrote Berlin, 'went beyond anything which anyone had ever described to me in spoken words.' This article was the text of a lecture in memory of Maurice Bowra that Berlin had given in Oxford, and was also published in longer form, on the day before it appeared in the *TLS*, in his book *Personal Impressions*.

Another lecture, published in July 1980, ended with an amusing story about the lecturer himself, Hugh Trevor-Roper. It was called 'History and Imagination', and was given on the occasion of his vacating his chair as Regius Professor of Modern History at Oxford to become Master of Peterhouse, Cambridge. The previous year he had become a life peer, taking the title Lord Dacre of Glanton. He said that twenty-six years earlier he had displeased Evelyn Waugh, who had subsequently written: 'One honourable course is open to Mr Trevor-Roper. He should change his name and seek a livelihood at Cambridge.' 'I am sorry that Mr Waugh is not alive,' said Trevor-Roper, 'to savour this little victory, which I would willingly concede to one who cared so much for "our rich and delicate language", the necessary vehicle and sole preservative, for us, both of history and imagination.'

In February 1980, Norman Stone – who a few years later would become Professor of Modern History at Oxford – took the opportunity, in reviewing a book by David Nicholls called *From Dessalines to Duvalier*, of drawing a vivid picture of 'Papa Doc' Duvalier, the ruthless dictator of Haiti, and of the day of his death:

> On the morning of his death, there was an eerie calm in the town; somehow even the dogs did not bark, or the cocks crow as they always, cacophonously, do. The first days of 1848 must have been something like that: there was a palpable 'Grande Peur'. On the radio, they played their classical record – Mozart's A minor quartet, K464, which had a crack in it, and played the same phrase again and again. No-one noticed this. We knew then that the old boy had finally gone, for classical music was never played except in times of national emergency, such as a hurricane, or an invasion-scare. Then, for hour after hour, the radio churned out recordings of those terrible Duvalier speeches, bloodthirstily meandering through all the clichés of twentieth-century tyranny: 'des anarchistes', 'le pep-leu', 'la politique que preconize Mon gouvernemon', 'contre les mersses democratiques' and so on. Everyone was amazed when the succession passed smoothly (with American manipulation) to Duvalier's teenage son . . .

This was another of the pieces which Gross considered to be among the best he published, particularly since it was on such an unusual subject for Stone.

The enlarged 'Commentary' section, now in the hands of Jeremy Treglown, published some robust articles on the arts. In February 1980, the journalist and author Richard West reviewed the film of Graham Greene's spy novel *The Human Factor*. He said that the story in the film was close to that in the book, but the detail was very inauthentic: for instance, when the British traitor arrives in Moscow he is given a little flat with cracked walls, whereas the real traitors were all given comfortable apartments, and his wife, supposedly South African, was not a Bantu or a Zulu as she should have been, but an Ethiopian. In March, John Bayley saw *Othello*, with Paul Scofield, at the Olivier

Theatre, and found its show of sympathy for all the characters quite destructive of Shakespeare's play. Scofield spoke in 'boneless, beautifully modulated cadences', and 'we are supposed to feel sorry for him, as we are today for all murderers, honourable or otherwise', while 'Iago could not be led hence to torture and execution – no, no, the prison psychiatrist will want to keep him under observation'. It was 'a production whose modern spirit this play cannot afford to bear'.

In January 1981, Hermione Lee wrote good-humouredly about the BBC TV version of Malcolm Bradbury's novel *The History Man*, but gave her readers a little help: 'People who mix up David Lodge's and Malcolm Bradbury's campus novels have to be reminded that *Changing Places* is the affectionate one that makes you laugh and *The History Man* is the unforgiving one that makes you wince.' In October that year, Norman Stone, back on his own territory, went to West Berlin to see an exhibition called 'Prussia: Striking A Balance', just by the Berlin Wall, which was the West Germans' reply to the East Germans' restoration of a statue of Frederick the Great in their half of Berlin. He found very little good art in it. There were portraits, but they ranged only from weaselly, frigid sixteenth-century faces to the grim, flinty countenances of the Prussian Enlightenment, reminiscent of the rows of worthies in the assembly hall in the Edinburgh Academy. However, the exhibition had been mounted with Prussian modesty and charm:

> As you enter it and look up, your eye is first caught by a horse's rump, suspended from a balloon. It is the nether end of a plastic replica of an equestrian statue of Kaiser Wilhelm I. The old party rather blearily waves a sword, but in his lifetime he was chiefly memorable for a meanness that could almost stand an exhibition of its own: he would solemnly mark his decanter, after he had had his glass of wine. This plastic Pegasus canters around above an assemblage of nineteenth-century industrial artefacts, in the middle of which there is a very large Krupps gun . . .

In February 1981 Anthony Burgess – a composer as well as a novelist, who had just been devising a musical version of James Joyce's *Ulysses* for his centenary the following year – reviewed a gigantic publishing venture: *The New Grove Dictionary of Music and Musicians*, comprising twenty volumes and 22 million words. Burgess found in it 'a brilliantly informed comprehensiveness mostly touched by the tentativeness of an age not so sure of itself as the expansive time of Grove I' – that is to say, Victorian Britain – and he pleaded for literary men to learn a little more about music: 'T.S. Eliot, who, as a man whose work was set to music and who wrote about the relationship between the two auditory arts, has an entry here, loved the later Beethoven quartets and yet probably did not know much about the Neapolitan sixth.'

While Burgess must have been browsing deep in the *New Grove* to write that review, *The Times* changed hands again. The new owner was Rupert Murdoch; the sale was agreed on 22 January 1981. Denis Hamilton and Rees-Mogg both resigned their editorships, and some time around then Murdoch happened to have a conversation with the General Secretary of the Trades Union Congress, Len Murray. Murray said that he felt the Fleet Street proprietors had always got the trade unions they deserved. Murdoch replied: 'Well, now perhaps the unions have got the proprietor they deserve.'

It was a warning of what was to come now that he was the owner. And he was the owner essentially because of what the unions had done to the Thomson organisation. Not only had the printers resumed all their old practices after the stoppage, but in July 1980 the National Union of Journalists, whose members had received their salaries throughout the stoppage, went on strike for a week over pay. For Kenneth Thomson, who had become the proprietor in 1976 after his father Roy had died, it was the signal to move. He was less attached to *The Times* than his father, and it had become an incubus to him. After the journalists' strike, he decided to sell. Rupert Murdoch's offer was generally agreed to be the most viable; the House of Commons debated it, the Monopolies Commission approved it, and Murdoch was in.

The supplements, along with the *Sunday Times*, were part of the deal, but the *TLS* was not affected, except in quite agreeable ways. Salaries went up; Gross gained more control over employment, especially of secretaries. But Gross was already considering leaving, and before the end of the year he had decided to resign.

He had maintained an extremely high standard of reviewing, helped by the fact that he had had no difficulty in discussing almost any subject with his contributors on an equal intellectual footing. He had decisively built up the range of American books reviewed, the number of American contributors to the paper and the American readership, and all of these were becoming more and more important. He had also been a punctilious and, when necessary, exacting editor. Victoria Glendinning said that learning under his guidance to subedit, check and rewrite contributions had been her real education. But he had been editor of the paper for seven years, and that was long enough for him.

Murdoch himself interviewed the candidates for the next editorship, who included John Sturrock, Claire Tomalin, at that time literary editor of the *Sunday Times*, and Paul Barker, the editor of *New Society*. He chose the relatively young Jeremy Treglown, whose appointment as editor from 1 January 1982 was announced in the last issue of 1981.

In Treglown's first issue, on that New Year's Day, there was a charming tribute to Gross. The political writer (and editor of R.H.S. Crossman's diaries) Janet Morgan had reviewed British Rail's Continental Timetable in the *TLS* the previous October, and had got involved in a correspondence in the paper over the correct name for an attractive little town in the Pyrenees, La Tour de Carol-Enveigt. Now, addressing her letter to the retiring editor, she suggested that the *TLS* should organise a special excursion to the town 'to reinvigorate exhausted readers and contributors' – and 'to mark the end of your distinguished time as editor, we might toast you where there is a wineglass symbol (buffet service of drinks and cold snacks), and make speeches after knives and forks in squares (tray meals)'. In spirit, many readers and contributors on both sides of the Atlantic doubtless joined that excursion.

Chapter Fourteen

The Trouble with Theory: 1982–90

W hen Rupert Murdoch bought *The Times*, he was required to give assurances to the Department of Trade that he would preserve its editorial independence. This requirement did not extend to the three supplements – the *Times Literary*, *Educational* and *Higher Education* supplements – as they were weekly, not daily publications, but Murdoch gave the same assurances with regard to them too. He also decided that he would keep all of them in existence. The *Educational Supplement* was the only one of them that made any profits, but these profits – which came from the many pages of advertisements for teaching posts in the paper – were potentially substantial, and indeed rose to remarkable heights after he bought it, even though for a time during the trades union picketing of Wapping, in 1986, some local education authorities boycotted it for advertising. Murdoch placed the supplements in a separate division in his organisation, and so for the first time they had a managing director – or publisher as he was initially called – of their own.

Just like John Gross, Treglown had to move his staff in the first year of his editorship. They left the Gray's Inn Road in August 1982 for some offices on the site of the Priory of St John of Jerusalem in Clerken-well, adjoining a sixteenth-century gateway. The issue of 13 August 1982 was the first to carry the new address: Priory House, St John's Lane, London EC1. Here they were to remain for the next eleven years.

But another, potentially far greater disruption was in store. Strikes continued to afflict *The Times* gravely, but Rupert Murdoch did not fail to follow up his threat to the print unions. He secretly set up a printing works based on the new computer technology at Wapping, organised a new system of distribution by his own lorries, trained a small number of journalists in the use of the new computers, and in an overnight coup on 24 January 1986 took his British newspaper empire out of Gray's Inn Road and Bouverie House down to Wapping, leaving most of the printing workers redundant. It was only electricians that he needed now. There was outrage in the print unions. Mass demonstrations took place around the new plant, which quickly became known as Fortress Wapping. But aided by Mrs Thatcher's union legislation, particularly the new restraints on picketing, Murdoch won the day. It was the end of the old-style printing industry in Britain.

The *TLS* had its problems during the week after the move to Wapping, and these were described to me by the publisher, Ian Trafford. The paper was at this time being set and filmed at a small plant in London, called Computer Graphics, and printed on the presses of the *Northampton Chronicle and Echo*. Although it was under threat from the unions, Computer Graphics kept going, and up at Northampton the management promised to do the same. On the first day after the Murdoch sackings, Trafford and Keith Young of Computer Graphics themselves drove up to Northampton with the supplement's film for printing, but the unions there were already talking about action, and finally, late in the night, refused to accept it. As dawn was breaking, Trafford and Young drove back to London, where they heard that there was a possibility that the *Kent Messenger* could help. They set off again to Maidstone, where they were put in touch with two men with presses at the back of a garage in Worthing. This place was given the codename 'John O'Groats' to try to conceal it from the unions; and here that week, the *TLS* was printed. The paper was a little late out, but the circulation was not much affected, partly because so many of the readers bought their copies on subscription.

Down at the offices in Priory House, life went on virtually the same as usual. There was no serious picketing there by the printers. Some reviewers, such as the left-wing Terry Eagleton, would not review for the *TLS* while the dispute lasted, but the paper could cope with that. Indeed, the only visible evidence of the great move to Wapping in the pages of the *TLS* is the absence of a printer's name on the back page of the issue of 7 February 1986.

In January 1982, Jeremy Treglown began making the changes that he had planned for the paper, backed by his knowledge of the proprietor's personal choice of him as editor. The position that Treglown inherited was not an easy one. In 1980, the year after the stoppage, the paper's average circulation per week had resumed at over 38,000, that is to say approximately what it had been before. Many readers, it appeared, wanted to catch up with the books which had not been reviewed while the paper was off the streets, and which were now being covered, as we saw, in long survey articles. But in the second half of 1981 the circulation slipped to under 31,000. The price had been put up to 50p in May 1981 – four years earlier it had still been only 25p – and this may have been a watershed for some readers. Many regular subscriptions had also been lost while the paper was not being published.

Further, seizing its opportunity, a rival to the *TLS* had sprung up in the year of the stoppage. This was the *London Review of Books*, founded by a group of writers and intellectuals on the model of the *New York Review of Books*, and edited by Karl Miller, with Mary-Kay Wilmers as his deputy (and also, as it later transpired, as the owner of the magazine). The *New York Review* had begun six years earlier (similarly inspired by a strike at the *New York Times*, with its influential *Book Review*) and was itself already something of a competitor with the *TLS*, on both sides of the Atlantic. Both these magazines freely used reviewers who also wrote for the *TLS*, and some writers, such as Christopher Ricks and Denis Donoghue, henceforth wrote almost exclusively for the new journals – partly because of Karl Miller's fiercely competitive spirit. It meant that outstanding reviewers were that much harder to find.

The *TLS* was also losing more money than before, partly because of the increasing cost of publishing and partly because at the Gray's Inn Road it had, probably correctly, been charged higher overhead costs by the management – and it was known that one thing Rupert Murdoch never contemplated with any pleasure was losing money. The move to Priory House, and the farming out of the make-up and printing which happened at this time, eased the situation in some degree. But the year of the stoppage had also seen the loss of most of the advertising for vacancies in libraries, because it had led to the librarians setting up their own journal. The *TLS* in fact became smaller now, because the number of pages it was allowed was henceforth strictly related to the advertising revenue it took each week. It was a challenging situation.

John Sturrock was still there as deputy editor, with special responsibility for foreign books. Many of John Gross's part-timers such as Victoria Glendinning and Rosemary Dinnage had left by now, mostly during the closure, though the philosopher Galen Strawson, who would become a Fellow of Jesus College, Oxford, still had an arrangement with the paper. The young poet Alan Jenkins had been brought in by Gross in 1981, and after Blake Morrison left had taken over responsibility for the poetry and the fiction.

Following the closedown of Ian Hamilton's magazine the *New Review*, three young women from his staff – Holly Eley, Amanda Radice and Mary Furness – had all been taken on by Gross not long before he left the *TLS*, and were kept on by Treglown. Other survivors from Gross's regime were Adolf Wood, who has already been mentioned and now had some of the responsibility for books on international politics; Lindsay Duguid, who had been looking after children's books, and two others who had joined just before Gross left, Richard Brain and Elizabeth Winter. In March 1982, Jeremy Treglown brought in a young writer, Alan Hollinghurst, to take charge of the arts reviews in 'Commentary', the job he himself had been doing for Gross. John Sturrock decided to go part-time in 1985, and Hollinghurst was then appointed deputy editor.

As in the past, everyone took part in the subediting and rewriting, which was extensive now, with more academics – who were not necessarily good writers – contributing, and those often tackling more difficult questions; and also with more foreign contributors. Umberto Eco told Treglown, on one occasion when he had made a contribution to the paper: 'I enjoyed your article, but I preferred my own.'

Treglown himself was thirty-five when he took over the editorial chair. Like many of the earlier figures in the history of the *TLS*, he was the son of a clergyman. He had been educated at Bristol Grammar School and Oxford, where he had subsequently become a lecturer in English at Lincoln College, and when John Gross persuaded him to join the paper he was a lecturer at University College, London. Eventually he returned to academic life. He was also an author. He had published a scholarly edition of the letters of the seventeenth-century poet Rochester in 1980, and would in due course write biographies of the children's author Roald Dahl and the novelist Henry Green.

From the start, he brought the staff together regularly to talk about the paper. He insisted that they should all read the publishers' catalogues of forthcoming books, and come up with suggestions for reviews that ought to be planned in advance and who might be asked to write them. One of his first aims for the paper was to extend still further the coverage of the arts in 'Commentary', and that soon showed in its pages. He was also keen to publish general articles and reflect British life and its debates more fully.

A good subject fell into his lap less than three months after he had become editor. A reader, D.A. Kendrick of London SW10, wrote on 26 March to draw attention to the many places in D.M. Thomas's novel *The White Hotel* where he had taken descriptions of events almost verbatim from Anatoli Kuznetsov's novel about the Ukraine, *Babi Yar*. Thomas wrote the following week to say that he had fully acknowledged his debt to Kuznetsov in the book, and that it was conceived as 'a synthesis of different visions and different voices'. James Fenton also sprang to Thomas's defence that week, arguing along similar lines.

Treglown made it the occasion to invite a number of writers to discuss the question of plagiarism in the issue of 9 April. Among the contributors were the novelist Ian McEwan, who declared that 'writers are in each other's pockets all the time' but not necessarily dishonestly, and the scholar Pat Rogers, who, citing eighteenth-century examples, said that 'the ingestion of other minds is a marked feature of the truly creative psychology'. There were one or two critical letters, but Thomas had not come out of the inquiry badly and he wrote a final, rather haughty letter on 30 April:

> Readers who admire *The White Hotel* think the letters attacking it silly; those who dislike the novel welcome the chance to say so, and are not going to be swayed by counter-arguments. I cannot imagine, therefore, that a prolonged correspondence is going to be fruitful; and I, at least, shall write no more.

The arrival of the year 1984 gave Treglown an occasion for looking back at George Orwell. On 6 January, Roy Harris, the Professor of General Linguistics at Oxford, contributed a long article. He applauded Orwell's abhorrence of the way in which men's inhuman behaviour in the twentieth century was so often concealed behind manipulated verbal facades, an abhorrence which had led to his invention of the repulsive 'Newspeak' in *Nineteen Eighty-Four*. But Harris argued that there was not really any such thing as a healthy, contrasting 'Oldspeak' or 'plain language' that directly reflected reality, and that it was naive of Orwell and other political writers to suggest that there was. Using language was always more complicated than that.

Treglown also acquired some unpublished letters by Orwell for that first issue of 1984. Most of them concerned Orwell's dealings with his publisher Victor Gollancz, who in the 1930s had made great difficulties over the anti-socialist aspects of Orwell's books. Gollancz, it appeared, had particularly disliked a scene in Orwell's novel *Coming Up for Air* that parodied a meeting of the Left Book Club. That was not surprising, as Gollancz himself had founded the club. In May 1984, in 'Commentary', Julian Symons reviewed Peter Hall's dramatic adaptation of *Animal Farm* at the Cottesloe Theatre, and complained that 'a timeless fable has been turned into a poorly told joke'. In February 1985, the young historian of Eastern Europe, Timothy Garton Ash, reviewed a number of books about Orwell, found most of them small-minded and biased, and reiterated firmly the view that *Nineteen Eighty-Four* was about Soviet Russia: 'In short, Orwell was an anti-communist socialist.'

There was a curious historical revelation in January 1987, when Lord Esher – writing as Lionel Esher – told the full story of the 'plot to save the artists' in February 1940. He described how his father and John Betjeman had drawn up a list of 'the pick of the creative artists under forty' – they included Evelyn Waugh, Benjamin Britten and Graham Sutherland – and his father had written to ask Oliver Stanley, the Secretary of State for War, to use them only for 'the safer forms of military service'. Stanley replied, rather drolly, that he agreed with Esher that to do this 'would not have a serious effect on the war effort of this country', but that he could not see his way to justifying the principle.

Lionel Esher commented that the failure of his father's scheme had in the event made no difference to the state of the arts in Britain, because none of the sixty-one artists named had died in action, and none of the writers and artists who had made most impact after the war – Kingsley Amis, William Golding, Philip Larkin, Anthony Powell, Francis Bacon and Lucian Freud, among others – had been on the list. However, he thought that 'the sceptics had been proved right for the wrong reasons'. A sad letter followed a week later to say that Esher had forgotten one of the composers on the list: Walter Leigh was killed in Libya in 1942.

Television had from time to time been discussed in John Gross's time, but now reviews of selected programmes began to appear regularly in 'Commentary'. The tone was very frequently sceptical, especially as the decade went on. The English lecturer David Nokes, reviewing London Weekend Television's adaptation of Waugh's *Scoop* in May 1987, said that 'like Lord Copper, the film seems to have got hold of the wrong Boot. Michael Maloney, dark-eyed and handsome, is more cavalry than gum-boot, and seems far more at ease in pith helmet and tropical suit than splashing after the questing vole in his muddy tweeds.' Jonathon Brown, reviewing Peter Brook's production of *The Mahabharata* shown on Channel 4 in December 1989, said that there was 'little point in denying that this is a Western drama, despite claims to have captured the myth, character and religion of India': the Krishna in the production had a voice 'warm with the Home Counties' tone of a children's television programme'.

Peter Kemp, reviewing the television coverage of the Booker Prize in November 1985, said that it had been better since LWT took over from BBC2. This was the year that the New Zealand writer Keri Hulme won the prize for her novel *The Bone People*, which had been reviewed in the paper two weeks earlier by Antony Beevor (later best known for his history of the battle of Stalingrad). Beevor thought that this story of a mute, unidentified boy, found by a Maori factory worker on the New Zealand shore after a shipwreck, began with disturbing realism but lost itself eventually in symbolism. Kemp (who thought better of the book) described the 'colourful climax' of the Booker dinner in the Guildhall, when, to accept the prize in the author's absence, 'a trio from the Spiral feminist collective – one got up in a dinner-jacket, the other two bedecked in traditional feather cloaks – advanced to the podium hand-in-hand and chanting', and he praised the 'faultless handling of the links' when, within minutes of the announcement that Keri Hulme had won the prize, Hermione Lee had managed to contact her in Salt Lake City and was conducting an interview.

Among the other arts, the best writing was perhaps found in the reviews of opera and painting. Peter Conrad, a Christ Church don, who had already been reviewing opera as well as writing literary reviews for John Gross, was deeply moved by Carlo Maria Giulini's conducting of Verdi's *Falstaff* in the famous production at Covent Garden in July 1982:

> Verdi's orchestra here constitutes a world – a thronging comic society, a thrivingly populous landscape. Its rhythmic energy and grace transcribe the ubiquitous manoeuvrings of the comic spirit . . . For Falstaff's monologues, the orchestra manages a discreet, whispering, overheard chamber music; it is intruding on his private self-scrutiny, and scarcely dares make audible his fears . . . [But] when the final crescendo swells up, it embodies, like the revivifying trill when Falstaff doses himself with wine, a brave victory over mortal alarm: it is the heroic recalcitrance of Don Giovanni, who refuses to repent or mourn.

Conrad's book on opera, *A Song of Love or Death*, was reviewed in February 1988 by Richard Osborne, who said that 'the book, aphoristic as ever', was 'brilliantly written and certain to offend those who balk at cleverness' – he knew a man at the BBC who had several times thrown the book across the room – but it was 'a uniquely vital and simulating study of the art'.

Patrick Carnegy was disappointed, on the other hand, by Peter Hall's production of Wagner's *Ring* at Bayreuth in August 1983: 'In *Rheingold*, gods, giants and Nibelungs blundered about on the inspiration of the moment . . . Wotan's great monologue completely defeated the producer, so that Siegmund Nimsgern probably wasn't the only one longing for "*das Ende*" at this point.'

Anita Brookner had written very attractively for John Gross about art exhibitions, and she went on doing so for Treglown. In April 1984 she reviewed the exhibition 'The Orientalists' at the Royal Academy, not liking many of the pictures, but characteristically turning the discussion to something she did admire. The nineteenth-century painters who made their pilgrimage to the Middle East, she wrote,

> failed in their most important task, which was to celebrate the glare and refraction of a dazzling light which greys down vistas and intensifies shadows. It is as if they had an opportunity to discover Impressionism and inexplicably failed to do so, preferring to concentrate on exotica like fantasias and odalisques, Moorish baths and harem kiosks, camels and seraglios, Turkish letter-writers and pilgrimages to Mecca, carpet bazaars and whirling dervishes. It is ironic that the most perfect realisation of the impact of the light is to be found in Flaubert's letters . . .

Another rewarding writer about art in the *TLS* in the eighties was Lawrence Gowing. In July 1988, soon after he had retired as Slade Professor of Fine Arts at University College, London, he contributed a long and memorable article about Rembrandt, in a series called 'NB' that Treglown instituted towards the end of his editorship. Gowing's subject was the moment when, with Hedrickje, the new model that Rembrandt found after the death of his wife Saskia, he turned 'to the beauty of the usual, the loveliness of what was normal, customary and relaxed'. When Hedrickje sat for him as Bathsheba, 'the customary undress was taken for granted as a natural part of the household scene . . . Model and painter both revealed a pleasure in familiarity which no-one had ever captured in its undefended generosity before . . . Nowhere else that I can remember in art have the features of a well-loved, mature face found their true scale without reticence or exaggeration. By comparison with this natural measure, Italian idealisation has no place for specific individual regard. The Ideal is constitutionally under-featured.'

Apart from this increased attention to the arts, Treglown also soon started a series of 'American Notes' by the journalist Christopher Hitchens. Hitchens was a provocative writer on the Left, and had a great deal of sport with American right-wing and capitalist institutions. For instance, in May 1984 he gleefully recorded some dissension in the ranks of a body called the Committee for the Free World. It had often attacked modern American novelists such as Gore Vidal and John Updike, but Saul Bellow had, rather surprisingly, been on its board. Now its director, Midge Decter, had written a forthright condemnation of Vidal in the Committee's newsletter, *Contentions*, saying that there were two main themes in Vidal's essays, a deep loathing of American society and a faith in the aesthetic superiority of homosexuality – and Bellow had resigned in protest against her article. The Free Worlders, commented Hitchens, were even tougher and more raucous than their predecessors in the Congress for Cultural Freedom.

Not all the readers liked Hitchens's column. In August 1986 a Canadian professor finally exploded at one of his articles. He wrote – not for publication – to Treglown saying that the straw that broke his back was Hitchens's comparison of the Library of Congress and the Lenin State Library, when he said that the schedule of opening hours in the two 'puts Washington well behind Moscow'. The professor agreed that the great Library of Congress should have longer hours, but surely, he said, Hitchens could have said something about the range of books available in the two institutions. The American libraries were monuments to democracy because they gave people the right to read and study various opinions. What did the Lenin State Library do?

Treglown continued publishing two regular features that Gross had introduced. One was a light-hearted column called 'Remainders', written each week by an antiquarian bookseller, Eric Korn, in which he mulled over books and buyers, told stories and made jokes. On April Fool's Day 1988, for example, he reported on some books that were eagerly sought by collectors. They included *Morgan Forced Her* by Howard Zend; *Up, Dyke!* by the Witches of Eastwick Collective, and Pat Moss on the Isle of St John.

The other was a competition, 'Author, Author', in which readers were asked to identify three quotations with a common theme. This fell into the hands of Alan Hollinghurst, with readers sometimes providing the quotations – and readers also, sometimes, not being able to recognise any of them. As for that long-standing *TLS* institution, the report on book sales and bibliographical matters, that was now contributed by H.R. Woudhuysen, a lecturer in English at University College.

Treglown also introduced a new layout for the paper. From 4 November 1983, the *TLS* reverted to a four-column page, and the rules breaking up the pages were mostly abolished. It gave the paper a much cleaner, more open look, and Treglown was justifiably pleased with it.

Books reviewed at this time were as varied in subject-matter as they had always been, and many of them were even more specialised than they had been in Gross's time. The reviews themselves were also sometimes more complex and difficult, especially as critical method began to make a stronger mark on younger academics. Some reviewers of fiction were now more inclined to take their readers on a kind of tour of a novel, pointing out interesting features that might easily be missed, rather than asking such questions – simpler questions, at least on the face of it – as 'What were the author's intentions?' ('The poor author wouldn't know anything about those!') and 'Is the book successful?' ('What criteria could we possibly use?'). To a much greater degree, the kind of fiction reviewing that Malcolm Bradbury called for in the seventies was making its appearance in the *TLS*.

Iris Murdoch's later, longer novels were themselves calling for hard thinking. Her novel *The Book and the Brotherhood*, about a young ex-Marxist trying to write a book on political philosophy and proving very trying to the comfortable circle of family and friends that are supporting him, was reviewed by Stephen R.L. Clark, Professor of Philosophy at Liverpool, in September 1987. The central question it posed, he said, was, 'How can we live in a world divorced from good?' Plato and Plotinus figured largely in it, 'as labels for an ideal of goodness never to be realised in the ordinary world'. But the book was neither a realistic novel, nor a systematic treatise of philosophy: 'what Iris Murdoch has created is an absorbing image of our present confusions'.

Clive Sinclair, a novelist himself, was much more critical of her novel *A Message to the Planet*, in October 1989. In this story of a Jewish magus and mathematician, whose amanuensis is convinced that the magus wanted to leave a message for mankind, Sinclair felt she had 'left the real world behind': 'None of Murdoch's characters seems to read newspapers, and most would go blind rather than watch television. Doubtless the avoidance of anything bearing a sell-by date is deliberate, but rather than create a timeless zone it merely reproduces the rarefied atmosphere of an Oxbridge common room.' Sinclair also blamed her for 'treating words with casual indifference' – and compared her to

Enid Blyton in this respect. This was not a good period for Iris Murdoch.

In May 1984, Kingsley Amis brought out a novel, *Stanley and the Women*, which seemed so critical of women that for a long time no American publishing house would take it on, such was the opposition of the women publishers' editors. The *TLS* reviewer, J.K.L. Walker, who was on the staff, did not take it so hardly. Here, he said, 'Amis excels himself in enjoyably passionate unfairness about women . . . the comedy stems from the misogyny'; and he called it 'perhaps the most skilfully written of all Amis's novels.' He believed it would survive unscathed its 'ritual burning by the feminists'.

In September 1986, Blake Morrison reviewed the Kingsley Amis novel that was to win the Booker Prize that year, *The Old Devils*, a story about some ageing Welshmen in their home town. He liked Amis's satire on the way Wales had changed for the worse, and also found the novel less misogynistic than might have been feared after *Stanley*. Quoting a Philip Larkin poem, he said *The Old Devils* was 'not untrue and not unkind'. But Michael Wood – less robust, or more sensitive – found fewer pleasures in Amis's *Difficulties With Girls* in September 1988. There was some 'splendid comedy' in it, but 'the book has a grim flavour finally, not desolate but shabby, confining, and it keeps reverting to Amis's crude old theme as to a hobbyhorse. All the women here but one are bitchy, selfish, vain, sex-starved and unreasonable, and the same goes for the feminine half of a homosexual couple.' The cumulative effect of Amis's novels was 'the sense they give of a strong intelligence working itself into a nasty corner'.

In April 1990 Lorna Sage, reviewing Amis's *The Folks that Live on the Hill*, had a different objection to make, though she noted the continued 'rumblings of the sex war' in the book. Harry, the uncle-like hero of the book who is the protector of a 'motley cast' of Londoners, hates and avoids saying serious things because – as she represented it – 'you spoil and desecrate and falsify them by naming'. She was therefore willing to credit this 'reluctantly literate' Harry with a kind of moral reticence. But as Harry was also Kingsley Amis's mouthpiece in the book, it meant that Amis too could content himself with using simple 'chums-and-chaps slang' – and that, she thought, was a dangerous strategy for a writer. This was a good example of a post-critical-theory review, asking the more radical questions about language that theory would suggest, but relating them to the questions that novel readers traditionally, or 'naturally', ask.

*   *   *

The late eighties revealed that William Golding's novel *Rites of Passage*, about an emigrant ship heading for Australia during the Napoleonic Wars, had been only the first part of a trilogy. The second volume, *Close Quarters*, was reviewed by David Nokes in June 1987. Colley, the parson, was dead by now, and Talbot, the young eighteenth-century gentleman and narrator, was at centre stage. Nokes saw the ship as a 'tightly rigged analogy for the human condition', with the passengers dancing and flirting 'as the green slime of Golding's symbolism spreads across the hull'. He thought that 'as a story-teller his touch never falters . . . but it is in the dark undertow of his metaphors that a feeling of strain and contrivance appears'.

However when the third volume, *Fire Down Below*, appeared in March 1989, Stephen Medcalf acclaimed the trilogy as a whole as a masterly novel. Its binding theme, he wrote, was

> the making of Talbot's soul – or perhaps the better word is character – so much so that one might call *Rites of Passage*, where he was shaken by Colley's death as he is never quite shaken again, the Inferno of this trilogy; *Close Quarters*, where he is first consistently presented as having the grace to feel ashamed and where he meets his Beatrice, the Purgatorio; and *Fire Down Below*, where he learns to look at the stars and which is the happiest of Golding's eleven novels, the Paradiso.

Peter Kemp reviewed another ambitious novel at length in August 1987. This was V.S. Naipaul's *The Enigma of Arrival*, the rather autobiographical-seeming story of a writer living and taking stock of himself in a cottage on what was once a great Edwardian estate in Wiltshire. Kemp had admired many of Naipaul's earlier books, but this 'exercise in self-assessment', as he described the new book, led him to feel that all Naipaul's books uncovered, in the end, the same pattern – a 'global view' of a 'nightmarish nature'. Naipaul's eye had 'travelled perceptively over a vast variety of scenes', but in his books 'sexual let-down lurks everywhere', 'society after society turns out to be a post-colonial catastrophe', 'the main cohesive force he detects in his journeyings is a repellent one: religion of the most regressive and superstitious kind', and 'travel seems not so much to broaden his mind as to deepen his presuppositions'. Everywhere what Naipaul really found was just 'the features of his own predicament' – a predicament that grew out of his own rootlessness and 'fear of extinction'.

This review enraged the American writer, Susan Sontag, from whom a letter appeared three weeks later. She said that 'most of what Kemp writes about Naipaul's work could be recast as a part of the description of a great writer with a tragic sense of the human condition and of contemporary history . . . his views, obsessions and his distress are those of a magnificent, important writer – one of the handful of that breed alive today'.

In September 1988, Galen Strawson reviewed an excellent novel that was easier to understand than any of these, even though one of its characters was 'a coherentish feminist, a "critical theorist" out of Sussex and Cambridge, a student of Barthes, Cixous, Derrida, Irigaray, Kristeva, Lacan, and so forth'. This was David Lodge's novel, *Nice Work*. Lodge in this book brings the young woman in question, Dr Robyn Penrose, into contact with the managing director of an engineering firm, Vic Wilcox, when she becomes her university's 'Faculty of Arts Industry Year Shadow' in his factory. They go, as Strawson put it with a cheerful dash of theory himself, 'through a classically ordered but modernistically canny minuet of binary oppositions', and, more simply, 'as the weeks go by, mutual hostility changes into unconscious respect and hidden liking'. Strawson found it a very enjoyable book, by an author 'accomplished at the comedy of difference', even-handed in his satire on the two characters, and optimistic because he is 'good at seeing what is good in things as they are'. He only regretted that 'Lodge's adjectives are often lazy or worse; his sentences lack shape or spring . . . Perhaps he is suffering from the Iris Murdoch syndrome, possessed by the story, neglecting the vehicle.'

With V.S. Pritchett, born in 1900, there was even less of an obvious problem. At any rate, Valentine Cunningham, saying that after the appearance of his *Collected Stories* in June 1982 no-one could doubt that he was 'the best living English short story writer', observed: 'Unflustered by anti-historicism and introspectiveness, Pritchett has kept up the honourable and important business of fiction as social observing. So that if you want England bungaloid or bombed, afflicted by ration-book or spiv, England stripping its pine, or getting into boutique antiques, Pritchett's stories are where the whole kaleidoscopic documentary delightfully unrolls.'

Anita Brookner, Beryl Bainbridge and A.S. Byatt all had big followings by now. Anita Brookner's *Hotel du Lac* was reviewed by Barbara Hardy, Professor of English at Birkbeck College, London, in September 1984, just before it won the Booker Prize: she said of this story about the woman writer Edith Hope, who is 'a tortoise, a wet, a Cinderella', that 'its strength lies in its images of loneliness' and 'it sympathises with the lovely pangs of impossible love', but that 'fortunately it keeps on laughing all the time'. Writing in December 1989 about Beryl Bainbridge's *An Awfully Big Adventure* (set once again in Liverpool), Lindsay Duguid thought that 'this story of an orphan finding a surrogate family in the raffish society of weekly rep' was like 'a dark version of J.B. Priestley's *The Good Companions*' – 'neither companionship nor true love are to be found among the backstage grime and casual behaviour'. A.S. Byatt had a great success in March 1990 with her long novel, *Possession*, which also won the Booker Prize. In the *TLS*, Richard Jenkyns said that this story of a scholar's pursuit of the truth about a Victorian poet 'restored the Victorians to honour, with an especial admiration for their emotional lives': it was 'a fine work, intelligent, ingenious and humane'.

But by now a new generation of novelists was crowding out the scene: Martin Amis, Julian Barnes, Ian McEwan, Graham Swift, Kazuo Ishiguro and Salman Rushdie.

The younger Amis gave his reviewers in the eighties quite a hard time as they struggled to separate what they had enjoyed in his books from what they were more doubtful about. In October 1984, Eric Korn reviewed *Money: A Suicide Note*, Amis's biggest success so far (he was now thirty-five). Korn first tried in his own prose to imitate the 'compelling, obsessive, obscene voice' of the book's narrator and chief character, John Self – 'this prole, this Goth, this foul-mouthed clockwork orange, this upstart . . . pawing and porning in New York' – which is where Self, in the story, has come to make a pornographic film. Korn went on to note Amis's 'surprise package' of a plot, his disgust at the corruption of sex by money (Self's fame is based on an 'unflinching use of flesh to sell'), his acknowledgement (for Amis appears in the story under his own name) of his sadistic feelings towards his horrible narrator. But Korn admitted that he found himself more interested in the 'diction and character' than in 'the structural wit, the metaphysics', and that the infighting and negotiations among the various members of the film's cast were 'the most uncomplexly entertaining parts of the book'.

Another young novelist, Adam Mars-Jones, reviewed Amis's book of short stories, *Einstein's Monsters*, in May 1987. A predominant theme of these stories was outrage at the very existence of nuclear weapons in the world, but Mars-Jones considered that Amis's style in them had the disadvantage of 'a too-constant intensity'. Amis could not help his own 'truculent brilliance' flaring up inappropriately in the middle of the very different style of his narrators. 'No one works harder on a sentence than Martin Amis,' wrote Mars-Jones, 'and no one stores up more pleasure for the reader with his phrasing. But sometimes it seems that the need to stamp each sentence with his literary personality defeats his ambitions as a literary artist.'

A poet who would shortly afterwards join the *TLS* staff, Mick Imlah, reviewed Amis's novel *London Fields* in October 1989. He too noted the subtle tricks of the narrative in this story of a woman novelist who knows she is going to be murdered, and who brings about the ending of her story in the way she wants. But what he felt was central to the book – 'frustrating for Amis as it might be' – was 'not the whole but the bits – the jokes and the farcical set-pieces and the exhilarating virtuoso prose – embedded in it'. The 'darker, more portentous, quasi-allegorical temper' of the novel was hard put to coexist with the exuberance of its author's style.

Martin Amis himself contributed to the 4,500th number of the *TLS* – or what, according to Jeremy Treglown, the circulation department insisted on calling 'the 4,500th anniversary number'. This was on 30 June 1989, and Amis wrote a review of a book called *Searching for Bobby Fischer* by Fred Waitzin, an account of a man's attempt to turn his son into a chess champion. He gave a zestful account of the book, and also threw in a brilliant description of a game he had played, and lost, against the world number three, Nigel Short, then aged twenty-four. Short's face

> was not so much ageless as entirely unformed: you felt it could still light up at the sight of a new chemistry set, or a choc-ice. But somehow his hands bestowed terrible powers on the white pieces. Those linked central pawns of his – oh, what they could *do* to me. They weren't *pawns* in the normal sense; they had grown, fattened; they were more like bishops, or rooks. No, they were like queens, I thought, as they worked their way into the very crux of my defence . . .

One does not feel that he would have said the same about his critics.

Amis's friend, Julian Barnes, did no better in the paper with his second novel, *Before She Met Me*, than he had with his first. Mark Abley, in April 1982, thought that the characters were 'paper thin' in this story of a man consumed by obsessive jealousy of his wife's past. However, *Flaubert's Parrot*, Barnes's 'extraordinarily artful mix of literary tomfoolery and high seriousness', got an excellent review from David Coward in October 1984. It is about a sixty-year-old man, Dr Braithwaite, who sets out to find the stuffed parrot that served as a model for the one that appears, hovering over a servant woman's head, at the end of Flaubert's story, *Un coeur simple*. Dr Braithwaite finds that his researches into relics that have survived in Normandy get him nowhere, and lead him into innumerable questions, mostly unanswerable, about the nature of the past, not least his own. The book, said Coward, 'positively jangles with cross-fertilising, self-seeding, memory-jogging, imagination-releasing resonances ... It is sober, elegant and wry. It works as literary detection, literary criticism and literary experiment.' The modern British novel found it easy to be clever and comic, but Barnes had also managed that much harder thing – 'he succeeds in communicating genuine emotion without affectation or embarrassment'.

Julian Barnes himself contributed some articles about Flaubert to the paper, notably a long review of Flaubert's *Carnets de travail*, in October 1988, in which he observed that while popular novelists find out everything they can about a subject, 'more sophisticated novelists pile up research like a compost heap, but then leave it alone, let it sink down, acquire heat and degrade usefully into fertilising elements'.

Barnes's last book of the eighties, *A History of the World in 10½ Chapters*, consisted of ten stories and a short reflection on love. It was reviewed by Michael Wood in June 1989. Wood's review was very much in the new vein, teasing out the complex feelings about such matters as human hopes and moral judgment that he found embodied in particular episodes and passages. He concluded that the book was above all making a claim for the importance of love, a claim 'animated by the accompaniment of live instances'.

In the *TLS*, Ian McEwan was regarded as having taken a step forward in his two novels at the end of the eighties. In September 1987, Michael Neve reviewed *The Child in Time*, the story of a man whose daughter disappears in a supermarket. Neve said that McEwan had been 'too implausibly horrified at life in his early work', but now he had written 'a courageous and socially enraged novel', in which he indicted 'a bored and cruel society that no longer has the power to look after its children'. His novel, *The Innocent*, about a young telephone engineer working in a Kafkaesque world in Berlin, was reviewed in May 1990 by Julian Symons, who wrote in similar vein: 'This book, like *The Child in Time*, shows a marked shift away from McEwan's earlier work, an attempt to blend the dark vision of his fantasies with an acknowledgement that a world of successful human relationships exists.'

Graham Swift's novel *Waterland* was reviewed by Alan Hollinghurst in October 1983. He was greatly impressed by this story of Tom Crick, a schoolteacher in the Fenlands who is struggling to make a lucid shape out of the history of that strange watery world, and at the same time trying to make sense of his own present confusions. In February 1986, Anne Chisholm reviewed Kazuo Ishiguro's *An Artist of the Floating World*, the memories of an old man in a provincial Japanese town a few years after the war: she thought this novel by a Japanese author writing in English 'unravels the old man's thoughts and feelings with exceptional delicacy', and that it delivered calm and instructive insights into modern Japanese history. Ishiguro's next novel, *The Remains of the Day*, about a butler in an aristocratic English household, won the Booker Prize in 1989. Reviewing it in May of that year, Galen Strawson said it was 'a strikingly original book, beautifully made', and, in its portrait of Stevens the butler, a tragic study of 'a man disciplined out of existence by an irresistible triunity – his father, his role, and his lovingly imperfect reproduction of his masters' language'.

Salman Rushdie's 'fantastical comedy' *Shame* was reviewed in September 1983 by Adam Mars-Jones. 'It crosses a chapati with a soufflé,' he wrote, and it was 'only due to Salman Rushdie's skills as a storyteller that it doesn't seem like a shotgun wedding'. When Rushdie's *The Satanic Verses*, the novel that led to his being sentenced to death in Iran for blasphemy against the Prophet, came out in September 1988, the *TLS* reviewer Robert Irwin did not anticipate any such outcome, but he did say that Rushdie was 'possessed by a story-telling demon', which might have been thought to prefigure uncannily the Ayatollah Khomeini's view of the matter. But Irwin wrote lightly about the book. This account of the life and fretful dreams of Gibreel, a Bombay movie star, contained, he said, marvellous things, including many 'enigmatic and engrossing parables'. In *The Satanic Verses*, Rushdie had 'created a fictional universe whose centre is everywhere and whose circumference is nowhere. It is several of the best novels he has ever written.'

When the blow fell, and the *fatwa* against Rushdie was pronounced the following February, the *TLS* gave a front page over to a declaration by over 700 writers, seventy of whose names, from Graham Greene to Arthur Miller and Chinua Achebe to Mario Vargas Llosa, were printed alongside. This statement, on 3 March, noted that the Ayatollah Khomeini had called on all Muslims to seek out and execute not only Salman Rushdie but also all those involved in the publication of *The Satanic Verses*, and with a show of boldness – or perhaps merely pomposity – it declared: 'We, in so far as we defend the right to freedom of expression as embodied in the Universal Declaration of Human Rights, declare that we also are involved in the publication.' It called on all world leaders to repudiate these threats, and to take firm action to ensure that they were withdrawn.

Such declarations did not achieve very much, and Rushdie went into hiding, protected by the British government. But the *TLS* followed the statement up the following week with a thoughtful article, called 'Too Important for Tact', by Jeremy Waldron, who would become the director of the Centre for Law and Philosophy at Columbia. Defending Rushdie against 'Khomeini's murderous anathema', he asked how we should conceive the idea of toleration and free speech in the modern world. We could not simply leave people alone with their faiths and sensibilities, because religions made rival claims about God and human life, and it was impossible to avoid criticising the tenets of other faiths without stifling one's own. But equally it was impossible just to debate each other's beliefs earnestly and respectfully, because religious disputation by its nature – and certainly by its history – entailed mockery, offence and insult. The only ideal to strive for was a world in which people were 'free to address the deep questions of religion and philosophy with all the resources they have at their disposal . . . That may mean that the whole kaleidoscope of literary technique – fantasy, irony, poetry, word-play, and the speculative juggling of ideas – is unleashed on what many regard as the holy, the good, the immaculate and the indubitable.' It was not an easy ideal to live with, Waldron concluded, but it was in that way that writers like Rushdie must be defended.

Meanwhile, two first novels noticed in the paper were Hilary Mantel's *Every Day is Mother's Day* and Alan Hollinghurst's *The Swimming-Pool Library*. Hilary Mantel's novel about a widow, her pregnant daughter and a social worker cast a 'malevolent eye', said Christopher Hawtree in March 1985, on 'suburban housing-estates, obnoxious children, squalid pubs, rebarbative mechanics and ignorant literati', and he relished the prospect of her devising further tortures for them. Alan Hollinghurst's book was about William Beckwith, a reckless young homosexual man in London in the days before AIDS, full of 'lurid and emphatic' scenes, astringently described, in clubs and lavatories, with the author succeeding in making us like Beckwith without approving of him. Michael Wood, writing in February 1988, said it was 'a deeply imagined, much thought on, elegantly composed work. Few novels in recent years have been better written, and none I know of has been more intelligent.' Hollinghurst's success with his novel enabled him to go part-time on the *TLS* shortly after.

There were also two Booker Prize winners from the old Commonwealth, both, as it happened, robustly reviewed by the poet D.J. Enright.

Schindler's Ark by the Australian writer, Thomas Keneally, became a world-famous film with its tale – only lightly fictionalised – of the German businessman, Oskar Schindler, who saved 3,000 Jews during the war. 'We are happy to hear of a triumph of good over evil once in a while,' wrote Enright in October 1982, even though the book was 'not a great literary novel in the class of Thomas Mann's *Doctor Faustus*, not the kind of book Grass or Böll might have created out of similar material. For better or for worse, symbolic overtones are rarely to be detected . . .'

Enright was less happy about the 1983 Booker winner, *Life & Times of Michael K*, by the South African J.M. Coetzee, a study of a very passive man who is asleep for much of the time. 'Kafka's K-characters,' Enright wrote in September, 'if not exactly masters of their fate, are comparatively brisk, alert and active,' but the only achievement of this K seems to be that 'he has passed through the guts of the state without being digested'. This 'barely living creature' was not enough for Enright.

However in July 1988 Dan Jacobson, a distinguished South African novelist himself, looked back at a novel of undoubted power, Alan Paton's plea for racial understanding in that country, *Cry, the Beloved Country*, which had been published forty years earlier. Trying to define its quality, he said that there were certain novels that cannot be adequately assessed in literary terms nor described wholly in the language of politics. 'Nor is the power they have to be wholly identified with the fervour of the *moral* homilies they contain. Rather, because they have no regard for those distinctions, they sometimes acquire a life in the mind of their readers that may best be described as proverbial.' And *Cry, the Beloved Country* was just such a book.

On the other side of the Atlantic, Saul Bellow was still the dominating figure among the novelists. Gabriel Josipovici sang his praises in a review of his new book, *The Dean's December*, in April 1982. He said that Bellow had discovered a form of fiction in which plot accounts for very little, but which is open enough to include almost anything – 'a long hard look at the whole of our civilisation as it now stands, or totters . . . Auden made poetry capable of bearing intelligence again, and Bellow has done the same for the novel.' In the new book very little happened – the Dean of a Chicago college, who has been fighting for the conviction of two black people who killed one of his students, goes to Bucharest with his Rumanian wife and in its dreary midwinter has time to ponder his life and times – but it was 'a far richer book than the sprawling and overlong *Humboldt's Gift*'.

In fact, Josipovici thought that this particular book did not break any new ground – though 'the ground cannot be gone over too often' – and that Bellow's insights were in some danger of turning into tricks of style. But there was one wholly new achievement – in the Dean's wife 'he has at last created a plausible and likeable woman'.

In February 1984, Clive Sinclair remarked on the 'manic energy' in Philip Roth's *The Anatomy Lesson* that was generated by the fictional fiction-writer Zuckerman's 'painful obsession with self', but did not appear to get much pleasure out of Zuckerman's comic misfortunes when, in this novel, he dreams of becoming a pornographer. Pearl K. Bell, the fiction reviewer for Norman Podhoretz's magazine *Commentary*, took on Gore Vidal's *Duluth* – the portrait of an 'Everytown, USA' – for the *TLS* in May 1983. She apparently shared the views that Christopher Hitchens attributed, as we noted, to the Committee for the Free World: 'When Vidal is consumed with indiscriminate loathing for an age that does not sufficiently appreciate his novels, for a political system he rejects out of hand as incurably corrupt, for a culture that he finds insufferably dull and second-rate, he is the wasp that fails to sting.' Anthony Burgess was gentler, but disappointed, when he reviewed Vidal's *Lincoln* in September 1984. Vidal, he said, was one of the most inventive novelists modern America had produced, but this historical novel about the Civil War was just 'the reduction of a tangle of complexities to a not over-long narrative in which the simple reader will learn the basic facts'.

Nor did John Updike get much better a reception in the *TLS* in the eighties. In January 1982, the satirical poet Carol Rumens, reviewing *Rabbit is Rich*, wrote that 'Updike, by being true to the extreme ordinariness of his character and the consumerism of his society, has turned himself into a bland reflection of both.' David Montrose, turning to another recurring Updike character, said of *Bech is Back* in January 1983 that 'the Bech stories are exactly what they seem: slight, elegantly written tales about a figure who merits better treatment'. The poet Craig Raine was much happier when he reviewed *The Witches of Eastwick* in September 1984: he thought that this story of a man-devil arriving in a small town on Rhode Island was a 'deceptively playful, intricate and absorbing look at feminism, evil and the cosmic set-up'.

Some American writers were appreciated more by *TLS* reviewers. In 1985, Lorna Sage enjoyed Alison Lurie's *Foreign Affairs*, about two American academics on sabbatical in London. Writing on 1 February, she said: 'it gives this dim, dreary new year a sudden shine', and she analysed the 'conspiratorial glow' with which it left the reader: 'You're assumed to be witty and literate, you're told (indirectly, of course) how very wide awake you are, and you're congratulated for being (on the other hand and after all) so sensible as to prefer your metafiction in traditional form. In short, the reader turns out to be a nicely rounded character, well-buttered with irony.' Another example, from this reviewer, of critical theory plundered for literary grace.

David Sexton, a young critic who would become well-known for his acerbity, thought *Lake Wobegon Days*, Garrison Keillor's stories of a small town in Minnesota where nothing much happens, 'wholly a success'. They constituted, he wrote in March 1986, 'a series of wonderfully comic responses to the problem posed by a Protestant faith that "in some way we were meant to be here", when "here" is a nowhere like Lake Wobegon'. In May 1988, John Clute described Raymond Carver's collection *Elephant, and Other Stories* as 'tales of anguish and torpor' among 'creatures of the hinterland', and called him 'the finest writer of short stories now active'.

But *The Bonfire of the Vanities* by Tom Wolfe was not approved of by Christopher Hitchens in March 1988. He acknowledged that this story of 'a rich and spoiled Wall Streeter . . . butchered to make a New York holiday' had 'touched a nerve in the general subconscious', but although it was an 'expression' of the debauched mores of Wall Street, it did not really seem to be a satire on them. In fact, reading the book, 'you could suppose that New York City over the past decade had seen the victimisation of the rich by the poor', while the underclass was shown living 'a boiling, pointless, vicious life', making animal noises across the tracks. It was not a portrait to please Hitchens, even though 'the city argot is well caught, the social absurdities are lovingly etched, and there is the best description of an Englishman awakening to a primordial hangover since *Lucky Jim*'.

On the still-divided Continent, writers could not escape from stubborn, older issues. In the same month as he was praising Saul Bellow, April 1982, Gabriel Josipovici also reviewed Günter Grass's new novel *Headbirths*, about two Germans (one of them Günter Grass himself) visiting China. He admired its combination of, on the one hand, simplicity and humility, and on the other 'commitment to the complex realities of the world'. Grass, he said, thought that German writers could live up to the heritage of the great émigrés, Mann and Brecht, only by 'stammering' – by false starts, by hesitations. But such modesty could bear its own fruit. 'Artists cannot pull down the walls men build, but they can make holes in them . . . walls around their countries, as in China; through the middle of their countries, as in Germany; around places they don't want us to examine too closely, such as nuclear installations; and around themselves' – and Günter Grass made such holes.

The Joke, the first novel by the Czech writer Milan Kundera, had originally been published in his own country as long ago as 1967, and there had been an English translation in 1969, but Kundera had promptly renounced that version in the *TLS*. In February 1983, Clive Sinclair reviewed a new translation which had been approved by the author. In his introduction, Kundera observed that both the Communists and the West had seized on *The Joke* as a political book, and he hoped that now it could be seen for what it really was, a novel about love. But Sinclair thought that this story, set in a small Czech town where the people live under Russia's gaze, was about more than eroticism. It was also about 'love of Czechoslovakia and its culture' – and it announced 'all the major themes that resonate through his later works: present absurdity, laughter, forgetting, the separation of love and sex, the boundary a person can easily cross beyond which everything is permitted and nothing has any value'.

In January 1987, Václav Havel, the playwright who would become President of Czechoslovakia after the fall of the Berlin Wall, was speaking more directly and politically about his country in an interview in the paper. Gorbachev was now in power in Russia, and Havel expressed a degree of optimism about events. He recalled how he had once said 'we are losing the sense of time – of what happened when'; but now, he told his interviewer, in Czech *samizdat* publications 'time is beginning to become evident again'. The following February, the Polish dissident Adam Michnik was writing still more challengingly: 'The debate about how to improve socialism has become irrelevant because nobody in Poland knows any longer what socialism is. Our discussions now concentrate on how to achieve freedom.' Michnik in turn would become the editor of the most influential paper in Warsaw after the collapse of Communism. These were voices from Eastern Europe that in the late eighties it was necessary, and good, to hear.

Meanwhile, one of the major Latin American novels of the decade, Gabriel García Márquez's *Love in the Time of Cholera*, was published in English translation, and reviewed in July 1988 by S.M.J. Minta. It was the story of a great and good man, Juvenal Urbino, a liberal doctor in a Colombian town, who for all his dedication never understands his own country – or his wife – and is 'blinded by the promise of a dream that is for ever future'. The novel, wrote Minta, is 'a vast celebration of all that Urbino is not: it is a novel in praise of spontaneity, sexual passion, disorder and vitality, a triumph of the uncertain, sprawling confusion of life over the comforting, dull precision of authority, a victory of the indigenous over the imported, old age over death, the popular over the learned'. The book displayed the same 'fidelity to life' as García Márquez's earlier *One Hundred Years of Solitude* (for which book, especially, he had won the Nobel Prize for Literature in 1982).

New poetry in Britain was not particularly remarkable in the eighties, but old poets went on exciting controversy. In December 1985 Gary Taylor made the case for attributing to Shakespeare a lyric, 'Shall I die?' in a Bodleian Library manuscript (Rawlinson Poetical Manuscript 160). Other scholars fell on him, objecting particularly to the fact that, as the American scholar Donald W. Foster wrote in a letter on 7 March 1986, Taylor had 'used his own revisions of the poem as evidence that Shakespeare wrote it'.

T.S. Eliot could not keep out of the pages. In his play *Tom and Viv*, produced at the Royal Court Theatre in February 1984, Michael Hastings took the line – as Hilary Spurling put it in her review – 'that Eliot connived at, if he did not actually contrive, a plot to have Vivienne Eliot [his first wife] certified insane and locked up for the last twelve years of her life'. The matter had already surfaced in the paper in an article about the play by Robert Hewison, and on 10 February Valerie Eliot, the poet's widow, wrote to say that it was Vivienne's own doctor who had proposed to her brother, Maurice Haigh-Wood, that she should be certified. Michael Hastings, in a letter on 17 February, said he had been somewhat taken aback by the hysteria which had greeted his play. The greatness of Eliot, Hastings wrote, was 'that he can withstand a glimpse at both the man and the work, which I believe are indivisible'.

In 1988, the first volume of Eliot's letters, edited by Valerie Eliot, was published. Reviewing them in September, Alan Jenkins also drew a connection between Eliot's marriage – which had begun, as the letters showed, so happily – and *The Waste Land*, 'six years and a nervous breakdown later, a poem of deathly apprehensions, of skewed, thwarted intimacies between men and women'.

In November of that year, Christopher Ricks raised another prickly question about Eliot – was he anti-Semitic? – in an extract from his book, *T.S. Eliot and Prejudice*. (It was not the first time the matter had been debated in the *TLS* – there was a big clash on the subject in Arthur Crook's time.) Ricks revered Eliot, but he conceded that there was an element of anti-Semitism in perhaps two of his poems. In 'Bur-bank with a Baedeker: Bleistein with a Cigar', the ugly note was just part of 'a maze of subtilised and elusive feelings' that could be attributed to dramatised personae in the poem (in this phrase, Ricks was quoting Eliot himself, discussing a play by John Middleton Murry); but in the 'Dirge' which was published posthumously there was a plain anti-Semitic note. However Eliot suppressed the poem, and we were in no position to say whether that was because he believed or disbelieved in what it implied. Moreover, Ricks concluded, 'Eliot – who believed in redemption and whose art is redemptive – came to contemplate the painful admission', in 'Little Gidding',

> *Of things ill done and done to others' harm*
> *Which once you took for exercise of virtue.*

Three English poets died at the end of 1985: Robert Graves (born in 1895), Geoffrey Grigson (born in 1905) and Philip Larkin (born in 1922). On 17 January 1986, the *TLS* printed tributes to the first two. The poet Fleur Adcock spoke of her feeling in her twenties that what Graves wrote was 'just poetry – a pure substance like distilled water', but she only allowed him now the grudging verdict: 'close to being a great poet'. Another poet, Peter Reading, commemorated Geoffrey Grigson, saying that he guided his readers towards 'items of best being' – a line from one of Grigson's poems – but Reading was cautious about praising the poetry itself too highly.

On 7 February there followed a long poem by Andrew Motion in memory of Larkin. One section told a delightful story. It described Larkin coming one lunchtime out of the library at Hull, 'half grinning, half scowling', and saying

> *Would you believe it . . .*

> *I'm reading the new Barbara Pym,*
> *and she says what a comfort*
> *poetry is, when you're grieving*
> *(but you were laughing):*

> *"a poem by T.S. Eliot;*
> *a passage by Thomas Hardy;*
> *a line by Larkin" . . . a line . . .*
> *And think what I did for her!*

When Larkin's *Collected Poems*, edited by Anthony Thwaite, came out they were reviewed by Blake Morrison, in October 1988. Morrison used evidence from many of the poems that had been rejected by Larkin himself, but that Thwaite had included, in order to argue that, although Larkin remained a bachelor, he was obsessed with marriage – 'as if his chief debt to Hardy were not a tone of voice but a conviction derived from the "Poems of 1912–13" that marriage is *the* poetic subject'. This volume, he concluded, should ensure that 'Larkin will never again be patronised as a dried-up toad squatting on modernism, but be seen as an original, obsessive, deep-feeling poet who consistently refused the consolations of conventional belief.'

The poet Geoffrey Hill was invited to review the second edition of the *Oxford English Dictionary*. Jeremy Treglown suggested he might discuss its literary uses, to writers or to critics. In the event, in April 1989, Hill wrote a remarkable essay. He acknowledged that 'most of what one wants to know, including much that it hurts to know, about the English language is held within these twenty volumes'. But, with an extraordinary combination of scholarship and feeling for the scope and power of words, he picked out many examples of word usage in great writers that the dictionary's definitions did not begin to comprehend. Some of these came from poems by Gerard Manley Hopkins (the centenary of whose death it was), such as the implications of 'pitch' and 'pitched' in Hopkins's agonised phrase 'pitched past pitch of grief', others from writers as different as Clarendon, Hobbes and Melville. Hill declared, in a resounding conclusion, his belief that 'the use of language is inseparable from that "terrible aboriginal calamity" in which, according to Newman, the human race is implicated', and wondered menacingly: 'In what sense or senses is the computer acquainted with original sin?'

1983 was a good year for D.J. Enright. In May, Anthony Burgess reviewed his anthology *The Oxford Book of Death*, and found it 'mostly heartening and sometimes even hilarious. To look death and its concomitants squarely in the skull is to take away a lot of the nastiness.' (It was, perhaps for that reason, a far more successful book than the publishers had feared it might be.) In September, Michael Wood reviewed Enright's *Collected Poems* and a volume of reprinted reviews and essays, *A Mania for Sentences*. Considering articles and poems together, Wood said that one underlying theme in them seemed to be that 'We all settle for less than all' – but that this was only a glum thought if you believed you could have everything. Poets like Sylvia Plath and John Berryman wanted 'the full horror, the wholly squandered bliss', but Enright had 'the humour and energy of a man who knows that settling for less than all may still leave us with quite a handful'. Wood particularly liked Enright's version of Milton in his *Paradise Revisited*: its tone was 'crisp, disrespectful, funny, and yet grim enough to remove all suspicion of frivolity'.

Seamus Heaney's *Station Island* was reviewed in October 1984 by Blake Morrison, who quoted Christopher Ricks's remark that he had become a 'trusted poet', meaning that he could be expected in his poems to do 'the decent expected thing'. Thus in one of the new poems, about eating lobsters, 'Heaney sounds much as he did when he ate oysters in *Field Work* and lets the meal become a similarly conscience-laden, question-filled debate on politics and aesthetics.' But Morrison thought that the new book, as a whole, was 'shaped to suggest a growth away from the reliable and familiar to the masked and alien'.

Neil Corcoran, reviewing *The Haw Lantern* in June 1987, found something quite different in the poems. He represented the book as 'very much of its literary-critical moment', that is to say very much a response to critics' current interest in the nature of writing and interpretation, with the poems largely about themselves and how they were written – 'the exchange between world and word, experience and text'. There was a strong sense in them, Corcoran thought, of how writing records a loss – it is 'elegy to experience'. However, if poetry (as Auden said) makes nothing happen, 'in Heaney it does at least make something "happen again"'. In Heaney, wrote Corcoran, writerly self-consciousness was not 'a nightmare of disabling confinement' – something of which 'modernism and post-modernism had given us numerous instances' – but 'the means of transforming the guilt and burden of writing into the freedom of responsible speech'.

This was a well-argued review that was also of its 'literary-critical moment' – but you would not have learned from it that in its main sequence of poems Heaney gave a beautiful description of his tender relationship with his mother – folding sheets together, peeling potatoes. Those poems were 'perhaps a little tired with their own facility,' said Corcoran.

The three poets whom the *TLS* particularly favoured in the eighties were another Irish poet, Paul Muldoon; the American poet John Ashbery, and the Russian poet, now also writing in English, Joseph Brodsky. The paper published a good number of poems by all of them – though some readers, and even the reviewers, found the first two hard going.

Mick Imlah, writing in September, called Muldoon's *Meeting the British* 'perhaps the most eagerly awaited poetry-book of 1987', and found it a 'difficult and delightful body of poetry'. Muldoon had recently gone to America – he had 'swapped his Irish origins for his Oregon' – and the book was largely about 'abandoned origins'. It found 'new and memorable metaphors for the process of our dissolving and disappearing', and though some poems were just baffling, the book as a whole – 'leaky, shining, overladen' – was a 'fascinating exercise in departure'.

Lachlan Mackinnon, reviewing *Madoc: A Mystery*, in October 1990, also acknowledged that while from Paul Muldoon 'we expect elusiveness, technical wiliness, sly humour and a wide-eyed amazement at the world, we also expect a quite unusual degree of difficulty when it comes to elucidation'. In this he was not disappointed, but after a good deal of struggle with elucidation he felt able to conclude that the book 'shows us a mind at work, teasing, improvising, listening, reading, loving, and his apparently impersonal narrative turns out to be a winning self-portrait. It is a dazzling achievement.'

Claude Rawson wrote a long article about John Ashbery's *Selected Poems* in July 1986. If Neil Corcoran had ventured to suggest that Seamus Heaney was responding to the current preoccupations of literary criticism, Rawson had no doubt at all about it in Ashbery's case. His article was headed 'A poet in the post-modern playground', and he wrote:

> Ashbery is in many ways a critics' poet, like many modern and post-modern masters, the product of a culture whose reading is shaped in the seminar-room and which accepts 'explication' (even defeated explication, which is a permanent invitation to more explication) as an essential part of its reading experience. This need not imply inauthenticity. It is a natural (and by no means the ugliest) product of the hegemony of university English departments over the literary consciousness of the more affluent regions of the anglophone world, and deeply rooted in the economics of (especially) American publishers, which have identified even for imaginative writers the profitability of the teacherly text.

After that cautionary opening he quoted Ashbery's reply when Kenneth Koch asked him if his poems had 'hidden meanings': 'No, because somebody might find out what they were and then the poems would no longer be mysterious.' That remark reflected Ashbery's 'poetics of surface . . . derived from Action Painting', and could also be read as 'an extreme formulation of the old modernist dogma of the irreducibility of poems to meanings', as well as containing 'an element of Dadaist tease'. Ashbery's focus in his poems was 'on a bravura artifice, a deper-sonalised surface crackling with "possibility", a brilliant randomness in which the analogy with Action Painting asserts itself with special force', said Rawson. That was as far as he was prepared to go in judgment on them.

Donald Davie was more forthright about Joseph Brodsky's poems in English. Reviewing the volume *To Urania: Selected Poems 1965–1985* in December 1988, he said that Brodsky did not seem to have realised how 'wavering and variable' the rhythms of English poetry were, compared with the 'emphatic and insistent' rhythms of Russian poetry. So Brodsky overloaded his English verse. 'The pounding Russian line can master and carry along with itself a clutter of exuberant tropes and physical detail,' but under such a weight 'the lighter English line stumbles and hesitates and is snarled'. Brodsky was a greatly gifted poet, so he deserved, as well as needed, honest appraisals and honest advice, Davie said, and in those circumstances, he added, 'the award of the Nobel Prize to him in 1987, when he was no more than forty-seven, may reasonably be thought not only premature but unkind'.

Not surprisingly, however, the *TLS* was glad to have Brodsky in its pages, to which he contributed a number of articles. One was a review in January 1987 of *Conspiracy of Silence: The Secret Life of Anthony Blunt*, by Barrie Penrose and Simon Freeman. Noël Annan had reviewed Andrew Boyle's *The Climate of Treason*, the book that exposed Blunt's treachery, back in December 1979, and had painted a subtle and com-plex picture of the Cambridge world in which the treachery began. Brodsky, bursting with hatred of the Soviet state, simply described the political climate in Cambridge in the 1930s as 'a climate of ignorance. Nobody seems to have told the young men of Cambridge that killing in the name of a social ideal is a contradiction in terms, that it is still murder.'

On 26 October 1990, the paper published a lecture by Brodsky, 'The Poet, the Loved One and the Muse'. There was a somewhat unhappy story behind this. Treglown had decided to institute an annual *TLS* lecture. Brodsky had been invited to give the first lecture, BBC Radio 3 had agreed to record and broadcast it, and it took place in the British Academy on 11 October. Unfortunately, Brodsky's Russian accent made him almost unintelligible, and the BBC felt obliged to scrap the broad-cast, even though it had been advertised in the *Radio Times* and the press. The lecture itself was a startling piece of writing, considering the current character of literary criticism in the West. It was a reflection on how the women that inspired poets came and went, but the poets did not care, as long as the Muse these women had temporarily embodied was still with them. Strangely and heartlessly romantic!

Australian poetry was surveyed by Clive James in a long article in an Australian special number in November 1987. He gently teased those Australian poets who still longed for recognition in Britain, suggesting that they would not get it however good they were, because 'the British nowadays have barely enough time to be concerned with their own poets'. He also mocked those new Australian poets of political national-ism whose work was like 'cold rice pudding'. But he praised Les A. Murray, who had already won the battle for international recognition, and Peter Porter, to whose *Collected Poems* the expatriate critic could point without guilt as 'the best example of what Australian poetry has to offer the world'. He picked out less familiar names such as Bruce Dawe, in whose work the Australian language had successfully swal-lowed the much larger American language 'like a snake swallowing a donkey', and Gwen Harwood, whose poetry 'moves and sings with deceptively simple formal elegance', as well as paying tribute to their predecessors A.D. Hope and Judith Wright, who 'should be Pleiadised' except for the fact that they had not stopped writing yet. He also mentioned David Malouf, who 'like Joseph Brodsky is a culture vulture with the range and cruising altitude of a condor'.

In the eighties, the *TLS* returned again and again to the debate about 'critical theory' – if, in the confused state of its own vocabulary, that was the correct name for it. In the review of D.J. Enright's poems and articles mentioned above, Michael Wood also put an argument against Enright's picture, in one of his *Paradise Revisited* poems, of human beings making their choice, good or bad, of language. Adapting a famous line of Milton's, Enright wrote: 'The words were all before them, which to choose'. Wood set against this remark Roland Barthes's assertion that 'language is fascist':

> For Barthes, the words only seem to be all before us. A lot of them have been chosen already . . . Language is fascist, he suggests, because it tells us what we are allowed to think, encloses us in an ideology we mistake for the world. This proposition can scarcely be true as it stands, or Barthes would not be able to utter it . . . And yet Barthes's notion does have a disquieting force – how many prejudices have we swallowed whole in mouthfuls of grammar or unexamined metaphor? – and it makes Enright's position look a trifle cosy.

This cautious infusion of 'theory' into literary criticism was very typical of the British response to it. Various reviewers in the *TLS* drew on critical theory's suspicion of what words are doing when we use them, without completely breaking with the common-sense view of our ability to choose our language rationally. Even Terry Eagleton, who along with John Sturrock had done as much as anybody in Britain to promote Barthes and his successors, revealed a not dissimilar approach – though in his case with a Marxist emphasis – when in a review of Elizabeth W. Bruss's *Beautiful Theories* in May 1983, he described the welcome that students gave to literary theory after the political turmoil of the 1960s.

> The sudden explosion of literary theory is at one with the crisis of liberal humanism; structuralism and the student movement were the prodigal children of the same distraught father . . . Fewer students were prepared to revere the traditional authority of critical judgments, given the political quietism they implied, the socially particular base from which they were launched, and the blandly intuitive impulses which shaped them. Fewer students, too, were ready to acknowledge traditional literature as a transcendental object, in a world where both mass culture and avant-garde art were busy undermining such received aesthetic categories.

Literary theory had, of course, by now gone far beyond those early excitements, and in October 1985, reviewing Robert Scholes's *Textual Power: Literary Theory and the Teaching of English*, Tzvetan Todorov, a Frenchman who had been one of the early exponents of structuralism, gave a brief, vivid history of its development in America. Until 1968, he wrote, American critics were mainly concerned with the question 'What does the text mean?' The arrival of structuralism did not, Todorov thought, change that scene fundamentally. Structuralism simply aspired to 'furnish a better answer to the same question, calling attention in this case to the internal construction of literary works'.

Now, though, under the name of 'post-structuralism', there had been a radical change. There were two forms of post-structuralism – 'deconstruction' and 'pragmaticism'. The answer to the question 'What does this text mean?' was, in the case of deconstruction, 'Nothing'; and in the case of pragmaticism, 'Anything'. Deconstruction said that it was impossible to know the world: 'only discourse exists, and discourse can refer only to other discourses'. But, for the deconstructionists, discourse was no better off than reality: 'the latter may be inexistent, but the former is necessarily incoherent'. And 'as no discourse is exempt from contradiction, there is no reason to favour one kind above another . . . Indeed, any behaviour that orients itself according to values (criticism, struggle against injustice, hope for a better world) becomes, in the deconstructionist perspective, quite pathetic.'

As for pragmaticism, whose most prominent representative was the American Stanley Fish, that at any rate produced more interesting criticism than deconstruction did. Critics and readers could at least choose their own meanings in what they read – something we saw the Lacanians doing at their conference back in 1978.

Todorov more or less left readers of the *TLS* to judge 'post-structuralism' for themselves after that exposition. In August 1987, Michael Edwards, reviewing *Post-Structuralist Readings of English Poetry*, edited by Richard Machin and Christopher Norris, went on to ask: 'Is post-structuralism not seriously flawed? . . . Deconstructionists find fractured subjects, dubious enunciations, wherever they look.' Deconstruction could be too glib in its determination 'to expose the shabby ruses of poets'.

Nevertheless the *TLS* published many articles in defence of critical theory in all its varied manifestations. John Sturrock wrote some of these; and rather amusingly, his own book *Structuralism* was criticised in his own paper in November 1986 for not making bold enough claims for its subject. The reviewer, Derek Attridge, Professor of English Studies at the University of Strathclyde, quoted Sturrock's remark that there was no need to fear that structuralism would be the death of humanism, since 'all that structuralism proposes to do is to establish the limits within which subjectivity must work'. Attridge commented that it was 'a little sad to see a once-fearsome dog with its teeth drawn'.

Sturrock had defended the original sources of the tenets of deconstructionism in the works of Jacques Derrida in an article in January 1982, but had criticised the American 'Genghis Khan school of Deconstructionists', as he called them, one of whom was Paul de Man. But de Man was in turn given an opportunity to express his views in a symposium, 'Professing Literature' in December 1982. He lived up to expectations by calling for 'theoretical ruthlessness', and urging departments of English in universities to change their rationale for teaching literature 'away from standards of cultural excellence that, in the last analysis, are always based on some form of religious faith, to a principle of disbelief that is critical in the full philosophical sense of the term'. De Man came under a cloud when some wartime writings of his as a student in Brussels were discovered and judged to be Fascist in character, but the American deconstructionist J. Hillis Miller defended him against the charge vigorously in the 'NB' column in June 1988.

The strongest attack on the whole movement came in John Bayley's review of Terry Eagleton's *Literary Theory* in June 1983. Bayley claimed that 'theory' was the conscious and deliberate enemy of literature. In the view of critics such as Eagleton, he said, 'English literature must now be abolished if England is to be saved. Theory, like a laser beam, will burn out all that dead tissue.' In Eagleton's book 'no author is treated as a person, in the fullest sense of art, with whom we learn to commune, whose world we can share. So far have things gone that a simple exclamation of pleasure from a perceptive critic about an author he knows and loves seems today like the past retrieved, the writer rediscovered.' Nevertheless he thought that 'most of the theories Eagleton expounds may soon seem outlandish curiosities'. It is not surprising how dismayed Bayley was when, as we have noted, Eagleton succeeded him in the Warton chair of English literature at Oxford in 1992.

The *TLS* was sometimes accused in these years of a campaign against literary theory, and Martin Walker of the *Guardian* actually wrote to Treglown saying various people he knew in 'the Eng-Lit field' had asked him to investigate the paper. They had suggested that there was 'a vast Murdochian conspiracy to purify Eng-Lit of structuralists and Leftists, with the *TLS* as the spearhead of a Thatcherite purge among the intellectuals'. Walker said that he thought it was all very silly, and it was not difficult to persuade him that there was nothing in it. The *TLS* in the eighties gave plenty of opportunity to the supporters of critical theory to express their views. Yet it is probably true that the bias of the paper, over the years, was hostile to theory. The *TLS*, after all, would have very little reason to continue if what the extreme deconstructionists believed were true. (But such an argument would, of course, have been a perfect example of what the deconstructionists, like Jean-Paul Sartre before them, would have scorned as bad faith.)

Roger Scruton continued to express his disbelief in the value of the whole critical theory movement. He wrote to Treglown telling him that it really was rubbish, like alchemy was rubbish, and that Treglown was wrong to be 'so neutral and stand-offish about this plague'. When reviewing George Steiner's book *Real Presences* in May 1989, Scruton declared that his attention was engaged on every page of the book, and that he was 'left in no doubt of the intellect and imagination which speak through this curious text', but he took the opportunity to deplore Steiner's tendency to 'defer to this rubbishy corpus of pseudo-science which tells the reader that the text is unreadable, that reference is impossible, that meaning is illusion and that nothing makes sense'.

Scruton had his own, opposing faith. In May 1986 he contributed a long essay to the paper called 'The Philosopher on Dover Beach'. It expressed his continuing belief in the 'sacred and miraculous' – in events such as smiles, when we understand the smile 'not as flesh, but as spirit, freely revealed', or in places where 'personality and freedom shine forth from what is contingent, dependent and commonplace – from a piece of stone, a tree, or a patch of water'. Nothing in the scientific view of things forbids the experience of the sacred, he claimed – and 'without the sacred, man lives in a depersonalised world, a world where all is permitted, and where nothing has absolute value'.

In the same vein, he had published a book earlier that year called *Sexual Desire*, in which he argued that the special character of human sexual intercourse was that it could be characterised by 'interpersonal intentionality', with the two people taking part each acting as 'a fully self-responsible individual, a free and moral agent'.

Galen Strawson, reviewing the book in February, acknowledged that this 'sexual Scrutonism' expressed an ideal of sexual intercourse and erotic love that Scruton was fully entitled to. But he felt that 'uninterrupted interpersonally intentional sex' was a relatively rare thing, and that Scruton too readily condemned the 'vast areas of innocent uncertainty, failure, imperfection, abnormality, honesty, exuberance and "animality" as more or less immoral, obscene or perverted'. There was a 'silvery sprat of Scrutonian good sense' swimming through the book, but on the whole reality ran rings round his ideal. Watching Scruton at work was like watching 'Procrustes trying to have his way with Proteus in the SCR.' It was a remark that might have applied, it must be said, to the theoreticians in all the current camps.

Modern feminism began to receive its full due in the *TLS* in the eighties, though in the academic world Women's Studies might be said to have begun seriously with Kate Millett's *Sexual Politics* in 1969, and the new feminism, in the wider world, with Germaine Greer's *The Female Eunuch* in 1970. In March 1988, Marilyn Butler, King Edward VII Professor of English at Cambridge, reviewed Carol Thurston's *The Romance Revolution*, which showed how the pre-1970s feminine ideal, 'the man-fixated virgin', had given way in popular romantic novels to the heroine busied with her career and her erotic adventures, 'dignified in Thurston's eyes because they are a metaphor for her struggle to find herself'. Marilyn Butler said the book was typical of the new feminist scholarship and criticism, which had challenged the old scholarly mainstream rather than joining it quietly. She saw the American women's movement as the source of this change, which had also produced the hard-hitting feminist books in the 1970s about nineteenth-century novels. After the impact of those, 'it seemed as though literature, and indeed woman, could not be read in the old way again', but she wondered if the momentum could be kept up. Women in the academic world were themselves beginning to demonstrate a resistance to feminist criticism.

Three months later, in June 1988, there was a special women's number of the *TLS*, in which Germaine Greer surveyed the history of university Women's Studies over the past twenty years. In its first vivacious period, which was 'rooted in the rebellion of clever daughters against the paternalist and patriarchal institutions that rewarded and distinguished them for the aggrandisement of masculine achievement', its main concern had been to 'identify and scarify sexism'. It had gone on to try to establish a canon of women writers for studying, but the best students had not proved to be particularly interested in that, and now the feminist academics were turning away from women's writing to the study of established male writers again – sometimes, perhaps, just because they were in search of tenure and were more likely to get it that way.

In this special number, eleven male writers were themselves invited to comment on the impact of feminism on them. Almost all of them paid tribute to the healthy influence of feminism on them, but almost all of them also expressed resistance to what they saw as its more extreme claims. The poet Douglas Dunn said that feminism had obliged most men of his generation to think more carefully of the women in their lives and writing, and that it acted as a kind of conscience on writers that prevented the invention of women as 'gratuitously caricatured, bad, boring or comic' – though 'only lickspittles would follow the party line'.

David Lodge more plainly declared his objection to the 'party line', taking as an example his use of striptease in his novel *Small World*. He said that, although doctrinaire feminists would think it impermissible to incorporate striptease into fiction 'except as an occasion for protesting against the exploitation of women entailed in that form of entertainment', for him striptease epitomised the paradox that 'desire can only be sustained by its own frustration'. He had had no qualms about portraying it prominently in his novel, which was also about other forms of disrobing and voyeurism. He would resist the attempt to set up a critical police state based on feminism, as on any other 'ism' – Marxism, fascism, or indeed Catholicism. (He is a Catholic himself.) The robust Germaine Greer would, one feels, have had little objection to this point of view.

The long E.H. Carr story, which had been so thoroughly entwined in the story of the *TLS*, came to an end at the beginning of the eighties. Carr died at the age of ninety in November 1982. To the last, he had been receiving a retainer of £250 a year from the paper, and contributing occasional short reviews. He had lived to see the publication of his massive *History of Soviet Russia* in its entirety – 6,553 pages, in fourteen volumes – with the last volume appearing in 1978.

It was reviewed in January 1980, as part of Gross's effort to catch up after the stoppage, by Alec Nove, the moderate left-wing Professor of Economics with a particular interest in Russia at Glasgow University. Nove was of course aware of the criticisms that had been made of Carr, and he went some way along with them. He agreed with Carr that there was an inevitability about the course that the Russian Revolution took – 'there was a dynamic force inherent in the revolution itself' – and that if Stalin had not come out on top in the power struggle, whoever had done so would have had to take actions similar to Stalin's. But he did ask if there were 'really no policy alternatives to a cruel and costly assault on the mass of the peasantry, i.e. on the majority of the citizens of the Soviet republic?' However, on this matter he would no go further than calling it a 'question which historians will debate for many decades'.

Nove acknowledged too that Carr could sometimes be reproached with 'having no regard for the unsuccessful'. However his review did not indicate any great regard for them himself. When in due course Stalin aimed at making Russia a mighty industrial power, said Nove, 'it was surely through no accident or personal whim that he ultimately had to slaughter the bulk of the old Bolsheviks, for he had to destroy the spirit and tradition of Bolshevism'. Nove concluded by calling the book a 'colossal scholarly achievement' and stating that 'the over-riding impression of any reader of Carr's great study must be one of ungrudging admiration'.

Carr did not live to see a review by Leo Labedz, the editor of the journal of East European affairs, *Survey*, in the *TLS* in June 1983. This was a review of a short posthumous book by Carr, *The Twilight of*

Comintern, 1930–35, and was arranged for the paper by Adolf Wood. There were conflicts between Treglown and Wood occasionally over the use of the fiercer right-wingers, such as Robert Conquest, to whom Treglown was not much attracted as contributors.

Labedz used the review as a peg for a devastating attack on Carr's whole approach to modern European history, and like a similar article in the *London Review* by Norman Stone earlier in the year, it made a great impact. (Melvin Lasky, the editor of *Encounter*, said to me: 'If there is one *TLS* review you must mention in your book, it is Leo's piece on Carr.') Labedz said that the underlying factor in all Carr's life and work was an 'intellectual love of power'. He thought Carr believed in appeasing Hitler and supported Munich; and he 'hardly concerned himself with barbarities' when it came to contemplating the course of the Russian Revolution. 'In the case of Hitler,' wrote Labedz, 'Carr kow-towed before the goddess of power in international relations; in the case of Stalin, he dressed her up as the goddess of history.' Labedz examined carefully the 'thematic meanderings' in the long *History* which, in his analysis, derived from the difficulties Carr experienced in maintaining his admiration for Stalin, and he concluded that 'to compare Carr's approach with Gibbon's is to register the contrast between his moral indifference and Gibbon's human concern, his blinkered pedantry and Gibbon's sovereign achievement in the sifting and validation of evidence'.

Labedz's review was sweeping and melodramatic in tone, but it is hard not to accept its essential correctness. Nove was one of those who wrote to the paper about it, finding 'this exercise of posthumous denigration offensive', but Labedz withdrew nothing when he replied in August, merely suggesting that Nove 'shares many of Carr's illusions and ambiguities'.

One of Carr's consistent foes, Leonard Schapiro, died in November 1983, and in July 1984 Richard Pipes, Professor of History at Harvard, took the opportunity to look back at his life when he reviewed his posthumous book, *1917*. It was Schapiro, Pipes said – implying 'not Carr' – who was 'arguably the greatest authority of his time on the history of the Soviet Communist Party', and Pipes drew an attractive picture of him as a man – a very different kind of man from Carr, also. Though Schapiro was born in Scotland, he had lived as a child in Russia. He was a gentle man, and a romantic, who loved Mozart and Turgenev and quiet country inns. Study of the Russian Revolution, wrote Pipes, who spoke from experience, 'has a relentless and depressing quality about it', and 'the historian who studies it tends to be overcome by its tragedy'. Schapiro himself saw no beneficial results rising from the events of 1917, and 'he bore his scholarship as a burden'. In the end he 'sought relief by abandoning the field on which his reputation rested' and devoted himself to his 'beloved Turgenev'. He returned to the history of the Party in this book, *1917*, out of a sense of duty – but the book had 'an air of melancholy resignation not evident in his earlier work'.

There was also a notable book about a man who 'looked more like one of Lenin's early collaborators than a Duke's son-in-law' – the prime minister Harold Macmillan. Peter Clarke, reviewing Alistair Horne's official biography of Macmillan in October 1988, said that it explained 'how this lonely and remote figure could put on the motley for the benefit of colleagues and public alike, with a disconcerting juxtaposition of throat-catching emotion and world-weary cynicism'.

The *douceurs de vie* found their place, if a relatively small one, in the paper. Hugh Trevor-Roper reviewed the 1990 edition of *Debrett's Peerage and Baronetage* in May of that year. He found that in the modern Debrett there was not much to be discovered about present peers that was not already in *Who's Who*, so he turned to the 'noble arms, crests and mottoes' of which Debrett gave a full account. Among the mottoes, he wrote, ' "Che sara sara" sigh the defeatist Russells', and 'I particularly like the plaintive cry of the Courtenays, "Ubi lapsus? Quid feci?" What distant temporary disappointments have occasioned these implausible hereditary laments, I cannot guess.'

Alan Pryce-Jones brought out an autobiography, *The Bonus of Laughter*, and it was reviewed by one of his old contributors, Alan Ross. He recalled how 'Pryce-Jones glided imperceptibly between high society and café society, among the very rich and celebrated, among struggling writers and impoverished eccentrics, and he gave equally, if briefly, of himself to each, charming, knowledgeable, generous, kind, elusive.' But he thought that readers of the *TLS* might be disappointed that 'there is little more than a couple of pages about the author's editorship of the paper. "Twelve very happy years passed quickly," he writes, before moving on to another topic.'

In December 1984, Jane Grigson, Geoffrey Grigson's wife and herself a noted author of cookery books, reviewed Elizabeth David's collection of her journalism, *An Omelette and a Glass of Wine* – 'yellowed cuttings that we have treasured in kitchen drawers, now clear again on the page'. She commented:

Mrs David has been more to us, I think, than Mrs Beeton was to aspiring Victorians. We hunted down proper pasta in long blue-wrapped packages and walked home with it tucked underneath our arms, a sign of revolt against macaroni-cheese (in those days we did not sniff glue, we ate it). We nervously tried out the new *courgettes* (italics of unfamiliarity), began dinner-parties with her chicken liver pâté or ended them with orange and chocolate mousse. We tried to make ratatouille taste of Provence . . .

The political writer Janet Morgan turned her attention in the Christmas issue of 1986 to the Garrick Club, in which *TLS* editors and contributors had had so many good times. Reviewing Richard Hough's history of the place, *Ace of Clubs*, she concluded that the real pleasure the members took in it was simply the business, not usual for them, of 'the kitting-out, smooth running and general conduct of a household . . . all innocent fun, a jolly doll's house, with steps up to the front door, and attics, a cellar, and good plain food and drink – lots of drinks and arguments with cook and disputes about household expenses ("I'm sorry to begin my annual campaign against the vegetables")'. Non-members, she advised readers, 'need not fear to go to the Garrick should they be invited, as they will immediately feel comfortable. Especially the women, for (and that is why they are excluded) it is like home life, only with men in charge.'

Meanwhile Victoria Glendinning had been imagining, and hoping, there was happiness in another social circle. Reviewing a batch of books about Princess Diana in June 1982, she observed their unreliability – 'Lady Diana passed her driving test the first time. Lady Diana failed her driving test the first time. As a child, she was devoted to her teddy, which has probably accompanied her to Highgrove. As a child, she never cared a rap for her teddy, which sat alone on a shelf' – but found agreement among all the authors on one thing – 'the total suitability of the match.' And that Lady Diana had fallen in love with the Prince, and that he had fallen in love with her 'in step with the rest of the world – or perhaps one step behind the rest of the world'. In 1982, she could hope that 'the fairy story will end in the proper way, and that the Princess of Wales and her Prince, and their son, will live happily ever after. It may be important to us, but it's far more important to them. *Honi soit qui mal y pense.*'

In the later years of his editorship, Jeremy Treglown introduced several other new features in order to open out the interest of the paper. In

October 1985, it instituted a *TLS*/Cheltenham Literary Festival poetry prize, with anonymous entries invited, and the winning poems, chosen by Alan Jenkins and a jury, were published in the paper. None of the winners was well-known, as was perhaps right, but none of them, unfortunately, became well-known subsequently. The following year, in September, eighty-four of the entries were selected and printed in the paper, also anonymously, and this time readers were invited to make the final choice. They did not do much better. However, the *TLS* won an award in 1985 under the Business Sponsorship Incentive Scheme for its sponsorship of the competition.

Two new columns were introduced early in 1988. On 1 January, a series of long, serious articles on general literary and publishing topics was begun under the title 'NB'. This was run by a new member of the staff, an American woman, Isabel Fonseca, who later became Martin Amis's second wife. (His first wife, Antonia Phillips, had also worked briefly on the *TLS* some years earlier, looking after art books.) Many excellent articles were published in 'NB', some of which have already been mentioned. Also, two weeks before this, a new style of dating the paper had been adopted, giving the whole following week – such as 'January 1–7' – rather than just the day of publication. Treglown thought that this would emphasise the topicality of the paper – and also allow him to review some books a week earlier without breaking the publishers' embargoes.

In February – on 'February 26–March 3' – a column called 'Freelance' made its first appearance. The idea behind this was to stress the point that the *TLS* was not only a home for academics but still also a forum for other writers and their interests. The poet Hugo Williams wrote the first column, a diary of his visit to the Arvon Foundation in Devon to teach a writing course to sixteen teenage boys and two girls from a Bromley comprehensive school. With their stereos, and their eagerness to read and write pornography, they gave him a hard time, but he managed to get them interested in a Paul Muldoon poem. Other writers, often poets including P.J. Kavanagh, contributed subsequent columns, but after Ferdinand Mount became the editor of the *TLS*, Williams wrote the column regularly for a number of years.

On 6 October 1989, readers found another small magazine bound up with their copy of the paper. It was called *Liber: A European Review of Books*, and was sponsored by five European newspapers, the *Frankfurter Allgemeine*, *L'Indice*, *Le Monde*, *El País* and the *TLS* itself, in each of which it was appearing, with the same contents, in the newspaper's own language. The editor was a Frenchman, Pierre Bourdieu, with his office in Paris, and Treglown was the *TLS* representative on the editorial board. The idea was that *Liber*, which would appear every two months, would bring together literary opinion from across Europe in order to encourage mutual awareness and understanding.

The new insert boldly tried to provide discussion of such authors as Heidegger and Böll, Eliot and Virginia Woolf, from different national viewpoints – for instance, in the first number Bourdieu himself offered an anthropological reading of *To the Lighthouse* – but it never attained any unity of character. The different intellectual assumptions of the contributors sat awkwardly side by side, especially in translation, where the contrasts of style were inevitably heightened. Bourdieu himself did not help matters. He was supposed to send articles submitted by each of the participating newspapers to the other representatives, but he would not do that if he did not like an article. Eventually, he sat for a long time on a critical article by Patrice Higonnet about the new Bibliothèque de France that Treglown had submitted, and this led Treglown to pull out of the project. In the end, all the members of the board became discontented with *Liber*, and it disappeared within a year after its first appearance.

As for the Higonnet article, that came out in May 1990 in 'NB'. It was a searching study of the way that the plan for the new Bibliothèque had abruptly changed from a 4-million-book library with general public access, and the rest of the books stored in silos outside Paris – President Mitterrand's plan – to a 12-million-volume library storing the entire French national collection – which the building could not properly house. Bourdieu's delaying tactics over the article were perhaps understandable from a patriotic Frenchman.

In 1990, Alan Hollinghurst went part-time in order to spend more time writing; he continued for a while to look after the poetry reviewing. Alan Jenkins was appointed deputy editor of the paper, while Lindsay Duguid took over the fiction reviewing. John Sturrock was still working part-time for the paper; besides his interest in foreign literature and critical theory, he was responsible for the reviewing of history and the social sciences, and was indispensable enough to be allowed also to act as an adviser to the rival *London Review*. Other members of the staff brought in by Treglown were Redmond O'Hanlon, James Campbell, Adrian Tahourdin and Anna Vaux.

By Treglown's time, the payment to contributors had risen to £75 a thousand words. It was not very much with which to woo contributors, and Treglown had to use the same arts as his predecessors to find good reviewers and other contributors. He managed it as surprisingly and successfully as they had done. However, the academics were often very slow to produce their articles, and some needed a great deal of chivvying. Once Treglown invited a group of reviewers to lunch, and only when it was over did he tell them that they were all there because they were six months late with their reviews. Generally speaking, he would not accept any reviews more than a year after publication of the book.

The price of the paper went up, in an almost annual series of rises, from the 50p it had been in May 1981 to £1.40 in November 1990. Library advertising had, as we have seen, virtually disappeared from the paper, and in these years British publishers also began to lose faith in the value of newspaper advertisements for their books. Much of what they continued to spend went to the popular *Sunday Times* book section. Only the American publishers continued advertising in the *TLS* in any significant volume: the influence of Frank Derry, with his bowler hat and umbrella, lived on.

Not much money was put into promotion of the paper. There were sporadic publicity campaigns in the United States, which usually led to a rise in sales, but the promotions were not sustained and the sales always dropped off again. The circulation of 31,000 that Treglown had inherited went down further in the eighties. By 1989, it was an average of 26,792 copies a week.

In these circumstances, it was not surprising that the *TLS* registered a loss, if not a large one, in most years. In the financial year 1987–88, for example, it lost £28,000. By contrast – and fortunately, no doubt, for the *TLS*, since it was under the same roof – the *Times Educational Supplement* made a profit of £4,348,000 in that year.

Towards the end of 1990, a new chief executive of the supplements (the title 'Publisher' had been dropped by now) made his appearance on the scene. This was Michael Hoy. Treglown and he did not get on. As had so often been the case in the past, the management attributed the paper's financial problems to editorial failings, while the editorial staff felt that their *raison d'être* was not understood or appreciated by important figures in the management. Treglown's decision to print the Rushdie protest on the front page of the *TLS* in March 1989 was not well thought of, if only because it exposed *The Times* to Iranian retribution, and another item on the front page led to what Treglown called a *casus belli* in October 1990.

The Czech poet Miroslav Holub, who had also had a distinguished career in medicine in his own country, was invited to write a review of two books, one on syphilis, one on AIDS. He wrote a brilliant and reflective piece, arguing that there was no simple opposition between humanity and disease. On the contrary, both our bodies and our society were what they were because of the effect on them of disease, and 'humanity would not exist if it had not been for the evolutionary pressure of death and illness'. Treglown made a lead of this article, under the title 'This long disease, our history', and flagged it on the cover in large capitals as 'SYPHILIS AND US'.

Hoy could not believe this would do anything except put readers off. Treglown believed – rightly, I am sure – that it was just the kind of subject to interest *TLS* readers, and that they would not be disappointed when they read the article. He went ahead and did what he wanted to.

By now, both parties were coming to the conclusion that it was time for a change. Treglown wanted to resume his academic career, and he gave up the editorship at the end of December. He had not misjudged his future: he went as a visiting professor to Princeton, and was soon afterwards appointed Professor of English Literature at the University of Warwick.

The new editor was the political writer and novelist, Ferdinand Mount. Hoy said he had 'the breadth of vision and literary perception the paper needed'. Mount, interviewed by *The Times* on 15 November just after his appointment had been announced, said that 'guarantees of independence have descended on my shoulders like dandruff', but that he did not want to tamper with 'the bedrock virtues of the paper – the comprehensive coverage, the adventurousness, the readiness to cover any book, no matter how obscure or difficult'. The spirit of Bruce Richmond was still, it seemed, protecting his *Literary Supplement*.

Chapter Fifteen

Debates and Deaths: 1991–2001

It had never crossed Ferdinand Mount's mind that he might edit the *Times Literary Supplement*, and when he was invited to take the job by Michael Hoy, his first thought was 'Not a good idea.' He had been asked about editing before, but apart from a year as literary editor of the *Spectator* in 1984–5, he had always preferred to remain a writer. However, when he woke up the next morning he suddenly felt he would like to do it.

At the time he was a political columnist on the *Daily Telegraph*. Earlier in his career he had been chief leader writer on the *Daily Mail*, and from 1982 to 1984 he was the head of Mrs Thatcher's Policy Unit. His grandfather was a baronet (and he would inherit the baronetcy from his uncle in 1993, though he has not used the title), while his mother was one of the great writing family of the Pakenhams. He had been educated, like so many of the earlier figures on the *Literary Supplement*, at Eton and Christ Church, with a spell also at the University of Vienna.

Although his career so far had been mainly as a political writer, he had also published several novels and indeed in his first year as editor he brought out a novel, *Of Love and Asthma*, that won the Hawthornden Prize. The following year he published a book on *The British Constitution Now*.

When he came to the offices in Clerkenwell, the staff of the paper at first seemed large and awesome, he told me, but he quickly saw what it was that he wanted to do with the paper. First and foremost he wanted, as we saw, to keep up its tradition of a wide coverage of books reviewed with scholarly rigour. But three other goals also quickly formulated themselves. He was determined to increase the circulation, now at its lowest since the end of the war; he wanted the contents set out in such a way that it would be easier for readers to find their way around them – although he saw the charm of the old 'self-conscious purposelessness' of its layout – and he wanted to broaden the *TLS* out into a journal of discussion as well as a review of books, thereby seizing 'a little more of the territory occupied by the *London Review* and the *New York Review*'.

The first goal was inevitably a long-term one. He felt that the management – all of them newspaper men, whose expertise was in selling papers in newsagents' shops and on the streets – did not understand the very different kind of promotion needed by a magazine, especially one with half its sales to subscribers, and also with half its sales abroad. He started pressing steadily for better and more sustained promotion through advertising and mail-shots, and for the relentless following-up of lapsed subscriptions, with particular attention being paid to the United States. After a year or two the circulation would begin to rise again from the 1990 average weekly sale of 26,414 that he had inherited.

He swiftly made some changes to the appearance of the paper. For the first time in its history, the pages in each issue were numbered from 1 to 32 (or whatever the last page might be that week), instead of the paper being numbered from 1 on the first page of the year to for instance 1248, on the last page of the year. Although he kept the four-column page and the generous spacing that Treglown had introduced, on 1 February 1991 he restored the fine rules between columns and beneath articles, and printed bolder headings at the top of each page giving the subject to be found on it, though he admitted that whether a book was (say) 'History' or 'Politics' it was sometimes hard to decide. (An occasional set of pages, usually in the summer and at Christmas, simply headed 'Books for Pleasure' solved some of the problems of classification.)

Mount also reorganised the middle of the paper, where the various features and columns, as opposed to the reviews, were by now traditionally located. He gave several pages to 'Arts', and laid these out without any column rules so that they were at once visually distinct from the other parts of the paper. He included in this 'Arts' section not only reviews of television, films and so on, but also reviews of books on the arts.

'Commentary', the heading under which the arts reviews were formerly printed, became the title of a distinct section in which long general articles on any cultural subject started appearing. In this 'Commentary' section there were also to be found the 'Freelance' column, now regularly written by Hugo Williams, and a new light-hearted and sometimes knuckle-rapping literary diary, for which Mount took over from Treglown the title 'NB'. This was written in the earlier years of Mount's editorship by David Sexton (as D.S.).

Photographs appeared more frequently in the paper from now on, and colour was used more and more as time went by, both on the cover and inside. There was also a change in appearance, which was dictated by circumstances, at the beginning of August 1991: the page-size became slightly smaller, as the printing moved back to News International's own presses at Wapping. In compensation, the number of pages went up from an average of 28 to 32 each week.

As it happened, the monthly magazine *Encounter* ceased publication just after Mount became editor of the *TLS*, and in that same issue of 1 February he wrote a tribute to it and its editor, Mel Lasky. He called it Britain's 'only memorable journal of ideas since the great quarterlies of the nineteenth century' (*Criterion*, *Scrutiny* and *Horizon* were too predominantly literary to qualify) and said that for the generation which grew up in the mid-fifties its famous anti-Communism was not its main attraction – though it was 'bound to be its central theme', for 'what else loomed so large in that bleak and viewless landscape of the times?' However, what the magazine really offered his generation, Mount continued,

> was the excitement of an intellectual Abroad ... To us brain-starvelings, *Encounter* was equivalent to the first whiff of garlic and baguette at Boulogne after the lifting of the travel allowance. And Mel Lasky himself, with his relentless energy and good humour (looking not unlike Lenin after a decent lunch) was an unstoppable, unmistakable foreign trafficker in ideas of the kind that we knew our English pastors and masters would dismiss as unsound ... At their best, *Encounter*'s pieces had a purposeful amplitude which never lost itself in vapour nor soured into vinegar. Where are we to find such stuff nowadays?

Mount concluded by saying *Encounter* 'may turn out to have been a rare excursion in English intellectual life, and one which is unlikely to be soon repeated'. But when he asked: 'Where are we to find such stuff nowadays?' I have no doubt he was thinking that he would like the answer to be: 'In my *TLS*'.

Moreover, it was a good moment, as it turned out, for an editor to take over a magazine with a purpose like that in mind. The nineties were a decade when more energy and imagination went into general political and cultural ideas, and into scientific thinking, than into poetry and fiction. No outstanding new poet or novelist appeared on the scene in the nineties, at least as far as we can see at present.

In October 1995, the paper published a list of 'the hundred books which have most influenced Western public discourse since the war'. It had been compiled by the Trustees of the Central and East European Publishing Project, a group of scholars and thinkers whose aim was to foster a 'common market of the mind' in Europe, under the chairmanship of Ralf Dahrendorf, the Warden of St Antony's College, Oxford. Not surprisingly the list consisted mainly of works by political and social thinkers, and philosophers in a broad sense, from Sartre in the 1940s to Havel in the 1980s. But, said the selectors, 'works of fiction are included only when they had a wider impact' – such as Orwell's *Animal Farm*.

That word 'wider' was surely significant. It was not surprising that novels about personal relationships or, for that matter, poetry making a direct appeal to the sensibility and emotions, were left out of the list as defined. But the implication of the word 'wider' was that such works belonged in a 'narrower' sphere. There was an implicit claim there, characteristic, I think, of the last decade of the century, that 'discourse' was now of greater importance than literature.

The new editor not only wanted to make the *TLS* more of a journal of debate; he also wanted it to tackle current political issues in Britain more directly than it ever had done before. A general election soon loomed, and in the spring of 1992 we find the paper publishing a head-on clash between Steven Lukes writing from the Left and Roger Scruton from the Right. At the end of March, Lukes, an Oxford don, wrote that the Left had 'a strongly egalitarian, liberal and anti-individualist political morality . . . Left-Right maps still make sense of our politics, and the Left is right'. The following week, Scruton replied: 'There is no evidence that we help the worse off by aiming for equality. Maybe those at the bottom are better off in a society where the successful are not constantly hampered by niggling egalitarians and where the creative can push ahead, so as to open the space into which the weaker can rise.'

Mount himself wrote about these political issues. He was – and is – a liberal conservative, drawing on the two main traditions of modern conservative thought – the practical view that only capitalist economies have any hope of creating prosperity, and the moral view that the

505

Conservative Party has a responsibility for the wellbeing of the whole nation. In a delicate way, he expressed these views in many articles in the *TLS* after he became editor.

On 25 January 1991, only three weeks after he joined the paper, he reviewed John Jenkin's book, *John Major: Prime Minister*. He attributed the 'destruction' of his old employer, Mrs Thatcher, largely to her failure in civility towards her colleagues (though he added that 'she remained infinitely thoughtful to those who worked *for* her'), and he praised John Major for characteristic reasons:

> Major's unmistakable ambitiousness has not turned his heart to stone. His view of society quite clearly owes as much to Adam Smith's *Theory of Moral Sentiments* as to *The Wealth of Nations* – and it was striking how instantly public opinion recognised this, before he had given the slightest hint of compensation for haemophiliacs who had contracted AIDS, and other such adjustments to the Thatcherite legacy.

In October 1953 Mount reviewed John Gray's book *Beyond the New Right*. He deplored the 'free market obsession' of the New Right thinkers, and praised Gray's essays as 'among the most distinguished analyses of our present condition now on offer' for their recognition that, while the free market was indispensable, the revival of the 'common life' of the nation, the co-existence of people living in peace, was what was important now, and that in particular the welfare of the weakest could not be 'left to the invisible hand: a society in which there is an abandoned underclass is ignoble, unlovely and graceless'.

Mount also sometimes approached political issues in more indirect ways. For instance in September 1991 he described the scene down the Towy Valley 'when the evening gilds the tide' – a view still as beautiful as it was when it was portrayed by the poet John Dyer in his 'Grongar Hill' in 1716 – and went on to regret the way in which Dyer was later scorned because he also wrote 'rhapsodies on the mills of Leeds and Bradford and their workhouses'. Mount thought it wrong that Dr Johnson's allegation of 'meanness' still stuck to images of trade and manufacture in Britain, and argued that the countryside could not be frozen, even though some people wanted to keep it as a scene of 'sedgy fields, rotting barns and silent villages'. He was glad that Grongar Hill was unspoilt, but glad too that down below in the valley there was a hum of activity, with the woods and parks a nature reserve and the castle a television studio.

Mount escaped criticism for using the *TLS* to publish his own political views, arguably because of the 'eclectic hospitality', as he puts it, that he gave in the paper to all sides of the debate. In fact, in all its spheres of 'discourse', the *TLS* appeared to be the only paper where authors of books were allowed to thrash points out at length with critical reviewers.

Major essays on political philosophy and philosophers were also frequently published in the nineties. Elie Kedourie, by now Emeritus Professor of Politics at London University, was an Iraqi scholar who had published many reviews of books on the Middle East in the *TLS*. In April 1988, another student of Middle Eastern affairs, Andrew Mango, reviewing Kedourie's *England and the Middle East*, had told the story of how Kedourie had withdrawn his DPhil thesis (which was what this book was) in Oxford in 1951, because the examiner had wished him to give a more favourable account of British policy in the Middle East. However, Kedourie was no radical, and had from early in his career taken a pessimistic view of progress in the Muslim Middle East. He had also interested himself in wider political questions, and in January 1992 contributed to the *TLS* a long historical essay on the nature of conservatism, in which he argued that its overriding goal should be the protection in a nation of a 'diversity of interests and a diffusion of power'.

The death of Michael Oakeshott, aged ninety, just before Christmas 1990, was followed in March 1991 by a long review by John Casey, the English don at Caius, of Robert Grant's book *Oakeshott*. Casey tried in his article to elicit Oakeshott's vision of an ideal state – a 'civil condition' – in which the individual could be free within a tradition of established practice. Oakeshott, he said, wanted to initiate people into what he called 'the conversation of mankind', his symbol for civilisation – and one of his whimsical notions was that civilised man was descended from a race of apes 'who sat for so long and so late in talk that they wore out their tails'.

Karl Popper's death in 1994 gave rise to an essay by the political philosopher Alan Ryan, who was later to become Warden of New College, Oxford. Ryan looked back at the way Popper's most famous idea – that what made a claim scientifically respectable was that it was open to testing – led for different reasons to his criticism of Freudianism and Marxism. The Marxists would not admit that Marx's predictions had been falsified, and the psychoanalysts never expressed their theories in a form that could be falsified.

Ernest Gellner, former Professor of Philosophy at the London School of Economics, took the opportunity to criticise Oakeshott and praise Popper – both luminaries of that institution – when he reviewed Ralf Dahrendorf's history of the LSE in May 1995. He called Oakeshott and his followers 'implausible troubadours of tradition' – who nevertheless made the School a more enjoyable place – and Popper the most important mind to have worked there. He made a similar point to Ryan's. Popper laid down the basic law of 'the republic of the mind':

> Decent people, when they say something, must have a sense of what it is which would damn their assertion. They may not always be able to identify it with precision, but they must recognise that it is there, and refrain from undue use of falsification-evading devices (whether inherent in a doctrine such as Freudianism, or attached to it after falsification, as in Marxism).

Isaiah Berlin died in 1998. On 29 May, the *TLS* published three tributes to him – by Bernard Williams, Avishai Margalit, Professor of Philosophy at the Hebrew University of Jerusalem, and Stuart Hampshire – that had been delivered at a commemoration in the Sheldonian Theatre, Oxford, on 21 March. Williams said that you could not pack Berlin's principal ideas into some academic or journalistic receptacle – 'the myriad images in his head of past worlds, of people living and dead and their thoughts, were not the right shape for receptacles'. Margalit said that 'Isaiah's family branches in all directions, and extends to the whole of the Jewish people. When Isaiah gossiped about the family, it was social history at its best. And when Isaiah talked about social history, it was as intimate as family gossip.' Hampshire said that he had been introduced to Berlin in 1935 to talk about Kafka, and they had been talking since then, more or less continuously, for sixty-two years.

These were private tributes to a man widely loved and revered. There had been an earlier 'celebration' of him, as it was subtitled, a book of fifteen essays by different thinkers, called *Isaiah Berlin* and edited by Edna and Avishai Margalit, in 1991. It was reviewed in July of that year by John Gray, who – in spite of what Bernard Williams had said – picked out what he saw as Berlin's 'master idea',

> that ultimate values are objective and knowable, but they are many, they often come into conflict with each other and are uncombinable in a single human being or single society, and that in many such

508

conflicts there is no overarching standard whereby the competing claims of such ultimate values are rationally arbitrable. Conflicts among such values are among incommensurables, and the choices we make among them are radical and tragic choices. There is, then, no *summum bonum*, no Aristotelian mean or Platonic form of the good, no perfect form of human life, which we may never achieve but towards which we may struggle, no measuring-rod on which different forms of human life encompassing different and uncombinable goods can be ranked.

And this principle of Berlin's even applied to 'liberty' itself: gains made in one class of liberties might be at the expense of losses in others, and even democracy and individual freedom might be incompatible.

A great historical event cast its colouring, of course, over all these political and philosophical discussions: the collapse of Communism in Russia. The Russian Revolution itself began to be scrutinised anew. Richard Pipes, the Baird Professor of History at Harvard, wrote an essay in November 1992 to mark the seventy-fifth anniversary of the Revolution. He said that in the 1960s, under Khrushchev, the Russians decided to seek accommodation with Western scholarship on the nature of the Revolution: 'The objective was to have Western historians accept the cardinal principle of Communist dogma, namely the legitimacy and inevitability of the October Revolution and the régime that issued from it, at the price of minor concessions in matters of detail and interpretation.' Pipes said that for a time, a revisionist school of Sovietologists that accepted this view acquired quite a dominant position in Western universities, but these accommodating scholars were rapidly being discredited by the opening up of Soviet archives, and had 'a bleak future'. It was now perfectly clear that 'the October [1917] coup was carried out by a band of fanatical intellectuals . . . who exploited the anxieties and hopes of a politically inexperienced population . . . It was an experiment on a mass scale unprecedented in audacity and uniquely catastrophic in its consequences.' Perhaps the time had come, Pipes concluded,

after two world wars, Hitler, Lenin, Stalin, Mao and Pol Pot, to abandon the whole notion of history as a metaphysical process that leads to a goal of which people are only dimly aware . . . I see only countless ordinary individuals who materialise in contemporary documents desiring nothing more than to lead ordinary lives, being dragged against their will to serve as building material for fantastic structures designed by men who know no peace.

The Cold War was also being reassessed. In January 1993 the military historian Michael Howard, in the course of reviewing a batch of books on the subject, asked a difficult question: during those forty post-war years 'was it really necessary for the West to arm itself to the teeth and indoctrinate two generations in a spirit of Manichaean hostility towards such a bumbling and inefficient adversary?' Only access to the Soviet archives would begin to answer that question. Nevertheless he believed that 'the policy of the West has been ultimately vindicated, not only by our victory, but by the fact that the War remained *Cold*; and that we are all alive to tell the tale'.

Howard, incidentally, had just retired as Regius Professor of Modern History at Oxford and taken up a professorship at Yale, and Norman Stone, another Professor of Modern History at Oxford, had looked back at Howard's decade in the Regius Chair when he reviewed his collection of essays *The Lessons of History* in September 1991. He noted that Howard had himself 'fought a doughty battle, though in elegant language', with the Campaign for Nuclear Disarmament, by establishing that it was not the 'Edwardian arms-race' that led to the First World War – an argument much used by the CND in their campaign against nuclear weapons.

Stone also dwelt on what was, in his hands, a lighter aspect of the Cold War, when he reviewed some books on spies in May 1995. Why were Guy Burgess's activities undetected for so long? There was a Hungarian Soviet agent, Theodor Maly, 'who recruited Anthony Blunt, as a spy, and through him others. England at the time had its freemasonry of men who had been in bed with one another – Blunt led to Burgess, who led to Harold Nicolson, who led (as his Bodleian papers reveal) to Sir Archibald Clark-Kerr, later Lord Inverchapel, and his Majesty's Ambassador to Moscow and then to Washington. That network saved Burgess from exposure for an unconscionably long time.'

Later in the decade, the young historian Orlando Figes gave one of the *TLS* lectures – which went on in spite of the Brodsky broadcasting fiasco – on 'The Russia of the Mind'. He spoke at the Hay-on-Wye Festival in May 1998, and his lecture was printed in June. He went back before the Revolution to suggest the Russian sense of nationhood was unique in that it was embodied entirely in its culture, 'in the values and ideas of its literature and arts', and had never been embodied in an actual state. The Revolution shattered Russia's national identity, and Russia as a nation only continued to exist in the minds of the exiles. He did not say so in the lecture, but readers saw in it at least a hope that that culture of the mind might find embodiment in reality at last.

As for the consequences in the rest of Europe of the fall of Russian Communism, Timothy Garton Ash contributed a long essay in May 1995, in which he dwelt on the relationship between what he called EU-rope, with its fifteen states and 370 million people, and 'the other Europe from which it was so long insulated by the Iron Curtain'. He was afraid that the very success, if it were achieved, of the 'Continental project' – that is to say, of a monetary union with a Franco-German core – might end up 'offering nothing to the rest of Europe knocking at our door'. It could mean that the leaders of EU-rope would become so completely preoccupied with their own internal reforms that they would 'not have enough time, energy and attention left for the parts of Europe where our actions might actually make the difference between democracy and dictatorship, war and peace. They'll still be fiddling in Brussels while Sarajevo burns.'

The *TLS* paid due attention to two remarkable books precisely about the burning of Sarajevo, and more generally the conflicts in the former Yugoslavia. These were *Bosnia: A Short History* (1994) and *Kosovo: A Short History* (1998), both by Noel Malcolm, an expert on Hobbes, a political columnist for a time with the *Daily Telegraph*, a linguist, a writer on music, and an outstanding scholar of Balkan history.

In *Bosnia*, which was very sympathetically reviewed by Dimitri Obolensky in April 1994, Malcolm argued that the independence of Bosnia as a multicultural nation would have been wholly feasible had the Serbs, under the leadership of Milosevic, not set out to destroy it, and had the West not intervened with an arms embargo which precluded the possibility of the Bosnians defeating the Serbs. He did not believe that the conflict between different ethnic groups in Bosnia had been inevitable, as some of his critics argued.

In Malcolm's Kosovo book, reviewed almost as appreciatively by Richard Crampton in April 1998, he argued that the role of Kosovo in Serbian legend and song was based on false history and that Serb claims over the territory could not be sustained. If a settlement of disputes were to be achieved there, 'blinkered views of the history of Kosovo' would have to be discarded by both the Serbs and the Albanians – who just as falsely believed that they had constituted the majority of the population since Ottoman days. Malcolm's views in this book were equally vigorously contested. But of course another, quite different solution was shortly afterwards imposed on Kosovo by the West.

*   *   *

Across the Atlantic, very different issues were the subject of debate, and the paper made a steady effort to focus on those. The forces opposed to each other there were essentially cultural opponents, and multiculturalism (with a very different significance from the one it had in Bosnia), feminism and 'dumbing down' were the new elements on the scene, not to mention critical theory, which we shall come to in a more strictly literary context later.

In September 1994, the British professor of English Claude Rawson, now at Yale, reviewed Diana Trilling's account of her marriage to Lionel Trilling, *The Beginning of the Journey*. He said that the book had 'an atmosphere of settling scores – not just with women and shrinks, but with parents, siblings, in-laws, all New York intellectuals between 1929 and the present, and Lionel'. But it also reflected what Diana Trilling had stood for for over half a century: 'an essential decency, a generosity of spirit and perspective, a continuous vigilance to preserve an unclouded mind among the trendies, the bigots, the unstoppable fetid battalions of the *bien pensants*'. Rawson remarked that the book 'reminds us how remote the liberalism Lionel defended is from the dominant modes of thought of both left and right'.

In April 1999, Kenneth Minogue reviewed two other books which looked back to that time, and in which Lionel Trilling appeared as a figure 'of great moral and intellectual seriousness'. These were Norman Podhoretz's *Ex-Friends*, subtitled *Falling out with Allen Ginsberg, Lionel and Diana Trilling, Lillian Hellman and Norman Mailer*, and Hilton Kramer's *The Twilight of the Intellectuals*.

Each author was 'faithful to the tradition of high intellectuality which flourished in mid-century America,' said Minogue – and each, 'while they deplore the lies and the posturings of the Communist intellectuals of that period', was 'little less dismissive about the present'.

What was this change that Rawson and Minogue both spoke of? Minogue said that Kramer provided the best perspective on how the new cultural milieu evolved:

> He takes 1959 as the crucial year in which the old political preoccupations began to give way to a new world 'devoid of inhibition, formality and other impediments to the unfettered expression of the self'. The crucial figure is identified as Susan Sontag, whose aim it was to eviscerate content in favour of identifying art's essence as style and form. The challenge to tradition was most evident in her 'Notes on "Camp"', in which she remarked that 'the whole point of Camp is to dethrone the serious'. It would be hard to find a more direct

challenge to Trilling's Arnoldian insistence on the moral responsibilities of culture.

One of the early denouncers of this new 'cultural milieu' had been Allan Bloom, whose book *The Closing of the American Mind* had been reviewed in Treglown's period as editor in July 1987. Minogue had also been the reviewer then – and his approval of Bloom had been challenged in the paper that September, in a rejoinder written, significantly perhaps, by Susan Sontag's son, David Rieff.

Rieff thought that it was extraordinary that Bloom should call education 'the taming or domestication of the soul's raw passions' and then 'totally identify civilisation with education'. He mocked Bloom's hatred of rock music, as seen in his portrait of a thirteen-year-old American boy 'whose body throbs with orgasmic rhythms; whose feelings are made articulate in hymns to the joys of onanism or the killing of parents; whose ambition is to win fame and wealth in imitating the drag-queen who makes the music'. Bloom asked if this was how the boy should be 'enjoying the liberties hard won over centuries by the alliance of philosophic genius and political heroism'. But Rieff said that Bloom hated humanity – 'the thirteen-year-old whom Bloom portrays as subhuman could be any kid who likes to dance', and 'however awful life is, it is better and richer than Bloom seems able to imagine'.

That exchange drew some of the battlelines. In May 1991, Joseph Epstein, the editor of *The American Scholar*, drew them in a slightly different, more provocative way. He was reviewing a book by Richard Brookhiser, *The Way of the Wasp*, and saw the main change in American culture as the fact that the WASP – the white Anglo-Saxon Protestant – was in retreat. 'One moment it was there, all intact, Waspdom and Waspocracy, stern and stout and seemingly built to last, and the next moment – poof! – a shambles.'

Brookhiser wrote that this was the result of the sixties student rebellion and the 'rush to ethnicity' that followed. 'In literature, Jewish and black novelists attracted most of the critical attention. Everyone featured and vaunted his own odd national ancestry. Such was the rush to ethnicity that two new groups were formed claiming something like ethnic status: homosexuals and women. The ethnics could dwell upon the pleasures of past oppression, while the Wasps were excluded from what one wag called "the joys of victimhood".'

Epstein, Jewish himself, thus allowed himself a little light mockery of the Wasps. But he did not hesitate to say that 'Wasp values made America a wealthy, independent, and immensely impressive country.'

He quoted Brookhiser on the Wasp qualities – 'success depending on industry; civic-mindedness placing obligations on success, and anti-sensuality setting limits to the enjoyment of it; conscience watching over everything' – and said that these were the qualities that had drawn people the world over to immigrate to the United States. Epstein concluded:

> Fashionable in the United States just now is the movement known as multiculturalism. Its official claim is that one culture is quite as good as another and ought to be honoured as such. Fair enough, one would think, except that in practice multiculturalism almost always turns out to be about the politics of oppression, and its villain inevitably turns out to be not merely the Wasp but white European (male is usually tossed in at no extra charge) culture. Its intellectual thrust tends to be anti-scientific, its philosophical position anti-enlightenment, its emotion liberationist and vengeful. If it really got going it could be most unpleasant. American Wasps are not likely to find much comfort in it, and neither will anyone else.

Other contributors to the *TLS* treated the issue with a little more scepticism. James Bowman, who also wrote a fairly regular article about America in the 'Commentary' section, reviewed a book called rather melodramatically *The Dictatorship of Virtue: Multiculturalism and the Battle for America's Future*, by the journalist Richard Bernstein, in June 1995. Bowman said it was one of the best of the spate of books 'purporting to chronicle the abuses of "multiculturalism" and "political correctness" on American university campuses – and, increasingly, in other places'. But he thought it was intemperate in tone. 'Many of the new revolutionaries are sinister and unpleasant people, but they have not as yet started guillotining their opponents.' He called for more laughter at such episodes as when, at the University of Pennsylvania, a black woman was excluded from a group called White Women Against Racism on the grounds that 'racism is a white problem'. But when he asked: 'Who killed the American sense of humour?' Bowman pointed a rather severe and traditional finger at the culprit: 'It is the democratic superstition that everyone's point of view, no matter how seemingly absurd, idiotic, self-contradictory, sophistical, self-deluded or insane, has equal value and a title to equal respect.'

The paper also reviewed the book *Dumbing Down: Essays on the Strip-mining of American Culture*, which gave a new phrase to the language. This was a collection of essays edited by Katharine Washburn and John F. Thornton, and was tackled by an American writer, Martha Bayles, in February 1997. She acknowledged that 'dumbing down' – the practice of simplifying writing so that it could be understood by the least sophisticated – and 'strip-mining' – the phrase the authors used in order to cover 'ignorance, vulgarity and the other things educated people complain about' – were pervasive by now in American culture 'from poetry to cyberspace'. But she saw the fault as lying at the top as well as the bottom: 'Cultural conservatives will remain ineffective as long as they confound high artistic standards with categorical dismissals of popular culture and the electronic media, or (worse) indulge in the furtive pleasures of racial, ethnic and class snobbery.' And they should also watch out for 'the fancy perversity of the cultural élite'.

A new recruit to the staff of the *TLS* was the classics don Mary Beard. She joined the paper as an adviser on books on classical literature and history, and often reviewed books herself. The nineties were a time of much classical reappraisal. In April 1996 she described Professor T.P. Wiseman's study of *Remus* as 'one of the best-written, most engaging and provoking books on ancient history to have appeared in the last fifty years'. Wiseman had dismissed every previous explanation of why the Romans chose the story of 'Romulus and Remus' as their foundation myth, and come up with the idea that Remus was only added to Romulus in the third century BC, when he was invented to represent the plebeian element in Roman politics. His name 'Remus', which came from the Latin for delay, indicated that the plebeians had to wait a long time before achieving their share of power. Mary Beard found this argument 'immensely enjoyable, often seductive'. Nevertheless, she thought that most of the book was nearer to fantasy than history.

Hugh Trevor-Roper, perhaps now the doyen of British historians, reviewed a book on Erasmus, *Man on His Own* by Bruce Mansfield, in February 1993 – a product, he said, of 'the great manufactory of the new Erasmus industry in Toronto'. The book, with a previous volume, *Phoenix of His Age*, studied the history of Erasmus's reputation since his death. The heroes of the book – whom Trevor-Roper seemed to admire too – were those 'perceptive critics who, beginning in England with Gibbon, saw Erasmus not merely as marking a stage in the Reformation of Luther and Calvin . . . but as the founder of "a second and more complete Reformation whose outcome has been the intellectual emancipation of the eighteenth century". Through their work, Trevor-Roper wrote with an air of approval, 'Erasmus became once again, in historiography, as he had once been in history, the leader of a cosmopolitan intellectual elite'. The reviewer could have justly claimed that he had contributed to that revaluation.

A long article in June 1995 commemorated the centenary of Lord Acton's inaugural lecture – on 11 June 1895 – as Regius Professor of Modern History at Cambridge. The article, by Roland Hill, who had just finished writing a biography of Acton, may evoke a memory of many of the reviews from the first years of the *Literary Supplement*. For the liberal Acton, said Hill, 'progress in the direction of organised and assured freedom was the characteristic fact of modern history', and he rejoiced that 'the deeds of modern men are done in open daylight'.

One successor of Acton's in that chair was G.M. Trevelyan, friend of Bruce Richmond's, who was the subject of a biography by a notable younger historian, David Cannadine. This was reviewed in October 1992 by Stefan Collini, Reader in Intellectual History at Clare Hall, Cambridge. Collini said that a reviewer might be forgiven for fearing that Cannadine's 'often remarked vivacity and wit would obscure the less snappy, though hardly less highly coloured, writing of his subject. But although no-one could describe Cannadine's prose as "chaste", it is, in this instance, at least irreproachably monogamous.'

Collini thought that all Trevelyan's major books were illuminated by Cannadine, especially his *English Social History*, seen 'not just as a thinly disguised broadside against mass society, but as a welcome displacement of attention from the world of politics that had become so unendurably alien and threatening by the 1940s'. Cannadine, who in other books had established himself 'the historian of the aristocracy', here linked Trevelyan's writing to his extensive work for the National Trust, and wrote with particularly authority on the changes after 1918, 'not just in the pattern of land-ownership but also of the land's cultural significance, as the aristocracy ceased to be seen as "the exclusive owners of 'the land' . . . and became instead the altruistic protectors of 'the countryside' on behalf of the community as a whole"'.

Another historian of Cannadine's generation was Linda Colley, his wife. In May 1997, when she was a Professor of History at Yale (where so many British academics were now going), she reviewed a book called *The Heritage Crusade and the Spoils of History* by David Lowenthal. She cited approvingly his view that the decline in religious belief was the essential backdrop to the 'massive appeal' of architectural or land-scape or family heritage to people since 1980. Just as nature-worship was embraced by liberal intellectuals such as Bertrand Russell and G.M. Trevelyan, who had lost their Christianity but retained a conditioned need for metaphysics, so people now who had ceased to believe that eternity was their 'future and only significant heritage', were searching for 'an attractive, usable and reinforcing past'.

She found this concern for heritage most attractive when it was not national but local in character – 'whatever our politics or ethnic identification, we can all agree to admire a coastline, enjoy a display of crafts, relish lovely architecture'. But she feared its appeal to 'both right-wing and left-wing little Englanders', and here she thought historians could be helpful in countering 'massaged presentations of the past'.

Andrew Roberts was another young historian who had attracted attention. His 'all-encompassing, broad-appeal blockbuster' on the life of the prime minister, Lord Salisbury, was described as 'excellent' by the historian Paul Smith in October 1999.

Simon Schama, who had been so admired in the years of John Gross's editorship, saw his reputation in the *TLS* slide. In November 1987, Jonathan Israel, the Professor of Dutch History at University College, London, had reviewed his book on Dutch culture in the Golden Age, *The Embarrassment of Riches*. He acknowledged that no-one could read the book 'without their capacity to enjoy and appreciate Dutch Golden Age art being immensely enriched and enhanced', but he had some severe strictures to make. The book had very little to say about the poor Dutch of the time, it did not place the religious ideas of the period in any historical context, and one did not need to be a Marxist to feel that there was too large a void between 'society' and 'culture' in the way he presented them.

Similarly, Schama's *Citizens: A Chronicle of the French Revolution* was adjudged to be 'fizzing with vitality and insight' by Colin Jones in July 1989 – but, the reviewer observed, Schama so much enjoyed running with the aristocratic hares that he refused to hunt with the revolutionary hounds. His book was distorted by its emphasis on the revolutionary violence, and its almost complete neglect of the violence used by the enemies of the Revolution.

Jonathan Israel came back to Schama in November 1999, when he reviewed his *Rembrandt's Eyes*. This time he was scathing. There was no real attempt in the book to describe Rembrandt's Amsterdam as 'a political, cultural, religious and economic environment' – just vivid impressions of such things as food and smells, ending up again and again as an 'accumulation of verbiage'. Again, in his account of Rembrandt himself, Schama tried to explain the greatness of his painting simply by reference to his personal psychology and 'the inner logic of his genius', not as part of a specially northern Netherlands artistic and cultural context, and he placed far too much emphasis, with little evidence, on Rembrandt's rivalry with Rubens. Israel ended with a tirade against the 'media hacks, publishers' agents and reviewers unfamiliar with the subject' who would undoubtedly be producing an 'orchestrated fanfare' for the book – but he did not believe that those forces 'could ever truly sweep scholarly values aside'. There spoke the enduring spirit of the *TLS*.

One other clash of historical approaches in the nineties was of a more abstract nature. In February 1993, Ernest Gellner, the Czech-born philosopher who was now William Wyse Professor of Social Anthropology at Cambridge, reviewed *Culture and Imperialism* by Edward Said, the Palestinian-born thinker who was now greatly revered on the Left, especially in the United States. Said's book was an attack on Western imperialism, and in particular on its 'ranking' of cultures with Western culture at the top, an attitude of mind that Said called 'Orientalism'. Gellner thought that what Said was offering in its place was 'a kind of unsustained, facile inverse colonialism', that took no account of the complex relationship between different cultures in the world. For one thing, should Said not be grateful that Western influence had actually made it easier for people throughout the world to make a 'free, individualist choice of identity', rather than having to accept a role that their own culture imposed on them?

The ensuing argument between them in the correspondence columns fell into a string of denials that each party believed what the other party claimed it believed. But a brilliant article that brought one item in the debate down to earth appeared in the paper in February 1995. One of Said's arguments was that Jane Austen's novel *Mansfield Park* showed that she, as well as Sir Thomas Bertram, was quite content to accept exploitation and slavery in Antigua as the source of wellbeing in the Bertram household.

In this article, 'The Silence of the Bertrams', Brian Southam, a publisher and Jane Austen scholar, examined closely the date of the events in the novel, and the progress of attempts in Britain at that precise time to abolish slavery. The state of the debate in the country in October 1812 – Southam's date for Sir Thomas's return to Britain – made it almost certain that when, in the novel, Fanny challenges her uncle Sir Thomas over the slave trade, and is answered with a significant 'dead silence', readers at the time would clearly have seen this a challenge by Jane Austen herself to the Sir Thomas Bertrams of Britain. Fanny Price and her creator, wrote Southam, were not, as Said would have us believe, 'friends of the plantocracy. At this notable moment, in the lion's den, Fanny is unmistakably a "friend of the abolition", and Austen's readers in 1814 would have applauded the heroine and her author for exactly that.'

Two twentieth-century novelists were also defended stoutly in the paper against criticism that had been widespread. Some MI5 documents about P.G. Wodehouse were released in September 1999, and Iain Sproat wrote an article the following month that seemed to prove decisively that the comic novelist had in no way been a traitor when he made his five famous broadcasts from Berlin in July 1941. The Germans had proposed initially that he should make some light-hearted broadcasts to America in the way that prisoners of war were allowed to send messages to their families. The point of the broadcasts would be, from the German point of view, precisely that Wodehouse was not a Nazi sympathiser or a collaborator. The talks, describing his capture and internment, would just show that the internees were keeping their spirits up, and it was thought by the Germans that they would make a good impression in America, which was not yet in the war. 'They contain,' wrote Sproat, 'not one single word of pro-Nazi or anti-British sentiment. Indeed they poked fun at the Germans.'

Goebbels later decided that there would be useful propaganda in representing Wodehouse as a traitor, and re-broadcast the talks to Britain, but Wodehouse never received any money from the Germans, and, Sproat pointed out, was completely cleared after the war by the Foreign Office, which in 1947 had written in one of the newly-released files: 'Mr Wodehouse made the celebrated broadcasts in all innocence and without any evil intent.' Many Jeeves-lovers were delighted and relieved by Sproat's article – but many of them must still have thought that Wodehouse had been very naive, which was something that Sproat did not say.

Nabokov's *Lolita* was also defended in the paper when a film of it was made in 1997. While the film was in production, Norman Podhoretz had written about the novel in his magazine, *Commentary*, suggesting that it was a dangerous force in the promotion of paedophilia. Precisely because it was such a literary masterpiece, it disguised the immorality of the desires and actions it described, and removed the taboo from the molestation of children. The philosopher Colin McGinn disagreed with this view of the novel in an article called 'The moral case for *Lolita*' in August 1997. He argued that while we may be 'entranced by Humbert's tumescent and smitten prose . . . we are never for a moment encouraged to approve of his actions. Nor, of course, does he come at all well out of his passion for nymphets: he ends his days in prison, soon to die of coronary thrombosis, alone, defeated and broken.' McGinn thought that this reading of the book was so entirely obvious 'that it is surprising that it needs to be said at all'.

Sex in Henry James came up in December 1996 – but in his life, not his novels. An American scholar, Sheldon M. Novick, argued in his book *Henry James: The Young Master* that James had had an active homosexual life from the age of twenty-two. Millicent Bell showed very convincingly that the key passage which Novick seized on in James's journal as an account of his first sexual experience – 'I had there [in the Cambridge of his youth] ... *l'initiation première* (the divine, the unique)' – was in fact an account of 'the crucial moment when he abandoned his studies at the Law School and began to write fiction'.

Sex in Christopher Isherwood – totally homosexual, and this time abundant – came up in August 2000, when a posthumous book by him was published: *Lost Years: A Memoir 1945–1951*. It was a 'raw' account, as the blurb truthfully claimed, of the numerous sexual comings and goings of that period – 'Andrew, Barry, Brad, Cliff, Denny,' etc., etc. – and startled the reviewer, the American conductor, music critic and Stravinsky expert, Robert Craft, who knew Isherwood well, but had no idea all this was going on. He found the book monotonous – 'The story is always the same, the pick-up, the flirtation, the dinner, bed.' And he seemed to be taking a kind of revenge on Isherwood when he included in his review a memory of his own, the première of *I Am a Camera* on Broadway: 'May I say that for some of the audience the most theatrical moment of the evening was the entrance of Stravinsky, escorted by Christopher down the central aisle, when the composer's old friend Marlene Dietrich left her seat and flung her arms round him, without noticing poor star-struck Isherwood.'

The nineties were also a decade of death among English novelists. Graham Greene died in 1991, and the *TLS* published three articles about him on 12 April. David Lodge, himself a Catholic novelist, described some meetings with Greene, and the change he had seen in him. At first Greene's novels, in spite of their evident compassion for suffering humanity, had in them the anti-humanist message encapsulated in T.S. Eliot's remark on Baudelaire, 'it is better in a paradoxical way to do evil, than to do nothing: at least we exist', and 'this abstract message . . . was invested with a vivid and persuasive concreteness in Greene's fiction'. But later it was obvious that Greene's faith was drying up, and that he was taking a more ambiguous view of the human condition, as expressed in the epigraph (from Thomas Hardy) to his novel *The Honorary Consul*: 'All things merge into one another – good into evil, generosity into justice, religion into politics.'

Peter Kemp noted the fascination that 'people with fault-lines running through them' held for Greene, and his 'aversion to holders of fixed positions' – as shown in the antipathy to statues, all spattered with bird-droppings or toppled to the ground, that was dotted through his novels. But David Pryce-Jones condemned Greene as a writer whose main characteristic was that he appealed to the self-pity in all of us. His novels were just variations on 'The Sorrows of Young Graham' – and even that repeated representation of himself as a victim, so appealing to many of his readers, was a caricature of the truth about this very successful man.

The protagonists of that memorable Booker night in 1980, William Golding and Anthony Burgess, both died in 1993. Lorna Sage wrote a tribute to Burgess that December. She said that he wrote compulsively, 'all the hours God gave', but she evidently could not find anything that he had written wholly satisfying. However, she ended tenderly: 'He hoped, perhaps, that if in this curious way he kept his head down, the Almighty might look the other way, and Art would creep in at the back door. If you identify writing with living so closely, you don't want to produce something too finished – after all, time will do that for you.'

In June 1995, Mary Lefkowitz reviewed the novel Golding had left unfinished at his death, *The Double Tongue* – the supposed memoirs of a priestess of Delphi in the first century. As a woman, the reviewer thought that the book successfully portrayed 'the isolation of a woman's life, her feelings of loneliness and despair'. As a classicist she found the book less persuasive. Sex was taken too prudishly and seriously for the ancient Greeks, and if Golding was suggesting that his priestess's religious doubts anticipated the arrival of Christianity, that was to attribute too great a prescience to her – 'the Greeks were not so eager for a new monotheistic religion as most people might suppose'.

Kingsley Amis died in 1995. His memoirs had come out in 1991, and were reviewed in March of that year by the humorous writer, Craig Brown. Brown wrote very entertainingly about them but was nevertheless drawn into disapproval. He found Amis's tone, 'decked in the chumminess, tetchiness and naughtiness of the lounge bar', extremely limiting. It produced 'very funny descriptions of self-aggrandising strangers', including Lord Snowdon, Arnold Wesker, Roald Dahl and Tom Driberg, who were 'wiped out with blissfully nasty anecdotes, related with his singular skill for the mimicking of affectation'. But when it was extended to old friends this bitchiness became repulsive. He had tailored the past 'so as to fit more comfortably his paunchy attitudes of the present', and 'respect, love, interest and understanding that he once held towards others are deemed never to have existed'. The review was headed 'Amis buys his round of poison'.

Two books that appeared not long afterwards seemed very relevant to these memoirs. In September 1994, David Horspool reviewed Amis's novel *You Can't Do Both*, about the adolescence of a boy with a South London background rather similar to Amis's. He thought it was rather verbose and not very funny, but that it 'succeeded in its main aim, of demonstrating the sort of adolescence that makes a man dedicate himself to "being a shit"'. When Eric Jacobs's biography of Amis came out the following year, the young critic D.J. Taylor, writing in June, said that it showed a pattern in Amis similar to that of his novels, which were mostly about 'people trying and failing, and failing bitterly, to put a brake on their selfishness'.

This biography by Eric Jacobs had also produced some interesting letters from him in the correspondence columns. In April 1994, Jacobs had written to say that the Bodleian Library would not let him see the letters written by Amis that they owned, in order, they said, to protect third parties, even though Amis had agreed to his reading them. In June 1995, just before the biography was reviewed, Jacobs announced that he had after all been able to see the letters, but only because Amis himself had asked for copies of them. Even so, Amis had had to pay for these copies of his own letters, and they had been sent him very slowly over a period of five months.

Jacobs had been asked by Amis to edit his letters as well, but a newspaper article that he wrote just after Amis's death turned Martin Amis against him, and in the end it was Zachary Leader who edited the letters. They were reviewed by David Lodge in May 2000 along with a new autobiographical book by Martin Amis, *Experience*, which was largely about the death of his father.

Lodge began by stressing how funny the letters were – he had not laughed so loud at a book so frequently for a very long time, possibly since reading Larkin's letters. He acknowledged that the letters were 'not going to change the minds of people who have already decided that the man who wrote them was boorish, bigoted, sexist and over-rated', but he said that was all the more reason that they should be read in tandem with Martin's memoir, 'in which exasperation and outrage are tempered by affection and intimate memories'.

Martin himself had observed of the tone of the letters to Philip Larkin that 'It was love, unquestionably love on my father's part', and Lodge speculated

> how different the development of post-war English writing might have been if Kingsley Amis and Philip Larkin had not happened to meet as undergraduates in war-time Oxford and become friends. In due course they introduced a new style, a new tone of voice, a new stance towards reality, in poetry and prose and redefined the concept of the writer's vocation.

In these letters, said Lodge, one could observe 'the gradual formation of what might be called the "poetics of the Movement"'. 'Do I hear a derisive snort from the spirit world?' he added.

As for Martin's book, Lodge said that it was full of delectable humour, and that 'some readers will be surprised by the personality of the author it reveals: tender, affectionate, even sentimental at times; a doting father, racked by guilt for breaking up his first marriage, thus visiting on his own sons the misery he and his brother suffered when their parents separated . . . The simultaneous publication of these two richly rewarding and intimately connected books, *Letters* and *Experience*, is a major literary event.'

Meanwhile, Martin's novels had been getting a mixed reception in the *TLS*. In September 1991, the novelist M. John Harrison had greatly admired *Time's Arrow*, the story, told consistently backwards, of a German doctor who had murdered people under the Nazis and subsequently gone to America. 'Telling the story backwards gives it the vigour of apocalypse,' the reviewer wrote: the book, 'predicated on the moral rage of the author', had more in common with 'the stark unprincipled conceits of Swift, Orwell or Huxley' than with those science fiction novels that reversed the arrow of time.

But Adam Mars-Jones, in a long review of *The Information* in March 1995, was disturbed by the very nature of Amis's originality, which had been 'to detach lyrical language from lyrical impulse'. This story of two rival novelists was 'full of commandingly vivid detail', but none of it was sensuous: 'Not a sensation enjoyed, hardly even a tune heard with pleasure, no food taken into the body without latent or patent disgust . . . It's as if Martin Amis wanted to leap directly from life to literary immortality without having to serve out his probationary period as a human being.' However the book deserved to be read – 'for the ride, if not the view'.

Iris Murdoch died in 1999. Her long philosophical book, *Metaphysics as a Guide to Morals*, had not been much regarded by Simon Blackburn, reviewing it in October 1992: he did not like its 'age-old device of exalting the mystery of the necessary and unconditional Good by debasing the everyday'. Lorna Sage made a somewhat similar criticism of Murdoch's novel *Jackson's Dilemma*, in September 1995: 'Once upon a time – though slapdash – she bothered to be plausible, but no longer. She doesn't describe the day-to-day ordinary world with conviction, nor does she observe a consistent distinction between what goes on in her characters' heads and what goes on in her own.'

Neither reviewer attributed any of the weaknesses of the books they were writing about to any illness of the author, but as the decade went on, it became manifest that Iris Murdoch was suffering from Alzheimer's disease. In 1998, her husband John Bayley published a short book about their marriage, and what it was like caring for her now that she was ill, called *Iris: A Memoir of Iris Murdoch*. Some people thought it rather insensitive of him to publish the book, and call it a memoir, while she was still alive, but an Oxford don and friend of the Bayleys, Katherine Duncan-Jones, gave it an admiring and tender review in October of that year: 'To his many adoring friends, John has always been the gentlest of men', and in the book he had been 'irresistibly honest about every aspect of the richly extraordinary life he and Iris have led together'. She called *Iris* 'a brave and a brilliant book, which makes Iris's fading seem only the latest and worst of many accidents that have somehow come right'.

After Iris Murdoch's death it fell to Lorna Sage to write a tribute to her in February 1999 in 'Commentary'. Lorna Sage dwelt on her 'celebration of human jumble', especially in the earlier novels, rather than her abstract ideas: 'The trick her novels aim to pull off is not to make order, but to complicate order in such a way that it starts to resemble living.' She was 'marvellously sensuous about skin, hair, eyes, clothes, pictures, possessions, food', but also wrote memorably about 'the inverse attraction of the revolting . . . Murdoch novels are decorated and furnished with a kind of perverse elegance: a Greek kouros and unwashed milk-bottles, plastic flowers and Shakespearean quotations.' She might have been, as a thinker, a kind of Renaissance neo-Platonist, 'the kind who would justify physical desire and the lust of the eyes by saying that the images were rungs on the ladder', which you would kick away when you became a Socratic saint. But it was the concrete detail of the novels, with their 'plots and portraits for provocation, seduction, consumption rather than contemplation', that clearly loomed largest for the author of this tribute.

Anthony Powell died in March 2000 at the age of ninety-four. D.J. Taylor wrote a fine tribute to him in the issue of 7 April. He was 'a comic novelist to end all comic novelists,' said Taylor, 'or rather a novelist who could write about serious things in an intensely humorous way without ever losing sight of his targets'. He dismissed the criticism, propagated once by Malcolm Muggeridge, that Powell's landscape was narrow – 'a high-class nightclub of Old Etonians, peers of the realm and whatnot'. In reality, Taylor wrote, 'the rooms through which Jenkins wanders, though always interconnected, are often startlingly distinct from each other ... Many of its sharpest portraits are of people on the way up, social entrepreneurs busily dismantling the barriers that disintegrating inter-war society has stacked, sometimes not altogether wholeheartedly, in their way.' And Powell did not make the 'fussy social judgments' of which John Updike had accused the modern English comic novel: 'with Powell, you feel, all judgments are provisional, cancelled out or modified by time. Some of the most terrific moments in the sequence – the most "like life" – come when a character declares himself, suddenly reveals a greater depth of experience or consequence than Jenkins has previously felt able to allow', such as Widmerpool taking charge of the drunken Stringham after dinner. Powell, concluded Taylor, 'was a great survivor – the last of that spangled generation of Edwardian toffs and rebels that took in everyone from Connolly and Orwell to Waugh. Death will find his reputation no less enduring.'

Muriel Spark had been in the doldrums in the *TLS*, but in September 1996 the novelist Shena MacKay praised the 'discipline and stylish wit ... an object lesson to the aspiring' in her twentieth novel, *Reality and Dreams*, about a megalomaniac film director and the daughter who hates him. Patricia Craig, in September 2000, said that *Aiding and Abetting*, in which Muriel Spark imagined what might have happened to Lord Lucan, 'will no doubt stand as the sharpest and most intriguing elucidation of the enigma'.

Beryl Bainbridge was writing ambitious historical novels again. In December 1991, the writer Francis Spufford reviewed her novel about Scott's fatal expedition to the South Pole, *The Birthday Boys*, and said that 'she succeeds wonderfully in navigating the story, with laughter and grief, as if it were happening fresh, for the first time, in all its brave absurdity'. But Jonathan Keates, schoolmaster and author, was less pleased with *Every Man for Himself*, her novel about the *Titanic*: 'the book's deeper layers are too easily allowed to go down with the ship'.

Salman Rushdie still appeared to be the leader – perhaps neck and neck with Martin Amis – of the new generation of novelists. On 8 November 1991, six writers commented on 'A Thousand Days of the Fatwa'. Nadine Gordimer called on the United Nations to take up Rushdie's case; Joseph Brodsky said that 'tolerance should not allow intolerance to shout down the class'; Hans Magnus Enzensberger raged that Iranian publishers had been invited to the Frankfurt Book Fair; Michael Frayn drew attention to the impossible situation in which the British Muslim community found themselves after the fatwa; the Hungarian-born poet George Szirtes said that pressure should be kept up, and Ferdinand Mount said that the support for Rushdie from British society – apart from the writers – had often been tepid and sullen, but Islamic fundamentalism had to be persuaded that it would remain outcast until it came to terms with Western standards of civility.

Meanwhile, in hiding for most of the time, Rushdie carried on writing, and his books were reviewed by some new voices on the paper. When his volume of short stories, *East, West*, was published, Pico Iyer wrote in September 1994 that 'beneath all the elaborate images and ornate arabesques and imaginative somersaults, one can see a novelist who is living, and acutely feeling, the mixed rat races he describes'. In September 1995, Orhan Pamuk reviewed *The Moor's Last Sigh*, a chronicle of the love and business affairs of four generations of a rich, grotesque Indian family. But although he thought that Rushdie was 'one of the most brilliant magicians of the English language writing today', he felt there was a problem – namely that 'Salman the verbal innovator too often rushes to offer help when Salman the fabulator loses his breath.' In *The Ground Beneath Her Feet*, Rushdie's novel about a rock group, Michael Gorra, in April 1999, found 'too much too-muchness . . . Rushdie's outsized style is the perfect instrument with which to describe the overdrawn symbolic world of music videos and stadium shows. Rock and roll could indeed have given him a grand subject had he not made it grandiose instead.'

Swift, McEwan, Barnes, Ishiguro and Hilary Mantel were all still writing steadily and being given due space in the paper, again often with the opinions of new reviewers. Graham Swift's *Last Orders*, which won the Booker Prize in 1996, received a long review from Oliver Reynolds in January that year. It consisted of the thoughts and memories of four men – an undertaker, an insurance clerk, a second-hand car dealer and a fruit-and-veg trader – as they make a journey in a car from London to Margate to scatter the ashes of a dead friend, while the author's voice was only 'a diffused radiance, something shimmering behind the words and thoughts of his characters'. Reynolds found the book engrossing, 'emotionally charged and technically superb'.

The same reviewer also wrote at length about Ian McEwan's *Enduring Love* in September 1997. He admired McEwan's 'immense gifts', but in this novel about a young couple whose lives are invaded by a religious maniac he had a sense of 'fiction threatened by background reading, of the novelist's bookcase toppling on top of him'. McEwan's *Amsterdam*, which won the 1998 Booker Prize, was described by Phil Baker in September of that year as an 'implausibly elegant black comedy'.

Julian Barnes did not do very well in the paper in the nineties (though he continued regularly to review tranches of Flaubert's letters for it). His novel about two men competing for a woman, *Talking It Over*, was 'skilfully executed but scarcely memorable . . . it won't bear much talking over', wrote Mick Imlah in July 1991, while in January 1996 Gerald Mangan thought that his volume of short stories, *Cross Channel*, mainly about 'characters whose Englishness accompanies them, like a sensible mackintosh, into the unpredictable depths of France', did not show much interest in French people for an author who was so admired in France, and in one story suggested Barnes's own sense of 'a failure to circumvent the clichés that still clog Anglo-French understanding'. *Love, etc*, Barnes's sequel to *Talking It Over*, was liked better by Mick Imlah, who wrote in July 2000: 'although, as before, what happens is entirely trivial, the psychological drama is constantly refreshed by Barnes's invention and intelligence'.

Pico Iyer, reviewing Kazuo Ishiguro's *The Unconsoled* in April 1995, called it 'one of the strangest novels in memory'. It was about a pianist's 'odd, sepulchral, maze-like journey through a nameless European country', with the strangers whom he meets turning to him for help that he cannot give them. Iyer found it a 'profoundly lonely and harrowing book', which certainly fulfilled Ishiguro's expressed desire never to be taken as a realist again. But sometimes the effects were so calculated that Iyer felt 'as if I were hearing about sadness rather than feeling it'. The American novelist Joyce Carol Oates reviewed Ishiguro's *When We Were Orphans* in March five years later. She surveyed his work in the style of an old-fashioned 'middle' in the paper, calling him 'one of our most eloquent poets of loss', but finding that this new novel, about a bewildered English detective in Shanghai in 1937, did not wholly succeed in linking its protagonist with the 'global, impersonal events' going on around him.

Hilary Mantel turned her attention to the French Revolution in a long novel about Camille Desmoulins, Danton and Robespierre, *A Place of Greater Safety*. David Coward wrote, in August 1992, that 'the plot is, of course, predictable – History got there first – but it is overlaid with crafty tensions, twists and high drama, and a detached irony sets the tone'. Peter Kemp, in March 1994, was more enthusiastic about her novel, *A Change of Climate*, in which an idealistic Christian couple become the victims of 'lacerating barbarity' in Africa, and return home, by now unillusioned, to Norfolk. 'Recounting how two traumatised but persistingly well-intentioned people struggle on to lead useful, unselfish lives,' wrote Kemp, 'it is crisp with wintry humour, and pulses with unstaunchable vitality.'

Some new novelists also made a mark. Pat Barker's *The Ghost Road*, which won the Booker Prize in 1995, was the third novel in a trilogy about the First World War which had begun with *Regeneration* in 1991 and continued with *The Eye in the Door* in 1993. Reviewing the trilogy in September 1995, Peter Parker said that unlike most recent novels about that war, 'it reaches beyond a meticulously researched account of life in the trenches, beyond the historical irony so well deployed by Siegfried Sassoon, right into the dark heart of the matter'.

A novel about the Second World War was a runaway success with the public: *Captain Corelli's Mandolin*, by Louis de Bernières. This was about a love affair on the island of Cephallonia between a Greek girl and an officer of the Italian occupying forces, the delightful Captain Antonio Corelli, musician and comedian. 'It portrays optimism in the face of adversity, and sometimes of inhumanity,' wrote David Horspool in April 1994. 'Humour and humanity make the chorus of voices telling the story harmonious to the ear.'

Finally, the Irishman William Trevor, long admired for his short stories, brought out a 1,261-page *Collected Stories* in 1992, which was hailed by Bernard O'Donoghue in November. Trevor's telling 'never risks overshadowing the tale' he wrote; his greatest skill was 'the tact and precision with which he manoeuvres between societies and dialects, especially between Ireland and Anglo-Ireland'. The book had claims to be seen as the best full collection since the 'master of the Irish short story', Frank O'Connor.

Gore Vidal's memoirs, *Palimpsest*, were reviewed by Karl Miller in October 1995. He clearly enjoyed them, but said that 'within the limits set by a laid-back Whig lordliness, the memoir is outstandingly scabrous and malicious'. Vidal contributed two notable long essays to the paper himself, about one of which very much the same could be said.

Vidal's four-page review, in October 1998, of some books on the American airman Lindbergh was provocative but not 'outstandingly' critical of anybody. He showed a great deal of sympathy for Lindbergh's opposition to America entering the Second World War, and for Lindbergh's hostility to Roosevelt at that period. Vidal's own father, Gene, was a colleague of Lindbergh's in the transcontinental airline, TAT ('an acronym, according, to cynics, for Take A Train'), and Vidal gave the inside story, as he saw it, of how with British help the WASP eastern establishment succeeded in taking America into the war. Vidal also gave his own explanation of why so many of the early fliers came from the upper Midwest:

> On my one visit to South Dakota [where his father, an Army flier, came from] I was conscious of an all-enveloping bowl of light, as if one were at the bottom of a vast goldfish bowl; odder still, the light also seemed to be coming as much from below as above. Then I noticed how flat the plain was that I was crossing, how tall sky and low horizon made a luminous globe. In such a landscape, aerial flight seems, somehow, inevitable.

Vidal's five-page essay on John Updike, 'Rabbit's Own Burrow', in April 1996 was, by contrast, outstandingly offensive. Nominally he was reviewing Updike's new novel *In the Beauty of the Lilies*, but he turned first to Updike's memoir *Self-Consciousness*, which had been published in 1989. Vidal said that when most fiction was 'mass-baked sugary dough', he had always hesitated before criticising even any 'halfway good' novelist. But lately he had noticed Updike tilting at him in the *New Yorker* for not sufficiently loving 'the good, the nice America', and becoming one of the 'whittlers and belittlers'. (We may recall the attacks made on Vidal by the Committee for the Free World in 1984 – although at that time Christopher Hitchens had reported that they had attacked Updike too.)

Vidal then proceeded to go through Updike's memoir demonstrating, to his own satisfaction at any rate, that throughout his life Updike had fretted about what 'normal, nice' people would think of him, that books had never meant much to him, that he had been an 'unctuous' supporter of Nixon at the time of the Vietnam war, and then just as strong a supporter of President Johnson when times changed: 'In the presence of Authority, Updike is like a bobby-soxer at the Paramount Theatre when the young Frank Sinatra was on view.'

As for the new novel, his 'big book', a story of four generations of

American life from 1910 to the 1990s, Vidal drew from it the conclusion that Updike believed 'that no matter how misguided, tyrannous and barbarous the rulers of one's own country have become, they *must* be obeyed; and if one has actually made money and achieved a nice place in the country, then one must be doubly obedient, grateful, too. Under Hitler, many good Germans, we are told, felt the same way.'

Meanwhile, other *TLS* contributors were reviewing an Updike that seemed to have absolutely nothing in common with Vidal's portrait of him. In February 1993, Galen Strawson described Updike's *Memories of the Ford Administration* as 'the product of a fast-breeding mind locked tight to the facts of the world', while in January 1999 the Cambridge don Bharat Tandon called his *Bech at Bay* 'the kind of work which gives *jeux d'esprit* a good name'.

In April 2000, Tandon reviewed Saul Bellow's short novel *Ravelstein*, the author's disguised tribute to his friend and hero Allan Bloom – the author of *The Closing of the American Mind*. Although he found 'sequences of great beauty and accomplishment' in it, he thought it in the end a rather unsatisfactory 'chamber piece'. What was perhaps the most remarkable work of American fiction of the decade, Philip Roth's trilogy, *American Pastoral*, *I Married a Communist*, and *The Human Stain*, had to wait until the last of these three books appeared before it received full recognition.

American Pastoral, about a Swedish-American sports hero in Newark whose daughter becomes a terrorist, was reviewed by Paul Quinn in June 1997, who called it a specimen of 'burglar-alarmed' fiction like Tom Wolfe's *Bonfire of the Vanities*, in danger of simplifying and mythologising America. In October 1998, Brian Cheyette reviewed *I Married a Communist*, the story of Ira Ringold, a Communist sympathiser who during the McCarthy era marries an American radio star. Taking a somewhat similar tone to Quinn's, Cheyette called Ringold another 'mythologised everyman who is buffeted and bowed down by the vertiginous excesses of American reality'.

It was only when *The Human Stain* appeared in Britain in May 2000 that this new vein of Roth's received a full blast of praise in the *TLS*. The reviewer, Michael André Bernstein, said that Roth himself had probably not foreseen how far afield his writing would range in the nineties, and how much of American life, history and politics his novels would set out to claim for their subject matter. The novels returned regularly to the streets and houses of the Jewish Newark that was so familiar in Roth's earlier books, but now Zuckerman, the narrator, was only a listener and occasional minor actor in the more intense dramas of powerful figures whose lives, in successive novels, are shattered by the collision of their private self-fashioning with the anti-Vietnam-war movement, the McCarthy era purges and, finally, the 'ecstasy of sanctimony' and collective self-righteousness, the most visible public enactment of which was the national fixation on the Clinton-Lewinsky scandal during the summer of 1998. What Roth has attempted in the trilogy is nothing less than the fusion of 'the American Jewish novel', among whose most skilled practitioners – and anarchic subverters – he has always been counted, with something like an updated version of what was once called 'the condition of America' question. Not even Saul Bellow has so powerfully melded these two central strands in modern American fiction, and uneven though the three books are (the middle one being by far the weakest), cumulatively the trilogy is a formidable achievement.

A cheering note on which to end almost a hundred years of slowly increasing interest in American fiction in the *TLS*.

Franz Kafka was re-examined by the Czech novelist Milan Kundera, in an article translated from the French, in May 1991. While he whole-heartedly applauded Kafka's friend Max Brod for bringing Kafka's novels to the attention of the world in the late twenties, he thought that Brod had launched a false image of Kakfa on the world, an image which the 'Kafkologists' had merely taken still further. Brod had portrayed the novels as essentially religious works, and Kafka as a kind of saint. Kafkology had continued to treat the books as solemn, philosophical works in allegorical form.

Kundera argued that, on the contrary, far from being a saint, Kafka was essentially a hard-headed comic writer, and, in the novel *Amerika*, a comic writer above all about sex. Even more importantly, he really was a novelist, not a philosopher, and what his novels had done, with their 'poetics of surprise', was to go 'beyond the frontier of the credible, not (in the manner of the Romantics) in order to evade the real, but to grasp it better . . . It was he who opened the breach in the wall of the credible; the breach through which many others followed him, each in his own way: Fellini, Márquez, Fuentes, Rushdie.'

Homage was also paid to one of those Kafka followers, Gabriel García Márquez, when Michael Wood reviewed his *Collected Stories* in September 1991. Wood also stressed the realism of Márquez's writing.

531

He quoted a story about a magician who was said to have been so good at embalming viceroys that 'for many years they went on governing better than when they were alive'. Wood commented that 'those dead viceroys, like the live ones, govern with our collusion, and not only in Latin America. Reminders of such facts do seem to have an old-fashioned ring; but they are also, given recent events in Eastern Europe and Russia, absolutely up to the minute.'

It was the older, or the dead English poets who were found to be the most interesting in the nineties. James Knowles, a lecturer at Newcastle University, discovered a masque by Ben Jonson written to celebrate the construction of a shopping arcade in the Strand in London in 1609. Robert Cecil, Earl of Salisbury, was the owner of this building, called the New Exchange, and James I formally opened it, naming it 'Britain's Burse'. Jonson's masque for the occasion, called 'The Key Keeper', and described as 'a comic harangue of welcome' to the King, contained characters speaking of magical products (such as suitable beards for various London officials) and also the real wealth of 'Indian wares' – exotic Chinese or other Asian goods – that would be on sale there. The name 'Britain's Burse' was significant: the exchange stood, Knowles concluded, writing in February 1997, 'as a monument to Cecil and James's projects to unify the kingdom, and to Cecil's policies towards the unification of trade, presenting an image of a world united through its links to Britain as the market of its goods, with the New Exchange as the crossroads of the new London, the renewed nation, and the new world'.

The centenary of Tennyson's death was noted in October 1992. Kingsley Amis observed how he had once seemed an 'intolerable Victorian' and how that had changed; he quoted T.S. Eliot's remark that he was 'the saddest of English poets'. The poet Tom Paulin continued to maintain that he was 'a morbid symptom, a pathological case'. Seamus Heaney wrote of the 'strong hypnotic frequency' of his verse, 'a note somewhere between that of the banshee and the turbine'.

Dylan Thomas made an appearance in a memoir by John Berryman, published posthumously in September 1993. Berryman had met him in England just before the Second World War, and recalled how scornful he was of all living writers, 'above all the two best relevant ones, T.S. Eliot and W.B. Yeats'. When Berryman arranged to meet Yeats for tea in the Athenaeum, Thomas took him to an afternoon drinking-club in Chelsea, hoping to get him so drunk that he would not be able to go.

T.S. Eliot appeared again, in the film of Michael Hastings's play *Tom and Viv*. Philip Horne, a Henry James expert and lecturer at University College, London, was very scornful of the film when he reviewed it in the Arts section in April 1994. It strained, he said, to be 'a romantic weepie, an epic of loving feminine sacrifice and loyalty despite male unworthiness' and its melodramatic portrayal of the wedding night of Eliot and his wife Vivienne, 'designed to blame Eliot as sexually squeamish and emotionally selfish' was 'a grossly intrusive and clichéd speculation'.

The *Selected Letters of Philip Larkin, 1940–85*, edited by Anthony Thwaite, were reviewed by Mick Imlah on October 1992. Imlah was not very attracted by them. His review was headed 'Selfishly yours, Philip', and 'what they restate, richly or poorly,' he wrote, 'are: the impossibility of letting another person into his life; his depression at writing so much less than he wished; his innate meanness . . . ; and above all, his consuming fear of ageing and death. Still,' Imlah conceded, 'self was his life; and in it he made not only – incidentally – hundreds of sharp and sad and funny letters to others, but also (and this was the paradoxical point of it) dozens of the most generally enjoyed poems of the century.'

Tom Paulin, in a letter on 6 November, voiced some of the even sharper criticism of Larkin that was being heard in the country, accusing him of race hatred on the evidence of some letters, and suggesting that Thwaite had deliberately omitted some compromising passages that would have provided even more substantial evidence of it. Thwaite replied the following week, stating that none of his cuts were intended to protect Larkin and that they had all been made to avoid repetition, to save space in what was already an extremely long book, or for legal reasons. In fact, said Thwaite, he had himself found some passages in the letters repulsive but had decided he must leave them in because there was no point in trying to present a sanitised Larkin. In any event he thought Paulin grossly exaggerated what Larkin himself called his 'gouts of bile'.

Outside the *TLS* there were more vigorous defences of Larkin, stressing the unfailingly generous humour of the letters, and Larkin's tendency to exaggerate and indeed caricature his 'reactionary' feelings in them. When Andrew Motion's biography of Larkin came out in April 1993, Ian Hamilton conceded that the letters showed Larkin to be 'a fairly unpleasant piece of work' but thought that 'the widespread outrage seemed excessive'. Larkin had 'turned his vein of coarseness to advantage in his work, setting it off against an equally strong vein of tender sentiment'. As for Motion's biography, Hamilton found it painstaking and intelligent, but thought that the author was 'too solemnly intrusive: he likes explaining things'.

A more subtle evaluation of Larkin appeared in the *TLS* in a long essay called 'Larkin and Money' by Barbara Everett, a research fellow at Somerville College, Oxford, in September 1997. She saw as one important element in his poems a profound respect, even a feeling of awe, for 'the job of work' in a world where 'the transcendental and ecclesiastical are removed from vocation'. Recalling that in his first *Who's Who* entry he gave his occupation as 'librarian' in the belief that 'a man is what he is paid for', and that his father was a Midlands City Treasurer, she wrote of his poem 'Aubade' – and of his poems generally:

> Through the vacant spaces of what Larkin called in a letter 'this absurd, empty life!' messengers move: not angels but postmen. They visit like doctors, curing as best they can. Letters are sent from friend to friend (or were, in Larkin's day). And poems are, of course, the letters that go furthest. 'A man is what he is paid for'; Larkin, the Treasurer's son, converts into vision the 'work' that 'has to be done'.

The relationship between Ted Hughes and Sylvia Plath leaped into prominence again in 1991–92. Ever since Al Alvarez had sown the seeds of the story of the suicidal poetess and her abandonment by her husband in the 1960s, the public hostility to Hughes, especially by extremist feminist groups, had grown. His name had even been chipped off her gravestone. Linda Wagner-Martin's biography, *Sylvia Plath*, in 1987 had expressed unremitting admiration for her and added to what Ted Hughes's family and friends considered serious misconceptions about her and Hughes. It was considered 'nauseatingly sentimental' by Mark Ford when he reviewed it in April 1988. The poet Anne Stevenson then wrote a book, *Bitter Fame*, that tried to give a more balanced account of the marriage, but this book was criticised in the *TLS* in October 1989 as rather chilly about Sylvia Plath and her supposed 'bad behaviour', by Diane Middlebrook, the Watkins Professor of English at Stamford – though the reviewer thought that the book gave an excellent account of Sylvia Plath's development as an artist, her creativity 'fuelled by fury'.

It was a book called *The Haunting of Sylvia Plath*, by Jacqueline Rose, that set off the new round of argument in the paper. The book argued that the picture of Sylvia Plath and her work that had been given to the world by Ted Hughes, from the editing of her posthumous volume *Ariel* onwards, had been a false one, with Hughes suggesting imperiously that he alone knew her 'true self' and trying to suppress other accounts. Now the Plath estate had denounced Rose's book as 'evil', and Rose's interpretation of one of Sylvia Plath's poems, 'The Rabbit Catcher', as an expression of 'sexual ambiguity' in the poet, had been called by Hughes 'grounds for homicide in some countries'.

Joyce Carol Oates reviewed the book in the *TLS* on June 1991. She found the book 'admirable in passion and integrity', and recorded her view that Rose's analysis of 'The Rabbit Catcher' was 'like most of the literary analysis in the book, both temperate and convincing'.

After some further acrimonious debate both in the *TLS* and other papers, Olwyn Hughes, Ted's sister and for a number of years the literary agent for the Plath estate, wrote a long letter on 29 March 1992, detailing what she considered her reasonable response to requests by Rose and others for permissions to quote from Sylvia Plath's work. She said that when she began acting for the Plath estate, she knew nothing of 'the snippets of vindictive and unjust rage in Plath's letters and comments. But these have been the myth's tiny seeds . . . Forests of fantasy have grown up around Plath. I have encountered in all this a lack of sensitivity and understanding that I would not have believed possible had I not been the unhappy witness of it.'

Jacqueline Rose replied on 10 April, stating that she had dealt fairly over quotations from Sylvia Plath's work. She stood by her interpretation of the poems, including 'The Rabbit Catcher', and insisted that her book was not a biography but a reading of Plath's work. Ted and Olwyn Hughes had privileged access to the sources, but this did not or should not carry with it 'a monopoly of interpretation on truth'.

Ted Hughes himself answered this letter on 24 April. Jacqueline Rose's 'strongly feminist' book had claimed that Sylvia Plath's 'sexual identity' had been 'distorted, reinvented, mispresented and violated by the way in which I have edited Sylvia Plath's writings'. On the contrary, Hughes wrote, in her interpretation of 'The Rabbit Catcher', Professor Rose 'distorts, reinvents etc Sylvia Plath's "sexual identity" with an abandon I could hardly believe – presenting her in a role that I vividly felt to be humiliating to Sylvia Plath's children'.

He was astonished, further, discussing the matter with her before the book was published, to find that she considered her interpretations were merely the 'reading of a poem' and implied 'absolutely nothing about Plath's lived identity as a woman'. He had asked her to consider how quickly her 'fantasy', as she now called it, would carry round the world. This was the supposedly 'illegitimate pressure' he had put on her: 'I was trying to get her to look into her heart, but the only effect I had was that she consulted her lawyer. And the passage remains in the book.'

That was effectively the end of this debate in the paper, though two years later a rather remarkable book appeared, not about Ted Hughes and Sylvia Plath but about the books about them. This was *The Silent Woman* by Janet Malcolm, which was reviewed in November 1994 by Lorna Sage. Janet Malcolm was critical of nearly all the Plath biographers, and of many other contemporary biographers too, as well as their readers, all seeking the illicit pleasures of 'voyeurism and busybodyism' – though she thought Anne Stevenson's *Bitter Fame* was a good book. Sage saw Janet Malcolm's book as an ambitious one, not really exposing myth-making and falsification, but claiming her own 'corner of our contemporary Parnassus'. It was the expression of an obsessive 'love-hate affair with writing, conducted from the sidelines'.

During the nineties, Hughes had also gone on writing and publishing himself, and two of his volumes of poetry were soon to achieve a degree of acclaim that he had not had for a long time. In the meanwhile he brought out a long exegesis of Shakespeare's work, *Shakespeare and the Goddess of Complete Being*. Here Hughes presented Shakespeare's work as an 'heroic, lifelong, patient attempt to rescue the Female – in some way or other to salvage the Goddess'. Marina Warner, reviewing it in April 1992, called it a dazzling reading of Shakespeare, and in general accepted the mythological style of this interpretation. However, she said, 'while the poet in the present day unswervingly faces the loathing, destruction and burial of the female in Shakespeare, and celebrates the reassembly of her scattered bones and the restoration of her shattered voice, as he sees it, through the last romances to the final consummation of *The Tempest*, he reproduces the axioms of that self-same misogyny ... The Shakespeare he has made, and vehemently, is a portrait of the artist as a man.'

Tales from Ovid, the first of the two volumes of poetry, consisting of twenty-four poems based on the *Metamorphoses*, was widely praised, but the poet Sean O'Brien, reviewing it in the *TLS* in July 1997, had misgivings about it: at times, he said, 'the large-scale competence of *Tales from Ovid* seems somehow industrialised and thus slightly flat and disappointing'. However, where Hughes succeeded, 'we can feel fortunate to have at our disposal these pungent, dynamic, distinctively northern versions of the Mediterranean epic'.

But Karl Miller was very happy with the poems about Hughes's seven-year marriage to Sylvia Plath in the volume *Birthday Letters*.

Reviewing it in February 1998, he mocked the poets 'who have said that poetry makes nothing happen, and is no place for the personal life, and that what the reader should care about is not "the thing said" but the way of saying it'. It seemed very possible that 'the thing said' here, and the way of saying it

> will make a difference to the way people feel about poetry, and about marriage, however unlikely it may be that the book will appease the blamers and defacers who have contributed to the *cause célèbre* of this particular marriage by demonising Hughes.

It was not a self-justifying book, and it contained 'no Lord Hughes of Life, giving out his authorised version'. But Miller found many tender and funny poems in it, and said that with Hughes's *Tales from Ovid*, they were 'an impressive recruitment and rejuvenation of his powers'. Miller was particularly eloquent about a poem towards the end of the book where Hughes is in the garden of their deserted West Country house, haunting it,

> peering into it as through a keyhole into a casket, the kind of keyhole that might be attempted by a blade of grass. But he 'did not know' that he had already lost the treasure from that casket. Treasures are apt, as here, to be magical, equivocal, ephemeral. In this thrilling poem he is about to discover that the good life is over. Paradise lost.

The nineties were a decade of the death of poets as well as novelists. Ted Hughes died in November 1999, and the *TLS* carried two tributes to him, both of them comparing him and contrasting him with Larkin. John Bayley called them 'our two great recent eccentrics in poetry' and 'as poets of our time . . . the two great freedom-givers', though as poets and personalities they had nothing in common. He said that Hughes had a 'spontaneity in his craft which came from some inner joy in the ceremonial powers of poetry', but he felt that 'his life in poetry was led astray, if not blighted by the Sylvia Plath connection. It seems to me as incongruous and life-disenhancing as if Philip Larkin had been married to and worked with Doris Lessing: the two kinds of genius, the two ways of making poetry and of looking at the world with it, were surely quite incompatible?' Anthony Thwaite quoted Larkin's description of Hughes – 'looking like a Christmas present from Easter Island' – and said that after the death of these two poets there were none left who achieved 'their combination of inevitability, memorability and availability'.

Donald Davie died in September 1995. In August 1991, Claude Rawson had reviewed his *Collected Poems*, saying that 'of all English poets now writing, he seems to me the most various in his responsiveness to the feel of regions, cultures and periods, English and other'. He had 'a sensitive cosmopolitanism that brings together, as he put it in the poem on Gloucestershire in his book *The Shires*, parochialism and *civiltà*.' Thom Gunn wrote a poem for him, 'To Donald Davie in Heaven', that appeared in March 1997, and was perhaps one of the most touching tributes to a literary critic ever written by a poet. He said that, like a fish in an unruffled fishpond, Davie drew to whatever came, thinking it something to feed on,

> *your appetite unslaked*
> *for the fortifying and tasty*
> *events of reading.*

And he imagined him entering Heaven, while

> *those who sought honour*
> *by bestowing it*
> *sing at your approach*
> Lo, one who shall increase our loves.

> *But maybe less druggy,*
> *a bit plainer,*
> *more Protestant.*

Thom Gunn himself received a new burst of acclaim in the nineties. When his *Collected Poems* came out in 1994, the poet Glyn Maxwell wrote in March that Gunn had always written from 'that lost and loving centre between brain and body, which thinks while it feels, and feels while it learns: that species of poetic consciousness, perhaps unique to him in contemporary verse, has never flinched from joy or mortality, and does not flinch from the lengthy raw detailing of hopeless sickness that has been so much of its work in recent times. The human frame, fighting its dirtiest war for years, has at least got its strongest poet in the lists.' This last reference was, of course, to AIDS, the depredations of which among his friends had been the main subject of Gunn's book in 1992, *The Man with Night Sweats*. Hugh Haughton had written of this book, in May of that year, 'the best of these poems are explorations of a profoundly amorous, companionable commitment to the world of bodily intimacy' and they had a claim to be 'some of the most authentic occasional poems of our time'.

Geoffrey Hill's long poem *The Triumph of Love* was reviewed in January 1999 by the American critic, Adam Kirsch. Hill was unafraid, he said, 'to treat the largest subjects in forceful tones, deploying erudition as a chastisement of ignorance'. But there was a danger to setting up as judge of the twentieth century, of which Hill did not seem sufficiently aware:

> It is impossible to write poetry on such a subject without engaging in rhetoric. Rhetoric is speech that is concerned primarily with the effect it is making, rather than with the truth or accuracy of what it says; in the passion of display, the rhetorical poet, like the orator, always has one eye on himself. And this is deadly both to poetry and to moral judgment, for it detracts from the objectivity, the selflessness, that both in their different ways require.

In the same year, Seamus Heaney brought out a translation into modern English of *Beowulf*. He said that in it he wanted to make the poem speakable by the 'big voiced Scullions' of his own Irish family, who uttered their words with a 'weighty distinctness'. But Tom Shippey, reviewing it in October, thought that this had led to a loss of complexity in the characters of the poem and their speech.

Joseph Brodsky died on 28 January 1996. Seamus Heaney wrote a poem for him, which appeared on 9 February. It was in the form of Auden's poem on the death of Yeats, which occurred on the same day in 1939, and Heaney spoke of the

> *Double-crossed and death-marched date*
> *January twenty-eight.*

Thus four famous public poets were brought together in the slight but solemn verse.

More poems by Brodsky had been printed in the paper before his death, including a long one, 'Vertumnus', on 4 October 1991. It recalled his meeting with the Roman god of the seasons in the winter snow, and whispered to him to come back now, a quarter of a century later, with the warmth from under the yellow floorboards of his New York apartment. In January 1997, the poet Michael Hofman wrote an affectionate tribute to this poet who was born in 'what he might have called "Theningrad"' during the siege in 1940, and for whom exile in an

America to which he felt passionate gratitude was 'not fate but opportunity'. The poetry of this 'autodidact and globetrotter,' wrote Hofman,

> is rare in our time for being the elaboration of an expansive and coherent body of thought and experience and reflection composed of, or dealing with, among other things time and space, mortality, personal virtue, geopolitics, silliness, rhyme, water, evolution, art in a mass society, things, mathematics, provocations, places. To get involved with him is to get involved in all that, and to have it come at you with the author's inimitable and irreplaceable urgency, eccentricity, wit and intellect.

Alan Jenkins, the former poetry editor and now deputy editor, and Mick Imlah the poetry editor after 1992, continued to back Paul Muldoon, and many poems by him appeared in the paper, including the three-page poem, 'Incantata', on 26 August 1994, a startling, highly-wrought work in memory of a woman friend. This poem appeared in *The Annals of Chile*, which was reviewed by the novelist Lawrence Norfolk that October.

Norfolk called it a 'beautiful and heartfelt elegy . . . Muldoon's most transparent poem for some time, and also his most musical'. But he gave particular praise to another long poem called 'Yarrow'. At first, he said, it gives 'an impression of something close to chaos: a maddening whirl of incidents and images, references and recherché allusions . . . [But] beneath its crazed activity and intermittent wackiness this is a fundamentally calm poem. The volume's earlier lyrics are gathered in its retrospective gaze . . . The genocides, successive invasions, and fertile miscegenations which are the annals of Chile (and Ireland) are also previsions of the individual lives which flicker, always and already extinguished, always and already alight, and which are sustained in this magnificent poem. "Yarrow" is a new kind of elegy, an elegy for the unborn and the dead alike.'

Nicholas Jenkins, a lecturer in English at Stanford University, reviewed Muldoon's next collection *Hay* in January 1999. He was equally enthusiastic about this book, calling it 'a motley, strangely cheerful collection of poems', in which, to quote one of the poems in it, Muldoon was making hay while he could still hit the nail on the head.

Hay, said Jenkins, 'stages middle Muldoon as someone inseparably identified with the burden of a particular personal and civic history, as represented here (inwardly) by floods of often desolating memories and (outwardly) by a welter of objects'. But it had a 'much less cryptic relation towards representation of Muldoon's own experiences'. However there was also an elaborate patterning of words and rhymes throughout the book, as in Joyce's *Ulysses*, which readers would need help in perceiving (and Jenkins recommended a book called *Reading Paul Muldoon* by Clare Wills). But Jenkins's conclusion was that '*Hay* memorably demonstrates that it is not the tightly woven fabric of an idealised textual or social order that creates meaning. Instead, it is the anomalous connecting "rhymes" and fertile instabilities in language that generate poetry.'

John Ashbery's poems also continued to appear regularly in the paper. In December 1991, Mark Ford reviewed his long poem 'Flow Chart', which was 200 pages long, and said Ford, 'constitutes his most exhaustive approach yet to his impossible goal of offering an all-inclusive transcription of the windings of consciousness, as it relates to the multiple environments of late twentieth-century American culture'. Ford saw the poem as an expression of Ashbery's scepticism about 'the single privileged moment, replete with poetic experience and neatly packaged for consumption . . . all his long poems may be seen as flow charts, abstract diaries recording emotional weather changes over extended periods of time, in which the act of continuing to speak is finally more important than any of the poems' specific illuminations'. The poem's fictions were 'fragments shored against the poet's impending ruin'.

However, in this review, as in many other reviews of poetry and fiction we have noted in the last two decades of the twentieth century, the author was more concerned with elucidating the work, than with giving an opinion about the value or interest of it to the reader, except perhaps through a generally sympathetic – or occasionally unsympathetic – tone.

Tim Kendall's review of Ashbery's collection *Wakefulness*, in August 1998, ran counter to this trend. He found pleasure, but distinctly small pleasure in the book. Ashbery's poems, he said, strenuously resisted the notion that poems possessed a *sense*, and the reader must be unworried about becoming lost in the book's whispering gallery of disembodied voices. But 'the little pleasures which these poems provide more than repay that trust'. However, even he admitted that in one of the poems that he found most satisfying – 'Laughing Gravy', whose nine lines were at once 'funny, enigmatic, anxious and desiring' – 'quite what wolves get up to in wolf factories, why they seem to be in mourning, and what relation they have to the rest of the poem, I really couldn't say'.

Finally, in the matter of poetry, in January 1995, Malcolm Bowie asked why poetry in English and poetry in French had drifted so far apart. The two neighbouring cultures had long had different expectations of their artists and intellectuals he said. 'Taking Philip Larkin and Yves Bonnefoy as representative grand figures, we could set a world in which people live in digs, do the pools, get married and wear Bri-Nylon nighties against one in which they wrestle with the Incarnation, read Hegel, stagger in pursuit of ghostly brides and wear the dark haloes of the death instinct ... When a necessary tension is lost in modern English poetry, we are left with gossip and gentility. When it is lost in French poetry, we are left with empty verbal grandeur. It is high time that dialogue between the two neighbouring traditions began again.'

In November 1991, the *TLS* published an extract from the afterword John Gross had written for a new edition of his book, *The Rise and Fall of the Man of Letters*. It was a strong attack on the presumptions and immodesty of critical theory. He wrote:

> To insist on the priority of theory over literature is bad enough. It is as though no-one were allowed to go to church without first taking a degree in theology. But, in practice, the situation is even worse, since a great deal of critical theory is devoted not so much to illuminating literature as to undermining it, robbing it of its autonomy ... Reading a poem or novel for its own sake becomes a mere naive prologue to the serious business of analysis.

Gross saw a Marxist political message as implicit in most critical theory – the idea that traditional Western values are illusory – and he singled out for its arrogance a passage from a booklet published in 1989 by the American Council of Learned Societies, 'Speaking for the Humanities'. This said:

> It is precisely because the teachers of the humanities take their subject seriously that they ... allow themselves to become professionals rather than amateurs – belle-lettrists who unselfconsciously sustain traditional hierarchies, traditional social and cultural exclusions, assuming that their audience is both universal and homogeneous.

And Gross quoted the reply of the American critic, Roger Kimball, to this: that what we are being asked to accept is that 'only your professional academic is canny enough to escape bondage to naive and intellectually crippling assumptions about social and cultural power. No mere Mencken or Orwell or Auden could do it, you see, because as amateurs and belle-lettrists, they were just too unaware of "traditional hierarchies" to tell us anything of value.'

In July 1994, the paper published a symposium by various writers and scholars on critical theory. John Bayley saw the literary theorists as skilful exploiters of the situation in universities, giving the impression that they were doing something more demanding and exciting than just patiently taking students through the beauties of *Beowulf* or *Paradise Lost*. But he was glad that outside, where 'its exclusiveness makes it as harmless as any other esoteric hobby', theory had little influence, and that people went on reading as they had always done.

Most of the symposiasts took the balanced view of theory that we saw prevailing earlier in Britain. Robert Alter thought that in the late 1960s the study of literature was 'under-conceptualised', but that theory should be ancillary to the reading of literature – 'a view that many would contest'. John Sutherland also said that 'no one who can remember the 1960s (or earlier dark ages) would deny that English departments are livelier for the advent of theory' but he regretted the alienation of general readers from literary criticism, the division that existed between a hieratic élite who understood theory and a sump class of undergraduates and sixth-formers who were supposed to be 'not yet ready for it', and the decline in the number of generalist teachers.

For Elaine Showalter, Professor of English at Princeton, 'the developments of feminist critical theory, gender theory, and its offshoots in gay studies and queer theory, have revitalised literary study', but she regretted that 'the difficult languages of high theory, such as Lacanian, have become a new orthodoxy as muffling as scholastic Latin'. John Sturrock, however, thought that 'our understanding of what we read is far keener for being of a theoretical kind' and that 'meanings can do no permanent harm to the texts that host them'. Terence Hawkes was the chief enthusiast for theory in the symposium: he thought it had enabled American literary criticism to 'escape from Englishness' and from the British love of 'deodorised and soothed-over presuppositions and prejudices'.

The French founding fathers, in spite of those alleged presuppositions and prejudices, were not neglected in the paper. In fact, in August 1995, in 'Commentary', Roy Porter criticised an earlier *TLS* review of one of Foucault's books. This was the review in October 1961 of Foucault's *La Folie et la déraison: Histoire de la folie à l'âge classique* by Sir Aubrey Lewis. Disregarding all Foucault's doubts about the definition and treatment of madness, Lewis had blandly accepted the book as a sound piece of research that bore out his own belief that the history of psychiatry had been one of progress and enlightenment. Foucault, on the contrary, had believed that 'madness' had wrongly been reduced to the purely negative concept of 'unreason', whereas traditionally – and rightly, in Foucault's view – it had always been thought to speak its own truth. Porter said that that view was now widely accepted, while the idea of psychiatry held by Lewis had come under fierce attack. 'So how should the historian evaluate Sir Aubrey's response?' asked Porter.

Was his Olympian calm in the face of Foucault's iconoclasm genuine and solidly grounded? Do we catch a certain professional complacency? Or was he just good at blocking out?

The possible origins of Foucault's own Nietzschean subversion of accepted ideas about reason and morality were discussed in a review by Mark Lilla in March 1993 of two books on him, *Michel Foucault* by Didier Eribon and *The Passion of Michel Foucault* by James Miller. This gave a vivid picture of his loneliness at the Ecole Normale, where he once chased a fellow student with a dagger, and the way in which he had to live his youthful homosexuality in the shadows, 'experiencing the shame, thrill, irony, self-hate, and hardening such a life inevitably brought with it'. But Lilla did not allow these revelations of Foucault's early life, or his own feeling that *Folie et déraison* was more a work of imagination than history, to undermine his belief in its originality and importance.

Jacques Derrida's personal life, or part of it, also got an airing in the *TLS*, when he visited Oxford in March 1992 to give a lecture along with some other French theorists in aid of Amnesty International. James Wood reported on the event on 3 April, but the correspondence that followed was mainly about his parenthetical remark that 'all of the speakers except Derrida gave their services free'. First it seemed that he had in fact donated his fee to the charity, then that he would get a fee for publication of his talk, then – on Derrida's own authority – that he would take a fee for neither.

Wood described Derrida, who had an audience of 1,400, mostly young, in the Sheldonian Theatre. 'Derrida looked foxy and prosperous.

He has a small head with a floury loaf of white hair laid over it. He squints analytically. [He wore] a dark green corduroy suit [and carried] a neat shoulder bag.' As for his talk, which was actually a conversation about deconstruction with the Oxford philosopher Alan Montefiore, that received prolonged clapping. It seemed to represent back-dated homage from several years of students, who 'were thanking him for bequeathing a new language of reading, for showing how texts may be read against themselves. Like Freud, Derrida has enabled people to look for what is *hidden*, and to see that what is hidden will return to mark what is already revealed.' But Wood deplored the 'alienating language' Derrida used – and even more the language, incomprehensible to most, of another speaker, Julia Kristeva. As her distinction between the symbolic and the semiotic came and went, 'of twelve people in my row, three were napping, one was reading a newspaper, two were doodling.' Frank Kermode, who spoke after the French theorists, seemed like an ambassador of that 'empirical tradition' of which they had spoken – 'mild, generous, witty and richly inconclusive'.

The two main British protagonists in the debate in the *TLS* were Terry Eagleton and, in the other corner, the polymath Raymond Tallis, a working doctor as well as a cultural critic, novelist and poet. Eric Griffiths, the English don at Trinity College, Cambridge, reviewed Eagleton's book *Ideology* in June 1991. He found Eagleton's definition of ideology fuzzy and his loosely Marxist belief that ideology could be a force in the material world unproven and unprovable. 'A Marxist,' he wrote 'could not but be ashamed of Eagleton's productions – their disgraceful sloppiness in formulation, the abeyance in them of any sense of history more detailed than that of a "quality" colour magazine, their self-publicising opportunism and political futility. A non-Marxist will find them just sadly unpersuasive.'

Eagleton had a chance to put his views on literary theory in the section of the paper devoted to the subject in July 1994. He concentrated on the nature of the theorist's objection (which was perhaps, rather, his own Marxist version of it) to the humanist: 'it lies,' he wrote, 'in the latter's assumption that culture is the chief surviving enclave of the human spirit in a degenerate world.' He believed that neither religion nor culture, 'its secular substitute', could 'redeem the time', and there was nowhere to go except to politics, 'which can actually transform the degraded conditions which brought about this fetishising of culture in the first place'. But as another don, John Butt, pointed out in a letter a fortnight later, Eagleton gave no indication of what that action should be.

Raymond Tallis's book *Enemies of Hope: A Critique of Contemporary Pessimism* was reviewed in November 1997 by Robert Grant, reader in English literature at Glasgow. Tallis's book was a criticism of every kind of argument that denied us freedom of consciousness and power to choose. These ranged from Freudian and Marxist arguments which, while approving of reason, denied that human behaviour was rational in its origins, to the 'revolutionary and nihilistic' assaults on reason and free will of writers such as Foucault and Derrida. Grant, while subjecting many of Tallis's ideas to close scrutiny in a long article, was broadly sympathetic to his belief in 'old lamps refurbished: roughly speaking, the liberal society we know, but globalised, with less poverty and disease, greater aesthetic and intellectual abundance, and no more nonsense of the kind he has devoted his books to exposing'.

Tallis was engaged in arguments on these themes in the correspondence columns throughout the decade. He tackled Eagleton directly in a review of his book *The Idea of Culture* in July 2000. He thought that all that was best in Eagleton's book derived from Raymond Williams's study of the relationship between culture and civilisation in his book, *Keywords*, in 1976. But in Eagleton these ideas 'keep on being brushed aside by outbreaks of politically inspired anger which make the narrative almost impossible to follow', and the politics behind the anger were difficult to pin down too. Tallis got no thanks for this review. A letter from Daniel W. O'Bryan, of Sierra Nevada College, Incline Village, Nevada, said that the review was not a review but an 'extended slur', accused Tallis of 'reptilian techniques', and claimed that 'Give me a book, and I could write a Tallis review in under an hour.'

There were also severely critical reviews in the paper of books written by two of its own regular reviewers on cultural matters. In January 1996, the American critic Robert Alter reviewed George Steiner's collection of essays *No Passion Spent* and a book of nine stories by him, *The Deeps of the Sea*. He pointed out and deplored Steiner's hyperbolic and sometimes poorly-based critical judgments, such as his declaration that the Hungarian poet Sander Weores was 'one of the master voices of the century', when Steiner could not even read Hungarian. He criticised even more strongly the 'errors consequent upon Steiner's pretending to knowledge he does not really possess', such as his incorrect observations on the nuances of some terms in the Hebrew Bible.

More generally, Alter acknowledged that Steiner had offered insights into many major writers – Dostoevsky, Sophocles, Rilke, Kafka and Celan – but felt that he was essentially a theological critic, only interested in such great questions as 'What purchase can the idea of redemption have in the stubbornly unredeemed realm of history?' which meant there was scarcely any room in his canon 'for Rabelais, for Sterne, for Stendhal, for Dickens, even for Joyce' – restorative writers who could scrutinise the mess of history with subtlety and humour. Steiner's fiction, said Alter, 'which exhibits remarkable stylistic and technical deftness, is mesmerised in the same way by historical catastrophe'.

Steiner was hurt by this review, but went on contributing to the paper, in both August 1997 and January 1999, for instance, writing about some matters to which he had given much thought, Heidegger's philosophy and his relationship with Hannah Arendt. About the latter subject he concluded, unsubdued in the sweep of his vision: 'It may well be that in centuries to come the Abelard-Eloise letters and the Heidegger-Arendt *Briefe* will circle one another, reciprocally illuminating and mapping, in their intersecting orbits, a cosmography of the thinking heart.'

The other contributor who was heavily criticised was Roger Scruton. The reviewer of his book *An Intelligent Person's Guide to Modern Culture*, in July 1999, was Eric Griffiths, who showed he could lay about him on the Right as well as on the Left.

Griffiths mocked Scruton's nostalgic version of the history of Western culture:

> For centuries, it seems, people lived in 'the old way of life – the rooted, pious, unquestioning and obedient life'. Then, the Enlightenment and the French Revolution happened; the worst excesses of that unfortunate movement have led inexorably to drug culture, Derrida and Oasis, which Scruton fumes about in the second half of his guide. If the reader will imagine a collaboration between the Hegel of *Phenomenology, VI* and the scriptwriters of *Monty Python and the Holy Grail*, he will have a fair sense of Scruton's manner and quality as a historian of culture.

One other general theme received a good deal of attention in this decade: feminism. In June 1991, Kenneth Minogue, reviewing a batch of books on the subject, expressed his doubt whether feminist theory, which was the dominant element of Women's Studies, really belonged 'in the cool groves of academe'. It was passionate and salvationist and knew in advance the conclusions it would arrive at. 'Academically, it is mostly unsophisticated. A little light generalising work is followed by polysyllabic decoration and some spray-on indignation.'

This review brought some outraged letters from women the following week, but in September 1992 a book about women novelists which drew on critical and feminist theory was warmly praised by Isobel Armstrong. This was Lorna Sage's *Women in the House of Fiction*, which set out to show that women writers had produced a range of narrative experiments and fictional innovations which were different from other modernist writing. Sage was hostile to the idea of a special kind of 'feminine' writing, but she interpreted what novelists such as Doris Lessing and Iris Murdoch were trying to do in the light of feminism, and she did so in 'precise and concrete writing'. She was especially eloquent on the work of Angela Carter, Joyce Carol Oates and Toni Morrison, but did not much like the self-consciously feminist writers, such as Kate Millett or Erica Jong, with their 'dogmatism, tendency to hysteria and "libertarian striptease"'.

When Camille Paglia, the rebel against feminism who believed that women were neither weak nor oppressed, brought out her book *Sex, Art and American Culture*, the *TLS* reviewer said that whenever Paglia spoke on campus she attracted 'unprecedented numbers of cheering, laughing students'. The reviewer, Christina Hoff Summers, Professor of Philosophy at Clark University, Massachusetts, writing in January 1993, went along with her against the trend of feminism. She noted Paglia's belief that civilisation was a male product, quoting her remark that 'If civilisation had been left in female hands we'd still be living in grass huts', and commented that 'Paglia's appreciation of what men have wrought is refreshing in these days of feminist harangues about "patriarchy".' The following January, when Paglia was visiting London, the 'NB' column quoted a still racier politically incorrect remark she had made: 'I'm so tired of making love with women, it takes forever. I'm too lazy to be a Lesbian.'

A symposium on feminism in March 1998, ten years after the one that Treglown had organised, mostly showed the kind of balanced attitudes that we saw in the symposium on literary theory. The historian Linda Colley said that she did not want to become a women's historian but that she would not now want to write a book in which women played only a negligible or token role. Roy Porter said that feminism had affected his practice as an historian in three ways. It had opened his eyes to areas of human experience utterly absent from his undergraduate training – 'beyond a few great queens, I doubt if women even figured in my finals'. Secondly, feminist scholarship in the last twenty years had been a key stimulus in the history of sexuality, the body and psychiatry: 'the wider history of medicine owes at least as big a debt to feminism as to Foucault (though why feminists pay such homage

548

to Foucault beats me).' But thirdly, he had been glad to counter the neo-misogynistic myths of those feminist historians who demeaned women as helpless victims. The most uncompromising feminist in this symposium was Andrea Dworkin. She declared that 'we will use means both legal and illegal to destroy whatever keeps male violence defended and in place. We know we have another 300 to 400 years of struggle.'

The paper also often turned its attention to paintings in these years. In October 1994, Marc Fumaroli, Professor of Cultural and Foreign Affairs at the Collège de France, revealed that Anthony Blunt, in his book on Poussin, suppressed the evidence of the painter's deep attachment to the Jesuits in his pleasure at portraying him as a kind of Enlightenment spy in Rome, 'apparently perfectly adapted to his surroundings, while in his heart betraying it for a cause known only to him and a few confederates'.

When the Vermeer exhibition opened in the Mauritshuis in the Hague in 1996, and thousands of Britons flocked across the North Sea to see it, Alan Jenkins wrote an evocative account, in April of that year, of the paintings in their museum setting:

> We are held simultaneously by an overwhelming sensuous immediacy, and an immense richness of suggestion. An exhibition guide tells us how, in maps, paintings within paintings, inscriptions on musical instruments, the instruments themselves, Vermeer employed the iconographic repertoire of his time . . . We might feel that we were thus equipped to 'read' the paintings, but we would be wrong. Their mood still seems ambiguous, poised between melancholy and a great joy; their meaning remains enigmatic, muted, beyond the reach of any intrusion . . . This is, in essence, Vermeer's vision of woman, in the great series of solitary, seated or standing figures of the 1660s . . . For him, the female subject was not to be grasped, mastered, possessed – not even by the eye.

Mount liked employing practitioners of the arts to write about them. One of the art critics the paper used most was the painter Julian Bell, who in February 1993 described the work of Paula Rego in reviewing a book about her by John McEwen. He said that she had always subverted canons, hierarchies and 'high art' through her insistence on the incontestably personal and visceral, and 'if she is seen as an exemplary figure, it is because her stance seems to embody anti-patriarchal hopes'. But in her work for the National Gallery restaurant, 'Crivelli's Garden', she had only met these hopes half-way:

> She has cunningly plucked all the female saints out of the predominantly male pictorial world around her and rewoven them into a quirky, tastefully understated, feminist heroic history incorporating many of the devices of the Old Masters. 'Everything I know is in this picture,' she claims.

In September 1992, there was a special number on 'Cities', and a number of writers were asked to describe the city that in their view came closest to perfection. Thom Gunn chose San Francisco with its street fairs, Peter Green – who had contributed many articles to the *TLS* on classical history and literature over the years – chose Athens, which in spite of its smog, traffic and incomparably scabrous yellow press, was the only city where he felt totally at peace with himself and the world, and Patrick Leigh Fermor chose Prague, which he had seen once only, in 1934,

> when the ice on the Vltava was breaking with loud bangs, and the fragments were jostling each other downstream between the fourteen cutwaters of one of the great bridges of the world . . . But the snow was intact over the hushed city, and it gave an unreal lightness to the tiers of flaunting and beautiful palaces, renaissance, baroque and rococo – with mantelling and fauna running wild in the colonnades, muscle-bound Atlases groaning under heaped lintels and the ghosts of toccatas and passacaglias just out of earshot.

The singer Ian Bostridge wrote about some books on Schubert in November 1997. He said that Schubert's carousing and contraction of syphilis under the influence of his friend Schober had, ironically, acted as a release from idleness and diverted Schubert's work into new channels. 'One of the special qualities of Schubert's mature style,' Bostridge wrote, 'is surely its eerie juxtaposition of the domestic and the savage, the dance interrupted by the angry outburst, the arrogant coexisting with the cosy.' In the same special Music number, Robert Craft, reviewing Peter Ostwald's book on Glenn Gould, recorded his own experiences of working with the pianist, a happier story than those he had to tell about Christopher Isherwood. After 1964 Gould retired from public performance for fear of infectious microbes spread by coughing audiences, and for eighteen years only played in recording studios. Craft described Gould arriving at a New York studio to tape a concert for television, in which Gould was playing Bach's D minor concerto and Stravinsky was conducting *Firebird*:

> The pianist arrived with the famous bag containing the wood blocks used to elevate the legs of his pianos, and the folding-chair substitute for a stool. He was swathed in scarves, wore a heavy coat, galoshes and sheepskin gloves, none of which was removed until a moment before he started playing. The studio was draughty, but I learned only later that he would have worn the same clothing indoors in midsummer. Warned of his hand-shaking phobia, I did not offer mine, but I noticed that he removed a glove to meet Stravinsky's extended arm . . .

As for television, that continued to receive regular but relatively sparse and rarely favourable notice in the paper. However, Mick Imlah reviewed the BBC's production of *Middlemarch* in February 1994 and said that 'its marriage of a wonderful book and an unusual budget set standards that anything similar will struggle to match in the future'. He took the modern view that one of the functions of such adaptations was to liberate characters from the moral or sexual prejudices of their authors, and thought that readers of the *TLS*, in particular, might feel that the rehabilitation of the scholar Casaubon was overdue, and be glad that 'we see him in the library of his lovely home rising above the impertinent taunts of his bride'.

Science had never been neglected in the paper, but it received particular attention in the *TLS* in this last decade of the century. In January 1994, a distinguished American biologist from Princeton University, John Tyler Bonner, looked back on sixty years of genetic and evolutionary studies. He said that the greatest biological revolution in his lifetime had been Watson and Crick's discovery of the structure of DNA, followed by the detailed understanding of how genes gave their orders, and all the consequent advances in medicine. The biggest revolution in the study of evolution was instigated by the London and Oxford biologist W.D. Hamilton. This was the series of ideas that led to the recognition, in the 'felicitous term' of Richard Dawkins, author of *The Selfish Gene*, that organisms are simply 'vehicles' carrying genes: 'The genes in our bodies are the ultimate survivors. The organisms come and go with each generation.'

In August 2000, Dawkins himself recalled W.D. Hamilton, in a eulogy he had given in New College Chapel, Oxford, after Hamilton's death. He remembered how a cheque from the Royal Society for £15,000 once blew out of Hamilton's bicycle basket because he cycled so fast, how at one time he wore a paperclip on his glasses to attach to a lock of his hair, because the glasses sat too heavily on his nose, and how in his scientific papers he would bury, in throwaway lines, ideas that in other theorists' hands would fill a whole article.

New studies of the brain were discussed by new experts in the field. Dan Sperber argued in December 1996 that social scientists – for instance, anthropologists who argued about the reasons why cultures were different – should abandon their suspicion of the natural sciences, and turn to such phenomena as the genetic 'architecture of the human mind' to look, at least in part, for explanations. In May 1997, Jerry Fodor, Professor of Philosophy at Rutgers, reviewed a book by Jeffrey L. Elman and others called *Rethinking Innateness*. Fodor stressed that even now nobody knew how the 'cognitive brain' works – no-one could look at a brain and make out whether it belonged to someone who knew algebra – but amongst theories about brains he preferred the belief that in some respects we were born with 'innate content' in them.

The astronomer Sir Bernard Lovell wrote in February 1994 about some books on the origin of the Universe (which he reverently spelled with a capital). He too looked back on the history of research into his subject in the twentieth century, in this case from Einstein's equations that predicted that the Universe was expanding, to Alexander Friedmann's solution of those equations and Edwin Hubbble's astronomical discoveries, and on to 'the almost unanimous belief of scientists that the Universe began in a big bang some ten or fifteen billion years ago'. Finally, in 1992, Lovell wrote, the Cosmic Background Explorer satellite had found the 'Holy Grail of cosmology', the irregularities in the primordial background from which, on that 'big bang' or 'primeval fireball' theory, the galaxies must have arisen. 1,500 people had worked on the satellite and the data it provided, under the direction of George Smoot, the author of one of the books he was reviewing, *Wrinkles in Time*.

Lovell also observed that 'the issue at stake today is the beginning' – and noted that the mathematician and physicist Stephen Hawking was one of those 'who seek an escape from the difficulty of a beginning by invoking the concept of imaginary time, in which the Universe has no beginning and no end, [and] imaginary time translates into real time at the big bang'.

Hawking had also predicted that in twenty years computers might take over altogether in theoretical physics. If that were so, concluded

Lovell, 'there are now only a few years left for theorists to discover the theory of everything'.

A challenging finale to an arguably over-theoretical decade.

By the middle of the year 2000, Ferdinand Mount had brought the circulation of the *TLS* up to over 35,000 – nearly 10,000 more than it had been when he began. Two-thirds of the readers were now overseas purchasers, and two-thirds of the readers were subscribers. The price had gone up, in the ten years he had been at the paper, from £1.25 to £2.20. Mount had kept up the pressure on the management to promote the paper, and there were now annual *TLS* lectures, a regular *TLS* presence at the Hay-on-Wye Festival and the London Literary Festival, co-operation with the Society of Authors over translation awards, and other such activities. There was also a crossword in the paper again, with very literary clues.

As for the other contents, Mount had sustained successfully his ambition to make the paper an organ of general literary and political discussion. Besides numerous essays of the kind already discussed in these pages, there was, for instance, a long series of articles called 'Election Excursions' in 1997, in which authors ranging from the chief inspector of prisons, Stephen Tumim, to the free-market economist Tim Congdon discussed issues germane to the forthcoming general election. No-one had been barred from the paper's pages because of their political persuasion.

The scope of the book reviewing and the arts coverage had been extended, and numerous new reviewers brought in. Merciless scholarly judgments had quite frequently appeared in the paper, but Mount had tried to avoid 'donnish sniffiness', as he put it, or 'dons jumping on the more popular books from a great height'. When a batch of books on the Royal Family had accumulated in June 1991, he invited Craig Brown to review them. Brown observed that 'for contemporary royal biographers, there is no division between what is interesting and what is uninteresting, for the less interesting anything is, the more it is worth cherishing'; and he concluded that, after reading all the books, one was forced to ask two questions about the royal family: 'If they are so ordinary, why are they so special? And if they are so special, why are they so ordinary?'

The impact of literary or critical theory on the universities, from which the majority of the reviewers now inevitably came, had been fielded well by the paper. The difficult debates that the subject provoked had been covered generously, and for the most part with a lucidity to which the matter did not easily lend itself. But there was a further problem which the paper had on the whole solved. It could scarcely avoid – nor would it have wanted to avoid – the impact of these new ideas about literary criticism on its own reviewing. But it had found many reviewers of poetry and fiction who, while influenced by critical theory or responding to its challenges, had not lost sight of the simple demand of readers of book reviews to be told if the book was worth reading and why.

The reviewing of children's books was one element of the paper, extremely important in earlier days, that was nevertheless dropped in the nineties. In two reader surveys that were carried out, this was the only category of books that the majority of readers now expressed no interest or pleasure in.

This history has not had much room to speak of all the innumerable invitations to review books that were turned down, and of the 'ghost TLS', as Jeremy Treglown has put it, that might have existed had all those invitations been accepted. But of course all its editors had their struggles and disappointments in trying to get the books reviewed in the first place. The reviews that appeared had rarely glided effortlessly on to the page, and during Mount's editorship one inducement – money – had not been of the greatest help.

By the end of the century the paper was generally paying about £100 a thousand words – very little compared with national newspapers – and many young reviewers began writing for the *TLS* only to move on somewhere else, while academics often wrote as much to advance their career through publication as for the pay they received from the paper. (They were also, of course, usually glad to get the books.) Nevertheless, as we have seen, many outstanding writers and thinkers were pleased to write for the paper simply because it was an intellectual organ of distinction in which they could express their ideas freely and at length.

Mount may have been daunted by the size of his staff when he first met it; nevertheless he increased it, giving more distinct responsibility for different sections of the paper to various members of it, though he kept a watchful eye on everything that was published. Many of the members of staff who were there when he arrived were still there in the year 2000, including Richard Brain, Mandy Radice, Adolf Wood and Keith Walker. Alan Jenkins was still deputy editor. Elizabeth Winter was now second deputy editor and in charge of Eastern European reviewing. Holly Eley looked after biographies, among other more far-flung subjects such as Japan. Lindsay Duguid was still responsible for fiction reviews. Adrian Tahourdin was in charge of foreign literature and the correspondence columns. Anna Vaux watched over feminist topics; she had married Galen Strawson, who still advised on philo-sophical works. John Ryle, who worked for the Save the Children Fund for half of each year, also had an arrangement with the paper. After David Sexton stopped writing the 'NB' column in 1996, it was taken over by James Campbell, who (as J.C.) kept up its witty, pungent commentary on literary life.

Mick Imlah, who had already been reviewing poetry, came in as poetry editor in 1992. After John Sturrock finally retired from the *TLS* in 1995, David Horspool, who had also joined in 1992, took over history reviewing, and was also the assistant fiction editor, while, as we have seen, Mary Beard advised on ancient history and the classics. The explorer Redmond O'Hanlon advised for a time on natural history. He was succeeded by Orlando May, my son, who was the first science editor the paper had had (and also its first rock and roll editor); after he left, he in turn was followed by Maren Meinhardt, who specialised in medicine and psychology. Giles Foden and Will Eaves had responsi-bilities in the arts sphere. Other new members of the staff were Lucy Dallas, Robert Irwin, Alix MacSweeney and Robert Potts. Maureen Allen was Mount's long-standing secretary. Nicola Walker was the production manager. 'She runs the paper,' Mount told me.

At the end of the century, the financial situation of the paper was 'moving towards washing its face', as Lucy Heller, the managing direc-tor, put it to me. There had been a distinct improvement in its fortunes when in October 1993 the editorial offices moved from Clerkenwell down to Wapping, where – rather late in newspaper history – the staff had to learn computer typesetting. The paper was already being printed by now, much more cheaply, on the News International presses.

The management organisation had also changed in the meanwhile. Philip Crawley had succeeded Michael Hoy as managing director of the supplements, and he was followed by James MacManus, under whom new educational enterprises on the internet were set up and Times Supplements changed its name to TSL Education. MacManus took charge of this larger institution, and Lucy Heller was appointed manag-ing director of the *TLS*. Sir Edward Pickering, the executive vice-chairman of Times Newspapers Limited, told me that Rupert Murdoch, the proprietor, was still completely committed to the paper.

There is no natural end to this book. Looking back in December

1999, the paper asked a large number of writers to choose their 'international books of the year – and of the millennium'. For their millennial book, most of the writers chose Dante, Cervantes, Shakespeare, the James VI Bible and other books that might have been expected from earlier epochs, but several named a book published in the lifetime of the paper, Proust's *A la recherche*. Luckily the *TLS* – or the *Lit Supp* – could hold its head high over its first review of that one.

But the paper was also, fortunately, still in a position to look forward. In 'Commentary', in April 2000, Ferdinand Mount wrote an article that was much remarked on, called 'Farewell to Pudding Island'. In it, he noted that a new generation of writers – Martin Amis, Salman Rushdie and Ian McEwan – had found England a stodgy place and hit out for New York. He thought, however, that this was 'a rather surprising moment for a British novelist in search of excitement to step westward'. America, he said, was wonderful, but it was so quiet, so orderly, so polite. By contrast, Britain at the turn of the century 'could be described as an almost insanely open-minded, casually reckless place'.

Perhaps the British had rediscovered the rôle they had before the British Empire taught them to keep their chins up and their upper lips stiff: 'that of a coarse, freebooting people whose licentiousness is controlled by a certain underlying self-discipline. Or alternatively, we are all going to the dogs. Or again, perhaps a subtle hard-to-grasp mixture of both. In either event, the British situation cannot exactly be said to be dull. One could even write about it.'

He would be too modest to say so, but I have no doubt that he thought, with pleasure, that in the new millennium the *TLS* would have plenty to write about too.

SELECT BIBLIOGRAPHY

Dictionary of National Biography, the twentieth-century volumes
   (Oxford: OUP)
*The History of the Times, Vol. III: The Twentieth Century Test, 1884–
   1912* (London: The Times, 1947); *Vol. IV: The 150th Anniversary
   and Beyond, 1912–1948* (London: The Times, 1952); McDonald,
   Iverach, *The History of The Times, Vol. V: Struggles in War and
   Peace, 1939–1966* (London: The Times, 1984); Grigg, John, *Vol.
   VI: The Thomson Years* (London: HarperCollins, 1995).
TLS 1962: Essays and Reviews from the Times Literary Supplement
   (Oxford: OUP, 1963), and subsequent volumes, *TLS 2–12, 1964–
   74*.

Aldington, Richard, *Life for Life's Sake* (London: Cassell, 1968).
Amory, Mark (ed.), *The Letters of Evelyn Waugh* (London:
   Weidenfeld & Nicolson, 1980).
John Bailey, 1864–1931: Letters and Diaries edited by his wife
   (London: John Murray, 1935).
Barker, Nicolas, *Stanley Morison* (London: Macmillan, 1972).
Bayley, John, *Iris* (London: Duckworth, 1999).
Boston, Richard, 'Tribute to John Willett', in 'Communications', the
   Journal of the International Brecht Society, Vol. 26, No. 1, June
   1997.
Brodribb, C.W., with an introduction by Edmund Blunden, *Poems*
   (London: Macmillan, 1946).
Buchan, John, *Memory Hold-the-Door* (London: Hodder and
   Stoughton, 1940).
Cecil, Lord David, *Max* (London: Constable, 1983).

Clutton-Brock, Arthur, *Thoughts on the War* (London: Methuen, 1914).

—— *More Thoughts on the War* (London: Methuen, 1915).

Crick, Bernard, *George Orwell* (London: Secker & Warburg, 1980).

Curtis, Anthony, *Lit Ed* (Manchester: Carcanet, 1998).

Edel, Leon (ed.), *The Life of Henry James*, three volumes (London: Hart-Davis, 1953–1963).

—— *The Letters of Henry James*. Vol. IV: 1895–1916 (Boston: Harvard University Press, 1984).

Eliot, Valerie (ed.), *The Letters of T.S. Eliot*, Vol. I: 1898–1922 (London: Faber & Faber, 1988).

Ellman, Richard, *James Joyce* (Oxford: OUP, 1982).

Gross, John, *The Rise and Fall of the Man of Letters* (London: Weidenfeld & Nicolson, 1969).

—— (ed.), *The Times Literary Supplement Companion: The Modern Movement* (London, HarperCollins: 1992).

Hamilton, Denis, *Editor-in-Chief* (London: Hamish Hamilton, 1989).

Harcourt Kitchin, F., *Moberly Bell and His Times* (London: Philip Allan, 1925).

Hirst, Francis Wigley, *The Early Life and Letters of John Morley*. (London: Macmillan, 1927).

Lago, Mary, and Furbank, P.N. (eds.), *Selected Letters of E.M. Forster*, two volumes (London: Collins, 1983–85).

Lee, Hermione, *Virginia Woolf* (London: Chatto & Windus, 1996).

Lubbock, Percy, *George Calderon* (London: Grant Richards, 1921).

Lucas, E.V., *Reading, Writing and Remembering* (London: Methuen, 1933).

McLachlan, Donald, *In The Chair: Barrington-Ward of The Times, 1927–1948* (London: Weidenfeld & Nicolson, 1971).

Middleton Murry, John (ed.), *Journal of Katherine Mansfield* (London: Constable, 1927).

Moberly Bell, E.H.C., *The Life and Letters of C.F. Moberly Bell*. (London: Richards Press, 1927).

Moore, Harry T., *The Collected Letters of D.H. Lawrence*, two volumes (London: Heinemann, 1962).

Morgan, Charles, *Reflections in a Mirror* (London: Macmillan, 1944 and 1946).

Mount, Ferdinand (ed.), *The Times Literary Supplement Companion: Communism*. (London: HarperCollins, 1992).

Murray, D.L., *Scenes and Silhouettes* (London: Jonathan Cape, 1926).

Nicolson, Nigel (ed.), *The Letters of Virginia Woolf*, six volumes (London: Hogarth Press, 1975–80).

Olivier Bell, Anne (ed.), *The Diary of Virginia Woolf*, five volumes (London: Hogarth Press, 1977–84).

Pardon My Delay: Letters from Henry James to Bruce Richmond (London: The Foundling Press, 1994).

Pound, Reginald, *Arnold Bennett* (London: Heinemann, 1952).

Powell, Anthony, *To Keep the Ball Rolling: The Memoirs of Anthony Powell*, four volumes (London: Heinemann, 1976–82).

Pryce-Jones, Alan, *The Bonus of Laughter* (London: Hamish Hamilton, 1987).

Richardson, John, *The Sorcerer's Apprentice* (London: Jonathan Cape, 1999).

Smith, Grover (ed.), *Letters of Aldous Huxley* (London: Chatto & Windus, 1969).

Stuart, Sir Campbell, *Opportunity Knocks Once* (London: Collins, 1952).

Thwaite, Anthony (ed.), *Selected Letters of Philip Larkin, 1940–1985* (London: Faber & Faber, 1992).

Treglown, Jeremy and Bennett, Bridget (eds.), *Grub Street and the Ivory Tower* (Oxford: OUP, 1998).

Webb, Barry, *Edmund Blunden* (New Haven: Yale University Press, 1990).

Wrench, John Evelyn, *Geoffrey Dawson and Our Times* (London: Hutchinson, 1955).

INDEX

Beaver, Harold, 397
Bechhofer, C.E. *see* Bechhofer
  Roberts, C.E.
Bechhofer Roberts, C.E., 118, 142–3,
  183, 210, 228; *This Side Idolatry*,
  168; *Through Starving Russia*, 143
Beckett, Samuel, 329; *More Pricks
  Than Kicks*, 201
Beeching, Canon H.C., 55
Beerbohm, Max: writes for *TLS*, 96;
  criticises Clutton-Brock, 121; V.
  Woolf on, 158; letter on W.H.
  Davies, 177; cartoon of *Times*
  editorial staff, 297; *Seven Men*,
  134; *Zuleika Dobson*, 76
Bees, Henry A.: *A History of English
  Romanticism*, 32
Beevor, Antony, 466
Begbie, Harold: 'Witenagemot'
  (poem), 25, 37
Belgion, Montgomery, 237, 239–40
Bell, Alan, 430
Bell, Charles Frederic Moberly:
  works at *Times*, 1–3; qualities,
  4–5; background, 6; and founding
  of *TLS*, 7–10, 18; demands total
  accuracy for chess column,
  15–16; and success of *TLS*, 17;
  and Thursfield's move from *TLS*,
  20–1; and *Encyclopaedia
  Britannica* reviews, 21; and Case,
  22; on Britain's 'few friends', 24;
  and advertisements in *TLS*, 38,
  48, 57; and publication of
  Victoria's letters, 57; in 'Book
  War' over cheap sale of books,
  58; founds Times Book Club, 58;
  and sale of *The Times* to
  Northcliffe, 60–3; Richmond
  complains to about reduced
  space, 63–6; death, 87; in
  Morison's *History of The Times*,
  297
Bell, Clive, 174, 320, 323; *Art*, 106

Bell, Ellen Moberly, 1–3
Bell, Gertrude, 84–5
Bell, Jessie, 118
Bell, Julian, 549
Bell, Kenneth, 139
Bell, Millicent, 520
Bell, Pearl K., 479
Bell, Quentin, 455
Bell, Vanessa, 133
Bellow, Saul, 468; *The Adventures of
  Augie March*, 333; *Dangling Man*,
  292; *The Dean's December*,
  478–9; *Herzog*, 396, 429;
  Humboldt's Gift, 429, 478; *Mr
  Sammler's Planet*, 396; *Ravelstein*,
  530
Beloff, Max (*later* Baron), 344, 368
Benham, Allen H.: *English Literature
  from Widsith to the Death of
  Chaucer*, 115
Benn, William Wedgwood (*later* 1st
  Viscount Stansgate): *In The Side
  Shows*, 139
Bennett, Arnold, 174; death, 201;
  Anna of the Five Towns, 33; *The
  Card*, 76; *The Grand Babylon
  Hotel*, 33; *Imperial Palace*, 201;
  The Old Wives' Tale, 76; *The
  Regent*, 76
Benson, Arthur Christopher, 56
Beowulf: translated by Heaney, 539
Beresford, J.D., 169–70
Beresford, John, 241
Berger, John: *G*, 388; *Permanent
  Red*, 388
Beria, Lavrenti, 371
Berkeley, Humphry: *The Life and
  Death of Rochester Sneath*, 422
Berlin Diaries (anon), 229
Berlin, Sir Isaiah: disputes with Carr,
  305; dislikes *Lucky Jim*, 331;
  reviews and articles, 345, 373;
  letters to Crook, 360, 369–70, 372,
  377; on Steiner, 377; on meeting

Buckingham, Bob, 441

Buckle, George Earl: edits *The Times*, 1–5, 14, 141; background, 6; letter from Richmond, 7; uses *TLS* space, 18–19; and Case, 22; and Northcliffe's acquisition of *The Times*, 60–3; resigns, 88–9, 123; reviewing in Great War, 101–2; continuation of Monypenny's *Life of Disraeli*, 103, 109, 141; and sale of *Times* after Northcliffe's death, 153; edits Queen Victoria's letters, 156; in Morison's *History of The Times*, 297

Burgess, Anthony, 360, 387, 406, 451, 457–8, 479, 484, 521; *A Clockwork Orange*, 360; *Earthly Powers*, 451

Burgess, Guy, 510

Burke, Edmund, 179

Burke's Peerage, 301

Burney, Fanny (Madame d'Arblay), 194

Burra, Peter, 227

Burroughs, William: *The Naked Lunch*, 359–60

Butler, Marilyn, 492–3

Butler, Samuel: *The Way of All Flesh*, 45–6

Butt, John, 545

Butterfield, Herbert, 304

Byatt, (Dame) Antonia S: *Possession*, 473; *The Virgin in the Garden*, 432

Byrne, Muriel St Clair, 269

Calder-Marshall, Arthur, 402; *The Watershed*, 281

Calderon, George, 70–3, 76

Callaghan, James, 446

Calvocoressi, Peter, 306

Cameron, J.M., 305

Campbell, James, 499, 555

Campbell, Roy: 'Flowering Rifle', 246; *Taurine Provence*, 202

Camus, Albert, 379; *La Peste (The Plague)*, 293, 312

Canetti, Elias, 377; *Auto da Fé*, 290

Cannadine, David, 516

Cannan, Gilbert, 96

Capes, Revd W.W.: *Scenes of Rural Life in Hampshire*, 12–13

Capper, J.B., 1, 3, 6, 14, 18–20, 63

Carey, Wymond: *Love the Judge*, 51

Carlill, H.F., 282, 299, 317

Carlyle, Jane Welsh, 160

Carman, Bliss: 'Coronation Ode', 26

Carne-Ross, D.S., 338

Carnegy, Patrick, 421, 467

Carpenter, William Boyd, Bishop of Ripon, 21, 24

Carr, Edward Hallett: reviews and articles, 228, 237, 242, 258–9, 264, 267, 273, 278–81, 287, 299, 304–5, 329, 341–3, 368, 402, 436; Isaiah Berlin criticises, 372; death, 494; *Conditions of Peace*, 259; *History of Soviet Russia*, 341–2, 368, 494–5; *Nationalism and After*, 280; *The New Society*, 342; *The Twilight of Comintern, 1930–35*, 494–5

Carr, Mrs E.H., 275

Carr, Herbert Wildon, 145

Carr, John Dickson, 454

Carter, Angela, 548

Carter, John ('Jake'), 209, 222, 349, 351–2, 403–4

Carter, John and Graham Pollard: review *Between the Lines* and denounce Wise, 294; *An Enquiry into the Nature of Certain Nineteenth Century Pamphlets*, 208, 294

Carver, Raymond: *Elephant, and Other Stories*, 480

INDEX

Fleming, Ian, 454; *Casino Royale*, 333; *Dr No*, 333

Fleming, Peter, 187–8; *Brazilian Adventure*, 209

Fletcher, Constance ('George Fleming'), 30, 34, 46, 51, 54

Flint, F.S., 128, 131, 138–9

Flower, Sir Newman, 302

Foden, Giles, 555

Fodor, Jerry, 552

Folliot, Bernadette, 305, 309, 311, 328

Fonseca, Isabel (*later* Mrs Martin Amis), 498

Foot, Michael, 425

Forbes, Alastair, 423–4

Ford, Ford Madox (Hueffer): *Joseph Conrad: A Personal Reminiscence*, 176–7; *Last Post*, 170; *The Good Soldier*, 110

Ford, Mark, 534, 541

Forman, Henry Buxton, 208, 294

Forster, E.M.: criticises Clutton-Brock, 121; disparages Valentine Chirol, 155–6; reputation, 174, 255; on Lowes Dickinson, 196; single review for *TLS*, 197; death, 382; Furbank's biography of, 440–1; *Abinger Harvest*, 227; *Anonymity*, 165; *Aspects of the Novel*, 166; *The Celestial Omnibus*, 75; *Howard's End*, 75; *The Longest Journey*, 51; *Maurice*, 382–3; *A Passage to India*, 155, 165; *A Room With a View*, 75; *Where Angels Fear To Tread*, 52

Forster, John, 169

Forster, Professor, 108

Fortescue, John, 118

Foster, Donald W., 482

Foster, Sir Michael, 21, 24

Foucault, Michel, 379, 450, 544, 546, 548–9; *La Folie et la déraison*, 380, 544

France: in wartime, 260, 264; liberated, 266; Brogan writes on, 280; *TLS* special number on, 322–3

France, Anatole: *Vie de Jeanne d'Arc*, 85–6

Frankfurt School, 448

Fraser, George S.: background, 289–90; poetry reviews, 289–90, 316–17, 335–7, 340, 391–2, 394; chooses poems for publication in *TLS*, 315; on literary criticism, 318, 323, 338; on Beckett, 329; leaders, 341, 389; teaches in Japan, 346; article on McDiarmid, 361; on Iris Murdoch, 384; obituary tribute to Eliot, 389; (ed) *Poetry Now* (anthology), 338

Frayn, Michael, 526

Freeborn, Richard, 373

Freeman, G.S., 214

Freeman, J.H., 212, 229–30, 259, 267

Freeman, John, 179

Freud, Lucian, 465

Friedmann, Alexander, 552

Fries, Felix, 247

Frost, Ernest, 330

Frost, Robert, 324; *Collected Poems*, 205; *New Hampshire*, 173; *Selected Poems*, 173

Fry, Roger, 174, 251

Fulford, (Sir) Roger, 323, 401

Fuller, Roy, 315

Fuller, S.R., 270

Fullerton, William Morton: *The American Crisis and the War*, 110

Fumaroli, Marc, 549

Furbank, P.N.: biography of E.M. Forster, 440–1

Furness, Mary, 463

Fyfe, Harry Hamilton, 8, 13, 17

Gallacher, William: *The Case for Communism*, 304

Millett, Kate, 548; *Sexual Politics*, 492

Milosevic, Slobodan, 511

Milton, John, 225, 488; Sparrow's spoof on, 412

Minogue, Kenneth, 512–13, 547

Minta, S.M.J., 481

Mitchell, Sollace, 449

Mitford, Nancy: *Love in a Cold Climate*, 309

Mitterrand, François, 499

Mitton, Miss G.E.: *The Lost Cities of Ceylon*, 111

Molony, J.C., 209

Moncrieff, C.K. Scott, 138, 174

Monroe, Harriet, 115

Montagu, Ivor, 254

Montaigne, Michel de, 160

Montefiore, Alan, 545

Montrose, David, 479

Monypenny, William Flavell: *Life of Disraeli*, 81–2, 103, 109, 141

Moore, Geoffrey, 324

Moore, George Edward, 121, 145

Moore, Marianne, 130, 324

Moore, R.W., 201, 285

Moore, T. Sturge, 121, 131, 167

Morandi, Giorgio, 375

Moravia, Alberto, 429

Morgan, Charles: turns up in court dress, 189; writes 'Menander's Mirror', 260–5, 269–71, 273, 277; and Murray's departure from TLS, 271; reputation, 323; *The Fountain*, 201; *Portrait in a Mirror*, 170; *Reflections in a Mirror*, 271

Morgan, Edwin, 376

Morgan, Janet, 459, 497

Morison, Samuel Eliot, 218

Morison, Stanley: Richmond writes to, 3; editorship of TLS, 185, 271–80, 282–5, 287, 294–5, 305, 422; designs Times New Roman

typeface, 193; advises on layout of TLS, 216; at Garrick, 222; and Murray's editorship of TLS, 234–5; and Barrington-Ward's editorship of Times, 258–9; Catholicism, 274, 283; character and background, 274–5; and Pryce-Jones's appointment to editorial staff, 287–8, 295–6; retires and takes up special duties, 296–7; visits America with Gavin Astor, 297; and payments to contributors, 346; and The Book Ring, 349; and Pryce-Jones's absences, 352; and Crook's appointment to editorship of TLS, 354; death, 402; *Four Centuries of Fine Printing*, 185; *The History of the Times*, 20, 152, 217, 247, 274–5, 295–6, 325

Morley, Frank, 3, 320

Morley, John, Viscount: article on Mill, 55–6, 81; reviews Monypenny's *Disraeli*, 81–3, 103; *Life of Gladstone*, 40–1, 55; *Recollections*, 113

Morley, Lacy Collison, 145

Morning Post, 10, 91

Morrah, Dermot, 244–9, 264, 275, 278

Morrell, Lady Ottoline, 115, 136, 236

Morris, James, 356

Morris, R.O., 143

Morris, William: 'The Hollow Land', 225

Morrison, Blake, 434–5, 438, 447, 462, 470, 484–5

Morrison, Herbert (*later* Baron): *Wartime Speeches*, 264

Morrison, J.F.D., 302

Morrison, Toni, 548

Mortimer, Raymond, 182, 323

Motion, Andrew, 483, 533–4

Wright, Judith, 488
Wright, Richard, 306
Wyndham, Francis, 310–11, 323–4, 329–30, 432

Yeats, William Butler: on appreciating poetry, 36; Virginia Woolf on, 158; recognition and reputation, 171, 245; Leavis on, 206; death and tribute to, 244–5, 539; accused of Fascist tendencies, 263; Dylan Thomas's hostility to, 532; *The Cutting of an Agate*, 132; *Ideas of Good and Evil*, 44; *Last Poems*, 245; *Later Poems*, 132; *Poems 1899–1905*, 54; *Responsibilities*, 111; *The Tower*, 172; *The Wild Swans at Coole*, 132; *The Winding Stair*, 205
Yorke, Henry *see* Green, Henry
Young, G.M., 252
Young, Keith, 461

Zilliacus, Konni, 282
Zola, Emile, 77, 287